D1394016

Performance

AUSTRALIA
The Law Book Company
Brisbane . Sydney . Melbourne . Perth

CANADA
Carswell
Ottawa . Toronto . Calgary . Montreal . Vancouver

Agents:

Steimatzky's Agency Ltd., Tel Aviv:
N.M. Tripathi (Private) Ltd., Bombay;
Eastern Law House (Private) Ltd., Calcutta;
M.P.P. House, Bangalore;
Universal Book Traders, Delhi;
Aditya Books, Delhi;
MacMillan Shuppan KK, Tokyo
Pakistan Law House, Karachi, Lahore

Performance

The Business and Law of Entertainment

by

LESLIE E. COTTERELL

LL.B., D.P.A., Solicitor

Third Edition

LONDON
Sweet & Maxwell
1993

First Edition   1977
Second Edition   1984
Third Edition   1993

Published in 1993 by
Sweet & Maxwell Limited of
South Quay Plaza, 183 Marsh Wall, London E14 9FT
Computerset by MFK Typesetting Ltd., Hitchin, Herts.
and printed in Great Britain by
Butler & Tanner Ltd,
Frome and London

British Library Cataloguing in Publication Data

A catalogue record
for this book is available
from the British Library

ISBN 0-421-471905

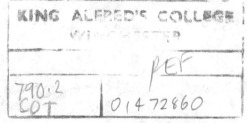

To my Mother and Father
in gratitude and remembrance

PREFACE to the THIRD EDITION

Since the last edition of this study in 1984 important changes have come about in the entertainment industry and to the law directly affecting entertainment so that a major revision of the text has been undertaken. Even so the structure of the book has not been altered. *Performance* is not a legal textbook but has been planned as a work of reference for those persons who need to know about the commercial and legal issues of the business of entertainment. The book is intended to serve the needs of those engaged in management, production and administration in the various branches of entertainment, and to offer guidance to artists, musicians, directors and producers, writers, composers and other creative persons in the pursuit of their profession.

In Parts 1 to 5 an account is given of the organisations representing managements and performers which negotiate minimum terms and conditions of engagement in the various branches of entertainment. A detailed survey is made of the principal collective agreements which embody those terms and make provision for the settlement of disputes. However, the survey does not include the industry agreements which apply to persons employed in technical and craft grades. An outline of the principles of contract law and of the law of employment material to persons engaged in entertainment is included, together with an explanation of the rights of performers in their performances now firmly established by law.

Part 6 is an outline of copyright law noting the works capable of protection, the rights which copyright protection confers, and the circumstances when protected works can legitimately be used without infringing copyright. The rules for dealing with copyright by assignment and licence and the remedies for infringing copyright are noted, as are moral rights which have been adopted into English law by the Copyright, Designs and Patents Act 1988.

Part 7 sets out to demonstrate and apply the principles of copyright law in a practical way. Consideration is given to the terms on which rights in literary, dramatic, musical and artistic works are granted or acquired for purposes of entertainment, and to the issues which can arise in the negotiation of agreements licensing the performance, use and exploitation of works and the products of the entertainment industry. The collective agreements prescribing the terms for commissioning new works and licensing the performance of existing works in the theatre and in the medium of broadcasting and film are reviewed. As film production is no longer confined to major enterprises there is included a brief outline of the agreements for the commissioning and making of films and independent productions for television broadcasting.

The system of collective licensing especially of the public performance and broadcasting and of the recording of musical works, the roles of the principal collecting societies and the functions and powers of the Copyright Tribunal are explained.

The restraints which the law imposes on what may be performed and the manner of performance—the boundaries of performance—are considered in Part 8.

Parts 9 and 10 are to serve the needs of those who provide and manage places of public entertainment. Of crucial importance are the enactments requiring places of public entertainment to be licensed, the procedures for the making and hearing of applications for the grant and renewal of licences, the terms and conditions upon which premises are licensed, and the powers of local authorities and the police to enforce the legislation and the conditions upon which licences are granted.

The terms and conditions of agreements whereby theatres, concert halls, arts centres and the like are licensed or made available to touring companies and promoters of entertainment of all kinds are considered in Part 10. The legal responsibilities of managers for the general management of places of entertainment and for the activities and performances given are outlined, and the relationship in law between the proprietors of places of entertainment and admission of audiences and other persons.

The principles of law governing the relationship of an agent and/or personal manager and his client, the customary terms of representation agreements and the provisions of the Employment Agencies Act 1973 and the Regulations made under it which apply in particular to the entertainment industry are reviewed in Part 11.

It may appear that the needs of the societies and clubs responsible for the provision of amateur performances and entertainment have been overlooked but that is not so. In particular the sections of the book about the use of copyright works and the licensing and management of places of public entertainment are as material to amateur entertainment as to commercial entertainment. The provisions of the collective agreements which specify the terms upon which professional artists are customarily engaged to perform with amateurs are noted in Part 3.

This study could not have been undertaken without the kind cooperation and assistance of the secretaries and officials of the associations, societies and organisations which variously represent managements, performers, authors and copyright owners, or who are otherwise connected with the business of entertainment. I wish to record my thanks for their help and advice given over quite a period of time, and for their permission to use the industry collective agreements and quote from their publications.

I also extend my thanks to the members of the editorial team at Sweet and Maxwell for their guidance in the preparation and presentation of the text. With their patience and skill I have endeavoured to ensure the material set down is correct to December 1992.

In conclusion I wish to record my appreciation of the encouragement and support I have had from my life long friends Hans and Helen Wessel in the writing of this study.

Leatherhead, Surrey.
January 1993   L.E.C.

CONTENTS

Part 5 THE PERFORMER AND THE LAW

Part 6 THE ELEMENTS OF COPYRIGHT

Part 7 THE COMMISSIONING AND USE OF COPYRIGHT WORKS

Part 8 THE PERFORMANCE

"Show business is like life. You don't know how long it's going to last so you may as well enjoy it while you can."—Frankie Howerd (1921–1992)

Part 1

INTRODUCTION

A. PERFORMERS AND MANAGEMENTS

It is often said that appearances count and as they certainly do in the world of entertainment it can hardly be wondered at that in this study attention is given first to the performer rather than to other persons contributing their artistic talents to the performing arts. It may be perfectly true that theatrical productions, concerts, films, television and so on begin with the original and creative work of authors, composers, producers, directors, designers, etc. but even so, central to all theatrical and other entertainment is the artist engaged to perform a part or play an instrument.

Despite the stories of the whims, fantasies and tantrums of impresarios, actor-managers, prima donnas, film stars, directors and others which make amusing reading and behind all the glitter and extravagance of showmanship, standards and rules of professional conduct exist which are generally observed by managers, producers and performers of all kinds in their dealings with one another. This situation has been brought about over the years through the endeavours of Equity and the Musicians' Union representing performers and the associations variously representing theatrical, film and television producers. Because of the role these organisations play in the subject matter of this study it is appropriate that at the commencement a brief description should be given of the two performers' Unions and of the theatrical Management Associations. Other associations representative of persons, companies and organisations variously engaged in or concerned with the performing arts and the business of entertainment are mentioned in the text.

Equity

British Actors' Equity Association (Equity) was constituted in 1930 and at first represented only the regular theatrical actor and actress. In 1967 the Variety Artistes' Federation merged with Equity so today Equity represents persons of differing talents engaged in all branches of entertainment and currently has a membership of about 46,000.

Any person who exercises professional skill in the provision of entertainment "whether as artist, producer, stage-manager, or in any similar capacity in the theatre, music hall, films, radio, television and the like media," is eligible for membership. If admitted, persons are normally first entered as provisional members and this status confers all the rights of full membership except the right to be elected an officer of the Council.

Full membership is granted to a provisional member of not less than 30 weeks standing and who satisfies the Executive Committee that he or she has had not less than 30 weeks professional experience. With film, radio and television engagements a week's professional experience means any period of six days during which an artist has been professionally employed irrespective of the number of days of actual work. Thus allowance is made for the different working arrangements in the mechanical media as compared with the stage. Engagements in clubs and cabaret for performance on less than four consecutive days are counted as a half-week's professional engagement.

Temporary membership of Equity can be granted by the Executive Committee for such period of time and upon payment of such fees as the Committee may decide. Visiting foreign artists are admitted to temporary membership for the duration of their engagement in the United Kingdom. In order to secure an engagement, artists who are nationals of a country outside the European Community require a work permit issued by the Department of Employment and apart from any other considerations possession of a permit is a condition of admission to temporary membership of Equity.

Election to membership in any of the above classes is by a majority vote of members of the Executive Committee present at a Committee meeting. It is the Executive Committee which is also empowered to fine, suspend or expel a member in accordance with the Rules of Equity.

The governing body of Equity is the Council composed of 67 members elected every two years by ballot of the members in full benefit. Candidates are elected in panels, meaning a general list of candidates, candidates representing members in the regions established by Equity and candidates representing the various sections of employment in entertainment. From among the members of the Council and by the members of the Council are elected the President, two Vice-Presidents and the Treasurer who with the full-time General Secretary comprise the Officers of the Association.

The Council is expressly enjoined "at all times to act in the best interests of the members in accordance with the objects of the Association and shall determine anything therein wherein the Rules are silent but in no case shall they alter or depart from the established constitution and Rules of the Association." Thus the Council is expressly empowered to issue all necessary instructions to members in pursuance of the Objects of the Association. It also has the obligation to elect 17 of its members to constitute, with the Officers of the Association, the Executive Committee to carry on the normal day to day management and direction of the affairs of Equity. Five members constitute a quorum for meetings of the Executive Committee.

Under the Rules the Executive Committee has specific duties cast upon it, namely, the admission of members, the negotiations with employers and their associations, and the investigation of all complaints made by or against members. It has the residual powers and duties "to take any action it deems fit on behalf of the Association and allowed by the Rules and not expressly reserved for decision by the Council," but all decisions of the Committee are required to be ratified by the Council.

In addition to the Executive Committee and to assist the Council, separate committees are appointed to deal with or advise on particular national issues and matters of special concern to the various sections of the profession and members of Equity. Also there are area committees to advise on local issues affecting members of a region. All these committees perform only an advisory role as the formulation of policy and negotiations with managements on the terms and conditions of employment rest with the Council acting as the representative of the whole membership of Equity.

In order to bring about a regular liaison between Equity officials and members undertaking engagements the Rules provide for the election of a deputy from among members working for a theatre, television or film company. Failing an election from among members a deputy may be appointed by the Executive Committee with the consent of the members concerned. Deputies serve as the representatives of the Equity members of a company or unit at meetings with a management and report to the officials of Equity any issues which require resolution. However, it is expressly laid down by the Rules of Equity that deputies cannot enter into negotiations with a management about general conditions of employment as such negotiations are the province of the General Secretary or persons appointed by him. Deputies generally perform routine functions especially in regard to membership of Equity by the inspection of membership cards and the collection of subscriptions.

The Rules make provision for the holding of annual general meetings and for the calling of special general meetings of members and prescribe the procedures to be observed and how meetings are to be conducted. Issues can be put to a ballot of the entire membership of the Association by referendum.

Musicians' Union

The Musicians' Union, which represents the vast majority of professional musicians, was established in 1921 by the fusion of the Amalgamated Musicians' Union and the National Orchestral Union of Professional Musicians. With a few exceptions membership of the Union is open to anyone who is following the profession of music in any of its branches, that is anyone who is engaged in performing, teaching or writing music.

There is no rule prescribing a minimum number of qualifying engagements or proficiency of performance. No attempt is made to control entry into the profession, for whereas persons may think they can act professionally without training or experience, the ability to play an instrument professionally will often have been proved through performing semi-professionally for some time with a youth or local orchestra or group.

Application for membership is made to the branch covering the area in which a musician resides or is musically employed and is accepted by the branch committee or branch meeting. If it is rejected the rejection must be reported to the Union's headquarters with an explanation. An entrance fee is payable as prescribed by the Executive Committee of the Union from time to time, as well as an annual subscription. Once admitted a member can always resign but only the Executive Committee of the Union can terminate a member's membership, by 13 weeks' written notice.

The Rules place certain obligations on members and those of particular importance are that members:

(a) do not accept engagements at less than the minimum rates or on less favourable conditions than those adopted by the Union;

(b) give and receive a written contract and complete all other procedures for such engagements and in such manner as specified by the Union;

(c) in regard to recording engagements, ensure the consent to the recording of their performance is given in the form authorised by the Union and thereby nominate the Union as their representative for any use of the recorded performance not specifically provided for in a collective agreement between the Union and the maker of the recording.

The undoubted strength of the Union rests on the sanction and observance of these obligations, the position of the branches as the emanations of the Executive Committee in supervising the contracts and engagements of members, and the authority given by the Rules to the Executive Committee to impose fines or suspend, or in extreme cases expel a defaulting member.

The management and direction of the Union rests with the Executive Committee composed of members elected from its nine districts in proportion to the number of members in each district; election is by ballot from among the members of a district. The district councils are formed from delegates from the branches within the area of a district, elected by ballot of the members. The branches, of which there are 130 throughout the country, each have a committee and officials are elected from among their members. The Union has a biennial delegate conference, delegates being elected from among the members of a district and in number proportionate to the membership of a district. Under the Rules the Executive Committee has weighty and extensive powers of government and control over the affairs and organisation of the Union, but the policy decisions of the delegate conferences are binding on the Committee.

The admission of musicians to membership of the Union and therefore the recognition of their professional status for the purpose of securing paid employment is not regarded as a problem that is likely to lead to under employment and overcrowding, but there is a measure of restraint in the admission of foreign musicians. A foreign musician who for at least twelve months preceding his application has been continuously resident in the United Kingdom can be admitted to membership with the express consent of the Executive Committee. An applicant who has not been so resident cannot be admitted unless he or she is entitled by law to seek and obtain employment here without the need for specific authorisation. A musician who is a national of another EC country or who does not require a permit from the Department of Employment to undertake employment is eligible for membership.

There is no real problem of "demarcation" as between membership of Equity and the Musicians' Union; professional performers may be members of both unions. The "grey" area surrounds the singer/instrumental performer and the pop groups. The guiding principle is that where the vocal or singing element of a performer's work is subordinate to the instrumental, *i.e.* the performer is more closely identified with the playing of an instrument, then that person is regarded as following the profession of music and so qualifies for membership of the Musicians' Union. When singing is the dominant element then that person as an artist can apply for membership of Equity.

Society of West End Theatre

The Society was founded in 1908 as an association to represent the interests of West End of London theatrical managements. Today the Society comprises individual persons and representatives of companies who are managers and proprietors of London theatres and producers of professional performances of plays, musical plays, opera, ballet and light entertainment on the London stage. Whilst the majority of members are connected with the commercial theatre the Society's membership includes representatives of all the national subsidised companies centred in London.

Membership is on an individual basis. An applicant's eligibility is first considered by the Society's Board of Management but election is by the Society in general meeting. As the Society is concerned to uphold professional and responsible standards of theatrical management, election is not a matter of course but rather depends upon the financial standing, integrity and reputation of the person seeking election. Moreover, in order to satisfy the rules of the London Theatre Council as explained in Part 2 below, persons are first elected as "deposit members" and on election required to make the deposits for future productions in compliance with those rules. In due course, with a proven record of management in accordance with the rules of the Theatre Council, members become eligible for election by the Society in general meeting as "non-deposit members."

The policy of the Society is laid down by its President and Board of Management, all of whom are elected annually from amongst all members of the Society, but subject to the directions of members given at regular general meetings of the Society. The administration of the Society's affairs is conducted by its Chief Executive and salaried staff.

From its inception the Society has been a centre for the discussion of all matters of concern to theatrical managers. It acts in co-operation with the Theatrical Management Association through the Theatres' National Committee but naturally concentrates on those issues of direct concern to its members and as they relate to London's traditional theatre land.

The Society is responsible for the negotiation on behalf of its members with Equity and the Musicians' Union of minimum rates of pay and conditions of engagement of artists and musicians for the West End theatre as outlined in Part 2 below. Likewise it negotiates with the Broadcasting Entertainment Cinematograph Theatre Union (BECTU) the rates and conditions of employment of theatre staff, technicians and craftsmen. The Society's officers assist in conciliation when issues arise in regard to the application of these collective agreements.

In more recent times the Society has actively undertaken to promote West End theatre by liaising with tourist and travel organisations and by providing a range of publications particularly the fortnightly London Theatre Guide. It also manages the half-price ticket booth in Leicester Square and the theatre gift token scheme.

Theatrical Management Association

The Association was founded in 1894 as a national organisation to represent the interests of managers of theatres and theatrical companies. In 1979 radical alterations were made to its constitution when the Council of Regional Theatre (which was founded in 1944 to promote the repertory movement) and the Association of Touring and Producing Managers (whose members were producers of light entertainment shows) merged with the Theatrical Management Association. Now with a membership of about 450 comprising individuals, companies, corporate organisations and local authorities the Association represents a wide range of theatrical enterprise encompassing live entertainment of all kinds—repertory, touring companies, resident shows, variety, ice skating—and the ownership and management of places used for public entertainment.

Membership

There are three principal categories of membership, namely, full, probationary and associate, the latter being for a member who has ceased to be actively engaged in theatrical entertainment. The distinctions are important not only because of their effect on members' voting rights and eligibility for election to the Council, but also because only full membership automatically confers "approved" management status and registration with the Provincial Theatre Council as explained in Part 2.

Applications for membership must be proposed and seconded by full members of the Association and supported with information as prescribed by the Council about the applicant's general business standing, organisation, theatre ownership and theatrical productions. The Council's Membership Committee considers each application and the category of membership to which an applicant should first be admitted. If the proposed membership receives the recommendation of the Committee and it is endorsed by the Council it is notified to all members of the Association and to the General Secretary of Equity. Unless an objection is raised within 21 days of the notice the applicant is admitted to membership. If under the Provincial Theatre Council's constitution Equity enters an objection which is upheld by the Theatre Council this results in the automatic rejection of the application. If objection is made by a member of the Association the matter is considered by the Council and the applicant is elected only if he receives a two-thirds majority of votes of the members of the Council present at the meeting and provided such two-thirds majority consists of at least three votes. If a member is first admitted as a probationary member then after two years an application can be made to the Council for full membership but the same procedure as for the initial application must again be followed.

Corporate members of the Association appoint a representative to attend, vote and speak at meetings which the member is entitled to attend. Individual members may also appoint a representative to attend and speak at meetings but a representative can vote only in the absence of the member.

When a full or probationary member ceases to be actively engaged in the entertainment business continuously for not less than one year the Council can request his resignation from the Association. If a member becomes bankrupt the Council has the power to terminate his membership and there are detailed provisions in the Rules about the expulsion of a member who acts in a manner prejudicial to the Association or contrary to the best interests of the theatrical profession.

Management

The general conduct and management of the affairs of the Association rest with the Council consisting of a minimum of four and a maximum of 15 elected members, together with the Association's President and two Vice-Presidents (one being the immediate Past President and the other being subject to annual election) who are ex-officio members. In addition, if they are not already members of the Council, the Chairman of the Industrial Relations Committee and the Chairmen of the Resident Managers', Commercial Producer's and the Grant-Aided Management Standing Committees are also *ex-officio* members. The Council is elected in one third rotation annually from among full members of not less than nine months standing and associate members who were formerly full members for at least nine months; election is by the members by postal ballot. The offices of President and Vice-President are confined to persons who are members of the Council and the appointment is held from one annual general meeting to the next. The incumbents are eligible for re-election and in the absence of any other nominations can continue in office but the President may not serve for more than three consecutive years except in the absence of any other nomination for President. When more than one person is nominated for election to either office a ballot of the members of the Association is conducted.

Meetings of the Council take place at regular intervals and four members present constitutes a quorum. The Council and Officers are assisted by an appointed full-time Chief Executive and staff. The consideration and discussion of issues affecting members are to some extent channelled through the three standing committees corresponding with the three broad areas of theatrical enterprise, namely:

(1) Resident Manager's Committee for members responsible for the administration and management of theatre buildings or other places of public entertainment directly involved in the commercial, local authority and university sectors;

(2) Commercial Producer's Committee for members responsible for the presentation and management of theatrical productions other than in the non-profit distributing sector; and

(3) Grant-aided Management's Committee for members responsible for the administration and management of productions and theatres in the non profit-distributing sector.

Each of the committees comprises nine members elected annually by and from among the members of the Association according to their category. On election a member is registered in the category appropriate to the member's activities but a member can change his category by notice to the

Secretary except during the eight weeks following an annual general meeting.

Meetings of the standing committees are held as required from time to time. Four members present constitute a quorum. The chairmen report to the Council on the meetings of their committees as any action proposed by a committee requires the authority of the Council.

In addition to the Standing Committees the Rules provide for a separate committee called the Industrial Relations Committee to deal with all trade union matters affecting members. The Committee is composed of nine members two of whom are appointed by each of the Standing Committees and three by the Council. The Committee is appointed annually but without any restriction on members being re-appointed. The Committee elects its own Chairman and Deputy Chairman the former becoming an *ex-officio* member of the Council during his term of office if not already a member of the Council. The Committee can exercise the powers delegated to it by the Council but cannot conclude any union agreement without the Council's prior approval and as to which the Rules of the Association are specific. Before there can be any ratification of a settlement of a union claim or revision of a union agreement the details must first be circulated to those members likely to be concerned. The Council must allow 14 days to elapse after the details are circulated to enable members to submit to the Chief Executive their comments and if 15 or more members do not approve of a settlement then a consultative meeting of members must be called and the Council must have regard to the views expressed at such a meeting.

The Rules make provision for the holding of an annual general meeting of the Association and the business then to be transacted. In addition provision is made for the holding of quarterly general meetings for the consideration of matters as required, for extraordinary general meetings for the alteration of the Rules and for the removal of a councillor, and for special meetings if requisitioned by one tenth of the members. Ten members present constitute a quorum but a quorum of 40 members entitled to vote is required to pass a binding resolution.

A referendum on any matter may be called by the Council other than those specifically reserved for decision by the members as prescribed in the Rules. One tenth of the members can request a referendum on submission of a form of questionnaire. Issues are determined by a simple majority of the members voting but there can be no reversal of the decision except by a two-thirds majority in a subsequent referendum which may not be held on the same or substantially the same question within six months of the initial referendum.

The funds of the Association are derived from entrance fees, members' annual subscriptions and a "performance fee" of an amount fixed at a general or extraordinary general meeting (held prior to January 1, of the year for which the fee is payable). The performance fee is payable by members per paid public performance at any auditorium licensed under the Theatres Act 1968 or other statute or operating pursuant to Letters Patent of the Crown. In addition, on the Council's recommendation and if resolved upon at a general meeting of the Association a special contribution to meet some special contingency can be levied on members.

Theatres' National Committee

The Committee comprises the Society of West End Theatre, the Theatrical Management Association and the Independent Theatre Council. It serves as the collective voice and representative body of theatrical management on broad political, economic and social issues as they relate to or affect the theatre, issues such as safety, theatre licensing, taxation, copyright and overseas tours. The Committee participates in union negotiations only in matters which have national significance.

B. CASTING AGREEMENTS

One of the recurring issues in the entertainment profession is the admission of new members when existing members often experience difficulty in securing regular employment and proper remuneration for their competence and skill acquired from years of experience. A musician must usually have achieved a fair standard of ability in performance and gained some recognition by other musicians before entering the profession; mere presence or good looks are no criterion for a musical career. No formal qualifications are necessary for entry into the acting profession and this remains so although there are opportunities for training at drama schools some of whose courses are accredited by the National Council for Drama Training and the Council for Dance Education and Training. It is not the purpose of this study to review the arguments for a restricted or unrestricted right of persons to enter the profession to exploit their artistic talents, or for managers to engage or employ whoever they choose. However, it can hardly be disputed that some measure of supervision is needed over entry to a profession where employment is mainly casual and freelance and the careers of those who are experienced and intent on making the performing arts their livelihood and life's work can be put at risk by those who have no experience and or commitment. As Ernest Clark, a past President of Equity once remarked, "One of the disadvantages of belonging to a 'glamour' profession is that by its very nature it attracts so many people to it that the competition within it for survival is unglamorous to the extent of being positively destructive."

In order to bring about an orderly admission of persons to the acting profession casting agreements have existed over the years in the various branches of entertainment. These agreements have never applied to persons appearing as themselves but even so they have been modified as a result of the Employment Act 1990 whereby it is unlawful to refuse a person employment because he or she is not a member of a trade union or is unwilling to become a member of one. Thus the essence of all the existing casting agreements is that in normal circumstances persons should not be engaged to perform a part or a role of some kind unless they are experienced professional performers.

Theatre

The Management Associations and Equity have made revisions to the Schedules to the collective agreements reviewed in Part 2 which deal with the casting of performers collectively called "artists". This expression includes understudies, assistant stage managers who are also engaged to act or understudy, and assistant stage managers not engaged to act or understudy known as technical ASM's. The basic premise of the casting agreements is that in the normal course of events a manager will not offer an engagement to any person who is not an experienced professional artist. Full or provisional membership of Equity constitutes proof of the required experience and attainment of professional status.

Nonetheless with the exception of the West End Theatre the Casting Agreements permit a manager to engage persons who do not meet the above criterion but up to the limit of a prescribed annual quota, and to engage registered graduates. A "registered graduate" is a person who has graduated from an acting or stage management course accredited by the National Council for Drama Training, or a dancing course accredited by the Council for Dance Education and Training, and whose name has been placed by his/her Drama or Dance School Principal on a register maintained by Equity for a period of two years from the day of his/her graduation. A certificate is issued to a registered graduate which constitutes proof of his/her status.

The prescribed annual quotas which apply for persons who are not registered graduates are as follows:

Provincial Theatre:

Resident Season or Provincial Theatre Tours—

300 newcomer places per year (of which 175 are reserved for registered graduates), to be allocated by TMA amongst its members as TMA thinks fit.

Non-Subsidised Repertory—

(a) artists—2 per manager

(b) technical ASM's—1 per manager

both (a) and (b) to be allocated by TMA amongst its members as TMA thinks fit.

Sessional Work for Tours or Seasons—

1 per manager.

Subsidised Repertory Theatre, TIE, and Young People's Theatre:

(a) artist—1 per manager

(b) technical ASM's—1 per manager

both (a) and (b) to be allocated by TMA amongst its members as TMA thinks fit.

The quota year runs from August 1. Except for the quota for Resident Seasons or Provincial Theatre Tours, if any part of a quota has not been allocated by TMA in a quota year it may be applied during the first four months of the next quota year.

If a manager wishes to engage an artist who does not satisfy the requirements—or to exceed the quota—then he must give reasons in writing to Equity. Within seven days of the receipt of the statement Equity must either consent to the engagement or reply that it considers the manager has not made out his case. In the latter event a manager can appeal to the Provincial Theatre Council which must meet within seven days of the notice of appeal. If the Council finds in favour of the manager, or fails to reach a decision the manager may proceed with the engagement. If the Council rules against the manager then he may not engage the person concerned. When Equity consents to the engagement of an artist, or the engagement is otherwise permitted as just noted the artist is deemed to be an "approved" artist for the purposes as explained in Section B of Part 2 below.

West End Theatre:

The West End Theatre Casting Agreement is for West End theatrical productions (excluding opera and ballet), and pre-West End tours and post-West End tours and applies to artists and stage management staff. It alone stipulates that to qualify for an engagement an artist must normally have not less than 30 weeks of professional experience. Full membership of Equity is deemed to be proof of such experience. No quota provisions are included in the Agreement. When a manager wishes to engage a person who does not satisfy this requirement the same procedure applies as described above except that (a) when the person to be engaged is under 21 Equity must respond to a manager's statement within 48 hours and (b) any appeal against a rejection by Equity is made to the London Theatre Council.

The collective agreements for other persons variously engaged for theatrical productions—for opera and ballet, as director, choreographer, designer—do not contain corresponding or equivalent casting provisions. However the agreements incorporate provisions whereby a manager undertakes that if the person engaged is not a member of Equity he/she will be encouraged to apply for membership, and that irrespective of such a person applying for membership he/she will not be engaged on terms less favourable than those set out in the applicable collective agreement.

Television Broadcasting

In the General Agreement between the BBC and Equity for the engagement of artists and performers in television programmes the BBC undertakes to endeavour to ensure that for the categories of engagements covered by the Agreement only professional performers are employed. When a person not having a professional status is to be engaged, or when an amateur, or amateur group of players, is to be employed to provide a contribution which in the opinion of the BBC a professional(s) cannot do, then Equity is to be informed as soon as practicable. Equity may make representations concerning the engagement and if necessary have the issue considered at a formal Casting Conciliation Meeting attended by the programme director or producer. Although it may not approve of the engagement at such a meeting Equity undertakes not thereafter to take any action to impede the BBC's choice and the production of the programme.

When non-professional performers are engaged in capacities covered by the General Agreement it is the practice of the BBC to apply its terms and conditions to such engagements. This principle does not apply to amateur choirs, talent spotting programmes, or to non-professionals used in accordance with the BBC's policy of reflecting the different interests of the community. Normally only professional artists are engaged as Supporting Artists and Walk-ons for programmes produced in London and the Regions.

Under the Main Agreement between the Independent Television Programme Companies and Equity for the engagement of performers it is stipulated that it is the policy of the programme companies, in so far as it is reasonable and practical, to offer engagements subject to the Agreement to experienced professional performers. It is also provided that amateur artists will not be used to supplant professional performers and that amateur performances of special significance will not be unreasonably opposed by Equity. A programme company has the right to broadcast performances by bona fide amateur artists from time to time provided that such artists have not previously appeared in a company's programmes as amateur artists within a year. An exception to this principle is made for amateurs appearing in competitive programmes provided only one series of such programmes is presented by a programme company in any one year.

There is no undertaking in the Supplementary Walk-ons Agreement about casting but when such artists are required for performances at the established studios of programme companies it is usual, but not necessarily so, for local professional artists to be engaged.

Television Commercials

In the Agreement made between Equity and the Associations representing the producers of commercials and the advertising business it is provided that in the normal circumstances where appropriate and practical engagements as "featured artists" are to be offered to experienced professional performers though casting decisions remain within the discretion of a producer and advertiser. Engagements for stunts/fights are to be offered only to suitably qualified stunt artists and arrangers, or suitably qualified professionals.

In Part II of the Agreement which is for the engagement of walk-on and background artists, only in regard to walk-on artists is there any stipulation concerning casting. Where practical engagements are to be offered to professional performers, but casting decisions remain within the discretion of the producer and advertiser.

Film Industry

It was in 1966 that the first formal agreement and understanding on the casting of artists to perform in cinematograph films was reached between Equity and the British Film Producers Association. At the present time the collective agreements between the Producers Alliance for Cinema and Television (PACT) (as the lineal successor to the B.F.T.P.A.) and Equity are under review. As for the provisions on casting the principle that in normal circumstances engagements for parts in films which come within the scope of the collective agreements are to be offered only to experienced professional performers is being adopted.

Part 2

ARTISTS, DIRECTORS & OTHERS

A. THEATRE ENGAGEMENTS FOR ARTISTS

Standard contracts of engagement for employment on the professional stage (often referred to as "Esher" contracts for reasons explained below) were first adopted in 1935 when the London Theatre Council was established. Over the years minimum terms and conditions of employment and rates of pay have been negotiated between the Management Associations and Equity and set down in a number of collective agreements.

There are now standard contracts embracing theatrical entertainment of all kinds, from straight plays, musical plays, opera, ballet, pantomine to ice shows, and according to the place of entertainment, from West End theatres to seaside summer venues and "Theatre in Education". Moreover the standard contracts distinguish the roles and services rendered by professional persons who variously contribute to a theatrical production, from leading or principal artists to chorus line, and for stage management, directors, choreographers, designers and fight directors. In addition there are especially approved contracts to meet the special requirements of particular managements such as the Royal National Theatre, Royal Shakespeare Company, the Chichester Festival Theatre, and the Royal Exchange Theatre, Manchester, and of the national operatic and ballet companies.

All performers, artists and stage management engaged for the professional stage are engaged in accordance with and subject to the rules issued by the London and Provincial Theatre Councils (outlined in Section C below) which require as a condition of engagement that a manager is an "approved manager" and an artist is an "approved artist." However, it needs to be stressed that none of the rules impose any restraint on a manager with regards to the actual production, a manager's choice of professional artist for a part, or how a manager may stage or direct a play, save only for rules about nudity.

The following is an outline of the crucial terms of the contracts for the various kinds of theatrical engagement.

COLLECTIVE AGREEMENTS FOR ARTISTS AND STAGE MANAGEMENT

The three collective agreements which cover and apply to most theatrical engagements throughout the country are as follows:

A. January 1990—Agreement between the Society of West End Theatre and Equity for the employment of performers, understudies and stage management for theatrical performances at West End theatres and for pre-London and post-London tours.

B. April 1991—Agreement between the TMA and Equity for the employment of performers, understudies and stage management but excluding supernumeraries for theatrical performances at Provincial Theatres and other venues licensed for theatrical performances in the United Kingdom (other than Subsidised Repertory, opera and ballet).

C. April 1991—Agreement between the TMA and Equity for the employment of performers, understudies and stage management (but excluding "supernumeraries") by subsidised managements during a repertory season or repertoire season.

A "subsidised management" is defined as "one in receipt of subsidy from the Arts Council or Regional Arts Council or Association (or similar body), a local authority, a university or any other public body or private charitable institution."

A "repertory season" is defined as "a number of weeks of performances of plays at a theatre(s) at which the same management is presenting plays with approximately the same company of artists and/or nucleus of a working cast."

A "repertoire season" is defined as "a repertory season during which plays are repeated at intervals."

A "supernumerary" (also known as a "super") is defined as "a person who appears as a background artist who is not engaged to employ specific singing or dancing skills and who does not speak individual lines." He should be rehearsed not more than once and should attend technical and dress rehearsals as required. His role must be capable of being taken by another person at very short notice. Before supernumeraries are engaged Equity is to be informed.

These three collective agreements are structured alike as they each include the forms of standard contract appropriate to the particular engagement, a first schedule of general terms and conditions of employment, and a second schedule whereby the engagement is subject to the rules of the London or Provincial Theatre Councils and the procedure to be followed by way of arbitration and conciliation if a dispute arises. The casting agreements and the Agreement between Equity and Theatres' National Committee on nudity and simulated sex acts on stage are also incorporated into each of the agreements.

The agreements are intended to operate for a specified number of years and thereafter until either a management association or Equity gives to the other the prescribed notice of its proposals for revisions. However, particular provisions of these agreements are expressly designated "financial provisions"; for example, those dealing with minimum basic rates of pay, subsistence, allowances for travel, meals and the like, holiday pay and supplements for extra duties and responsibilities. These provisions are subject to annual review effective from January for the West End Theatre Agreement and April for the Provincial Theatre and the Subsidised Repertory Theatre Agreements. When new minimum rates are settled they become part of the terms of the collective agreements and therefore engagements already contracted become subject to the new minimum rates as well as, of course, all subsequently contracted engagements.

The standard forms of contract of engagement are devised to meet the general requirements of the areas of work they respectively cover but special provisions can be inserted to take account of any exceptional requirements or conditions of an engagement provided such variations are not less favourable than the prescribed minimum rates or terms and conditions of employment.

Unless it is impossible to do so normally a manager must issue the appropriate contract prior to an artist's first day of rehearsal. Three copies of a contract should be prepared since, apart from the manager and artist each having signed copies, a copy is required to be sent to Equity. The following is an outline of the various forms of contract of engagement.

West End Theatre

There is one standard form of contract which provides for one out of a possible 10 different kinds of engagement covering both principals and chorus for a play, or alternatively one out of three different kinds of engagement for a review. An artist must perform at such theatres in the West End and in the provinces before the first performance in the West End, as a manager requires. The total number of weeks during which an artist can be required to perform in the provinces may not exceed eight, except for musicals. With musical plays a total of 12 weeks of tour is permitted and which may be both before and after the West End run but any post-West End tour may not exceed four weeks and its duration must be notified to an artist before the ending of the West End run.

The period of the engagement must be specified and for this there are three options as follows:

1. For the period of rehearsal and run of the play provided that:

   (a) the engagement may be terminated by either party at or after 12 months (15 months for musicals) from the date of an artist's first paid performance by not less than four weeks notice in writing so as to expire after the last performance on a Saturday;

(b) a manager gives not less than two weeks notice of the termination of the run of the play or pays two weeks salary in lieu of notice;

(c) for an artist engaged solely to understudy an engagement may be terminated at any time after it has subsisted in the West End for 13 weeks by the artist giving not less than six weeks prior written notice at any time after the seventh week together with written evidence of an offer to him and his acceptance of another theatrical, television or film engagement as a principal. After 20 weeks from the first West End performance the artist is entitled to give the required six weeks notice unconditionally.

2. For the period of rehearsal and thereafter until either party gives to the other not less than four weeks written notice at any time after the artist's first performance in the West End.

3. For a specific period of time but for not more than 12 months or for the run of the production whichever shall be the shorter, provided the manager gives not less than two weeks notice of the termination of the run. (The provision of the above paragraph for understudies applies to "walking understudies" engaged on this basis.)

Normally an engagement begins on the day an artist first attends the theatre to read or rehearse following a call by a manager. The form of engagement must specify the date for the start of rehearsals (or not more than seven days thereafter) and the date of the first paid performance (or not more than 14 days thereafter), and the number of performances in a week, namely eight if the production is once-nightly, 12 if twice-daily or twice-nightly, or two performances on any one day.

The artist's salary at the agreed weekly rate is to be stated and is expressed as exclusive of such allowances and additional payments as may be due under the general conditions of the engagement. Where the artist's agreed weekly salary is above the stipulated minimum then during the initial rehearsal period for up to five weeks (seven for musicals) a manager is entitled to pay the artist less than his salary but not less than the minimum rate.

Provision is made for an artist to be paid a retainer for up to two weeks where there is an interval between the time of an artist's last performance in a production in the provinces under an engagement on a non-West End Theatre Contract and the start of rehearsals under a West End Theatre engagement. Also if during the non-West End Theatre engagement an artist rehearses for the West End presentation of a production a daily rehearsal supplement is payable.

Provincial Theatre

There are four separate standard contracts of engagement for performers appearing at Provincial Theatres namely:

1. for Resident Seasons in provincial theatres;

2. for Provincial Theatre Tours;

3. for Non-Subsidised Repertory at provincial theatres;

4. for Sessional work for tours or seasons in the provinces, *e.g.* children's theatre, studios, workshops, etc.

The forms of engagement for each of the first three categories of engagement distinguish between principals and chorus and for each of these two classes there is detailed the particular kinds of performance for which an artist can be engaged. For Sessional work there is one list of seven kinds of performance. The title or kind of production or presentation must be entered on the form and the place(s) of performance as appropriate. The date of the commencement of the engagement must be entered (but this can be varied by a manager by up to seven days either side by giving not less than eight weeks prior written notice) and the duration of the engagement specified.

There are provisions common to all four contracts about the duration of an engagement but there are important differences with regard to the giving of notice of termination. So an engagement may be for:

1. the period of rehearsal and the duration of the season or tour subject to a manager giving not less than two weeks written notice of termination or paying two weeks salary in lieu;

2. the period of rehearsal and then until either party gives not less than an agreed specified number of days notice in writing (but not less than 14) at any time after the artist's first performance, the notice to expire after the last performance of the working week; (*N.B.* this provision does not apply to Repertory engagements)

3. the period of rehearsal and then for a specified number of consecutive weeks;

4. (Repertory engagements only) the period of rehearsal and then until either party gives not less than an agreed specified number of days notice in writing (but not less than 14) the notice not to expire before the last performance of the production in which the artist is rehearsing or performing on the date the notice is given;

5. (Repertory engagements only) the period of rehearsal and on tour as specified in the form of engagement.

The rate of weekly salary payable to artists is variable for the rehearsal period and actual performances. The rehearsal salary which must be specified is payable from the commencement of the engagement and then for the first five weeks of preliminary rehearsals. Thereafter, but in any event from the day of an artist's first performance, the stated weekly performance salary becomes payable. The salaries are exclusive of subsistence and touring allowances and any other sums payable under the general conditions of engagement.

Each of the separate contracts also makes provision as required for special payments for particular duties and the number of performances to be given in a week namely, eight if once-nightly, 12 if twice-daily or twice-nightly. The contract for Provincial Theatre Tours alone makes provision for "weeks out" (but for not more than one week per complete five weeks of an engagement) with the payment of a minimum salary and other mutual terms.

Subsidised Repertory Theatre

There is one standard form of contract whereby an artist is engaged to perform at a named theatre or in such theatres and towns as a manager may require. An engagement may be to play a specific part or parts, or to play as cast, or to play as cast and to understudy if required, or to play as cast and in addition undertake the duties of assistant stage manager, or to play as cast and understudy if required and in addition undertake the duties of assistant stage manager. Separate from these five kinds of engagement is an engagement as an actor/teacher to assist in the devising and presentation of programmes, workshops, demonstrations, courses and pre-production sessions and to devise and/or take part in performances of plays.

The period of an engagement commences on the date entered on the contract and continues for either—

(a) an indefinite period but terminable by either party giving an agreed specified number of days notice (but not less than 28 or in the case of Theatre in Education, 56), the notice to be in writing and not to expire before the last performance of the production in which an artist is appearing at the date when the notice is given, or

(b) a guaranteed specific number of consecutive weeks.

The agreed rate of weekly salary is to be inserted in the contract, this being exclusive of subsistence and any other payments due under the general conditions of engagement.

Stage Management

Each of the three collective agreements described above includes a standard form of contract for the engagement of artists as stage management which are similar to the contracts for performers. The precise services to be rendered, rates of pay and the number of performances to be given in a week must be specified by a manager. The West End contract provides for the combined appointment of company manager and stage manager but not for the services of a company manager alone. It and the Subsidised Repertory contract precludes the inclusion of services as understudy at any level of stage management.

The contracts provide for the commencement, duration and termination of an engagement in much the same terms as the contracts for performers as noted above. The West End contract exceptionally permits an artist to terminate an engagement on grounds of betterment, *i.e.* by providing written evidence of an offer and acceptance of another engagement when a production has subsisted for 13 weeks. Four weeks notice of termination is required; it can be given at any time after the ninth week of a run of performances. An artist is also entitled to terminate an engagement if during it more than 80 per cent. of the cast has been changed. Notice must be given in writing to expire on the Saturday of the fourth week of performance by the new cast.

Appendices to the schedules to the West End and the Provincial Theatre Agreements set out the terms and conditions of employment special to stage management covering for example, rehearsal periods, hours of work, Sunday working hours and the transfer of duties to a more senior level. Also there are provisions dealing with extra services such as preparing a prompt script or acting edition of a play, auditioning, preparing for a production other than that named in the contract, and acting or understudying by assistant stage managers. For all such services additional payments are due.

Both of the appendices prescribed the minimum team or complement of stage management staff to be appointed for a production. Also prescribed are the limitations on a member of the stage management team acting or understudying when only a minimum stage management staff is appointed.

There is no appendix to the Subsidised Repertory Theatre Agreement dealing with stage management as the schedule of conditions of engagement applies to both performers and stage management. However, the schedule prescribes for the engagement of the minimum of stage management staff.

COLLECTIVE AGREEMENTS FOR OPERA AND BALLET

There are separate collective agreements between the Society of West End Theatre and the Theatrical Management Association (jointly) and Equity for opera singers, for guest opera singers, for dancers and for stage management for opera and ballet. Many of the provisions of these agreements are like those of the foregoing three theatrical collective agreements. Minimum terms and conditions of employment and rates of pay are prescribed for the various engagements and standard forms of contract are made part of each of the agreements.

Each of the collective agreements is approved by the London and Provincial Theatre Councils which have the like standing and authority with regard to the approval of managers and artists and the settlement of disputes as under the theatrical collective agreements. There are separate "house" agreements for a few opera and ballet companies which provide for special rates of pay and conditions of employment but on terms no less favourable than under the collective agreements.

Opera Singers

The Collective Agreement for opera singers of May 1991 prescribes the minimum terms and conditions of employment for singers engaged to perform roles, to understudy, or as members of the chorus. The standard form of contract of engagement between a management and an artist provides for:

(a) a description of the services to be rendered,

(b) the period of the engagement and the commencement date (but which may be on some other day not more than two weeks before or one week after that date at the discretion of the manager), and

(c) the amount of the artist's weekly salary.

Throughout the period of the engagement a manager is entitled to an artist's exclusive services but may not unreasonably withhold consent to an artist performing for a third party provided that the publication of the artist's name is accompanied by due acknowledgment to the manager. An artist is required before signing his contract to give to a manager written particulars of all engagements previously entered into which have to be fulfilled during either the rehearsal or the performance period of the engagement.

Opera singers are engaged on the basis of their attending a number of working sessions, a session consisting of three hours. A "working session" means a performance, a rehearsal, a call for costume fitting, or a nominated dress rehearsal. A "nominated dress rehearsal" is a rehearsal nominated as such by a manager. It may be either of four hours duration (with a performance on the day if required), or of six hours with no performance on the day. It counts as two working sessions and one hour of overtime is automatically payable. There may not in the aggregate be more than one nominated dress rehearsal per month of an artist's engagement, or 12 in any one year.

An artist may not be required to render services for more than two working sessions on any one day; a break of at least one hour is to be allowed between sessions. An artist performing a principal part or role may not normally be required to rehearse during the afternoon of the day on which he performs.

The agreed weekly salary is for an artist's attendance at up to 10 sessions Monday to Saturday, and up to 11 sessions in a pre-production week when a company gives no public performance. This number of sessions includes the performances an artist is to give in a week, the number of which must be entered in the contract. The number may not exceed six, but for short performances, *i.e.* performances of 90 minutes or less, the limit is eight. A minimum of one-sixth of an artist's weekly salary, or pro rata if the number of performances contracted is less than six, is payable when an artist consents to rendering his services in excess of the prescribed number of sessions. It is also payable when an artist gives more performances in a week than as specified in the contract but only one-eighth of the weekly salary is payable for a short performance.

An artist cannot be required to rehearse on more than three Sundays in each period of three months. A rehearsal session on a Sunday counts as two sessions at the rate of one-fifth of the artist's weekly salary.

Guest Opera Singers

The Collective Agreement of March 1992 prescribes the terms and conditions of employment of guest artists for opera, meaning those singers who are engaged to perform a specific role in a particular operatic production. It has to be recognised that for star opera singers and especially those of international standing their terms of engagement are often individually negotiated by a manager with the artist's agent. Moreover, issues outside the provisions of the Agreement arise and need to be agreed upon, such as the appointment of the music director and engagement of other artists to appear in the production, publicity, arrangements for any broadcast relay and links with recording companies.

The standard form of contract provides for an engagement as a performer or "cover" (understudy) and for there to be inserted:

(a) the date(s), time(s) and place(s) of performance;

(b) the role(s) to be performed and in what language;

(c) the period during which or the dates on which there are rehearsals;

(d) the fees payable which may be specified separately for learning/rehearsals/performance/cover, or else an inclusive fee negotiated.

Minimum rates are prescribed being a minimum weekly salary and session fee, a minimum performance fee, a minimum cover fee, and a minimum inclusive fee.

The Agreement makes provision for "working sessions" in terms as in the Agreement for opera singers. An artist singing a principal role may not be called upon to rehearse on the day he/she performs except in an emergency. Solo music calls if made at the request of the artist do not count as working sessions or qualify for payment but any other calls by a manager are treated as working sessions and qualify for payment.

Under this Agreement a manager is not entitled to an artist's exclusive services during his engagement. However, an artist may not perform or otherwise render his services to any third party without the consent of the manager but which is not to be unreasonably withheld. At the time of the signing of the contract an artist is to declare in writing all engagements already entered into to be fulfilled during the rehearsal or performance period. If an artist resides overseas then the town in which the management company is based is deemed the artist's base for the purposes of the payment of travel and other allowances for tours and the like. The arrangements for the artist's travel from his home overseas to the town in which the company is based is a matter for individual negotiation.

Ballet

The Collective Agreement for ballet and dance artists of July 1990 between the Society of West End Theatre and the Theatrical Management Association (jointly) and Equity applies only to professional dancers. The employment of student dancers at any theatre is subject to special negotiation between an individual management and Equity.

The standard form of contract of engagement between a management and an artist provides for:

(a) a description of the services to be rendered, embracing rehearsing, understudying, playing or dancing as required, or specific roles;

(b) the commencement and duration of the engagement which may be continuous for up to 52 weeks (inclusive of any holiday period);

(c) the amount of the weekly salary for which a minimum rate is prescribed.

An artist's services are exclusive to a manager during the period of an engagement. Thus if an artist wishes to perform or otherwise exercise his talents for the benefit of any other company, institution or person a manager's consent is required but may not be unreasonably withheld.

The negotiated weekly salary is for an artist's services for a maximum of 33 hours in a week (Monday to Saturday). These weekly hours are inclusive of rehearsals, a maximum of eight performances (a performance counts as three hours), travel time, costume fittings, placing, photocalls and company promotional work. If an artist is required to give more than eight performances in a week then for every additional performance one eighth of the weekly salary is payable. When the additional performances result in the basic 33 hours being exceeded then the fee for an additional performance is one sixth of the artist's weekly salary. Supplementary fees are payable for performances on statutory holidays. A full week's salary is payable for a broken week occurring at the commencement or termination of an engagement unless a mid-week start or end is at the request of an artist when one sixth of the weekly salary is payable for each day worked.

An artist must attend a minimum of four one-hour classes a week and a manager must provide not less than one class on each working day except on matinee days when an artist's attendance at a "warm up" is optional. A manager's consent is required for an artist's attendance at private classes to count towards the prescribed four minimum attendances. With engagements for a period of 52 weeks or more there should be rehearsal periods totalling five weeks during the engagement. There may not be more than one designated dress rehearsal for each ballet per season.

Normally an artist should be released from a class or rehearsal on a performance day two hours before the rise of the curtain but this rest period may be waived by agreement between the manager and the artist(s). The two hours may be reduced to one and a half hours for tours on a nightly basis, or on the first night of a touring date. If travel time exceeds three hours there should be an interval of two hours between arrival and a rehearsal. An artist's working day may not be more than 12 hours from the time of first call (inclusive of travel and break time and time at class, rehearsal and performance) to the time of final release. No class or rehearsal may start before 10 a.m. and no rehearsal (other than a designated dress rehearsal) may last beyond 9 p.m. accept in an emergency.

The Agreement specifies those services which are subject to overtime payments and the rates applicable according to when the services are rendered; also when travel time counts as working time or attracts overtime payment. There are special provisions governing touring and subsistence payments, illness, for payment for necessary treatment due to injury sustained at work, and the making by a manager of a video recording of a rehearsal.

There are two appendices to the Agreement the first of which relates to the non-renewal of an artist's contract after a continuous period of employment of at least 52 weeks on the grounds of "capability." Capability is assessed "by reference to skill, aptitude, health or any other physical or mental quality." Procedures are prescribed for any dispute in this regard. The second of the appendices provides for the retirement of ballet dancers by discussion between an artistic director, administrator and the artist concerned.

There is no standard or collective agreement for the engagement of guest ballet artists corresponding to that for guest opera singers described above. Such engagements will need to be individually negotiated and any special terms and conditions agreed. Where only the essential terms of an engagement are on record if any issue should arise concerning the engagement then it is likely the standard conditions would be deemed to apply.

Stage Management for Opera and Ballet

The Collective Agreement for Stage Management for opera and ballet of April 1991 between the Society of West End Theatre and the Theatrical Management Association (jointly) and Equity prescribes the minimum rates and conditions of employment of stage management and the minimum team to be engaged on a production.

The standard form of contract of engagement between a manager and an artist provides for:

- (a) the services to be rendered, that is one of four capacities namely, company and stage manager, stage manager, deputy stage manager or assistant stage manager;

- (b) the commencement and duration of the engagement which may be continuous for up to 52 weeks (inclusive of any holiday period);

- (c) the amount of the weekly salary.

Throughout the period of the engagement a manager is entitled to an artist's exclusive services but may not unreasonably withhold consent to an artist performing for a third party provided that the publication of the artist's name is accompanied by due acknowledgment to the manager. An artist is required before signing his contract to provide a manager with written particulars of all engagements previously entered into which have to be fulfilled during either the rehearsal or the performance period of the engagement.

The stage management team for an opera normally comprises one stage manager, one deputy stage manager and one assistant stage manager; for ballet there must be at least one stage manager. By agreement between a manager and Equity the minimum team may be reduced for opera or augmented for opera and ballet according to the needs of a particular production or the special circumstances under which a production is to be presented.

The weekly salary payable to an artist is for his services for a total of 44 hours rendered Monday to Saturday between 9.00 a.m. and midnight exclusive of breaks but inclusive of travel. The Agreement contains detailed provisions for the payment of overtime and for the payment of additional sums for work outside the hours of 9.00 a.m. and midnight, when breaks are not taken during these hours, for work on Sundays and statutory holidays and for travel on a Sunday. The time worked for which overtime is payable does not count towards the basic 44 hours whereas, by inference, time worked for which additional sums are payable does. A full week's salary is payable for a broken week if occurring at the commencement or termination of an engagement unless a mid-week starting or end is at the request of an artist when one-sixth of the weekly salary is payable for each day worked.

If on account of absence the duties of a senior artist are required to be undertaken by another artist, then that other artist is entitled to be paid not less than the appropriate minimum rate of the senior grade unless such absences are occasional and do not exceed 24 hours at any one time. If an artist is required to appear in a performance on stage in a costume designed for the production a special supplemental fee is payable for each performance. If an artist is required to wear a particular form of formal dress a standard weekly sum is payable by a manager as a contribution to the cost.

The Agreement provides that in the normal course of events a manager will not engage a person who has less than 30 weeks professional experience as a company and stage manager, or stage manager, or deputy stage manager, or a person who has no professional experience as an assistant stage manager. These provisions are qualified to the extent that a manager has the right (a) to employ one assistant stage manager per stage management team per year who has no previous professional experience, and (b) to appeal to the appropriate Theatre Council if Equity shall have rejected a manager's request for any exemption from these provisions.

OVERSEAS TOURS

When a theatrical production (including opera and ballet) is to tour overseas the provisions of the Collective Agreement between the Theatres' National Committee and Equity of August 1987 apply by way of addendum to an artist's original contract of engagement. Where a production is assembled for an overseas tour only, without prior presentation and performance in the United Kingdom, then normally artists are contracted initially under the Provincial Theatre Agreement. In its schedule there are set out the minimum conditions to be observed in such matters as accommodation, subsistence, travel arrangements, insurance and rest periods. As soon as reasonably practicable a manager must supply Equity with full details of the itinerary for the tour with details of the proposed travel arrangements and subsistence and which Equity may comment on within two weeks of receiving the details.

The Collective Agreement incorporates a standard form which must be signed by a manager and artist with the date of the artist's original contract of engagement inserted and thereby extending the engagement on the terms therein set out (unless expressly varied) for the duration of the tour which must be specified together with the countries where performances are to be given.

As in the course of a tour the local conditions of employment and rules of a performers' union may need to be observed, the Agreement makes allowance for the modification of the Equity standard terms and conditions accordingly. Thus where an artist is required to perform on a Sunday the performance counts as part of the aggregate of performances to be given for the agreed contracted weekly salary. Normally an artist cannot be called upon to perform, rehearse or travel or attend any other call for more than six consecutive days and then only exceptionally without additional payment.

An appendix to the Agreement makes provision for the recording for broadcasting locally in news bulletins and magazine programmes of rehearsals, performances and backstage activities and for the payment of fees and repeat fees. These provisions will apply unless there are like provisions under the rules of the local performers' union.

GENERAL CONDITIONS OF THEATRE ENGAGEMENTS

It has been shown above that the schedules to the collective agreements prescribe the minimum rates of pay and contain the detailed terms and conditions of employment which attach to a contract of engagement. The terms and conditions are obligatory and may not be altered or omitted or added to except for (a) special stipulations relating to an artist's position in billings and advertisements, (b) special stipulations due to the exceptional requirements of particular engagements or other exceptional circumstances, and (c) special stipulations for conditional cancellations or postponements of contracts. If a complaint is made to or by a management association or Equity that these provisions are not being fairly adhered to the matter falls to be investigated by the appropriate Theatre Council under the conciliation procedure.

These schedules contain provisions such as may be found in any like collective agreement on working conditions. Thus there are paragraphs covering minimum salaries and fees, the services to be rendered, hours of work and times of attendance, overtime, travel time, subsistence, holidays, work on public holidays, illness and absence from work. In addition, there are provisions special to the theatre dealing with such matters as costume and make-up, publicity, billing, production photographs, minimum rehearsals, understudies and cast changes, short run guarantees, touring and broken weeks during tours, a production being cancelled, the suspension and omission of an artist from a performance, and the manner in which complaints that contracts are not being fairly observed are to be dealt with.

Although many provisions of the schedules to each of the collective agreements are alike there are important differences of detail. Some provisions are special in that they reflect the differing needs and working arrangements in the branch of the theatre covered by a particular collective agreement.

As the schedules comprise many pages and paragraphs it is impractical to review each of them here but there are some provisions which are common, or for all intents and purposes common, to all the schedules and merit particular attention and comment.

Exclusivity

All the collective agreements confer on a manager the right to an artist's exclusive services during the continuance of the engagement but some concession is allowed under the West End Theatre Agreement for an artist performing at another West End theatre during the rehearsal period and under the Provincial Theatre Agreement for "weeks out" on tours. The provisions concerning exclusivity of an engagement are all qualified to the extent of allowing an artist to accept other professional engagements with a manager's consent, such consent not to be unreasonably withheld.

A right to a person's exclusive services means there is a complete bar on that person rendering his professional services to a third person or on his own account, even gratuitously. If an artist engages in the making of records or programmes for public broadcast or in advertising commercials there is an infringement of a manager's right to the artist's exclusive services although the theatrical engagement may not be in the least affected. However, if an artist engages in some other activity, such as authorship, outside his profession of acting then no objection can be made to such pursuits so long as they do not conflict with or impair his ability to render the services he has contracted to perform.

By accepting an engagement an artist is deemed to imply that he is free to accept it and has no obligations to a third party which would preclude him from properly performing his services. Provisions to this effect are expressly included in the Subsidised Repertory and the Provincial Theatre Agreements. Accordingly if an artist has a current professional commitment of any kind which is likely to overlap the period of the proposed theatrical engagement the commitment ought to be disclosed even though it may not clash with or be detrimental to the theatrical engagement. Conversely, by accepting the theatrical engagement an artist could jeopardise an existing engagement if it was contracted on the basis of his rendering his exclusive services.

Barring and Restrictions

The engagement of a leading celebrity may be made subject to the acceptance by that artist of certain restrictions on his future appearances immediately following the engagement, such as not performing within a specified radius within a given time, or not performing the same role for another management or in some other medium, or not appearing on television or radio broadcasting. All such barring provisions which restrict an artist pursuing his profession and earning his living are viewed critically in law. Even so a manager has a right to protect his legitimate interests and protect both the investment in a production and his obligations to the company of artists and others engaged for the production.

It is not easy to say precisely what restraints would be allowed as essentially the issue rests on the particular circumstances at the time. However, the principle is clear that restraints are not easily tolerated and if they are challenged the onus will rest on the management seeking to enforce them to justify them.

A special term might also be introduced requiring an artist to disclose his appearances—especially on television—before the commencement of the contracted engagement. Obviously this cannot affect the pre-existing engagements but a material misrepresentation by an artist in this regard could render him liable for breach of contract.

Use of Services

If an artist is engaged to rehearse and perform or otherwise render his services then provided he is, in the rather hallowed expression, "ready, willing and able" to render his services he is entitled to receive the agreed remuneration until the engagement expires or is suspended or is terminated in accordance with the terms of the contract. Exceptionally events may happen which frustrate the engagement entirely or result in its suspension such as the cancellation of a performance or closure of a theatre on account of circumstances of force majeure. The collective agreements variously provide for these contingencies and the obligation of a manager to make any payment to an artist.

In the event of a manager failing to produce or abandoning the production of a play or other theatrical production for which an artist has been engaged, compensation is payable to the artist in settlement of all claims against a manager. Under the West End and Provincial Theatre Agreements the amount of compensation is calculated according to the number of weeks' advance notice given of the abandonment before the start of rehearsals and the stipulated number of weeks of an artist's performance salary consequently payable. The shorter the period of notice the greater the number of weeks of salary payable. Under the Subsidised Repertory Agreement there is payable either a sum equal to four weeks' salary (eight weeks for Theatre in Education), or the entire salary if an artist is engaged for a guaranteed period. All three collective agreements provide that whatever sum is payable it may be reduced by the amount an artist earns from other engagements during the period of the cancelled engagement since an artist has the responsibility to mitigate his loss from the breach of contract.

When a production has commenced its run but is withdrawn prematurely an artist's rights are governed by his contract of engagement. With a fixed term contract the balance of his aggregate salary is payable as if the engagement had run its full term. Where an engagement is open ended *e.g.* for the run of the play or for the season, then the provisions of the collective agreements guaranteeing minimum payments, in addition to any payments accrued due when notice is given, become crucial. Under the West End Theatre Agreement payment of an artist's salary is guaranteed for six weeks inclusive of rehearsals; eight weeks if a production opens out of London. The guarantee does not apply to seasons anticipated to be of less than six weeks, or to temporary cast replacements or understudies. Under the Provincial Theatre Agreement a minimum of two weeks' performance salary is guaranteed. With engagements under the Subsidised Repertory Theatre Agreement unless due notice is given an amount equal to an artists' salary is payable as if notice had been given. It is to ensure the enforceability of these obligations that managers are required to be approved and registered by the Theatre Councils as explained in Section C below.

In the past the courts ruled that the opportunity for an artist to perform and advance his professional standing was as much part of the consideration and inducement for him to accept an engagement as the fees or salary payable. By preventing an artist performing, unless on account of his own fault, a manager was in breach of an implied term of the contract that the artist would be allowed to perform so consequently giving grounds for the artist to claim damages. This legal nicety has been over-come in as much as the collective agreements provide that a manager may suspend an artist from any performance or number of performances regardless of his appearance having been advertised but must continue to pay the artist's salary. The reasons for the suspension must be notified to the artist in writing and reported to Equity and Equity can request the appropriate Theatre Council to consider and adjudicate on the manager's decision.

Manner of Performance

Each of the collective agreements stipulates, in much the same way, that an artist is to perform his services diligently and competently, to play the part as directed by the manager and not to insert in or omit any words or business from the artist's part not approved by the manager.

The legal sanction of the first element of this undertaking is hard to assess as actual proof of its breach would not be easy. One serious instance alone may be sufficient to demonstrate that an artist has failed to honour the obligation or the failure may be shown by a course of conduct over a period of time. Failing in diligence and not performing as directed are issues of fact which if established may justify the termination of an engagement. Where an artist has been cast but his performances are not as expected that would not necessarily amount to a failure by the artist to honour the undertaking unless he showed a serious lack of professional competence. In such a situation a manager may perhaps omit the artist from performances and report this to the appropriate Theatre Council in the way mentioned above but not terminate the engagement.

The second and third elements of the undertaking are important because disregard of them can have critical legal consequences for both artist and manager beyond the ambit of the contract itself. In Part 8 below the legal aspects of the giving of a performance are considered at length but suffice it to note the provisions of the Theatres Act 1968 which render a person liable to prosecution if a performance is obscene, or provokes a breach of the peace or by the provisions of the Public Order Act 1986 incites racial hatred. It is the person who presents or directs the perform-ance who is liable to prosecution and not the performer unless the latter person performs otherwise than as instructed by the director of the play. In any proceedings brought under the Acts the script is material evidence of what was performed and so if an artist makes changes to his part without approval and does not perform as directed it follows that he places himself at a risk if a performance is held to have contravened the Acts.

The undertaking not to insert in or omit any words or business from a part without a manager's approval is also important because if the changes should be defamatory of a person both a manager and artist may be liable for damages for libel. If the changes are not approved then an artist would be in breach of his undertaking and liable to have his contract terminated and forfeit any indemnity he might otherwise have from a manager for the claims of a third party. Indeed he may be liable to indemnify the manager for loss suffered by the manager.

In both the West End Theatre Agreement and the Provincial Theatre Agreement there is a provision whereby a manager expressly represents that a production does not violate the law and that the manager will defend and indemnify an artist if a claim or charge is brought against him on account of a breach of the law or the rights of a third party. This provision, although re-assuring by its presence, is little more than declaratory of what can reasonably be inferred by a manager's offer of an engagement, namely that he has the right to cause the production to be performed and by performing it as directed the artist will not be infringing any person's civil rights or be in breach of the law. The manager as the provider of the scripts and material can reasonably be assumed to have obtained the necessary licences of copyright owners and to have resolved any other legal issues likely to arise from the performance of the material, such as libel or any contravention of the Theatres Act.

If the material is provided by the artist then it is legitimate for a manager to require to be satisfied about these same matters and to obtain an express indemnity to avoid the risk of liability to others. Only the Subsidised Repertory Theatre Agreement covers the situation of an artist including in his performance material not supplied by a manager. Still the manager's consent is required but when it is given it imports a warranty by the artist that he has the right to use the material, that it does not infringe copyright and that the artist will indemnify the manager should this not be so. However the warranty does not extend to the material not being defamatory and so an additional express indemnity from the artist may be required if the content of the material should justify one.

Billing and Advertising

The forms of engagement do not provide for artists to be accorded billing and publicity. The collective agreements variously but not consistently provide for artists' names to be announced in programmes or cast lists. Any agreement concerning the form, position, size or extent of the credit and publicity to be given to an artist therefore needs to be annexed to the form of engagement.

The relevant provisions of the collective agreements are as follows:

(a) **West End of London**—Where the names of all the artists (other than children) appearing in the production are not billed on a poster or otherwise, the manager must place in the Front of the House a board on which the names of all artists (other than children) appearing in the production are listed in alphabetical order.

For cast replacements the order may be varied at the manager's discretion. An artist has the right of approving all biographical material to be included in programmes. Any errors in the programme must be corrected by a slip or reprint as soon as practical. Once an artist has left a production his name and photograph are to be dropped from all advertising and publicity as soon as reasonable and practical and his replacement properly advertised.

All understudies are to be listed in programmes if they so require.

If there is a change of cast, other than a change of ensemble parts in large-scale musicals, the programme must be slipped with the name of the replacement or understudy and the character portrayed as well as the name of the actor being replaced. An announcement from the stage of a cast change is permissible only in an emergency. Written notice in reasonable size of a cast change is to be displayed in the foyer and remain there until the audience has left the theatre.

(b) **Provincial Theatre**—The manager has the sole right to determine the inclusion and/or the position of the artist's name and the size and nature of the type on all bills, programmes and advertisements. Programmes are at all times to show the current cast and stage management other than in emergencies or for an understudy replacement when the programmes are to be slipped showing the name of the artist appearing. If biographies are included in programmes an artist, if reasonably available, has a right of prior approval. A manager must endeavour to ensure that all publicity for a production relates only to the current cast.

(c) **Subsidised Repertory Theatre**—The provisions are virtually the same as for the Provincial Theatre except that with regard to cast changes an announcement may be made to an audience or the programme slipped and written notice exhibited in the foyer and at the box office of the theatre.

(d) **Opera and Ballet**—The Agreements provide simply that a manager has the sole right to determine the inclusion and/or the position of the artist's name and the size and nature of the type on all bills and advertisements and its position in the programme.

Production Photographs

The West End Theatre and the Provincial Theatre Agreements make provision for photographic calls and for a manager to have the right to exhibit and reproduce photographs of artists.

During the rehearsal of a production photographic calls are deemed part of rehearsal time. After a production has opened an artist can be required to attend one photographic session without payment but all subsequent calls are subject to the payment of a minimum sessional rate. A session is four hours inclusive of time for make-up and dressing.

The copyright in production photographs commissioned by a manager will normally belong to the manager but the collective agreements stipulate that a manager must use his best endeavours to ensure that photographs are not published for any purpose other than for publicity or advertising the production or the season of which it forms part. Any extended use of photographs requires an artist's prior agreement.

The West End Theatre Agreement contains additional provisions about photographs for cast replacements and artists required to pose nude. When there are cast changes (except due to illness or holidays) then any photographs displayed containing four or less members of the cast are to be replaced. If an artist leaves a cast he can request the photograph to be removed and if a manager unreasonably refuses the request the artist is entitled to have the matter considered by the London Theatre Council. If any photograph on display contains three principal artists who have left the production, then the photograph must be removed immediately.

If an artist is required to pose for photographs involving any element of nudity a manager must first obtain the artist's consent. No such photographs can be released for publication or display without first obtaining the artist's written consent and, with a West End engagement, a signed copy being deposited with Equity.

Recording and Broadcasting of a Production

An artist is engaged to rehearse and perform a part on the stage before an audience so that any other use or exploitation of his services needs his express approval. This principle has been fortified by the reforms to the law brought about by the Copyright, Designs and Patents Act 1988 so that an artist's consent is required for any recording or broadcasting of his performance. Performers' rights are considered in Part 5.

The collective agreements variously provide for the recording of the whole or a part of a rehearsal for playback during rehearsals. In addition, solely for the archival purposes of a manager, but subject to the unanimous consent of the artists concerned (not to be unreasonably withheld), there may be a video recording made of a performance.

Individual or group voices may be recorded or pre-recorded by a manager to supplement or augment a production, and artists may be recorded on video or film for use in a production. The recordings may only be used for the duration of the production. When there is a cast change then if the contribution of an artist who has left the cast is publicly identifiable the material concerned must be re-recorded. In addition a manager may record crowd noises or snatches of dialogue or lyrics that could otherwise be performed live without extra payment provided the recording is made during normal rehearsal hours.

Radio and television broadcast relays of a theatrical production or rehearsal are subject to the general agreement between the Theatres' National Committee, Equity, the BBC and the Independent Television Programme Companies. The making of original cast record albums of musical shows is subject to the Agreement between the British Phonographic Industry (acting on behalf of record companies) and Equity. The making of films or video tape recordings for sale is subject to special agreement between a manager and artists. For all these wider uses of an artist's services additional fees are payable in accordance with the collective agreements considered in Part 4.

Absence and Misconduct

If an artist absents himself from any rehearsal or performance without good cause such as illness or accident then he is in breach of his contract. In all the collective agreements there are provisions dealing with the consequences of an artist so absenting himself. Ordinarily a manager is entitled to deduct one sixth of the artist's weekly rehearsal salary for absence from a rehearsal, and one eighth from the weekly performance salary for absence from a performance. With engagements under the Subsidised Repertory Agreement for an absence from a rehearsal the deduction is one sixteenth of the artist's weekly salary.

More stringent action may be taken by a manager. An engagement can be terminated forthwith on account of absence or at once reported to the appropriate Theatre Council. The summary termination of a contract of employment is a most extreme course and so in such an event the artist has the right exercisable through Equity to appeal to the Council which has the power to reverse the manager's decision or to direct such penalty as it thinks fit.

Compliance with the terms of an engagement and the observance of proper professional standards of conduct are further and more subtly secured by a provision in the collective agreements whereby if the conduct of an artist is such as to bring the company or management into disrepute then the management can either cancel the engagement or report the matter to the appropriate Theatre Council. A Council can award such penalty as it thinks fit and its decision is binding on the management and the artist. Whether an artist's conduct is such as to justify his summary dismissal and the termination of the engagement is a matter of law. A court or industrial tribunal might view the matter differently from a management. If this provision is invoked then the second alternative open to a management is to be preferred unless the circumstances are quite exceptional. Charges of intemperance are required to be dealt with at the time of the allegation and the artist concerned medically examined as soon as possible.

Arbitration and the Settlement of Disputes

Where parties by the terms of their agreement have laid down a procedure for dealing with disputes, that procedure must be adhered to, since as a matter of law, the provisions detailing how issues are to be resolved are as much a part of the agreement as the substantive terms. One party cannot of its own volition ignore those provisions and take legal proceedings in the courts, but from that it does not follow that one party alone cannot have recourse to the courts to ensure the procedures and rules contained in such provisions are correctly applied.

All the collective agreements (including those for directors and others considered in Section B below) contain provisions substantially alike, prescribing how an issue or dispute between an artist and a manager which cannot be settled between themselves is to be dealt with.

The general principle is that disputes which arise between an artist and a manager, or their respective representatives, concerning an artist's contract and the construction or application of the provisions of the relevant collective agreement (which form part of the contract), are to be referred to the London or Provincial Theatre Council as appropriate for a ruling which may be either a decision or recommendation. The constitution and role of each of the Councils in the affairs of the professional stage are considered more particularly in Section C below.

Certain disputed issues are expressly reserved for referral to and decision by a Theatre Council, for example: reports of the suspension of an artist from any performance or an artist absenting himself from a performance (except for illness or accident), complaints of professional misconduct, complaints that the provisions of a collective agreement are not being fairly observed. When complaints of this kind are made to a Theatre Council they must be adjudicated and settled in accordance with the procedures and powers of the Council as laid down in its constitution and the relevant collective agreement. Normally a decision must be given within seven days of a complaint being lodged unless Equity and the Management Association agree to an extension of time.

Where the issue is one on which a Theatre Council may give a recommendation, as distinct from a decision, then if either the artist or manager is unwilling to accept the recommendation the matter may then be referred to two arbitrators, one to be appointed by each party in accordance with the Arbitration Act 1950 as amended. One arbitrator is to be nominated by the manager and the other (to be appointed by the artist) nominated by Equity. This provision in no way affects or restricts the right of either of the parties from applying to the court for relief by way of injunction or an order for specific performance.

Nudity on the Stage

With the changes which have come about in recent years in attitudes towards matters of sex and nudity and how these may be presented on the stage, a revised agreement was made between Equity and the Theatres National Committee in January 1971 about personal appearances and simulated sex acts at auditions and performances, to help preserve the dignity of performers in their profession. This Agreement is annexed to each of the collective agreements so its terms are part of an artist's terms of engagement. The Agreement is reproduced here:

1. In respect of any production in which there is nudity and/or sex acts, all artists shall be informed in writing of this fact and of the general nature and extent of such nudity and/or acts prior to the conclusion of the contracts of engagement.

2. Where nudity and/or acts of a sexual nature are required of a performer in the course of a production, the performer must be so advised in writing, clearly indicating the extent of the requirements, including the degree of nudity and/or the nature and extent of any such acts required, in advance of his or her entering into a contract and the script must be submitted to the performer if he or she so requests prior to his or her being contracted.

3. No performer may be required to disrobe in whole or in part until after he or she has been auditioned as an actor, singer or dancer, etc.

4. Nudity or semi-nudity at auditions may be permitted only if:

   (a) an official Equity observer or an observer agreeable to Equity is present;

   (b) the direct professional and artistic interest of all persons present has been agreed between Equity and the Management.

5. No sex acts shall be required of any performer at any audition.

6. (a) Photographs depicting artists in the nude, partly nude and/or sex acts, shall not be used for purposes other than direct publicity for the production, other than by the express written consent of the artist.

   (b) The Manager undertakes that the prints and negatives of such photographs will be destroyed at the conclusion of the production.

7. In the case of an artist arrested or charged with any offence arising from his or her performance as directed, the management will do all that is legally possible to assist the artist.

8. For the purpose of these regulations:

   (a) "Acts of a sexual nature" and "sex acts" shall mean "any act which if performed in public would be regarded as an indecent act;"
   (b) "Nudity" "semi-nudity" and "disrobe" shall mean "to be in a state of undress which if in public could be regarded as indecent."

Any dispute arising in relation to the said regulations shall be referred to the appropriate Theatre Council, which shall meet within 72 hours of such reference, and whose decision shall be binding on the parties. Failing such a decision, the dispute shall be referred for a binding decision to the independent Chairman or Vice-Chairman of the Theatre Council or, should this be impracticable to an independent person appointed by the Theatre Council for the purpose.

B. THEATRE ENGAGEMENTS FOR DIRECTORS, OPERA PRODUCERS/DIRECTORS, CHOREOGRAPHERS, DESIGNERS AND FIGHT DIRECTORS

Until 1976 the only collective agreements between the Management Associations and Equity were for the engagement of artists and stage management; now there are the following collective agreements for other persons rendering creative and artistic services.

A. October 1983 between the Society of West End Theatre and Equity for the employment of freelance directors and assistant directors for theatrical productions of plays, musicals, revues and pantomime intended for initial presentation at a West End Theatre (including any pre-West End tour).

B. May 1990 between the Theatrical Management Association and Equity for the employment of directors and assistant directors for theatrical productions covered by the TMA/Equity Agreements for Performers and Stage Management in the Provincial Theatre and Subsidised Repertory Theatre.

C. January 1987 between the Society of West End Theatre and the Theatrical Management Association jointly and Equity for the employment of resident producers and staff producers (collectively "Resident Producers") and freelance producers for new productions of opera or substantially new productions of revivals of operas at theatres in the United Kingdom. The title "producers" includes the title "Directors."

D. December 1990 between the Society of West End Theatre and Equity for the employment of choreographers for theatrical productions, (including any intended pre-West End tours) intended for presentation at a West End theatre other than theatres operated by the Royal National Theatre and the Royal Shakespeare Company, the Royal Opera House; opera and ballet productions at the Coliseum, Dominion and Sadler's Wells theatres.

E. October 1989 between the Theatrical Management Association and Equity for the engagement of choreographers for theatrical productions intended for initial presentation at theatres covered by the TMA/Equity

Agreements for Performers and Stage management in the Provincial Theatre and Subsidised Repertory Theatre.

F. April 1989 between the Society of West End Theatre and Equity for the employment of designers of theatrical productions (excluding variety productions for which artists are engaged on Variety and Allied Entertainments Council Contracts) intended for presentation at a West End theatre other than the Royal National Theatre, the Royal Shakespeare Company, the Royal Opera House; opera and ballet productions at the Coliseum, Sadler's Wells; Royal Court Theatre and Donmar Warehouse.

G. March 1992 between the Theatrical Management Association and Equity (with the Broadcasting and Entertainment Trades Alliance) for the engagement of set, costume, set/costume and lighting designers for theatrical productions intended for presentation in the United Kingdom other than under the SWET/Equity Collective Agreement for designers (F, above).

H. February 1989 between the Theatres' National Committee and Equity for the engagement of fight directors for theatrical productions when a significant amount of choreographed fight moves are required.

Like the collective agreements for artists and stage management these agreements comprise a schedule setting out the minimum fees and terms and conditions of employment, and standard forms of contract of engagement. Each of the Agreements is for a fixed period of time but provisions covering such matters as minimum rates of pay and subsistence are subject to annual review.

There is no requirement for persons engaged under any of these agreements to be "approved" like with the engagement of performers and stage management but the Theatre Councils have a role in the settlement of disputes which may arise between individuals and a management. All these agreements provide that if a person engaged in any of the capacities covered by them is not a member of Equity he is to be encouraged to apply for membership. In any event no person is to be engaged on terms less favourable than as set out in the applicable agreement.

The agreements accommodate the practice well established in the entertainment business of a person's services being made available through a loan-out company. When this occurs a director is required to counter-sign the contract of engagement and to guarantee the performance of the obligations entered into on his behalf by the loan-out company. Payments due in accordance with a contract can be validly paid by a manager to a director or to the company.

DIRECTORS

West End Theatre

The Collective Agreement of October 1988 for directors and assistant directors engaged for the West End theatre is somewhat different from the Collective Agreement for directors employed in the provincial theatre as it reflects the differing needs and working arrangements in the two areas. In the West End directors are engaged freelance for a named production, but in the provinces a director may be engaged either for a single production, or as a resident director for a period of time. The extent of a director's commitment to a management will depend on the type of engagement offered but any services required of a director beyond those of directing a production need to be specifically agreed upon and written into the contract of engagement.

The engagement of a West End theatre director begins on the signing and exchanging of the contract and continues until the close of the production unless otherwise mutually agreed. A manager is entitled to a director's exclusive services during the period beginning on the first day of rehearsals until the conclusion of the first press night performance.

The date for the commencement of rehearsals, of the first paid performance, and of the West End press night must be specified in the contract of engagement. The start of rehearsals can be advanced or deferred by a manager by up to 14 days either side of the stated commencement date. The first paid performance can be deferred by a manager by up to 14 days. In addition a manager can postpone a production for a maximum of six weeks by notice in writing before the start of rehearsals. In this event and within seven days of the receipt of the notice a director must inform the manager if he elects to withdraw from the engagement or accepts the new date. When a director accepts the new date and continues with the engagement, then if the new date is at least seven days later than the date first contracted, an additional quarter of the director's initial or preparatory fee is payable forthwith. If a director does not accept the new date then the engagement is terminated and both parties are released from all further liability under the contract.

If a manager cancels a production before the start of rehearsals there is payable to a director in addition to any sums already paid to him but in satisfaction for all claims by him, a quarter of the initial fee if notice of cancellation is given 10 or more weeks before the projected start of rehearsals, one-half of the initial fee if five or more weeks' notice is given and three-quarters if less than five weeks' notice is given.

The remuneration of a director is made up of three elements, namely an initial or preparatory fee, a weekly touring fee and a weekly supervisory fee. Each of these fees is negotiable but minimum rates are prescribed. For special or seasonal productions in the West End and for productions in the West End of less than 75 minutes playing time excluding intervals, reduced minimum rates are prescribed.

The preparatory fee is payable in instalments, one quarter is due on the exchanging of the contract, one-half on or before the first rehearsal and the last quarter on or before the first paid performance of the production. When only the minimum rate is paid the fee is increased by 20 per cent. for each week the rehearsal period exceeds four; for musicals five weeks. The weekly touring fee is payable for each week a presentation is on tour prior to the West End opening; two instalments of the fee are payable even if there is no pre-opening tour. The weekly supervisory fee is payable for every week during which the production is performed in the West End as compensation for a manager's right to require a director to be reasonably available after the first press night to supervise auditions and rehearsals for cast replacements. When a director is called on to render these services in excess of 30 full or half-day calls in any six months period he is entitled to additional daily or half-day remuneration. In the Agreement a week is defined as Monday to Sunday.

Provision is made in the standard form of contract for the payment of a percentage share of gross receipts in lieu of the weekly fees but the sums paid must not be less than the prescribed minimum weekly rates. "Gross receipts" are defined as "the gross box office receipts less library and party booking discount, credit card commission and VAT or other tax or the equivalent thereof." It is also provided that in any week in which the production plays below the certified "break even" figure, a director shall not unreasonably refuse to waive his remuneration in the same ratio as the manager, author and all others (except artists) in the West End production creative team waive their remuneration. However this waiver is conditional on a director being paid not less than the prescribed minimum weekly touring or weekly supervisory fee, as the circumstances may be.

Assistant Directors

The appendix to the Collective Agreement contains the general terms and conditions of employment and minimum rates of pay for assistant directors and the standard form of contract of engagement.

An assistant director is contracted for a specific production for performance once-nightly or twice-daily or twice-nightly. A manager has a right to a director's exclusive services throughout the period of the engagement and for the services to be performed in the provinces as well as in the West End from the date nominated by the manager as provided for in the form of contract of engagement.

An engagement can be on any one of three basic terms, namely:

(a) for the run of the production but subject to two weeks notice by a manager of the termination of the run, or payment of salary in lieu.

Either party can give notice of termination at or after the expiration of 12 months (15 for musicals) from the date of the first paid performance but not less than four weeks prior notice in writing is to be given and to expire after the last performance on a Saturday;

(b) for a specific number of weeks, or for the run of the production whichever period shall be the shorter but subject to two weeks notice;

(c) until the engagement is terminated by either party giving at any time not less than two weeks' notice.

However an assistant director is entitled to terminate his engagement at any time after it has continued in the West End for 26 weeks by giving four weeks prior notice and providing written evidence of an offer and his acceptance of a position as director of another theatrical, television or film production. There are also detailed provisions for the right of a manager to terminate an engagement on account of a director's illness or a director failing to supply a medical certificate.

An assistant director is remunerated at a weekly rate. If he is required to work on a Sunday or public holiday an extra one-sixth of the minimum weekly salary is payable. If he renders any services beyond the duties of assistant director, or for another production, or renders services prior to the commencement of the rehearsal period or after the termination of the run of the production a director is entitled to additional payment.

Touring allowances are payable, also allowances or expenses for late night travel and for Sunday travel when travelling from one venue to another. The personal expenses of an assistant director reasonably incurred when required by a manager to travel in connection with a production are to be reimbursed.

Unlike directors, an assistant director has no entitlement to additional remuneration when a production is re-mounted or presented overseas. Like directors, if a manager for any reason does not present the production an assistant director is entitled to a compensatory payment. Thus there is payable either the salary for the period of the contract, or the sum amounting to his weekly salary multiplied by the number of weeks of prior notice of abandonment in accordance with the scale set out in the Collective Agreement, whichever amount is less.

Provincial and Subsidised Repertory Theatre

The Collective Agreement of May 1990 for the employment of directors and assistant directors for theatrical productions intended for initial presentation in provincial and subsidised repertory theatres is structured like other collective agreements.

There are two schedules each setting out terms and conditions of employment, the first for Subsidised Repertory Companies and TIE Companies attached to Subsidised Repertory Companies, the second, for Commercial Tours, Seasons and Repertory. To each of the schedules is appended the standard forms of contract of employment. This is for both freelance directors engaged for an individual production for a specified period of time, and for resident directors engaged for an indefinite period or guaranteed period. In addition and correspondingly, there are appendices and forms of engagement for assistant directors. A third schedule sets out the minimum fees and salaries payable for the various categories or kinds of employment.

The Agreement sets out in detail the duties and responsibilities of a director and for which the director's fee is paid. The duties range from the preparation of the background, context and meaning of the play, to the responsibility for all artistic and performance aspects of a production as approved by a manager. Inclusive of the payment of the fee is the right and licence for a manager to exploit the products of a director's services as provided in the Agreement. With freelance directors certain duties are specified which are normally to be rendered pre- and post the period of exclusive engagement and for which an additional payment known as "exclusive services payment" is payable. The special role of artistic directors of subsidised repertory companies is recognised in that the duties may include membership of the board of management, responsibility for general programming policy and a right to delegate responsibilities to a subordinate director. Where an artistic director is entitled to sabbatical leave, he is entitled to undertake remunerative work for a third party.

A manager is entitled to a freelance director's exclusive services from the day of first rehearsal until the final performance of a production on the Saturday of the week in which the first press performance takes place, or as may otherwise be agreed and stated in the contract of engagement. A manager may postpone these dates for a maximum of six weeks by written notice to the director and who within seven days of receipt of the notice must indicate to the manager whether or not he wishes to remain contracted to the new dates. If he agrees then one-half of the director's fee is again then payable. If the director does not accept the revised dates the contract is deemed cancelled subject to the director being paid such proportion of his director's fee and exclusive services payment according to the number of weeks' prior notice of cancellation as specified in the Agreement.

The services of a resident director are exclusive to a manager throughout the period of the engagement except for the concession allowed for artistic directors noted above. An engagement may be for an indefinite period but terminable by either party giving not less than four weeks' notice in writing (or payment of salary in lieu if the notice is given by a manager), the notice not to expire before the first public performance of the production for which the director is then currently responsible. The period of notice for artistic directors is 13 weeks. Alternatively there may be an engagement for a guaranteed period of consecutive weeks but which must be not less than six weeks but for artistic directors not less than 13 weeks.

The fees payable to directors are negotiable but subject to minimum rates. For freelance directors engaged for individual productions by sub-sidised repertory companies, there is payable a director's fee as to one-half on the date of the signing of the contract, one-quarter on or before the first day of rehearsal, and one-quarter on or before the first press/paid performance. There is payable for each week of the period of exclusive services an exclusive services payment which may be paid weekly, or as a fee calculated by the number of weeks of the period of exclusivity. This is paid in two instalments, one-half on or before the first day of rehearsal and the remainder on or before the first press/paid performance. There is a third payment (except for peripatetic companies), namely a weekly touring fee for every week a production directed by the director appears at a non-West End theatre other than as may be stated in a director's contract.

For freelance directors engaged for individual productions by commer-cial repertory companies the same pattern of a director's fee and exclusive services payment applies. A third payment may be agreed which may be a specified percentage of the weekly gross box office receipts (less library and party booking discount, credit card commission and VAT), or a fixed sum payable (in addition to any other payments) each week during which performances of the production continue from the week commencing as specified in the contract. With engagements for commercial tours and seasons two fees are payable. First an initial fee of which one-quarter is payable forthwith following the signing of the contract, one-half on or before the first rehearsal, and the remainder on or before the first paid performance. The second fee is a specified percentage share of the weekly gross box office receipts or else a specific weekly sum (whichever may be the greater but not less than the prescribed minimum rate), for the seventh and subsequent weeks of any tour.

When only the minimum rate of director's fee is paid by any company, if the play is "a difficult play"—meaning U.K. premieres and plays which are being performed in the U.K. for the first time in over 50 years, or which being incomplete or corrupt require editorial work by a director— the director's fee may not be less than 120 per cent. of the minimum rate. Also if a director attends after the period of his exclusive engagement to supervise auditions and rehearsals of cast replacements, a daily fee of one-sixth of the weekly exclusive services payment is payable.

For resident directors engaged by subsidised repertory companies there is payable a weekly salary. An agreed director's fee is payable for a production for which a director directs rehearsals which commence within five weeks of the start of the engagement. If a director is required to direct more than five productions in any 52 week period then in addition to the weekly salary, for each extra production there is payable a negotiated director's fee. A resident director is also entitled to a weekly touring fee for every week a production directed by him appears at a non-West End theatre.

For resident directors engaged by commercial repertory companies a weekly salary is payable. In addition if a director is required to direct more than five productions in any 52 week period for each extra production there is payable a negotiated director's fee. This fee is also payable in respect of a director's first production if the rehearsals thereof commence within three weeks of the start of his engagement. A third payment may be agreed being a specified percentage of the weekly gross box office receipts, or a fixed sum (in addition to other payments) for each week during which performances of the production continue from a week as specified in the contract, as from a specified date.

Each of the standard forms of contract provide for the payment of subsistence, travel costs and incidental expenses in accordance with the detailed provisions of the schedules.

Assistant Directors

The two separate appendices and forms of contract of engagement provide for the employment of assistant directors in rather like terms as for directors but certain of the provisions of the schedules covering directors, such as those dealing with billing and transfers of productions (considered below), do not apply to assistant directors.

An assistant director may be engaged either for a definite number of consecutive weeks, or else for an indefinite period. Throughout the period of the engagement a manager is entitled to an assistant director's exclusive services. An engagement of indefinite duration may be terminated by either party giving the agreed number of days written notice, but if given by a manager it may be terminated by the payment of salary in lieu of notice. The required minimum periods of notice are—four weeks for subsidised repertory, eight weeks for TIE and two weeks for provincial commercial theatre. If notice is given by an assistant director it must be given to expire on the Saturday of the week in which the first public performance takes place of any production on which he is engaged when giving the notice. With both kinds of engagement the start date may be changed by a manager to a date seven days either side of the contracted date provided eight weeks' prior notice is given of the alteration.

All resident assistant directors are subject to engagement on a weekly salary basis but assistant directors engaged for individual productions may be engaged on the basis of either a weekly salary, or the payment of a fee. If the latter the fee must amount to a sum not less than that equal to the minimum weekly rate payable to an assistant director multiplied by the number of weeks (or part weeks) of the engagement. The fee is payable in instalments, namely, one-quarter on the exchanging of the contract, one-half on or before the start of the engagement, and the last quarter on or before the first performance.

Subject to an assistant freelance director's reasonable availability a manager is entitled to his services pre and post the exclusive services period to assist with or supervise auditions and/or rehearsals for original or replacement casts. For each day or part of a day's attendance one-sixth the contractual weekly salary or pro rata the engagement fee is payable.

If a manager for any reason fails to produce a production for which an assistant director has individually been engaged (*i.e.* as a freelance) then in addition to sums accrued due at the time there is payable an amount calculated according to the number of weeks' salary (or pro rata for engagements on the basis of a fee) and the number of weeks' advance notice is given of the abandonment of the production: 10 weeks or more, two weeks' salary; five weeks or more but less than 10, three weeks' salary; less than five weeks, four weeks' salary.

Subject to some important exceptions, but not materially so in regard to working conditions, the provisions of the schedules applicable to directors also apply to the engagement of assistant directors.

GENERAL PROVISIONS OF THE COLLECTIVE AGREEMENTS FOR DIRECTORS

The schedules to the West End and Provincial Theatre Directors' Collective Agreements both provide for the payment of expenses, subsistence, holiday entitlement, illness and other like matters relating to working conditions. There are other provisions of the schedules which deal with the special status and interests of a director which justify particular attention. They concern both freelance and resident directors and where appropriate the provisions are in virtually identical terms.

Casting

Unless otherwise provided in a director's contract of engagement, the casting of a production is a manager's exclusive right and responsibility but it is stipulated that a manager is to consult with a director and have regard to his views on the selection of performers. Whenever possible the engagement of other creative persons such as the designer, choreographer, musical director is also subject to advance consultation with a director. The responsibility for casting may be delegated to a director but that does not absolve a manager of responsibility for the observance of the terms of the collective agreements (reviewed earlier) for the employment of artists, the agreement about nudity on the stage and policies of integrated casting and equal opportunities. When casting is so delegated it is incumbent on a manager to ensure that the director is informed on all these matters.

Copyright

The schedule to the West End Theatre Agreement provides that the products of the services of a director shall be assigned to the manager but that does not affect the right of a director to negotiate for additional fees for his contribution to a play. A director's rights in regard to the production being presented in another medium or transferred to another theatre are noted below.

The schedules to the Provincial Theatre Agreement provide that the rights of copyright in the products of a director's services rendered in the course of an engagement remain his property. A manager has the exclusive licence to exercise all the rights exercisable by the director in the products of his services for the duration of the manager's licence from the author (or other owner of the copyright) to perform the work being produced. Where no such author's licence is required the duration of the manager's rights is by implication for the run of the production, and is then for a period of 24 months after the end of the initial run of the production (including its run in repertory where appropriate). In regard to the right of a manager to reproduce or exploit the production in another medium, this element of the director's licence is subject to the condition that if a manager enters into an agreement with any third party to undertake the exploitation the stipulations noted below must be observed.

A manager is to allow a director to make and keep for his own use a copy of the prompt script by the end of the week including the press night.

Production in Another Medium

On account of the differences between the two Agreements concerning the ownership of the copyright in a director's services there are some differences in the Agreements providing for the presentation of a production in another medium, that is, on film, television, cassette or by any other media coupled with the right to adapt the production for such purposes.

Under the terms of the schedule to the West End Agreement and despite the assignment of copyright, a manager's right so to deal with a production is subject to the director's consent, not to be unreasonably withheld. It is also subject to a manager fully consulting the director whenever reasonably possible as to the treatment of the production in the new medium. If the director disagrees with the treatment that does not prevent the manager proceeding with the reproduction and its exploitation, or permitting any third party so to do. However, unless the director is a "star director" the director can require his name to be withdrawn from the production in the new medium but that does not deprive the director of his entitlement to any payment due under his contract of engagement for the reproduction. The schedule is not specific about the payments due to a director for the reproduction of a production. A "star director" is a director who by a stipulation in the contract of engagement is entitled to have his name billed in the same size as the title of the production and/or its main star.

Because under the provisions of the Provincial Theatre Agreement, as noted above, a manager is entitled to exercise all the rights of copyright in the products of a director's services, it follows and it is expressly provided in the schedules, that a manager has the exclusive right to reproduce and exploit the production produced on film, television, cassette or by any other media, and to adapt the production for such purposes. Others may be sub-licensed to exercise all or any of these rights. However, these rights of a manager are subject to the observance of important conditions.

For a period of 36 months from the date of the press night a director has, at the discretion of the manager either of the following rights:

(a) A right of first refusal to direct the production in the new medium provided the director can show a reasonable degree of experience in the chosen medium. A reasonable degree of experience means "at least one previous production directed or co-directed by the director in the said medium. "If a director does not have this experience he is to be offered the right to direct the play together with a co-director who is reasonably experienced in the medium.

(b) A right to be paid a compensatory fee of an amount not less than the minimum fee payable to a director under the Union agreement applicable to the chosen medium. If there is no such Union agreement the fee is to be settled in consultation with Equity. The director also has the right in such circumstances to be given full credit in the publicity attached to the production in the new medium. He also has the right to withdraw his name from the publicity without prejudice to his right to receive the compensatory fee.

It is further provided that if a dispute arises over the application of the above provisions the dispute is to be dealt with by the appropriate Theatre Council on the understanding that unless the minimum compensation has been offered to the director, that is where the circumstances arise as in (b) above, no action will be taken respecting the transfer to the new medium until agreement has been reached between the parties.

Transfers of Productions between Theatres

Under the Provincial Theatre Agreement there is provision for a director to receive additional fees where a manager transfers a production from one area of the initial production to another. This arises where a repertory production is transferred from a subsidised repertory theatre to a commercial provincial tour (or season), or to the West End, and where a commercial production is transferred from a commercial season to a tour, or to the West End. The payment to which a director is entitled is a percentage of box office receipts as mutually agreed from performances of the production during the period of the transfer. Alternatively before the transfer there may be mutually agreed a sum payable for each performance or week of performances of the production during the period of the transfer but of an amount not less than:

(a) for transfers of five weeks or fewer weeks, 10 per cent. of the relevant minimum director's fee applicable to the theatre(s) at which the transfer is to be presented for each week of such performances;

(b) for transfers of six or more weeks, 50 per cent. of such relevant minimum director's fee.

With this alternative then all other of the contractual conditions applicable to the theatres at which the transferred production is presented apply, such as for a director to render additional services subject to his availability on a daily basis for cast replacements and the like on payment of the daily fee and expenses.

Where the transfer is to a West End theatre then under terms of the West End Theatre Agreement if the director also directs the production he is entitled to be paid not less than the difference between the remuneration he received for his initial direction and the minimum fees due to a director as provided for in the West End Theatre Agreement. If the director is a resident director then his remuneration is deemed to be his salary for the number of weeks for which the production was first rehearsed. If the director is not invited to direct the West End production or is unable to do so because of a prior commitment, the director is entitled to one-quarter of the minimum fee and guarantee prescribed in the West End Theatre Agreement.

The transfer to a provincial tour or season of a West End production is also provided for in the West End Theatre Agreement. Where a play having first been presented in the West End, (and similarly where a play has first been presented at a provincial theatre has been transferred to the West End) transfers to or is licensed to be presented on a provincial tour or season with the majority of the same final cast following or within three months of the end of the West End run, a manager is bound to use his reasonable endeavours to ensure the director of the production is offered the first opportunity to direct the extended presentation. If the director so renders his services there is payable by the manager of the tour or season for the duration of the tour or season the fees or percentage of gross box office receipts as were paid to the director during the West End run of the production.

If the West End production requires to be remounted the manager of the tour or season is to offer the director the appropriate minimum fee payable under the Provincial Theatre Agreement. If the director is not available he is entitled to receive one-quarter of the fees due under the West End Theatre Agreement.

Other Transfers and Revivals

Under the West End Theatre Agreement if a manager licenses the presentation of a production in a country overseas with the majority of the final West End cast the manager is to make reasonable endeavours to ensure the director of the production is invited to direct the overseas production. If the director is not so invited not less than the prescribed minimum fee is payable to the director for each week of the overseas presentation. Under the Provincial Theatre Agreement the payment due to the director is a sum not less than one-half of his fee.

Note that the following provisions appear only in the Schedules to the Provincial Theatre Agreement.

When within 12 months of the first press night of a production a manager produces or co-produces at any U.K. theatre a substantially different presentation of a production (or permits a third party so to do), the manager is to ensure that the director of the original production is offered the opportunity to direct the new production. If the director is available but not offered such opportunity he is entitled to be paid not less than 25 per cent. (or, if the original production was a U.K. or world wide premiere, 50 per cent.) of the minimum director's fee prescribed in the Agreement relevant to the new production as well as not less than 25 per cent. (or, as above, 50 per cent.) of the minimum guaranteed weekly payment (if any) payable under such Agreement.

If a production is revived by a manager within one month of its final performance with the same cast, a manager is entitled to the director's services on a daily basis to assist with auditions, cast replacements and rehearsals subject to the director's availability and the payment of one-sixth of the director's contracted weekly exclusive services payment for each day of attendance plus expenses. When the revival is later the director is to be given the first option to re-direct the production. If the casting of any of the substantial parts of the revival is different from the original production there is to be a minimum of one week's rehearsal. If the revival is to start more than six weeks after the last performance of the production the period of re-rehearsal is to be agreed between a manager and director. When a director is involved in the re-casting then for each day or half day of attendance the one-sixth payment as above is payable.

Scripts

It is a manager's responsibility to provide all scripts and music for a production and to acquire all licences necessary for its performance. All such material remains the property of the manager and should be returned by a director when requested.

Billing

The standard entitlement of a director to billing is "to normal credit on all posters and programmes over which the manager has control." Except for a star director, a director has the right to have his name withdrawn from the billing if a manager makes substantial changes to the production without his consent, or requires changes to be made but which the director is unwilling to implement. Where a director requires his name to be withdrawn from billing this is to be done forthwith from hand written bills and posters outside the theatre and from other printed matter when such matter is next altered. The withdrawal of the director's name at his request does not affect his entitlement to the fees and payments due to him.

Legal Protection of Directors

As explained in Part 8 below the civil and criminal law can affect the content and presentation of a theatrical production. The laws of libel must be regarded but in particular the provisions of the Theatres Act 1968 under which a prosecution may be brought on the grounds that a performance is obscene, or provokes a breach of the peace. The Public Order Act 1980 should also be borne in mind under which a prosecution may be brought on the grounds that a performance incites racial hatred. It is the person who presents or directs the performance rather than the person who takes part in the performance who is liable to prosecution and a penalty, regardless of whether he was actually present at the performance. Ordinarily a director will be deemed to have contracted and undertaken not to render his professional services in a way likely to lead to the risk of a manager being liable to any civil proceedings for infringing another's rights or to prosecution under the Theatres Act or other criminal law.

Both of the Collective Agreements deal with the risk of infringement of civil rights and prosecution under the criminal law. If a complaint is made that a production is in violation of the law or statutory requirement, or if a claim or charge (either civil or criminal) is made against a director acting in accordance with his contract, a manager must defend the director at his own expense and indemnify him against any loss or damage. However, if a manager warns a director in writing that his treatment of a production is likely to bring about such a complaint or claim or charge and the director ignores the warning, then the manager has no obligation to protect the director. A director is to co-operate with a manager in every reasonable way to assist him in defending any action against the director.

Exclusivity

There are no provisions in the Collective Agreements which prevent a director exercising his talents as he chooses. Unless the written terms of his engagement provide otherwise, there can be no objection to a director rendering his services to another theatrical manager or in another media except when, as noted above, a manager is entitled to a director's exclusive services. In the absence of an express provision a director cannot be restrained from rendering his services to any other theatrical manager at any time or place after the period of the engagement, or indeed from directing another presentation of the same play or entertainment by another theatrical management or for another media.

OPERA PRODUCERS/DIRECTORS

The Collective Agreement of January 1987 for opera producers/directors provides separate standard contracts of engagement for a freelance producer for a "single production" and for a resident/staff producer "for other than a single production." The title "Resident Producer" means a producer engaged for more than one production under the same contract and includes an artistic director (if required to produce), consultant director, director of productions, production director, assistant production director and resident producer. The title "Staff Producer" includes a senior staff producer, staff producer, assistant producer, associate producer.

Minimum salaries and fees are prescribed for Resident/Staff Producers and for freelance producers but the rates vary according to the category of the company. The minimum fee payable to a freelance producer engaged by one of the premier companies—Royal Opera House, English National Opera, Glyndebourne, Scottish Opera, Welsh National Opera and Opera North—is assessed on the basis of a rehearsal period of six weeks or less, meaning the period beginning on the Monday of a week in which rehearsals start and ending on the Saturday of the week in which the first press night performance is given. If the period exceeds six weeks then an additional 16 and two-thirds per cent. is payable for each further week of the rehearsal period. A manager and producer may mutually agree to calculate the six weeks as an aggregate rather than consecutively. For an engagement by any other company the minimum fee payable to a freelance producer is assessed on the basis of a rehearsal period of six weeks or less (calculated consecutively and not aggregated). If the number of weeks is exceeded then for each additional week of the rehearsal period 16 and two-thirds per cent. of the fee is payable.

Freelance Producers

The contract for a freelance producer must specify the date for the commencement of rehearsals, but which can be advanced or deferred by a manager by up to 14 days either side of the stated date. Similarly the date of the first paid performance of the production must be stated but which a manager can defer by up to 14 days. In addition these dates may be postponed by a manager for a maximum of six weeks by notice in writing to a producer before the start of rehearsals. In this event and within seven days of the receipt of the notice a producer must inform the manager if he accepts the new dates or wishes to withdraw from the engagement. If a new date is accepted and is at least seven days later than the original then the first quarter of the producer's fee (as below) becomes payable again forthwith. If a producer elects to withdraw the contract is cancelled and both parties are released from all further liability under the contract.

The engagement fee is negotiable but subject to a minimum sum. The fee is payable in four instalments, namely, one-eighth on signature and exchange of the contract, or not later than 24 months before the first rehearsal (whichever is later); not less than a further one-eighth on the signature and exchange of contract, or not later than 12 months before the first rehearsal (whichever is the later); not less than one half on or before the first rehearsal, and the balance of the fee on or before the first paid performance.

A subsistence allowance may be negotiated in lieu of the subsistence payments due in accordance with the provisions of the schedule to the Agreement.

A manager is entitled to the exclusive services of a freelance producer until the conclusion of the final performance of a production on the Saturday of the week in which the first press night performance takes place, unless otherwise agreed in writing at the time of the engagement. It is also a term of the engagement that before the start of rehearsals a producer will discuss the production with the designer at the times as may be agreed but so as to enable the designer to meet the contractual dates for the delivery of designs and drawings.

Resident Producers

The engagement of a Resident or Staff Producer is either for a guaranteed period of consecutive weeks (which may not be less than 13 for a Resident Producer), or for an indefinite period, but which may be terminated by either party giving in writing not less than four weeks' notice. If the notice is given by the producer it must be given so that it does not expire before the first press night performance of the production for which he is responsible at the time of giving the notice. A manager is entitled to terminate the engagement by paying four weeks' salary in lieu of notice.

A Resident or Staff Producer is paid a negotiated weekly salary but subject to the minimum rates. A subsistence allowance may be negotiated in the same way as for a freelance producer.

A resident producer is deemed to be engaged exclusively by a manager and so a producer may not render his professional services for any other person without a manager's consent, but this may not be unreasonably withheld.

General Provisions

Included in the schedule to the Agreement are provisions of general application. The copyright in the products of a producer's services is assigned to a manager. However, if a manager exercises the right to transfer a production from a lower category house to a higher one, or to transfer it overseas, or arranges for its sale to another management, or for its presentation in another medium—film, television or videocassette—or for its revival at a date not less than two years after the last performance of a series of performances, then on any of these happenings a producer has a right to receive additional fees and/or the right to be offered an engagement for a revival, or for the production in another medium.

The casting of a production is a manager's exclusive right and responsibility but, where practical, a producer is to be consulted and his views given consideration. A producer is entitled to be consulted before a manager gives permission for a principal artist to be absent from a rehearsal.

A producer is entitled to be accorded normal credit on all posters and programmes over which a manager has control. If a manager requires substantial changes to be made to a production but which a producer is unwilling to make, or a manager makes substantial changes without a producer's consent, a producer is entitled to withdraw his name from the production and have his name removed from posters at the theatre and from other printed matter. For a re-production of the same production based on that production's original producer's conception and interpretation, the words "this production rehearsed by" are to be inserted in the credit.

CHOREOGRAPHERS

West End Theatre

The Collective Agreement of December 1990 for choreographers makes provision for choreographers and assistant choreographers with standard forms of contract for each engagement. An engagement is for a particular production so the name of the person intended to be engaged as director, the provisional date for the commencement of rehearsals and the number of weeks of rehearsal, the date of the first paid performance and of the first press night are all to be inserted in the contract.

The day on which rehearsals are to start may be changed by a manager to a date within 14 days of either side of the date stated in the contract. Furthermore before the start of rehearsals, by notice to the choreographer, a manager may postpone the specified day by up to six weeks. In this event, and within seven days of the receipt of the notice, a choreographer must indicate whether or not he wishes to continue with the engagement. If he accepts the new date and if this is at least seven days later than the original date then an additional one third of the basic fee (as explained below) becomes payable forthwith. If the choreographer withdraws the contract is cancelled and both parties are released from all further liability under the contract.

The basis for the remuneration of a choreographer is the payment of a fee and a royalty. The fee is for the services rendered preparatory to the start of rehearsals, such as auditioning, casting and pre-production meetings, and a number of weeks of rehearsal. The minimum rates prescribed are in amounts to reflect the days of preparation and duration of the rehearsal period; they distinguish between engagements for (a) choreography and musical staging for musicals, and (b) choreography and/or musical staging for plays. The fee is payable in three equal instalments, on the signing and exchanging of the contract, on the first day of rehearsals and on or before the first press night.

The royalty which is payable can be paid in one of three ways:

(a) A fixed sum, but which may not be less than the minimum rate, for each week of the run of the production but which is automatically increased when the run exceeds five years.

(b) A percentage of the gross box office receipts but so that not less than the minimum weekly rate as above is received.

(c) A fixed sum for each performance at a rate not less than the highest priced seat in the house for the production, but with provision for some flexibility when, in any week after the opening week, the "break even" figure is not reached.

When an engagement is for a season of eight weeks or less a manager need not pay more than two-thirds of the minimum initial or preparatory fees and the weekly royalty fee. A manager and choreographer may agree that in lieu of paying the fees as above for an engagement, by the payment of not less than the minimum initial fee plus 52 weeks of the prescribed minimum weekly royalty fee the choreography may be used by a manager for a (renewable) period of five years.

If a choreographer is required to appear in a production then he must also be engaged and paid in accordance with the appropriate collective agreement for performers.

If for any reason a manager abandons the production at any time after the signing of a contract a choreographer is entitled to be paid up to and including the next one-third instalment of the basic fee and all agreed expenses.

When only a small amount of choreography and musical staging is required there may be a sessional engagement, a session being of three and a half hours duration. A choreographer's attendances are as mutually agreed with a manager but normally is for attendance at the technical and dress rehearsals and two performances, one of which may be the press night. A minimum sessional fee is prescribed and is payable for at least the four sessions.

General Conditions of Employment

Unless otherwise agreed in writing at the time of the engagement a manager is entitled to the exclusive services of a choreographer from the first day of rehearsals until the conclusion of the first press night performance as specified in the contract. This date may be varied by a manager by seven days' previous notice subject to a choreographer's agreement and availability. During its run a manager is entitled to request a choreographer (subject to his availability) to visit the production.

The casting of performers is the exclusive right and responsibility of a manager. However, a choreographer has the right to be directly involved in the casting of those artists (including replacements) whose performance consists substantially of dancing, but otherwise he is to be consulted on casting and due account taken of his views. It is a manager's responsibility to provide adequate and suitable rehearsal facilities with a temperature of at least 65°F (17°C) to be maintained.

The Agreement contains detailed provisions respecting a choreographer's entitlement to billing. In addition to the normal entitlement, credit is to be given on such items as record sleeves, publications and other merchandise.

The choreography may not be altered or cut after the first press night of the West End production without the written consent of the choreographer, but which may not be unreasonably withheld. If a manager makes substantial changes to the production without a choreographer's consent, or requires substantial changes to be made but which a choreographer is unwilling to implement, the choreographer has the right to have his name withdrawn from the production. This does not prejudice a choreographer's right to payment up to and including the next one-third payment of the basic fee. Also a choreographer has the right to have his name removed from theatre posters, programmes and from other publicity.

Copyright

An important and distinguishing provision of the Agreement is for the protection of the copyright in the products of the services of choreographers. Among the works capable of protection under the Copyright, Designs and Patent Act 1988 (considered in Part 6) is a dramatic work which is defined as "including a work of dance or mime" and which is recorded "in writing or otherwise." Thus the Agreement provides that the copyright in a choreographer's work for a production, if recorded in notation or otherwise by or on behalf of the choreographer, is vested in the choreographer unless assigned to a manager. The standard form of contract of engagement makes special provision for this.

The copyright may be assigned to a manager absolutely but subject to the payment to the choreographer of at least double the minimum basic fee.

When the copyright is not so assigned then by the payment of the fees in accordance with the contract a manager acquires certain rights in the choreography for the duration of the initial run in the West End only.

Even so this may include a pre-West End tour of a maximum of eight weeks (12 weeks for musicals) and a post-West End tour which takes place within three months of the West End run.

The rights a manager acquires unless modified by the contract, are to incorporate and/or utilise the products of the choreographer's services for the purposes of the production as defined by the contract and as presented on the first public performance (or on the date on which the final payment falls due or such date as is agreed between the parties) as follows:

(a) Public performances of the production.

(b) Recording or causing to be recorded rehearsals and/or in performances for rehearsal and/or archival use and for short excerpts for the purposes of promotion, publicity and documentary use, subject to the payment to the choreographer of the fees due pursuant to the relevant Collective Agreements between Equity and the broadcasting companies also applying to the choreographer.

(c) Recording or permitting a recording or live relay by any third party of the production or of a production based thereon, for the purposes of broadcasting or otherwise exhibiting by television or any other media including such as film and video provided that no recording is made or exhibited without the fees or payments being first agreed in writing with the choreographer and with advance consultation with Equity. If a dispute arises concerning the payments to be paid the matter is to be settled by arbitration.

(d) Authorising third parties to exercise all or any of the foregoing rights subject to a manager requiring a third party prior to the exercise of any such rights to enter into a written agreement with the choreographer as regards the fees and payments to be made by the third party to the choreographer. A manager is to provide basic written details of the rights so licensed and a choreographer is not to unreasonably refuse to reach agreement with a third party.

(e) If a manager stages the production overseas using the original choreography a royalty is payable to the choreographer. If the choreographer undertakes any work on the production a further fee and royalty are payable to him.

Assistant Choreographers

The appendix to the Agreement sets out the terms and conditions for the engagement of assistant choreographers in the West End theatre. Most of the general terms and conditions applicable to the employment of choreographers apply but not in particular the provisions on casting and copyright and other uses of the products of a choreographer's services.

An engagement is for a named production and can be for any one of three basic terms, these being the same as for assistant directors as noted above. A weekly salary is payable throughout the engagement at not less than the minimum rate which may not be less than the lowest salary paid to dancers in the production. For work on a Sunday or statutory holiday one-eighth of the weekly salary is payable for each block of four hours or part thereof.

Provincial and Subsidised Repertory Theatre

The Collective Agreement of October 1989 for the engagement of choreographers for the Provincial and Subsidised Repertory Theatre was the precedent for the West End Theatre Agreement. As the terms and conditions and the standard forms of contract of engagement are very much alike in the two Collective Agreements only the material differences are noted here.

An engagement is for a specified production which is to be named in the contract with the opening date and the date for the commencement of rehearsals. The provisions for the deferring and postponing of these intended dates as described above apply. Likewise a basic or initial fee is payable for the services rendered by a choreographer together with a royalty which may be either a fixed sum (the equivalent of not less than one per cent. of the initial fee) or less than the prescribed minimum (whichever is the greater) for each performance, or alternatively a percentage of the gross box office receipts to take effect not later than six weeks after the official opening night. The minimum fees variously payable are according to a scale depending on the category of theatre or production as prescribed in the Collective Agreements for performers.

Where only a small amount of choreography and musical staging are required an engagement may be on a daily basis and for which minimum daily rates are prescribed.

The basic or initial fee covers the preparatory work and for the attendance of a choreographer on up to three days for auditioning, casting and pre-production meetings, and up to two weeks of rehearsals. Thereafter either the prescribed additional weekly rate or daily rate becomes payable. A daily rate is also prescribed for any day or part of a day for rehearsals conducted by a choreographer before the start of the rehearsal period, for any day or part of a day when services are rendered in excess of the three days for auditions etc., and for any attendance for the purposes of post-production duties.

Unless otherwise mutually agreed with a manager, a choreographer must attend at least one production meeting before the rehearsal period, and visit a production at least once subsequent to the week in which the first paid performance takes place. Any additional post-production visits are subject to mutual agreement. For these attendances the daily rate and a choreographer's expenses are payable.

The copyright in the products of the services of a choreographer are vested in the choreographer unless assigned to the manager by the payment of at least double the appropriate minimum initial fee. Where there is no such assignment then the payment of the fee(s) is inclusive of the manager's acquiring the like rights as in the West End Theatre Agreement noted above (excepting the rights under paragraph (e)) for the United Kingdom and the rest of the world "for the period of copyright," save as may be expressly modified in the contract of engagement.

Even so additional fees are payable to a choreographer in two situations. First, if the run of a Subsidised Repertory production is extended for more than three weeks immediately following its initial run, or is revived following a gap of at least four weeks then a sum equal to 10 per cent. of the initial fee is payable to the choreographer for the extension or for each revival—not to exceed two. These payments do not include payment for any services required of the choreographer for any of these purposes.

Secondly, if the production is transferred to the West End the choreographer is entitled to at least half the contracted initial fee and a weekly royalty of not less than the prescribed minimum. For these payments a manager is entitled to the choreographer's services for up to six days prior to the West End opening. If the choreographer is not available then an alternative choreographer is to be mutually agreed and the substitute remunerated from the payments otherwise due to the choreographer.

Assistant Choreographers

The appendix to the Agreement sets out the terms and conditions for the engagement of assistant choreographers. Most of the general terms and conditions applicable to the employment of choreographers apply but not the conditions about copyright, transfers and casting.

An engagement is for a named production and can be for any one of three basic terms, these being the same as for assistant directors as noted above. A weekly salary is payable throughout the engagement at not less than the minimum rate which may not be less than the minimum salary payable to deputy stage managers under the appropriate collective agreement. For work on a Sunday or statutory holiday one-sixth of the weekly salary is payable for each block of four hours or part thereof.

DESIGNERS

West End Theatre

The Collective Agreement of April 1989 for the engagement of designers comprises a schedule of terms and conditions of employment and a standard form of contract of engagement. A designer is engaged freelance for a specific production to be identified in the contract with the date and place of the first paid performance. The date can be advanced or deferred by a manager within a margin of seven days either side of the stated date provided a manager gives eight weeks' previous notice of the change.

A designer's remuneration comprises an agreed basic fee and additional payments. The basic fee is subject to minimum rates which vary according to the kind of production—major musical, musical, straight play—and the kind of designer services contracted—set, costume or lighting designer. Where a production is for a season of eight weeks or less a manager is not bound to pay more than two-thirds of the prescribed minimum fee. The basic fee is payable in three equal instalments, on the signing of the contract, on completion of the designs and working drawings, and on or before the first paid performance.

The additional payments may be (a) a fixed sum which is payable for each week of the run of the production but at a rate not less than the prescribed minimum, or (b) a percentage of the gross box office receipts but so that not less than the equivalent of the minimum weekly rate is paid, or (c) a fixed sum by way of royalty for each performance at a rate not less than the highest priced seat in the house for the production. There is provision for some flexibility in the payment of these additional payments when, in any week after the opening week, the break even figure is not reached but even so not less than the minimum weekly fee is payable to a designer. The parties may agree that in lieu of these additional payments and the payment of fees for the further use of the designs as noted below, a designer will receive the minimum weekly fee for 52 weeks. This alternative arrangement also covers the use of the designs for a (renewable) period of five years.

Where a designer is responsible for two or more aspects of design such as both sets and lighting, then the applicable minimum initial and weekly fees are aggregated and payable to the designer.

If for any reason a manager abandons the production at any time after the signing of a contract a designer is entitled to be paid up to and including the next one-third instalment of the basic fee and all expenses incurred up to that time.

When a manager requires a designer to travel in connection with a production his reasonable expenses are to be reimbursed at minimum rates.

General Conditions of Engagement

The contract of engagement must specify the duties and work to be done by the designer, the dates for the delivery of preliminary and final drawings and designs, information about the budget and its allocation between production costs and the construction or supply of sets, costumes, properties, special effects and lighting.

At the time of the signing and exchanging of the contract a manager is to provide the designer with as much technical data and particulars of company personnel as is then known. The script and other relevant material are to be made available at the earliest opportunity but not less than eight weeks prior to the first technical/dress rehearsal unless otherwise mutually agreed.

When costumes are to be designed full details and information about the cast is to be provided as soon as practical but not less than six weeks prior to the dress rehearsal. A designer is to have the opportunity of at least one preliminary and one final individual fitting of costumes prior to the dress rehearsal. Calls for costume fittings are to be at times as mutually agreed between a manager and the designer.

A designer is committed to attend all fit-ups, technical and dress rehearsals and to be present at the first public performance of the production unless otherwise agreed. Also he is to be available on other occasions as may be mutually agreed up to and including the day of the first public performance. If substantial design services are required after the first West End press night they are a matter for separate negotiation between a manager and designer; any other design services are subject to mutual agreement.

A designer's entitlement to credit is precisely defined in the Agreement. It is to be announced in the specified order for settings, costumes and lighting when more than one designer is involved in a production.

A designer other than a lighting designer, is entitled to be consulted regarding the design of posters, programme covers and other related material for the production where elements of his work are used. If a manager or a third party wish to reproduce for merchandising purposes (as distinct from publicity purposes including programmes and brochures) aspects of a designer's designs, any such use is subject to agreement between the designer and manager or third party. All photograph calls by a manager involving sets, costumes, etc. for press and publicity purposes are to be made in consultation with the designer.

The designs created by a designer and which have been approved by a manager and director may not be altered after the opening of the West End production without the written consent of the designer, which consent is not to be unreasonably withheld. If a manager makes substantial changes to a production without a designer's consent, or requires substantial changes to be made but which a designer is unwilling to implement, the designer has the right to have his name withdrawn from the production and have his name removed from theatre posters and from other printed material without prejudice to his right to receive the payment of the initial fee.

Copyright

The ownership of the rights of copyright in the products of the services of a designer and the use of the designs are matters which are important to both a designer and a manager. The standard form of contract makes provision whereby the parties can agree either for the assignment of the copyright in the designs to the manager for a period of time, or for the reservation of all rights by the designer subject to the limited rights of a manager to use the designs for the production.

For there to be an assignment of copyright then, in addition to the payment of the initial fee a manager must also pay to the designer a sum equivalent to at least twice the initial fee. By this payment a designer is deemed to have assigned to the manager all rights of copyright and all other rights whatsoever throughout the world in the designs for the period expiring 10 years from the date of the last West End performance of the production. No other sums as would otherwise be due on account of any extended use or exploitation of his work are payable during this period.

Unless the form of contract is amended and the payment made as noted above all rights of copyright in his designs are automatically reserved by a designer but he has the obligation to make his work available to a manager for any reasonable purposes until such time as the production is abandoned. All designs, models, working drawings and plans remain a designer's personal property and must be taken due care of when in a manager's possession.

Where a designer reserves and retains the copyright in his work a manager acquires the exclusive rights in the designs for the purpose (and for the period of) of the initial run of the production in the West End. This period may include an eight weeks' tour (or 12 weeks for musicals) of which a maximum of four weeks only may be a post-West End tour. If for any post-West End tour further work is required to be carried out by a designer then (apart from the weekly payment due as noted above), an additional fee is payable as negotiated between a manager and designer but at a rate not less than one-third of the designer's contracted initial fee. Implicit is the right to use the designs as and to the extent noted above in regard to publicity unless otherwise expressly stipulated in the contract.

Where a production is moved from one theatre to another within the scope of the Agreement, then provided the interval of time between the move does not exceed four weeks, the move does not break the initial run, but during the interval the contracted weekly fee continues to be payable to the designer. If because of the move additional work is required a designer is entitled to be paid on a daily basis at a mutually agreed rate.

Other Uses of Designs

The rights which a manager acquires in a designer's work are for the initial presentation and performance of the production on the stage. Any other or extended use of a designer's work is generally subject to his consent and the payment of additional fees. The main exception to this of course is where the 10 year assignment has been effected as noted above. Accordingly, the making of any film or video recording or television broadcast of the production is subject to a designer's written consent, this not to be unreasonably withheld where there is the offer of an appropriate payment. Should this be in dispute the parties can have the issue referred to arbitration by the London Theatre Council. The same principle applies where a manager desires to mount the production overseas using the designer's work.

Should a production or a substantial part of a production be reproduced or sub-let in the United Kingdom using the original designs the designer's consent must first be obtained (not to be unreasonably withheld) and a new agreement made under which not less than the minimum weekly fee will be payable unless additional work is required for the production.

If a production, first designed by the designer, is reproduced in or outside the United Kingdom within 18 months of the first press night in the West End and new designs are required, then the manager of the original production is enjoined to make every reasonable endeavour to ensure that the designer is invited to design the reproduction. If not so invited the designer is entitled to receive one-third of the relevant minimum basic fee.

A manager has the right to dispose of the "physicals," the sets and costumes. When they are sold for use in another totally different production a manager is to ensure the items are not used in the form as they were used in the production, and is to inform the designer of any such disposals and to whom the set and/or the costumes have been transferred.

Where a production has originated in a theatre not within the scope of this Agreement and a designer's original designs are to be used in a production in a theatre which comes within its scope the use is subject first to a designer's agreement and to the making of a contract between the designer and manager and for the payment of not less than 75 per cent. of the minimum fees due in accordance with this Agreement.

Assistant Designers

There is no separate contract or schedule for assistant designers but by mutual agreement between a manager and the designer an assistant may be engaged. A minimum weekly salary equivalent to that payable to an assistant stage manager under the Collective Agreement for performers is payable. An engagement automatically terminates unless otherwise expressly provided in the contract, following the final performance of the production on the Saturday of the week in which the first press night performance is given.

Provincial and Subsidised Repertory Theatre

The Collective Agreement of March 1992 between the Theatrical Management Association, Equity and the Broadcasting, Entertainment, Cinematograph and Theatre Union (BECTU), is for the employment of designers for theatrical productions outside the scope of the foregoing West End Agreement. It is structured like other of the collective agreements with schedules of terms and conditions of employment and minimum rates for (a) freelance engagements for individual productions, and (b) engagements on a continuing basis *i.e.* for resident designers. For each category of engagement there is a standard form of contract.

Freelance Engagements

The basis for the employment of freelance designers for individual productions is like that for West End theatre designers. An initial or basic fee is payable in three equal instalments, namely, on the signing of the contract, on the approval of working drawings or final designs and on or before the first press or paid performance, whichever is the earlier. In addition there is payable either a fixed sum (but not less than 2 per cent. of the relevant minimum fee) for each performance or week of performances, or else a percentage of the box office receipts in respect of each week of performances given under the management of the manager. The additional payment may not apply if a manager is in receipt of revenue funding from the Arts Council, Regional Arts Authority or a Local Authority.

The minimum rates payable are set out in the appendix to the schedule, the scale making allowance for the various categories of companies or theatres (subsidised and commercial) and the kind and scale of a production including opera and ballet. The minimum fees are combined for set and costume designers; there is a separate rate for lighting designers. As the prescribed rates are regarded as so minimal that they are normally exceeded, in a footnote to the appendix it is provided that the rate is to be increased by 40 per cent. where there are separate designers for sets and costumes but the division of the total amount is a matter for agreement between the designers and a manager. Also where a designer is engaged for only sets or costumes the fee is to be not less than 70 per cent. of the combined minimum rate. If for any reason a production is abandoned by a manager after the signing of the contract a designer is entitled to the next third instalment of the initial or basic fee plus all agreed expenses incurred up to when notice of the cancellation is given.

Where the run of performances of a subsidised repertory production extends four weeks beyond the initially intended period a further 10 per cent. of a designer's engagement fee is payable. Also if such a production is transferred to a tour of commercial theatres the designer is entitled to receive from the manager of the tour such percentage of box office receipts from performances during the tour as may be mutually agreed. Alternatively the parties may agree to the designer receiving a sum for each performance or week of performances during the tour, the amount being not less than 50 per cent. of the appropriate category minimum if a tour is of five weeks or more, or 10 per cent. if less than five weeks.

If there is a revival of a production using a designer's original designs at a theatre under a different category from that stated in the designer's contract (the categories as set out in the appendix referred to above) the designer is entitled to a further fee. The fee due is not less than the difference between the minimum prescribed in the appendix for the category applicable to the initial production and the minimum prescribed for the category applicable to the reproduction. Where only some elements of redesign and/or additional design are required, if the work is undertaken by the original designer or another it is for the parties to agree a fee. Except where it is agreed the amount of work involves less than five days commitment, this fee may not be less than 20 per cent. of the minimum rate for the applicable category of theatre.

General Conditions of Engagement

A designer is on first call to a manager during the period as specified in the contract of engagement and so is required to keep the manager informed of his whereabouts and how he can be contacted. After the period of first call then any additional services required are a matter of separate negotiation between the parties. Provision is made for the payment of expenses as approved by a manager when a designer is required to work in a town more than 25 miles from his normal residence and for the reimbursement of a designer's incidental expenses; an agreed fixed allowance may be paid. If a manager requires a designer to provide models the costs are payable by the manager.

The schedule sets out in some detail the respective duties of a designer and manager. A designer is to attend all fit-ups, technical and dress rehearsals and be present at the first public performance, modify any designs as may be required to satisfy statutory and local authority regulations, not order materials without due authorisation from a manager or manager's representative.

Unless otherwise mutually agreed a manager is to ensure that scripts and other relevant material such as musical score, ground plans and technical data are available at the earliest opportunity but not later than six weeks before the first day of rehearsal. Where a designer is engaged to design costumes, details of the cast and measurements are similarly to be provided six weeks before the date of the first dress rehearsal and arrangements made for individual cast fittings. Where there are cast replacements a manager is to endeavour to ensure the original costume design is used. If there is a revival of a production then a manager is to give as much advance notice as possible to the designer and any attendance by the designer in connection with the revival and payment for his services is subject to negotiation between the parties.

A designer is entitled to be accorded credit on all posters and programmes over which a manager has control and in which the director is announced; the designer's credit is to be in type not less than 50 per cent. of the type used for the director.

Designs approved by a manager and director may not be altered after the opening of the production without the written consent of the designer. Furthermore a manager may not make unreasonable changes to the design of a production. If agreement on changes cannot be reached but changes are made by a manager a designer is entitled to have his name withdrawn from the production. This does not prejudice his financial contractual rights except that if royalty payments are due they cease only when the designer's name has been removed from bills and posters and programmes or an insert made in programmes.

Copyright

The ownership of the copyright in the work of a designer belongs to the designer. Exceptionally it may be assigned to a manager absolutely in perpetuity provided that the amount of the initial or basic fee paid to the designer is at least twice the appropriate minimum rate. Ordinarily by the payment of the fees in accordance with the contract a manager acquires the right and licence to incorporate and use the products of the designer's services for the purposes of the production named in the contract and as presented on the first public performance, (or on the date when the final instalment of the basic fee falls due, or on such date as mutually agreed), as and to the extent as follows unless expressly modified in the contract.

(a) Public performances of the production.

(b) Recording rehearsals and/or performances (subject to Equity's agreement) for rehearsal and/or archival purposes only, and/or use of such recording for promotional purposes subject to the relevant agreements between Equity and the broadcasting companies for performers also applying to designers.

(c) Recording or permitting a recording or live relay by any third party of the production or a production based thereon, for the purposes of broadcasting or otherwise exhibiting by television or in any other medium including film and video provided the fees payable to the designer are first agreed to by him and subject to advance consultation with Equity. If a dispute arises concerning the fees to be paid there is provision for the matter to be settled by arbitration.

(d) A manager may authorise a third party to exercise any of the above rights and if so the designer is to be supplied with written details of the rights licensed and a manager is to ensure that the third party first enters into a written agreement with the designer for the payment of the fees due to him. A designer may not unreasonably refuse to reach such an agreement.

All designs, models, working drawings and plans remain a designer's personal property and must be taken due care of when in a manager's possession. A designer must at all times make these items available to a manager until such time as a production is abandoned. A manager has the right to dispose of sets and costumes but must ensure they are not used in the form they were used in the original production.

Resident Designers

The terms and conditions of employment and minimum rates of pay for designers engaged on a continuing basis are set out in the second of the schedules to the Agreement. The standard form contract of engagement annexed provides for the insertion of details of the theatre or "place of engagement" a designer is to serve and in what capacity—Head of Design, Designer (Resident or Associate), Assistant Designer and Lighting Designer. The functions and duties of these categories of designers are generally described in the schedule. The frequency of productions, the date of the commencement of the engagement and of the first public performance of the first production for which the designer is to be responsible are to be inserted in the contract. A designer may undertake freelance work with the permission of a manager which is not to be unreasonably withheld.

An engagement may be either for a guaranteed number of consecutive weeks, or for an indefinite period. If the latter the engagement is terminable by either party giving the number of days of notice as stated in the contract (which may not be less than 28 for Subsidised Repertory and 14 for other engagements), and so given as not to expire before the first public performance of the production for which a designer is responsible at the time of giving notice.

A designer is paid either a fixed amount per week throughout the period of the engagement, or else a retainer of a fixed amount per week throughout the engagement and an additional negotiated fee for each production for which a designer is responsible. Minimum weekly rates for the various categories of designers are prescribed in the schedule. Where a designer is remunerated on the basis of a weekly retainer and fee for each production the total of the payments must represent an average reimbursement for the weeks worked of not less than the relevant minimum weekly salary. A designer is entitled to a subsistence allowance as prescribed in the TMA/Equity Collective Agreement for Stage Management/Performers.

Additional payments become due to a designer on a transfer or extension, or revival of a production. If a subsidised repertory production is transferred to a tour of commercial theatres the designer is entitled to receive from the manager of the tour such percentage of box office receipts from performances of the production during the tour as is mutually agreed. Alternatively the parties may agree to the designer receiving a sum for each performance or week of performances during the tour, the amount being not less than 50 per cent. of the appropriate category minimum if a tour is of five weeks or more, or 10 per cent. if less than five weeks.

When a production is presented by a manager at his base theatre for more than three weeks beyond the initially intended period, a designer is entitled to a further fee as mutually agreed, but which may not be less than two weeks' current minimum salary per period of further presentation. However, if the designer's engagement is still subsisting the fee is payable only if the further presentation is at a theatre different from that named in the contract. When the fee is payable it covers all performances during the period of further presentation. A designer is also entitled to an additional fee when a production is co-produced and toured by a manager with another subsidised repertory manager. The fee may be mutually agreed but may not be less than two weeks' current minimum salary.

The standard form of contract makes provision for the parties to agree upon the ownership of the copyright in the services of a designer. Unless there is an assignment of the entire copyright to a manager then the manager's rights in the designs are as detailed above for designers engaged for individual productions.

The schedule prescribes in detail a designer's working time and hours.

Other of the provisions are like those in the first schedule for freelance designers in regard to such matters as a designer's involvement with the production of posters and photographs, a designer's entitlement to billing, the rights of a manager and designer respecting alterations to designs, the reimbursement of expenses and the payment of allowances, the use and care of drawings and models, and a manager's rights to dispose of sets and costumes.

As back stage staff at subsidised and commercial provincial theatres may render services as lighting or sets or costume designer, the Agreement provides that when they do a sum additional to their salary becomes payable. The sum is as mutually agreed with a manager but may not be less than half the fee of the appropriate freelance designer fee. Where such a person's basic annual salary exceeds the aggregate of the appropriate BECTU minimum salary plus the appropriate number of the sums for designs undertaken over the year then no further payment is due. If the basic annual salary does not exceed such aggregate then any shortfall is payable at the end of the year.

FIGHT DIRECTORS

The Collective Agreement of February 1991 between the Theatres' National Committee and Equity prescribes minimum terms and conditions for the engagement of fight directors for theatrical productions when a significant amount of choreographed fight moves is required. Persons who are on Equity's Fight Directors' Register are most often engaged. However, a person who is not on the Register but has had previous professional experience as a fight director with the manager, or has previously worked with the director may be engaged and Equity so informed.

A standard form of contract is required for each production and is separate from any other engagement a fight director may also undertake such as stage management. Details of the production, the venue, the commencement of rehearsals and the first paid performance are to be entered and the agreed fees. For the services of a fight director there is payable either a sessional fee, or a negotiated overall fee for pre-rehearsal meetings, rehearsals and post-production visits. A performance fee may also be payable.

A session is of three and a half hours for which a minimum rate is prescribed according to the category of theatre, namely:

(a) West End Theatre, Royal Shakespeare Company and major Opera and Ballet companies,

(b) Provincial Commercial Theatres and major Subsidised Repertory Theatres, and

(c) smaller Subsidised Repertory Theatres.

A manager has the right to use and permit the use of the products of the services of the fight director in other presentations of the production. When the presentation is by another management in another theatre of a higher category as above, the difference between the fees paid by the originating manager and what would have been payable had the succeeding management first presented the production is payable to the fight director. If the production is presented in any other medium (apart from use for archival or publicity purposes) the fight director is entitled to at least the fee specified in the collective agreement applicable for the chosen medium, or as may be agreed in the absence of such an agreement.

A fight director is contractually required to visit a production at least once subsequent to the week of the first press night. For additional visits requested by a manager, and especially for the purpose of auditioning and supervising rehearsals for understudies and cast replacements, the sessional fee is payable. The form of contract stipulates that a fight director is to be accorded credit in all programmes over which a manager has control and in other printed material as agreed by a manager.

A manager is responsible for the provision of suitable and separate rehearsal space, of suitable protective equipment for performers engaged in fight sequences, and for the care and safety of weapons. A fight director has the duty to advise a manager in writing of any particular safety concerns arising from any proposed fight. Except in an emergency a fight is not to be substantially altered after the first press performance without the consent (not to be unreasonably withheld) of the fight director, and with rehearsals if mutually deemed necessary. If a manager requires substantial changes without a fight director's consent or which a fight director is unwilling to implement, a fight director has the right to withdraw his name from the production but without prejudice to his right to be paid all contracted fees.

In the event of a manager for any reason (other than circumstances beyond his control) abandoning a production a fight director is entitled to all fees due under the contract up to and including the date of abandonment. If a production is abandoned after the first day of rehearsals the full overall fee remains payable, or if a specific number of sessions had been agreed, the fees for those sessions.

The arbitration and conciliation provisions of the main collective agreements are deemed to be included as part of the Agreement. Any issues arising over the Agreement or dispute between a manager and a fight director are referable to the appropriate Theatre Council.

C. THE THEATRE COUNCILS AND THE CONCILIATION PROCEDURE

Before explaining the roles of the Theatre Councils in the system of collective bargaining and conciliation it may perhaps be helpful to touch on the history of their inception although this may well be known to some readers. In 1934 members of Equity sought the inclusion in their West End theatrical contracts of a term whereby they would not be required to work with performers not in membership of Equity but when this was refused, 86 leading actors and actresses solemnly declared in writing "we will not enter into any engagements with theatre managers on conditions which would deny our right to refuse to work with non-members of Equity." This declaration and example came to a head in 1935 when the Ivor Novello musical play "Glamorous Nights" was about to be first produced in London at the Theatre Royal, Drury Lane. The management would not concede that the cast should be drawn solely from members of Equity and so engagements were refused by Equity members. The impasse was broken by the intervention of the government of the day which brought about conciliation between the Society of West End Theatre and Equity by the setting up of the London Theatre Council and the appointment of Lord Esher as its first Chairman—hence the reference to "Esher" contracts.

Constitution and Objects

The functions and role of the Council were laid down by its constitution dated February 15, 1935 to which both the Society of West End Theatre and Equity subscribed and the instrument has remained unchanged. The establishment of the Council led to a new approach and philosophy respecting the employment of talented and creative people not only in the theatre but in other spheres of entertainment, although many might contend that the full fruits of this have been slow in ripening. However, the setting up of this formal structure had repercussions in the film industry, broadcasting and variety entertainment. In 1943 the Provincial Theatre Council was constituted on the pattern of the London Theatre Council for theatres and managements operating outside the West End.

The constitution, rules and procedures of the London Theatre Council are embodied in the Agreement of February 1935 (as amended) between the Society of West End Theatre (SWET) and Equity, and those of the

Provincial Theatre Council in the Agreement of April 1942 (as amended) between the Theatrical Management Association (TMA) and Equity. As the constitutions of both councils are virtually the same what follows covers both Councils.

The objects of the Councils are declared to be:

(a) to secure the largest possible measure of co-operation between producing and theatre managers and artists for the safeguarding and development of the Theatre as part of the national life;

(b) to secure the recognition of mutual interests and obligations, to devise ways and means of settling any differences that may arise and generally to bring together the experience and different points of view of those engaged in connection with theatres as managers and artists;

(c) to secure complete organisation of managers and artists and to resist the action of those who would seek to avoid their mutual obligations or would injure the standard conditions of employment by offering or accepting engagements on less favourable terms;

(d) to approve, maintain and enforce Agreements concluded between the Society of West End Theatre/Theatrical Management Association and British Equity ("Approved Agreements").

The Council comprises an equal number of representatives of management and artists its members being nominated by SWET/TMA and Equity. The officers comprise an Independent Chairman nominated by the Secretary of State for Employment; the Council appoints an Independent Deputy Chairman. The Presidents for the time being of SWET/TMA and of Equity serve as Vice-chairmen, and the Chief Executive and the General Secretary of these organisations respectively, as Joint Secretaries of the Council.

The Independent Chairman or the Independent Deputy Chairman presides at meetings of the Council which they are asked to attend. Neither of them is entitled to vote but have power to advise, to make a recommendation or give a binding decision thereat as the Council requests.

The constitution provides for three types of meetings of the Council. First an annual general meeting and secondly for ordinary meetings to be held as and when jointly agreed by SWET/TMA and Equity, or when called by the Independent Chairman on the application of either Joint Secretary. The Independent Chairman must take note of but is not obliged to accept any objection by the other Joint Secretary to such an application. The third type of meeting is a conciliation hearing. SWET/TMA and Equity are represented at meetings (as distinct from conciliation hearing considered below), by such of their members as each of them determine. Most often the Council operates through an executive committee with two members representing management and artists, and a non-voting chairman.

The principal functions of the Councils are to institute and maintain the system of the registration of managers and artists as "approved", and to serve as the forum of conciliation for the settlement of disputes.

Registration of Managers

The system of approval of managers rests on a manager's membership of SWET as a non-deposit member, and/or as a full member of TMA; such managers are deemed "approved managers". (The rules for membership of these Associations are noted in Part 1 above.) Other managers must seek approval by making application to the appropriate Theatre Council and complying with its rules as outlined below.

On account of the exemption from the deposit rules which membership of the TMA confers, under the rules of the Provincial Theatre Council the TMA before admitting a manager into full membership is first to enquire of Equity whether Equity is satisfied with the candidate's credentials. If TMA fails to make such enquiries and after a candidate's election evidence is brought forward that the manager member's professional record is unsatisfactory, Equity can appeal to the Provincial Theatre Council to demand the member complies with the deposit rules. No such rule applies for non-deposit members of SWET.

A manager who does not have approved status on account of not being a member of the appropriate Management Association, or if a member not of the prescribed category as above, must make individual application to the appropriate Theatre Council for registration. A management is required to give information on the form provided about its legal status, its banking arrangements and the names of persons for business references. Full details are required concerning the type of production to be presented, the number of artists and other personnel to be employed and an estimate of the total weekly salaries payable, the date of the first rehearsal and place of first presentation. With the application there is payable a registration fee and from time to time depending on the duration of the run of the production, a nominal service charge.

By making the application a manager gives certain undertakings, in particular first to deposit monies with the Council in accordance with the detailed rules set out in the form of application, and secondly to engage performers and stage management *i.e.* artists on terms and conditions not less than the minimum provisions of the current applicable collective agreement.

The sum to be deposited is of the amount equal to the aggregate of the artists' rehearsal salaries (or one week's performance salary whichever is the greater), and two weeks of their performance salaries (plus VAT on the salaries of artists registered for VAT) and the employer's National Insurance contributions for the artists. The deposit is payable not later than 14 days before the first rehearsal of the production. The rules also provide for the depositing of additional sums during a production to meet any increases in the minimum rates payable under the collective agreements or if the salaries of the cast are otherwise increased during the run of a production.

At the absolute discretion of the Council and provided no recourse has had to be made to the deposit to meet any claims by artists, the deposit in respect of rehearsal salaries (less a sum equivalent to one week's performance salary) may be returned to a manager following the opening of the production. The balance of the deposit is returnable at the termination of the production. Put briefly, the like principles apply for the deposit of monies in respect of the employment of directors, designers and choreographers and their assistants.

Registration of Artists

As for the registration of performers, full membership of Equity automatically confers the status of "approved artist" and registration with both Theatre Councils, but for provisional members of Equity this status is limited to the Provincial Theatre Council. The way of securing "approved" status for a performer who is not a member of Equity is as described in the review of the Casting Agreements in Part 1 above.

Since it is rare for a manager to wish to engage a person who is not competent and professional, and as most professional artists are members of Equity and so eligible for registration, it is customary for managements to send cast lists to Equity to check on artists' membership and thereby ensure compliance with the Casting Agreements and the procedure of registration.

For the discharge of their functions as regards the registration of managers and artists, the rules of the Theatre Councils also provide that a Council has the power to refuse, suspend or cancel the registration of any manager or artist and to issue directions as to the engagement of artists. However, the Theatre Councils have no right or power over what theatrical entertainment is produced, who produces it, or who performs in it provided the registration requirements are complied with. Furthermore as the system of registration has been devised to secure the organisation of both managers and artists in accordance with the objects of the Theatre Councils the rules also provide:

(a) Managers have the right to select their own artists and to be the sole judges of an artist's suitability for their particular requirements at the time of engagement.

(b) Neither Equity nor its members may take any action to impede or endanger a production or run of a production provided that all the artists engaged are registered as approved artists at the time of engagement and that all artists are engaged in accordance with the approved relevant collective agreement.

(c) If during the run of a production (or the rehearsals) a manager ceases to be an "approved manager" by ceasing to be a non-deposit member of SWET or a full member of TMA, it is open to a Theatre Council to decide whether or not the production is to cease being presented by such a manager, or presented subject to the manager placing a deposit in an amount as the Council may decide.

Conciliation and the Hearing of Disputes

The negotiation of minimum rates of pay and the terms and conditions of employment, in other words, the negotiation of the provisions of the collective agreements rest with the Management Associations and Equity. The only function of the Theatre Councils in the formation of the agreements and the standard forms of contract annexed to them is to take formal note of their making since it is the function of the Councils to ensure their observance.

The system of registration and approval of managers and artists as just noted is the first of the ways the Theatre Councils discharge this duty. The other is through acting as the forum for the hearing of disputes and claims respecting compliance or non-compliance with the terms of the Collective Agreements as variously noted above. The rules for the conduct of hearing such disputes are set out in the schedule to each of the Councils' constitution.

A written submission must first be made to the appropriate Joint Secretary setting out the substance of the claim which is then forwarded to the defendant for comment.

A hearing is before a Panel which is to comprise a Chairman and not less than four members drawn in equal number from members of SWET and Equity if the matter is before the London Theatre Council, or of TMA and Equity if before the Provincial Theatre Council. The Joint Secretaries select the Chairman and respectively select the other members of the Panel. Normally the chairmanship alternates between a representative of SWET/TMA and Equity. The Joint Secretaries, or each Council by the unanimous agreement of its constituent bodies, may invite the Independent or the Deputy Independent Chairman of the Council to be the Chairman of a meeting and whose special powers are as noted above.

At a hearing the parties have the right to be present and conduct their case in person, or through a representative of their respective organisation, or through a lawyer. Witnesses can be called by the parties (the intention to do so should be indicated in the initial written submission), who may be questioned by the claimant and defendant and by the Panel. The Panel has the right through the Chairman to put questions to any person present at any stage of the hearing. The Chairman may also on the recommendation of the Panel, call or permit to be called any other persons as a witness and who may be questioned by the claimant, the defendant and the Panel.

The Joint Secretaries are entitled subject to the Chairman's permission to put questions to the parties, witnesses and other persons present at the hearing. They are to give such advice as the Chairman and/or other members of the Panel may require in connection with the conduct of the proceedings.

Neither the Chairman nor the Joint Secretaries may vote at a hearing and the Chairman does not have a casting vote. Decisions of the Panel are made by each of the sides constituted by the SWET and Equity members (or TMA and Equity members) casting one vote. The decision of each side is determined by a majority of the votes of the members of that side. Where a side is of even number that side is to determine its procedure for deciding how to vote if there is no majority.

Apart from the special rules which apply to claims arising under the Casting Agreements, a claim does not succeed unless both sides of the Panel vote in its favour. However, except as may be specifically provided in the provisions of the appropriate collective agreement, the Panel is entitled to decide in respect of any claim whether to make a recommendation or a binding decision. The Panel may take such action or reach such decision as it deems proper including making financial awards and the cancellation, suspension or refusal of the registration of a manager or artist. If a financial award is made the Panel is to prescribe when the award is payable and the consequences of non-payment.

Regarding claims under the Casting Agreements, as noted when considering their terms, a decision is to be made within seven days following the receipt of a complaint, and the claim succeeds if the Panel either finds in favour of the claim or fails to agree.

D. VARIETY AND LIGHT ENTERTAINMENT

In the business of variety and light entertainment there is not the same integrated organisation of managers and performers as there is in the theatre except for the managers and performers who are members of their respective associations affiliated to the Variety and Allied Entertainments Council of Great Britain as explained below. There are many factors which militate against the acceptance of standard terms and conditions of employment and a regular procedure for the negotiation of minimum rates and the settlement of disputes.

First there is an immense diversity of acts and performers. There are differences in content, duration, novelty and presentation of acts. There are differences of professionalism, some performers being very casual in their engagements and often confining themselves to a limited area as they are not dependent on their earnings for their livelihood, whilst others are wholly committed to a career in entertainment. There is a diversity in the places and conditions of performance ranging from front rank theatres, cabaret clubs and dance halls to holiday centres, community halls and public houses. There is diversity in the kinds of management engaged in presenting light entertainment, *e.g.* proprietary clubs, members' clubs, charitable organisations, working men's clubs, municipal authorities. There are managements whose primary business is presenting a bill of celebrated and very professional artists as compared with those managements presenting entertainment when often the one-night stand and unknown or semi-professional performer is regularly accepted. Then also there are managements whose concern is predominantly the presentation of "live" entertainment in contrast to those managements such as of restaurants and clubs for whom the engagement of performers and the provision of entertainment are but a part and not necessarily a major part of their business and the amenities they provide. Despite this predicament of variety entertainment there has been brought about over the years a degree of organisation of management and performers to establish orderly relations between the two sides which certainly requires more than a passing reference in this study.

Variety and Allied Entertainments Council

The inception of the Variety and Allied Entertainments Council in 1955 was the voluntary action of the management associations and the Variety

Artistes' Federation (which subsequently merged with Equity), and not the result of government intervention. The constitution of the Council, the arrangements for the negotiation and approval of standard contracts and the procedures for the settlement of disputes however, correspond closely with those of the London and Provincial Theatre Councils. The Council now comprises six management associations, namely, the Entertainment Agents' Association, the Institute of Leisure and Amenity Management (the association representative of municipal entertainment), the Society of West End Theatre, the Theatrical Management Association, the National Association of Licensed House Managers and the Association of Circus Proprietors of Great Britain and one performers' association, namely Equity. Each of these seven affiliated associations is entitled to appoint a representative to serve as a member of the Council. The Chairman of the Council is elected from among the members of the Council and is not an independent person appointed by the government. The Council has joint secretaries representative of management and performers.

The Council approves the adoption of the standard contracts negotiated between the management associations and Equity and which are outlined in the following Section. By maintaining a register of approved managers, agents and artists—the lists of full members kept by the individual affiliated associations according to the rules constitute the register—the Council monitors the making of engagements and the observance of the provisions of the various standard contracts.

The associations affiliated to the Variety and Allied Entertainments Council are national organisations, but managers and agents engaging artists need not be in membership or indeed qualify for membership of any one of them. Furthermore the contracts described in the following Section are not necessarily the most suitable as light entertainment artists are engaged by many kinds of organisations and by individuals to appear at many different venues for both public and private performances. Because of the casualness with which many engagements are made—a booking may rest on a telephone call—and in order to avoid the risks and abuses which can result from this practice, Equity has provided for the use of its members a National Standard Contract for casual engagements.

The parties insert details of the date, place and time of performance, the number and length of spots and the fee to reflect what has been verbally agreed. The contract is deemed to be accepted only when it is signed and returned within 14 days, or if not so exchanged no written objection to its terms have been made and the artist, in response to a call from the management, rehearses or performs.

Under the general terms it is stipulated that a manager is to provide an adequate supporting sound system and competent musicians necessary for any accompaniment of the artist. An artist is not obliged to take part in any sound or television broadcast from the venue whether or not during a normal performance. If an artist agrees to any such broadcasting he is free to negotiate a separate fee with whomever is responsible for the making of the broadcast. When an engagement is agreed directly between a management or employer and an artist no commission is payable, and in no circumstances may commission be deducted from a fee without an artist's consent. There is included a provision whereby any dispute arising between the parties may be referred to a joint arbitration committee.

E. THE STANDARD CONTRACTS OF THE VARIETY AND ALLIED ENTERTAINMENTS COUNCIL

When an artist is being contracted to perform in variety and light entertainment usually the engagement will be subject to the rules of the Variety
and Allied Entertainments Council (VAEC) and one of the standard
contracts described below will be applicable. Yet doubts can arise
whether an artist ought not instead to be contracted according to the rules
of the London or Provincial Theatre Council. The criterion is that when an
artist is to perform a named or identifiable role or part then he should be
contracted on the appropriate "Esher" standard contract. When an artist
is appearing as himself and performing his own material—in the sense
that even if it is scripted the material does not involve him appearing in a
named role—or is performing his own dance routine or other speciality,
then normally the engagement should be contracted on the appropriate
VAEC approved standard contract. There is an exception to this principle
for a "produced show," meaning a musical or other light entertainment
with co-ordinated and supervised direction, settings, choreography and
style (and perhaps built around a celebrity) presented at a theatre. In this
situation then, although an artist may be performing his own material
and engaged for an act "as known," the appropriate "Esher" standard
contract will apply.

There are three standard contracts approved by the VAEC namely:

(1) for engagements at clubs, cabaret and venues such as public
    houses;

(2) for engagements by local authorities for children's and similar
    entertainments;

(3) for engagements for "produced" variety, cabaret or "floor shows"
    and for pantomimes presented at ballrooms, hotels, clubs and tours
    of clubs (but not theatre tours or theatre seasons).

The first two of the standard contracts are markedly different from the
"Esher" standard contracts as they do not contain provisions about hours
of work, rehearsal times, overtime rates, meal breaks, or subsistence
allowances. Minimum rates are prescribed only for the engagement of
children's entertainers (Contract No. 2). The standard contract for artists
performing in "produced shows" (Contract No. 3) as will be seen below

resembles both in form and terms and minimum rates, the "Esher" standard contract for engagements for the commercial Provincial Theatre.

Contracts for Individuals or Groups

Engagements contracted on either Contracts Nos. 1 or 2 are for individuals or groups to perform "as known" or as might be particularly described. In the schedule made a part of each contract there is provision for the insertion of the days and dates of the engagement, the venue(s), times of rehearsal, the number, times and duration of the performances to be given and the salary or fee payable for each performance. Additional provisions may be inserted as especially negotiated but not so as to detract from the basic conditions of engagement. Thus terms may be added about billing and publicity, the engagement of supporting artists and backing musicians, the particular use or placing of sound amplification, lighting and other equipment or effects, and other appearances when an artist is engaged for a period of time. A separate schedule applies to the engagement of circus acts "as known."

The somewhat different ways and circumstances of booking variety engagements as compared with those for the regular stage have already been remarked upon but now uniform terms have been included in the standard contracts about the payment of commission and the signing of contracts. If a contract is made without the intervention of an agent a management is not entitled to charge or deduct commission; if a contract has been negotiated by an agent then commission can be deducted only on the artist's written authority. When an engagement is for only one week or less than a week an artist is entitled to payment forthwith on the completion of the engagement. But when the period of the engagement is for more than a week an artist is to be paid on a weekly basis. As for the contract itself, it reflects the terms and conditions verbally agreed and is deemed to be accepted only when it is signed and returned within 14 days, or no written objection is made to its terms within this period, or the artist rehearses or performs in accordance with its terms in response to a call from the management.

General Conditions of Engagement

The detailed conditions of an engagement run to many pages. An artist undertakes that he will perform professionally and in the manner and style by which his act is generally recognised, and that the content of his performance will not infringe copyright or be contrary to law. An artist cannot be obliged to take part in any broadcast from the venue whether or not during a performance but if he does he is free to negotiate with the broadcasting organisation for an additional fee. Similarly there can be no recording or filming of an artist's performance for any purpose without his consent.

Because the acts which are performed and the conditions under which they are performed can be so varied the contracts contain an undertaking by an artist that his performance will not be dangerous to himself, the audience or other employees at the venue and that he agrees to indemnify the management for any damages or loss which arises as a result of his default. It is therefore advisable for an artist to have proper and adequate insurance cover to meet any liability on this account. Similarly an artist is required to undertake to ensure that all equipment, properties, scenery, etc. brought by him for his performance complies with the safety rules and regulations prescribed by statute generally and by public authorities licensing places of entertainment. As this statutory liability is strict a management has a very real interest in enforcing compliance with this undertaking.

During the period of an engagement at the request of a management and with the artist's consent (not to be unreasonably withheld) an artist may be transferred to appear at any other venue owned or controlled by the management and in emergency to appear as a replacement provided this does not cause any breach of the artist's undertakings to another management. Any additional expenses incurred by the artist must be paid and the fee payable for the appearance as a replacement for another artist negotiated prior to the performance.

Regardless of an artist having been advertised or announced as appearing a management has an absolute discretion to exclude him or his performance in whole or in part without giving any reason. In such an event and provided the artist is ready, willing and able to render his services as contracted a management must pay to the artist his full contracted fees or salary and by such payment the management is discharged from all claims by an artist on account of his having been billed to appear. The issue of an artist's performance being questionably decent, or his being fit to appear, or of his act attaining the standard required by a management, or of his otherwise being in breach of a term of his contract may therefore be resolved by a management paying off an artist. On the other hand, issues such as whether a management was justified in withholding the payment of fees on any grounds, or an artist being in breach of contract are matters which would fall to be dealt with in the way laid down in the standard contracts.

Somewhat detailed provisions provide for the non-appearance of an artist on grounds of sickness, and an artist's failure to perform and the rights of a management to terminate the engagement. There are also included important conditions respecting an artist's commitments, the giving of exclusive services and his appearances for other managements.

An artist warrants that he has no commitments so as to preclude him from fulfilling his scheduled performances and will not undertake any such commitments. The engagement, that is when it is for a specified period of time, is on the basis of the artist giving his exclusive services to a management so that except for any existing engagements disclosed at the time of the offer of the engagement, an artist contractually undertakes not to exercise his talents for any third party without a management's consent not to be unreasonably withheld. To overcome any devious avoidance of these conditions there is also included an undertaking by the artist that he has not concealed any change of professional name or description.

A barring provision is included which precludes an artist performing at other venues within a defined radius and for a specific period of time both before and after an engagement. The extent and duration of the bar is on a fixed scale related to the amount of an artist's salary or fee. The contracts allow an artist to appear or "double" at another place during the engagement when this is expressly agreed to at the time of making the engagement. The barring provision applies only to places of "live" performance so that radio and television engagements are not affected. However it needs to be borne in mind that any broadcasting engagements during the period of the engagement, even if they do not in the least interfere with the contracted scheduled performances, need to be disclosed or consented to by a management otherwise an artist will be in breach of his warranties and the stipulation for his exclusive services.

Contract for Produced Shows

Contract No. 3 for produced shows of variety, cabaret, floor-shows and pantomime presented at ballrooms, hotels, clubs and tours of clubs (but not at theatres), in structure resembles the contracts for engagements for the regular stage. There is a standard form of contract, a schedule of minimum conditions of employment and a second schedule whereby the engagement is made subject to the rules of the VAEC which provide for the registration of managers and artists and for the hearing and settling of complaints. The contract and conditions do not apply to artists performing "as known"; such artists are engaged on individually negotiated fees and terms of employment.

The standard form of contract of engagement permits the individually negotiated terms to be inserted: the services to be rendered whether as entertainer/compere, comedian, singer, dancer, chorus or understudy; whether the engagement is for once-nightly or twice-nightly performances that is eight or 12 performances respectively in a week; the place of performance. The duration of the engagement is from the agreed commencement date for the period of rehearsal and thereafter:

(a) for the duration of the season, subject to a manager giving two weeks' written notice of termination or paying two weeks' salary in lieu, or

(b) until either party gives to the other at any time after the artist's first performance 14 days written notice of termination but so that the notice expires after the last performance in the working week, or

(c) for a guaranteed number of consecutive weeks but with a manager having the option to extend the period by up to four weeks subject to giving not less than four weeks written notice prior to the ending of the guaranteed period.

Throughout the engagement a manager is entitled to an artist's exclusive services.

The Contract prescribes minimum rates of weekly salary. One rate is applicable for the period of rehearsals up to a limit of three weeks. A separate rate applies from the date of an artist's first performance and this rate also becomes payable if the rehearsal period exceeds three weeks. If an artist is absent on a rehearsal day for another engagement which a manager has consented to, one-sixth of the weekly rehearsal salary is deductable. One-sixth of the weekly rehearsal salary is payable per day of a broken week at the commencement of the engagement, that is, the rehearsal period; a full week's performance salary is payable for a broken week occurring at the end of an engagement.

When an artist is engaged for once-nightly performances, for every performance in excess of eight one-eighth of the weekly salary is payable except that if an additional performance is given on a seventh day then one-third of the weekly salary is payable. When an artist is engaged for twice-nightly performances the weekly salary is for 12 performances but if an additional performance is given one-twelfth of the weekly salary is payable unless the performance is on a seventh day when one-sixth of the weekly salary is payable. When a performance is given on a public holiday supplementary fees are payable and for which a minimum is prescribed. If no performance (or no matinee performance) is given on a public holiday no deduction from the weekly salary may be made on that account.

Both the weekly rehearsal salary and the weekly performance salary are in respect of a week of six days (including Sunday) consisting of 48 hours in total including costume fitting. The Contract contains detailed provisions on rehearsal hours, breaks during working periods, rehearsals on a seventh day, and rehearsal time following the first performance of a show and for emergency cast replacements. When overtime is payable it is at one and a half times an artist's hourly rate. It is payable when more than 48 hours are worked in a week, or more than eight hours are worked on a day or after nine hours from the time of an artist's first call on any day.

Any rehearsal time after 11 p.m. is at the rate of three times the artist's hourly rate. An artist must attend all rehearsals after the first performance without additional payment but normally the rehearsal time is to be limited to nine hours a week or an aggregate of 36 hours in the first four weeks of the run of the production: for understudies 12 and 48 hours apply respectively.

In addition to the payment of salary if an artist is required to rehearse and perform 25 miles or more from his address a standard rate of subsistence is payable for the first nine weeks of the engagement (except if the artist lives and works in the Greater London area), or a touring allowance when on tour.

General Conditions of Engagement

As remarked above, the Contract is like the "Esher" standard contract for the Provincial Theatre and so incorporates many of the general provisions to be found in that Agreement. A manager has the right to exclude an artist from performances or to prohibit the whole of an artist's performance. Subject to any special stipulation in a contract of engagement a manager has the sole right to determine the inclusion and/or the position of an artist's name and the size and nature of the type on programmes and advertising, but, except in an emergency, programmes should announce the current cast. No part of a rehearsal or performance may be broadcast or recorded without the consent of Equity but a manager has the right (without such consent to record a rehearsal or any part thereof for playback during rehearsal. Other general provisions provide for holiday entitlement and sickness, the transfer of an engagement in an emergency, the use of understudies, the payment of commission, the failure of a manager to produce the show and situations of force majeure.

All the standard contracts considered above include provisions for the settling of disputes over the application of the contracts and the observance of their terms but the procedures laid down are not consistent. However, the general practice is for parties through their respective associations or individually to refer issues to the VAEC and for the decision of the VAEC to be final and binding. Even so parties are at liberty to rely on the strict wording of the separate contracts for the settlement of disputes and so they can have recourse to formal legal proceedings.

Standard Contract for Overseas Engagements

Apart from the above three standard contracts approved by the VAEC there is the Standard Contract approved by Equity and the Entertainment

Agents' Association for the engagement of dancers and chorus to perform in produced shows assembled for touring overseas. Artists engaged for such shows performing their own "act as known" contract on terms and conditions individually negotiated with a management.

From the date an artist first performs in public the artist's negotiated full weekly salary is payable, the payment being for the agreed number of performances but not exceeding 12 in any week. The working hours during the weeks of performance may not exceed 48 and no performance may exceed three hours. If more than 12 performances are given in any week one-twelfth of the salary is payable for each extra performance; the number of extra performances in a week may not exceed four. If an artist performs on a seventh day then the performance counts as an extra performance and one-sixth of the salary is payable for the performance. The duration of an engagement (throughout which a management is entitled to an artist's exclusive services), is normally for a specified number of weeks but the Standard Contract provides for various extensions to the initial term as may be agreed between the parties.

When rehearsals are in Great Britain prior to the start of a tour an artist's weekly salary and working conditions are governed by the rates and conditions set out in the Provincial Theatre Agreement; the Standard Contract prescribes the working conditions for rehearsals abroad. Rehearsal time is limited to 48 hours within a six day week, and a rehearsal day may not exceed eight hours within a 10 hour day. Overtime is at time and a half of an artist's hourly rate (calculated on the artist's weekly rate as above) but for rehearsals on a seventh day payment is twice the hourly rate. No rehearsals are to take place on the day of arrival at a venue. Rehearsals after the production of the show are limited to nine hours in a week except for emergency rehearsals needed for cast replacements. During the period of rehearsal overseas before the first performance of the show a management must provide an artist with travel and lodging or an allowance in lieu thereof, plus an expense allowance at not less than the prescribed minimum rate. A management must also provide transport from an artist's home address to a specified place and thereafter throughout the tour and until the return to the artist's home address. Travel time at the commencement or termination of the engagement counts as part of the period of an artist's engagement.

Crucial to the effectiveness of the Standard Contract—certainly as regards the artist—is the pre-condition that a management must deposit with Equity the amount of an artist's salary for two weeks plus the cost of the return fare from the farthest point of the tour. These monies are properly payable before the contract is signed and exchanged but until payment is made the obligations of the artist are unenforceable. The counter-signature by an Equity official of the Contract is evidence that a management has satisfied the deposit requirements.

Reciprocal agreements between Equity and performers' unions in other countries exist to ensure the observance of minimum rates and conditions of employment prevailing in their respective countries. Thus the Standard Contract stipulates that where the terms and conditions of employment of artists in a country within the tour are more favourable to an artist than those provided for in the Standard Contract then the local conditions are to apply.

F. THE SMALL SCALE INDEPENDENT THEATRE

Traditionally the theatre has been not only a place for entertainment but also a forum for the exposition of new ideas and the airing of controversial issues. In recent times this latter purpose has become more apparent with the growth in the number of groups or companies committed to exploring and developing new ways of theatrical production and presentation, and to performing often in unconventional theatrical surroundings and before audiences of young people and communities with special needs. So there has emerged a perceived independent or "alternative" theatre somewhat apart from the established or regular theatre.

Despite the independence of small scale theatre companies organisations exist as centres for the discussion of issues of concern to constituent members and to act as their representatives in negotiations with other organisations just as has happened in the established theatre. For the purposes of this study the Independent Theatre Council must be especially mentioned as it performs many of the functions of the Management Associations of the established theatre noted above as well as seeking to maintain and improve the level of funding for its members.

INDEPENDENT THEATRE COUNCIL

The Independent Theatre Council is a democratically constituted organisation based on the holding of a minimum of three General Councils a year from amongst at least 10 per cent. of the voting strength of the members of the organisation or 10 voting members of which five must be those of member companies, whichever is the lower. The general affairs of the Council are managed by an Executive Committee of not less than six or more than 20 members elected annually at a General Council meeting. The work of the Council is co-ordinated by a full-time administrator. Membership of the Council is open to both companies and individual theatre workers and subscriptions are graduated according to the economic standing of members. Companies applying for membership must supply information about their management structure with details of any relationship with any sponsoring body, an outline of their current method of funding and financing generally, the field of work being pursued and the type of venue or audiences served so as to satisfy the Council that the company or group conforms with the objects of the Council and can observe the duties of membership.

The Council negotiates with Equity minimum rates of pay and conditions of employment and together with the two organisations have established a system and procedure for the settlement of all disputes which arise between their members. As with the regular theatre these matters are contained in collective agreements. For a company or group to qualify for participation in this system it must be incorporated as a limited company or as a limited company with charitable status, or be registered as a charity, or be a co-operative. In addition evidence of sufficient financial resources to cover its obligations to performers must be provided and a deposit of £200 paid to a joint account of the Council and Equity as a contingency against default. This deposit is refunded on request at any time a company for whatever reasons ceases to use the collective agreements. Membership of the Council confers the status of "Approved Manager" and thereby a management is obligated to comply with the collective agreements between the Council and Equity.

There are two such agreements, namely, the Small Scale Touring Contract and the Producing Venues Contract both of April 1989. These Contracts subsist for a number of years but the financial provisions are subject to annual review. There is one common standard form of contract of engagement annexed to the Contracts. Although there are differences in detail between the two Contracts, in practice the Touring Contract is most often used and only its provisions are reviewed here. As its title indicates the Producing Venues Contract applies only to a company resident at a fixed place.

TOURING CONTRACT

By the terms of the Casting Agreement, which is one of the appendices to the Touring Contract, in the normal course of events a manager may not engage persons who are not experienced professional artists in excess of the prescribed annual quota; full or provisional membership of Equity is deemed proof of the necessary professional experience. The quota provisions are:

   (a) two persons per quota year per company provided that at any time not more than one-third of the company comprises newcomers; this proviso does not apply to a company on being given Approved Management status;

   (b) 40 persons per quota year to be used as a contingency pool for the use of existing companies given Approved Management status for the first time, the allocation being made by the Council to companies; this number is additional to the quota referred to in (a) above.

The "quota" year is a year commencing April 1. Any person so engaged, if not a member of Equity, is to be encouraged to apply for membership.

Should a quota be exceeded by a manager wishing to engage an artist who has no previous professional experience, the reasons must first be notified in writing to Equity who must reply within seven days. If the request is rejected a management can appeal to the Small Scale Theatre Council which must then meet within seven days. If the Council finds for the management or fails to reach a decision the engagement may proceed but not otherwise.

Terms of Engagement

In the standard form contract of engagement, which should be signed and exchanged before the start of an engagement, the kind of services to be rendered are to be specified—to play specifically named parts, to play as cast, to participate in workshops, or to undertake stage management duties. An artist may be engaged to undertake other duties as may be mutually agreed and noted in the contract. An engagement may be for either a fixed term or for an indefinite period terminable by either party giving the agreed number of weeks' written notice (but not less than three).

The weekly salary (which is exclusive of allowances and other payments to which an artist may be entitled), is for a working week of six days (Monday to Saturday or Tuesday to Sunday). A working week consists of 45 hours for rehearsals, performances, participation in workshops, travel, costume fittings and other incidental duties. For dancers these hours include teaching and participation in classes and all preparations for them. There is a limit of 12 hours to a working day inclusive of rest and meal breaks: a working day begins at the time of first call to the assembly point or place of rehearsal whichever is the earlier. When free time is mutually agreed upon it does not count as working time or as part of the 12 hour day. Travel on a day of performance is limited to six hours.

An artist cannot be required to perform more than twice on any day. The maximum number of performances which may be given in any week of a full length play is seven, but if the company is performing in the same venue for a whole week eight performances may be given. The maximum number of performances which may be given of a short play in any week is 10. A short play is one lasting for up to one hour and 10 minutes. This latter rule also applies where the total time actually spent at any one venue (exclusive of breaks) is two hours and 40 minutes. With workshops which involve public participation and/or an audience an artist cannot be required to take part in workshops, or in workshops and performances for more than six hours on any day, the time excluding breaks and intervals but including the "half". Also an artist cannot be required to take part in workshops at more than two venues on any day.

Schedules of tours are to be issued at least two weeks in advance. No tour may exceed three weeks without returning to a company's base for a minimum of 48 hours free of all calls (but which may include a free day). The turn round time may be four weeks if a company stays in one venue for at least two weeks, or stays at each venue for at least five days.

An artist is entitled to one free day in every seven consecutive days except in an emergency. When this occurs another free or rest day must be given and payment made for the hours worked at one and a half times the hourly rate. Other provisions of the Contract prescribe for the payment of overtime at twice an artist's hourly rate when the prescribed breaks are curtailed and for time off or the payment of overtime if the hours worked in any week or day exceed the permitted maximum. Unlike the collective agreements for artists engaged in the regular theatre there is no provision for the payment of supplementary fees for working on a Sunday. If an artist is required to work on a public holiday either a day off in lieu must be given or overtime paid at twice the hourly rate for the hours worked calculated in minimum quarter hour blocks and with a minimum payment as for four hours worked.

No company member can be required by a manager to drive but when this is agreed upon special provisions apply. When distances on a tour entail more than two hours travelling time there are to be two drivers per vehicle; no driver is to drive for more than three hours on a performance day. A driver is entitled to additional break time at a venue. When a driver has driven for one and a half hours prior to arriving at the performance venue he is to be excused from the "get in" or given an extra break of 30 minutes on arrival; conversely on departure from a venue he is to be excused the "get out".

Provision is made for the payment of fares, the cost of overnight accommodation and meal allowances, and for the payment of a subsistence allowance for the first 16 weeks of an engagement when an artist is required to rehearse and perform more than 25 miles from his home and the provisions for the payment of the touring allowance or for a manager to provide overnight accommodation do not apply.

Dancers

In the appendix to the Contract provision is made for dancers. All reasonable endeavours are to be made by a manager to provide warm and suitable rehearsal facilities. A manager is required to provide and an artist to attend a minimum of four classes each of at least one hour per week; additional classes may be scheduled by a manager. At his own expense an artist may attend other classes but subject to a manager's consent if these classes are to be counted in the prescribed minimum of four per week. A manager may occasionally request an artist to teach a class which request is not to be unreasonably refused.

Included in the appendix is a detailed provision setting out the obligations of a manager to provide or pay for the cost of treatment for any injury an artist might sustain whilst at work during the engagement. In addition to the general provision respecting costume a manager is required to provide all specialist footwear.

Stage management

The appendix to the Contract for stage management stipulates that the provisions of the Contract concerning hours of work, breaks, overtime and driving apply to stage management. Normally a minimum of two persons (only one of whom may act or understudy) is to comprise a stage management team. When a touring production has four or less performers and provided the set and lighting and sound rig are uncomplicated the team may be one stage manager.

General Conditions of Engagement

Throughout the period of an engagement a manager is entitled to an artist's exclusive services; any waiver of this right is subject to a manager's consent not to be unreasonably withheld. If an artist deliberately absents himself from a call without good cause a manager is entitled to make a pro-rata deduction at the hourly rate from the artist's salary; in an extreme case a manager may terminate the engagement.

No part of a rehearsal or performance may be broadcast or recorded for any commercial purpose without the consent of Equity. A manager is entitled to record a rehearsal for playback during the rehearsal or for other private purposes. A performance may be recorded for archival purposes subject to the consent of the company members and prior notification to Equity. Artists' photographs taken during photographic calls may be used only for publicity for the production in which the artists appear or for the general publicity of the company. If the latter use is to occur after the completion of the production this is subject to the artists' consent not to be unreasonably withheld.

Unless in the form of engagement there is a special stipulation regarding an artist's entitlement to credit, a manager has the sole right to determine the inclusion and/or position of an artist's name, and size and nature of type to be used on all bills, programmes and advertisements. Generally, the current cast and stage management are to be shown in all programmes.

A particular provision on costumes is that if an artist is required to use his personal belongings (clothes, "props," musical instruments, etc.) details of these are to be supplied to the management which is responsible for providing adequate insurance cover. The amount of the fee to be paid to the artist for the use of his belongings is to be agreed between the artist and management prior to the use of the property.

The Agreement between the Theatres' National Committee and Equity on nudity and simulated sex acts applies and is incorporated as an appendix to the Contract.

If a management for any reason fails to produce the production there must be paid to an artist in satisfaction of all claims of the artist under his contract of engagement, three weeks' salary (or the weekly salary for the number of weeks of the engagement where the engagement is for a definite period), together with all accrued rehearsal and other payments due to the artist up to the date when notice is given of the management's abandonment of the production.

The Producing Venues Contract contains a short run guarantee whereby if a management produces the production for which an artist is engaged then despite the production not running for three weeks the management must pay to the artist three weeks performance salary and any other payments accrued and due as if the run had lasted three weeks. Where an artist has been engaged for a definite period then he must be fully compensated as if the production had run for the term of the engagement.

The Touring Contract stipulates that if a management terminates a tour by giving due notice and recommences the tour within the next four weeks but does not re-engage an artist on the terms as before, if an artist is aggrieved on the grounds that such recommencement does not constitute a new tour he may within three weeks after the start of the tour refer the matter to Equity for arbitration in the manner outlined below.

Conciliation

The procedure for resolving any grievance which may arise in the course of an engagement, or dispute over the application or interpretation of the provisions of the Contracts are set out in appendices to the Contracts. Ordinarily any issue is to be dealt with by internal enquiry by a management and an artist or his representative. Otherwise an issue can be referred to the Small Scale Theatre Council. If a manager wishes to terminate an artist's engagement the reasons must be given in writing and the artist given the opportunity to make a reply. If the dismissal is to stand but the artist wishes to contest it the matter is to be reviewed by the company's management body or representatives but either party may refer the matter to the Small Scale Theatre Council for final decision.

The Small Scale Council consists of two members of both Equity and the Independent Theatre Council all sitting as individuals, and a non-voting chairperson chosen at alternate meetings from Equity and the ITC. A person from both Equity and the ITC attends in the capacity of joint secretary but has no vote. If at a meeting a unanimous decision is not reached there may be a majority vote but in the event of a tied vote the issue can be referred to two arbitrators.

Part 3

THE MUSICIAN

A. INTRODUCTION

There is an immense and diverse repertoire of music and many persons competent to perform it, and there are many purposes for which music is performed. The conditions upon which professional musicians undertake to render their services reflect the differing ways of music making, the places of performance and the purposes or uses of a performance. In this Part attention is given to the engagement of professional instrumental musicians for live performances as ordinarily understood. The issues and limitations which arise in regard to recorded performances are considered in Part 4.

A professional musician may perform as a solo artist but most often as part of a group—a large symphony orchestra, theatre orchestra, show band, small classical ensemble, or jazz or pop group. The places of performance are innumerable ranging from the grandeur of the opera house and the formal atmosphere of the concert hall, to the leisure of the park bandstand, the revels of the cabaret, club or pub, and to the arena of a pop festival. There is a diversity of purposes for which music is performed just as there is a diversity of styles of musical performance to suit those purposes. So a musician's performance may be the focus of attention or serve as an accompaniment to another artist's performance. It may be to entertain, to serve the occasion or to give atmosphere to surroundings; it may be ephemeral or rendered permanent by its being recorded.

Musical composition and performance are creative pursuits and both would be the poorer without innovation but there is concern that the modern devices for reproducing electronically the sounds of musical instruments could jeopardise the employment opportunities of musicians. This is a factor which has led to the inclusion in many collective agreements of a stipulation that electronic instruments are not to be used in a manner to displace or reduce the employment of conventional instrumentalists where they would normally be engaged.

There is no system corresponding to that existing in the theatre for the approval and registration of musicians and managers, although the Musicians' Union maintains a register of "approved contractors" for musicians engaged to perform for the mechanical media as noted in Part 4 below. Thus in numerous places solo musicians, duos or groups may be engaged casually and irrespective of whether the performer is a professional or semi-professional musician. However, the sanction for the maintenance and observance of regular conditions of employment and minimum rates of pay for musicians rests on the fact that there are about 40,000 professional musicians in membership of the Musicians' Union and who by the rules of the Union as noted in Part 1 above are under an obligation not to accept engagements at less than the prescribed minimum rates, or on conditions inferior to those prescribed in the standard contracts.

Incorporated Society of Musicians

The Incorporated Society of Musicians (ISM), as the professional association for musicians, also plays an important role in protecting the interests of its members in their various pursuits. The governing authority of the ISM is its Council which is elected by the full members of the Society. The Council appoints an Executive Committee which together with *ex officio* members of the Council and the salaried officials conducts and administers the affairs of ISM. There are specialised sections within ISM each having a committee of elected representatives to review and advise on the issues affecting the particular sectional interests of members. There are three sections, Performers and Composers, Private Teachers, and Music in Education.

As the objects of the ISM include the promotion of the interests of musical performance, particularly classical and serious music, (and as the ISM is a society of musicians wholly engaged in the profession of music) it has adopted a code of ethics to further its objects and to uphold the integrity of members in their dealings as amongst themselves. By the ISM's rules of membership the Council has powers to ensure members observe the code.

The ISM publishes a range of recommended minimum fees, including rates for concert and recital engagements, and negotiates agreements on terms and conditions of employment to assist its performing and composing members in their own negotiations. As a professional association it does not engage in collective bargaining. The Agreements negotiated by the ISM with the BBC for television and radio broadcast engagements (reviewed in Part 4 below) contain standard contractual terms of engagement for performers and although basic minimum fees are included, performance fees are a matter for individual negotiation between the BBC and a member.

Because of the range and diversity of music making and musical performances and on account of the various means and techniques for the recording and reproduction of performances, the ISM and the Musicians' Union have a Joint Standing Committee with the object of complementing and co-operating with each other on matters of mutual concern.

B. THE MUSICIAN IN LIGHT ENTERTAINMENT

With the vast amount of music making, it follows there is an immense number of engagements so that frequently bookings are made and dates fixed with the least formality. This may be commendable where goodwill and fair dealing exist between the persons concerned but as these qualities can be found wanting when the time of reckoning arrives only then is the value of a written record of the booking acknowledged. A formal document is not necessary as a simple letter confirming the booking, the date, place and duration of the performance and fees payable will usually suffice. Even so for the benefit of its members the Musicians' Union has produced a numbered series of standard contracts (obtainable from Branch Secretaries) some of which have been agreed with associations representing managements regularly engaging the services of musicians. In addition to these standard contracts there are "house" or individual company agreements negotiated by the Musicians' Union for particular places of entertainment. There is no one collective agreement with standard rates and conditions of employment between the Musicians' Union and the various associations representing pubs and clubs, or cabaret club proprietors, or social and working men's clubs as their ways of business and needs differ.

In the business of live musical performance, when musicians perform in combination, most often it is the leader of the group or band who organises and negotiates the terms of engagements. It is the leader as "contractor" who undertakes with a management or "engager" to provide the services of musicians as required to perform and fulfil the engagement and to be responsible for their remuneration in consideration of the management's undertaking to pay the agreed engagement fee. The formal legal commitment rests between the management and the leader. It follows that the musicians engaged to perform are properly the employees of the leader and subject to his supervision and direction. The manager or engager has no formal standing in relation to the individual member of a group, the services he performs or responsibility for the payment of his services.

Standard Form Contracts—General

Most of the standard form contracts provided by the Musicians' Union are for contracts as between a management and a leader and provide for the insertion of details of an engagement, including the fee payable and setting out the basic terms and conditions of that engagement. Only for engagements which are likely to be for a period of time, and not one-night stands, such as provincial theatre engagements (as noted more particularly in the following Section C), and holiday centre engagements is there a second or "back-up" standard form of contract as between a leader and individual musicians. In addition to specifying the details of the engagement—the place, weekly fees, duration—these contracts incorporate the terms and working conditions negotiated and agreed between the Musicians' Union and the respective management associations.

In all these instances where a leader/contractor undertakes with a management or engager to provide the services of musicians, on account of the legal relationships noted above it is necessary for the leader to ensure there is placed on the management the obligation to make payments to the leader in terms sufficient for the leader to satisfy his obligations to the individual musicians and to comply with the general conditions of a musician's engagement as prescribed by the Union. Where there is no standard form of contract as between a contractor/leader and individual musician then it is for the persons concerned to make such written record of an engagement for the reasons remarked on above.

Many engagements in the field of light and popular musical entertainment are on a casual basis of one-night stands for which there exists the national minimum "gig" rate and conditions of employment promulgated by the Union. The rate is annually reviewed and it is possible for a rate higher than the national minimum to be adopted by a local District of the Union. The engagement fee is calculated on a half-hourly basis with a minimum fee equal to an engagement of three hours duration inclusive of breaks; a higher rate becomes payable when an engagement extends beyond midnight. For an engagement which begins after midnight then a special supplementary rate is payable—in addition to the normal after midnight rate. When a performance extends beyond the time booked overtime is payable calculated at rates higher than the regular pre- and post-midnight rates as applicable. If musicians accompany a cabaret or play for dance demonstrations or competitions an additional fee for each musician is payable. Where more than 20 miles are travelled in total in performing an engagement (using a central point determined by each Branch within a District to calculate the mileage), a distance fee is also chargeable as compensation for travel time in addition to the reimbursement of a musician's actual travelling expenses.

Contracts—Nos. 3, 5 and 7

Three Standard Contracts numbered 3, 5, and 7 have been promulgated by the Musicians' Union for bands or groups performing in dance halls, ballrooms, restaurants, social and proprietary clubs and cabaret clubs. The contracts are between the engager and the leader, there being no formal supporting contract for use by the leader and an individual musician. Contract No. 3 is for a single casual engagement of a band or group to perform for dancing, or cabaret accompaniment, or stage show, or background music as agreed by the engager and the leader. The latter undertakes to provide a combination of musicians for the kind of musical performance contracted, for the period of time at the venue and on the day as specified. (This contract can be used for gigs when no other form or note to confirm a booking is to hand or applicable.) Contract No. 5 is similar but is for engagements of indefinite duration and subject to two weeks notice in writing which can be given by either party after the final performance in a week. The days and times of performance in a week are required to be inserted in the schedule. Contract No. 7 serves for engagements particularly at cabaret clubs and like venues for performances on the dates and at the times within a week or shorter period as specified in the contract.

With all three contracts the fees are expressed as "inclusive" so it follows that, in agreeing the amount with an engager, a leader must take into account the rates and any supplementary payments which may be due to the musicians engaged by him and any increases in basic rates which may be promulgated if the engagements are some time ahead. The contracts place on the engager the responsibility for providing a piano in good playable condition when one is required, for ensuring the availability of any equipment or instruments required by performers (other than those to be engaged by the leader in fulfilment of his undertaking), and for ensuring so far as possible a safe supply of electricity at the venue. The rates of pay and terms of engagement are negotiable as between the leader and the individual musicians but at rates not less than the national minimum gig rates.

For variety shows, stage band shows and Sunday night concerts, special national rates apply but with differentials according to the audience capacity of the venue. The rates cover a single show with a maximum spread of three hours plus a rehearsal of three hours on the same day, or two performances and a single rehearsal all on the same day. A half concert fee is payable for any extra rehearsal. Overtime is payable for each quarter of an hour or part thereof for extra time at a rehearsal and performance. A "doubling" fee of 20 per cent. of the concert fee is payable for the first additional instrument and a further 15 per cent. for each additional instrument in the customary way. Distance fees are payable for engagements over 15 miles from a musician's centre of employment and travel expenses, porterage, subsistence, late return and overnight allowances are payable as the circumstances may be.

Contract Nos. 11 and 12

For the engagement of solo musicians to perform for dancing, cabaret accompaniment, stage show and background music the Musicians' Union has promulgated two Standard Contracts, Number 11 for a casual engagement and Number 12 for a continuing engagement. These contracts are as between the engager and the musician, the fees being subject to individual negotiation. Provision is made for the insertion of details of the venue, date and duration of a performance and the fee payable for the casual engagement. For a continuing engagement there is provision for a schedule of performances, any variation and any additional performances being subject to mutual agreement. The fee payable is expressed at a weekly rate. Being a continuing engagement it may be terminated only by either party giving two weeks' written notice such notice to be given after the final performance in any week. The general provisions covering such matters as the facilities to be provided by the engager are as in other like contracts.

Profit Sharing Contracts

A "profit sharing" form of contract has been promulgated by the Musicians' Union for musicians engaged casually as a group and where the members are to share equally in a percentage of the revenues arising from the event. The contract is as between a "promoter" and the group, the venue, date and duration of the actual performance time being specified. There is provision for the group to receive a stated percentage of the box office receipts (but not less than 50 per cent.), with details of the capacity of the venue and ticket prices/sales to be inserted. It is an express term of the contract that the promoter is to give the group reasonable access to the records of box office ticket sales to enable the group to verify the amount of the remuneration payable. As the "profit sharing" contract is intended for use primarily where a group is the sole or featured performance, there is a further stipulation that the inclusion of any other performance within the event is subject to agreement between the group and the promoter. Other of the provisions of the contract such as the facilities to be provided by the promoter are as in other of the contracts noted above.

Service Bands

It is fitting to mention here the arrangements for the engagement of Service Bands to perform at private functions and for public performances particularly in parks and resorts. The restrictions under Queen's Regulations on Service Bands accepting paid engagements are currently as follows:

"(a) Before entering into a contract to play in public, officers administering a band are to satisfy themselves that:

(i) The musicians are not to be employed to assist any political party or to become involved, even passively, in activities of a partisan or controversial nature.

(ii) The proposed fee is not below the commercial scale accepted in the locality by civilian bands or equal performances. There is no objection to the acceptance or rates higher than the current commercial rates by bands able to command them.

(iii) The acceptance of the engagement by an orchestra or dance band does not displace a civilian combination which has a long standing record of previous employment for the particular occasion. (A "long standing record of previous employment" is considered to exist where the same civilian band has been employed for the particular engagement on three consecutive occasions out of the preceding five or fewer occasions).

(b) The only acceptable evidence that a private engagement complies with the conditions detailed in this regulation will be a certificate (Form F/BAND/221) signed by the sponsor of the entertainment. This certificate is to be completed before a contract to fill an engagement is signed."

As a result of negotiations between the Musicians' Union and the Ministry of Defence an informal agreement has been reached that a "long standing record of previous employment" could be interpreted to apply either to the same civilian band or a similar combination of individual players, so as to take account of musicians appearing under different band names.

C. THE MUSICIAN IN THE THEATRE

The collective agreements about to be considered lay down minimum rates and conditions of employment for musicians engaged to accompany theatrical productions as distinct from "featured musicians" when soloists, groups or orchestras are engaged to appear as themselves and contracted on separately negotiated terms, and orchestral musicians and soloists performing on the concert platform. There are two principal collective agreements, one for West End theatres between the Society of West End Theatre and the Musicians' Union and one for provincial theatres between the Theatrical Management Association and the Union for musicians engaged to accompany musical plays, operetta, pantomime, variety and spectaculars. There is a third collective agreement between the Theatrical Management Association and the Union for musicians employed for touring opera and ballet performed at provincial theatres and at West End and other London theatres as part of an unbroken tour. When there is a casual season of opera and ballet in London a special agreement is made and approved by the Musicians Union.

The procedures for the approval and registration of managements and artists established by the Management Associations and Equity through the setting up of the London and Provincial Theatre Councils do not apply to musicians performing in the theatre, but the collective agreements with the Musicians' Union prescribe a conciliation procedure. A few theatres and opera houses and companies have orchestras with a staff of permanent salaried members whose terms and conditions of employment are separately negotiated between the management and the Musicians' Union to suit the particular needs of individual managements and where standard contracts of the kind now to be considered are inappropriate.

THE WEST END THEATRE AGREEMENT

The Collective Agreement between the Society of West End Theatre and the Musicians' Union was revised in October 1991 and sets out the general conditions of employment at theatres managed by members of the Society. The standard minimum weekly rates are subject to annual revision based on the Retail Prices Index. It is a term of the Agreement that the

Society recognises the Union as the sole representative organisation for musicians and music directors engaged in West End theatres and strongly recommends those musicians and music directors employed to become or remain members of the Union.

There is no standard form of contract for the engagement of musicians annexed to the Agreement. The general practice is for orchestral musicians to be engaged by letter stipulating the amount of the weekly production salary and according to a musicians' classification and whether the engagement is for once-nightly or twice-nightly performances. Subject to any special terms which may be agreed between the individual management and musician the engagement is automatically subject to the general provisions of the Agreement.

Conditions of Engagement

The basis of employment is a weekly engagement for which a "weekly production salary" is paid at a rate according to whether the engagement is once-nightly or twice-nightly. The rates are standard for all musicians but supplements are payable. A leader is entitled to a supplement of 20 per cent.; for a musician to double any two instruments 15 per cent.; to treble in the woodwind and brass sections 15 per cent.; for percussionists there is automatically a supplement of 15 per cent.

A once-nightly engagement is for eight performances over six weekdays and a twice-nightly engagement for 12 performances. Performances means and includes matinee and/or evening performances and rehearsals. A once-nightly performance is of three hours duration before a paying audience; a twice-nightly is a maximum time of four hours and 40 minutes. Rehearsals are of three hours duration. All these times are inclusive of the time allowed for intervals during a performance, the time between the performances twice-nightly, and during a rehearsal as follows:

(a) not less than 15 minutes—

    (i) during each three hour rehearsal;

    (ii) during each once-nightly performance, but if the performance does not exceed two hours there need not be an interval;

    (iii) between twice-nightly performances

(b) not less than 10 minutes during each of the twice-nightly performances;

(c) not less than 30 minutes between a matinee and evening performance.

If less than the maximum number of performances is given before a paying audience in the week the production opens still the whole weekly production salary is payable to a musician except when he is engaged for a limited season, *i.e.* a season not exceeding six weeks including a broken opening week, when the salary can be pro-rated accordingly for the first week.

The Agreement does not expressly stipulate that the working week commences on a Monday but this is the accepted custom and interpretation as it does provide that a musician's engagement is terminable by either party giving to the other on a Saturday not less than two weeks' notice unless the engagement is for a limited season or other fixed term.

When services are rendered in excess of the maximum covered by the weekly production salary then additional payments fall due, as follows:

(i) If the performance time exceeds the above limits overtime is payable weekly in arrear—computed in five minute units at one and a half times pro-rata the once-nightly or twice-nightly performance rate respectively. The orchestral steward maintains a written record of running times of all performances (from time of call to time of conclusion of exit music) and if the maximum running time is exceeded then the excess or overtime is checked and agreed with the stage manager.

(ii) For additional performances there is payable one-eighth or one-twelfth of a musician's weekly salary respectively for each extra once-nightly or twice-nightly performance, except that for an additional matinee performance under a twice-nightly engagement the payment due is calculated as one-tenth of the weekly salary.

(iii) For additional rehearsals, that is any rehearsals which may be in addition to eight (or 12) performances or rehearsals in a week, one-eighth of a musician's weekly salary is payable for a rehearsal of up to three hours. Time in excess of three hours for a rehearsal is paid pro rata in minimum 30 minute units.

(iv) For short rehearsals of up to two hours during the run of a production there is payable a standard fee calculated at the once-nightly performance rate, that is, one-sixth of a musician's minimum once-nightly weekly salary. For a rehearsal call of less than two hours a minimum calculated as for one hour at pro rata once-nightly performance rates is payable. A one hour rehearsal call is deemed to include the period elapsing between the opening of the theatre to the public for the performance and curtain up. Moreover, to qualify as a short rehearsal the rehearsal must either immediately precede the opening of the theatre to the public for a matinee or evening performance, or immediately follow such a performance. Only the music currently being performed in the production can be rehearsed.

(v) For rehearsal time after midnight, for rehearsals on a Sunday, and for rehearsals and performances on a statutory holiday the rates payable are doubled.

The Agreement provides for other payments to musicians:

(vi) If a musician is required by a manager to play either outside the area defined by a manager (normally the orchestra pit) prior to the first paid performance of a production, or to play within the acting area of the production (normally the stage), an additional fixed sum according to whether the engagement is once-nightly or twice-nightly is payable for each performance.

(vii) Porterage payments for the prescribed instruments at the set rates are payable at the commencement and end of a run of a production.

(viii) A weekly subsistence allowance is payable to a musician for each week he is required to play for a production in a theatre outside the Metropolitan Police area.

(ix) Provision is made for holiday entitlement for a musician who completes four weeks' continuous service with the same management to accrue at the rate of one and a half day's pay for each complete period of one week's service.

No deductions may be made from a musician's weekly production salary because a theatre is closed on a statutory holiday. Special provisions apply for extra performances given during a Christmas week to replace performances which would otherwise be given on the day of the week Christmas Day falls.

A musician cannot be called to render services sooner than 10 hours after the end of a late night rehearsal or performance. Absence from any rehearsal or performance except due to illness is subject to a manager's consent.

A manager is entitled to alter scheduled rehearsal times during the 21 days prior to the production's first paid performance in the West End subject to his giving not less than 14 days notice. If as a result a musician has to cancel or decline an engagement then providing he supplies evidence of this satisfactory to a manager he is entitled to be compensated for any reasonable loss of remuneration.

At the first call for rehearsal in the orchestra pit a management is entitled to 30 minutes to allow for the arrangement of the orchestra's seating; no additional payment is due to musicians for this time. This same rule applies for the first rehearsal at theatres outside the Metropolitan Police area when a production is on tour, but only when local musicians are recruited for the performance at the theatre.

The number of musicians employed in any musical production may not be reduced after the opening night except that if the production is transferred to a smaller theatre the number of musicians may be reduced to a number appropriate for the particular theatre but not then further reduced after the opening night at the smaller theatre.

Recorded music may not normally be used in theatres without the permission of the Musicians' Union. Recorded music may be used for curtain up and scene changes for non-musical plays, and for the playing of national anthems. However, the Agreement provides that instruments and devices incorporating pre-recorded sounds or providing sounds by electronic means can be used in productions provided they do not replace or reduce the employment of conventional instrumentalists on engagements carried out under the Agreement where conventional instrumentalists may reasonably be expected to be used.

A disciplinary procedure is laid down for when a musician's conduct or performance is questioned. A manager, or his representative, is to caution a musician in the presence of the accredited orchestral steward, or failing which in the presence of another member of the orchestra as the musician may choose. Written confirmation of the caution is to be given to the musician and a copy retained by the management. The caution is to be disregarded for disciplinary purposes after one year if it relates to performance, and two years if it relates to conduct, but subject to satisfactory conduct or performance. In the event of further complaint the foregoing procedure and rules apply; if there is a third complaint it is competent for a management to dismiss the musician and for the Musicians' Union to be advised accordingly. Only for gross misconduct may a musician be summarily dismissed.

Conciliation

The conciliation procedure laid down in the Agreement provides that when a dispute concerning its interpretation cannot be resolved between a management and a musician after reasonable time then at either party's request the matter is to be referred to a Conciliation Board consisting of an equal number of representatives from the Society of West End Theatre and the Musicians' Union. The Board's decision which is to be given within not more than seven days of the issue being referred to it (unless otherwise agreed between the parties), is final and binding on the parties. If the Board cannot reach a unanimous decision either the Society or the Union can request a further meeting of the Board under an agreed independent chairman, or if one cannot be agreed upon, under a person appointed by the Advisory Conciliation and Arbitration Service (ACAS). The power of the chairman is limited solely to the making of a recommendation unless the Society and the Union specifically agree that the chairman shall have power to make a binding award.

THE PROVINCIAL THEATRE AGREEMENT

The Collective Agreement between the Theatrical Management Association and the Musicians' Union was revised in February 1992 and sets out the conditions of employment for musicians engaged to perform at theatres in any part of the United Kingdom except the West End, where the proprietor of the theatre or the producing management responsible for providing the orchestra is a member of the Association.

The Agreement does not apply to the employment of musicians for tours of opera and ballet as there is a separate collective agreement for such tours. A theatre proprietor is not bound by the Agreement in respect of amateur musicians performing without payment when a theatre is let for bona fide amateur performances.

It is a term of the Agreement that the Association recognises the Union as the sole representative organisation for musicians and music directors engaged in members' theatres and strongly recommends those musicians and music directors employed to become or remain members of the Union.

There are expressions used in the Agreement which need to be especially noted:

"production week"—means a week during which either:

(a) the production is performed before a paying audience or an invited audience by the management in writing or admitted by ticket; or

(b) any rehearsal for the production which finishes later than 5.30 p.m.

"weekly production salary"—means the salary payable in each production week (at not less than the rates prescribed by the Agreement) to cover a musician's services for:

(i) a once-nightly engagement with a maximum of eight performances per week on the six weekdays, or

(ii) a twice-nightly engagement with a maximum of 12 performances per week on the six weekdays and where the first performance starts at 6 p.m. or later.

(iii) a twice-daily engagement with a maximum of 12 performances per week on the six weekdays where the two daily performances take place within a period of not more than six hours between 10 a.m. and 5 p.m.

"performances" means any one of the following:

(a) matinee and/or evening performances lasting for up to three hours for a once-nightly engagement;

(b) performances of up to two hours and 20 minutes each for a twice-nightly engagement;

(c) rehearsals not exceeding the performance times according to the type of engagement and taking place before midnight.

Included in the expression "performances" are interval and break times which must be allowed as follows:

(i) 15 minutes during a once-nightly performance (or rehearsal);

(ii) 10 minutes during each performance of a twice-nightly engagement (or rehearsal) but excluded is the period of 10 minutes prior to curtain-up when a musician is required to be in attendance at the place of performance.

Musicians' Contracts of Engagement

Unlike the West End Theatre Agreement there is annexed to the Agreement the Standard Form of Contract No. 4A agreed between the Theatrical Management Association and the Musicians' Union. It should be used when musicians are engaged individually by a theatre proprietor, company management, or contractor/leader. The negotiated terms need to be inserted, namely, the weekly production salary, the date of commencement and termination of the engagement, the place of performance and the number of performances according to whether the engagement is once-nightly or twice-nightly. If the engagement is one for continuous employment throughout the year a stipulation for a period of notice of termination by either the manager or the musician can be inserted. The other clauses of the Contract reflect the terms and conditions of employment all as contained in the Agreement.

When a theatre proprietor or company management engages a contractor/leader to provide a combination of musicians then Standard Contract No. 4 will apply, the contractor/leader undertaking to engage and present the number and combination of musicians as mutually agreed and on the terms of employment according to the Agreement. The financial considerations and legal implications of this contractual arrangement are explained in Section B above.

General Conditions of Engagement

Although the prescribed minimum rates are applicable to all musicians without distinction (save for doubling) the Agreement provides that music directors and key musicians with special responsibilities in a production are entitled to negotiate higher fees individually with a management.

The basis for the employment of all musicians is a weekly engagement once-nightly or twice-nightly or twice-daily for the number of performances as above; for each kind of engagement the prescribed weekly production salary is payable. If additional performances or rehearsals are given in any week in excess of the permitted maximum then for each extra evening or matinee performance or rehearsal there is payable one-eighth or one-twelfth of the weekly production salary according to whatever is the basis of a musician's engagement. In the calculation of the weekly production salary there is to be included any additional payments for "doubling" and/or performing outside the orchestra pit (but not overtime payments), but subject in any event to the payment of the minimum rates for extra performances or rehearsals as stipulated in the Agreement.

If in the first production week less than the maximum permitted performances are given, that is, eight performances (once-nightly) or 12 performances (twice-nightly or twice-daily) and meaning by definition actual performances or rehearsals, then instead of the full weekly production salary being payable one-eighth or one-twelfth (according to the type of engagement) of the salary is payable for each performance given subject to payment being made for not less than five performances (once-nightly) or eight performances (twice-nightly or twice-daily).

When performance and rehearsal times are exceeded then overtime becomes payable for every extra 30 minutes or part thereof. Payment is at a rate calculated by dividing a musician's weekly production salary (including any additional payments for doubling and/or performing outside the orchestra pit) by 48 on an eight performance once-nightly engagement, or 56 on a 12 performance twice-nightly or twice daily engagement, multiplied by one and a half. Minimum rates of overtime are stipulated in the Agreement. Overtime is computed weekly and payable not later than the Friday of the next following week, but overtime occurring at additional rehearsals and/or additional performances must be computed for each such additional rehearsal or performance instead of being computed weekly. When any rehearsal extends beyond midnight then for the extra time payment is at double rates.

Pre-opening rehearsals can be paid for separately pro rata in exactly the same way as for an additional rehearsal as noted above, but if a rehearsal lasts beyond 5.30 p.m. it will result in the starting of the first production week.

Sundays are treated separately from weekdays. The payment for a Sunday performance is at double time and is additional to a musicians weekly salary. Irrespective of whether the engagement is once-nightly or twice-nightly or twice-daily, one-eighth of a musician's weekly production salary (including payments for "doubling" but no other additional payments) multiplied by two is payable for a rehearsal of up to three hours. If the rehearsal exceeds three hours then for the extra time payment is calculated differently; the weekly production salary is divided by 96 if a once-nightly engagement, or by 112 if a twice-nightly or twice-daily engagement, and the result multiplied by two and a half for each quarter of an hour or part thereof of overtime. The payment for Sunday rehearsals is subject to the minimum rates as prescribed by the Agreement.

When a visiting production company does not require the services of musicians who are resident at the theatre the musicians must still be paid their basic weekly production salaries for the period of lay-off.

The Agreement makes special provision for "doubling" whereby a musician is entitled to an additional 25 per cent. of his weekly production salary if he is engaged to play two instruments. Percussion instruments have their own four separate "doubling" categories. Two pairs of instruments namely piano and celeste, organ and celeste, are treated as one instrument. For the woodwind/reed section a musician can be engaged to play up to three instruments when the "doubling" rate is 35 per cent. of the weekly performance salary.

If a musician is required by a manager to play either outside the area defined by a manager (normally the orchestra pit) prior to the first paid performance of a production, or to play within the acting area of the production (normally the stage), or to play in costume (as distinct from the usual form of evening dress), a musician is entitled to an additional fixed payment of an amount according to whether the performance is once-nightly or twice-nightly but subject to a weekly maximum payment.

A musician is entitled to refuse to render his services for Sunday performances and on a Good Friday and Christmas Day when the theatre is closed under its ordinary licence but open under a special licence. When a theatre opens on either of these days or on any other statutory holiday a musician is entitled to double time for performing on any such day.

Where a theatre is closed on a Christmas Day or Good Friday then one-sixth of a musician's weekly production salary is to be deemed to have been earned on each such day so there cannot be any deduction from his salary for the day of non-performance. But if a Christmas Day or Good Friday falls in a week when the first public performance of the production is not given until after the Monday in that week, then one-sixth of the musician's weekly production salary can be deducted subject to payment being made in respect of such week for not less than five performances (once-nightly) or eight performances (twice-nightly). There are variations to the foregoing for theatres in Scotland.

A musician is entitled to porterage for the prescribed instruments at the set rates as laid down in the Agreement at the commencement and end of an engagement. Where a musician's home is situated 20 miles from the theatre at which he is engaged to perform, then he is entitled to be reimbursed the cost of his second class fare at the commencement and end of his engagement and reasonable additional travel expenses when a musician is not entitled to porterage payments. If the engagement is for less than 52 weeks a subsistence allowance is payable at the prescribed rates. Where an engagement is for a touring production a musician is entitled to be reimbursed his travel expenses at the commencement and/or end of a tour, and during the tour to be paid the prescribed touring allowance and travel expenses.

The normal dress for a musician is evening dress or other similar attire. A musician cannot be required to engage in any "patter" or "gags" or the like in the course of a performance other than comedy instrumental effects.

A musician is entitled to holidays with pay amounting to one-half day for each week of continuous service with a management. Payment in lieu of holidays not taken is calculated at one-twelfth of the weekly production salary including additional payments for "doubling," performing out of the orchestra pit, additional performances and rehearsals (but not any overtime or Sunday rehearsal payments). The maximum holiday entitlement in any year is twenty-four days.

A musician may not absent himself from any rehearsal or performance without the consent of the manager except for reasons of illness. A musician is entitled to payment at the rates prescribed in the Agreement during certificated sickness provided he has been employed by a manager for not less than two consecutive weeks.

A musician engaged for a theatrical production is not under an obligation to permit his performance to be broadcast or recorded and a management must have the prior agreement of the Musicians' Union to any such broadcast or recording. If there is a radio or television broadcast relay then a musician is entitled to receive additional fees in accordance with the collective agreements made between the Union and the broadcasting organisations considered in Part 4 below.

Use of Recorded Music

Detailed provisions have been incorporated into the Agreement concerning the use of recorded music. In principle recorded music is not to be used in any production without the agreement of the Musicians' Union but the Union's prior approval is not required in four kinds of situations:

(i) where the recorded music is genuinely in the action of the play, *e.g.* switching on a radio or television or putting a record on a record player provided that this is an incident in which the duration of the music does not exceed two minutes;

(ii) curtain up and scene changes music for non-musical plays provided the use of recorded music does not displace any existing
employment,

(iii) music contained in an effects film as part of a theatrical performance
provided that the film maker had obtained the necessary authori-
sations for the incorporation of the music in the film;

(iv) the use of recorded music for puppet or mime performances provided that (a) the recording has not been made in contravention of
the provisions of the Copyright, Designs and Patents Act 1988
which confer rights on performers and (b) the performances come
within the productions for which musicians are engaged to perform
the other musical elements in the production, or where the puppet
or mime performance is put on in an educational establishment or
other venue during the day primarily for school children.

When any of these situations arise a producer must report the use of
recorded music to the National Office of the Musicians' Union and the
Theatrical Management Association within one month on the form
annexed to the Agreement. In any other circumstances when it is
intended to use recorded music a producer must supply details of the
proposed use on the form annexed to the Agreement to the Union and the
Association not later that 14 days before the first rehearsal. Recorded
music may not be used without the Union's agreement but which is not to
be unreasonably withheld.

As in the West End Agreement it is provided that instruments and
devices incorporating pre-recorded sounds or providing sounds by electronic means can be used in productions provided they do not replace or
reduce the employment of conventional instrumentalists on engagements carried out under the Agreement where conventional instrumentalists may reasonably be expected to be used.

Sunday Concerts

The Agreement makes provision for musicians engaged on a weekly basis
to render their services at a theatre for Sunday concerts. These services
are wholly separate and apart from those within the meaning of "production week" and "performances" as noted above. The services may be
rendered on any Sunday during the period of an engagement and on the
Sunday prior to the start or following the ending of an engagement.
Standard concert fees are prescribed:

(a) for one performance of up to three hours and one rehearsal of up to
three hours (both on the same day),

(b) for two performances each of up to three hours and one rehearsal of up to three hours (all on the same day).

The rates are variable according to the audience capacity of the venue. The fees cover performance on one instrument only. The "doubling" fee is an additional 20 per cent. of the appropriate concert fee for the first additional instrument and a further 15 per cent. is payable for each subsequent additional instrument. A fixed rate of overtime is payable for each 15 minutes or part thereof by which a performance or rehearsal exceeds three hours. If extra rehearsals are called half the concert fee is payable. No additional travel and subsistence payments are due to musicians on account of a Sunday concert.

Although the above provision is expressed as applying only to musicians engaged by a management on a weekly basis by custom it is applied to casual musicians engaged to perform with weekly salaried musicians at a Sunday concert. Indeed it has become the practice to apply the rates for orchestral musicians assembled ad hoc for a Sunday theatre concert.

Conciliation

If a management and musician are in dispute as to the interpretation of the Agreement and cannot resolve the issue then either can request that the matter be referred to a conciliation board. The board consists of an equal number of representatives of the Theatrical Management Association and of the Musicians' Union and a decision must be given within 28 days of the dispute being referred to the board and is final and binding on the parties to the dispute.

THE TOURING OPERA AND BALLET AGREEMENT

The terms and conditions of employment of orchestral musicians to accompany opera and ballet performed at provincial theatres and performed at West End or other London theatres as part of an unbroken tour, are contained in a separate Collective Agreement for Touring/Ballet Orchestras between the Theatrical Management Association and the Musicians' Union and which was revised in April 1991.

Conditions of Engagement

Engagements can be for a tour of either indefinite duration but subject to termination by two weeks written notice by either party, or for a specific period. In addition an engagement can be for a single performance as may be needed on account of the particular requirements of a musical score or when a musician is recruited locally on a casual basis. The Agreement provides for the classification of musicians but only to the extent of distinguishing "principals," "sub-principals" and "other musicians." A minimum weekly production salary is payable but the rate applicable to a musician depends on his classification. Lower rates are prescribed for "listed" companies, that is, small established companies included in the list annexed to the Agreement with the approval of the Musicians' Union. Provision is made for single performance fees but the rate payable is similarly variable according to a musician's classification and whether the engagement is at the standard rate or that applicable to a "listed" company. A standard supplementary fee is payable to a musician required to perform on stage in any week of his engagement.

Supplementary fees are also payable for "doubling" as usually understood. If a musician is engaged to play two instruments a supplement equal to 10 per cent. of the minimum salary according to the musician's position in the orchestra is payable for each week of the engagement. Alternatively a musician may be engaged to perform more than one instrument during any one or more weeks of his engagement and for each additional instrument played there is payable 25 per cent. of the musician's weekly salary (including the on stage supplement when payable but excluding overtime payments) for each additional instrument played. This manner of payment can be applied when a musician engaged to play two instruments is required during any time of his engagement to play a third instrument.

The weekly production salary is for services rendered at up to eight sessions per week during the six weekdays and one seating rehearsal held on the first performance day of the week. A "session" means matinee and evening performances and rehearsals of not more than three hours each. A "seating rehearsal" is a session not exceeding one hour held within three hours of the first session of the week to arrange musicians in the orchestra pit for balancing of sound but not to play to rehearse artists. The rate payable for a single performance includes payment for a seating rehearsal held before the one session for which a musician is engaged.

When additional sessions are required then one-eighth of a musician's weekly production salary is payable. If supplementary fees are payable for "doubling" or performing on stage these fees are added to a musician's weekly production salary (or single performance fee) for the calculation of the payment due for an additional session. When a session exceeds three hours then for each 15 minutes (or part thereof) a musician is paid at time and a half pro rata to his weekly production salary, or for a single performance engagement one-twelfth of the session rate. If a musician is required to perform on a public holiday double time is payable and if a musician is not required to work on such a day one-eighth of the weekly production salary is still deemed to have been earned on that day. Although not expressly mentioned in the Agreement the provisions of the Collective Agreement for the Provincial Theatre covering interval and break times are tacitly adopted and count towards the three hours of a session.

General Conditions of Engagement

A basic weekly touring allowance is payable (or at one-sixth per day for five or fewer days touring) but the exact amount is variable according to the towns or cities toured and changes in the Retail Price Index during the period of an engagement. A manager is obliged to provide transport or to pay the equivalent of the cost of a musician's second class rail fare at the commencement of the engagement and return to his home town at the end and to pay for transport from place to place during a tour. The transportation of instruments and baggage is to be provided by a manager but at a musician's own risk. Where a musician by agreement with a manager travels independently then payment for the porterage of large instruments is also to be agreed with a manager. Unlike the Collective Agreement for the Provincial Theatre the Agreement does not provide for Sunday sessions or rehearsals but provides for payment for travel on a Sunday. For each 30 minutes (or part thereof) of travelling time in excess of three hours a musician is entitled to double his half hourly rate, that is, one twenty-fourth of his weekly production salary, or one-third of the single performance rate. Travel time is calculated from the company's base on scheduled train times or the actual travel time when travelling by coach.

A musician is entitled to holidays with pay at the rate of one half-day for each week of service with the same management. Payment in lieu of holidays not taken is due at the end of an engagement at the rate of one-twelfth of a musician's weekly production salary. If a musician is absent due to certified illness he is entitled to payment of his weekly production salary at the end of the week in which the absence first occurs and thereafter to his salary for a further aggregate period not exceeding two weeks in any one year. A manager is entitled to deduct National Health Sickness Benefit from a musician's salary. A musician cannot substitute a deputy in his place for any rehearsal or performance or normally absent himself without the approval of the management.

A musician is under no obligation to permit his performance to be broadcast and a management is precluded from arranging any radio or television broadcast without the prior agreement of the Musicians' Union. If any broadcast is approved then regardless of the payment ordinarily due to a musician in accordance with the terms of his engagement a manager must also pay to him the fees due in accordance with the rates agreed between the Union and the broadcasting organisations. The use of recorded music in substitution, amplification or augmentation of a performance requires the approval of the Union.

There are no standard forms of contract of engagement as there are for ordinary provincial theatre engagements but even so a letter or other written memorandum of the essential terms of an engagement should be exchanged between a management and musician.

House Agreements

Separate "house" or company agreements negotiated with the Musicians' Union apply to the national operatic and ballet companies and when London seasons of opera or ballet are presented by these companies. When a casual season of opera or ballet is presented by a management in London and which is not part of a whole tour then the employment of accompanying musicians is in general subject to the Collective Agreement for the West End Theatre. However, special weekly production salaries and overtime rates apply. A Sunday session counts as an additional session to the eight weekday sessions and is at double time. Single performance engagements are permitted.

THE REHEARSAL PIANIST

The engagement of a pianist for rehearsals and auditions is generally on a casual basis and individually agreed upon with the engager but national conditions and rates are promulgated by the Musicians' Union from time to time.

For all engagements of pianists for rehearsals other than rehearsals for performances broadcast from or recorded at studios, there is a prescribed basic hourly rate for casual engagements with a minimum call of two hours. For a weekly engagement a minimum rate is prescribed for a 30 hour week within five consecutive days or five specific days within a period of seven days with a finishing time of 6 p.m. on each day. Rehearsals continuing after or beginning after 6 p.m. and any hours in excess of the basic 30 are subject to the hourly rate as for a casual engagement. Work on a Sunday or public holiday is at double time.

Musicians performing as accompanists at auditions are similarly engaged at a prescribed casual rate but with a minimum call of three hours, or else on a weekly basis when all the conditions relating to hours of work for rehearsal pianists apply.

D. THE ORCHESTRAL MUSICIAN

Instrumental musicians who perform as members of symphony orchestras, light orchestras and bands are most often engaged on a casual and freelance basis rather than for a period of time at a weekly salary. There are exceptions as where regular members of an orchestra in return for undertaking to fulfil all or most engagements contracted by the orchestra's music director or a management receive some preferment in the form of higher sessional rates and/or a profit participation or other financial stake in the orchestra.

The principal regional symphony orchestras, a few chamber orchestras and the various orchestras of the BBC have a permanent and salaried staff of playing musicians. The terms and conditions of employment for the members of these orchestras are negotiated by the respective managements individually with the Musicians' Union and often in consultation with representative members of each orchestra.

The leading London symphony orchestras have their own individual and distinctive structure of corporate membership with a board of management elected by the playing members. The members are self–employed and freelance but generally they are bound to accept a percentage (roughly 80 to 85) of all engagements secured by the orchestra's management, and to perform at concerts promoted by the management so that the management has first call on a member's professional services. The payment of members is on the basis of a sessional fee according to a scale assessed on various factors, such as a member's position in the orchestra or section of the orchestra and seniority.

Association of British Orchestras

The Association of British Orchestras represents the major orchestral managements, and managers of chamber orchestras, specialist orchestras and ensembles. The membership of the Association includes corporate organisations such as the BBC and the National Federation of Music Societies. With the exception noted below, the Association is not directly engaged in the negotiation of the terms and conditions of employment of orchestral musicians. It acts in an advisory capacity in such matters but perhaps more importantly undertakes enquiries and conducts seminars on issues such as variously affect concert management and the promotion and financing of concert performances of classical and serious music.

National Collective Agreement for Casual Concert Engagements

In October 1990 a revised national Collective Agreement was made between the Association and the Musicians' Union setting out the minimum rates and the terms and conditions on which musicians who are members of the Union are engaged casually for orchestral, choral and other similar concerts promoted by or given by orchestral managements and by concert societies in membership of the National Federation of Music Societies.

The fees payable to a musician are assessed on two counts. The first is that named orchestras are classified into four groups with a fifth group for orchestras of music societies in membership of the Federation. The rates are to scale the highest payable being for engagements by orchestras in group one. Secondly, the rate payable by a management within any one of the groups is according to a musician's placing in an orchestra, that is, as "section principal", "principal", "sub-principal" or "rank and file".

A musician's casual concert rate is for a concert of up to three hours' duration with a rehearsal of up to three hours on the same day. Both three hour sessions are inclusive of interval time of not less than 15 minutes. Where because of the work performed no interval occurs during the concert 15 minutes is automatically added to the performance time and if this results in the total time exceeding three hours the extra time counts as overtime.

For schools and educational concerts the concert rates are varied. If the concert engagement with or without a rehearsal is contained within a total of three hours then 60 per cent. of the applicable rate is payable; if two concerts with or without a rehearsal are given within a total of six hours then only one fee at the applicable rate as for a regular concert is payable. A half hour break must precede a concert. The overtime rate is half the regular overtime rate.

When a concert or rehearsal exceeds three hours, overtime is payable at time and a half (one-eighth of the applicable rate), for each 30 minutes or part thereof up to a maximum of one hour's overtime. For an extra rehearsal 50 per cent. of the musician's applicable rate is payable. If a rehearsal or extra rehearsal is on a day other than the day of performance 50 per cent. of the applicable rate is payable together with other fees as may be due such as "doubling" and "out of town" fees, plus a standard expenses payment. This standard expense supplement is also payable when the only or final rehearsal is on the performance day and the scheduled start of the rehearsal is six hours or more before the commencement of the concert.

If a musician is required to play more than one instrument an additional

10 per cent. of the musicians' concert fee is payable for each additional instrument; minimum payments are prescribed according to whether a whole or half concert fee is being paid. A musician cannot be required to play more than three instruments at any session. If by "doubling" a musician performs an instrument at a higher position, for example by "doubling" plays in the position of sub-principal, his concert rate becomes that for a sub-principal, the "doubling" fee being payable additionally. Keyboard instruments and percussion instruments are dealt with and grouped separately so that additional fees are not payable for playing more than one of the instruments listed within either of the groups. A scale of porterage payments is appended to the Agreement which applies unless an orchestra management arranges for the transport of instruments.

When a concert engagement is beyond 15 miles from the recognised central point of a musician's normal centre of employment an "out of town" fee is payable at a standard rate calculated on the total return mileage necessarily travelled to fulfil the engagement. For very long distance engagements the "out of town" fee is subject to special agreement and if a sea journey is involved a further sum becomes payable.

When an engagement is beyond the 15 mile radius a musician's second class return rail fare is payable unless alternative transport is provided: alternative transport is not construed as meaning the use of a musician's own car or the shared use of another musician's car. Where alternative transport is provided it must include provision for the conveyance of instruments. Coach travel may not exceed a total of 250 miles in any period of 24 hours.

If an engagement entails an overnight stay, or the time of a musician's return to his normal centre of employment by coach or other public transport would be after 2 a.m., subsistence is payable at standard rates unless hotel accommodation is provided. When the time of a musician's return to his centre is between midnight and 2 a.m. a standard scale of late return payments applies. If a musician's time of departure from his normal centre of employment for an engagement is before 8 a.m. a standard supplement is payable for each hour or part thereof.

The Agreement makes special provision for orchestral tours in the United Kingdom. A tour is defined as an "engagement comprising more than one performance and which involves the musician in two or more consecutive nights away from his normal centre of employment." The "out of town" fee is payable only in respect of the first and last days of the tour, that is the days on which a musician leaves and returns to his normal centre of employment. In addition to concert fees and overnight subsistence payments (or the provision of hotel accommodation) a standard touring supplement is payable for each day of the tour except for the days when the "out of town" fee is payable. There must be not less than eight hours free time before the time of first call on any day of the tour, that is a call for the orchestra collectively for travel, rehearsal or performance. If a call is before 8 a.m. the standard early call supplement mentioned above is payable. On the days during a tour when a musician is not required to perform, a half concert fee is payable; it is also payable on the opening day of a tour but not on the return day unless the time of return to a musician's centre is after 1 p.m.

The engagement of musicians and the fees payable under this Agreement are for concert performances in the ordinary way so that any extended use of the services of musicians is subject to special agreement. If a concert is to be relayed and broadcast or recorded then additional fees become payable according to the collective agreements providing for the broadcasting and recording of performances reviewed in Part 4.

Conciliation

The Agreement makes provision for the settlement of disputes about its interpretation which cannot be settled at local level. A dispute is to be referred to the Secretary of the Association of British Orchestras and the General Secretary of the Musicians' Union who are required to meet as soon as possible but within 10 days of the reference. If the Secretaries are unable to agree and to resolve the dispute the matter is then to be referred to a single arbitrator, being a person of standing acceptable to both parties. If agreement on the choice of arbitrator cannot be reached within seven days the procedure is to be regarded as exhausted.

Musicians' Union Casual Concert Rate

The national Collective Agreement does not apply where an orchestral management or concert society is not in membership of the Association or the Federation, for example where an orchestra is assembled ad hoc, and so the Musicians' Union has promulgated separate rates and conditions of employment which are contained in Standard Contract No. 9A for the purpose of casual concert engagements.

Although the prescribed minimum rates are lower than those under the Collective Agreement between the Association and the Union the general conditions of employment are much the same including the payment of "out of town fees," but there are differences of detail. Separate rates are prescribed for "principals," "sub-principals" and "rank and file" to cover the concert and one rehearsal on the performance day, both the concert and rehearsal being each of up to three hours' duration inclusive of an interval of 15 minutes. There is no special stipulation about a concert being continuous and without an interval but otherwise the provisions of the Collective Agreement governing overtime payments and supplements for extra rehearsals apply. The same conditions for reductions in the rates payable for schools and educational concerts apply.

The fee for "doubling" is 15 per cent. of a musician's concert fee for each additional instrument; a musician may not be required to play more than three instruments in a session. If a musician is required to "double" on an instrument normally classified as a principal instrument the "doubling" fee is payable in addition to the principal's rate for the engagement. Other of the standard supplementary fees such as "out of town" fees and the provisions about transport and subsistence described above apply. There is one standard supplementary payment for a late return (that is between midnight and 2 a.m.); payment for a morning call does not become due unless the time of departure is before 9 a.m. and in lieu of a standard hourly supplement a musician is entitled to overtime at time and a half for each 30 minutes or part of thereof for the early call.

The provisions of the Collective Agreement concerning tours outlined above apply to casual orchestral concert tours but with two exceptions. In lieu of the touring supplement a daily rate of subsistence is payable for meals and other expenses on each day of the tour (excepting the first and last days for which the "out of town" or "distance fee" is paid), and the time for the morning call and additional payment due is as noted in the previous paragraph.

When negotiating for the engagement of an orchestra for a concert performance often many of the same issues which arise in the negotiation of contracts for the engagement of solo performers as outlined in the following Section E will arise. Furthermore it needs to be borne in mind that the total fee negotiated between a concert promoter and orchestral management must at least make allowance for overhead expenses of management and the sessional fees and disbursements which will be payable by the orchestral management to the individual members of the orchestra.

E. THE INSTRUMENTALIST AND SINGER IN THE CONCERT HALL

The musician who performs in the concert hall may be a soloist or member of a small ensemble or group with its own established identity and reputation. The solo musician or group may be pursuing a career in the area of classical music or that of light, jazz or pop music but in the context of this study this distinction is immaterial. It is also immaterial whether the place of performance is a concert hall as such or another place of public resort and performance—theatre, civic building, cathedral, stately house, park or lake-side "bowl" or stadium.

Solo musicians or groups as freelance and independent professional performers are free to negotiate fees and conditions for the engagement of their services by concert managers and promoters and societies and festival organisations on such terms as they judge best and to their advantage. There are no prescribed standard minimum rates and conditions of engagement although fairly regular and customary practices exist in the various areas of musical performance. The Incorporated Society of Musicians (ISM) provides for its members a standard form of agreement for concert engagements for solo instrumentalists, singers, accompanists, conductors and chamber ensembles and recommended fees.

The Contract of Engagement

The elements of an independent solo musician's contract for a concert engagement are intrinsically simple, namely to play and perform the instrument and works for a management or concert promoter at a stated place and time for the fee as mutually agreed. However, depending on the professional standing and critical acclaim attaching to a musician—and here the concert solo-singer and vocal group can be bracketed with the musician—there may be special terms which need to be agreed as conditions for the engagement; for example, the proximity both in time and place of other engagements, the risk of conflicting radio and television broadcast appearances, the identity of other solo artists appearing in the same concert, tie-ups with record releases, the right to make any recording or broadcast of the concert performance and the payment of the fees for such extended use of the performer's services.

There are other matters material to an engagement which according to the circumstances will need to be decided and agreed upon, such as the programme content and a proper description of the concert performance, the amount of rehearsal time required and the time and place when rehearsals are to take place; the provision and tuning of instruments and of acoustic and amplification equipment; the nature and extent of publicity and promotion including the provision of biographical notes and reproduction of photographs and identity of the party to be responsible for the compiling, printing and timely delivery of programmes; the position and order of artists in both publicity and actual concert appearances; the payment of travel and accommodation expenses. If only a fee is payable for the engagement then on payment a management will have discharged its obligations but where a performer is to receive a share of the profits from a concert promotion, then provisions need to be included in the contract whereby the management undertakes to keep proper records and accounts with a right for them to be inspected and checked by the performer or his representative.

The standard form of contract for concert engagements recommended by the Incorporated Society of Musicians (ISM) provides for the payment of a negotiated fee for the performance together with one rehearsal on the same day not exceeding three hours' duration and with at least an hour's break between the rehearsal and performance; any additional rehearsals required by a management attract a further fee. An artist cannot be required to rehearse before an audience except by prior agreement. Provision is also made for the payment of a travel allowance and overnight subsistence allowance when an artist is unable to return to his home by midnight. If payment of the fees and allowances is delayed an artist is entitled to claim interest on the total sum until it is paid. Other practical details are provided for such as the provision of publicity material by the artist, billing, dressing room facilities and the responsibility of the promoter for the payment of any fees due to the Performing Right Society. Also included is a stipulation that there is to be no broadcasting or recording of any kind of the performance without the written consent of the artist.

The ISM's form of contract provides that if after an engagement has been agreed a concert is cancelled by the promoter, then provided notice of the cancellation is given in writing more than four weeks before the concert date only 75 per cent. of the fee is payable but if given later than four weeks the whole fee is payable. If due to illness or other circumstances beyond his control the artist is unable to fulfil the engagement no liability attaches to the artist but an alternative engagement may then be agreed upon.

Professional Chorus Singers

There is no collective agreement between any management association and Equity or the ISM for concert engagements of professional chorus singers but both Equity and ISM promulgate minimum rates and conditions which are adhered to by choral managers.

The rates are according to scale and take account of the size of the chorus—the larger the choir the lower the rate—with a special rate for choirs or ensembles of eight or less. The differences are to reflect the weight of importance usually attached to the performance of a small group than a large one, and the likely complexity of the works performed by an ensemble.

The fees promulgated are standard for all singers. The concert performance fee is for a concert of two and a half hours; a supplement is payable for each additional period of 15 minutes or part thereof. In addition a rehearsal fee for a rehearsal of three hours on the performance day is automatically payable. For rehearsals on a day previous to the performance the rehearsal rate is doubled. For each period of 15 minutes or part thereof in excess of three hours a supplement is payable but if a rehearsal exceeds 30 minutes the full rehearsal fee becomes payable.

When a concert is broadcast or recorded, in addition to the concert fee there are also payable fees at the rates prescribed in the collective agreements described in Part 4 below.

For engagements at a place beyond 15 miles of the recognised central point of an artist's regular centre of employment an "out of town" fee is payable according to the mileage necessarily travelled by an artist to fulfil an engagement. The cost of travel and a supplement for late night return (after 11.59 p.m.) are payable; a meal allowance and the cost of reasonable overnight accommodation are also payable as the circumstances may be.

Unless circumstances arise outside his control, a concert promoter is liable for the payment of the fees due to an artist unless due notice of the cancellation of a concert is given. Provided more than four weeks' notice is given only 50 per cent. of the fees due is payable, if two weeks' notice is given then 75 per cent., but if less than two weeks 100 per cent. of the fees is payable. Promoters are not contractually bound for engagements which are 'pencilled' in but only when confirmed orally or in writing.

Equity has instituted a code of practice for choral managers which is contained in the form of agreement entered into by a manager with Equity.

A choral manager undertakes to offer engagements only to singers with professional experience. Full or provisional membership of Equity is a way of demonstrating such experience. When on account of the particular circumstances this undertaking cannot be fulfilled, a choral manager is required to consult Equity before engaging non-professional singers.

The services of professional singers may be provided to augment non-professional choirs provided the concert for which they are engaged is promoted by the (amateur) choir or choral society. Professional singers may not be made available to perform with non-professional singers in studios and the like.

Choral managers should obtain terms and conditions of engagement for singers not less favourable than the minimum terms currently in operation. In negotiating engagements with concert promoters and agents and others, managers are enjoined to ensure payment is made of all the fees due so that managers can account to singers within 30 days of the completion of an engagement for the fees due to them. If there is any default on the part of a promoter or the like in making payment Equity is to be informed. If cancellation fees are not paid Equity is to be informed. Managers are also required to account to singers promptly for all royalties, repeat fees and any other additional fees as received.

F. THE PROFESSIONAL MUSICIAN AND ARTIST WITH AMATEUR PERFORMERS

Throughout the country there are many thousands of societies, associations, clubs, variously undertaking non-commercially the promotion and presentation of festivals, concerts and theatrical entertainments of all kinds. Concert performances by entirely professional musicians may be sponsored and promoted by music societies, but it is the engagement of professional musicians and artists to conduct, accompany or supplement musical performances by amateurs, and to direct and appear in productions of opera, operetta and musical plays which is considered below.

Many of the societies undertaking concert and theatrical productions are in membership of the National Federation of Music Societies and the National Operatic and Dramatic Association which are charitable organisations of long standing. Because of the scale of the activities of their members and the amount of the revenues thereby generated, both of these organisations secure advantages and concessions for their members in such matters as comprehensive insurance, access to and the hire of scores and scripts, and arrangements for the payment of performing right fees. These organisations play an important consultative role in many of the aspects of live entertainment but as regards the negotiation of the terms and conditions of the employment of professional performers by their members, only the National Federation of Music Societies is a party to any collective agreement, namely, that with the Association of British Orchestras and the Musicians' Union for the casual engagement of orchestral musicians.

The engagement of a celebrity professional musician to conduct an orchestra and choir, or to perform as a solo instrumentalist or singer at a concert organised by a music society will need to be negotiated by the organising committee with the musician (or his agent) in the same way as for any other professional engagement as explained in the preceding Section E. Similarly with the engagement of a visiting orchestra, the terms and arrangements will need to be negotiated with the orchestral management and these will be very much governed by the rates and conditions applicable to the employment of orchestral musicians as outlined in Section D above. If professional instrumental musicians are engaged to augment an amateur orchestra the minimum rates and conditions as for casual orchestral concert engagements promulgated by the Musicians' Union will be applicable.

Where professional musicians are engaged to accompany amateur productions of opera, operetta and musical plays at theatres whose proprietors are members of the Theatrical Management Association and at other theatres and cinemas (except in the circumstances explained below), the rates and terms contained in the Collective Agreement for Provincial Theatres will apply so that musicians should be contracted on Contract No. 4A. When amateur productions are at theatres and cinemas with a seating capacity of less than 500 and provided not less than 12 professional musicians are engaged, then, with the Union's approval, the special reduced promulgated rates referred to below can be applied.

Amateur productions in venues other than theatres and cinemas are subject to special rates and terms promulgated by the Musicians' Union and for these engagements the Union has provided Contract No. 8A. Engagements are for a stated period and place of performance and for each week not less than the minimum promulgated salary is payable. Payment of the weekly salary covers six calls that is, rehearsals and performances each of up to three hours' duration; for any additional calls a standard rate is payable. Overtime calculated for every 30 minutes or part thereof is at the rate promulgated by the Union. Double rates are generally waived for rehearsals and performances on a Sunday but otherwise the general conditions of engagement are those contained in the Collective Agreement for the Provincial Theatre. When professional choral singers are engaged to supplement an amateur choir the rates promulgated by Equity and terms of engagement outlined in Section E above apply.

When professional singers and artists are engaged to perform roles in amateur theatrical productions the minimum rates and conditions prescribed in the Collective Agreements for the Subsidised Repertory and Provincial Theatre outlined in Part 2 above apply.

Part 4

THE PERFORMER AND THE MECHANICAL MEDIA

A. INTRODUCTION

The expression "the mechanical media" has come to be used to describe collectively radio and television broadcasting, the cinematograph film industry in its various branches—films made primarily for cinema or theatrical exhibition, television films, documentaries, advertising, video cassettes—and the record industry. It is in this sense that the expression will be used in this study.

The technical facilities and resources needed for the creation of the products of the mechanical media and the means required for those products to be exploited, necessitate both major capital investments and extensive commercial organisation. Consequently in contrast to the multiplicity of managements and enterprises engaged in the provision of "live" entertainment, the direction and conduct of the business and management of the mechanical media is concentrated in a relatively few corporations and international conglomerates which often have interests reaching far beyond the bounds of entertainment and the performing arts. This phenomenon affects the resources available for production and the methods of promotion and marketing of the output of the mechanical media. More especially it accounts for the diversity of issues which impinge on the terms and conditions upon which the persons with their various talents and skills are employed in the entertainment industry.

In this Part an attempt is made to give a coherent account of the terms and conditions upon which professional performers are regularly engaged or their services contracted in the various branches of the mechanical media. Because of the output and pace of production of programmes for radio and television broadcasting and of films of all descriptions, it follows there has to be prescribed minimum rates of pay, hours of work and conditions of employment. With the potential for the exploitation of the products of the film and television industry, the matter of the rights exercisable in the products of the services rendered by creative persons are a crucial element in the negotiations between managements and unions.

In the past film producers had virtually absolute and unrestricted rights of exhibition in a film but since film production has become directed more towards serving the needs of television than the cinema that is not so. Films and television programmes are variously exploited world wide. They are distributed and sold to the general public as videograms, made available for viewing "non-theatrically" and by "trapped audiences" (meaning briefly viewing for instruction by cultural organisations, and viewing in aircraft and other forms of transport). The potential for the exploitation of programmes and films has also been enlarged by cable and satellite broadcasting. These changes in the film and television industry have resulted in managements and unions agreeing on the payment to artists, musicians and writers of additional fees or royalties according to the more extended use of the products of their services.

In the recording industry there are no established standard minimum rates and conditions of engagement for professional performers negotiated between management representatives and the Unions apart from the exceptions noted below. The manufacture of records and their promotion may be highly concentrated but this is in marked contrast to the enormous amount of available talent so ready and willing to make recordings and which defies any organising. Thus it is that the individually negotiated recording contract with a royalty calculated and paid according to a record company's business and trading policy is the common practice of the industry. The exceptions alluded to concern the engagement of professional sessional musicians and singers and the making of theatrical cast record albums of musical shows. For these performances there are collective agreements between the Performers' Unions and the British Phonograph Industry which represents the managements of the recording companies.

The collective agreements which govern the terms and conditions for the employment of performers in the various branches of the mechanical media are copious in detail and their labyrinthine provisions with footnotes of explanation and meaning make daunting reading. In the following Sections an explanation of these agreements is attempted but when any dispute or issue arises then recourse must be made to the agreements themselves (and the intervening changes) for the resolution of the matter.

B. TELEVISION AND THE ARTIST

The Broadcasting Act 1990 has brought about major changes to radio and television broadcasting and especially to commercial television broadcasting. The Independent Television Commission (ITC) has been constituted in the place of the Independent Broadcasting Authority. As from January 1, 1993 programme companies become regional licensees and wholly responsible for the programmes they broadcast; the ITV Channel becomes the Channel 3 service. The Channel Four Company also then becomes a separate and independent corporation constituted under the 1990 Act.

Some of the established programme companies have had their franchise for their respective region renewed by the ITC whilst new companies have been appointed for those who have not. It follows that new collective agreements to operate as from January 1, 1993 will need to be negotiated by the programme companies and the Unions representing performers of all kinds, writers and owners (or representatives of owners) of copyright works. For the time being the existing collective agreements outlined below will continue to be applied but it remains to be seen how drastically these agreements are altered as a result of the changes which are emerging to commercial television broadcasting.

The BBC as constituted by Royal Charter and the licence under which it is empowered to transmit programmes is not substantially affected by the provisions of the Broadcasting Act 1990. The BBC because of the scale of its operations, its range of programmes and employment of artistic talent of all kinds stands apart from other broadcasting organisations. Moreover, it is in the unique position in that its income is derived mainly from the general public licence fee and is not dependent on the sale of advertising time or sponsorship. Even so the BBC is not insulated from the expansion and changes in broadcasting resulting from the Act.

A role has been accorded by the Government for independent producers to provide programmes for the BBC and ITC networks. The way of commissioning independent productions has been modelled on the practice of the Channel Four Company and the terms of the agreements for these productions are considered in Part 7 below.

For the majority of persons performing in the programmes transmitted by the BBC and the ITC their minimum fees and conditions of employment are governed by collective agreements negotiated by the BBC with

Equity and the Musicians' Union and correspondingly by the representatives of the programme companies with Equity and the Musicians' Union. The basic fees paid are for certain limited rights of transmission; supplementary fees or royalties are payable for repeat transmissions in the domestic services, for transmissions overseas, and for other extended uses of recordings of programmes. In the following paragraphs a broad outline is given of the structure and terms of the principal collective agreements for the engagement of performers. The collective agreements detailing the terms and conditions of employment of production staff, technicians and craftsmen are not dealt with; the collective agreements for writers are considered in Part 7.

THE BBC AND EQUITY TELEVISION AGREEMENT

The Collective Agreement between the BBC and Equity for artists engaged to perform in television broadcast programmes was much revised in July 1992. It is divided into 13 sections the first five detailing the different kinds or types of engagement. The remaining seven sections deal with matters of general application such as the broadcasting of excerpts of productions from theatres and the relaying of productions produced independently of the BBC, repeat transmissions and the payment of repeat fees, the sale of programmes for overseas transmission and exhibition to non-paying audiences, the general conditions of employment, and the Casting Agreement. Section 12 provides for the employment of Supporting Artists and Walk-ons (which is considered separately below). The last section 13 provides for the duration and nature of the Agreement, namely, that it is binding in honour and does not give rise to any legal obligations between the parties.

Artists are engaged under one of the five prescribed classes of engagement for each of which minimum rates and terms of service are prescribed. The five sections classifying engagement are:

Section 1: Artists exercising dramatic skills in plays, features and light entertainment shows etc.; Dancers and Skaters (whether solo or in a group); Solo Singers (when taking part in at least one act of operas, operettas or musicals).

Section 2: Variety acts, including Specialty Acts, Solo Light Entertainment Singers, Pop Singers and Pop Groups.

Section 3: Stunt or Fight Arrangers and Stunt Performers.

Section 4: Choreographers.

Section 5: Chorus Singers.

For each of the five classes of engagement minimum rates are specified but the fees payable to an artist are open to individual negotiation according to the criterion as set out in the Agreement, namely, such factors as "the nature and weight of the artist's constribution, the number of programmes to be recorded, the length of the engagement, and the artist's status and earning power in television and elsewhere". The basis of all engagements is that for the negotiated engagement fee the BBC is entitled to an artist's services as laid down in the Agreement and by paying the fee, to transmit or permit the transmission of the artist's performance in the relevant programme, whether live or recorded, once only from every transmitter of the relevant BBC channel either simultaneously or at different times in different BBC regions.

Terms of Engagement

Section 1 The current Agreement has brought about a major change in the way artists, especially those within this section, are engaged. Hitherto artists were contracted under different categories for each of which a prescribed minimum fee was payable for a prescribed number of days of attendance. These categories have been dispensed with and now with certain exceptions artists are engaged on a weekly basis for a uniform commitment of attendance and work. A minimum weekly fee is prescribed but for engagements exceeding one week there is a scale of minimum fees at rates according to the number of weeks of the engagement and the duration of the programme. The sum of the weekly fees constitutes an artist's engagement fee.

The commitment for a week's engagement is attendance on six days, but for engagements of two weeks or more attendance on five days per week (including the first). A working day may be for the purposes of rehearsal or recording or travel, or in any combination of these services. If an artist is required to work on more than the prescribed days an additional standard daily rate is payable for each extra working day but at a reduced rate when only a travel day. Subject to his availability in an emergency an artist's engagement may be extended beyond the agreed number of weeks and for each additional day's work an agreed daily fee is payable.

There are special provisions which allow for "split attendance" when an artist's services may not be required continuously during a period of engagement. This may be reflected in the negotiated weekly fee and when the BBC will have first call on an artist's services and not be entitled to his exclusive services. Special provision is made for artists engaged to perform in serials rehearsed and performed within a seven day period.

For educational, religious, documentary, features, instructional, critical and magazine programmes artists may be engaged on a daily basis. A minimum fee is prescribed for five hours work in an overall period of six hours for a maximum aggregate of 10 minutes transmission material. One day engagements may likewise be agreed for artists engaged to perform minor contributions to a programme which can be rehearsed and recorded on a single day. A minimum fee is prescribed for up to eight hours work in an overall period of 10 hours. There are special provisions for engagements for voice-only performances, for closed-circuit exercises and for puppeteers. Provision is also made for the use of an artist's appearance in opening and closing sequences of series and serials, and for the use of trailers of a programme.

Section 2 Artists performing as variety acts, solo light entertainment artists, pop singers and pop groups are engaged for a negotiable fee to cover two days work. Minimum rates are prescribed on a scale according to the number of artists comprising the act or performance. A standard fee is payable to each artist for an additional day of work whether for rehearsal and/or performance. When artists are engaged for a programme produced in a region or in London but transmission is excluded from the London Region, the engagement fee may be reduced by 25 per cent.

Light entertainment singers, pop singers and pop groups may be engaged for the recording of opening and/or closing music on the basis as above but the fee covers the right of unrestricted use of the recording as a signature tune for a programme for a period of six months from the date of the first transmission. The six month period is renewable by additional payments equal to the original engagement fee.

Section 3 Stunt or fight arrangers and stunt performers are engaged on a daily basis for rehearsals and performance and for reconnaissance when necessary. A separate fee is payable when an arranger also performs. All stunt work fees are negotiable to take account of (a) the number of times the artist is required to perform the stunt, and (b) the degree of hazard involved, but subject to minimum rates. If an artist is required to supply any properties this also is to be taken account of in the negotiation of the engagement fee. Standard supplementary fees are payable for waiting days on location or travel days when it is not practical for an artist to return home. If a stunt performer is required to appear in vision to establish or confirm the character performed in the stunt and which requires work beyond that expected of a Walk-on the engagement fee is subject to further negotiation and at an increased minimum rate.

Section 4 Choreographers are engaged on virtually the same terms and conditions as dancers, that is, as artists engaged under section 1. A weekly fee which is negotiable subject to a minimum rate is for up to six working days within a week; an additional two days may be added to the week at a minimum fee of 25 per cent. of the agreed weekly fee. Provision is made for short engagements to direct simple dances for which a minimum payment to cover not more than three work days is payable.

A choreographer's working hours are as for dancers engaged for the production. No payment is due for rehearsal overtime but when a choreographer is present at a recording then overtime is payable corresponding with the payment paid to the dancers. The copyright existing in a choreographer's work rests with the choreographer subject to the rights of the BBC under the terms of an engagement.

If a choreographer is required to perform in the production then an additional fee as for an engagement under section 1 is payable. If a dancer is required to assist a choreographer, a standard supplement to the dancer's weekly fee is payable.

Section 5 Chorus singers may be engaged on a sessional or weekly basis or a combination of both. A "main" session consists of up to five hours work over seven hours for both rehearsal and performance (which may be alternated), for which a standard minimum fee is payable. For each 15 minutes or part thereof of overtime a standard fee is payable. An additional rehearsal session of three hours (for which a separate fee is payable), may be booked for the same day as, or prior to the main session. There may be up to one hour's overtime at this rehearsal session at a special rate, but if the hour is exceeded a whole additional session is deemed to have commenced at the start of the overtime. If at an additional rehearsal session any recording is made a daily standard supplement is payable.

The Agreement provides for the engagement of singers for a shorter main session of three hours at reduced rates providing the singers are out of vision and the music is recorded in its entirety in advance of the final recording of a programme by other artists.

An engagement on a weekly basis may be contracted at a standard minimum fee for six days work in any consecutive seven days. Working hours, overtime and other conditions of engagement are as for other artists engaged under section 1. A weekly engagement may be extended for up to two days for each of which a main session fee is payable. Pre or post the period of a weekly engagement additional recording days may be booked as for a main session.

For the recording of signature tunes for opening and/or closing music the payment of the sessional fee is inclusive of payment for the right of unrestricted use of the recording as a signature tune for six months from the date of first transmission. The six month period is renewable by additional payments equal to the original total sessional fee(s).

General Conditions of Employment

The Agreement sets out conditions of employment which apply to most engagements; the particular exceptions have been noted in the above Sections.

The hours of work and overtime during an engagement are:
(a) in the studio:
    (i) On the principal (or nominated) performance day, a continuous period of 12 hours to include up to 10 hours of work. Thereafter overtime at a standard rate is payable for each 15 minutes or part thereof.

    (ii) On other working days if used for pre- or post-recording including rehearsal, a continuous period of 10 hours to include up to eight hours work and a meal break of not less than one hour. Thereafter overtime at a standard rate is payable for each 15 minutes or part thereof. If the working day is for rehearsal only, a continuous period of eight hours to include up to six hours work. Thereafter a standard rate of overtime is payable per hour or part thereof.

(b) on location:
A continuous period of nine hours to include up to eight hours work and a meal break of not less than one hour. An aggregate of up to one hour's travel time may be scheduled over and above the nine hours without additional payment. Thereafter overtime at a standard rate is payable for each hour or part thereof.

Night work is either work scheduled to extend beyond midnight, excluding overtime, or to begin between midnight and 7 a.m. A special supplementary fee is payable for night work and a special rate of overtime applies but otherwise night work is part of the terms of an engagement. If night work continues unforeseen into day work time the hourly rate for overtime applies. When day work extends unforeseen into night work it counts as overtime for which a special standard hourly rate applies but no other supplementary fee is payable. If an artist is called early, but not before 5 a.m., an additional standard fee is payable and the hours worked thereafter count towards the work day.

Time spent in costume and make-up preparation counts towards the overall work period. Rehearsal and performance may be alternated and spread throughout a working day as may be required. Only in exceptional circumstances is an artist to be required to work on more than six consecutive days. It is the normal practice for a work period not to exceed five consecutive hours and for there to be a rest between work on the same engagement of not less than 10 hours, but usually 12 hours.

Standard fees are payable for attendance at read-throughs, and for attendances at photographic sessions and costume fittings when these occur before the start of an artist's engagement period. Payment of an artist's weekly fee normally covers his appearance in a trailer but if an artist is required to take part in a trailer after the engagement period a standard fee is payable. Recorded trailers may be broadcast without limitation.

The BBC undertakes to use its best endeavours to fulfil any arrangements made concerning an artist's billing but by so doing the BBC does not make a contractual commitment to accord billing whether on the screen or in the *Radio Times*.

Without his prior consent the use of still photographs of an artist taken by the BBC in the course of an engagement is limited to use in programmes and for promotional activities including use in BBC publications.

An artist's travelling time to and from a location begins with his time of departure from the appropriate railway station, terminal or assembly point nominated by the BBC, and ends with his time of arrival on returning to the departure point. There are detailed provisions concerning travel arrangements, allowances and the payment of expenses and evening dress allowance.

Broadcasting of Excerpts of Theatrical Productions and Concert Performances

The relaying live or recorded of performances by professional artists at theatres, concert halls and other places of entertainment is as noted in Part 2 always subject to their consent and any broadcasting of the whole of a theatrical production is subject to the approval of Equity. Section 6 of the Agreement provides for the broadcasting of only excerpts of up to 10 minutes from productions of other managements.

Excerpts are normally recorded at an artist's place of work but if more practical at the BBC's studios or other location when the excerpt may be transmitted live. A recording is to be completed within a call time of three hours including an artist's travel time. No excerpt may include the denouement of a play, consist of a complete work, or interfere with the theatre presentation of the production.

The fees payable for an artist's services are according to a scale which takes account of the transmission time of the excerpt and the kind of programme in which the excerpt is included, which are: (a) news bulletins and news items in news magazines, and (b) magazine, feature and documentary programmes. If an excerpt is over five minutes (it may not exceed 10) artists are engaged as for a one day engagement as provided for in section 1 of the Agreement.

Directors and stage management staff who are especially called by the BBC to attend the recording, or appear in the transmitted excerpt or in the opinion of the BBC make a significant contribution to the recording are paid the like fees as the artists.

Excerpts of over 10 minutes transmission time may be made of concerts in which an artist's contribution is musical or narration to music, of concert performances of opera, and of solo concert performances by singers (with or without backing chorus); also of special functions such as championships, pop concerts and festivals. For all such excerpts a minimum fee is payable to each artist and a minimum for each chorus singer.

Relays from cathedrals and churches are subject to rates agreed for lay clerks by the Incorporated Society of Musicians but Equity represents the lay clerks of Westminster Abbey, St. Paul's Cathedral and Westminster Cathedral. For ordinary services payment is at the rates as for chorus singers (section 6 above), but for the relay of special services 150 per cent. of the rates apply.

Relaying of Opera and Ballet Productions

Section 7 covers the transmission live or recorded of a public performance of opera and ballet rehearsed and produced by a company independently of the BBC. A scale of fees for the various categories of artists adopted by the opera/ballet company and length of production is prescribed but for principals the fees are negotiable. The fees for directors (and staff producers of a company if engaged by the BBC for the broadcast programme) are also subject to negotiation.

The basis of an engagement is three work days (two rehearsal and one recording day) out of seven if required; supporting artists and walk-ons are paid on a daily basis. Each artist is contracted individually and no firm commitment is made until complete agreement is reached with all those involved in the production.

Offers of engagement by the BBC are normally made to the artists to appear in the production not less than two months before the performance date and there is an obligation for a response within seven days. If agreement cannot be reached with an artist (provision is made for arbitration when fees are negotiable), a management with the approval of the BBC has the right to re-cast a part so that the broadcasting of the production can proceed. If the recording of the opera or ballet is repeated or transmitted overseas then as for any other programme additional fees are payable to the artists concerned.

Repeat Transmissions of Programmes

The extent to which the broadcasting of recorded programmes may be repeated in the BBC's Domestic Service is governed by section 8 of the Agreement. Generally the right is limited to repeat the broadcasting of a recording twice on either of the BBC's channels and in different regions at different times within three years from the date of the original transmission subject to the payment of a repeat fee.

The payment to a performer for each repeat transmission is based on "the residual basic fee" which is usually 100 per cent. of an artist's total engagement fee, but may not be less than 80 per cent. There is excluded from the calculation of the residual basic fee the payments made for any of the following services: additional work days, overtime, retainer fees, expenses, read-through, photographic session, costume fitting, night work fees, trailers after the final date of an engagement, reconnaissance by stunt performers and the supply of costumes or properties.

The standard repeat fee payable is 80 per cent. of an artist's residual basic fee but there are variations. For drama and light entertainment programmes repeated more than two years but less than two and a half years after the original transmission, the repeat fee is 90 per cent. of the residual basic fee; if the repeat is more than two and a half years but within three years of the original transmission the fee is 100 per cent. of the residual basic fee.

When a programme is repeated within one week of the original transmission the repeat fee is 50 per cent. of the residual basic fee provided payment is guaranteed at any time before the first transmission; accordingly it is payable whether or not the repeat transmission takes place. If there is a second repeat the normal repeat fee is payable but if a third repeat is given within one week of the second transmission the repeat fee is 50 per cent. of the residual basic fee.

For particular categories of artists and performers such as chorus singers, voice only performances and theatre excerpts, there are special provisions respecting the percentage of the residual basic fee payable for a repeat transmission.

Continuing education programmes may be repeated five times over a period of five years from the date of first transmission. For these repeats 50 per cent. of an artist's residual basic fee is payable but for the fourth 100 per cent. is payable. Schools programmes may be repeated seven times within the same five year period when 50 per cent. of the residual basic fee is payable for each repeat except for the fifth and seventh when 100 per cent. is payable.

Use of Extracts of Recorded Performances

Flashbacks of an artist's performance may be used for the purposes of continuity between one episode of a series or serial and another; one minute of a previous episode may be used in the next without any additional payment. For any other use of flashbacks standard fees are payable to an artist according to the duration of the flashback and whether or not the artist appears in the episode in which the flashback is used. The fee paid for a flashback is additional to an artist's engagement fee and so forms part of the calculation of an artist's residual basic fee.

In principle extracts from programmes may be included in later pro-grammes without restriction of the time within which any extract may be used or its duration. Extracts from variety performers and specialty acts are limited to two minutes unless the prior consent of the artists has been obtained, and may not include whole acts or the climax of an act. An artist's consent is required for the use of an extract to criticise or ridicule the artist's performance, or the performance is of an explicitly sexual nature.

Standard fees of an amount calculated according to the minutage used are payable to artists for the use of extracts. By the payment of 100 per cent. of the extract fee at the time of the first use of the extract, no further payment is due if the programme incorporating the extract is repeated at any time. Similarly by the payment of 100 per cent. of the extract fee on the first occasion of any sale of the programme (as below) no further payment is due to an artist on account of the wider exploitation of the programme incorporating the extract.

Extracts of up to one minute may be used in programmes of an histor-ical or reminiscent nature without the payment of any fee to an artist. The making and transmission of compilation programmes, that is pro-grammes consisting entirely of extracts from previously transmitted pro-grammes featuring one artist, or an established group of artists, or a programme series, is subject to the consent of the artists involved and to the payment of a fee but not less than the prescribed minimum.

Section 8 also provides for the broadcasting in any period of 12 months and in place of "bought in" material of (a) up to 52 out of time repeats, and (b) out of time repeats aggregating in transmission time not more than 150 hours per year. A special scale of percentages of artists' residual basic fees applies for these out of time repeats. The scale of percentage payments is according to whether a transmission is during peak time or off peak time, and when the programme was made. The fees increase according to the number of years elapsing since the year when a programme was made.

Overseas Transmission of Programmes

Following the balloting of its members Equity, in recent years, negotiated initially with the programme companies of the ITC and subsequently with the BBC a radical change in the way artists are paid for the sale and broadcasting of programmes overseas. Hitherto payment for such usage was by reference to the fees paid to an artist for an engagement and according to the country of sale a percentage of an artist's fees was payable. A quite elaborate scale of percentage payments for particular countries and territories of the world and stipulating the number of transmissions and in some instances identifying particular networks and stations within a country (notably the U.S.A.) formed part of the collective agreements. This system continues to apply in respect of engagements contracted with artists by the programme companies before January 1, 1988 but with the BBC it continues to apply to those engagements where the final recording or performance date was before October 31, 1989.

In the Supplement to the Agreement, the BBC, BBC Enterprises Ltd. and Equity have agreed to the adoption of a system of royalty payments like that of the programme companies. The system applies to all Television Drama Group output and Regional drama, to all Light Entertainment output, and all other drama output including that of school broadcasting and children's programmes.

All Equity type artists (but excluding Walk-ons and Supporting Artists) share in a royalty of 17 per cent. of the gross income accruing to BBC Enterprises in respect of the exploitation of a programme, the royalty being shared among the artists appearing in the programme in the proportion to their individual total residual basic fees (as above). With co-productions not giving rise to income for BBC Enterprises the royalty is based on a notional income derived from standard rates for the particular form of exploitation published in "Variety."

The Supplement provides that the royalty system applies to all media of exploitation and covers "any means of distribution now known or hereafter developed including but not limited to cable television satellite broadcasting and terrestrial broadcasting whether in the United Kingdom or overseas but in respect of the following forms of exploitation existing agreements continue to apply while in force unless otherwise agreed, namely, videograms, simultaneous retransmissions in Europe."

The exploitation of any programmes falling outside the categories listed above is subject to the earlier existing scheme for the payment of additional fees. Also where BBC Enterprises wishes to exploit a programme not covered by the Agreement a special arrangement is to be made with Equity. Flexibility in the application of the new royalty scheme is provided for by agreement with Equity when necessary according to the particular circumstances.

Unless at the time of negotiating an engagement a stipulation is included in an artist's contract to the contrary, the BBC has automatically the right to exploit the recording of an artist's performance in a programme in accordance with the terms of the Agreement as above. There is no limitation on the time within which any exploitation of a programme may take place or restriction on the extent of the exploitation such as the number of transmissions which may be made.

Section 10 of the Agreement makes special provision regarding programmes made specifically for Eurovision (EBU) and/or Intervision (OIRT). For such a programme there is added to an artist's engagement fee a supplement which is a percentage of his engagement fee of an amount as set out in the Agreement for each country transmitting the programme. One transmission either live or deferred is permitted in a country within 30 days from a transmission in the United Kingdom. This transmission may be either the original transmission or a repeat transmission by the BBC. Programmes not made specifically for EBU and/or OIRT transmission when broadcast in the foreign territories of the EBU are treated as for any other overseas sale of a programme.

Other Exhibitions of Programmes

Section 9 of the Agreement provides for "non-paying audience rights"—otherwise known as non-theatric exhibition rights—and which are defined as "the right of exhibition of material to audiences not making any specific payment to see or hear the material in question and coming within the following categories of audience:

(a) in educational institutions (e.g. universities, colleges, schools, evening institutes);

(b) educational classes and gatherings held by companies and other bodies not being educational institutions;

(c) in clubs and other organisations of an educational, cultural, religious, charitable or social nature (e.g. drama study groups, film societies, churches, professional associations, women's institutes, the British Council and any other Government Agencies."

Prints or tapes may be supplied either direct to users or through recognised film societies or film libraries.

The fees paid to artists for this use throughout the world are a percentage of an artist's total residual basic fee (as above) at rates according to the territories covered and the programme classification set out in the section. Payment of the fee is for unlimited exhibitions for seven years. The period may be extended for a further seven years by the payment of the percentage of an artists' residual fee at the rates then current. The classification is between programmes in which Equity members provide:

(a) the major ingredients—drama productions including Shakes-pearean plays, classic series or serials, and dramatised documen-tary programmes, and

(b) only a minor ingredient such as in further education and schools series, feature or documentary programmes or series. Also included in this latter category are drama programmes of not more than 30 minutes' duration provided by the BBC's Television Schools Department regardless of Equity members providing the major ingredient.

Section 9 also provides for closed circuit exhibitions of programmes to visitors at hotels, to passengers in aeroplanes, ships, buses and trains provided no specific charge is levied to view a programme, and for exhibitions at construction sites and oil rigs. One per cent. of an artist's total residual basic fee is payable for each of these five uses and which payment is for a three year term but the extent of the coverage depends on which one of the particular uses is licensed, *e.g.* for hotels one per cent. per 5,000, for aircraft one per cent. in respect of each airline using the facility.

An innovation to section 9 made by the current Agreement is for the release of programmes for theatrical exhibition. By the payment of 50 per cent. of an artist's residual basic fee on the first release of a programme on account of a royalty of 20 per cent. from the income received by BBC Enterprises, a programme may be shown theatrically in the United King-dom and in all overseas territories (including in the U.S.A.) provided that:

(a) the exhibition takes place within a total period of 18 months before and 18 months after the first transmission in the United Kingdom,

(b) the duration of the exhibition of a programme does not exceed three consecutive months in any territory,

(c) exhibitions in the United Kingdom are limited to 30 cinemas and which are not all in the same cinema circuit.

The exploitation of programmes by the sale and hire of videograms to the public is the subject of a separate agreement as noted below.

SUPPORTING ARTISTS AND WALK-ONS

The terms and conditions upon which Supporting Artists and Walk-ons are engaged are now contained within the Agreement in section 12 and not in a separate agreement as in the past. These artists are defined as follows:

"(a) A Supporting Artist is not required to give individual characterisation in a role nor to speak dialogue beyond crowd noise or reaction.

(b) A Walk-on is not required to give individual characterisation in a role but may be required to impersonate an identifiable individual, to accept individual direction and to speak a few unimportant words (unscripted) where the precise words spoken do not matter."

Supporting Artists and Walk-ons if called for auditioning are paid an attendance fee. If between the time of the BBC's offer of employment and the first day of work an artist is offered a better engagement then every endeavour is to be made for him to be released to accept the better offer. When during rehearsals the work for which an artist has been engaged is developed to such an extent as to bring about a variation of the category of engagement an artist is expected to undertake the work provided he is re-contracted on the appropriate higher level if possible before the performance is given.

Supporting artists are paid a standard rate for each day of attendance but at a higher rate for night work. Walk-ons are paid for each day of attendance but at higher standard rates; one rate for rehearsals days and one for recording days and at different rates for night work. For both categories of artists if two or more programmes are recorded on any one day (multi-episodic recordings), an additional 50 per cent. of the applicable fee is payable for that day.

A working day or night is eight hours spread over nine. Night work is either work scheduled to extend beyond midnight or to begin between 10 p.m. and 7 a.m. Time worked in excess of the standard working hours is overtime and standard rates per hour or part thereof are prescribed for day and night work both for rehearsals and recordings. These rates are higher for Walk-ons when recording. If day work extends into night work, that is after 12.15 a.m., night work overtime rates are payable, and if night work extends beyond 7 a.m. night work overtime rates remain payable.

Performers required to exercise special skills are entitled to an additional standard payment for each day they are required so to perform. These special skills are defined as driving vehicles, riding horses, fencing and other skills as designated in the engagement. Artists required to appear nude or semi-nude (if female) are paid the special skills supplement. If required to simulate sexual acts which may or may not involve nudity the fee is negotiated individually. If costume fittings do not take place on a working day an attendance fee is payable.

By the payment of the attendance fees the BBC acquires all rights and for all purposes in the contributions of Supporting Artists and Walk-ons to a programme. Only Walk-ons are entitled to any additional fees and these are limited to payments for repeat transmissions of a programme in either of the BBC's channels and for the use in other programmes of extracts from programmes.

The number of repeat transmissions and the period within which they may be made are as in section 8 of the Agreement as outlined above. In principle 100 per cent. of a Walk-on's total recording fee for a programme is payable for a repeat, but the entitlement to enhancement (to 110 per cent. and 120 per cent.) and liability to reduction for certain programmes applies as for other artists as in section 8. For out of time repeats a Walk-on's fee is increased by a percentage on a scale according to the date when a programme was first made. A standard fee is payable for the use of extracts at rates according to the minutage; the extract may be used in any programme category without restriction of time or percent. of programme length. The same requirement as stipulated in section 8 for the consent of an artist to the use of an extract in certain programmes applies to walk-ons.

Performers required to provide evening dress or other clothing not normally in use by them are entitled to standard daily hiring fees according to the number of outfits they provide. Hair styles may be specified at the time of engagement and a supplementary fee may be payable if this is a special requirement. If an engagement entails unusually strenuous work or work in unusually discomforting conditions then a special additional payment may be negotiated.

THE VIDEOGRAMS AGREEMENT

In 1986 the BBC, BBC Enterprises Ltd., Equity and the Musicians' Union made a collective agreement—the Videograms Agreement—for the making, distribution and sale to the public world wide of videocassettes and videodiscs of BBC programmes incorporating contributions of their members.

An artist's consent is required to such an extended use of the recording of his performance but this is normally given as a term of an engagement. An artist may negotiate special terms as a condition to the giving of consent in lieu of the standard terms of the Videograms Agreement. No consent is required from artists engaged as Supporting Artists and Walk-ons since as noted above the BBC acquires all rights for all purposes in their performance. No formal consent is required from musicians as under the terms of the BBC/Musicians' Union main Agreement consent to the use of the recording of a musicians' performance extends to any agreement in force made between the BBC and the Musicians' Union, the Videogram Agreement being such an agreement. Prior to the release of a videogram of a programme incorporating any performance of artists of the type for which Equity and the Musicians' Union are recognised, the title of the programme and the names of all the relevant artists whose performances are included in the videogram are required to be notified to the Unions.

The BBC may edit or abridge an artist's contribution to a programme for the production of a videogram and may dub an artist's spoken word in foreign languages for the purpose of making versions of a videogram for the overseas sale.

Payment to artists for the videogram right is based on a royalty of 15 per cent. of the adjusted trade price meaning the suggested retail price of a videogram less VAT, dealer discount and wholesale/distribution costs and 7½ per cent. of that net retail price in respect of other rights owners. A further reduction of £1.50 is allowed when the suggested retail price is less than £10. The royalty rate of 15 per cent. is subject to increase up to a maximum of 18 per cent. as stipulated in the Agreement. When BBC Enterprises licenses a third party to sell videograms then from the total income it receives from licensees there is first deducted 7½ per cent. in respect of other rights owners and 28½ per cent. of the remaining net income is applied in the payment of royalties.

The royalties arising as above are divided between artists in the proportion that an artist's total fees (excluding expenses) for the original engagement bears to the total of the fees paid to all other of the qualifying artists engaged for the television production. Where only a part of an artist's performance is included in a videogram that does not affect his entitlement to share in the royalties but no share is payable to an artist whose performance is not included in the videogram. Where a videogram is a compilation of two or more programmes the royalty payable to each artist is based on the total fees paid to an artist in respect of each performance actually incorporated in the videogram.

The Agreement makes provision for the payment to artists of specific amounts by way of advance on royalties and for detailed accounting at regular intervals to Equity and the Musicians' Union of the sales of videograms.

An agreement in similar terms between the BBC, BBC Enterprises and the Incorporated Society of Musicians (ISM) provides for the production and exploitation of videograms of performances by artists making an ISM contribution to a programme.

From the total income received by BBC Enterprises from the sale and/or hire by its licensees of individual videograms of programmes containing any ISM contributions there is first deducted 7½ per cent. for the payment of fees to rights owners. From the net remaining income a royalty is payable on a scale rising from 2½ per cent. to 10 per cent. according to the proportion the ISM type contribution bears to Equity and Musicians' Union type contributions. The resulting royalty is then divided between all the artists making ISM type contributions in the proportion each artist's fee bears to the total of the fees paid to the artists making ISM type contributions to the programme reproduced in the videogram.

THE TELEVISION PROGRAMME COMPANIES AND EQUITY TELEVISION COLLECTIVE AGREEMENTS

The negotiation of the collective agreements between the programme companies of the ITC and the Unions representing artists, musicians, writers and other persons employed by the companies is conducted by the Labour Relations Committee of the Independent Television Association. The Association is the trade association representing the collective views and interests of the programme companies. The Labour Relations Committee although financed by the Association stands apart from it as the Committee operates under the general direction of the companies and is responsible for industrial relations at national level. The collective agreements are subscribed to by each of the programme companies jointly as one party and by the appropriate Union as the other party.

There are two Collective Agreements for the year beginning January 1992 between the programme companies and Equity, namely, the Main Agreement setting out the minimum terms and conditions for the employment of members of Equity for television broadcast programmes (excluding television commercials), and the Walk-ons Agreement.

The Main Agreement covers:

1. Performers, meaning artists exercising dramatic skills in plays, features, documentaries, light entertainment, readings and other types of programmes.

2. Ice skaters.

3. Dancers.

4. Singers.

5. Speciality acts.

6. Choreographers and assistant choreographers.

7. Stunt arrangers and stunt performers.

8. Puppeteers, *i.e.* performers who exercise artistic skill in the manip-
   ulation of three dimensional figures to simulate living movement;
   this definition does not apply to movements solely achieved by
   electric remote control or stop frame animation.

9. Broadcasters in entertainment programmes in the following
   categories:

   (a) disc jockeys;

   (b) quiz masters;

   (c) hosts/hostesses;

   (d) compères/masters of ceremonies;

   (e) regular chairmen and regular members of panel games;

   (f) regular presenters of children's programmes.

Persons who appear as themselves rather than as performers and
instrumental musicians are not engaged under the terms of this
Agreement.

As part of the Agreement the companies declare it to be a policy so far as
reasonable and practical to offer engagements within the scope of the
Agreement to experienced professional performers. If, when engaged,
such a performer is not a member of Equity it has become the custom and
practice to inform Equity of the engagement. Equity acknowledges the
right of companies to broadcast performances by bona fide amateur
artists from time to time.

Programme Engagements and Contracts

An artist is engaged to perform a named part for a particular programme
and to render services at studios and locations as required during a stated
period of time which normally spans the rehearsal period to the final day
of production. Prior to the start of an engagement an artist can be called to
attend for one day for a read through for which payment is made as for a
rehearsal day.

Throughout the contracted period of the engagement there is payable
to an artist (a) a fixed sum for each rehearsal (or standby) day, and (b) a
fixed sum for each production day. In addition there is payable a fee
which is known as "the programme fee" which is negotiable for every
artist but minimum rates are prescribed.

When the terms of an engagement have been settled the standard form
contract signed on behalf of the engaging company should be despatched

within four days, to the artist for counter signature and return within four days of its receipt. When special terms have been negotiated, for example to take account of any exceptional requirements of the part, or for an artist's release to fulfil another engagement, to specify a particular form of credit or to limit any overseas exploitation of the recording of an artist's performance, such terms need to be reflected in the contract. If an artist fails to return a contract counter-signed within four days of its receipt or before the first day of the engagement, or fails to make a statement of objection to the terms offered but still renders services, then the artist is deemed to have accepted the engagement on the terms set out in the contract.

It is by the payment of the programme fee that a company acquires the right to transmit or permit the transmission of an artist's performance in one out of the first five of the six transmission areas set out in the Agreement. Furthermore it is the programme fee which provides the basis for the calculation of the payments due to an artist for any extended transmission of a performance over the independent television network and any repeat transmissions. For any other use of the recording of an artist's performance a royalty is now payable as noted below. The first five of the transmission areas are:

(1) London—the regional area licensed to Carlton Television Limited for week-days and to London Weekend Television Limited at weekends.

(2) Midlands—the regional area licensed to Central Television Limited.

(3) Lancashire—the regional area licensed to Granada Television Limited.

(4) Yorkshire—the regional area licensed to Yorkshire Television Limited.

(5) The rest of the United Kingdom—the remaining regional areas of the ITC licensed to other programme companies and appointed by the ITC.

When a programme is transmitted in more than one of the above five transmission areas 100 per cent. of the programme fee is payable for each additional area but payment for four areas automatically covers the right to transmit in the remaining fifth area. Thus by the payment of 400 per cent. of an artist's programme fee the performance can be transmitted once simultaneously or non-simultaneously over the entire independent television network.

The sixth transmission area identified in the Agreement is Channel 4, the network operated by the Channel Four Television Corporation. For the transmission of a programme on Channel 4, 400 per cent. of an artist's performance fee is payable.

General Provisions on Working Conditions

There are agreed guidelines for the number of rehearsal and production days for a programme. Scripts are to be delivered to artists three days before the start of rehearsals. There should be a read through by all the cast who have speaking parts prior to any rehearsal or performance and prior to any recording. There should be one day of rehearsal for each six minutes of programme length. For a drama production of 90 minutes (*i.e.* slot time) there should be not less than 15 days of rehearsal and three days in the studio of which one need only be an afternoon or evening run through on the set: for productions of 60 minutes—10 days of rehearsal and two days in the studio: for productions of 30 minutes—five days of rehearsal and one full day in the studio. The normal maximum number of production days should be for programmes exceeding 60 minutes—five days, exceeding 30 minutes—four days, for under 30 minutes—three days.

There are different guidelines for series and serials. For a 60 minute weekly series or serial produced on a fortnightly turnround with continuing characters, for the first 13 episodes there should be not less than 10 days of rehearsal; when there are more than 13 episodes continuing characters should have a minimum of five days' rehearsal and the remainder of the cast 10 days. For bi-weekly or daily serials artists should be given as much preparation as possible.

The guidelines are relevant in the negotiation of an artist's programme fee so that when the rehearsal period is eight or more consecutive days an artist is fairly remunerated for the whole of the engagement period. If an artist is engaged to appear in more than one episode of a series or serial or programme of a similar format and gaps occur between the completion of work on one episode and the commencement of work on another and during which time an artist is not required to render services, then the gaps are to be taken into account in negotiating the programme fee if the gaps are of such duration as to inhibit an artist accepting other work.

A normal engagement is the rehearsal period calculated from the first day of rehearsal to the final day of production, but there are refinements. There may be location work prior to rehearsals and when the working hours noted below apply. The Agreement makes provision for a break between the completion of the location work and the start of the rehearsal period when an artist is not required to render services. When the break is of six weeks or less a standard weekly sum is payable for each week of the break with a daily rate for a broken week but of not more than five out of each seven consecutive days. No payment is due when the break exceeds six weeks.

The daily rehearsal rate is payable in respect of five days out of seven consecutive days but if an artist in fact rehearses on more than five consecutive days the payments due for the sixth and seventh days are at progressively higher rates. The rehearsal payment is not payable on days when an artist is absent due to illness or other causes, or if he has been notified by the company that his attendance is not required on a particular rehearsal day and he accepts another engagement for that day. A rehearsal day is of six hours excluding two hours for meal or rest breaks and then overtime is payable at hourly rates.

Production days are days on which an artist is recorded (sound or vision or both), or performs for the transmission whether in a studio or on location. A production day in the studio consists of up to nine hours, including two meal breaks each of one hour, during which rehearsal and/or recording may take place. A standard rate of overtime is payable for each additional hour or part thereof. A company may extend an artist's working day by up to one hour at the beginning of the day for make-up and costume fitting for which overtime at the standard rate is payable. The standard production day payment is at a higher rate for work on a seventh consecutive working day or public holiday.

A production day on location, that is work outside an established television studio, consists of up to 10 hours during which up to eight hours of rehearsal and/or recording may take place; one hour for a meal break and one hour travelling must be allowed. Overtime for each hour or part thereof is payable at the standard rate. Days spent in travelling to and from a location and days spent on location without an artist rehearsing or recording attract a separate standard payment.

Nightwork, whether in the studios or on location is work scheduled to extend beyond midnight, or to commence between midnight and 7 a.m. Payment for night work is at one and a half times the production day payment; overtime is paid at the rate of one and a half times the daytime overtime rate.

When an artist is engaged for a network production a minimum guaranteed weekly rate is payable. A week for the purpose of this provision is a period of five days out of a period of seven; all additional days are at one-fifth of the weekly rate. Under this provision an artist's total earnings are to be divided by the number of weeks of his engagement to give an average weekly earnings figure. If this is less than the minimum the difference is payable for each week of the engagement. Furthermore, for the purpose of calculating repeat payments, the amount of the difference in the weekly earnings is to be added to the artist's programme fee.

The total of an artist's earnings, for the purposes of the above provision, comprises all rehearsal and production day payments, the programme fee, overtime payments and any payments made in respect of work on location and the commencement of the rehearsal period of up to six weeks. Where there is a break between work on location and the commencement of the rehearsal period of less than six weeks, the number of weeks of break count towards the number of weeks of the engagement for the calculation of the average weekly earnings.

Special Categories of Programmes and Performers

Although the foregoing is the basis on which most artists are engaged for most television programmes the Agreement contains special provisions and conditions for particular programmes and particular artists.

The Agreement applies to the production and use of schools and adult educational programmes but makes special provision regarding the payment of programme fees, the number of repeat transmissions and the time within which repeats may be made. Without the consent of Equity these programmes may not be transmitted other than at times normally reserved for their transmission, namely, off peak hours.

Although the Agreement does not apply to children the general understanding and custom of the industry that child performers are paid at half the rate of adults is endorsed. But for children appearing in schools programmes no payment is due when the children appear in learning/teaching situations where no dramatic skill is required, or as children in demonstrative situations.

Series and Serials

For series and serials and for programmes of a similar format an artist may be engaged on a weekly basis provided such programmes are transmitted three or more times in a week and before 7 p.m. (8 p.m. on a Sunday) or after 11.30 p.m. Such an engagement must be for a period of not less than eight consecutive weeks. A minimum weekly rate is prescribed for specific transmission areas or for a network transmission. The weekly rate is for five working days in any period of seven days; a working day is of six hours with overtime thereafter at an hourly rate for each hour or part thereof (exclusive of performance times and meal or rest breaks). There are special rates for work on a sixth day. The number of performances in a week is limited to five. An artist's programme fee for each separate programme is calculated by multiplying an agreed rate (a minimum is prescribed) by the number of days on which an artist rehearsed but did not perform and deducting the resulting amount from the weekly payment. The balance is then divided by the number of programmes and the resultant figure is the artist's programme fee.

Artists may also be engaged for a single day at the studio consisting of up to nine hours work with two meal breaks each of one hour for an inclusive payment. A minimum rate and overtime rate are prescribed. An artist may be required to rehearse and/or record the artist's part for inclusion in not more than six episodes of a series or serial or programmes of a similar format. The inclusive payment is for one network transmission (which may be simultaneous or non-simultaneous). One-quarter of the inclusive payment counts as an artist's programme fee for the purposes of paying repeat fees.

Artists may be engaged expressly for the purpose of performing in opening and closing sequences of a series or serial. Rehearsal and production day payments, and overtime, are payable as appropriate together with a minimum programme fee. The recorded performance may be included in up to 13 episodes of the same series or serial or programmes of a similar format. For each additional 13 episodes (or lesser number) 100 per cent. of the programme fee is payable.

Trailers and Promotions

For the making of trailers an artist who agrees to appear in character outside the contracted period may be paid a production day payment. If the trailer is pre-recorded or transmitted live during the period of an artist's engagement then no additional payment is due. Trailers compiled from extracts from a programme may not exceed 5 per cent. of the running time of the programme and may not be used for any purpose other than for the advertising and promotion of the programme.

An artist may be engaged solely to appear in a promotion trailer of up to three minutes' duration. Rehearsal and production day payments are payable and a negotiated programme fee the latter entitling a programme company to transmit the trailer twice in the area covered by the programme fee. Up to three extra transmissions may be made subject to the payment of 40 per cent. of the programme fee for each transmission.

Voice-over Artists

For the purpose of recording in sound only an artist may be engaged for a voice-over session of four hours but spread over five hours to allow an hour's break. The session may be extended by up to two hours when overtime is payable for each hour or part thereof. If the two hours are exceeded a new session is deemed to have begun as from the start of the overtime. The session can be conducted as a continuous rehearsal/recording of a performance. Minimum programme fees are prescribed according to whether a recording is for inclusion in up to six or 13 documentary, educational, religious, critical and magazine programmes; also according to whether a recording is for incorporation into up to 13 programmes or episodes of a series or serial, or a programme of a similar format of any category other than the foregoing. For a drama programme there can be a two hour session for which a minimum programme fee is prescribed.

Singers

Singers performing out of vision may be engaged for a session of three hours when rehearsal/recording may take place. A minimum programme fee is prescribed and an hourly rate for overtime for each hour or part thereof. Unpaid breaks are to be allowed if a session exceeds four hours. For rehearsal time prior to the start of a session, or on a day prior to the recording day an hourly rate is payable. The fees paid are in respect of only one transmission area. Special provisions apply for the payment of repeat fees.

The Agreement makes special provision respecting the fees payable to singers performing in vision in groups of nine or more, to choreographers and assistant choreographers, to dancers and to artists performing a specialty act, meaning any act of an individual or group (but not singers) which is available as a rehearsed entity ready for performance prior to the engagement. Apart from prescribing particular minimum programme fees minimum payments are also especially prescribed for these categories of artists.

Stunt Performers

An appendix to the Agreement sets out the provisions governing the casting and employment of stunt/fight arrangers and stunt performers. It reflects the terms and conditions for the engagement of these artists set out in the Collective Agreements for Cinema and Television Films considered below. Engagements are on the basis of a negotiated daily rate; a minimum rate is prescribed subject to there being a two days' engagement. Stunt arrangers are usually paid at an appropriately higher rate than stunt performers.

The programme fee is negotiated to reflect whether or not a stunt arranger is required and the nature and number of stunts to be performed. Provision is made for reconnaissance when requested by a company and for work on more than one programme or episode on any one day when supplements to the daily salary become payable. The provisions of the Agreement respecting hours of work etc., and the uses of any recording of a performance apply as for other artists but overtime is at the rate of one-fifth of the negotiated day or night rate. If the transmission of a programme is repeated the basis for the payment of repeat fees to stunt arrangers and performers is four times the negotiated daily rate when an engagement is for work of up to seven days. If the engagement is for work in excess of seven days the foregoing basis applies but the amount is increased proportionately.

Broadcasts of Theatrical Productions

The television broadcasting of theatrical and similar productions presented by an outside management in which Equity members perform is subject to special agreement with Equity as pointed out in Part 2. However, this approval is not required for excerpts of up to 15 minutes from a production especially staged for the purpose of television broadcasting and on the basis that artists are engaged on the terms and conditions of the Main Agreement. If a choreographer (or assistant) is engaged on the theatre production then only if the dancers are seen in vision is the choreographer (or assistant) similarly subject to the Main Agreement. Stage management grades in the production are entitled to be paid the appropriate daily rates as agreed between Equity and a company. The theatre director of a production and the designer are also similarly entitled to payment unless the excerpt is for inclusion in critical, magazine, news magazine and like programmes reviewing theatrical and similar productions when no payment is due.

There are concessions approved by Equity for interviews and short recordings of rehearsals and general backstage activity of theatre productions made for news and topical magazine programmes. Interviews can be made with an artist's consent without payment or for an agreed nominal fee. For recordings of parts of rehearsals and the like, nominal standard fees are prescribed by Equity and the duration of transmission times, namely two minutes for news programmes and up to three minutes for an item included in a magazine programme. If these limits are exceeded or if a recording is used in any other category of programme then artists must be contracted strictly in accordance with the Main Agreement at not less than the minimum rates and conditions.

Use of Extracts of Recorded Performances

Extracts from the recording of an artist's performance may be used in instructional, critical, magazine and similar programmes provided the extract does not exceed four minutes. In educational programmes extracts may be up to five minutes. Standard fees are payable according to an extract not exceeding one minute or exceeding one minute. The use of extracts from the recording of a programme after the time when it may be repeated, or before its transmission is subject to the consent of Equity. The use of an extract in a critical programme is subject to an artist's consent.

If an extract from an artist's performance in a programme is incorporated into another programme as a flashback or flashforward the artist is entitled to additional payments. A standard fee is payable at a rate set according to whether or not the artist is engaged for the programme in which the extract is incorporated, and according to the duration of the flashback or flashforward.

Repeat Transmissions of Programmes

Programmes may not ordinarily be transmitted in any area more than three times or repeated after five years from the date of the first transmission in the United Kingdom without the consent of Equity. For series and serials which have a finite number of episodes and where the final episode is transmitted not later than 26 weeks after the date of the transmission of the first episode, the five year period commences from the date of the transmission of the final episode.

When a programme is transmitted a second or more times in any region an artist's programme fee is again payable. If the repeat transmission occurs after two years from the date of the original transmission 150 per cent. of the programme fee is payable; if after four years 175 per cent. is payable. In addition for each repeat a standard supplement is payable at the rate prescribed according to whether an artist's engagement was of less than or more than six weeks' duration. The Agreement permits up to 52 network out of time repeats (*i.e.* repeats beyond the five years as above) in a year. An artist's consent is required for such a repeat. For the sixth and every additional year from the date of the first transmission of such a programme a further 25 per cent. of an artist's programme fee is added to the 175 per cent. referred to above. Repeat fees are payable within seven days of a repeat transmission.

The foregoing are the principles which govern the payment of repeat fees but there are refinements. For any repeat of a programme the transmission of which begins at or after 11.30 p.m. but before the starting time of franchised breakfast television only 33⅓ per cent. of an artist's programme fee is payable. Special provisions apply to the calculation of repeat fees to artists engaged for sound recordings only, singers engaged to perform out of vision and artists engaged for a single day. For specified programmes which are to be repeated within a week the terms on which repeat fees are payable may by arrangement between a company and Equity be varied.

Overseas Transmission and Other Uses of Programmes

A company's right to use or permit the use of a recording of an artist's performance otherwise than by television broadcasting in the United Kingdom is subject to an artist's consent not being withheld. If an artist's performance is not to be made available for transmission in a particular country or is not to be used in a specified medium of exploitation permitted under the Agreement, the restriction needs to be precisely written into the form of engagement.

As already noted in the survey of the BBC and Equity Television Agreement above a radical change in the way artists are paid for the extended use of recordings of their performances was introduced into the Agreement in fairly recent years. The change became applicable to contracts entered into on and after January 1, 1988. The system of paying additional fees for overseas transmissions as a percentage of an artist's programme fee continues for contracts made before January 1, 1988 but for any other use of recordings of artists' performances made under those contracts the fees payable are as if the contracts had been made on January 1, 1988.

Under the Agreement now in operation a company may use or permit the use of a recording of an artist's performance in any or all media (as defined below) in the United Kingdom and overseas. A programme royalty of 17 per cent. of the gross receipts from sales is divided between artists in proportion to their original programme fees. In respect of those programmes where the aggregate original earnings of Musicians' Union members exceed the aggregate original earnings of Equity members a royalty of 21 per cent. is divided between performers in proportion to their original earnings.

"All media" is defined as:

"inclusive of any and all means of distribution, transmission or exploitation now known or hereafter developed including (but not by way of limitation) cable television, videograms, satellite broadcasting, terrestrial broadcasting, non-theatric and closed circuit television whether in the United Kingdom or overseas, excepting only original transmissions and repeats on ITV and Channel 4, and theatric rights."

The Agreement makes special provision for the payment of fees for artists engaged for recording in sound only, singers performing out of vision, and artists contracted for one day engagements.

Royalties are to be accounted for not later than 28 days after the receipt by a company of the payment for an overseas transmission or not later than 28 days after the known first transmission in the relevant area whichever is the earlier. In respect of sales of programmes for other uses payments may be aggregated and made at reasonable intervals but not exceeding three months. Provision is also made for certified audited statements of receipts to be provided from time to time, for a company to endeavour to recover all payments due from a defaulting purchaser. Where appropriate alternative arrangements may be agreed between a company and Equity for the payment of royalties.

For Eurovision transmissions which are direct or deferred relays of programmes, the provisions of the Agreement between the European Broadcasting Union and the International Federation of Performers applies.

General Conditions of Engagements

The Agreement details the general working conditions for all engagements. The following provisions merit particular attention:

1. Subject to an artist's professional engagements an artist may be called upon to attend a post-synchronisation session of up to four hours for the post-synchronisation of his own voice to his previously recorded visual performance. For these services a minimum sessional fee is prescribed.

2. Unless an artist is engaged to perform his own repertoire, as for example speciality acts which are available as a rehearsed entity ready for performance (except for camera rehearsals and band calls), a company has the sole right to decide the manner in which an artist's personality is to be presented, how a part or role is to be portrayed, how the artist is to dress and appear. But if there are to be any changes to an artist's physical appearance which might be of a semi-permanent nature, as for example hair style or abnormal make-up requirements, these must be the subject of special stipulation included in the form of engagement. An artist's voice may not be dubbed unless especially agreed upon and provided for in the contract of engagement.

3. "Still" photographs taken of an artist during the course of an engagement for the promotion of a programme or use in the programme itself cannot be used for commercial purposes such as for book publications of television dramas or in merchandising without the artist's consent. These conditions are further emphasised by the obligation of a company to take such steps as are reasonable to prevent any illicit use of recordings or reproductions of an artist's performance.

4. An artist has no automatic right to be accorded billing or credit for his performance. Any agreed credits (including billing in publications issued by or reasonably within the control of a company) must be defined in the contract of engagement.

5. An artist is required to provide all such modern dress and footwear as he may possess and may normally and reasonably wear, but otherwise a company is to provide all visible modern dress and all character, period or special costume. If an artist is required to supply and wear evening dress a standard daily allowance is payable by the company. If an artist is required to attend for costume/

wig fitting on a day other than a rehearsal or production day, a standard daily fee is payable plus reasonable out of pocket expenses.

6. A company is not obliged to use an artist's services and it has the right to curtail or withdraw a performance and any publicity regarding it. However, a company's obligation to pay all the contractual fees due to an artist cannot be avoided unless an engagement is cancelled or terminated on account of an artist's conduct. Equity is to be notified in writing of the circumstances giving rise to such action.

7. If an artist supplies material to be performed by him a company can require evidence of the necessary copyright clearances for its use. Also a company has the absolute right to reject and without the need for an explanation any part of an entertainment submitted by an artist. If as a consequence an engagement is cancelled the fees than accrued due remain payable. Where in the form of engagement it is provided that an artist's performance shall be seen and approved by a representative of the company then if all or any part of the entertainment is rejected the artist is to submit other substituted material promptly.

8. An artist is entitled to the payment of the cost of his travel by public transport (or a car mileage allowance) between the centre of the towns listed in the Main Agreement and the place beyond the specified radius (London, Charing Cross, 10 miles, other towns, seven miles) where he is required to rehearse or perform if the place is not a permanent studio in which performances for transmission are normally given. When an artist is called at a time before or detained beyond the time when public transport is not available then private transport must be provided or reasonable living accommodation and meals provided. Where an artist works at a centre or on location away from his usual base then his second class return rail fare is payable. A standard overnight subsistence allowance is payable for each night an artist is required to remain away from his usual place of residence and meal and out-of-pocket expenses are payable at locally agreed rates. If an artist is required to remain away from his home for more than 14 consecutive nights the amount of subsistence is then subject to individual negotiation.

9. If the production of a programme is prevented or interrupted by reason of any cause beyond the control of a company an engagement may be cancelled subject to the payment of all monies accrued due to an artist up to the time of cancellation. Instead the engagement may be postponed or other arrangements agreed upon between a company and the artist.

10. In the event of an artist being unable to rehearse or perform on account of illness or other like incapacity this is to be immediately notified to the engaging company. Subject to its first consulting Equity the company is entitled to terminate the engagement on payment to the artist of all fees accrued due up to the date of incapacity.

WALK-ONS AGREEMENT

The Agreement between the programme companies and Equity for artists engaged as walk-ons specifies three categories of engagement and the services to be performed as follows:

Walk–on 1 (extra)—"a performer who is not required to give individual characterisation nor to speak any word or line of dialogue except that crowd noises are not deemed to be dialogue in this context."

This definition is further amplified in that an artist so engaged is a person or member of a group contributing to the overall authenticity and atmosphere of a scene. The individual or individuals in the group may be dressed in clothing identifiable with the calling or trade selected for each by the director, who may direct each individual to move as required on the set. Crowd noises can include community singing of well known songs where the words do not have to be learned and also congregational hymn singing of well known hymns from hymn books.

Walk-on 2 (non-speaking)—"a performer not required to give individual characterisation but who is required to impersonate an identifiable individual subject to individual direction."

This definition is further amplified in that the artist may be required to perform in medium shot or more closely, a special function peculiar only to the trade or calling that his character is supposed to represent; e.g. a bus conductor collecting fares on a bus, a policeman on point duty, a bar tender serving drinks; and/or at the time that his movements are recorded he has a direct relationship with the actor who is performing his own part as set out in the camera script of that particular shot. It is also stipulated by way of explanation that movement on the set or display of interest in something taking place and any business done in unison with other Walk-ons (extras) does not entitle a Walk-on 1 (extra) to payment as Walk-on 2 or 3.

Walk-on 3 (speaking)—"a performer who in addition to carrying out the functions set out for Walk-on 2 is required to speak a very few unimportant words where the precise words do not matter."

When during rehearsals a performance is developed so as to bring about a change in the category of engagement, a performer is expected to undertake the work provided he is re-contracted on the appropriate basis if possible before the performance is given.

The fees payable to artists for their attendance are according to the category in which they are engaged. Walk-ons 1 are paid a standard fee for attendance on both rehearsal and recording days. Walk-ons 2 and 3 are paid standard fees, but at separate rates, for each day of attendance but at higher rates for a recording day. If artists render services on more than one programme or episode of a series or serial on an attendance or recording day, the fee payable is one and a half times the appropriate rate.

A working day or night is eight hours spread over nine hours. The rates of pay for night work are consistently one and a half times an artist's applicable day rate. Hours worked in excess of eight constitute overtime at one and a half time the relevant hourly rate according as the overtime occurs on a working day or night.

Calls where rehearsing or recording commences before 7 a.m. attract the night rate for all the hours of the call. Calls before 7 a.m. for the purpose of travelling only to a place of work attract payment at the night overtime rate for each hour or part thereof falling before 7 a.m. but the payment for the rest of the day is at normal rates. Calls for work which is scheduled to extend beyond midnight are at night rates for all the hours of the call. If a working day extends beyond midnight for each hour or part thereof falling after midnight the night overtime rate is payable. For attendance on a sixth consecutive day or night the rates are one and a half times an artist's applicable rate; for a seventh day it is double the rate. Higher rates are payable for work on public holidays.

Walk-ons called for auditioning are paid a standard attendance fee. Artists are not normally contracted more than seven days before the first working day (14 if needing time for costuming). If in the interim a performer is offered a better engagement then whenever practicable he is to be released from the contract.

Standard supplementary fees are payable to artists performing special skills (driving, sports etc.), for strenuous work, for two or more changes of costume on any day, for supplying special dress, for costume fittings at times other than during a normal attendance day, and for complying with special requirements in the way of physical appearance, particularly hair style. Artists required to appear nude are engaged in the category of Walk-on 2 and if required to simulate "the sex act" Walk-on 3. Artists are to be informed of the requirement when offered the engagement.

The attendance and recording fees paid to walk-ons are for one transmission of a programme in all areas of Channel 3 or on Channel 4. Only Walk-ons 2 and 3 are entitled to an additional payment when a programme is repeated in the United Kingdom, namely, 25 per cent. of the payments received for recording (but excluding overtime payments), for a repeat in any one area within two years of the first transmission and

37½ per cent. after two years but within five years of the first transmission. Payment for four areas allows a repeat over all five areas of the ITV network. For a repeat on Channel 4 the appropriate rate payable is equal to that paid for the network (*i.e.* 100 per cent. or 150 per cent.).

With schools' programmes no additional payment is paid to Walk-ons 1 for any repeat transmissions. With Walk-ons 2 and 3 the initial payment is for two transmissions in an area provided the second transmission takes place within a period of two weeks. By the payment of 50 per cent. of the original payment to an artist (excepting overtime payments) a third transmission may be screened during the school term or holiday period.

Residual or additional fees are not payable to walk-ons as paid to other artists when programmes are transmitted overseas or otherwise exploited.

The use of extracts from recorded programmes in other programmes (in the same way as for artists under the terms of the Main Agreement) entitle walk-ons to a standard payment according to the minutage. Walk-ons 2 and 3 are entitled to additional standard payments for flashbacks and flashforwards according to the minutage and precise use. Special provisions provide for the engagement of walk–ons to appear in opening and closing sequences for a series, and in promotional trailers.

There is no restriction on the use of "still" photographs for promotion or merchandising in which walk-ons appear. Any other use of a "still" in which a Walk-on 2 or 3 appears requires the consent of the persons concerned; if a Walk-on 1 is identifiable then where practicable the person's consent is to be obtained.

A travel supplement is payable for each day of attendance at a studio or place of rehearsal beyond the relevant fixed radius prescribed in the schedule to the Agreement, but at a lesser rate for attendance within the radius. When persons are assembled by a company and taken to a location the working day begins at the time of assembly and ends at the time of dispersal after the return journey. If persons travel independently to a location the working day begins at the time they would be required to be at an appropriate main place of departure in time to reach the location and ends at the time of return to the main place of return. The ordinary fares payable for the return journey are payable by a company or else a car mileage allowance paid. If a person is called at a time or detained after a time when public transport is not available then transport must be provided by a company, or else overnight accommodation.

DISPUTES PROCEDURE

The two Collective Agreements make provision for the settlement of disputes arising between an artist and a company or between a company and Equity, and for dealing with any complaint of misconduct by an artist. Where issues cannot be settled by negotiation and informal discussion between officials of a company and Equity on behalf of an artist or its members generally, then the dispute can be referred to a Joint Standing Committee consisting of three representatives of Equity and of the programme companies. If then a settlement is not reached the issue is to be referred to two arbitrators, one nominated by the company and the other appointed by the artist but nominated by Equity. The arbitrators so nominated appoint an umpire. Their decision is binding on both parties. This procedure does not affect or preclude the right of the parties to apply to the courts for relief by way of injunction.

C. TELEVISION AND THE MUSICIAN

The basis for the employment of professional musicians in television broadcasting as in other branches of entertainment is the session and the payment of a sessional fee. The Collective Agreements between the Musicians' Union and the BBC and the programme companies have much in common as both provide for various categories of sessional engagements with minimum rates but there are important differences of detail and application. Both Agreements make the important distinction between a session for the performance of music for a programme which at the time of the session is being transmitted live or pre-recorded, and a session where the music being performed and recorded is for subsequent use and incorporation into a programme.

The category of session booked governs the rate of fee payable, the working hours, the amount of music which can be performed or recorded and the manner or extent to which pre-recorded music may be included in a programme. Other provisions provide for repeat transmissions and for the overseas transmission and other uses of recorded programmes, for the relaying of public performances of concerts and other live or pre-recorded entertainment. The various sessional rates and other supplements prescribed apply to all musicians without distinction but extra allowances are made for "doubling" and in some instances such as with symphony and chamber orchestras, musicians designated "principals" or "sub-principals" receive higher sessional rates.

Apart from these two main Collective Agreements for the television broadcasting of musical performances there are in addition agreements negotiated by the BBC with the Musicians' Union and the Incorporated Society of Musicians for the engagement of musicians performing the repertoire of chamber music and musicians engaged as instrumental and vocal soloists, conductors, choral conductors, and church musicians. These collective agreements are considered separately below.

THE BBC AND MUSICIANS' UNION TELEVISION MAIN AGREEMENT

This Agreement applies to the engagement of sessional musicians, that is musicians engaged as required as distinct from those musicians performing in the BBC Staff Orchestras who are contracted on a permanent basis.

The Agreement is divided into six parts. Part I is in eight sections detailing the eight categories of sessional engagements which can be booked.

The Sessions

1. Basic session of five hours for the rehearsing and then performance in or out of vision of music for a programme of up to 60 minutes duration. The working time is four hours as one hour is allowed for rest and a meal break between the rehearsal and actual performance. If extra rehearsal time is required then the duration of the rehearsal and rate of additional fees payable depend on whether the extra rehearsal is immediately before the performance or separate from the session such as on a preceding day. If the working time or the amount of music transmitted or recorded exceed the limits as above additional fees at standard rates become payable.

2. Discontinuous recording session of three hours for a programme of up to one hour when performance and rehearsal may be alternated as required. The music may be recorded either simultaneously with, or in its entirety in advance of the recording of the performances of other artists appearing in the programme. This session does not apply to variety light entertainment programmes when an audience is present.

3. Selective pre-recording session of three hours (but four hours for opera, ballet and serious music) on any one day prior to the day of final performance. Not more than 50 per cent. of the total running time of a programme may be recorded except if an artist is required to dance or move in production numbers then up to 80 per cent. may be recorded: the remainder of the session can be for rehearsal time. At a session on the day of final performance one hour may be used to make a selective pre-recording of not more than one-third of the musical content of the programme; the remainder of the session can be for rehearsal time.

4. Signature tune session of three hours for the recording of opening and/or closing music, national anthems, identifying items and special instrumental effects for a named programme series: not more than one signature tune may be recorded at a session but different versions or treatments of it may be recorded.

5. Incidental or linking music session of three hours for a single programme or episode, or for multi-episodes for a series or serial: up to 60 minutes of music may be recorded. For opera, ballet or serious music the session may be of four hours' duration.

6. Session for short items rehearsed and produced by an outside

organisation: under this section short items or excerpts from theatrical or any other entertainment can be transmitted but only in special programmes such as news, magazine, documentary, educational religious and critical programmes. The duration of a session and the sessional rate payable depend upon the aggregate duration of the items to be recorded. If not exceeding a total of five minutes of music an hour's session, if over five but not exceeding ten minutes then a two hour's session will apply.

7. Broadcasts of public concerts: A standard fee is payable to each musician for a transmission of up to three hours; a standard supplementary fee is payable for each 30 minutes or part thereof in excess of the three hours. The fee is inclusive for any simultaneous radio broadcasting of a concert but fees payable for any repeat or overseas transmissions of a concert are as noted below.

A distinction is made between a concert promoted by the BBC and one promoted independently. Concerts promoted by the BBC can be recorded in their entirety for a deferred transmission but the first transmission must be within six months of the date of the concert.

With concerts not promoted by the BBC, when a recording is made for later broadcasting, the standard fee is for a recording of only one hour's duration; a supplement of 10 per cent. of the standard fee is payable for each hour or part thereof in excess of the first hour. The recording must first be broadcast within six months of the date of the concert.

Regardless of whether a concert is promoted by the BBC rehearsal fees are payable only for those rehearsals required by the BBC. The rate for a three hour rehearsal is variable according to whether the rehearsal is on the performance day or a previous day, but a standard supplement is payable for each 30 minutes or part thereof by which a rehearsal exceeds three hours.

8. Broadcasts and recordings of opera, ballet and similar musical productions which are cast, rehearsed and presented by other organisations and performed at outside locations either with an invited audience or without an audience. The musicians can be engaged for a basic five hour session (as above) for the first hour of recording and with overtime rates as appropriate, or for two or more such sessions with appropriate overtime and additional performance rates as the circumstances may require. The discontinuous recording session and selective pre-recording session (as above) may be used only where both rehearsal and recording are required for the recording of the production. There is provision for retakes on grounds of quality or serious artistic or technical faults and any discarded recorded music does not count towards the

duration of the material recorded in a session. Most other of the provisions of the Agreement apply to this category of engagement as they apply to the foregoing seven including the provisions for the payment of additional fees for repeat and overseas transmissions considered below.

The Agreement provides that where programmes are pre-recorded then the re-recording of sections of a performance is a matter for decision of the programme producer or conductor which may be on the grounds of quality in addition to serious artistic or technical faults. Where there is any retake of any music, then the duration of the discarded recordings does not count towards the duration of the material recorded in the session.

The standard fees payable to musicians are prescribed for each of the sessions, the rates being for a network transmission but provision is made for reduced rates when a programme is for regional transmission. By the payment of the fees due the BBC has the automatic right to incorporate the performance of music in the programme for which it was recorded but otherwise the use of tape recordings is strictly controlled by the terms of the detailed specifications of each of the sessions. These provide for example, for the payment of additional fees to musicians for the use of tapes at rehearsals of a programme at which they are not present, and for the erasing of the tapes.

Contractors who on behalf of the BBC assemble musicians for sessions and undertake the monitoring of their contracts of engagement and attend to the payment of all the fees due to them, are paid an assembly fee for their services. In principle 10 per cent. of the basic fee multiplied by the number of musicians engaged together with 10 per cent. of all other supplements paid to musicians in the course of an engagement (except porterage and out-of-town fees) is paid to a contractor. Also 10 per cent. of the amounts paid to musicians for any repeat broadcasts and for overseas transmissions or other exploitation of recorded programmes is paid to a contractor.

General Provisions

Part II of the Agreement contains the more general terms of engagement and working conditions. Provision is made for the payment of an additional standard fee for night work that is, any work between midnight and 9 a.m.; for the payment of out-of-town rates for engagements beyond 16 miles of the recognised city centre where a musician is normally based; for the payment of fees for "doubling" and additional fees when an audience is present at a rehearsal or discontinuous recording session; for the payment of porterage, subsistence and travel allowances.

Other provisions allow for the showing of trailers without additional payments; for the use of extracts from programmes (but subject to various additional payments) in programmes for schools, and in religious, educational, documentary, critical and like programmes; for cross media usage (meaning the use of extracts of recordings for television in radio broadcasting and visa versa), and for the making of backing tracks (meaning the recording of an orchestral accompaniment in advance of the performance by the other artists for a programme). Provisions are also included for the general reduction of the standard rates when a programme is transmitted in one BBC region or area only and for the payment of the balance if and when a programme is subsequently transmitted in another region or network.

Repeat Transmissions

Part III of the Agreement provides for repeat transmissions in the United Kingdom of recorded programmes and for their broadcasting overseas and other exploitation.

A recorded programme may be repeated without limitation of time or number on either of the channels of the BBC and in different regions at different times. Additional fees are payable for each repeat transmission these being a percentage of a musician's "performance fee." The performance fee is the aggregate of a musician's session fee, additional performance fees (that is, the extra payments made when the working time of a session is exceeded or the permitted amount of music performed or recorded is exceeded) and "doubling" fees. The fees paid for rehearsals or selective pre-recordings are not aggregated.

There is a scale of percentages of a musician's performance fee payable which applies to the repeat transmission of most programmes, namely, 50 per cent. for each of the first two repeats, 100 per cent. for the third repeat then 50 per cent. for each of the fourth and fifth repeats and 100 per cent. for the sixth repeat, the same pattern applying for successive repeats. For repeat transmissions of continuing education and schools programmes the pattern is modified so that most often 50 per cent. of the performance fee is payable.

Exploitation of Programmes

The most important of recent changes to the Agreement has been the introduction of a system of royalty payments for the extended and wider use of programmes complimentary to that established under the Equity Agreement for artists. No longer is the exploitation of programmes limited in time nor the amount of additional fees linked to specific forms of exploitation.

The new system of payment covers all categories of programmes and their exploitation in all media except as noted below. The Agreement also covers cable television, satellite broadcasting and terrestrial broadcasting whether in the United Kingdom or overseas. However, the existing agreements for the sale of videograms and commercial records of programmes and for the supply of programmes to British Sky Broadcasting continue to apply while in force.

Musicians' Union-type artists share in a royalty of five per cent. of the gross income accruing to BBC Enterprises from the exploitation of programmes. In respect of concerts (including rock concerts) which do not involve contributors making Equity-type contributions the share is in a royalty of 17 per cent. of the gross income. The royalties are shared among artists in proportion to their performance fee. With co-productions not giving rise to income for BBC Enterprises the royalty is based on a notional income derived from standard rates for the particular form of exploitation published in "Variety."

The exceptions referred to above are opera, ballet, concerts in which Equity-type artists are contributors, and "Top of the Pops" and similar chart-orientated programmes. Musicians' Union-type artists are paid as if they shared together with Equity-type artists in a royalty of 25 per cent. of the gross income accruing to BBC Enterprises. The royalty is shared among all such artists in proportion to the total performance fees of Musicians' Union-type artists and the aggregate fees of Equity-type artists who performed in the particular programme.

With the release of audio tape, records and compact discs of music programmes the rates prevailing under the Agreement between the Musicians' Union and British Phonographic Industry are paid.

Part III of the Agreement makes special provision for the simultaneous or deferred relay of programmes for Eurovision (EBU) and/or Intervision (OIRT). A supplementary fee of a fixed percentage of the fees earned for performance and rehearsal is payable for each country of transmission in accordance with the prescribed scale. A deferred relay must take place within 30 days of the BBC transmission.

Self-contained Pop Groups

Part IV of the Agreement provides for the engagement of established "self-contained" groups presenting their own act and having gained recognition as a group prior to the broadcast. These provisions apply to groups working in the field of pop, beat, rock, folk and similar music and whose performance is predominantly instrumental (including such instruments as electric guitars, electric keyboard, organs, drums and front line instruments) with or without a vocal element in their performance, bands, organists, drummers, pianists and musicians generally whether accompanying or presenting a musical act. Such performers are represented by the Musicians' Union. Those artists whose performance is not predominantly instrumental, that is non-instrumental vocalist and harmony groups, are represented by Equity so that their engagements are subject to the Agreement between the BBC and Equity.

A minimum performance fee (which is inclusive of "doubling" and porterage) is payable to each musician for an aggregate of four hours work in 12 hours on the day of final performance (or recording) for an aggregate of one hour's performance, plus a three hour session (including any recording) on one other day. If the aggregate of one hour's performance on the final performance day is exceeded a supplement to the perform-ance fee is payable for each additional six minutes (or less). If there is any recording on the day previous to the final performance day a further supplement is added to the performance fee for each 30 minutes or part thereof of recording. If extra rehearsal time is needed outside the four hours on the final performance day or the three hour session on a previous day for each 30 minutes or part thereof of extra time a standard additional fee is payable.

Other Parts of the Agreement apply to musicians engaged under this Part IV with minor modifications, but payments for repeat transmissions are calculated on 75 per cent. of the performance fee, and the share of the royalties from other transmissions and exploitation of a recording of a performance is 25 per cent. as noted above.

Pianists and Music Directors

Parts V and VI of the Agreement contain the standard rates for rehearsal pianists and musical directors. Engagements of the former can be on the basis of nominated days with minimum daily earnings or a guaranteed six day week of 40 working hours (with specified times) for a standard fee. Audition sessions are separately rated. Fares and subsistence are payable as for orchestral musicians.

For musical directors the work entitlement is the same as for musicians but the rates payable are at least twice the standard rates paid to the individual musicians playing under the musical director. Other parts of the Agreement variously apply to musical directors, as for example the payment of additional fees and royalties for repeat transmissions and exploitation of recorded programmes. If in lieu of a musical director a playing musician directs an orchestra a supplementary fee is payable to such a musician.

THE BBC AND MUSICIANS' UNION TELEVISION CHAMBER MUSICIANS AGREEMENT

This Agreement sets out the standard conditions and minimum fees for musicians engaged for the performance of chamber music as the description is generally understood. The Agreement applies to engagements where chamber music is performed by three or more instrumentalists with one musician only to each part, the performance having been already rehearsed so that the performance is the musicians' collective interpretation of a work rather than as directed by a conductor. When musicians perform in duo or as solo instrumentalists or accompanists playing chamber music their engagement is subject to the Agreement with the ISM considered below.

A musician's performance fee is negotiable but there are prescribed minimum rates for both network and regional ("opt-out") transmissions which cover both rehearsals and the live broadcast or pre-recording. Rehearsals and recordings may be alternated during a session as required. The working period is 10 over twelve hours on the performance day but when a performance is before 1.00 p.m. work may start on that day at 9 a.m. with an aggregate of four hours having been worked on the previous day. A standard rate of overtime is payable per hour or part thereof. When additional days of attendance are required supplementary fees are payable to musicians whose performance fee is below a fixed amount (at present £1,515) for attendance for an aggregate of six hours of work in eight hours. Travelling and subsistence allowances and porterage are payable according to the terms of the Main Agreement.

The Agreement provides for a short session at reduced rates for particular programmes such as education, religious, documentary, instructional, critical and magazine programmes. The fee covers five hours of work in an overall period of six hours for a maximum aggregate of 10 minutes of material, but with documentary and religious programmes the transmitted items may not exceed 25 per cent. of the whole programme. Rehearsal and recordings may be alternated as required during a session.

Like the Main Agreement, the Chamber Musicians' Agreement provides for other kinds of sessional engagements such as for the performance of signature tunes and incidental music. For engagements for schools programmes two-thirds of the normal fees is payable.

Concert Relays

The Agreement makes special provision for the live broadcasting or recording for later transmission of public concerts before a paying audience and which apply whether or not the concert is promoted by the

BBC. Apart from the fee which is paid to a musician by the concert promoter a musician is entitled to a fee equal to 75 per cent. of his concert fee (excluding payments made for rehearsals, expenses and the like) but subject to a minimum payment. Where a concert is pre-recorded for later transmission, the broadcasting fee is not payable until the programme is first transmitted. If the concert is for charity and the artist receives no fee or a much diminished fee then an assessed fee is payable for the broadcast transmission. When a performance is being simultaneously transmitted by radio and television the fee is inclusive of the radio broadcast.

Separate from the foregoing there may be included in magazine, critical, religious, documentary and educational programmes recordings of short extracts, not exceeding five minutes, from productions rehearsed and produced independently of the BBC and for which a minimum fee is prescribed.

Repeat Transmissions

The payment of the fees due to a musician for his attendance and performance entitles the BBC to transmit the programme once throughout the United Kingdom, or if an "opt-out" engagement then once in the specified region. In the event of such a programme being transmitted on network the "opt-out" fee is made up to the network fee. As provided in the Main Agreement, trailers of up to two minutes may be made and brief extracts included in historic and reminiscent programmes without additional fees.

Unless otherwise stipulated in a musicians's contract of engagement there may be repeat broadcasts of recorded programmes in the United Kingdom without limitation on the number or time within which the repeats may be made. The fee payable for each repeat transmission is 50 per cent. of a musician's performance fee but the fee is increased according to a scale of percentage increases over the years following the first transmission; for example after three years a 10 per cent. increase, after six years a 15 per cent. increase.

Overseas and Other Uses of Recorded Programmes

The entitlement of musicians to additional payments by way of royalties for the broadcasting overseas and any other extended use and exploitation of recorded programmes is as provided in the Main Agreement. The special provisions governing international relays—EBU and/or OIRT transmissions—and supplementary payments also apply.

THE BBC AND INCORPORATED SOCIETY OF MUSICIANS TELEVISION AGREEMENT

In this Agreement there is prescribed the general conditions of engagement and minimum fees to apply to solo instrumental musicians, instrumental and vocal duos playing chamber music, conductors of symphonic and orchestral concerts, conductors of operas and ballet, choral conductors, accompanists and church musicians. Solo singers are also within the scope of the Agreement but if they perform as principals in opera, musical plays or in light entertainment their engagement will be subject to the terms of the Agreement between the BBC and Equity.

The Agreement is in virtually the same terms as the Chamber Musicians' Union Agreement whereby an engagement may be for a network or "opt-out" regional transmission. The performance fees are negotiable and although the minimum fees are a little higher, other of the provisions of the Agreement in particular covering hours of work, additional attendance days and any supplementary payments are the same as provided for in the Chamber Musicians Union Agreement. Likewise the provisions for one day short sessions and the recording of incidental music. There are identical corresponding provisions for the relaying live and the recording for later broadcasting of public concerts before a paying audience, including the provision for the broadcasting live (or recorded) in magazine, educational and such like programmes of short items taken from productions rehearsed and produced by organisations other than the BBC.

The Agreement makes provision for church organists, lay clerks and choir boys/girls taking part in broadcasts live or pre-recorded of services at cathedrals and churches of similar status. The fees for organists and assistant organists are negotiable but minimum fees are prescribed. For lay clerks and choir boys/girls there are standard fees but which vary according to whether the transmission is network or regional, and whether the session is of standard or short duration. Additional standard fees are payable for rehearsals on the day previous to the relay or recording. The prescribed fees are for broadcasts of regular services; higher fees may be paid for special occasions. The payment of the programme fees for a television broadcast are inclusive of payment for a simultaneous radio broadcast relay. A special minimum rate is prescribed for professional organists only at churches of less than cathedral status.

Lay clerks at Westminster Abbey, St. Paul's Cathedral and Westminster Cathedral are represented by Equity as noted above.

United Kingdom Transmissions

As with other engagements the payment of the performance fee entitles the BBC to broadcast an artist's performance by every means once from each transmitter in the United Kingdom, or if it is an "opt-out" engagement then once in the agreed region. The Agreement makes provision for the extended use and exploitation of any recording of an artist's performance for which additional fees are payable. Any restriction on the further use of a recording as provided for in the Agreement must be the subject of special stipulation in an artist's contract of engagement.

There is no limitation on the number or the time within which there may be a repeat transmission in the United Kingdom of a recorded performance. For each repeat transmission there is payable 50 per cent. of an artist's original programme fee (that is, excluding payments for rehearsals, overtime, additional attendance days and expenses). The amount of the repeat fee payable is increased after three years from the date of the first transmission by 15 per cent., after 10 years by 25 per cent. and after 25 years by 50 per cent.

Overseas and Other Uses of Recorded Programmes

The system of royalty payments for the overseas broadcasting and other uses of recorded programmes which applies to engagements subject to the Collective Agreements between the BBC and Equity and the Musicians' Union has not been adopted for engagements subject to this agreement. For the broadcasting overseas of a recording of an artist's performance a scale of percentage payments based on an artist's performance fee is payable for particular overseas territories, for example, British Commonwealth 25 per cent., Continental Europe 48 per cent., U.S.A. (excluding a major network) 50 per cent. The payments permit a specified number or "block" of transmissions, eight in each country of the British Commonwealth, two in each country of Continental Europe, eight in the U.S.A. (as defined above). If a further "block" of transmissions is licensed the appropriate percentage payment becomes payable. For sales of programmes for exhibition to non-paying audiences such as at universities, colleges, societies, 30 per cent. of an artist's performance fee (but 25 per cent. if music is a minor ingredient of a programme) is payable which permits a recording to be shown in this medium world wide for seven years following the payment. For sales to "trapped" audiences (hotels, ships etc.) one per cent. of an artist's performance fee is payable for use within three years of the payment.

The special provisions governing international relays—EBU and/or

OIRT transmissions—and supplementary payments referred in the Musicians' Union Main Agreement form part of this Agreement.

The exploitation of programmes in the form of videograms is subject to a special agreement between the BBC, BBC Enterprises and the ISM. The written consent of an artist is required for the exercise of videogram rights and the terms individually negotiated. Nonetheless the Agreement prescribes for the payment of minimum royalties calculated as a percentage of the recommended retail price (less certain deductions) to be shared between artists. If there are Equity artists and Musicians' Union artists contributing to the videogram then the royalty is shared in the proportions of the contributions of ISM, Equity and Musicians' Union artists to the videogram. Where BBC Enterprises enters into a licensing agreement with third parties for the sale and/or hire of videograms a different scale of royalties applies based on the income received by BBC Enterprises.

THE TELEVISION PROGRAMME COMPANIES AND MUSICIANS' UNION COLLECTIVE AGREEMENT

The Agreement of October 1991 for the employment of musicians for programmes produced by the programme companies of the ITC in its structure is similar to that of the Main Agreement between the BBC and the Musicians' Union. A musician can be engaged for any one of a number of sessions; each session has specific conditions, rates and uses of the performances. It is important to understand that, save for the exceptions as noted, the payment of the sessional fee entitles a programme company to broadcast a musician's performance once over the transmission areas of:

(a) any two programme companies provided only one of the two is one of the five major programme companies; or

(b) any five of the smaller programme companies.

For the wider transmission of a programme standard supplementary fees (network supplements) are payable, the rates varying according to:

(a) the category or kind of session for which a musician was engaged, and

(b) whether there is a full or partial network transmission over the regions of the ITC or Channel 4.

A partial network transmission (for the purposes of the Agreement) is a transmission over all the areas of the nine smaller programme companies. Programmes may be transmitted simultaneously or non-simultaneously but any separate regional transmission must be completed within nine months from the date of the first transmission.

The Sessions

The categories or kinds of session for which musicians can be engaged are briefly as follows:

1. Basic session of four hours work spread over five hours to permit of an interval between the end of rehearsals and the start of the performance. The performance may be in or out of vision, transmitted live, or pre-recorded for subsequent transmission but the performance time may not exceed one hour. A session may be extended to provide more than one hour's performance time when extra payment becomes due for each six minutes or part thereof by which the session is extended.

    Provision is made for additional rehearsal time which may be immediately preceding or following the rehearsal time allotted within the session. The additional rehearsal time may be separate from the actual four hour session. The fees payable for the additional rehearsal time depend on the length of the interval between a rehearsal and the performance or recording session. If there is a rehearsal on a day when there is no performance or recording session, a standard hourly rate is payable but with a minimum payment as for a three hour rehearsal session.

    Selected items of music may be pre-recorded in sound or vision provided the recordings are as continuous as technical and artistic requirements allow. The total length of the recording of the selected items may not exceed 20 per cent. of the scheduled transmission time of the programme and the programme itself may not exceed one hour's duration. An extra supplement is payable to musicians for this facility at rates according to whether the recording is in vision or sound only.

2. Discontinuous sound only recording session. This may be of three hours for the rehearsal and sound recording of up to 20 minutes of music for subsequent incorporation into a specified programme of up to one hour's duration. By payment of a supplement a session can be extended up to 30 minutes to secure the permitted maximum of 20 minutes of recorded music. The facility of an additional rehearsal does not apply but a session can be extended by up to one and a half hours at the time of a musician's engagement by the payment of an additional fee for each half hour booked. In each

such half hour an additional three minutes and 20 seconds of music may be recorded.

There may alternatively be a three hour session, but at a higher rate, for the continuous or discontinuous recording of up to one hour's music in sound and vision, or vision only for subsequent incorporation into a specified programme of up to one hour's duration. The session may be extended by up to 30 minutes by payment of a supplement for each 15 minutes or part thereof by which the session is extended.

If the recording session is incomplete in that vocal parts are to be added at a separate session, then 50 per cent. of the appropriate session fee is payable to each musician when the recording is completed. This further fee is not payable when 20 or more musicians were engaged for the initial recording session.

3. A session of three hours for the recording of a signature tune and or up to 20 minutes of programme item identification music for use in a specified programme or series of programmes. The session may be extended in order to complete the recording of the music required by the payment of an additional fee for each six minutes or part thereof the session is extended. The sessional fee is variable according to whether the programme is for network or partial network transmission. When both a signature tune and 20 minutes of music are recorded at a session 100 per cent. of the sessional fee is payable. Appendix A of the Agreement stipulates that signature tunes for all programmes involving four or more episodes are to be especially recorded except for schools programmes broadcast during school hours, and pre-school programmes.

Payment of the fee gives the right of unrestricted transmission of the programmes in the United Kingdom for two years from the date of the first United Kingdom transmission, and for 10 years unlimited overseas use in all media except videogram form. If the fee first paid was for non-network or partial network transmissions only, network transmission rights may be acquired by the payment of a supplement. By payment of 75 per cent. of the appropriate fee within four weeks of the date of the final recording session (50 per cent. for educational programmes) there may be unlimited transmissions of a programme in the United Kingdom for five years from the date of the first United Kingdom transmission. The two and five year periods may be renewed by the payment of additional fees at the rates (or calculated at the rates) current at the material time. When there is a repeat transmission of an episode from a series, a repeat fee is payable as distinct from a renewal fee.

4. A session in or out of the studios for the rehearsal and recording discontinuously, in sound or in sound and vision of items from

productions rehearsed and produced by other organisations, for inclusion in magazine, news, documentary, educational, critical and such like programmes. A session may be up to two hours for the recording of items aggregating 10 minutes, or up to one hour for items aggregating five minutes, but this latter facility applies only when 10 or more musicians are involved. There are different rates for each of the sessions, payment of the applicable rate giving one transmission of the programme.

5. A session of three hours to rehearse and record discontinuously up to one hour of incidental music for inclusion in series or serials or anthology programmes. A session may be extended by up to one hour to complete the recording; a standard supplement is payable for each 15 minutes or part thereof by which the session is extended. The session rate is variable according to the number of episodes for which the music is recorded, and according to whether the programmes are for full or partial network or for transmission in a single area of the ITC.

6. The engagement of musicians for a session for the recording of featured musical items for inclusion in more than one programme (multi-programme session) is subject to agreement between a programme company and the Union as the need arises.

7. A special sessional engagement for established self-contained groups has been recognised in the same way as under the BBC Main Agreement. A basic performance fee is payable to each musician which is inclusive of "doubling" and porterage but the network supplement becomes payable when appropriate. An engagement may comprise a three hour session followed by a nominated performance day. On the day of the three hour session up to 20 minutes of music may be recorded in sound only continuously or discontinuously and without any limitation on any member of the group overdubbing his own performance. The session may be extended to allow the full 20 minutes of music to be recorded but a standard supplement is payable for each 15 minutes or part thereof the session is extended.

The session on the nominated performance day is of four hours spread over 12 and during which up to one hour's performance may take place in vision and be transmitted live or recorded continuously or discontinuously. The use of the recordings made at the previous three hours' session as above in the course of the production of the programme does not attract additional payment. If the performance time exceeds one hour then for each extra six minutes or part thereof an additional standard supplement is payable to each musician. Rehearsal time in excess of the four hours also attracts extra payment for each musician for each 15 minutes or part thereof of additional rehearsal time. Any rehearsal time required outside the sessions as above has to be treated as an additional rehearsal session in the same way as a rehearsal extending beyond a regular basic session of five hours described above.

8. Separate provisions of the Agreement cover the relaying of concerts or other entertainments in which musicians perform. A standard fee is payable to each musician for the relay which may not exceed one hour without the prior agreement of the Musicians' Union. The relay may be of a programme given before an invited audience and therefore pre-rehearsed, or of a regular public performance which if not transmitted live must be transmitted within two weeks of the recording. A concert relay in excess of 12 in any year is subject to the approval of the Union, so to overcome this rule musicians will be engaged by a programme company and paid the rate as for an ordinary basic five hour session independently of the engagement by a concert promoter.

There are other provisions of the Agreement directly relevant to the conduct of the sessions which need to be noted.

When in any session a musician overdubs his performance then for each extra line of sound added there is payable 125 per cent. of the appropriate sessional fee for the first overdub, and 140 per cent. for each further overdub. When a musician is required to participate in or contribute to a visual recording other than as part of a performance such as at a basic session (session No. 1 above) a standard supplement is payable for the first hour then for each additional six minutes or part thereof of the visual recording.

The use of sound tapes of music recorded at the sessions is subject to strict control. Where tape recordings are used at rehearsals at which the musicians are not present an additional standard fee is payable for each hour of use. Similarly when tape recordings are incorporated into the visual recording of a programme in the absence of the musicians an additional standard fee is payable after the first hour of the visual recording. Special rates and terms apply to the making and use of backing tracks for light entertainment and non-light entertainment programmes.

No additional payments are due for the use of music recorded under the Agreement in programme promotion trailers broadcast on Channel 3 or Channel 4.

The fees payable to musical associates and music directors are negotiable but the Agreement prescribes an hourly rate for musical associates. Music directors are entitled to not less than twice the standard rate paid to the individual musicians engaged for the session for which the director is engaged. Musicians engaged only for rehearsals are paid at rehearsal rates as for a basic rehearsal session of three hours. An appendix to the Agreement sets out the scale of fees payable to arrangers for general orchestration, choral scoring, keyboard scoring and the rates payable to copyists. There is also provided as an appendix the fees payable for the use as backing tracks of commercial records in conformity with the British Phonographic Industry (BPI) and Musicians' Union Omnibus Agreement referred to in Section G below.

The Agreement provides for the use of extracts from a company's programmes in other of its programmes. A nominal payment is stipulated for a three minute extract in schools programmes and two minutes in documentary, religious, critical and such like programmes. The use in other kinds of programmes of extracts of up to three minutes from programmes of a company's programmes, or programmes of another programme company or other organisation is subject to the payment of the fees as payable to musicians engaged for the recording of short items (session No. 4 above) and notice of the use of the extracts to the Musicians' Union.

Repeat Transmissions

Programmes made under the Agreement may be repeated up to three times in the United Kingdom over all or any of the stations of the ITC simultaneously or non-simultaneously, or on Channel 4 within a period of five years from the date of the first transmission in the United Kingdom. No additional fees are payable for a repeat transmission made within seven days of the initial transmission but otherwise for any repeated broadcast payments are due.

Ordinarily for each repeat transmission there is payable to a musician 60 per cent. of the fee for that session which gives the highest remuneration. In calculating the amount due there is included any additional amounts paid for any extended performance or recording time but no other supplements other than partial or network supplements as applicable. A programme company may elect to pre-empt the first repeated transmission by paying to a musician at the same time as the payment for the original transmission musician 30 per cent. instead of 60 per cent. of the fee as above.

There are different provisions for the repeat transmission of schools and adult educational programmes. There may be up to six repeat transmissions but within five years of the date of the first transmission. No fee is payable for the first repeat made within seven days of the original broadcast. Otherwise the fees payable are a percentage of the original fee paid the percentage depending on the time when the payment is made. No fee is payable for the fourth or sixth repeat if made within seven days of the third and fifth repeat transmission respectively.

A programme company undertaking the making of a compilation programme may either negotiate for special rates with the Union or pay 60 per cent. of the basic session fee current at the time of the transmission of the compilation programme in respect of each programme from which extracts are taken and pay a network supplement if the programme is shown in more than one area.

Overseas and other Uses of Recorded Programmes

The provisions of the Agreement for the television broadcasting overseas and other uses of recorded programmes have been much altered in recent years and in part to complement the new system of royalty payments adopted for performers as already noted. Thus a programme company can elect to pay either a combined use fee or a royalty.

The combined use fees are according to scale the rates payable depending on:

(a) for which territories of the world the rights are acquired, namely, (i) the world, (ii) U.S.A., (iii) Europe, (iv) Commonwealth, (v) Rest of the world; and

(b) the time when the fee is paid after the final session.

The rights acquired by the payment of the combined use fee are for the exploitation of a programme in all media except for repeats on ITV or Channel 4 and any theatrical exhibition. The rights are in perpetuity except for a series of programmes when the period of exploitation is limited to 10 years from the date of the first transmission of the programme in the United Kingdom.

The system of royalty payments gives the same rights of exploitation as above but without limitation of time or reference to territories of the world. Royalties are not payable in respect of non-theatric and closed circuit television use.

A royalty of 4 per cent. of gross receipts from programme sales is payable to musicians which is divided between the musicians in proportion to their original sessional fee. In respect of those programmes where the aggregate original earnings of Musicians' Union members exceed the aggregate original earnings of Equity members, a royalty of 21 per cent. is divided between the performers in proportion to their original earnings.

The expression "original earnings" means the payment to performers made under the applicable Collective Agreement by programme companies but exclude:

(a) repeat payments, overseas residual payments and in the case of programmes not originally transmitted in all companies' transmission areas, subsequent payments for transmissions in other companies' transmission areas; and

(b) payments intended to reimburse actual expenditure incurred by a musician, including subsistence payments, travel payments, and musicians' porterage payments.

For those programmes involving only members of the Musicians' Union and where the programme consists of at least 40 per cent. of featured music a royalty of 17 per cent. of gross receipts from programme sales is payable and to be divided between musicians in proportion to their original sessional fees.

Note that for programmes made before January 1, 1988 the method of residual payments based on a percentage of sessional fees according to the country of sale and number of transmissions continues in operation.

The Agreement provides for the accounting and payment of use fees and royalties to musicians at three monthly intervals.

General Conditions of Engagements

The Agreement contains provisions of general application including a stipulation that by accepting an engagement under the terms of the Agreement a musician gives such consent as may be necessary under the Copyright, Designs and Patents Act 1988 or any variation thereof and for the purposes of the transmission of his performance. The Agreement makes provision for such payments as porterage, travel and subsistence allowances, there being a schedule of town centres for the assessment of additional transport expenses.

When a musician is required to play more than one instrument a standard "doubling" fee is payable for the first additional instrument; a lower standard fee is payable for each subsequent instrument played. There is no restriction on the number of instruments a musician may be required to play at a session. The "doubling" fee is not payable for a rehearsal held on the day of the main recording session but is payable for a rehearsal on any other day.

In an appendix, but as part of the Agreement, there is reproduced the agreement reflecting the understanding between the programme companies and the Musicians' Union on the use of commercial gramophone records in programmes. On behalf of its members the Union gives consent to the dubbing of recordings of performances given by its members under the terms of the Collective Agreement between the British Phonographic Industry and the Union (reviewed in Section G below), into television programmes for all purposes and all sales and licences of those programmes throughout the world in all media.

The companies undertake not to dub such commercial records in programmes where music is a normal feature of programmes and when musicians might reasonably expect to be engaged to perform music required for programmes. Records are not to be used to provide sound tracks for miming or other performances by artists except as agreed between the companies and the Union. The companies also agree to pay 30 per cent. of the annual expenditure on licences from phonographic performances for the broadcasting of records to the Union for the benefit of its members.

Disputes Procedure

The Agreement includes provision for the settlement of disputes over the application and interpretation of the Agreement. With disputes between an individual musician and a programme company the issues are first to be referred to accredited representatives of the particular company and the Musicians' Union, meaning for the matter to be settled at studio floor level; otherwise the matter must be referred to a conference between appropriate representatives of the company and the Union. If the matter remains in dispute it is referred to a Joint Conciliation Committee. The Committee consists of three representatives of the programme companies and three of the Union, the companies providing the Secretary. On receiving notice of a dispute the Committee is required to meet within three days but sooner if practicable. If then a dispute cannot be resolved the issue may by mutual agreement be referred to ACAS or to arbitration, the decision of an arbitrator being binding on both parties.

THE RELAYING OF PROGRAMMES TO EUROPE

The broadcasting organisations and authorities of most European countries and some few other nearby countries are members of the European Broadcasting Union and by an agreement between it and the International Federation of Performers programmes can be relayed from a member country to other countries who are members of or associated with the Union, or the transmission can be deferred for up to 30 days following the initial transmission in the originating country. Thus programmes produced by both the BBC and the programme companies may be relayed to European countries simultaneously with their broadcasting and transmission in the United Kingdom, or deferred. A supplementary fee is payable to "performers" meaning, in short, the freelance artists and musicians covered by the various collective agreements just reviewed. The amount of fees payable is a fixed percentage of the initial fees actually paid to a performer for rehearsing and performing in a programme according to the scale laid down in the Agreement for the various member countries of the Union.

The distinction between an overseas transmission of a recorded programme and a relayed or deferred transmission made under this arrangement with the European Broadcasting Union lies in the fact that a relayed or deferred transmission must carry the "Eurovision" identification symbol; no such identification symbol is included in an ordinary overseas distribution and transmission of a recorded programme.

D. RADIO BROADCASTING— BBC

Radio broadcasting is both a national and local service provided by the BBC and contractors of the Radio Authority. Because of the diversity of programmes and differences in the areas of transmission inevitably the terms and conditions upon which persons are engaged to perform are correspondingly numerous and varied. It is hardly practical in this study to review all the kinds of engagements which may be offered but recognising the prodigious output of the BBC it follows that the main agreements made by the BBC with the principal organisations representing professional performers need to be considered.

THE EQUITY AGREEMENT

This Agreement sets out the general terms and conditions for the employment of professional artists and performers for all programmes—drama, comedy, musical, documentary, educational—broadcast in the domestic and world services of the BBC and whereby recordings can be used by the BBC's Transcription Services. The Agreement broadly distinguishes (a) actors exercising dramatic skills and variety performers, and (b) ad hoc chorus singers and solo light entertainment singers, and pop groups whose performance is predominantly non-instrumental.

It is a term of the Agreement that the BBC undertakes to make every endeavour towards ensuring that only professional performers are employed in broadcast programmes. When a person not having a professional status is to be engaged, or when an amateur, or amateur group of players, is to be employed to provide a contribution which in the opinion of the BBC a professional(s) cannot do, then Equity is to be informed as soon as practicable. Equity may make representations concerning the engagement and if necessary have the issue considered at a formal Casting Conciliation meeting attended by the programme producer. Although it may not approve of the engagement at such a meeting Equity undertakes not thereafter to take any action to impede the BBC's choice and the production of the programme.

Nonetheless the BBC's need to broadcast the work of amateurs and amateur productions as part of its obligations as a national broadcasting organisation is expressly recognised. Amateur choral groups may not normally be employed in the broadcasting of professional productions of the BBC but the broadcasting of entertainments produced independently of the BBC which include amateur performers is not a breach of the general undertaking. Apart from the BBC's annual Promenade Concerts the use of amateur choirs in concerts in London promoted and relayed by the BBC is limited to 20 occasions in any year with choral groups of 90 or more.

Engagement of Actors and Variety Performers

With the engagement of artists within this category a distinction is made betwen engagements for programmes for the regular network radio of the BBC's Domestic Service and those programmes which are for regional radio, BBC Local Radio, the vernacular services (World Service), BBC English (World Service), or the Open University. The following relates only to standard engagements for network radio of the Domestic Service except as otherwise stated.

An artist's engagement fee is negotiable. Minimum rates are prescribed but in negotiating a fee account may be taken of an artist's professional standing and value to broadcasting and to the weight of an artist's contribution to a programme. All fees which may be payable to an artist in addition to the engagement fee are at standard rates.

Payment of the engagement fee is for two broadcasts of the programme in the Domestic Service, thereby allowing one repeat broadcast as of right, and one simultaneous transmission overseas. Where an artist is engaged for a programme initially for the World Service the fee is for two cycles of broadcasts. One cycle means three broadcasts within a seven day period to enable the programme to be heard throughout the world.

The standard engagement is of nine hours inclusive of not less than two hours for meal and rest breaks. Overtime is payable for each 15 minutes or part thereof of additional time. If there is a rehearsal previous to the performance day a fee is payable for six hours of rehearsal spread over eight hours; overtime is payable for excess time. The Agreement makes provision for variations to the standard working engagement. There may be half-day engagements and at reduced rates for school and continuing education programmes and World Service programmes. Special provisions and terms also apply to such programmes as multi-episodic drama programmes, and for item recordings, that is for artists engaged to record material for inclusion in religious talks, anthology, magazine, music and non-drama educational programmes.

The relaying of theatrical productions is subject to the agreement of both Equity and the Theatres' National Committee. However, provision is made for the recording of parts of rehearsals or performances and of general back stage activity for news bulletins and news items in news magazines; only if an item exceeds two minutes is a standard fee payable. For the recording of items for inclusion in topical magazine programmes and recordings for schools and continuing education programmes at schools where Theatre in Education companies are working, a minimum rate is prescribed for items up to three minutes in length; if an item exceeds this time the regular minimum payment as for a regular half day engagement is payable.

When for technical reasons it is not possible to make a recording at an artist's place of work a five minute contribution to a topical magazine programme may be recorded at the studios. A minimum fee is prescribed and the recording must be completed within two hours of an artist's arrival at the studio.

Extracts of current productions may be recorded at a theatre or rehearsal room of up to five minutes. A minimum fee is prescribed and the call time may not exceed three hours. If a theatre director is required by the BBC to attend the recording the director is entitled to the same minimum fee as payable to the artists.

Extracts from recordings of programmes may be included in other programmes excepting drama and entertainment programmes, but "flashbacks" may be used in serials. An extract may not exceed four minutes (five for schools programmes) and if the extract is for inclusion in a critical programme an artist's permission must first be obtained. The right to use extracts is for the period within which the recorded programme may be repeated. The fees payable are according to the minutage of the extract. Extracts may be used without payment in programmes of an historic or reminiscent nature and as trailers.

Generally there is no limit on the time within which programmes may be repeated in either of the Services, but repeat fees become payable when there is a third or more repeat in the Domestic Service, and a third or more cycle in the World Service. When a programme first broadcast in one Service is later broadcast in the other repeat fees are payable. If a repeat is in the Domestic Service and a fee is payable then 33⅓ of the performance fee is payable for a repeat within three years of the first broadcast and if after three years the same percentage is payable but of an artist's performance fee current at the time of the repeat. For repeats in the World Service a different formula applies.

Engagement of Solo and Chorus Singers

The terms on which solo light entertainment singers and chorus singers are engaged are in some important respects different from those of other artists.

For solo singers a minimum performance fee is prescribed for an engagement of three hours performance and three hours rehearsal on the performance day. When there are additional rehearsals and where the rehearse/record technique is used the provisions as below for chorus singers apply as do those provisions on broadcasting and repeat rights.

Professional chorus singers engaged ad hoc for a studio performance (concert performances are treated separately below), are engaged at standard rates which are scaled to reflect the size of a chorus and the hours of the performance time. If the size of chorus is four or less and the person contributes significantly to a programme a standard supplement is payable to each singer; this does not apply to a backing group. When a performance is of exceptional complexity fees above the standard rates may be negotiated.

The sessional fee is inclusive of a three hour rehearsal on the day of performance. If the rehearsal time is exceeded overtime is payable for up to 30 minutes and if the performance time is exceeded the fee at the rate for the next level of the scale of performance time is payable. For an additional rehearsal the rate payable is according to whether the extra rehearsal is on the performance day or a day previous. Overtime is payable for up to a maximum of 60 minutes but if the hour is exceeded another rehearsal session is deemed to have begun.

When studio performances are pre-recorded rehearsal and performance may be combined and the rehearse/record technique used. There are limitations on the amount of programme music which may be recorded depending on the duration of the session. If the session is of three and a half hours, music for a programme lasting up to 30 minutes may be recorded; if of four hours then music for a programme lasting more than 30 minutes may be recorded. If the time allowed is exceeded then overtime is payable for each 30 minutes or part thereof to a maximum of one hour for a three hour session and to a maximum of 30 minutes for a four hour session.

The Agreement makes provision for other kinds of sessions, such as for the recording of light music for item use, the making of backing tracks, the recording of national anthems and tunes of particular national significance, of signature tunes, opening and closing music and special effects and jingles. Special provisions apply to singers engaged to augment the BBC Singers.

The payment of the engagement fee is for one transmission once in the Domestic Service and simultaneously overseas. Alternatively for the World Service, by the payment of 35 per cent. of the performance fee, repeats may be given as required over the cycle period of seven days of the first broadcast in the World Service. The recording of a programme may be repeated in the Domestic Service by the payment of 50 per cent. of a singer's performance fee. If the repeat is more than three years after the date of the first transmission the repeat fee is calculated on the performance fee current at the time of the repeat broadcast. The fees ordinarily payable for repeat transmissions in the World Service are 20 per cent. of the performance fee for each of the first five repeats and 10 per cent. for each repeat thereafter.

Relays of Public Concerts and Opera

The following terms apply to concert and opera performances given before a paying audience.

For the broadcasting live or recording for a deferred transmission of a public concert promoted by the BBC the fee payable to a solo singer is negotiable. For ad hoc chorus singers a standard concert fee is payable at rates according to the size of the chorus plus a standard fee for the relay. For a concert not promoted by the BBC in addition to the fees payable by the concert promoter a relay fee is payable by the BBC which for a solo singer is negotiable (subject to a minimum rate) but for chorus singers is a standard rate.

For the broadcasting live (only) of performances of opera from opera houses normally 50 per cent. of the performance fee paid by the opera company to solo artist is payable for the relay. A standard fee is payable to chorus singers. Nominal payments are also paid to a company for the services of producers, and stage management.

By the payment of the performance fee for the broadcasting of a concert or opera there may be one relay transmission in the Domestic Service and a simultaneous transmission overseas. If the World Service originates the broadcast the fee covers one transmission in the World Service. A relay is still deemed to be live if the recording of a performance is broadcast on the same day as the performance.

If the overall length of a concert or of an opera (including intervals) exceeds three hours overtime is uniformly payable for each 30 minutes or part thereof. With concerts a balance test may be made during a rehearsal without additional payment.

International relays of concerts and opera to members and associate members of the European Broadcasting Union may be made simultaneously with the BBC's transmission in the Domestic Service, or a relay may be deferred for up to 30 days from the original transmission. For such relays no additional fees are payable to chorus singers.

General Conditions of Engagements

If because of a technical fault recorded material is required to be re-recorded outside the time of an engagement, then provided the amount of material to be re-recorded does not exceed five minutes, and provided an artist is not required to make a special journey to the studio or other place of recording, only a fee equivalent to a rehearsal fee is payable.

If an artist is required to work outside the BBC area in which he normally works his travel expenses, and if an overnight stay is involved then subsistence at current rates is payable. If an artist is required to attend a photographic call a standard fee is payable at a rate according to whether the call is on a rehearsal day or other day requiring the artist's special attendance. A supplementary fee is payable to an actor who is required in the performance of a play to sing a song unless the item is short and sung in character and as part of the action of the play. A standard allowance is paid for artists who are required to wear evening dress when performing at the studios but not when performing at a public event.

There are no undertakings contained in the Agreement for the giving of credit to artists either in the broadcasting of programmes or in publications announcing their broadcasting.

The Agreement makes detailed provision for the licensing of recordings of certain of the above performances by the Transcription Service and the payment of additional fees to artists and singers, and for the making of programmes expressly for the Transcription Service.

London Cathedral Choirs

When services at Westminster Abbey, St. Paul's Cathedral and the Westminster Cathedral are broadcast their lay clerks are paid fees as for ad hoc chorus singers, except that for special services the fees are increased 50 per cent. When a service is also transmitted by television live or deferred, then the fees for the radio relay is additional to the fee payable for the television broadcast. Lay clerks and church musicians in other cathedrals and churches who perform at services which are broadcast are paid fees in accordance with the Agreement between the BBC and the Incorporated Society of Musicians as noted below.

THE MUSICIANS' UNION AGREEMENTS

There are two agreements prescribing the terms and conditions for the engagement of freelance orchestral and instrumental musicians as distinct from those musicians who are members of the permanent orchestras of the BBC. The Main Agreement is first considered and the second which applies only to chamber musicians later.

The Main Agreement distinguishes classical from light musical performances as there are separate sessions and rates for each one. A third category of sessional engagement is that for self-contained pop groups.

Symphony Orchestras and Chamber Orchestras

For live or pre-recorded studio broadcast performances there are three basic engagement units namely:

(a) performance up to one hour and rehearsal with a maximum of four hours work in an overall period of five hours;

(b) performance up to two hours and a rehearsal lasting up to three consecutive hours at any time on the same day;

(c) performance up to three hours and a rehearsal lasting up to three consecutive hours at any time on the same day.

For each of these engagements there are standard rates of pay but they vary for "principals", "sub-principals" and other orchestral players. Supplementary fees are payable for each 30 minutes or part thereof of extra rehearsal time. For an additional rehearsal (of up to three hours) the fee payable depends on whether the extra rehearsal is on the performance day or on a day previous. When a performance exceeds three hours a supplementary fee is payable for a maximum of 30 minutes or part thereof of excess time. Unlike the basic engagement fees all these supplementary fees are at uniform rates for all orchestral players.

Where there is a pre-recording of a programme the whole of the period allocated to final rehearsal and performance may be used for discontinuous recording, that is, given over to the rehearse/record technique. The time allowed for discontinuous recording is three hours plus the actual programme time; for a programme lasting 30 minutes or less the maximum time allowed is three and a half hours. The studio rates for sessions as above are payable but if the time allowed for discontinuous recording is exceeded then overtime is payable at a standard rate for each 30 minutes as part thereof.

The fees paid for performances are for the initial transmission of the complete programme in the Domestic Service. Only by the payment of the repeat fee may a recorded performance subsequently be used as an item recording and included in other programmes.

Light Orchestras, Dance Bands and Groups

There are three categories of sessional engagements namely:

1. Live broadcasting or studio pre-recording. The session is four and a half hours with up to three hours of rehearsal, a break of 30 minutes and a performance time of one hour. If the hour is exceeded a supplementary fee is payable for each additional 15 minutes up to a

limit of 30 minutes. If the performance time exceeds one and a half hours but not two hours then two session fees are payable for a working period of nine hours comprising two hours performance, six hours rehearsal (with a 15 minute break during each rehearsal period), and a 60 minute break. There may be extra rehearsal time and an extra rehearsal on the same day as the performance day. A supplementary fee is payable for each 30 minutes of extra rehearsal time. An extra rehearsal is of up to two and a half hours duration for which a supplementary fee is payable with a further supplement for each 30 minutes this rehearsal time is exceeded. If a rehearsal on a day prior to the performance day is required the basic sessional fee is payable.

2. Discontinuous pre-recording (rehearsal and performance being alternated as required). The session is of three and a half hours comprising up to three hours of rehearsal and a performance time of 30 minutes. Any breaks allowed do not count towards the session time. The session may be extended to three and three quarter hours when up to 45 minutes of music may be recorded; supplementary fees calculated in units of five minutes are payable. If the performance time exceeds 45 minutes a whole new session is deemed to have started from the expiration of the initial three and a half hours session.

3. Item recording session. The duration of the session and conditions for any extension of additional performance time are the same as for the preceding category of session, but with this session the items recorded may be used in any programme.

The sessional rates for all three categories of engagements differentiate between principals and dance bands musicians to whom one rate is payable, and other musicians to whom a lower rate is payable but the supplementary fees when payable are uniform. The rates payable for the first and second categories of these sessional engagements are the same. For the third session the rates are higher on account of the varied uses which can be made of the recordings and because the fee is inclusive of payment for two transmissions, but there is a time limit within which the transmissions may take place. The first broadcast is to be within one year of the first transmission of the first item to be broadcast; the time limit for the second broadcast is one year from the date of the first item to be re-broadcast. The Agreement provides for the facility of recording symphony and chamber orchestras and by the payment of 100 per cent. of a musician's fee the whole or parts of a recorded performance may also be treated as item recording once provided any broadcast is of the whole of a work. This use may be repeated by the payment of the repeat fee.

Other kinds of sessions are provided for, such as for the recording of national anthems and music of national significance, identifying items, opening/closing music, signature tunes, for the recording of short items for magazine, documentary, critical, religious and such like programmes where the performances are given by musicians already engaged by outside organisations, *e.g.* a theatre company.

The Agreement makes provision for the recording of backing tracks under strict supervision and for the tapes to be erased after the completion of the complete programme for which the recordings are made. The use of the technique of layered recordings (i.e. the recording of different groups of musicians at different sessions) is subject to the process of overdubbing not being used for more than four items in any one session and to a musician not being required to overdub his own performance. At any session where a performance is pre-recorded then the re-recording of sections of a performance is a matter for decision by the programme producer or conductor which may be taken on the grounds of quality in addition to serious artistic or technical faults. Where there is a retake of any music then the duration of the discarded recordings does not count towards the duration of the material permitted to be recorded at a session.

Concert Relays

For the relaying live or the recording for deferred transmission of public concerts of music or opera before a paying audience a relay fee is payable to musicians whether the concert is promoted by the BBC or another organisation. The relay fee is additional to a musician's concert performance fee. The working conditions are as follows:

(a) for symphony orchestras and chamber orchestras—a standard relay fee for a concert of up to three hours and a standard overtime rate for each 30 minutes or part thereof;

(b) for light orchestras, dance bands and groups—a standard relay fee for a concert of up to two hours and a standard overtime rate for each 15 minutes or part thereof up to a maximum of one hour's overtime. The rates applicable to light orchestras are higher than those for symphony orchestras.

When the relay is transmitted simultaneously in the World Service no additional fee is payable; a transmission is treated as simultaneous provided the broadcast commences during the Domestic Service transmission.

If the concert of music to be relayed includes music requiring performances by chorus singers the provisions of the Equity Agreement will apply to those singers. The engagement of solo singers is dealt with below.

Balance tests are permitted during a concert rehearsal for which no additional payment is due to musicians but if a special rehearsal is required by the BBC then a standard supplementary fee is payable for a rehearsal of up to three hours with overtime for each 30 minutes or part thereof. A higher fee is payable for a rehearsal called for a day prior to the performance day.

Repeat Transmissions

All recordings of studio performances and of recordings of public concerts may be re-broadcast but the number of repeat transmissions is limited to two in the Domestic Service. (Exceptionally programmes of serious music may be repeated a third time.) Subject to the payment of repeat fees there are no restrictions on repeat transmissions in the World Service. Musicians may be contracted for a re-issuable recording whereby additional transmissions of a recorded performance can be made. Programmes which are primarily literary, dramatic, documentary (including light entertainment programmes) when the musical element is subsidiary may be repeated as required subject to the payment of repeat fees.

For the repeat broadcasting of a programme a standard fee is payable to all musicians without distinction except for self-contained pop groups and the repeat broadcasting of item material by light orchestras as noted above. When the repeat occurs three or more years after the date of the first transmission the fee payable is at the rate prevailing at the time of the repeat transmission and not at the time of the engagement.

Recordings of programmes originated by the BBC and of concert performances promoted independently of the BBC may be made available by the BBC's Transcription Service to broadcasting organisations for unrestricted transmissions overseas. For this use a standard supplementary fee is payable.

Self-contained Pop Groups

A special category of engagement is recognised for established "self-contained" groups presenting their own act and working in the field of pop, beat, rock, folk and similar music. The guidelines for performers to qualify for this particular kind of sessional engagement are the same as for television engagements outlined above.

A session may be either (a) three hours rehearsal and three hours of performance on the same day, or (b) a discontinuous session (that is rehearse/record alternatively) of three and a half hours for the recording of up to 30 minutes music or for the recording of item music.

For each of the sessions there is a fixed rate which is inclusive of "doubling" and porterage payments. Supplementary fees at fixed rates are payable in the following circumstances. If a continuous performance exceeds three hours up to an additional 30 minute performance time is allowed for which a supplementary fee is payable. When there is a discontinuous session the session can be extended to three and three quarter hours when overall 30, 40 or 45 minutes of music may be recorded. For each extra five minutes of session time or of music recorded in excess of 30 minutes a supplementary fee is payable. When the recorded music exceeds 45 minutes a new session is deemed to have started. Fixed supplementary fees are also payable for extra rehearsal time and for an extra rehearsal of three hours at rates according to whether the extra rehearsal is on the performance day or a day previous.

For repeat transmissions of performances recorded in either sessions (a) or (b) above a fee of 50 per cent. of the performance fee is payable for each repeat transmission in the Domestic Service. Groups may be contracted for a re-issuable recording as mentioned above. For a repeat transmission in the World Service 35 per cent. of the performance fee is payable for all uses within seven days of the first transmission in the World Service or 20 per cent. for separate uses. For the unlimited use of a recording in the Transcription Service 125 per cent. of the performance fee is payable; alternatively by the payment of lesser percentages for particular territories limited rights for four years may be acquired.

The Agreement provides for the relaying live or recording for deferred broadcasting of public concert performances by groups in generally the same terms as for the relay of other concerts as noted above. A standard relay fee is payable for a concert of up to three hours. Provision is made for the extended use of recordings in the Domestic and World Services and the Transcription Service. Repeat fees are payable and at the rates as for repeats of recordings of studio performances.

Rehearsal Pianists and Music Directors

Special provision is made for rehearsal pianists and music directors. Pianists may be engaged for one day of four hours with overtime at an hourly rate, or for audition sessions, or for a guaranteed six-day week of 40 working hours with specified times of attendance. Music directors are engaged usually on the basis of their receiving fees of a minimum of twice the rate of the fees payable to the musicians appropriate to the category of the session for which they are engaged. Minimum rates apply for repeat transmissions. When players also direct, in lieu of payment as musical directors a supplementary fee is paid additional to their sessional fee.

General Provisions

The Agreement stipulates that a musician may not be required to play more than three instruments at any session. Where a musician is required to play (or be prepared to play) more than one instrument, for each instrument a standard additional fee is payable. Provision is made respecting "doubling" for certain instruments in the customary way. A scale of porterage payments is included in the Agreement.

Supplementary fees are payable for night work (*i.e.* for work between midnight and 9 a.m.); an out-of-town allowance is payable for engagements at places 15 or more miles from the recognised centre of the city in which musicians are based. A standard supplement is payable when an audience is present at a rehearsal.

The Agreement renders engagements subject to international relaying in accordance with the Convention of the European Broadcasting Union. Performances may be broadcast to member countries simultaneously with the initial transmission, or within 30 days thereafter, without the payment of additional fees.

Local radio broadcasting is provided for so that by the payment of the performance fees according to the category of session, a performance can be broadcast by up to four stations simultaneously, or non-simultaneously provided the transmissions are made within 30 days of the initial broadcast. Provision is made for broadcasts to be made by more than four stations and for the repeating of local radio broadcasts.

THE CHAMBER MUSICIANS' AGREEMENT

This Agreement contains the terms and conditions for the engagement of chamber musicians where chamber music (as generally recognised) is played by three or more instrumental musicians with one (only) to each part and where each musician contributes his own interpretation of the music rather than under the direction of a conductor. These engagements are also on the basis that musicians have already rehearsed and prepared for the performance for which they have been contracted.

The standard engagement is for the performance of the music as agreed (which may be pre-recorded for deferred broadcasting) with one rehearsal normally not exceeding three hours on the day of the performance. If an extra rehearsal is required by the BBC previous to the day of performance an additional fee is payable. Engagement fees are negotiable but separate minimum rates are prescribed for transmissions on the Domestic Service network and London (other than Greater London Radio), for a single region and for local radio.

The technique of rehearse and record may be used but if for this purpose more than one session is required (a session may not exceed three hours plus the transmission time), additional fees are payable according to scale relative to the basic fee for the first session. If the recorded performances are for more than one programme separate fees for each programme are payable except for engagements for recordings for item transmission.

There is no restriction on the time or number of repeats which may be given of a recorded performance. For each repeat 50 per cent. of the original performance fee is payable but the fee is increased after three years from the date of the first transmission by 15 per cent., after 10 years by 25 per cent. and after 25 years by 50 per cent. No additional fee is payable for a simultaneous transmission in the World Service but for each of the first five repeats 20 per cent. of the performance fee is payable and for each further repeat 10 per cent. By the payment of 100 per cent. of an artist's original fee the whole or parts of a recorded performance may also be treated as item recording once provided any broadcast is of a whole work. This use may be repeated by the payment of the repeat fee.

For the broadcasting of a public concert before a paying audience there are two principle provisions. If the concert is promoted by the BBC the concert may be relayed live on payment of 50 per cent. of a musician's concert performance fee; the concert may be recorded for deferred broadcasting without payment until transmission. Repeat fees are payable as above. Where a concert is promoted by another organisation if the concert is relayed live or is recorded and transmitted later on the day of the performance 50 per cent. of a musician's concert fee is payable. A concert may be recorded without payment for subsequent transmission but a regular studio contract carrying the musician's normal studio fee must first be issued before the transmission of the recording. For further transmissions fees are payable as under a normal studio contract.

The remainder of the Agreement is similar to the Main Agreement reviewed above. It provides for special sessions for the recording of item music, short items for inclusion in magazine, documentary, educational, religious and critical programmes, for the recording of national anthems and other tunes of particular national significance, and opening/closing music and signature tunes. For each of these sessions various standard rates and terms apply. With all studio engagements if music is performed for schools programmes two thirds of the appropriate fee is payable provided a minimum payment (at present of £63) is paid to solo artists other than accompanists for whom the usual sessional rates apply. The general conditions of engagements are as in the Main Agreement.

THE BBC AND INCORPORATED SOCIETY OF MUSICIANS RADIO BROADCASTING AGREEMENT

The engagement of musical soloists and duos (whether instrumental or vocal), conductors, accompanists and church musicians to perform for radio broadcast programmes is subject to the terms and conditions of this Agreement.

Terms of Engagement

The fees for the broadcasting live or pre-recording for later transmission of studio performances are negotiable, but minimum rates are prescribed according to the extent of the transmission—network, single region, or local radio. The fee is inclusive of one rehearsal period of up to three hours on the day of performance. If a second rehearsal session is required on the performance day an additional 25 per cent. of the fee (but subject to a maximum) is payable. For extra rehearsals on days prior to the day of performance additional fees are payable at prescribed rates according to the amount of the performance fee and the number of extra rehearsals.

Payment of the basic fee entitles the BBC to broadcast a programme by any means once from each transmitter in the Domestic Service and simultaneously in the World Service. A transmission is deemed to be simultaneous if the transmission in the World Service commences on the same day as the broadcasting of the programme in the Domestic Service. With a regional (or "opt-out") and local radio engagement the fee covers one transmission in the region. As a Collective Agreement it follows that if any of the rights which the BBC has in a performance are to be curtailed, such as repeat rights, a special stipulation will need to be included in an artist's contract.

When a programme is repeated in the Domestic Service 50 per cent. of the performance fee (but not rehearsal or other payments) is payable. There are no restrictions on the number or time within which programmes may be repeated but the amount of the repeat fee is increased by 15 per cent. when the repeat transmission is three years after the initial broadcast, by 25 per cent. after 10 years and by 50 per cent. after 25 years. Fees for repeat transmissions in the World Service are at the rate of 20 per cent. of the performance fee for each of the first five repeats and then 10 per cent. for each additional repeat. Alternatively by paying 40 per cent. of the performance fee there may be three transmissions in the World Service within a seven day period. For the use of a recording in the Transcription Service 100 per cent. of the performance fee is payable.

When a performance is to be pre-recorded the whole of the period allocated to the final rehearsal and performance may be treated as a combined rehearsal and recording session when the discontinuous or rehearse/record technique may be used. The session may not exceed the three hours rehearsal time plus the transmission time of the programme. If more than one session is required to complete the performance and recording of the programme then additional fees are payable for each extra session unless the basic fee payable to a musician exceeds (at present) £450. The amount payable for repeat transmissions of programmes so recorded is calculated on the aggregate of the fees paid. Where this technique is used for separate programmes, separate fees are payable for each programme.

An artist may be expressly engaged for an item recording session when the material recorded may be used in various programmes. Depending on the amount of music to be recorded an artist's normal fee may need to be enhanced. The items recorded may be repeated in the same programme(s) or in other programmes on payment of the normal repeat fee. There is a time limit for the use of repeats of 13 months from the date of the first transmission. There is no limit on the number of repeats of all or any item provided the repeat fee is paid for each round of repeat usage; the repeat fee is due on the use of the first item in the round. By the payment of an artist's repeat fee the whole or parts of a recording of any other performance may also be treated as an item recording once provided any broadcast is of a whole work.

Concert Relays

Performances of public concerts may be relayed live or recorded for later transmission, the fees payable being additional to the concert fee paid to an artist by the concert promoter of the concert. If the concert is promoted by the BBC a performance fee equal to 50 per cent. of the concert fee is payable if the transmission is live. If a recording is made for later transmission not until the recording is broadcast is the fee payable. The provisions as outlined above for a studio engagement apply to repeat transmissions and broadcasts in the World Service of concert performances.

When the concert is not promoted by the BBC a fee equal to 50 per cent. of the concert fee is payable for a live transmission. The performance may be recorded and count as a live transmission provided the recording is broadcast on the same day as the performance. A concert may be recorded without payment for a deferred transmission, but before the transmission a regular studio contract will need to be issued and fees paid accordingly.

If a concert is for charity for which an artist receives no fee or a much reduced fee, a studio fee (as fairly agreed) is paid for the relay. When there is a simultaneous radio and television broadcast of a concert the performance fee paid for the latter covers the radio transmission.

Church Musicians and Church Recitals

Minimum fees are prescribed for organist/directors of music, assistant organists, lay clerks and choir boys/girls for the broadcasting of services from cathedrals and churches of similar status. The rates differ according to whether the broadcast is of a regular church service or a service especially arranged for broadcasting. For special national occasions higher fees are paid. The fees include payment for a rehearsal on the same day as the service but additional fees are payable for rehearsals on a previous day. If there is a simultaneous radio and television broadcast the fee paid for the latter covers the radio transmission.

The Agreement makes provision for the payment of fees to professional organists at churches of less than cathedral status.

For the broadcasting of recitals of music taking place in churches solo artists are entitled to fees of not less than the minimum prescribed for a basic studio engagement as mentioned above. Lay clerks and choir boys/girls are entitled to fees as for a service especially arranged for broadcasting. If there is a simultaneous radio and television broadcast the fee for the latter covers both transmissions.

The lay clerks of Westminster Abbey, St. Paul's and Westminster Cathedral are subject to the Equity BBC Radio Agreement.

Piano Accompanists

Piano accompanists are subject to special provisions of the Agreement. If an accompanist is engaged for a recital the minimum fees and other terms of engagement as for a soloist apply. For accompanying artists at other performances a standard fee is payable for a rehearsal of up to three hours with a performance on the same day not exceeding one hour. Overtime is payable at an hourly rate if either or both of these times are exceeded. Supplementary standard fees are payable for extra rehearsals at different rates according to whether the rehearsal is of up to three hours on the day of the performance or two hours on a day prior to the performance; there are rates for overtime. Standard rates also apply for other services, namely, for audition sessions, playing music to conductors etc. during sessions, and for rehearsals only.

General Provisions

Other provisions of the Agreement provide for the use of extracts from recordings of BBC programmes on payment to a musician of a standard supplementary fee in religious, instructional, schools and magazine and such like programmes and in critical programmes provided an artist's permission is first obtained. Extracts can also be used in such like programmes of performances promoted by organisations independently of the BBC on payment of a negotiated fee.

A musician may be engaged for studio performances for schools programmes when two-thirds of the basic fees are payable except for solo artist for whom a minimum is prescribed, and for accompanists who are entitled to the standard rate. Artists may be engaged for recording opening/closing music, signature tunes and like purposes on the same basis as for schools programmes except that by the payment of the fee the BBC acquires all rights in the recording.

The Agreement renders performances subject to international relaying in accordance with the Convention of the European Broadcasting Union. Performances may be broadcast to member countries simultaneously with the initial transmission, or within 30 days thereafter, without the payment of additional fees. The Agreement also provides for the recording of a programme to be made available by the BBC's Transcription Service to organisations for unrestricted radio transmissions overseas. For this use a fee equal to an artist's performance fee is payable. The right for the commercial exploitation of a recording as an audio-tape or compact disc does not form part of the Agreement and therefore is subject to individual agreement and negotiation.

An evening dress allowance is payable to artists who are required to wear evening dress at a concert before an invited audience. Travel and subsistence allowances when payable are notified to artists at the time of engagement.

Local Radio

Artists may be engaged for sessions in the usual way for local radio broadcasting by the payment of the prescribed minimum fees. A performance can be transmitted once by up to four stations simultaneously, or non-simultaneously within 30 days of the first transmission. By paying 100 per cent. of the fee a further four stations may likewise broadcast the programme.

By the payment of the repeat fee calculated in the same way as for the repeating of a broadcast in the Domestic Service as noted above, a programme can be repeated by the four stations and in the corresponding manner as the initial broadcast. Also by the payment of the repeat fee as for a repeat in the Domestic Service, up to four local radio stations may give a non-simultaneous broadcast of a programme first transmitted in the Domestic Service.

E. FILMS, TELEVISION FILMS AND VIDEOGRAMS

Central to the business of the film industry in times past was the production of feature cinema films with star artists and supporting casts, studio sets and locations which might be lavish in both spectacle and expense, plus the extravagance of promotions to entice eager audiences into large and numerous cinemas. Despite some outstanding productions expectations of a sustained revival and return to that era to benefit British studios has not yet come about. Even so the industry is not in a state of atrophy as in recent years there has come about a new direction and impetus in response to the demand for television films, the commissioning of television programmes from independent producers, and for the supply of commercial advertising films, documentary and instructional films and videograms.

The business and legal considerations which attach to the making of films and independent television programmes are explored in Part 7 below. Here there is to be considered the industry collective agreements applicable to artists and musicians engaged for the purpose of performing in films of various descriptions. It is relevant to note that in the 1960's the demand for the production of films made especially for television and international exploitation led to the making of separate collective agreements for these films. The film industry was used to the production of films as films but television was an intrusion on established ways. The reasons for there being separate agreements for cinema films and television films was in part due to the different ways of scheduling production but more especially the differences in the extent and ways of exploitation. These differences are narrowing, so in time there may be simply two collective agreements, one for the engagement of artists and one for musicians.

The organisation which represents the interests of British feature film and television film producers is the Producers Alliance for Cinema and Television (PACT). It was constituted in 1991 as the newly formed trade association and successor to both the British Film and Television Producers Association (which was the successor to the British Film Producers Association founded in 1938) and the Independent Programme Producers Association which had been established as a separate organisation to represent the interests of those producers primarily engaged in the production of television programmes. Being the successor to these associations for simplicity PACT is named as the party to the collective agreements considered below.

The membership of PACT comprises companies and individuals engaged in the production of films of all descriptions and regardless of the intended primary usage. In addition its membership includes a category or group for those engaged in the financing and distribution of films, and a category or group for those providing services and facilities for the production of films. A separate category of membership (affiliates) is for persons otherwise connected with the film industry.

The affairs of PACT are directed by its Council of 27 members which includes representatives of the particular groups or categories of members within PACT, and the provincial regions. The administration and management of PACT is conducted by a Chief Executive, and salaried staff. As a trade association PACT functions to promote and protect the interests of its members by providing a number of services including training and advisory services. Of particular importance is the Department of Industrial Relations which on behalf of members of PACT conducts the negotiations with the Trade Unions on the terms and conditions of employment in the film industry and on minimum rates of pay. The Department provides a continuous service of advice on the application of the various collective agreements and all other matters relating to employment.

THE PACT AND EQUITY COLLECTIVE AGREEMENTS

There are two Agreements both of January 1989 (but as amended) setting out the minimum terms and conditions for the engagement of artists (but excluding instrumental musicians and crowd artists) in the film industry. The first, the Cinema Film Agreement, is for engagements for films produced primarily for theatrical (cinema) exhibition which in its structure and crucial terms has an origin dating from 1947. The second, the Television Film Agreement, has much in common with the first and so in the following pages the various kinds of engagements which may be offered under respectively the Cinema and the Television Film Agreements are outlined. As the more general provisions attaching to an engagement are virtually the same in both Agreements these are reviewed together. The procedure for the settlement of disputes which is common to both Agreements is noted last.

Before considering the kinds of engagement there is first to be noted those provisions common to both of the Agreements which prescribe the procedures to be observed preparatory to any drama film production being undertaken. PACT (through its Industrial Relations Service) and Equity (through its authorised representatives) both participate in these procedures together with representatives of the Broadcasting Entertainment Cinematograph Theatre Union (BECTU) representing technical and craft personnel.

First, normally four weeks before the start of principal photography of a production, a producer must furnish PACT and the Unions with details of the planned production, in particular details of the budgeted cost and sources of finance. Since film production is undertaken ad hoc in order to secure the financial interests of the persons variously contributing to the actual production of a film it is then for PACT and the Unions to decide whether a letter of financial guarantee from a third party will be acceptable for this purpose. Alternatively a producer may be required to place monies in escrow with PACT sufficient to cover two weeks salaries for all the cast and members of the film crew. For this purpose there is a ceiling of £1,500 per week to the salaries of individual artists. Where there are to be overseas locations, the cost of return air fares is included in the calculation of the amount to be placed in escrow. Receipt of the letter of guarantee or monies paid in escrow is to be reported to the pre-production meeting as mentioned below.

When, in the absence of a satisfactory guarantee, monies are placed in escrow a statement is to be provided apportioning the sums as between each of the Unions representing artists and technical personnel. The amount placed in escrow may be varied or augmented in the light of the production plans and schedule considered at the pre-production meeting. Where there is a co-production the British co-producer is required to put in escrow the appropriate amount for the British cast and crew.

An application by a producer to withdraw the monies in escrow cannot be made earlier than two weeks before the end of principal photography. The release of the monies apportioned as between the Unions has to be authorised by the appropriate Union and PACT. Sufficient monies must be left in escrow to cover the post-production period. If for whatever reason a production ceases before the end of the scheduled period of principal photography the escrow monies are dealt with in the way described.

The second of the procedures to be followed is the convening of a pre-production meeting by the producer not later than 10 days before the commencement of principal photography of a film at which authorised representatives of Equity and the other Unions are normally present. At the meeting the overall budget is presented with the production schedule; PACT (through its Industrial Relations Service) reports on the receipt of the letter of financial guarantee or monies in escrow. The function of the meeting is to ensure compliance with the various industry collective agreements and working conditions generally. In particular hours of work, issues of health and safety and insurance, the provision of supporting services and facilities, arrangements for travel, accommodation and subsistence for when filming on location, and the post-production schedule are reviewed.

ENGAGEMENTS UNDER THE CINEMA FILM AGREEMENT

Unlike theatrical or television engagements whereby an artist's exclusive services are contracted by a management or company, in the film industry artists are contracted for a stated fixed period of time on "first call." This basic distinction is a reflection of the practices and techniques of filming as an artist's performance may not be photographed in natural sequence but arranged and spread over a period of time according to the shooting schedule. As an artist is not committed to render his services exclusively to a producer then subject to the overriding needs of a producer if a performer is not required during the period of first call he is free to accept other engagements and render his professional services to a third party. Apart from the few special kinds of engagement noted below artists are contracted on the basis of either a daily or weekly engagement for which there are separate forms of contract and conditions of employment. If an artist is engaged for two or more guaranteed periods each period counts as a separate engagement.

Daily Engagements

The precise period of first call, the guaranteed period, must be entered together with the amount of the agreed daily salary (a minimum rate is prescribed) and the amount of the guaranteed sum, this sum being the multiple of the agreed daily salary and the minimum number of days during the period of first call when an artist may be required to render his services. If during the guaranteed period of first call an artist renders services on additional days it follows the daily salary is payable for each such day.

In addition to the guaranteed sum the following supplementary payments in respect of each week of the guaranteed period or part thereof are payable:

(a) where the guaranteed period exceeds one day but an artist is entitled to payment of salary for one day only, the supplement payable is the amount equal to the negotiated daily salary which is subject to a maximum of £125;

(b) where an artist is not entitled to any salary payment the supplement payable is the amount equal to twice the minimum negotiated daily salary which is subject to a minimum of £125;

(c) where the guaranteed period is one day only, or where an artist is entitled to payment of salary for two or more days no supplement is payable.

A producer is entitled to extend the period of first call by written notice to an artist given not later than three days prior to the last day of the guaranteed period. Normally an extension may not be for a period longer than the initial period of first call. An artist cannot generally avoid or demand to be released from the possibility of a producer exercising this right of extension unless to be free to accept a bona fide offer of another engagement. Then an artist may request in writing to be released on a specific date and a producer must make a reply in writing within 24 hours or on the next working day. If a producer fails to make any reply his consent is deemed to have been given. If consent is not given a producer is deemed to have extended the period of first call up to and including the date requested by the artist to be released.

In the event of an artist agreeing to a period of first call after the expiration of the initial period (and any extension of it which may have occurred) a wholly new and separate engagement arises and must be contracted.

Calls for attendance are normally to be made not later than 8 p.m. on the day preceding the attendance. When an artist is called to the studios or location but is not required to rehearse or perform, if he is released within five and a half hours only half of the daily salary is payable but otherwise a whole daily salary is payable.

Where an artist engaged on a daily basis is required to travel to a resident location there is payable for each day one and a half the daily salary. When at a resident location the daily salary is payable although an artist may not have been required to render any services. If an artist is engaged for a location abroad the engagement must be on a weekly basis if the engagement involves a stay of more than two nights on the location.

Weekly Engagements

The period of first call, the guaranteed period, must be stated in the form of engagement but a producer is permitted by the provisions of the Agreement to advance or defer the contracted starting date by as many days (but not exceeding seven), as there are complete weeks in the guaranteed period. The artist's agreed weekly salary (a minimum rate is prescribed) must be entered and a daily rate which may not be less than one-quarter of the agreed weekly salary but in any event not less than the prescribed minimum daily rate.

In each week of the guaranteed period the weekly salary is payable but when the engagement is for more than one week then if the last week of the guaranteed period is a broken week, meaning a period of three consecutive days or less, a producer has the option of paying either the weekly salary or the daily salary for each day of broken week. If during the guaranteed period an artist is released at his request for any day or half-day a proportionate amount calculated on the daily salary is deductible from the payment of the current instalment of the weekly salary.

A producer may extend the guaranteed period but normally not for a period greater than the initial period of first call by giving notice in writing to the artist (or by recorded delivery post) not later than three days before the expiration of the guaranteed period. An artist cannot generally avoid or demand to be released from the producer's right so to extend the period of first call. The weekly salary or payment as for a broken week (as the circumstances may be) is payable throughout any extension of first call.

Second Call Services

From the time an artist accepts an engagement whether daily or weekly, until the first day of the guaranteed period he is on "second call" meaning that subject to his professional commitments he can be called upon to render his services for script reading and rehearsals, camera tests, costume fittings, still photograph calls and publicity. Similarly after the period of first call an artist is on second call until the completion of the film to render services for retakes, the dubbing of his voice and post-synchronisation. For services rendered on second call a half-day's or whole day's contracted daily salary is payable to an artist according to the kind of services rendered and the duration of the attendance or stand by.

Only reasonable expenses are payable to an artist for attending for the taking of publicity stills. For rehearsals or script readings if the period of time for these services does not exceed one-half the guaranteed period, then one-half of the contracted daily or weekly salary is payable for each such day or week of rehearsal; the full daily or weekly salary is payable for any further rehearsal time. When a script reading is nominated as such the daily rate is payable. For camera tests, wardrobe fittings and the like normally one-half of the contracted daily salary is payable for each attendance day up to a maximum of one-quarter of the weekly salary.

When second call services are rendered after the guaranteed period and particularly services required to complete the photographing and recording of an artist's part a full daily salary is payable when an artist attends for work following a call which may be made up to 8 p.m. on the day previous. A half daily salary is payable when an artist is required for stand-by following a call but if less than 24 hours notice is given a full daily salary is payable. A half daily salary is payable for an attendance of up to five hours for post-synchronisation but otherwise a full daily salary is payable.

Special Categories of Performers

(1) Principal Artists

Although engagements cannot be on terms less favourable than as provided in the Agreement and normally the conditions attaching to an engagement cannot be altered even so the Agreement permits the standard conditions to be varied for artists whose salary exceeds £770 per week or part thereof.

In such circumstances a producer and an artist may mutually agree to vary the commitments respecting first call and second call and working hours, make special provision about the presentation and treatment of an artist's role and performance and the promotion and publicity to be accorded an artist. Also special provision may be made concerning insurance and the entitlement of a producer to assign the right to the artist's services to a third party.

(2) Stunt Performers and Stunt Arrangers

The engagement of stunt performers and stunt arrangers is subject to special rules in an appendix to the Agreement. A stunt is defined as a "special performance requiring the use of skill and involving physical risk to the performer and/or any person working with the performer." Whether a performance is a stunt is solely for a producer to decide but if a decision is disputed the Agreement provides for the issue to be referred to the Joint Secretaries of the Joint Films Council for consideration by a Conciliation Panel. The Panel is to consist of an equal number of representatives of PACT and Equity and the meeting is to be within 48 hours of the reference excluding a Saturday, Sunday and declared holidays.

An engagement must first be offered to persons who are on the Equity Register of Stunt Performers and no artist can be obliged to work with any stunt performer or arranger who is not a permanent or temporary member of the Register. Exceptions are made for a person performing a stunt incidental to the performance of his or her part, and for the established double of a star artist performing a minor stunt for the star provided the Joint Secretaries are informed. If for the performance of a particular stunt there is no suitable registered stunt performer available a producer may engage a performer not on the register provided the Joint Committee for Stunt Performers established under the Joint Films Council is first notified of the intention so to do. The Committee is enjoined not unreasonably to refuse temporary registration as a stunt performer to the person appointed whether or not he is already a member of Equity.

Stunt performers and arrangers are contracted subject to the provisions of the Agreement like other artists but as varied by the provisions of the appendix. Separate minimum daily and weekly rates are prescribed for stunt performers and stunt arrangers but these are inclusive of the use fees which are payable to all other artists as explained below. When engagements are on a weekly basis the daily rate is one-quarter of the weekly rate. If services are required outside the guaranteed period additional fees are payable as follows: for rehearsal or performance the daily rate; for attendance for wig and costume fitting a standard fee is payable; for consultations with arrangers the fee is negotiable; for all other attendances the half daily salary is payable. Overtime payments are at the rate of one-seventh of the daily rate for each hour or part thereof. One-half of the daily salary is also payable for night work except at a resident location and for work on a seventh day and on statutory holidays.

The negotiated daily and weekly salaries will normally be settled for the stunt work as described at the time of the engagement or following an inspection of the site. However, it may be that during the engagement a particular stunt is required which merits an adjustment of the agreed fee. If the fee is increased the extra amount is not added to the contracted daily rate for the calculation of overtime and premium payments. If there is a dispute about the reasonableness of the fee at the time of execution of the stunt having regard to the written description the work is to be performed and the issue referred to the Joint Secretaries to convene a Conciliation Panel. However, a performer cannot be obliged to undertake a hazard which could not reasonably have been foreseen from the written description of the stunt.

A contract for the engagement of a stunt performer or arranger must contain a warranty that the performer is professionally competent to undertake the act or work contracted, and is insured at his expense to a level and extent not less than that fixed by Equity and reported to the Joint Committee for Stunt Performers. There may not be included in the contract any provision the effect of which would in any way abrogate any rights the performer may have by common law or statute in respect of loss, injury or damage arising out of the performance of the contract. The required stipulations to be included in all engagement contracts are:

"The Artist acknowledges that the engagement is to render services of a hazardous or dangerous nature and warrants that he/she is professionally competent to undertake the act or work contracted. The Artist also warrants that he/she is currently insured as required by the Agreement."

In the contracts of stunt arrangers an additional stipulation is required to be included:

"The Stunt Arranger undertakes that he/she will take no financial advantage from the selection or engagement of Stunt Performers or advising thereon other than his/her agreed fee as a Stunt Arranger."

As already noted stunt performers are normally required to be selected from performers listed in the register and this provision serves to prevent improper discrimination in the selection of performers.

For each engagement of a stunt performer and arranger a producer is required to make fixed payments to Equity at the rates prescribed in the Agreement to be applied by Equity in improving the benefits payable to members of the register under the group personal accident insurances held in the name of Equity.

(3) Choreographers

The employment of choreographers and manner of their engagement is the same as for regular artists, but in the standard form of engagement there is to be included a special stipulation as follows:

"It is understood and agreed that the Artist employed as a choreographer shall perform as a dancer if the needs of the film so require; in consideration of which agreement the Associate guarantees to pay to the Artist such use fees as may be payable under the Agreement whether or not the Artist appears in the film."

(4) Session Singers—Sound Track Recording

Solo and session singers who appear in vision in a film must be engaged in accordance with and are subject to the Agreement without variation or exception. Singers who are engaged only for sound track recording are subject to the Agreement but the following special rules apply as their engagement is on a sessional basis. A prescribed standard minimum fee is payable for a basic session of three hours and during which up to 20 minutes of material may be recorded. With the payment of the basic fee there is also to be paid nominated pre-purchased use fees one of which must include at least one of the two theatrical use fees as explained below.

A session may be extended by a total of 30 minutes and for each additional 15 minutes or part thereof a standard additional fee is payable and during which one and a half minutes of material may be recorded. If a session is to be extended this must be notified at the time otherwise any further working results in the commencement of a new session. Not more than two extended sessions may be worked on any day. The total amount of recorded material may be averaged out over a number of sessions but if the average exceeds the permitted standard amount or minutage of recorded material a standard additional fee is payable for each three minutes of extra recorded material.

If a singer is called before 8 a.m. or detained after midnight a standard supplementary fee is payable. If a session takes place on a public holiday the sessional fee is increased 100 per cent. and the additional payment for excess time is at a higher standard rate.

If session singers are required to overdub their performance, for the first dub an additional 125 per cent. of the appropriate fee is payable; for any subsequent overdub 140 per cent. If the performance is issued and released on record or pre-recorded audio tape a session singer is entitled to an additional fee at the British Phonographic Industry rate for every 20 minutes or part thereof of the recorded singing incorporated into the record.

(5) Revoicing and Commentary

Artists who render their services in revoicing or delivering commentary out-of-vision are subject to and entitled to all the provisions of the Agreement except as necessarily varied because such artists are engaged on a sessional basis like sessional singers. A session is of four hours but may be extended by a total of 30 minutes. A prescribed minimum fee is payable for the session and for each extension of 15 minutes or part thereof a standard additional fee is payable. With the payment of the basic fee nominated pre-purchased use fees are payable as with session singers. There is no limit on the amount of material which may be recorded in a session. This special provision for out-of-vision recording does not apply to artists who are engaged for the post-synchronisation or dubbing of their own part.

General Conditions of Engagements

The general terms and conditions of employment set out in the Agreement with few exceptions apply to all engagements. The provisions governing working conditions and hours of work can be varied by special agreement at the pre-production meeting mentioned above.

A working day or night is 10 hours including a break of one hour for a meal; normally a working day commences between 7 a.m. and 10 a.m., but otherwise at 10 a.m. Night work is work especially called as such and scheduled to extend beyond midnight. Dawn calls are calls at times when normal working is not possible or practical—such as for exterior/location shooting. It may commence at 4 a.m. and continue until 9 a.m., or at 5 a.m. until 10 a.m. Overtime applies when the terminal hours is exceeded as if a normal day had been worked.

For weekly engagements a working week is seven consecutive days beginning on the first day of an artist's period of first call. An artist may be required to work on more than five days but normally on not more than six. If an artist is required to work on a sixth and seventh day the daily salary is payable for each day in addition to the weekly salary. On resident locations of two or more weeks the working days can be aggregated over the whole period of the location time subject to an average of five days work in each week. If the average is extended then for each extra day the daily salary is payable.

When a continuous working day is agreed upon the working day is of eight hours normally between 7 a.m. and 7 p.m. without interruption for a formal meal break; overtime runs from when work exceeds the eight hours and should not, save in emergencies, exceed two hours. During a continuous working day short breaks are to be allowed according to operational requirements.

Time engaged in make-up, hairdressing and wardrobe counts as part of a working day. If the time taken for make-up etc. is a half hour or one hour then if shooting continues beyond the normal working time by the equivalent amount of time an artist is paid at straight time for the extended time.

Overtime is limited to four hours a day unless otherwise agreed. Even so an artist can be requested to work an additional 15 minutes at the end of a working day or night without payment to complete a "take"; if the minutage is exceeded the whole time counts for overtime. On resident locations if an artist is engaged by the week working hours and overtime may be aggregated over the week. Overtime is payable at the rate of one third of an artist's daily rate subject to a minimum rate. Artists engaged on a daily salary who are required to render services on nightwork (excepting on a resident location), or on a seventh day, or on a public holiday are paid an additional one-half of their daily salary.

There are detailed provisions setting out the respective obligations of producers and artists for the cost of travel and payment for travel time. These depend upon the situation of a studio or other designated place of work, whether a location is a non-resident or resident one, and the time of a call or release at the end of a working day and the availability of public transport. Only if an artist cannot reasonably return from a designated place of work or non-resident location to the artist's home each night is there an obligation on a producer to provide and pay for reasonable accommodation and board. Any travel by air to and from a resident location is to be provided by a producer and times are prescribed for when shooting can commence after a flight.

If the production of a film is prevented or interrupted for any cause beyond a producer's control a producer can elect immediately to suspend an artist's engagement for the duration of the event, or alternatively to terminate the engagement provided notice of this is given in writing within five working days of the event (whether or not the engagement has already been suspended) and the producer pays to the artist all accrued fees for the services rendered. When this provision of the Agreement is invoked a producer must inform Equity.

If a producer suspends an engagement and the suspension continues for three consecutive weeks the entitlement to an artist's services on first call then ceases. This consequence can be avoided by a producer giving to an artist within this time written notice of the desire to retain first call and during the continuance of the suspension paying to the artist the fees he would be entitled to receive on first call.

When the suspension of an engagement is lifted the period of first call is automatically extended by the period of suspension unless this would prevent an artist from fulfilling a commitment entered into before the suspension; in these circumstances an artist continues on second call. It follows that if there is a delay or interruption in production only by not suspending an engagement but exercising the right to extend the period of first call as necessary can a producer be assured of retaining an artist's services. If an engagement is suspended and during the suspension an artist wishes to enter into another engagement he must first consult the producer with a view to the artist being available to complete his part.

The Exploitation and Uses of a Film

A producer has the absolute right to decide how a film is to be promoted, advertised and exploited subject to complying with the provisions of the Agreement noted below about "use fees." If there is to be any restriction of a producer's rights in this regard it must be an express term of an artist's contract of engagement. An artist has no right to any particular screen or advertising credit unless provided for in the contract of engagement. A producer is entitled to use the name, photographs and biography of an artist in the publicity for a film but not without an artist's written consent in connection with the merchandising of other commercial goods. If any photographs showing an artist in a state of nudity or semi-nudity are to be used this must be especially stipulated in the contract of engagement; an artist has the automatic right to reject up to half of such photographs selected by a producer for such use.

A producer has the right to use extracts from a film, including extracts from the soundtrack incorporating an artist's performance and "still" photographs of an artist for the legitimate promotion of a film, but extracts may not be used in other films or other visual or sound recordings or broadcast programmes without an artist's consent. An exception is made for session singers as noted above.

In addition to the fees contractually payable to an artist in the course of an engagement in order for a film to be publicly exhibited and exploited in any way "use fees" are also payable unless an artist's performance is not included in the film released for exhibition. "Use fees" are a percentage of an artist's "total applicable salary," meaning the aggregate of the daily or weekly salary (or session fees where applicable) paid to an artist during the guaranteed period and any extension thereof and most of the fees paid for services rendered on second call. Payments for camera tests and the like incidental services or for stand by are not included, neither are any overtime or premium payments.

Use fees are payable according to the medium of exploitation of a film and are a percentage of an artist's total applicable salary as follows:

(a) Theatrical exhibition:

    (i) U.S.A. and Canada—50 per cent.

    (ii) Rest of the World including the U.K.—50 per cent.

(b) Non-Theatric exhibition:

    By the first payment for either theatrical exhibition as in: (a) above the right of non-theatric exhibition throughout the world is automatically acquired.

(c) Free Television broadcasting:

    (i) U.S.A.—Major Network—45 per cent.

    (ii) U.S.A.—other than Major Network—20 per cent.

    (iii) Rest of the world (excluding the U.K.)—15 per cent.

    (iv) U.K.—20 per cent.

(d) Pay Television Broadcasting:

    (i) U.S.A.—30 per cent.

    (ii) Rest of the world (including the U.K.)—8 per cent.

(e) Videogram sales:
    25 per cent. for unlimited sales world wide.

There is no limitation on the time within which any of the uses need to be acquired except that one of the two (territorial) theatrical exhibition uses as above must be guaranteed and the 50 per cent. of an artist's total applicable salary automatically paid with the performance salary. Generally but not necessarily so, with a feature film use fees are paid to artists on the completion of a film in order to secure clearance for all media of exploitation as above. Only in the United Kingdom is there any limitation on the extent of the free television broadcasting of a film. The payment of the use fee covers transmissions either separately or simultaneously in all or any television region three times but any second and third transmission must be within five years of the first. Special provisions apply for pay television broadcasting in the United Kingdom.

An appendix to the Agreement makes special provision for the registration at the Joint Films Council of low budget British films whereby the payment of use fees may be deferred except for the payment of the 50 per cent. of the performance salary for either of the theatric rights as above, and 20 per cent. for the United Kingdom free television rights. Any deferment can be only until a film has recouped revenues equivalent to two and three quarter times its certified budget where this is not more than one million pounds but if over that but not more than one and a half million pounds the multiplier is two and a quarter.

The exercise of any rights of exhibition, transmission or other exploitation of a film not provided for in the Agreement is subject to agreement between a producer and Equity. The terms of any agreement so made then become part of an artist's contract of engagement.

ENGAGEMENTS UNDER THE TELEVISION FILM AGREEMENT

The first Collective Agreement for films made primarily for television broadcasting was made in 1957 following the inception of commercial television broadcasting in this country. In subsequent years it was revised and then replaced by the current Agreement of January 1989 the provisions of which have remained unchanged apart from increases in minimum rates of pay.

The purpose of the Agreement as set out within its provisions is to lay down "the minimum terms and conditions for all artists (excluding instrumental musicians and crowd artists) employed in *productions* produced primarily for exhibition over television and by methods and techniques commonly used in the British film and television industry: (it applies) to productions irrespective of the source of finance, of the means of production, or of the ultimate use." Although the Agreement is primarily for the making of television films in fact its scope is much wider because the rights of exploitation a producer has in a production include theatrical release, non-theatric exhibition rights and rights of sale or rental to the general public of videograms.

Since the Agreement was formulated the number of companies engaged in the production of television films (especially as a result of the extensive commissioning of independent productions by the programme companies of the ITC and by the BBC), has greatly increased. Moreover the diversity or extent of television exploitation and the opportunities for the international marketing and exploitation of productions have advanced. As a result it is possible the Agreement will be revised in the fairly near future. The changes are not likely to be radical so far as the kinds of engagement and working conditions are concerned but there may be introduced a system of royalty or profit apportionment for performers similar to that now established for the wider exploitation of television programmes.

The Agreement does not apply without the prior approval of Equity to the making of the whole or part of any production currently or recently presented in any theatre or other place of entertainment with the same, or substantially the same cast. It does not apply to productions which are not primarily British.

It has already been remarked that there is much in common in this Agreement with the Cinema Film Agreement both as regards the general provisions on working conditions and practices including the distinctions between first and second call services. The major differences lie in the way artists are contracted and remunerated and the rights of exploitation acquired by a producer in the products of their services. These rights are outlined below but what most distinguishes their definition and exercise from those set out in the corresponding provisions of the Cinema Film Agreement is that after the expiration of 10 years calculated from the date of the commencement of the principal photography of a production any further exploitation of the production becomes subject to any revenue sharing or royalty arrangements agreed between PACT and Equity in operation at the material time. This provision has been devised to prevent the practice of a "buy out" of an artist's entitlement to residual payments arising in the future.

Types or Categories of Engagement

The various kinds of engagement which can be offered to an artist are broadly as follows:

(a) for a single production or episode of a series, or

(b) for a serial or long production capable of being shown in segments or instalments, or

(c) for a series, or

(d) for multiple use, that is for opening and closing sequences and library shots.

An engagement can be any one of eight according to the requirements of a producer and for each kind of engagement there is a standard form of contract with particular conditions of employment and fees payable. There are prescribed minimum rates in particular a daily rate of £150 and a weekly rate of £600. For an artist engaged on a daily basis there is a prescribed minimum earnings aggregate fee of £268. By the payment of the fees to an artist in accordance with the contract of engagement a producer automatically acquires certain television and exhibition rights in the film incorporating the products of an artist's services; additional rights can be acquired by the payment of use fees as explained below. There are special conditions applicable for the engagement of stunt performers and arrangers, artists engaged for revoicing, voice-overs and commentary, and for session singers.

Engagement for a Single Production or Episode of a Series

(1) Engagement by the day: This engagement most resembles the pattern of an engagement for a feature or cinema film. The period of first call must be specified but the actual start date can be varied by one day either side of the contracted starting date. The period begins on the first day following a call when an artist attends to render services in the rehearsing, photographing or recording of the artist's part. Failing a call a producer is deemed to have called and an artist to have attended on the day after the specified contracted starting date. A producer has the right at any time during the period of first call to give written notice to extend the period of first call.

The daily rate or salary must be specified in the form of engagement and the amount of the minimum aggregate earnings. For each day of the period of first call and any extension the daily salary is payable except that:

(a) for calls on public holidays one and a half times the daily salary is payable;

(b) when an artist is called without working because of weather conditions and is released before the lunch break, or if a night call at or before midnight, then 30 per cent. of the daily salary is payable (but 40 per cent. when the call occurs during an extended period of first call) but the period of first call is automatically extended by the number of days lost;

(c) when on any day of the period of extended first call an artist is not called to render services 40 per cent. of the daily salary is payable.

(2) Engagement for nominated days: The form of engagement must specify an artist's daily salary and minimum aggregate earnings and the days of first call, four of which may be consecutive. The days cannot be varied or added to without an artist's consent. Apart from the nominated days an artist is not under obligation to render any services on any other days except (but subject to his professional commitments), services for photographic and sound tests, make-up tests and such like pre-production activities prior to first call. For these services 50 per cent. of the daily salary or the standard sum for these attendances (whichever is less) is payable. The contracted daily salary is payable for each nominated day whether or not the artist renders any services, plus the exploitation fee.

(3) Engagement by the week: The agreed weekly fee must be specified together with a daily rate (which may not be less than a quarter of the weekly rate). The period of first call must be specified and throughout it the weekly fee is payable. If the period of first call is not less than two weeks and terminates in a broken week (that is a period of three consecutive days or less), a producer may pay either the weekly rate, or the amount of the daily salary for each day thereof as for an engagement by the day but subject to the rules as noted above.

A successive period of seven consecutive days counting from the day of commencement of first call constitutes a week's engagement. The form of engagement must specify if the engagement is for a five or six day week otherwise it will be deemed to be for a five day week; for work on a sixth day the daily salary is additionally payable. If in an emergency an artist is required to and consents to working on a seventh day the daily salary is augmented by 30 per cent. Work on a public holiday attracts an additional supplement of 30 per cent. of the daily salary.

The commencement of first call may be varied by a producer by one day either side of the contractual date, or two days if the period of first call is two weeks or more. At any time during the period of first call a producer may by written notice to the artist extend first call for a number of weeks and/or a broken week and throughout the extension the weekly salary (or daily salary for a broken week) is payable.

(4) Engagement for separate periods: This category of engagement can be contracted when there are to be separate periods of work with not less than a scheduled gap of seven days between one period of first call and the next. The periods of first call must be specified but may be on a daily or weekly basis or combination of both. The provisions noted above for engagements either by the day or week apply to each period of first call except that the day of commencement of the second or a subsequent period of first call may be deferred by only one day at the option of a producer. Any extension of the period of first call is subject to an artist's written consent. During the scheduled gap an artist is entitled to a retainer of one daily salary for each week or part thereof but during the gap period a producer is not entitled to any services from an artist. The retainer does not attract an exploitation fee.

Engagement for a Serial or Long Production

Such an engagement is for a production which has a continuing story and is made on one continuous shooting schedule but capable of transmission in more than one segment or instalment. An engagement is treated as if for a single production and when any one of the four kinds of engagement as above may be used but the form of engagement must contain the following special stipulation:

"The Artist's performance may be incorporated into more than one separately transmitted segment or episode."

In addition to the fees contractually payable to an artist under which-ever one of the four kinds of engagement an artist is engaged for, each episodes, segment or instalment of the production into which an artist's performance is incorporated entitles the artist to a further payment. The sum payable is the amount of an artist's aggregate earnings divided by the number of episodes, segments or instalments into which the serial or long production is divided but subject to a minimum guaranteed amount.

When an artist is engaged by the day the guaranteed amount is £268 per episode, segment or instalment when the number of days worked is the same as or more than the number of episodes into which an artist's performance is incorporated. When the number of days worked is less than the number of episodes into which an artist's performance is incorporated the guaranteed sum is £236. When an artist is engaged by the week the minimum guaranteed sum is the amount being 50 per cent. of an artist's weekly salary for each episode, segment or instalment into which an artist's performance is incorporated.

Engagement for a Series

(1) Engagement by the day: This engagement is applicable only to an artist engaged for a single part for incorporation into more than one episode of a series. The conditions of the engagement are the same as for an engagement by the day for a single production or episode as noted above except as follows.

For each episode into which any part of an artist's performance is incorporated an artist is entitled to an additional payment. The amount payable is the aggregate of an artist's earnings divided by the number of episodes but subject to a minimum guaranteed amount. The guarantee is £268 per episode when the number of days worked is the same as or more than the number of episodes into which an artist's performance is incorporated. When the number of days worked is less, the guaranteed sum is £236 per episode.

(2) Engagement by the week: Where an artist is to perform a part which lasts for the whole or substantially the whole of a long series there will generally be the need for a long-term commitment by both producer and artist to ensure the latter's availability according to the shooting schedule.

The form of engagement must specify the duration of the engagement and the number of weeks of first call which number in aggregate may not be less than three out of four weeks of the period of the engagement. The remaining weeks count as break periods when an artist is on second call and any request for him to render services is subject to his not being otherwise professionally committed. The amount of the weekly salary and of the daily salary—which may not be less than a quarter of the agreed weekly rate—must be entered in the form of engagement. For each week of first call the negotiated weekly salary is payable.

The date of the commencement and length of the period of first call may be varied by up to three days either side of the nominated starting date if the period of first call is less than 13 weeks, but up to seven days if the period is 13 weeks or more.

Not less than six days prior written notice must be given by a producer of the beginning and duration of a break period. If an artist attends to render any services during a break period the artist is entitled to payment calculated on the daily salary rate. If an attendance is for retakes, or added scenes or post-synchronisation only, the break period is not thereby ended, but if the attendance is for any other purpose the break period ends and the producer is obliged to pay the artist as though he had been continuously employed on first call during the break period. If a break period begins or ends on a day other than the first day of any week of an artist's engagement then the artist is paid on a daily pro rata basis for the services rendered during the broken week.

A producer can extend the period of the engagement by written notice to an artist not later than one week before its expiration. The permitted extension is three weeks where the original engagement is 15 weeks, five if more than 15 but less than 30, and seven if for more than 30 weeks. For every week of extension the weekly salary is payable except for a broken week at the conclusion of the extended period when a producer has the option of paying the amount of the daily salary for each day of the broken week.

A producer may include in the contracts of up to three artists engaged for the production a declaration that the performance by the artist is essential for its sale and distribution and a special stipulation that the artist undertakes not to accept without the written permission of the producer (for which no charge may be made or unreasonably withheld) any engagement beginning within the following periods after the expiry of the original period of first call. If the contracted period of first call does not exceed 15 weeks the restriction may be six weeks, if more than 15 but less than 30 weeks eight weeks, and if more than 30 weeks the restriction may be up to 10 weeks. If when sought a producer withholds permission and requires the services of the artist within the period as applicable then the period of first call is deemed to have been extended until the artist completes the services required by the producer. The weekly (or daily salary for a broken week) as above is payable throughout the extension of first call. When the number of episodes in which an artist appears exceed the number of full working weeks of the engagement, at the end of the engagement or after each 13 weeks (whichever period is the shorter) a producer must pay to the artist for each extra episode a sum equal to the artist's weekly salary.

The form of engagement is to specify whether an artist is engaged for a six or five day week. If an artist engaged for a five day week is required to work on a sixth day the daily rate is payable for that day. A "broken week" is three consecutive days or less in the week following the final complete week of the period of first call or any extension thereof. An artist can be required to render services in more than one episode on the same day.

Multiple Use—Engagement by the Day

This category of engagement is restricted to artists required to rehearse, photograph and record for the production of:

(a) announcements or scenes for the purpose of opening and/or closing a production, or the episode, segment or instalment of a production, or

(b) library shots for incorporation into more than one film, or segment or instalment of a long production.

The amount of the agreed daily salary and the guaranteed minimum aggregate earnings which may not be less than £268 must be specified in the form of engagement. At the conclusion of the engagement there is also payable a sum equal to the amount of the artist's daily salary but subject to a minimum of £214 which entitles a producer to incorporate the artist's performance in up to 13 episodes of a series, or into the segments of a serial or long production. By paying the sum a second time the performance can be included into a further 13 episodes of the same series.

Apart from engagements for multiple usages above the Agreement also makes provision whereby a producer, for the purposes of audience continuity, recap shots and flashbacks, is entitled to incorporate any part of an artist's performance, but not exceeding two minutes, in up to 13 episodes of a series, or into segments or instalments of a serial or long production by the payment of a fee of £54 for each such use.

Where an artist has been engaged under any other of the above types of engagement, for example, by the day or by the week, a producer is also entitled for the purposes of opening and/or closing a production, or segment or instalment of a production, to incorporate any part of an artist's performance or performances into not more than 13 episodes of the same series, or into segments of instalments of a serial or long production. A sum being the amount equal to an artist's daily or weekly rate is payable subject to a minimum of £215. By paying the sum a second time the same part or parts of an artist's performance may be so used for a further 13 episodes of the same series.

Special Categories of Performers

(1) Stunt Performers and Stunt and Fight Arrangers

The engagement of stunt performers and stunt arrangers is subject to special rules as set out in appendix TC to the Agreement. These rules are the same as for engagements under the Cinema Film Agreement as noted above.

Stunt performers may be engaged on a daily or weekly basis for which minimum rates are prescribed. The form of engagement must specify the rate to apply and if applicable the adjustment fee. If the engagement is weekly it is deemed to be for a five day week unless stipulated as being for a week of six days. Additional use fees are payable as for other performers.

The salary which is negotiable will normally be settled on the basis of the description of the stunt given at the time of negotiation. However, it may be and especially when an engagement is for a period of time, that a particular stunt devised on a location merits an adjustment of the agreed rate. If the fee is adjusted the extra amount is not added to the contracted daily rate for the calculation of overtime and other premium payments. If there is a dispute about the reasonableness of the fee at the time of execution of the stunt having regard to the written description, the work is to be performed and the issue referred to the Joint Films Council.

However, a performer cannot be obliged to undertake a hazard which could not reasonably have been foreseen from the written description of the stunt.

Stunt and fight arrangers may be engaged on a daily or weekly basis. Minimum rates are prescribed but unlike other performers the rates are inclusive of all uses and rights in the production as set out in the Agreement. Other special rules apply to stunt arrangers. Overtime payments are at the rate of one seventh of the daily rate per hour or part thereof; a premium of one half the daily rate is payable for nightwork, except on resident locations, and for work on a seventh day or on public holidays. If a stunt arranger renders services outside the period of the engagement the daily rate is payable for any rehearsal or performance; half the daily rate is payable for any other attendances but attendances for consultations are subject to individual negotiation. A stunt arranger may be engaged for a series or serial on terms that he will be available for consultation over a period of time but subject to other commitments. Payment for these services may not be less than minimum rates.

(2) Revoicing, Voice-Overs and Commentary

Artists who render their services in revoicing or delivering commentary out of vision are engaged on a sessional basis on the special terms as set out in appendix TD to the Agreement. These provisions do not apply when an artist is required to render services for the post-synchronisation or dubbing of the artist's own part.

A session is of four hours' duration with a break of 15 minutes for which the prescribed minimum fee payable is currently £145. A session may be extended by up to 30 minutes on payment of the prescribed fee for each 15 minutes or part thereof of the extended time. If there is a second consecutive session a meal break of one hour is to be allowed. An artist is entitled to be paid use fees like any other artist.

Payment of the sessional fee entitles a producer to incorporate an artist's performance into a single production, or episode, segment or instalment of a series, serial or long production. If the performance is used in more than one episode of a series, or more than one instalment or segment of a serial or long production then for each one such additional use 50 per cent. of an artist's sessional fee is payable. If the performance is for multiple use, or for the purposes of audience continuity, recap shots of flashbacks, or for stock shots 50 per cent. of an artist's sessional fee is payable for the incorporation of the performance or material in up to 13 episodes of the same series, or into segments of a serial or long production; by the payment of another 50 per cent. of the sessional fee the material may be included in up to another 13 episodes of the same series.

(3) Session Singers—Sound Track Recording

Singers engaged for sound track recording only and not required to appear in vision are engaged on a sessional basis on the special terms set out in appendix TE to the Agreement. If a singer is required to appear in vision then the singer must be engaged as required on a regular contract like any other artist.

A session is of three hours duration with a break of 15 minutes for which the prescribed minimum sessional fee payable is currently £145. A session may be extended by up to 30 minutes on payment of the prescribed fee for each 15 minutes or part thereof, but if a producer does not give notice of the extension at the end of the session then any further working time is deemed to constitute a new session. There may not be more than two extended sessions on any one day. If a singer is called before 8 a.m., or detained after midnight a standard supplementary fee is payable. If a singer performs on a public holiday the sessional fee is doubled and a higher fee is payable for extended sessional time. A singer is entitled to use fees like any other artist.

In a session up to 20 minutes of vocal music or material may be recorded and up to one and a half minutes of additional material during each 15 minutes of extended sessional time. The minutage may be averaged out where there are successive sessions but if the average is exceeded then a standard fee is payable for each additional three minutes of recorded material. If a singer is required to overdub his own performance the minimum sessional fee is doubled.

Payment of the sessional fee entitles a producer to incorporate a singer's performance into a single production, or episode, segment or instalment of a series, serial or long production. The same provisions as above for artists engaged for revoicing apply to a session singer where there is any multiple use of the performance.

General Provisions on Working Conditions

The provisions of the Agreement setting out the standard working conditions and hours of work have much in common with the corresponding provisions of the Cinema Film Agreement and as set out above. Moreover with minor exceptions the provisions apply to all of the engagements reviewed above. There are some important differences and these are noted in the following paragraphs.

Like engagements under the Cinema Film Agreement so too under this Agreement, from the time an artist accepts an engagement until the beginning of the period of first call an artist is on second call for purposes other than the principal photography and main sound recording of his part but subject to any previous professional commitments. The period of first call does not begin unless the day(s) of rehearsal run(s) consecutively and without a gap with the commencement of the period of first call. If before the beginning of any period of first call an artist is required to travel to a designated place of work but without being called upon to render any services and cannot return to his normal place of residence on the day of travel, a travel day payment is payable and the period of first call is deemed to commence on the following day regardless of whether the artist then renders any services.

After the period of first call an artist is on second call until the completion of his part or parts in the production. Thereafter, but of course on the basis of second call, an artist may be required to render services for retakes, added scenes and post-synchronisation.

For attendances for photographic and sound tests, make-up tests, story and other conferences and such like matters 30 per cent. of an artist's daily rate is payable subject to a maximum of £74. If the attendance is for costume or wig fittings or for publicity or "still" photographs the daily rate is payable. When an artist is called for the rehearsal of his part for each day or part thereof the daily rate is payable but the period of first call does not thereby begin unless the day(s) of rehearsal is/are consecutive with the commencement of the period of first call.

For other services rendered on second call the payments are as follows. The daily rate is payable when an artist:

(a) stands by on first call until after 1 p.m. or the lunch break, whichever is the earlier;

(b) is called to and attends the designated place of work, whether or not photographed;

(c) attends at the designated place of work and renders services in the rehearsal, photographing or recording of the part;

(d) attends for more than four hours and/or both before and after the lunch break for the purpose of pre-recording sound, post-synchronisation or the making of still photographs to be reproduced in the production.

Thirty per cent. of the daily rate is payable when an artist:

(i) stands by on first call and is released before 1.30 p.m. or the lunch break, whichever is the earlier;

(ii) attends for a half day not exceeding four hours either before or after the lunch break for the purpose of pre-recording sound, post-synchronisation or the making of "still" photographs to be reproduced in the production.

Calls are normally to be made no later than 8 p.m. on the day previous to the day an artist is required to render services; only in emergency is an artist obliged to accept a later call. If a call is cancelled the fee due remains payable unless notice is given 48 hours in advance.

As already noted working days and hours etc. are as for engagements for cinema films. However, when overtime payments are due payment is on the basis of one ninth of an artist's daily rate times one and a half for each hour or part thereof subject to a maximum of £54. Overtime payment may be excluded by special stipulation in the contract of engagement of artists engaged at rates of £3,215 per week or £804 per day.

Although under some of the engagements reviewed above a producer may extend the period of first call, in order that the right is not unduly burdensome or used indiscriminately the Agreement contains provisions governing a producer's exercise of the right. If an artist has a bona fide offer of another professional engagement which he wishes to accept he is entitled to request, in writing, to be released as from a given date from his obligation to accept an extension of first call. If a producer fails to reply in writing within 24 hours (but with due allowance for weekends and public holidays), he is deemed to have consented to the release. If a producer declines to release the artist then he is deemed to have extended the period of first call up to and including the date of release requested by the artist.

In the event of a production being prevented or interrupted for any reason outside a producer's direct control the producer may either cancel the production or an engagement but always subject to the payment of all moneys accrued due to an artist at the time of cancellation. Alternatively a producer may make other arrangements with an artist by way of postponement and the like as may be practical to fulfil the engagement. A producer is to inform Equity when these provisions of the Agreement are invoked.

Rights of Transmission and the Payment of Use Fees

The payment by a producer of the fees due to an artist in accordance with the contract of engagement (and supplementary fees which may have become due in the course of an engagement) is made not only for the services rendered by an artist but also for certain rights of exhibition of the production incorporating an artist's performance. The rights automatically acquired by a producer are:

(a) to transmit and broadcast the production by television
  (i) in the U.K. once either separately or simultaneously in all or any of the television regions,

    (ii) throughout the rest of the world except the U.S.A. without restriction;

(b) to exhibit the production theatrically throughout the world except in the U.K. and the U.S.A.;

(c) to exhibit the production non-theatrically throughout the world without restriction.

Any additional transmissions or theatrical exhibition of a production is subject to the payment to an artist of additional use fees as set out in Appendix TA of the Agreement.

The use fees are a percentage of an artist's aggregate earnings and the payments which count and do not count in the calculation of an artist's aggregate earnings are listed in Appendices TF and TG of the Agreement. Briefly these are the total of the contracted daily or weekly salary paid to an artist together with any supplementary fees paid for additional working days and as may have been paid to artists engaged for a serial or long production or series. Overtime and other premium payments such as for night work do not count. The following payments made for services rendered on second call are included:

(a) when an artist is called to and attends at the studios or location whether or not photographed;

(b) when an artist likewise attends for the rehearsal, photographing or recording of a part;

(c) when an artist attends for the purpose of pre-recording sound, post-synchronisation or the making of still photographs for reproduction in the production.

The additional uses which may be secured and the use fees payable calculated as a percentage of an artist's earnings are as follows:

(a) Additional transmissions in the U.K.:

a second transmission	35%:	minimum £86
a third transmission	35%:	minimum £86

A repeat transmission may be made either separately or simultaneously in all or any television region but within five years of the date of the first television transmission. After this period any additional transmission is subject to agreement with Equity.

(b) For transmissions in the U.S.A.:

1st prime-time transmission	75%:	minimum £214

2nd prime-time transmission	25%:	minimum £70
Thereafter per transmission	15%:	minimum £38
1st Non prime-time transmission	25%:	minimum £70
Thereafter per transmission	5%:	minimum £11
Syndication	15%:	minimum £38
Public Broadcasting Service	10%:	minimum £27

(c) Theatrical exhibition in the U.K. and the U.S.A.

The exhibition of a production theatrically in the United Kingdom is conditional on there being included in an artist's contract a special stipulation confirming such use and to the payment of a use fee of 10 per cent. with a minimum of £16. Exhibitions are limited to 10 cinemas and to take place within a total period of nine months before and three months after the first transmission in the United Kingdom for a duration of not longer than three consecutive months. Any general theatrical release of a production is subject first to negotiation with Equity and likewise any theatrical release in the United States of America.

(d) Other media of of exploitation.

World Videogram—meaning any form of videodisc or cassette offered for sale or rental to the general public for domestic viewing—a use fee of seven and a half per cent. with a minimum of £16.

World Pay Television—meaning systems for which subscribers pay directly for each programme or for a defined service (but not a service of relay of free television) the use fees are:

(i) where the initial use is for transmission on pay television outside the U.K., or its secondary use is for transmission on pay television anywhere in the world including the U.K. 20 per cent.: minimum £54

(ii) where the initial use is for transmission on pay television in the U.K. 30 per cent.: minimum £80

There is also included in the Agreement a provision whereby an extract (not exceeding three minutes in length) from an artist's performance in a production may be included in a United Kingdom television programme of an instructional, education, critical, magazine or similar nature on payment of a standard fee of £40. Any use in a critical programme is subject to an artist's consent.

Although ostensibly there are no restrictions or limitations on the exercise of the rights automatically acquired in a production, except in the United Kingdom and the United States as detailed above, there is an entrenched provision of the Agreement limiting the use of a production to 10 years calculated from the date of the commencement of principal photography. It is envisaged that after the 10 year period any further exploitation will be in accordance with revised revenue sharing or royalty arrangements. In the absence of such arrangements the further exploitation of a production will be allowed but subject to terms to be agreed between a producer and Equity.

The Agreement expressly stipulates that the exercise of any rights of transmission, exhibition or use of a production not provided for in the Agreement is subject to agreement between the producer and Equity and when agreed the terms are deemed to be part of the original contract as between a producer and an artist.

GENERAL CONDITIONS OF CINEMA AND TELEVISION FILM ENGAGEMENTS

The provisions of the Cinema Film Agreement and the Television Film Agreement respecting the use of an artist's services, the manner of performance and presentation on the screen and entitlement to credit and publicity are in essence the same.

When accepting an engagement an artist is required to warrant that to the best of his knowledge and belief he is in a state of health that will enable a producer to effect insurance under normal conditions. If an artist is unfit for work or due to illness cannot perform for three consecutive days following and including the date of a call, a producer can either terminate the engagement subject to the payment of accrued fees, or suspend the engagement for the period of an artist's absence and extend the period of first call by the equivalent of the period of absence but subject to the artist's existing commitments.

An artist may be asked to provide all such modern dress and footwear as he may possess and normally wear otherwise a producer is to provide all other visible modern dress and all character, period and special costume and footwear.

An artist cannot be required to undertake work which involves an unreasonable degree of risk unless this is expressly agreed to. The test of unreasonableness must be subjective and considered in the light of the particular circumstances. When an act is one which is dangerous or hazardous as to amount to a stunt as defined above, then the provisions of the Agreement about stunt performances will apply. When a performance involves a degree of risk then the producer's insurance indemnity cover must be adequate and the terms and conditions must be in accordance with the agreement between PACT and Equity governing the insurance of artists performing in films. Whenever artists work outside the United Kingdom a producer must effect insurance cover as required by the terms of the Agreements.

A producer has the sole right to decide the manner of an artist's portrayal of the part or role for which he is engaged and how he is to be presented on the screen. Any limitations on this inherent power of a producer must therefore be expressly agreed upon and made a term of the artist's contract of engagement. Any performance which is hazardous or which involves an unreasonable degree of risk is subject to special arrangement. If the make-up and presentation of an artist is to be exceptional and likely to involve changes in his physical and personal appearance such as might be of a permanent or semi-permanent nature, then the artist is to be informed of this and a special stipulation included in the form of engagement.

A producer is entitled to lengthen, shorten or re-write an artist's part entirely as he chooses, to eliminate it and to substitute another artist in the place of the artist. A producer is not bound to use an artist's services or exhibit the performance for which he was contracted so that no compensation is payable to an artist in either event, a producer's obligations being only to pay the fees due in accordance with the contract of engagement provided the artist is willing and able to render his services as contracted.

Under the Cinema Film Agreement a producer has the right to dub an artist's voice in English and any other language. The right to use a double in an artist's place for photography or the recording of his voice is subject to prior agreement and to there being a special stipulation included in the artist's form of engagement.

Under the Television Film Agreement the right to dub an artist's voice must be expressly reserved in the form of engagement. If not reserved nonetheless a producer has the right to dub in foreign languages, also for retakes and added scenes if an artist is not available when reasonably required to render service for such purposes. The right to use a double is subject to there being a special stipulation in the form of engagement. In its absence a producer may use a double in scenes which in the producer's opinion would impose an undesirable risk on an artist, and in scenes which do not involve the use of professional skill in dramatic interpretation and in which no feature identifiable as other than that of the artist appears on the screen. A producer has the absolute right to use a double for retakes and added scenes if an artist is not available when reasonably required to render services for such purposes. No double may be used in scenes involving nudity, semi-nudity or simulated sex acts unless especially provided for in an artist's form of engagement.

Provisions about nudity and simulated sexual acts are included in the Agreements in much the same terms as for theatrical engagements. The expressions "acts of a sexual nature" and "simulated sex acts" mean "any acts which if performed in public would be regarded as "indecent". Where in the portrayal of a part an artist is required to appear nude or perform acts of a simulated sexual nature an artist must be informed in writing in advance of the contract being concluded of the degree of nudity and/or nature and extent of any simulated sex acts required and be supplied with a copy of the relevant parts of the script. A special stipulation is required to be included in the form of engagement namely,

> "The Artist hereby acknowledges that he/she has been informed that there will or may be included in the production nudity and/or simulated sex acts as defined in CC 12 of the Agreement."

If an artist is subsequently "unwilling" to perform any of the scripted scenes a producer may employ body doubles. In the event an artist is unable to perform, the engagement of body doubles must be discussed between the producer and the artist and the contract of engagement amended in writing to reflect the artist's consent.

There are provisions in the Agreement for restricting the presence of persons in the studios during the filming of scenes of nudity and the like and for the destruction of such filmed material not required for inclusion in the completed film. If an artist is charged with any offence arising from the performance as directed, a producer is required to do all that is possible to assist the artist in answering any charge. Should an artist judge the assistance to have been inadequate the matter is to be referred to the Joint Films Council.

THE JOINT FILMS COUNCIL AND THE SETTLEMENT OF DISPUTES

The arrangements and procedure for the settlement of issues and disputes which arise concerning or in the course of a production is common to both the Cinema and the Television Film Agreements. There is constituted the Joint Films Council which is representative of both PACT and Equity and whose objects are to promote and maintain the production of cinema films and television productions, to consider issues and disputes between members of both parties arising out of the interpretation and operation of the two Agreements, and to make recommendations concerning any additions or amendments to the Agreements.

At meetings of the Council there is equal representation of both PACT and Equity excluding the Chairman whose appointment so far as possible alternates between the two parties. The Chairman has no vote. There are two Joint Secretaries one of whom is the General Secretary of Equity and the other the Director of Industrial Relations of PACT.

A decision of the Council is reached by the affirmative vote of each of the two sides considered and taken separately. If a vote is unanimous then it constitutes a settlement to be accepted by the parties.

The procedure for the settlement of all disputes is laid down in the Agreements. In the first instance a dispute is to be dealt with locally by representatives of PACT and Equity which if not resolved is then to be considered by representatives at official level of PACT and Equity. In the event of a failure to reach agreement at this stage either party to the dispute may refer the issue to the Joint Secretaries of the Council to arrange a conciliation meeting and agree the terms of reference.

The conciliation meeting is to take place within 72 hours (excluding Saturday, Sunday and declared holidays) and chaired by a representative of either PACT or Equity as jointly agreed. Also there must be present at least two representatives of each of the parties who have no direct involvement in the dispute, and cannot gain a direct advantage from any decision of the meeting however construed or arrived at.

If no agreement is reached at the conciliation meeting the matter is then to be referred to the Council within 72 hours (excluding Saturday, Sunday and declared holidays). The Council has power to determine the dispute if the vote on each side of the Council is unanimous. Failing a unanimous decision the matter is then to be dealt with by arbitration in the form decided by reference to the Advisory Conciliation and Arbitration Service (ACAS).

The Agreements provide that while the foregoing procedure is in operation no stoppage of work, lock-out, ban on overtime either of a partial or general nature, or any departure from normal working is to take place or be authorised.

CROWD ARTISTS IN CINEMA AND TELEVISION FILMS

The Collective Agreement of January 1992 between PACT and Film Artistes Association for the employment of crowd artists, stand-ins and doubles in cinema and television films is somewhat different from past such agreements.

The operation of the Agreement is restricted to the employment of professional artists for work within a radius of 40 miles of Charing Cross, London. Where filming takes place in actual public surroundings persons of the general public may be photographed subject to an appropriate number of artists being engaged to perform in proximity to the cast performers and provided there is no substantial creative direction of the public.

The basic requirement of persons engaged as crowd artists and stand-ins is that they perform and render services to set the atmosphere of the scenes as a producer may direct. This may include general and/or individually directed movement, group and individual activities, mass and/or individual reactions, audible and inaudible (mimed) sound, vocal and conversation effects. Also that artists work with such properties and wear such clothing, make-up, wigs and hair styles as a producer may direct.

For each of the three kinds of artists, crowd artists, stand-ins and doubles the Agreement details the particular services which may be required to be rendered, the conditions under which they may be rendered and the manner of performance.

For all artists a standard basic daily rate is payable. There are also premium hourly rates, overtime rates and special rates for attendance on public holidays. Correspondingly there are rates for night work. In addition to the standard rate the Agreement provides for the payment of a supplementary service fee at a rate according to the particular service to be rendered, and a supplementary performance fee at a rate according to the particular kind of performance to be given.

Thus in addition to the basic standard fee (currently a daily rate of £56 and a night rate of £70) there may be payable to an artist a fee for example, for rendering services in inclement weather (natural or induced) or for providing extra clothing when a fee of £9.13 will be payable; for doubling for a cast actor or actress, or wearing special clothing a fee of £15.29; for special hair dressing a fee of £24.53; for lookalike double £36.74. There may also be payable a fee for engaging in particular activities such as, swimming or driving when a fee of £12.21 will be payable; for dancing or horse riding £21.45; for specially directed performance as an individual or in a group of not more than four artists £27.50; for participating in a fight sequence £36.74.

If any services are required to be performed nude or semi-nude this is to be notified to an artist in advance and a supplementary fee agreed. An artist is not bound to accept a call and may not be penalised for refusing a call requiring a state of nudity. If an artist attends a call without being informed of this requirement he or she may refuse to perform but by doing so does not forfeit his or her entitlement to the basic standard fee.

If artists are called for auditions, or for costume fittings (other than when attending for photography and performance) fees are payable at rates according to the duration and place of attendance.

The Agreement makes provision for five types of engagement:

(1) Standard day—a working period of any eight consecutive hours (except for meal breaks) between 7 a.m. and 8 p.m.

(2) Standard night—a similar working period between 4.30 p.m. and 6.30 a.m.

(3) Continuous working day call—a working period of any seven continuous hours between 8 a.m. and 7 p.m.; after the seventh hour overtime is payable.

(4) Shift call—a work period of any four continuous hours taking place between 6 a.m. and 1 p.m., or 1 p.m. and 11 p.m.

(5) Multi period call—a contract for an artist's attendance on more than one call as specified and for which fees are payable irrespective of whether the artist is called.

When overtime is to be worked this is to be notified not later than one hour before the ending of the working time, that is, after eight hours for a standard day or seven hours for a standard night engagement. A producer is automatically entitled to require work to continue for 15 minutes after the normal finishing time for the purpose of completing a "take" but subject to the payment of half the overtime rate. Minutage in excess of the 15 counts as regular overtime. If overtime continues for longer than one and a half hours after the finishing time on a standard day or night call, a second meal break of one hour must be allowed but which does not count for payment as a working hour unless expressly curtailed by a producer. The overtime rate is payable in half hourly instalments when an artist's call extends before 7 a.m. or after 8 p.m. on a standard day call, or before 4.30 p.m. or after 6.30 a.m. on a standard night call, or before 8 a.m. or after 7 p.m. on a continuous working day call.

A producer may cancel a call and avoid the payment of fees excepting multi period calls if the cancellation is made before 5.30 p.m. on the day before the call is due to take place; otherwise the payment of fees is due whether or not a member attends the call. If a member attends a call which is then cancelled by a producer the full basic fee is payable. But if the cancellation is due to weather conditions or other cause beyond a producer's control and is within two hours of the time of the call only half the basic rate is payable.

Travel allowances are payable for places of work beyond a 10 mile radius of Charing Cross, London. For places of work beyond this radius transport is to be arranged by a producer or else there is payable one hour of the hourly rate and the fare by public transport. When the working time ceases at a time when public transport is not available a producer must provide for the transport of members or provide overnight accommodation.

Except when calls are at the principal established film studios, a producer must provide appropriate meals and refreshment but when this is not practical a standard meal allowance is payable. Meals at studios are at the cost of members.

The Agreement makes provision and specifies the procedure for the settlement of disputes arising from the application of its provisions and the engagement of members. If no settlement is possible locally the matter is to be dealt with by officials of the Association and the Union. In the event of a failure to agree on a resolution of the matter it is then to be referred to a Joint Council but thereafter to the Advisory, Conciliation and Arbitration Service (ACAS) for conciliation and/or arbitration.

THE ENGAGEMENT OF MUSICIANS

The Collective Agreement made in January 1987 between PACT and the Musicians' Union has not been renewed with the result that both PACT and the Union have each promulgated their own Agreements setting out the terms and conditions for the employment of musicians in the production of films. Annexed to both Agreements is a form of payment voucher for the purpose of putting on record the attendance and services rendered by a musician, the use fees paid and the rights acquired in a recording. Both Agreements provide for a producer engaging musicians directly and individually or through a contractor.

No distinction is made in either Agreement of the kind of film for which a musician is engaged, whether primarily for theatrical release or broadcasting by television as was so in the past. The core of an engagement remains the session during which a specified amount of music may be recorded. According to the rate of fee paid for the services rendered a producer acquires certain rights of exploitation in a film.

PACT Agreement

Under this Agreement there is a minimum payment of £100 per day for a call which sum counts towards hourly fees at rates which vary according to the rights chosen to be acquired. For example, payment at the rate of £60 per hour is for all media rights world wide including gramophone recording rights; payment at the rate of £30 per hour is for United Kingdom television broadcasting rights, namely, two transmissions (six for educational programmes). Any of the payments automatically give non-theatric rights worldwide. Additional rights or uses can subsequently be acquired on payment of the applicable hourly rate current at the time of acquisition. The hourly rates are subject to further variation when the aggregate number of hours per engagement exceeds 199, meaning the total number of hours of employment of musicians for a production. If the total of hours amounts to 200 but less than 599, in lieu of the hourly rate of £60 as above, the rate is £45; if the total hours is 600 or more the rate is £30.

Each engagement or call is on an hourly basis, with a minimum call of two hours, for rehearsal and recording. Overtime is payable when the duration of the original period of call is exceeded for which a standard fee is payable and when up to five minutes of music may be recorded during the first extra 15 minutes and one and a half minutes at each subsequent 15 minutes. Where there is a break of more than three hours (excluding an hour's meal break) between the end of one rehearsal/recording session and the next the minimum call payment is again payable. An average of 10 minutes of music per hour may be recorded at a session.

Musicians' Union Agreement

The Agreement provides for a basic sound recording session which can be of three hours during which 20 minutes of music may be recorded, or of three and a half hours for 23 minutes of music, or four hours for 26 minutes of music. The current minimum basic recording fee for each of these sessions is £109.35, £127.60 and £145.80 respectively. There is a standard rate of overtime of £10.95 per 15 minutes or part thereof when one and a half minutes of music may be recorded. Overtime at any session is subject to the agreement of the musicians and may not exceed 30 minutes.

The payment of the session fee and any supplements as may be due entitles a producer to incorporate a musician's performance into the specified film and to exploit it in any one of six ways in addition to worldwide non-theatric use which is automatically acquired. Thus for example there may be acquired two network free terrestrial television transmissions within the United Kingdom and Channel Islands either simultaneous or non-simultaneous. Any other of the six rights or uses can be purchased as required by the payment of a standard 25 per cent. of the fees paid for a musician's services but at the rates prevailing at the material time. Alternatively a producer may opt at the time of engagement to pay a combined use fee which is a total buy-out for all media worldwide in perpetuity including the release of the music on records for sale to the general public.

The Agreements Generally

The two Agreements are otherwise not so very different in content or meaning although there are differences in promulgated payments. In both Agreements provision is made for multi-episodic use, for the engagement of self-contained groups, for short sessions for the recording of short items for inclusion in programmes such as documentary, education, magazine and religious programmes, for miming engagements at an hourly rate subject to a minimum call of four hours, and for separate rehearsal calls. Other provisions stipulate in the usual terms for "doubling", overdubbing and supplements for performing in vision, at unsocial hours and on statutory holidays at double rates. Under the Musicians' Union Agreement work on a Sunday is at time and a half.

Provision is made for porterage, for travel expenses incurred by musicians whose normal place of work is in the Greater London Area for engagements beyond 30 miles of Charing Cross, but 25 miles under the Musicians' Union Agreement. Both Agreements stipulate for the payment of fees to musicians on the day of completion of an engagement or else where musicians have been engaged through a contractor, for payment to the contractor.

Both Agreements provide for the relaying or filming and recording of concerts. Fees are at hourly rates but distinguishing between limited use or a combined use but excluding any use of a recording in the medium of record sales to the general public.

VIDEOGRAMS

The various Collective Agreements reviewed above apply to what may be described as the main stream of film production, that is, films produced primarily either for theatrical exhibition or for television broadcasting. Any exploitation in the form of videograms (videocassette or videodisc) for sale and hire to the general public, and for which an additional use fee is payable, is usually a subsidiary consideration in the undertaking of a production.

For the production of wholly original videograms (or films) not intended for commercial exploitation in the accepted sense, such as for purposes of promotion of an enterprise, cause or interest or for purposes of training and instruction, there is no collective agreement for the engagement of professional musicians, or for the engagement of artists for a videogram made for private viewing only. (If it is for public exhibition or for retail sale and hire to the general public an artist's engagement is subject to the Cinema Film Agreement).

The Musicians' Union has promulgated standard terms and conditions for the recording of performances for inclusion in videograms in much the same terms as in the promulgated Agreement outlined above. There is provision for a basic session of three hours during which 20 minutes of music may be recorded and for which the current rate is £80. But provision is also made for when a videogram is produced with the intention of its being made available to the general public; in that situation the session fee is £90.

For the engagement of an artist to perform a role in a videogram for exhibition before private audiences Equity has promulgated a form of engagement. This provides for the payment of a negotiated daily fee, but at a rate not less than minimum rates, for the days as specified when an artist is to be on first call for the rehearsing and recording of his part. A working day is of 10 hours and other of the working conditions are similar to those in the Cinema Film Agreement. Where an artist is required to learn scripts in advance of the engagement a half daily fee is payable for each ten pages of dialogue or part thereof. Where the dialogue is technical or complicated for other reasons auto-cue facilities may be provided.

Payment of the contracted fee is inclusive of payment for the right of a company to exhibit or permit the exhibition of the recording before non-paying audiences for a period of three years. The term can be renewed by payment of 100 per cent. of the aggregate of the fees first paid. The videogram may also be used for such purposes as point of sale exhibition, sales exhibition and the like for viewing by the public subject to the prior consent of the artist and to the payment, for each three months of use, of 100 per cent. of the aggregate of the fees first paid.

F. TELEVISION COMMERCIALS

PERFORMERS—THE AFVPA, EQUITY, IPA AND ISBA AGREEMENT

A new Collective Agreement between the Advertising Film and Video-tape Producers Association (AFVPA), Equity, the Institute of Practitioners in Advertising (IPA) and the Incorporated Society of British Advertisers (ISBA) took effect in November 1991 for the engagement of performers for the making and use of television commercials. The Agreement is for a term of four and a half years, but the basic fees are subject to annual review. It has been devised to cater for the presence of a number of commercial channels and in doing so has introduced a new system for the payment of use fees for commercials calculated on the size of the viewing audience as measured by the British Audience Research Board and not as in the past on the number of times a commercial is transmitted.

The expression "television commercial" is given a precise meaning in the Agreement, also the manner and extent to which a commercial can be exhibited. A television commercial is a picture "made for the purpose of advertising a specific product or groups of products, or a service or groups of services for showing by such television programme companies which may from time to time operate under licence from the appropriate regulatory authority." Shopping guides and magazines are also within the definition but other promotion films of over six minutes duration are expressly excluded from the scope of the Agreement. The expression "picture" is "deemed to include a recording of a performance made by any process for transmission through the medium of television; but any recording by any process which is made of, or simultaneously with, a direct transmission of a performance is expressly excluded from the ambit of the Agreement."

The Agreement applies principally to "Featured Artists" (in the following paragraphs referred to simply as artists), there being separate provisions for the engagement of other categories of artists.

The Agreement defines a "Featured Artist" as "someone who is seen or heard (excluding background speech or noise) in a commercial whose individual role plays an essential part in the telling of the commercial story." The following are expressly excluded from the definition:

(a) Persons carrying on their own normal daily occupations, whether at their normal place of work or at the studio, or at the location, and not being further identified with the commercial message or product to the exclusion of the use of a featured artist;

(b) Instrumental musicians;

(c) Walk-on artists and Background Artists (as defined in Part II of the Agreement);

(d) Artists whose performance appears in the commercial although they are physically obscured.

As it is the advertising agency acting in accordance with the requirements of his client advertiser of a product or service who undertakes the supervision of the making of a commercial, it is the agency which negotiates an artist's fees. For this reason under the Agreement the agency is regarded as the employer of the artist and so responsible for the payment of studio fees and use fees. If an agency, as the owner of the copyright in the commercial, assigns any rights in it, the Agreement requires it to be a condition of the assignment that the assignee or purchaser undertakes to comply with the provisions of the Agreement—in effect to pay use fees. Notice of the assignment is to be given to the artist or his agent (or to Equity) and only then does the agency have no further liability to the artist.

To accommodate the need for agencies to consult their clients over the choice of artists according to their availability and the arrangements for the making of a commercial, the Agreement makes express provision for the "pencilling-in" of artists. The duration of the "pencilled" booking is to be agreed but not until an engagement is confirmed is there any obligation on either party. If an artist has an alternative offer which he desires to accept he should first notify the agency which must then either confirm the booking or release the artist, unless a further time is agreed within which the booking is to be confirmed or not. Where an artist decides to cancel a "pencilled" booking he should give immediate notice of the decision; if an agency so decides notice should be given within 24 hours so that an artist is free to accept other work.

Uses of Commercials

Television commercials made under the Agreement are primarily for transmission in the United Kingdom. Commercials may be transmitted overseas subject to the consent of the artist and the payment of additional fees calculated as a percentage of an artist's basic studio or session fee according to scale for individual countries or territories of the world as set out in schedule 5 of the Agreement.

No part of an artist's performance may be used or transmitted in connection with any product or service other than that specified in the form of engagement except with the consent of the artist and Equity.

Any ancillary use of a commercial such as for cinema, radio, press or advertising, or for inclusion in a film or television documentary or other programme is conditional on terms being first agreed between the producer, advertiser and artist. The use of any "still" photographs of an artist performing in a commercial in any other form of advertising or promotion of a product or service, or on the packaging of goods is subject to the consent of the artist and agreement on the payment of a negotiated fee. If a line drawing is made of an artist which is clearly a reproduction of the artist's likeness taken from a commercial "still", then such line drawing is to be regarded as a "still" for the purposes of the foregoing stipulation.

Categories and Conditions of Engagements

Artists are engaged for a fee, the "basic studio fee", (but for voice-over artists and out-of-vision singers the "basic session fee") which is payable for each working day, a working day being a period of nine hours plus a one hour meal break. Minimum rates are prescribed but fees are negotiable to take account of the weight of the artist's contribution to the commercial, his professional status, earning power in other areas and his value to the commercial.

All engagements are to be contracted on the form of engagement as annexed to the Agreement and must specify the number of commercials for which the artist has been engaged with details of the products or services to be advertised. Special stipulations may be agreed to take account of any exceptional requirements of the engagement provided these do not detract from the minimum terms and conditions laid down in the Agreement. An artist can be required to provide, prior to an engagement, complete and accurate details of all his engagements for television commercials in the preceding three years listing the advertiser, the product(s) or service(s) for which he performed and the date of each engagement. By signing the form of engagement the artist confirms the information so supplied.

An artist may be engaged for either:

(a) nominated days when for each day the basic studio or session fee is payable, or

(b) for a specified period when the basic studio or session fee is payable for each day an artist attends to render his services (working day), and 50 per cent. of the fee for every other day on standby unless the artist at his request is released from standby; the form of engagement must specify the number of guaranteed working days.

If an artist attends for a half day rehearsal and no recording takes place 50 per cent. of his basic studio fee, or the minimum basic studio fee for a visual artist if greater, is payable, but if the rehearsal time exceeds four and a half hours the full basic studio fee plus meal allowances is payable. When an artist is required to undertake voice work such as post synchronisation directly related to his visual performance on a day other than a visual recording day, 50 per cent. of his basic studio fee is payable for each two hour session. This payment does not qualify for use fees. For wig and costume fittings on days outside the period of engagement a standard fee is payable.

When required to work outside the United Kingdom an artist is to be insured by the advertiser or producer of the commercial upon terms and conditions as agreed from time to time between Equity, the AFVPA and the IPA.

The Agreement contains detailed provisions about working hours and conditions. A working day or night is normally of nine hours exclusive of an hour's meal break. Time runs from when a performer is called or attends at the studios or location to render services. Time spent in make-up, hairdressing and wardrobe is part of the working day. If an artist is required to render services for a "dawn call," meaning between 4 a.m. and 7.30 a.m. then for the time he renders services up to 7.30 a.m. (when normal working begins) he is entitled to one-fifth of the basic studio fee for each hour or part thereof so worked; this supplement does not affect any entitlement to be paid overtime when the number of hours worked is exceeded. Night calls are calls scheduled to extend beyond midnight or to commence between midnight and 4.00 a.m. Night calls attract a supplementary fee of 50 per cent. of the basic studio fee. Day calls commence between 7.30 a.m. and 12 noon and any call to render services after 12 noon is deemed to be for 12 noon for the purpose of calculating overtime. A call to attend on or after 4 p.m. is deemed to be for night work unless specifically stated otherwise and overtime is payable as from 10 p.m. that is, 10 hours after 12 noon.

Work on a Sunday or public holiday attracts an additional premium payment of 50 per cent. of the basic studio fee. Overtime is at the rate of one-fifth of a performer's basic studio fee and is payable for each hour or part thereof of overtime. If required to complete a take and provided no further overtime is worked for the day, 15 minutes overtime is automatically allowed without attracting overtime payment. Overtime which occurs after midnight (unless a night call) is at the rate of one-third of the basic studio fee. Overtime during night calls and when occurring on a Sunday or public holiday is calculated on the total of the basic studio fee and the additional night fee or premium payment as the circumstances may be. Premium payments and additional night call fees do not qualify for use fees.

An artist who is called for auditions is not entitled to payment for the first call or for videotape or photographs taken during the audition. If a performer is recalled (even on the same day as the first call) a reasonable amount to cover travel and out of pocket expenses is payable; a minimum is prescribed.

Like engagements for other kinds of filmed performances, a producer has the right to present and direct an artist as he may decide, to edit a performance and to omit the performance from the completed commercial. The right to use a double may be the subject of special agreement but otherwise a producer has no right to use a double except in scenes which in the opinion of the producer would impose an undesirable risk on the artist, or the scenes do not involve the use of professional skill in dramatic interpretation and in which no feature identifiable as other than that of the artist appears on the screen. Unless expressly provided for in the form of engagement a producer has no right to use a double in an artist's place in scenes involving nudity or semi-nudity. A producer has no right to dub an artist's voice unless this right is expressly reserved by a producer in the form of engagement, or the dubbing is for the purpose of retakes or added scenes required at a time when the artist is not reasonably available.

An artist cannot be required to render services of a hazardous or dangerous nature or which will involve an unreasonable degree of risk unless he has been specifically engaged for such services. If an artist is engaged for such services this must be the subject of a special stipulation in the form of engagement and the producer must effect insurance for the artist to a level not less than that required of stunt performers registered with Equity. Engagements primarily for stunts or fights are to be offered only to performers who are registered as stunt performers at Equity.

The "Life" and Exploitation of Commercials

Without express agreement to the contrary between an advertiser and artist a commercial may not be transmitted after the expiry of three years from the date of its first transmission. If station transmissions are suspended for reasons outside the control of the contracting parties, or if the use of the commercial is limited to test areas then an extension of time may be justified.

In addition to the basic studio or session fee payable to an artist for his attendance and services in the making of the commercial there is payable a transmission fee and use fees. The former is the sum equivalent to 100 per cent. of the artist's basic studio or session fee and is due following the first transmission of the commercial on any channel. By paying the fee the advertiser acquires the right to unrestricted access to and showing of the commercial on any and all television channels—terrestrial, satellite, cable or any other means. This transmission fee is a single once only payment but when a commercial is made for and transmitted only in a single ITV area accounting for less than 10 per cent. of United Kingdom individuals (aged four and over) the transmission fee is treated as a non-refundable advance on use fees.

Use fees are payable as a percentage of an artist's basic studio or session fee (BSF) for each transmission (including the first) of the commercial. No longer is the payment of use fees based on the number and areas of transmission but on audience viewing as measured and calculated according to a scale with four separate and declining or reducing rates as the commercial gains a larger cumulative audience. For the payment and calculation of use fees the Agreement provides:

"(a) The use fees payable to the Featured Artist for each transmission of the commercial (including the first) in which the artist appears shall be calculated by reference to the number of U.K. individuals aged four and over, reported to have viewed the commercial transmission by the audience measurement service operated by the Broadcasters' Audience Research Board (BARB). Viewing shall be defined as "consolidated viewing" (*i.e.* live viewing plus normal VCR playback viewing within 168 hours of the recording).

(b) The audience as defined in (a) above for all the transmissions of the commercial on all U.K. television services (irrespective of the signal delivery system) in each calendar month shall be accumulated to arrive at a total number of individual (aged four and over) viewing occasions.

(c) The total number arrived at in (b) above shall then be expressed as a percentage (TVR) of the total number of U.K. individuals aged four and over. The resulting figure is the Network TVR (TV rating) delivered by the commercial among U.K. individuals aged four and over.

(d) The use fees payable shall then be calculated according to the following scale which provides for four separate and declining rates as the commercial gains a larger cumulative audience:

Stage	Network TVR Band	Rate per Network (per cent. of BSF)
1	Between 0 and (including) 200	7.41%
2	Between 200 and (including) 400	3.68%
3	Between 400 and (including) 800	2.42%
4	over 800	1.64%

(e) If the commercial achieves a cumulative Network TVR of 800, all subsequent Network TVRs achieved during the life of the commercial shall be calculated at the Stage 4 rate of 1.64 per cent. of the BSF per Network TVR."

The Agreement contains very precise rules for the payment of fees by a producer/advertiser. Studio or session fees are payable in respect of worksheets/invoices received by the fifteenth of the month, not later than the end of the month; for those received after the fifteenth not later than the fifteenth of the following month. Use fees and the first transmission fee are payable by an advertiser not later than the end of the second month following that in which the transmission of the commercial occurs. When the payment of fees is delayed an additional payment of 1½ per cent. compound of the sum outstanding for each month or part thereof is payable by a producer/advertiser. Where payment of fees has been delayed a residual power is vested in Equity to give notice to an advertiser or an advertiser's assigns that unless the fault is rectified within 14 days of the notice the right to transmit the commercial ceases but subject to resort to the disputes procedure by a producer/advertiser.

An artist is entitled to receive notice of the first transmission of a commercial, and to be notified if it is not to be used or the artist's performance is cut out entirely as then no transmission or use fees will be payable unless guaranteed in the contract of engagement. If a commercial is shortened during its life time this does not affect the right of an artist whose performance remains included from receiving use fees. If with an artist's consent a commercial is edited and used to produce a new or different commercial a new contract of engagement with a basic studio fee should be agreed and use fees paid accordingly.

Barring Provisions

Provisions are included in the Agreement specifying the extent and terms upon which any bar can be imposed on an artist appearing in other commercials. The period of the restriction must be set out in the form of engagement but the period cannot exceed the life of the commercial. The extent of the bar must be specified that is, whether it is limited to appearances in commercials which advertise products or services competitive with those the subject of the advertisement for which the artist is being engaged, or is a general bar so that the artist may not appear in any commercial. The period of the bar can begin on a date as mutually agreed but if this date is not the same as the date of the artist's first studio or location day then any appearance in other commercials made for other advertisers before the start of the bar does not constitute a breach of the agreed restriction.

The right of a producer to request an artist to supply details of his engagements has been mentioned above but the Agreement further provides that there is a duty on an artist throughout the period of a bar, whether limited or general, and during the interval of time between the signing of the form of engagement and the commencement of the bar "to inform the advertiser of recent, past, present or proposed future employment which would affect the imposition of the bar or its duration or effectiveness as far as the advertiser is concerned." Whether this duty would be construed as applying to employment other than in the making of a commercial is doubtful.

The barring fee payable to an artist is negotiable and separate from his entitlement to use fees. Unless otherwise expressly agreed the barring fee is payable within one month of the commencement of the barring period. However, no such fee is payable when as a condition of an engagement an artist is only required to undertake not to perform for any person, (other than the advertiser by whom he is engaged), in a character part solely associated with the advertiser's products or services, or in such a part created for the advertisement.

Special Categories of Performers

In schedules 2, 3 and 4 of the Agreement special provisions are made for three categories of performances namely, voice-overs, out of vision singers, and stunt performers.

(1) Voice-overs: Engagements are for a session of one hour. The fee is negotiable but there is a prescribed minimum. If commercials are made for more than one product during a session a separate contract must be made for each product. Use fees are payable in the ordinary way based on the negotiated fee. A session of one hour, for test commercials may be negotiated subject to a minimum fee.

Engagements may also be for a "tag" meaning an appendage added to the opening or closing of a commercial solely for including information such as specific dates, areas, dealers or price changes. If tags are recorded by an artist during the session for which he is engaged for a commercial a supplementary fee of one-tenth of the negotiated session fee is payable for each tag. When tags are recorded at a separate session a negotiated fee is payable (at not less than the prescribed minimum) and for each additional tag one-tenth of the sessional fee is payable. These payments to the artist do not count towards use fees as the commercial so adapted is deemed an original commercial for the purpose of the payment of use fees. If another artist is engaged to record a tag the basic or agreed sessional fee (excluding any supplementary payments for additional tags) is used for the calculation of use fees in the ordinary way, that is, the session fee is not divided by the number of commercials for the purpose of calculating use fees.

(2) Out of Vision Singers: Engagements are for a session of up to two hours during which up to three minutes of music may be recorded to cover any number of versions of a commercial provided it is for one product. If commercials are made for more than one product during a session a separate contract and fee must be agreed for each commercial. Sessional fees are negotiable but a minimum rate is prescribed. Use fees are based on the session fee and a special stipulation must be included in the form of engagement whereby a singer authorises and empowers Equity to collect use fees.

Up to 30 minutes of overtime may be added to a session but only for completing the permitted three minutes of recorded music; overtime is payable at a fixed rate for each 15 minutes or part thereof. Where extra recording time is required it can only be acquired on the basis of a further session of which the singer must be given prior notice.

No mechanical means of double-tracking, overdubbing etc., may be used in order to reduce the number of singers required for a session but tracking may be used to produce an artistic effect by a supplementary payment of not less than 50 per cent. of the session fee and 50 per cent. of the overtime fee if tracking is done during overtime.

A singer may be engaged to appear in vision miming to his singing in which event the provisions of the Agreement will apply in the normal way and a negotiated basic fee is payable to cover both performances. If a separate recording session is required then a sessional fee is also payable but it does not attract use fees. If a singer performs as both a solo singer and a group singer in the same commercial during the same session and a fee for the solo performance was not negotiated in advance of the session, the session fee is to be increased automatically by not less than 50 per cent. and the use fees calculated on the higher rate.

When a singer is engaged for a test or "demo" session the fee is negotiable but may not be less than 60 per cent. of the minimum rate. Any public transmission of the recording is conditional on the session fee being re-negotiated and a new contract issued.

(3) Stunt Performers: An engagement as a stunt performer or arranger in normal circumstances is to be offered only to a member of the Register of Stunt Performers and Arrangers kept by Equity and only in exceptional circumstances may other persons be engaged. Engagements are subject to the regular provisions of the Agreement but for individual stunts a separate stunt fee may be payable but which does not count towards the studio fee and so does not attract use fees. The special conditions and undertakings for the engagement of stunt arrangers and stunt performers contained in the Cinema Film Agreement and Television Film Agreement are reflected in the schedule to this Agreement.

Employment of Walk-on and Background Artists

Part II of the Agreement provides for the engagement of walk-on and background artists.

A "Walk-on" is defined as an identifiable non-speaking artist (except that background speech or noise is not to be deemed to be speaking in this context), who is required to act individually in medium shot, or more closely, a special function peculiar only to the role, trade or calling that the character is supposed to portray and/or who, at the same time that his/her movements are recorded, is subject to individual direction and has a direct relationship with an actor (*i.e.* visual featured artist) who is performing his/her part as directed.

A "Background artist" is someone who is not required to give individual characterisation nor to speak any word or line of dialogue except that background speech or noise is not to be deemed dialogue in this context. Furthermore a "background artist" is a person or member of a group contributing to the overall authenticity and atmosphere of a scene. The individual or individuals in the group may be dressed in clothing identifiable with the role, calling or trade selected for each by the producer or advertiser, and may be directed by the director to move and/or react as required on the set. Crowd noises can include community singing of well known songs where the words do not have to be learned.

Where practicable only professional performers are to be engaged as walk-on artists but casting decisions remain at the discretion of the advertiser/producer.

Annexed to the Agreement is a form of engagement where details of the engagement and fees payable are inserted. The minimum rates prescribed are:

(a)	Walk-on artist	£150
(b)	Background artist	£75 for calls up to and including 10 artists
		Negotiable for calls of over 10 artists.

Use fees are not payable to these artists.

The general conditions of employment and hours of work for these categories of performers are in principle the same as for artists engaged under Part I of the Agreement. An artist called to a first audition is entitled to his reasonable travel expenses. If more than one commercial is to be made on a day or night engagement the artist's agent is to be notified of the number so that the fee can be fairly negotiated; likewise if an artist is to undertake strenuous work or work under stressful conditions. A standard supplementary payment may be due when an artist is required to provide more than one outfit or to have his hair cut very short by the standards of the day.

Disputes and Conciliation Procedure

If a dispute arises between an artist or artists and a producer and/or advertiser on a matter arising from the Agreement or an engagement, the matter is first to be referred to Equity to seek to resolve the issue in consultation with the producer or advertiser. If the matter is not resolved it is to be referred in writing to the AFVPA and/or the IPA and/or the ISBA as appropriate who may if considered desirable meet with Equity and the parties concerned. If no such meeting takes place within 14 days of the reference, or takes place but the issue remains unresolved then the matter is to be referred to a Joint Conciliation meeting in accordance with the rules contained in schedule 6 of the Agreement. The meeting is to be assembled within 21 days of the reference.

The meeting is to comprise an equal number of representatives from both sides and each providing an official to act as Joint Secretaries. Each side is alternately to provide a Chairman but who has no vote. A decision of a Joint Conciliation meeting is arrived at by the affirmative vote of each of the two sides considered separately. In the event of a meeting being unable to reach a decision the matter may be referred to arbitration the hearing to take place within the next 56 days.

An important stipulation of the disputes procedure is that the time-limits are to be adhered to strictly. If a party fails to do so then any party may issue to a defaulting party a "notice of compliance." The notice must state the decision sought and if within 28 days of the notice the defaulting party does not comply with the conciliation procedure the decision sought then becomes effective.

MUSICIANS—THE IPA AND MUSICIANS' UNION AGREEMENT

In the production of commercials much use is made of library and other such pre-recorded music but for the making of original recordings of performances of music for inclusion in commercials a Collective Agreement between the Institute of Practitioners in Advertising and the Musicians' Union was made in 1977 and continues in force but with revised rates. As in other of the collective agreements to which the Musicians'

Union is a party there is included a stipulation that electronic instruments and devices incorporating pre-recorded sounds or producing sounds by electronic means are not to be used to displace or reduce the employment of conventional instrumentalists in circumstances where they may reasonably be expected to be used. These devices may be used to produce sounds which cannot be produced by conventional instruments.

The Agreement provides for a choice of three recording sessions during each of which a specific amount of music may be recorded for a standard fee. The basic session is of one hour when up to three minutes of music may be recorded for inclusion in not more than two different commercials as required by a producer. A standard supplement is payable for each 20 minutes or part thereof of overtime. If the recording is incomplete because another element is required to be added only two minutes of music may be recorded at the session. Alternatively a musician may be engaged for a session of one and a half hours on the conditions as just noted except that no overtime is allowed. If the time is exceeded it follows that a whole new session begins. A third kind of session is one of three hours only—no overtime is permitted—when up to nine minutes of music may be recorded for up to six different commercials. If the recording is incomplete only six minutes of music may be recorded.

For each of the three kinds of session there is a prescribed standard sessional rate payable the amount of which depends on whether the commercial is for (a) television and cinema use only, or (b) television, cinema and radio use. The payment of the sessional fee allows unrestricted use throughout the world for the life of the commercial—three years from the date of first transmission or broadcast—and if the fee for television and cinema use only has been paid clearance for radio can subsequently be obtained by the payment of a standard supplement.

The music recorded can only be used for the product or service advertised or for a series of films produced to advertise the same product or service; it cannot be used for another advertisement. With the consent of a musician given at the time of the recording session and the payment of an additional standard fee for each three minutes of music, the recorded music may be reproduced and used in another medium, for example, in records and audio cassettes. If this consent is required after the recording but in any event only within the life of the commercial a higher supplementary fee is payable.

The Agreement makes provision for a musician to over-dub his performance subject to the payment of enhanced rates as normal. "Doubling" is permitted up to a limit of three instruments (with exceptions being allowed for particular groups of instruments as customary) subject to the payment of the supplements as usual. Provisions are included for the payment or porterage, for fares to and from studios beyond five miles from the main line terminal as appropriate, and for the payment to or from a musician's residence if a musician is called before or detained after public transport is available or else for the payment of overnight accommodation and meals.

The Agreement makes special provision for the recording of music for commercials to be used in a third world country at a concessionary rate. A session is of one hour when up to three minutes of music may be recorded for inclusion in not more than two commercials. If the commercial is used in any other country a supplement is payable which thereby also permits the advertisement to be used world wide in television and cinemas. Subject to a musician's consent and the payment of the additional supplement as explained above the music recorded may be used in another medium.

A one hour session for the recording of music for radio advertising only is also covered in the Agreement. Three minutes of music may be recorded for inclusion in not more than two commercials but if the recording is incomplete only two minutes may be recorded. The session may be extended by up to 20 minutes on payment of a standard supplement. The fee paid for the session secures world rights for the commercials.

Where a person is required to act the part of the musician for the visual element ("dummy work") a musician is normally to be employed unless the action requires a special character to appear. A standard fee is payable for a day's performance not exceeding eight consecutive hours (inclusive of a one-hour meal break), between 8 a.m. and midnight. Overtime is payable at a standard rate for each hour or part thereof but at an increased rate for work between midnight and 8 a.m.

G. RECORDS AND AUDIO CASSETTES

The limitations placed on the exploitation of television programmes, films and videograms as explained in the previous Sections are but a further application of the principles established in the past by the Musicians' Union with record manufacturers regarding the use and exploitation of gramophone records. Not only is the Union concerned about the observance of minimum conditions of employment and rates of pay for its members but also the impairment of employment opportunities by the unrestricted playing of records and pre-recorded tapes in places of entertainment and public resort, their use in broadcasting, and their reproduction in another medium.

The distinct and individual copyright in a gramophone recording was established by the Copyright Act 1911 and in a leading case before the Courts in 1932 the separate right of public performance in a recording was recognised with the result that the proprietor and managers of theatres, cinemas, ballrooms, restaurants and places of public resort no longer had an unlimited supply of music or entertainment for the mere price of a record. The outcome of this was the establishment of Phonographic Performance Limited as a company representative of record manufacturers which now serves to license on behalf of its members the public performance of records in the catalogues of its members (see Part 7).

Approved Contractors

Apart from musicians who are regular members of established orchestras, the engagement of musicians for recording sessions has traditionally been on a freelance and casual basis. This has already been demonstrated in the review of the collective agreements covering broadcasting and film production. Even where a series of recording sessions is arranged it can happen that a musician's total involvement in the production of a record is as little as one attendance at a two-hour session. Engagements for gramophone recordings and for recordings for films and broadcast programmes can be booked very informally so that abuses can occur especially with the collection and payment of exploitation fees and royalties due in accordance with the provisions of the various collective agreements. For the recruitment of session musicians "fixers" evolved, but the Musicians' Union established a system of "approved contractors" to assume the role of an employer or agent in much the same way as contractors who supply a combination of musicians to perform in light entertainment as noted in Part 3.

Persons recruiting and supplying session musicians are accorded the status of approved contractors by the Musicians' Union if they enter into a formal agreement with the Union by which they undertake to accept and observe all the obligations of a principal in oral and written contracts of engagement of members of the Union. Other terms of the Agreement are designed to ensure that all the collective agreements are properly observed; that contractors pay fees due within 28 days of a musician's attendance at a session or within 10 days of the receipt of payment from an engager; that contractors keep proper records and accounts respecting the collection and payment of residual and other supplementary fees due under the collective agreements; that contractors or their authorised representatives are present at all sessions to assume responsibility and ensure that only Union approved recording techniques and practices are used.

As an approved contractor and by the terms of the Agreement with the Musicians' Union where a third party is in default of an obligation or undertaking to a contractor, for example in the payment of session fees, the contractor is eligible for assistance from the Union in legal proceedings for the recovery of whatever may be due. A contractor also has the benefit of prior notice from the Union of a defaulting recording, film or other engaging company.

Because a number of approved contractors are incorporated as a company the Musicians' Union has introduced a second version of the approved contractor agreement. Under this the directors of the company are required to sign individually and personally and undertake to abide by the terms of the Agreement with the Union.

Fair Listed Record Companies

In the past the making of records was confined to a few companies so that the Collective Agreement about to be considered was sufficient to establish and maintain regular conditions of employment and rates of pay in the recording industry. Today with the new techniques and increase in the facilities available for recording very often records are made by small independent producers and managers of groups with the actual marketing of a recorded performance being effected by a tape-lease deal with a record company. Many of these smaller recording companies are not members of British Phonographic Industry (the record producers' trade association) and subject to its rules respecting the observance of industry collective agreements.

In order to fill this gap the Musicians' Union has sought to enforce the minimum rates and conditions established with British Phonographic Industry by requiring such record producers to subscribe to individual agreements with the Union for recognition and acceptance as "fair listed" record producers. By such an agreement a record producer undertakes to use only the recording techniques and practices approved by the Union; to ensure that the consent of the performers to the recording is in the form prescribed by the Union; to seek to engage only members of the Union at not less than the regular rates and engage musicians either directly or through the Union's approved contractors; to pay the fees due to musicians within 21 days of the recording date. Furthermore, in order to ensure that the public performance of the records produced is controlled in accordance with the practice of the record industry a record producer also undertakes:

(a) to become or remain a member or associate member of Phonographic Performance Limited so that the public performance and broadcasting of records of the recording are placed under the control of the Company; or

(b) to ensure that the records produced are placed under the control of a member company of Phonographic Performance Limited for the purposes of public performance and broadcasting; or

(c) to assign the United Kingdom broadcasting and public performance rights in the recording to the Union free of charge for the Union to retain but not exercise without the approval of the record producer.

Finally, the record producer undertakes to prevent recorded performances from being used for dubbing in films, audio-visual records, television films, library records or otherwise without the consent of the Union.

THE BPI AND MUSICIANS' UNION COLLECTIVE COMMERCIAL GRAMOPHONE RECORDING AGREEMENT

The "Omnibus" Agreement of September 1989 between the British Phonographic Industry and the Musicians' Union combines three agreements. The first is the Session Rates Agreement which is of long standing for the making of commercial records and within its provisions takes account of the techniques of recording and use of electronic instruments. The second and third agreements are respectively for the use of records as backing tracks in the production of television programmes, and for the making and use of music videos.

The Session Rates Agreement

Like the collective agreements reviewed above for radio and television broadcasting and film production, this Agreement prescribes the length of sessions, the amount of music which can be recorded and the rates payable. Musicians who are featured soloists or independent self-contained groups are most often contracted on terms negotiated individually by a record producer as outlined below, but the engagement of sessional and "backing" musicians is normally upon the terms of this Agreement.

The Agreement divides recording sessions into three categories:

(a) Part I—a standard session for all recordings of music of all kinds other than recordings made by orchestras subject to Parts II and III;

(b) Part II—a session expressly for recordings by "listed" symphony, opera and ballet orchestras; and

(c) Part III—a session expressly for recordings by "listed" chamber orchestras.

The "listed" orchestras are specifically named orchestras most of whom are well known; the lists are revised from time to time.

Part I Category Sessions

A standard fee is payable to all musicians at rates which vary only according to the length of the session booked. A session can be of four, three or two hours during which a maximum of 20 minutes of music (10 if a two hour session) may be recorded for inclusion in the issued recording. An interval of 20, 15 and 10 minutes respectively is to be allowed during a session and not more than two hours is to elapse without a break. Work on a Sunday is at time and a half; work between midnight and 8 a.m. and work on a statutory holiday qualifies for double rates.

A session can be extended with the agreement of the musicians to complete the recording of a work or title begun during the booked session. A three hour session can be extended by 15 or 30 minutes for which a standard rate of overtime is payable, but a 15 minute extension cannot be further extended as then a new session is deemed to have started. A two hour session can be extended but by 15 minutes only and for which a standard rate of overtime is payable. No overtime is permitted at a four hour session as it is a term of the Agreement that if a musician is booked for a four hour session then he must be guaranteed a minimum of three sessions of which not less than two must be of four hours' duration.

Following customary practice there may be "doubling" of up to three instruments at a session. A supplementary fee is payable at the rate of 25 per cent. of the basic fee for one additional instrument and 40 per cent. for two. The supplement is payable if a musician plays more than one instrument, and it is payable if a musician having been specifically requested to double and attends ready to do so but in fact is not called upon to double.

In the jargon of the recording industry expressions are used, "over-dubbing," "multi-tracks," and "incomplete recordings" which are material not only to the manner of the making of a record but also to the terms and conditions upon which musicians are engaged and these are reflected in the Agreement. Included is the expression "sampling," the process of producing records which consist of segments from other recordings or the use of pre-existing instrumental sounds as input to synthesisers and which can pass as an original recording; it is a practice which neither of the parties to the Agreement condones.

"Over-dubbing" is achieved by use of multi-track recordings where the contribution (or lines of sound) from either individual musicians or sections of musicians are recorded on separate tracks on the recording tape. The tape is played back and further contributions (or lines of sound) are added on other separate tracks to build up a "vertically" complete recording. When this process is done at different sessions it is regarded as an "incomplete recording." However, where a musician follows this process within a session and adds another contribution(s) (or line(s) of sound) on a separate track parallel to his first contribution, he is then over-dubbing his own performance. This process can be followed a number of times but for each additional contribution (or line of sound) an enhanced sessional rate is payable. It is possible for a musician to over-dub his own performance during a session yet there may still be an incomplete recording.

Where the facility of over-dubbing is required of individual musicians or sections of a group, a session may only be of three hours; a two-hour session may not be used to record performances for subsequent over-dubbing or for over-dubbing tracks previously recorded. A maximum of four titles may be recorded at the three-hour session but no overtime is permitted. For the making of backing tracks where no over-dubbing takes place or is to take place subsequently musicians may be engaged individually for either a two hour or three hour session. A musician may over-dub his own performance but for the first over-dub he must be paid an additional 125 per cent. of the appropriate session fee and for each subsequent over-dub an additional 140 per cent. of the appropriate session fee.

When there is an instrumental accompaniment for a vocalist who records in more than one language, the initial track recording of the accompaniment can be used for the production of other language recordings with the approval of the Union and subject to each musician included in the initial track recording being paid an amount equal to the current three hour session fee for each additional language recorded.

The use of electronic devices—"synthesisers"—in the course of performances is acknowledged. The Agreement expressly provides that a musician who is part of a group, or an established solo performer and uses synthesisers as part of his act, or when a synthesiser or like electronic instrument is used to make electronic sounds as opposed to recreating the sound of other instruments, then nothing in the Agreement is to be construed as restricting the use of synthesisers or limiting the exploitation of records incorporating their performance. On the other hand the Agreement affirms that synthesisers should not be used in circumstances where it would be reasonable to expect instruments in the accepted sense to be used.

Part II and III Category Sessions

These Parts of the Agreement are for "listed" symphony and opera house orchestras, and for "listed" chamber orchestras respectively. The general working conditions as described above such as interval time, the payment of "doubling" fees and premium rates (but Sunday sessions are excluded) apply, but there are some important differences and differences of detail between the two Parts.

The fees payable to musicians are at rates according to a musician's place in an orchestra and to the length of the session booked. A session can be of three or two hours' duration when 20 and 10 minutes respectively of music may be recorded for inclusion in the issued recording. The duration of the sessions can be extended and overtime paid similarly as noted above for a Part I category session.

With a Part II category session of three hours the maximum recording time of 20 minutes may be increased by up to two units of each three minutes of extra recording time; additional fees are payable for each unit or part thereof. This provision does not apply to a Part III category three hour session. The two hour session under both Part II and III categories may be booked only for the completion of work (including re-takes), or for the accompaniment of singers. There can be no extension to the limit of 10 minutes of recorded music.

Where a block or series of three hour sessions has been booked and provided the booking has been contracted six weeks before the first session the 20 minutes of recording time for each of the contracted sessions may be pooled. If there is recording time remaining this surplus may be used for the recording of additional works but the surplus time cannot be aggregated to any further session required to complete the recording of the additional works. Also, such surplus time cannot be used for re-recording elements of works recorded at a session previous to the block or series of sessions, or to rehearse works. If a musician is booked individually for one or more particular sessions within a block of pooled sessions he must be paid according to the amount of music recorded at the session(s).

The provisions for over-dubbing and backing tracks are qualified in as much as these techniques are permitted as a means of achieving better technical standards, or to overcome the absence of a singer due to illness. Where the facility is required all the musicians taking part are to be engaged for a three hour session. Up to four titles may be recorded in any one session but overtime is not permitted. When no over-dubbing takes place or is to take place later, individual musicians may be engaged for either a two hour or three hour session.

Only under Parts II and III of the Agreement can musicians be provisionally booked for sessions but a booking must be either confirmed or cancelled not later than six weeks prior to the provisional or "pencilled" recording date. Furthermore by agreement between an orchestral management and a recording company a session or series of sessions may be postponed on account of the illness of a conductor or soloist but the matter is to be reported to the Musicians' Union. The sessions are required to take place within 18 months from the date of the postponement or within 12 months from the date originally fixed for the session if the repertoire and/or the artists are changed. All the musicians who were originally booked for the sessions must be offered re-engagements for the replacement sessions but those who are not available are entitled to be paid their fee for the originally booked sessions less the amount of any fees received from other professional engagements carried out during the period of the original sessions. This stipulation applies to musicians who are not regular members of the orchestra concerned and to any regular members who before the replacement sessions may have left the orchestra.

Part IV of the Agreement makes provision for porterage payments at rates according to four groupings of instruments. These do not apply to symphony orchestras when an orchestral management provides transportation and charges the recording company session fee.

Under Part V of the Agreement a record company may record a concert performance live but subject to special conditions. The details of the concert and the items recorded are to be notified to the Musicians' Union. A recording company may record up to three performances of the same concert. A standard fee is payable to each musician for each 20 minutes of music included in the final record of the concert performance plus one additional session fee; the total of these payments must not amount to less than the prescribed minimum payment for the recording. A copy of the recording is to be supplied to the Musicians' Union.

Part VI of the Agreement stipulates the fees payable to musical directors unless they are contract artists and in receipt of record royalties when consequently the provisions of the Agreement do not apply to them. Ordinarily musical directors are entitled to a minimum fee equal to twice a musician's general sessional rate. In addition if a musical director is required to render consultancy services before and/or after a recording session an additional fee at a fixed half-hourly rate is payable. Standard rates are prescribed for arrangers according to the number of arranged parts and titles, but arrangements of medleys and choir parts are subject to individual negotiation. Standard rates are also prescribed for copyists.

An integral part of the Agreement is the form of consent required to be signed by musicians. It is in the following terms but a slightly different version applies for musicians who perform as members of one of the listed orchestras under Parts II or III of the Agreement.

> "I hereby give consent, in accordance with the requirements of the Copyright, Designs and Patents Act 1988, [and subject to the payment of the contractual fees] for my performance of the work or works listed above to be recorded for the purpose of producing sound recordings for the following:
>
> (1) Supply to the public;
>
> (2) Public performance and broadcasting to such extent as is licensed by Phonographic Performance Limited;
>
> (3) Incorporation into any record, including the soundtrack of a cinematograph film, to be used solely for paid commercial advertisements of duration not exceeding two minutes advertising supply to the public under (1) above.
>
> I hereby confirm that the Musicians' Union is authorised to act as my representative in all matters concerned with any uses not specified above of the sound recordings produced under this authorisation wherever in the world such uses occur or are contemplated."

The Backing Tracks Agreement

This Agreement enables recording artists and session musicians principally in television programmes to mime to recordings of their performances made by record companies or to sing live to backing tracks.

Although not parties to the Agreement the BBC and the programme companies of ITC and Channel 4 as producers and broadcasters of programmes have a material role in the operation of the Agreement since by the use of backing tracks there is avoided the need for new recordings to be made under the terms of the relevant Collective Broadcasting Agreement. The programmes in which miming and singing to records may take place are listed in the Agreement but they are revised as need arises. Programmes based on the record sales charts are automatically approved programmes. Only exceptionally may a performer mime to the performance of another artist or musician.

The Agreement prescribes the procedure for when a record company intending to make a record available for use and feature in a programme provides the Backing Tracks Clearance form to the Musicians' Union. Particulars of all artists and musicians whose performance is included in a record are to be given distinguishing those who are signed and contracted to the record company and those who are not, *i.e.* those who are casually engaged as session musicians and singers.

Apart from copyright clearances (considered in Part 7 below), the right to use the record as a backing track is by the payment of a fee by the broadcaster to each of the musicians whose performance is included in the recording. The fees payable are at the rates as provided for in the collective agreements between respectively the BBC, the programme companies and the Musicians' Union as outlined above. It is the broadcaster who is responsible for the payment of the fees for the use of the record as a backing track.

The Agreement makes provision for a musician to mime to a record or backing track for the purposes of a personal appearance in circumstances where it would not be practicable for a live performance to take place and provided no broadcasting of the performance is made. If a recording of performances by non-contracted musicians (that is, casual session musicians) is used, the performance is limited to three songs. Payment of the use fees to the non-contracted musicians is subject to agreement between a record company and the Musicians' Union in each particular case but is exclusive of any fee payable for a musician's appearance.

The Music Video Agreement

In 1983 the BPI and the Musicians' Union made an agreement supplementary to the then existing Commercial Gramophone Recording Agreement, for the making of "promos" as a result of the growing practice of dubbing recorded performances in the soundtrack of films made expressly for the promotion of the record itself and the artists concerned. That agreement has been replaced by the Music Video Agreement which is the third of the agreements comprised in the Omnibus Agreement.

A record company is required to notify the Musicians' Union of the making of a music video and provide particulars of the artists and musicians whose performance has been recorded, distinguishing those who are contracted to the company and those who are not. By the notification a company undertakes to pay the incorporation and use fees as due in accordance with the Agreement plus a five per cent. collection and distribution charge to the Musicians' Union. The incorporation and use fees (except the filming fee referred to below) are all payable to the Musicians' Union for it to distribute to the musicians concerned. If any such fees are payable to contracted musicians, *i.e.* musicians exclusively contracted to a record company, the fees are paid directly to the musicians by the company.

The Agreement provides that on the making of a music video and the dubbing of the recorded performance of artists and musicians in the soundtrack there is payable to each musician a standard incorporation fee of £50. To every musician who attends a filming session for the making of the music video a filming fee is payable at a standard rate of £25 each hour or part thereof; this fee is payable by a record company direct to the musicians concerned. To every musician whose performance included in the sound recording is included in the music video a further £50 use fee is payable for the exploitation of the music video in the United Kingdom without restriction by means of television broadcasting of all kinds, non-theatrically and not limited to juke boxes, and theatrically when shown to non-paying audiences. The payment confers a right of unrestricted use for a period of five years calculated from the date of the first showing of the music video on television in the United Kingdom.

By the payment of a further use fee a music video can be similarly exploited world wide outside the United Kingdom for a period of five years from the date of its first showing in any country outside the United Kingdom. The exploitation period of five years can for both areas be renewed by the payment of the use fees at the rates current at the time of renewal.

For the sale and hire of music videos to the general public—usually as a combined sequence of music videos in the form of video cassettes and video discs— a single standard fee for each music video is payable to the Musicians' Union for distribution to the non-contracted musicians like other of the use fees as above.

Where a musician has over-dubbed his performance the incorporation and use fees are payable in respect of each over-dub. If a music director has participated in the recording which is dubbed into the soundtrack of a music video 200 per cent. of the incorporation and use fees are payable in respect of his services. Where the number of musicians who performed in the making of a sound recording exceeds 40 the fees payable as provided for in the Agreement as above are open to special negotiation. Provision is made for the substitution of musicians in the making of a music video but no substitution may take place without the written consent of the musician who performed only on the sound recording. The musician is paid all the fees as if he had been engaged for the making of the music video and the substitute is paid the use fees due in accordance with the Agreement and the fee for attendance at the film session.

THE LIBRARY MUSIC AGREEMENT

Apart from the recording of music for the manufacture and sale of records and cassettes to the general public music is performed and recorded for what may perhaps be conveniently described as industry use, that is, for use by producers and enterprises of many kinds engaged in the business of entertainment. In this way music publishers have been enabled to promote their catalogues and music users have an immediate and wide source of recorded music which they can use according to their particular needs. To cater for this practice there exists the Library Music Agreement which has become recognised in the music business. It is not strictly a collective agreement as each agreement is signed separately by the Musicians' Union with the company engaged in the production of library music.

The standard form agreement stipulates that a company will engage musicians in membership of the Musicians' Union and that all engagements will be made by the company or through an approved contractor. Recording sessions are of three hours during which there is to be one break (being an aggregation of five minutes for each hour of the session) and when up to 20 minutes of music may be recorded. A standard rate is payable to each musician. Overtime is permitted for the completion of a work or title commenced during a session subject to the agreement of the musicians concerned. The fees payable for recording sessions, overtime, "doubling", over-dubbing, and the fees payable to musical directors and rates for arrangers and copyists are all generally in line with those as provided for in the Commercial Gramophone Recording Agreement. Companies undertake to provide the Musicians' Union with full details of each recording session—the musicians engaged, consents, the fees paid and the works recorded.

Crucial to the Agreement are the provisions which define the uses of library music. It is also stipulated that producers of the recordings by notice on record sleeves inform users of the permitted uses, and in respect of copyright protected works, of the need for licences from copyright owners or collecting societies for the reproduction and public performance and broadcasting of the recorded works. The uses are as follows:

(a) radio and television broadcasting, but not as an accompaniment to vocal featured music or choreography; in the United Kingdom library music may not be used in broadcasting where the music is featured and not merely background without the consent of the Union;

(b) film-making, but not for inclusion in a major feature film unless the use is incidental and additional to the music specially performed and recorded for the film;

(c) theatrical, provided the use is incidental and not used as an accompaniment to a performance or to replace "live" musicians;

(d) advertising commercials both television and radio provided the use is for background only and is not in any way featured;

(e) licensing as a whole or in part to a commercial industrial concern or establishment where the use is for background purposes only and does not displace "live" musicians or the practice of having music specially recorded for the like purpose;

(f) record and cassette release for retail sale to the general public subject to each musician being paid the sessional fee at current rates for each 20 minutes of recorded music reproduced in the record, but this does not apply to "spoken word" records when the music included is not featured music;

(g) original videogram productions provided the music is not featured;

(h) as themes and signature tunes, but where there are collective agreements between the Musicians' Union and third parties respecting the recording of such items the Union is to be informed and each musician who performed in the original recording, paid the fees in accordance with the applicable collective agreement for the recording of such items.

By subscribing to the Agreement a company agrees to take all practical steps to prevent the unauthorised use of library material and to report any infringement of which it has notice to the Musicians' Union. No liability attaches to a company for any consequential loss to the Union or its members arising from any unauthorised use or infringement of a recording.

THE BPI AND EQUITY COLLECTIVE GRAMOPHONE RECORDING AGREEMENTS

Singers and other artists who are featured in records are contracted individually by record companies on terms as outlined below. For session and chorus singers there is a collective agreement between the BPI and Equity which provides for a three hour and a two hour session with a maximum recording time of 20 and 10 minutes respectively. When more than one session is booked the recording times may be aggregated.

Minimum fees are prescribed for each session. For recordings of non-classical music there is one rate for sessional singers. For recordings of classical music the rates distinguish choruses of up to 20 members and choruses of over 20 members. For classical recordings the Agreement provides for a three hour rehearsal session for which a standard fee is payable. When a chorus exceeds 60 members the fees are normally negotiated for both rehearsals and recording sessions.

The duration of the sessions and the rates prescribed are inclusive of the intervals to be allowed, not less than 15 minutes for a three hour session and 10 minutes for a two hour session. At any of the sessions there may be overtime to complete the recording of a work begun at the session for which there are separately prescribed rates for session singers and choruses. Payment is for each 15 minutes or part thereof with a maximum permitted overtime of 30 minutes for a three hour session and 15 minutes for a two hour session. If the permitted overtime is exceeded a new session is automatically deemed to have started.

Double rates are payable for work between midnight and 8 a.m. and for work on a statutory holiday. For Sunday work the rates are time and a half. A session singer may overdub his voice; for the first overdub an additional 125 per cent. of the appropriate fee is payable and for each subsequent overdub 140 per cent.

CAST RECORD ALBUM AGREEMENT

There is a separate Collective Agreement between the BPI and Equity for the production and release of cast record albums, that is of recordings of current musical plays and popular musical stage shows and for which the artists appearing are engaged under a standard "Esher" theatre contract. The Agreement does not apply to opera stage productions.

The arrangements for the studio performance and recording of a theatrical production and the terms of engagement and rates payable to artists and chorus are as set out in the Collective Agreement for sessional singers as above. In addition to the sessional fees paid to the individual artists a royalty is payable to Equity on record sales during the 25 years from the date a recording is first released. Equity allocates the royalties it receives to the artists whose performance is recorded.

The royalty is paid on 90 per cent. of the royalty base price—which is variously calculated as prescribed in the Agreement—of each record sold and regardless of whether the record is a single or long play record, cassette or compact disc. The royalty rate on records sold in the United Kingdom is five per cent. rising to five and a half per cent. on sales in excess of 75,000 copies and to six per cent. on sales in excess of 150,000. The royalty on sales overseas is three per cent. These rates apply to records which are re-issues or "revivals" of recorded performances made in the past. The royalty provisions are qualified in the customary way of record royalty agreements providing for reduced rates for certain sales such as budget price and record club sales, the circumstances when no royalties are payable, such as promotional copies. A packaging allowance of 20 per cent. per disc applies to sale of compact discs.

There is included in the Agreement a restrictive provision, but in customary terms, that no artist whose performance is featured in a recording may make any further recordings of the material contained in the record during the period of five years from the date of the issue of the record without the consent of the record company concerned.

The sessional fees and royalty payments are only for the members of the cast taking part in the recording and making of the cast album. The accompanying musicians who may or may not be the regular orchestral musicians for the production are engaged on the terms of the BPI/ Musicians' Union Collective Agreement noted above. Composers, lyricists and book authors receive negotiated royalties. The theatrical producers or management of the recorded production normally have a participation in the profits accruing to the recording company after all costs of the production and manufacture and royalty payments have been met from the revenues from the sale and exploitation of the record.

RECORDING CONTRACTS FOR FEATURED MUSICIANS AND ARTISTS

The contracts of record companies with artists, meaning in this context chiefly solo singers, pop groups, and solo instrumentalists concern the making of an item of merchandise for a market which can be capricious and where competition is acute in a business which has international ramifications. Moreover, the number of young singer/song-writers, musicians and groups aspiring to embark on a career in entertainment and emulate the success achieved by established artists needs no emphasising.

The signing of untried and unknown artists entails an investment by a record company of both time and money on studio and promotion costs and thereby incurs financial risks. Like with any commercial enterprise to minimise the latter and maximise the return on the investment is at the heart of the negotiations by a record company with an artist or more likely his agent/manager. For an artist what is critical are his career prospects and professional standing within a commitment which could last a number of years. These are recurring issues so that the terms of recording contracts are fairly consistent although individual companies may have their own particular conditions of engagement.

Furthermore differences exist between contracts made with a leading record company and contracts made with a record producing company when master recordings are leased to a record company for promotion and distribution. A record company will have a number of contracted artists and commitments to them so in the planning of promotions they are likely to be given preference whereas the promotion of recordings of a record producing company is entirely optional. Thus only artists of proven worth are apt to be signed directly to a record company.

Exclusivity

A recording contract will commit an artist exclusively to a record company for a number of years as it is the company which has the right to decide to bring a contract to an end by not exercising the next successive yearly option. There will be an obligation on an artist to make a minimum number of recordings and often for at least one album in a year, and for the record company to provide and pay for all facilities and services required for the making of the recordings. In this connection, provision should be made for sufficient notice of recording arrangements and studio dates to take account of an artist's other professional engagements.

Unless an artist is established, the record company will have control over the choice of the record producer, the studio, and approval of the material to be recorded, or if the artist is a singer/songwriter the material to be used. An artist's commitment is satisfied only when the master recording is "commercially suitable for release to the public," an expression clearly open to argument in its interpretation and application.

There is likely to be provision for the release of singles to canvas the potential demand for an album and an artist's popularity. Allowance is made for the time required for the actual release of an album and assessment of its likely commercial success in the calculation of the time within which a company's option must be exercised to retain an artist under contract. If the option is not duly exercised then an artist is released from any further obligations particularly that of exclusivity.

Royalties

The figure for the royalty rate inserted in a contract may be attractive but of equal importance are the provisions setting out how the royalty is to be calculated and what expenditures by prior deduction are to be recouped from accrued royalties. Royalties are usually based on the retail or dealer price of full price records, but then the variations begin—the price in the country of manufacture or of actual sale, on net sales or with an in-built deduction for returned and damaged records, and an allowance (an invariable practice) for the cost of packaging. Income will also be affected by provisions for reduced royalties or alternative definitions of royalties for budget or mid/low priced records, sales to record clubs, mail order sales and sales with other merchandise promotions. An artist may have a percentage of net receipts from particular outlets such as a selling-off of record stocks as a "cut out," meaning when a record is deleted from a catalogue. These provisions vary according to the commercial policies of conglomerates in the music business and to accommodate the differences encountered in world record markets.

The fixed royalty rate will also apply to the coupling or inclusion of a recording in a compilation. The actual amount payable in respect of such records will be proportionate and calculated according to the amount the recorded performance bears to the total playing time of the coupling, or in the proportion the number of bands or tracks comprising the artist's recorded performances bears to the total number of bands included in the composite record.

An escalation of the royalty rate is not likely to occur as each option is exercised but rather will depend upon a record attaining a stated volume of record sales on a full price label. Royalties are normally accounted for at six monthly intervals payment being due within 90 days of the end of the accounting period and accompanied by a statement in fair and reasonable detail with explanations as appropriate. An artist should have the right of periodic audit of the accounts of record sales.

Material to an artist and in part as an inducement to his signing with a record company is the amount payable as an advance on royalties; usually a matter of negotiation. The initial advance and any later payments on the exercise of an option by a record company will be recoupable from all royalties or other such payments which may accrue due to an artist from the sale of all records made and issued pursuant to a contract and not from the sale of only particular records. Royalties from the sale of successful records serve as an insurance against a company's loss of recording costs spent on unsuccessful records.

All the expenses incurred in the making of a record are normally the responsibility of the record company but are a first charge on the royalties payable to an artist. Studio costs, the cost of technicians, and of editing transcription and the like are obvious items of expenditure. But costs can increase with the engagement of backing session musicians and singers, fees for arrangers and copyists so that it might be necessary to negotiate a ceiling on recording costs which can be recovered out of the royalties payable to an artist. If a record producer is engaged freelance and is remunerated on a royalty basis it is unlikely his services will count as an item of expenditure in the production of the recording.

The royalties payable to copyright owners for the recording of musical works and lyrics protected by copyright, that is, the reproduction or mechanical copyright fees, are the liability of a record company. The royalties or fees vary from country to country according to its national laws. What is often a matter of contention and resisted by a record company is the payment of such royalties where a singer and/or musician/ composer has control of the publishing of his recorded work and so participates in the receipt of the mechanical royalties derived from the exploitation by the record company of his record.

Promotion costs are a record company's liability since it has no obligation to release and promote a record. It decides the budget and direction of promotion, the extent of distribution of promotional copies of records (on which no royalties are payable), television and point of sale advertising, trade advertisements, and publicity in the way of appearances by an artist. Depending on the professional standing of an artist, terms may be negotiated on his having rights of approval of the artwork and lay-out of record sleeves, the credits to be given to other artists, the producer and other persons contributing to the making of the recording, and the form and extent of the promotion to be given to the record when released. The direct involvement of the artist in the promotion such as by making personal appearances, studio and concert performances are matters which may also require to be provided for especially where overseas sales are a major consideration in the whole enterprise. When an artist is to be involved with promotion then provision needs to be made about his availability and the payment or sharing of costs.

Copyright

It needs to be understood that the record company being the maker is the owner of the copyright in the recording and so is at liberty to deal with it or not to deal with it as the company chooses, subject only to the terms of an artist's contract. It can decide when a recording is to be released, the label under which it is issued, the territories of the world in which it is released, the manner of its marketing and promotion, whether it is coupled with the recordings of other artists, used in a compilation, and re-issued after an interval of perhaps years. Only by the inclusion of express stipulations in an artist's contract can there be any limitation on the exercise by a record company of any of these inherent rights from its ownership of the recording. These issues are as important to a record producing company as to a record company because any contractual limitations imposed by an artist on the exploitation of a recording may jeopardise the making of a tape leasing agreement with a record company which undertakes the promotion and distribution of a record.

Other Legal Considerations

There are two further important legal considerations to note. The first affects artists contracted as a group where the members performing as a unit is the inducement for their being engaged. If a group breaks up problems of replacement arise, and the commitment of both the record company and individual members of the group are affected. The consequences of such an event occurring are matters to be negotiated between a company and a group, and as between the members of the group individually. Persons cannot be made to perform but can be restrained from performing in breach of their obligations.

The second consideration is that of the restrictions which may be placed on an artist or group re-recording in the future the musical works first recorded by a company bearing in mind that after the expiration of a contract the record company will continue to have the right to promote or re-issue the recording. A company which has invested in the making and promotion of a record has a perfectly fair and legitimate interest in seeing that an artist or group after an engagement or after the expiration of an exclusive recording contract does not re-record the same musical works for a rival company. Thus it is usual for there to be a five year bar on an artist's repeating a recording of a work for another record company. This restriction has hitherto applied only to the making of commercial gramophone records and tapes and not to ephemeral recordings made for the purposes of radio and television broadcasting, or to recordings made in the course of the production of cinematograph films.

An exclusive recording contract frequently stipulates that before entering into a commitment to appear in a film an artist is to procure from the film producer an undertaking not to issue to the general public soundtrack records or tapes derived from the film which include any recorded performance by the artist without the approval of the record company. The recording by the artist for the film and the use and exploitation of his performance by the exhibition theatrically or by television or video cassette of the film would not constitute a breach of his obligation not to re-record a work or a repudiation of his exclusive commitment as a recording artist to a record company. With the growth in the distribution for sale and hire to the general public of video cassettes of films and of television programmes and the like, record companies may seek more stringent undertakings respecting the making and marketing of video cassettes of performances of their contracted artists. However as has already been remarked the courts view critically provisions in contracts of personal service which inhibit a person exercising and exploiting his skills or talents. Thus it will require the presence in a contract of clear words to render the making, distribution and sale to the general public of videograms of an artist's performance in a film, or of a videogram of a live concert performance or television broadcast performance a breach of a barring clause.

The making of a video-promo of an artist's performance has in recent years become a feature of record advertising and promotion campaigns. Now it is normally a term of an artist's contract to be willing to appear in vision and be available for the making of a video-promo if required to do so. The costs of making a video-promo are considerable for in addition to the direct studio costs there has to be reckoned the fees payable to non-contracted artists, that is fees due to session musicians and singers as noted above, director's and designer's fees and, print and distribution costs. As all these will be borne initially by the record company it is for the company to decide on the advantages of making a video-promo. As a new item in promotion budgets the cost will be sought to be recovered as to 50 per cent. from record sales and 50 per cent. from the royalty income paid to the artists from the commercial exploitation of the video-promo.

Another commercial element which has entered into recording contracts is the potential income or share of income which may be derived from merchandise variously produced and featuring a recording artist. A record company, like a film company, will justifiably require the right to use the name, biography and photographs or other reproductions of an artist on record sleeves and in other forms of promotion of a record. The right is now being extended to merchandise produced under licence by a record company in return for an artist's entitlement to receive a share of the licence income. The justification for this practice is open to argument but may result in an acceleration in the recoupment of recording costs from record royalties and thereby benefit the artist. Even so, if a merchandising provision is included in an artist's contract it should not be made exclusive otherwise an artist will be precluded from granting the like rights to any third party which might engage his services in any other capacity.

In the foregoing survey of individual artists' recording contracts the issues and terms most likely to affect featured groups and pop artists have been underlined because it is in the world of light music and pop recording where the most intense commercialism exists. Although the catalogue of classical music recordings is to a considerable extent supported by the popular record market commercial factors are important in the making and output of these records. The contractual terms for classical recordings are not fundamentally different from those already considered except that recording costs are not usually recoupable from artists' performing the classical repertoire. Where an orchestra is engaged the orchestral management may receive a payment separate from the standard recording sessional fees which the individual players will receive in accordance with the recording industry's collective agreement with the Musicians' Union as explained above. Rather depending on the international standing of recording artists, conductors and orchestras, restrictions may be imposed on the manner of the exploitation of a recording, in particular its issue on a low priced or budget label, and coupling with other recordings.

TAPE-LEASE OR FRANCHISE AGREEMENTS

The role of the record production company has already been alluded to and so it is appropriate to consider briefly the nature and scope of tape-lease or franchise agreements.

A record producing company (in the following paragraphs simply referred to as "a producer"), may engage a number of artists and bear the recording costs as an investment with the intention of negotiating with individual record companies for the release of the recordings. A tape-lease agreement may be made with a record company judged most likely to promote and exploit a single or number of the recordings advantageously by reason of the company being established in a particular territory or market, or having expertise in the promotion of a particular kind of music or style of musical performance. There may alternatively be a franchise whereby a record company has the exclusive right or first option to acquire the distribution rights in the recordings of certain or all the artists contracted by a producer but for the recordings to be released under the name or label of the producer.

Whether the arrangement is one of tape-lease or franchise, in both instances it is important for the contracts to be complimentary to those agreements made by a producer with artists. A producer must ensure that its obligations and liabilities to its artists are matched by the terms and conditions on which recordings are made available to a record company. Conversely, the undertakings of the producer given to the record company must be sustainable by the terms and conditions of the contracts made with its artists. This is especially so with a franchise agreement where a record company has rights or interests in future recordings.

All the considerations touched on above regarding artists' contracts are relevant to the terms of a franchise agreement. The obligations as between the producer and record company on the number and times of delivery of master tape recordings, quality control, the provision of material and artwork required in support of the promotion of a recording, the time of manufacture and release of records, the territories and the duration of an agreement and any sell-off period are matters to be covered. There should also be set out the rights of the parties where without wilful default by either party the time within which any of their respective obligations are to be satisfied is exceeded so that for example, options become extendable.

The costs incurred by a producer in the making of recordings will normally be recoverable only from the royalties received from the record company undertaking the promotion and distribution of the records. Accordingly the amount of the advance payable by the record company will represent the only guaranteed sum obtainable by a producer provided it is expressed as a non-returnable advance unless refundable in exceptional circumstances. Like the recording contract of an artist (whose entitlement to royalties may or may not be in like terms), the provisions of a tape-lease or franchise agreement detailing royalty rates, the basis for the calculation of the payments due and when to be accounted for are negotiable. Where a record company has the right to select what recordings it will manufacture then provisions may be included specifying the manner and extent of promotion and exploitation to be undertaken with penalties for any failure to do so to the detriment of the producer which is the owner of the recording.

Rights and Consents

A record company before embarking on the promotion of a record and incurring costs of manufacture and distribution can justifiably require and ought to have proof of a record producer's rights in the master tape and evidence to support any undertakings (which may or may not be included in the agreement) respecting such matters as an artist's or group's exclusivity, options for further recordings, availability for promotional appearances and the like. Precise and accurate information in the form of cue sheets will need to be supplied to a record manufacturer about the ownership of the copyright in the works recorded in order for the record company to pay to the owners of copyright works the fees due for the reproduction of the works, that is, the mechanical royalties. Furthermore, a record manufacturer may require to be satisfied that all regular sessional fees due to singers and musicians have been paid and that all studio costs and like expenses incurred in the production of the master-tape have been paid and all the required consents given in accordance with the Copyright, Designs and Patents Act 1988 so as not to put at risk or inhibit the production and marketing of the records.

Often the standing and reputation of a record company are material to the choice of company licensed by a record producer but without an express prohibition there is no bar to a record company's assigning or sub-licensing the rights and benefits it has acquired under a tape-leasing agreement. If the royalty advance is small, or if rights are granted which exceed the regular rights to manufacture and sell records, such as rights to the services of a group or an artist to make appearances and contribute to the promotion of a record, then any rights of assignment or sub-licensing should be viewed critically.

A tape-lease agreement confers proprietorial rights or interests in property, meaning the copyright in the master tape; the rights granted have a worth and asset value to a record company for so long as the franchise subsists. If a record company becomes insolvent then these rights, being part of its assets, will fall to be dealt with or disposed of by the company's liquidator in the same way as any other of its assets. Moreover, the royalties accrued and payable will be treated no differently from any other of the company's debts due to its creditors. Thus to protect the proprietorial rights and interests of the record producer it is usual for an agreement to stipulate for the automatic determination of the grant and the reversion of the rights in the master-tape to the record producer in the event of the record company becoming insolvent or being wound up on account of its indebtedness. There may be other reasons for premature termination, such as a substantial breach of the terms of the agreement.

Part 5

THE PERFORMER AND THE LAW

A. CONTRACTS OF ENGAGEMENT

In this Section A an endeavour is made to bring together the various strands and basic principles of the common law which underlay the contracts not only of artists but also of other persons such as writers, composers, and producers (considered more particularly in Part 7 below), who contribute to entertainment and the performing arts. The laws enacted by Parliament covering employment generally and those which relate especially to entertainment are considered in the following Sections.

It is important to understand that although the collective agreements made between management associations and trade unions contain detailed standard conditions of employment, every engagement rests on a separate and individual contract made between the company or management engaging a person's services and the person rendering his services. The contract will most often incorporate by reference the standard conditions but these are minimum conditions so that the rights and interests of the parties to the contract may be expressly negotiated according to the particular circumstances and it is the terms as agreed between the parties to the contract which count in law.

It is not essential for a contract of engagement to be in writing to be binding on the parties. A contract may be wholly verbal or it may be wholly written, or partly both. In addition it may arise and be implied by law from the conduct of the parties. A collective agreement may prescribe the manner in which individual engagements ought to be contracted just as they prescribe minimum conditions and these rules of industry practices will be of persuasive importance in resolving any dispute about the making of a contract and the terms of an engagement. Where an engagement has been agreed to partly verbally and partly in writing the combined elements will form the contract and although the written element will be preferred the verbal element could constitute the critical variation of the written part.

The difference between a contract **of** service (or a contract of employment) and a contract **for** services is important in law for many reasons. As will be seen it is material to the application of much of the employment protection legislation considered in Section D below. The distinction is very relevant in the assessment of liability to income tax, registration for VAT, national insurance contributions, entitlement to social security benefits, the vicarious liability of an employer to a third party for the wrongful acts of his employee in contrast to the primary liability of a self-employed person for damage caused to another person.

The distinction between a contract of service and a contract for services is one of fact and when this has been in issue the courts have looked rather at the substance and not the form of the contract. In other words the courts take particular notice of the amount of independence from control a person has regarding how work is to be done, whether the person performing the services is to provide the necessary gear or equipment or assistants, the manner of payment (whether a lump sum or regular stated payments) and whether there is any assumption of financial risk. The extent of control by the engaging party over what and how a job is to be done or a service performed is very material, but because a person has a professional status that is not enough to settle this point as today qualifications and expertise are prerequisites for the performance of many services. Thus the courts have come to approach the issue by also enquiring whether the person engaged is an integral part of the enterprise regardless of his title or status, whether the work and the way it is performed is integrated into the business as a whole or is but an ancillary contribution to it. How a person demonstrably conducts his business affairs to show he pursues his profession or occupation separately and apart from any enterprise which may engage his services is also material in deciding the issue.

Right to Perform

Many theatrical and film personalities and others connected with entertainment have ensured that their names if not their fame will be known to judges and lawyers through the reports of their legal proceedings. Indeed some may have contributed more to legal precedent than they did to entertainment! One notable precedent concerns an American actress Fay Marbe. In 1926 she was engaged by George Edwards to appear at the now legendary Daly's Theatre in London but her appearance was cancelled because another leading lady—evidently more esteemed by the management than Fay Marbe—would not tolerate being overshadowed by the visiting artist. Here was applied a principle recognised by the courts, namely, that where the opportunity to render the services contracted is as much a condition of the engagement as the payment of remuneration, then by wilfully preventing the performance or rendition of those services there is a breach of contract. The principle was applied to a writer who was engaged to write the screenplay version of a novel and whose work was wrongfully refused which resulted in the writer being deprived of the screen credit he would otherwise have received. Also it was applied to a writer who was an expert on jade and whose contracted article was withheld from publication when an essential feature of the arrangement was that the article would be published so as to afford the writer the opportunity to enhance his reputation. Generally there is no necessary implication of contracts of personal service that the person engaged must actually be given work to do, the payment of the agreed salary or fee being the essential obligation of the employer. But where the contract is about the doing of a specific job, the performance of a role or part, or where a special skill is involved and it is necessary to maintain it by practise and application, then the deliberate denial of the opportunity so to perform or practice a skill or art in the way contemplated may constitute a breach of contract.

In other cases like that of Fay Marbe the proposition has been advanced that the denial of the opportunity to perform resulted in damage to the artist's reputation which should be compensated. The preferred view is that any claim for compensation in such circumstances rests not on damage to reputation since that is already established, but rather on the grounds of loss of publicity and the opportunity of advancing a professional career which the engagement offers. However, the principle highlighted by the case of Fay Marbe is very often nullified by the inclusion of a stipulation in most contracts of engagement that a management will not be bound to make use of the services of an artist and that if it elects not to use them no liability will attach to it and no compensation will be payable to the artist for any alleged loss of publicity or opportunity for him to enhance his professional reputation or standing, the management's obligation being only to pay the remuneration as may be due to the artist in accordance with the terms of the contract.

Restrictive Terms

The unique value which a management may attach to the services and creative talents and attractions of an artist may be reflected by the inclusion in a contract of provisions which prevent an artist from engaging in any professional activity during the currency of an engagement and for a period of time after (and even possibly prior to) an engagement. To some extent this is justifiable especially when talent has been nursed and where there has been considerable financial investment in a production whether it is a stage presentation, a film or a record. When considering artists' contracts above it was remarked that restrictions may be placed on an artist's appearance within a stated area or radius or particular medium during a prescribed period of time. Similarly restrictions may be placed on a writer, composer, director, designer and the like rendering professional services in a particular sphere for a stated time. A right of first refusal to engage services or to acquire rights in a work may be imposed, or successive options on services may be secured as part of the terms of the initial engagement. All such provisions must be clear and precise in their meaning to be enforceable because of their inhibiting and restrictive effects.

Persons who are parties to a contract are at liberty to make what bargains and on what terms they choose and no enquiry will be made by the courts as to whether the benefits and burdens are evenly balanced. However, with contracts of personal service, the courts have inclined to scrutinise the fairness of the terms particularly in the light of the bargaining strengths of the parties. The music business has gained some notoriety in this development.

The courts are most likely to intervene on the grounds of an unconscionable bargain when there exists a fiduciary relationship between the parties, as for example, between a manager and artist, where one party reposes the management of his affairs in another party. Where there is such a relationship then if one party conceals his interests which conflict with or are inimicable to the interests of the other and to his properly discharging the obligations he has purported to assume, this will lead to an inference of his having taken an unfair advantage of the other party so that the contract will be voidable. A great disparity in the obligations between the parties to a contract are suspect and are most often the result of an abuse of a fiduciary relationship.

Provisions of contracts which seriously restrict or jeopardize a person's pursuit of his profession and opportunity to earn his living are viewed more critically. Proprietary interests in the results or products of a person's services, such as a film, or record or commercial advertisement, can be protected even to the extent of compensating a person for not pursuing his profession in some specific way. Even so any restrictions must be justified by the particular circumstances and to protect the legitimate interests of the party engaging and paying for the services rendered. Contracts engaging a person's exclusive services are inherently restrictive as the person is prevented from rendering any professional services to another. But that does not necessarily invalidate the contract as the distinction has been drawn between the total absorption of a person's work and abilities from their being rendered totally unproductive.

In recent years there have been instances of songwriter/record artists' contracts being challenged on a number of grounds and held to be so oppressive and unreasonable as to be unenforceable. It is not so much the actual or potential length of the period of exclusivity which has led to contracts being set aside by the courts, as the grossly disproportionate bargaining power of the artist and the oppressive terms imposed, such as acquiring total control over artists and sole power to release the products of their services. More particularly it has been the absence of any real and meaningful obligations and undertakings on the part of a record company (or promoter/manager) which has resulted in contracts being set aside. Obligations have been imposed on artists to record, to perform and to assign over the copyright in their works but there have been no undertakings by the company to promote and exploit their recordings and works, no guarantee of any kind of reward for the services performed and rights granted, or right for a songwriter/recording artist to retrieve his works after a period of time and find other outlets for the exploitation of his works.

Assignments of Rights

Another example of the special rules applied to contracts of personal service is that as personal skill, ability or confidence are involved the parties can insist upon personal performance by each other. The one who is engaged to perform a service can insist that the service is rendered only to the party which engaged him. As to be expected, the person who engages another to render a service can insist that only that person performs it. An artist who is engaged to perform, or a writer or the like who is commissioned to write or create some work cannot be compelled by a management to perform or produce a work for another. Accordingly very often a contract will expressly provide that a manager or producer is entitled to assign and transfer the benefits of the contract and so be able to make over to a third party the services of an artist as these are what benefit a management.

When such an assignment occurs a management will remain bound and liable for the observance of the obligations undertaken by him and owed to the artist, so consequently an undertaking should be secured by the management from the third party or assignee for the due fulfilment of the obligations owed to the artist. The artist remains unaffected by the assignment but if there is any default by the third party, then although the artist cannot claim twice over for the default he can have recourse to both the management which first engaged his services as well as the third party for the recovery of compensation for any default or breach of contract.

The third party, the assignee of the right to the services of the artist, will stand in the place of the management and be entitled to secure the performance of the services and compliance with any ancillary undertakings by the artist such as restrictions on the rendering of services to anyone else. However, for the assignee's or third party's rights to be enforceable directly against the artist there are formalities to be observed. There can be no partial assignment of the right to the artist's services; it must be absolute and unconditional, it must be effected in writing and written notice of the assignment given to the artist whose services are assigned. If there is any defect in these formalities then in effect the rights to the artist's services and the enforcement of the artist's undertakings can be secured only by the management and not directly by the third party. Furthermore, any such assignment does not defeat any claim of the artist against the management outstanding at the time of receipt of the notice of assignment.

As an alternative to the assignment of the right to an artist's services there may be a loan-out of his services provided that the right to do is conferred on a management by the terms of the contract. When an artist's services are hired to another the terms of the hire are as between the lender and the hirer as the artist has no formal legal standing in the transaction but has only the duty to perform his services as and to the extent agreed between himself and the management making available his services. If there is any dispute between the hirer and the artist, then formally it rests to be resolved between the management and the artist on the one hand and the management and hirer on the other according to the terms of the two respective contracts. Neither the hirer nor the artist can bring any claim based on the other's contract with the management as only the parties to a contract can sue and enforce the terms of a contract.

Irrespective of whether a right of assignment is included in a contract where the services rendered result in an end product such as a film or recording, the management engaging an artist is entitled to possess, use and exploit the product of the services rendered as his property as he decides. The services performed and the resulting product are two distinct entities. However, services may be rendered on special conditions apart from those relating to remuneration and working conditions; it is the consents which a performer gives respecting the use and exploitation of the products of his services which count. The terms of the consent are as much part of the contractual bargain between a management and an artist as any other of the contractual terms and are enforceable as such despite a management's ownership of the product of an artist's or other performer's services. The same principle applies to writers and others whose copyright works are reproduced or exploited as will be seen in Part 7 below.

While the benefits of a contract may be assignable the obligations and liabilities undertaken cannot be assigned to a third party. As has already been explained where a management has assigned the benefit of a contract it remains liable if the assignee defaults in observing the management's obligations to the artist, musician, writer etc.

A fundamental principle of the law of contract is that with rare exception only the parties to a contract can enforce it and sue for any breach of its terms. This means that an artist can sue a management or a film producer for fees but not the financial backers of a management or a completion guarantor or distributor of a film. This rule is of great significance in the mechanical media as the payment of royalties and residual fees is primarily the liability and responsibility of the producer or organisation which engaged the artist just as much as the payment of the artist's engagement fee. A distributor may undertake and agree with a producer to pay all residuals due to artists and others, yet although such an undertaking is intended for their benefit as they are not parties to the contract they cannot directly enforce its provisions. Moreover, there is no principle of law which in the ordinary way of commerce can compel a management or producer to take proceedings against a third party such as a distributor to enforce compliance with the terms of a contract intended to benefit persons who are not parties to it. The only safeguard is the inclusion of a term in the contract of engagement whereby a management or producer undertakes to institute proceedings against the third party on the latter's default, but in practice such an undertaking is unlikely to be given unless so qualified as to be of doubtful value.

Suspension and Termination

Long term contracts of engagement or contracts of uncertain duration often present special difficulties when circumstances arise which result in one party wishing to terminate the engagement. To some extent the problem is less critical in the theatre and "live" entertainment when recasting can take place during a run. The theatre standard contracts deal with the situation arising from an artist's illness or injury and contingencies which can interrupt or bring about the termination of a run. The collective agreements relating to performers in films, television film series and television and radio broadcasting also deal with these issues. Even so where a production entails an outlay and investment of capital, where the time and energy expended in a production remain always at risk until the production is complete and "in the can", special considerations may apply to the engagement of leading performers, writers, producers and directors.

A right of termination for *force majeure* is apt to be included in contracts but this alone is of doubtful value as expressions acceptable for property insurance and the like are not necessarily acceptable in the context of contracts for personal services. Only in extreme cases does the law intervene to relieve parties of their mutual undertakings by holding that a contract has been frustrated, where without the fault of either party its performance has become so onerous, so impossible due to unforeseen and changed circumstances that to hold the parties to the agreement would in fact be to hold them to a contractual relationship very different from that which they had made or intended. Where provision is made for a right of suspension or termination of an engagement then provision should be made to deal with the consequences of this—entitlement to future earnings or royalties or profits; substitution of performers, directors etc; rights to credit and publicity; the use and manner of exploitation of the material which has been produced or acquired before the suspension or termination; the rights of the parties during a period of suspension as distinct from termination; and the period of notice either must give to cancel a suspension or terminate the engagement entirely.

Breach of Contract

It is a common misconception that because one party does not or has not strictly complied with the terms of a contract, that entitles the other to terminate it; that is not so. Any breach of contract as a matter of law confers on the injured party a right to claim damages but that party must remain ready and willing and able to perform and continue with his part of the bargain and allow the defaulting party to make amends. Only a fundamental breach, one which goes to the core of the agreement, discharges the innocent party from further liability or obligation to observe the contract and to treat the other party as having repudiated the contract.

What constitutes a fundamental breach of contract depends on the particular circumstances as can be gathered from the terms themselves as reflecting the intention of the parties respecting the performance of their mutual undertakings. The extent or seriousness of the refusal of one party to perform his express undertakings is material in deciding whether or not there was such a fundamental breach of contract as to justify the other party treating the contract as terminated. Also relevant is how radically different was the actual performance (or material the non-performance) of an undertaking from that agreed upon. The mere delay in payment of money or lateness in the performance of a duty does not necessarily constitute a fundamental breach of contract. Time is not of the essence of a contract unless it is expressly made so or is obviously so.

Whether there has been a fundamental breach of contract is basically a question of fact, but by way of illustration of the problem two examples drawn from the entertainment business can be cited although they arose many years ago and when conditions of theatrical engagements were somewhat different from what they are today. When an artist was engaged to play a leading part in a stage play as from the beginning of its run but due to illness she could not perform until a week after the season had started so that a substitute had to be engaged, the producer was held to have been justified in refusing to continue with the engagement, the undertaking to perform from the first night being regarded as a condition of the agreement the breach of which entitled the producer to treat the contract as terminated. In another case when a singer was engaged for a season and undertook to rehearse for six days before the opening but arrived only three days in advance the producer sought to terminate the contract. It was held that the breach was not fundamental as the rehearsals were subsidiary to the main purpose of the engagement but although the producer could not terminate the contract he was entitled to be indemnified for any loss suffered by the breach of the contract.

The normal remedy for breach of contract is the payment of damages as the remedies of either a decree of specific performance or injunction will be granted by the courts only where the award of damages does not fairly compensate an injured party. This is particularly so with contracts for personal services which are never specifically enforceable for the common sense reason that the courts cannot supervise their performance; the law cannot compel a person to write a play, or sing "Norma"! However, as has been aptly remarked, the performance of personal services may be "encouraged" when the terms of the contract are susceptible to enforcement by way of injunction. Terms which are negative in their meaning, requiring inaction rather than positive action are capable of being enforced by injunction. An artist who has undertaken to perform at a stated time and place cannot be compelled to perform, but if also the artist has agreed not to sing or perform elsewhere during the period of the engagement, that undertaking may be enforced by injunction with the result of inducing or encouraging compliance with the agreement to perform.

Provisions of agreements of the kind noted above restricting or barring appearances before or following an engagement may be enforced by injunction. Even so an injunction will not be granted if the result would be to compel a person to render specific services. If an artist who is not employed full time is required to undertake to render his professional services wholly to one person and to no one else in any capacity, then it is unlikely an injunction would be granted to restrain him rendering services to another as otherwise he would be driven and compelled to render the specific services contracted. This kind of situation is to be contrasted with one where a film company engaged an actress on the basis that she would not act for another film company; an injunction was granted when she attempted to breach the restriction as the contract did not inhibit her rendering her professional services in other branches of entertainment. Although subject to technical rules and the discretion of the courts, the remedy of injunction can have surprising application. It was granted to prevent a pop group breaking up and to enable a record company to make a recording of the group. In the particular circumstances, if the recording had not then been made the opportunity to make the particular recording would have been lost for ever, but once the recording had been made disputes about rights of exploitation could be resolved later.

Taxation

At the risk of greatly over-simplifying a complex law and one often seemingly inconsistently applied, by way of footnote it may be useful to point out some of the very basic principles of income tax law of general application and the special rules which affect non-resident entertainers.

At the commencement of this Section the differences in law and the consequences of those differences between a contract of service and a contract for services were noted, but for the purposes of liability to income tax, or more correctly the basis upon which a person's liability to tax is assessed, the differences are becoming marginal for those engaged in entertainment.

There is a great diversity of working conditions and practices spread across the vast number of occupations throughout the country, but for tax purposes there are only two categories of persons who render personal services, namely, those who are employees and liable to tax under Schedule E (PAYE) and those who are self-employed (freelance) and liable to tax under Schedule D. The distinction does not depend on how a person chooses to regard himself or how an income tax official chooses to, but is based on an objective view of the characteristics of an engagement according to criteria which the courts have established and elaborated in a number of cases. A person's tax status is not determined simply by virtue of his profession but by the nature and conditions of his employment. A few cases may be cited by way of illustration. A once famous actress was variously engaged to appear on the stage, in films and broadcasting. All the activities were separately and independently pursued and for which there were successive contracts with various managements to do or perform particular acts. These contracts were held to be contracts for services and so the actress was assessed on the basis of what is now Schedule D.

A relatively more recent case involved a professional ballet dancer who was engaged by the Sadlers Wells Company under a standard contract to rehearse, understudy, play and dance when and where required by the company at a regular salary for a minimum period of 22 weeks full time, and thereafter subject to notice on either side. The dancer had previously been freelance and this engagement permitted him to perform professionally for others when not required by the Company. This was held to be a contract of service so that he was assessable under Schedule E.

A trapeze artist was engaged by a circus management and in addition to performing her act she also agreed to help in moving the circus from place to place and to perform the duties of usherette. On the facts this was held to be contract of service so that Schedule E applied.

A writer was engaged for three years by a film company and in each of those years for 12 to 16 weeks he was to render his entire and exclusive services to the company and write whatever stories, screenplays etc. it required and the entire copyright in all the material written by him during these weeks was to belong to the company. Because the writer was otherwise free to pursue his writing and career as he chose, this was held to be a contract for services and so he was assessed under Schedule D.

A television researcher's appointment was held to be consistent with his being an employee as his services were exclusive to the company, his work subject to approval by the programme producer, his pay was computed on an annual basis and working conditions were standard. Because there may have been grounds for regarding him as self-employed for tax purposes they were not conclusive in resolving the issue.

A member of an orchestra who was a shareholder in the orchestra's managing company and was remunerated by participating in the profits of the company by virtue of his shareholding, was held to be self employed and not an employee of the company.

The distinctions between a contract of service and a contract for services are often finely drawn—as the above demonstrate—but it is from the Sadlers Wells case that stems the practice made uniform since 1990 for theatrical performers engaged under Esher Standard Contracts to be assessed to tax under Schedule E. (An exception is made for those who, having already had three years of Schedule D status, are given reserved Schedule D status.) Thus all managements are required to make tax deductions and returns in accordance with the Taxes Management Acts like any other employer. It remains to be seen if, because of the existence of other standard terms of engagement for artists particularly in radio and television broadcasting and films, the like rules for the automatic deduction of tax on the basis of PAYE will be introduced. Engagements in the media unlike those in the theatre are more often of short duration, with broken periods of engagement and do not invariably engage an artist's exclusive services.

Perhaps the most contentious issue over the two Schedules is the treatment of expenses. With Schedule E for an expense to be allowed it must have been incurred wholly, exclusively and necessarily in the performance of the duties of the office or employment. Expenditure incurred merely to enable a person to perform the duties, or to perform them more efficiently does not satisfy the test. By an amendment to the tax laws made in 1990 the commission payable to agents by an artist assessed under Schedule E is allowed as a deductible item of expenditure to a limit of 17.5 per cent., as under the Employment Agencies Act 1973 agents are entitled to charge their commission to an artist whereas normally commission is chargeable only to employers.

The treatment of travel, accommodation and like expenses by the Inland Revenue is arguably severe. Neither the cost of travel to fulfil an engagement, nor the cost of accommodation when an artist necessarily remains away from his normal place of residence is deemed to be incurred in the performance of the duties of the employment. If these expenses are reimbursed they must be declared as they count as part of an artist's total remuneration. There is, in contrast, the situation where an artist is engaged for a tour from a base and returning to the base when in the performance of the duties an artist is necessarily required to incur the expense of travel and accommodation. If such expenses are not paid by a company, they are an allowable expense to be set against an artist's earnings. A tour such as a pre-London tour of a production is not treated in the same way as there is no actual established base from which it begins and to which it returns.

Musicians, composers, authors, writers, directors, choreographers and designers are most likely to be freelance and independent as most often their engagements are casual. Even so their status as self-employed persons or employees, whether an engagement can be regarded as a contract for services or one of service, and whether they are subject for purposes of tax to Schedule D or E, must rest on the terms of a particular contract and the inference to be drawn from them. It should not be overlooked that for purposes of taxation a person can have both professional independence as well as employment status at the same time, *i.e.* have an income or profit from a profession, and earnings or emoluments from an employment.

Value Added Tax. VAT is a system of taxation separate from Income Tax. Individuals, partnerships, companies, associations and charities engaged in the business of supplying goods or professional services (broadly) of whatever kind in the United Kingdom are potentially taxable persons. Business is widely defined so that persons rendering freelance (not as employees) artistic and creative services, or who grant rights of copyright in their works for payment, may be subject to the rules requiring persons to register with HM Customs and Excise and account for output tax on their supplies less input tax on certain of their purchases.

The obligation to register arises when the taxable supplies, the charges or fees of the business or profession, exceed the threshold of £36,600 in any preceding 12 months, or it is expected that within a given 30 day period taxable supplies will exceed this amount. Persons who reside abroad, who do not "belong to" or are not based in this country are exempted from registration. However, from January 1, 1993 in compliance with EC Directives the exemption will not apply to persons who are nationals of member states of the European Community. Such persons who perform in this country, so making a taxable supply may need to be registered.

Taxation of Foreign Artists. An innovation to the tax laws introduced in 1987 applies to a person who or organisation which makes a payment to an entertainer (and incidentally sportsman) who is a non-resident for his services as an entertainer in the United Kingdom. The payer is required by law to "withhold", *i.e.* deduct, from any payment due to the entertainer connected with such services an amount calculated at the standard rate of income tax and to account to the Inland Revenue for the sum deducted. This obligation corresponds in principle to the revenue laws of other countries such as the USA. The detailed rules for the withholding of tax from a payment are set out in the Income Tax (Entertainers and Sportsmen) Regulations 1987 (S.I. 1987 No. 530).

The definition of entertainer is somewhat generalised. It refers to persons who give performances in their character as entertainers in any kind of entertainment which is or may be available to the public or any section of it and whether for payment or not. What constitutes a performance is not clearly defined but emerges from there being a performance of a "relevant activity" by an entertainer in his character as entertainer, a performance on or in connection with a commercial occasion or event of any description for which the entertainer might receive or become entitled to receive anything by way of cash or any other form of property. Certain such activities are mentioned in the Regulations.

Performances are not confined to live performances on stage, concert platform or arena. Any form of recorded performance on film, video or record and any performance on radio or television falls within the regulations. Moreover, performance is not restricted to the performance of a role, a "specialty" or variety act, or musical performance. Any engagement in which an entertainer appears by virtue of his profession as a performer in entertainment, as a celebrity, counts such as appearance on chat shows. Any appearance designed to promote commercial sales or activity by advertising or endorsement or sponsorship of goods or services also counts as a relevant activity within the regulations.

All payments made directly or indirectly in respect of the performance of a relevant activity have to be accounted for, including all expenses which may have been paid on behalf of or reimbursed to an entertainer, such as travel, accommodation, per deims. (If such expenses are paid by the engaging company they will not be allowed in the computation of the company's liability to tax). In addition to the fee directly payable to an entertainer for his performance or appearance, all supplementary fees or payments however described—residuals, royalties, share of profits—are subject to withholding tax. An exception is made only for royalties payable on the sale of records and audio cassettes. Residuals which are payable for a performance before May 1, 1987 are also exempted.

Where an entertainer's services are contracted through the medium of a loan-out or service company so that all payments for his services are payable to the company, the payments are deemed to be payments to the entertainer and so within the regulations. The fact that another person or company and not the entertainer is entitled to receive payment does not alter the liability of the payer to make the deduction of withholding tax.

A person who or organisation which makes any payment covered by the Regulations is required to make a return of the payments and account to the Inland Revenue for the tax deducted within 14 days of the next quarterly period prescribed for the making of returns. Where the total payments due to an entertainer from a payer during any tax year amount to £1,000 or less, payments can be made without deduction of tax but a return of the payment must still be made. Where by the terms of the contract further payments may be due the obligation to make the deduction cannot be avoided. When tax is deducted a certificate of the payments made and tax deducted signed by the payer should as a matter of course be given to the entertainer or other recipient of the payment. There are prescribed forms for the making of returns and certificate of tax deducted. The Regulations make provision for written application to be made to the Inland Revenue by an entertainer and payer, together or singly, for an arrangement whereby an amount which approximates more closely to an entertainer's final liability may be deducted from a payment. An application must be made not later than 30 days before the payment is due to be made. If an arrangement is agreed a certificate authorising the agreed deduction of tax is issued by the Inland Revenue, but not until the certificate is produced should a payer withhold tax at any rate other than the rate prescribed in the Regulations.

Withholding tax does not apply to services rendered outside the United Kingdom. If an entertainer is engaged for a tour when only some appearances are to take place in the United Kingdom then two contracts may legitimately be issued by a management. One may be for the non-United Kingdom appearances and the other for the appearances here, the total remuneration being fairly apportioned between the two contracts so that only the fee attributable to appearances in the United Kingdom is subject to withholding tax. The same arrangement can be applied where an entertainer is engaged to appear in a film with the studio production taking place here but with locations overseas.

It needs to be understood that withholding tax is a payment on account of an entertainer's potential liability to British tax. At the end of a tax year it is open to both the entertainer and the Inland Revenue to review his tax liability which will be assessed in accordance with the tax laws as generally applicable. It is at that stage when reliefs and allowable items of expenditure incurred in the pursuit of his profession, such as agent's commission, expenses and the like, become reckonable and an entertainer's liability to tax finally assessed. The existence of double taxation treaties between this country and the country of an entertainer's residence is further likely to lessen the burden of taxation.

The Regulations apply only to entertainers, not to playwrights, authors, composers, producers, directors, choreographers and so on. Yet because of their generalisations still it may not be certain such persons are outside their scope. If a singer/songwriter produces his own recording, or a leading actor directs a stage production or film in which he also appears, or similarly a choreographer both dances and produces, then should the functions be separately contracted corresponding to the separate contracting of an artist to perform partly in the studio and at an overseas location? And how are the regulations to be applied when any such persons appear to promote their work—as entertainer or producer? The obligation and liability for the payment of withholding tax rests on the payer so that where there is doubt the issue should be referred to the Foreign Entertainment Unit of the Inland Revenue in Birmingham.

B. RIGHTS IN PERFORMANCES

A major reform of the law for the protection of performers against the illicit recording or use of recordings of their performances has been brought about by Part II of the Copyright, Designs and Patents Act 1988 ("the Act"). It has repealed the Performers Protection Acts 1958 to 1972 which had been enacted to comply with parts of the Rome Convention of 1961 for the protection of performers, producers of records and broadcasting organisations. These statutes provided for criminal prosecutions but did not give performers rights of civil action against persons who illicitly recorded or broadcast or otherwise exploited their performances. The Act has rectified this anomaly and given remedies corresponding to those for infringement of copyright; it has also conferred rights on those who have exclusive recording rights in artists' performances. The Act is about rights in performances rather than rights of performers since not only performers have rights under its provisions.

The Act does not confer any copyright or other proprietary rights or ownership in a performance. The rights it does confer are separate and independent of any rights of copyright and moral rights in any work performed, and the rights in any broadcast, and in any film, or sound or other recording made of a performance.

Performers' Rights

The rights granted by the Act are personal to a performer and are infringed by any person who does any of the following acts without the performer's consent in respect of the whole or a substantial part of his performance, namely:

(a) makes a recording of a performance otherwise than for his private and domestic use;

(b) broadcasts a performance live;

(c) shows or plays in public or broadcasts a performance by means of a recording which was, and which a person knows or has reason to believe was made without the performer's consent;

(d) imports into the United Kingdom otherwise than for his private and domestic use, or in the course of business, possesses, sells or lets for hire, offers or exposes for sale or hire or distributes a recording of a performance which that person knows or has reason to believe is an illicit recording.

"Recording" in relation to a performance means a film or sound recording made directly from a live performance, or from a broadcast of a performance, or directly or indirectly from any other recording of the performance. The reference to broadcasting is to be understood as meaning broadcasting and a cable programme service as defined in the Act.

"Performance" for the purposes of the Act has its normal and straightforward meaning, namely:

(a) a dramatic performance (which includes dance and mime);

(b) a musical performance;

(c) a reading or recitation of a literary work;

(d) a performance of a variety act or any similar presentation;

and which is, so far as it is, a live performance given by one or more individuals. As the rights are personal it follows they are severally and jointly enforceable whether the performance is one of a double act, group or combined orchestra.

There is no definition of performer. There is no requirement concerning the quality of a performance or standing of the performer—professional or amateur—or that any payment be made by any audience or persons viewing a performance, or for a performer to receive any payment or other consideration for his performance. However, the Act does lay down certain pre-conditions for the rights and protection given by the Act to be enforceable.

A performance must be a "qualifying performance," meaning one given by a qualifying individual or one which takes place in a qualifying country. By section 206 of the Act, a "qualifying individual" means a British citizen or a citizen or subject of, or an individual resident in, a qualifying country. A "qualifying country" means the United Kingdom, another member state of the European Community, or another country (as designated by Government order), which grants reciprocal rights to performers.

Consent

Unlike the Performers' Protection Acts there is no requirement that a performer's consent to another doing any of the above acts in respect of his performance must be in writing. The Act does not prescribe the manner or form in which a consent is to be given except that it may be given in relation to a specific performance, a specified description of performances, or to performances generally. Where there is more than one performer giving a performance then the consent of each is necessary for the purposes of the Act.

Where there is an infringement of a performer's rights by making a recording (except for private purposes) or live broadcast of a performance without his consent, if it is shown that at the time a person believed on reasonable grounds that consent had been given damages are not recoverable by the performer but that does not deprive him of other redress under the Act. It remains to be seen what grounds the courts will accept as evidence of the existence of reasonable belief that consent has been given. Where an artist attends and performs in a broadcasting studio, film studio, film location or sound recording studio there is a reasonable inference of his having consented to the broadcasting, filming or recording of his performance.

Rather more difficult is the situation of "secondary infringements" as when a recording is shown or played in public or broadcast. A performer's rights are infringed by so doing only if a person knew or had reasonable grounds for believing the recording was made without a performer's consent. Knowledge can in law be imputed; it is not enough simply not to ask where to do so would be reasonably prudent and would be expected. This is material in present times in view of the extent of the exploitation of recorded performances in many forms.

Although one may be left to infer consent, the reality and extent of the consent may come to be judged from the contractual terms on which a performer was engaged.

Furthermore, as the Act expressly makes it an offence for a person to represent falsely that he has authority to give consent on behalf of another, unless he believes on reasonable grounds he was so authorised, it seems a person can give consent on behalf of a performer as was permitted under the repealed legislation but which required the consent to be in writing. Thus when reliance is placed on a vicarious consent it should be had in writing. Rather like the rules of "fair dealing" with copyright works so the Act (by section 189 and in schedule 2) correspondingly specifies acts which may be done yet not infringe a performer's rights. The schedule is extensive but the following are the most material and salient of the permitted acts which have the effect of curtailing a performer's rights:

1. dealing with a performance or recording for the purposes of criticism or review of the performance, the recording or the work performed; also for the purpose of reporting current events;

2. the incidental inclusion of a performance or recording in a sound recording, film or broadcast; or anything done in relation to copies

of or the playing, showing or broadcasting of the sound recording, film or broadcast. Where a performance or recording comprises performance of both music and words (sung or spoken) the one is not to be regarded as incidental to the other;

3. the copying of a recording of a performance, the playing or showing of sound recordings, films broadcasts and the recording of broadcasts in the context of actual education, instruction or examination;

4. the showing or playing in public of a broadcast under conditions where no payment is actually made to see or hear the broadcast is not an infringement of a performer's rights in the performance or recording included in the broadcast, or in the sound recording or film which is broadcast;

5. the recording of a performance for the purpose of broadcasting, is not *per se* an infringement of a performer's rights provided no other use is made of the recording and the recording is destroyed within 28 days of being first used for broadcasting;

6. the recording of a performance for the purpose of supervision, record and control of programmes made by the BBC or under the rules of the ITC and by programme contractors.

An innovation of the Act which allows consents to be dispensed with arises under section 190. The Copyright Tribunal is empowered to allow a person wishing to make a recording from a previous recording of a "performance" (note, not a "qualified performance") to make a recording where (a) the identity or whereabouts of a performer cannot be ascertained by reasonable enquiry; or (b) a performer withholds his consent without adducing good reasons. Where the Tribunal gives the required consent then if the applicant and performer cannot agree on the payment to be made, the Tribunal is empowered to make an order as it sees fit. Because the right of consent conferred by the Act applies retrospectively to performances given before August 1, 1989, this section may be of use where hitherto the further exploitation of programmes has been prevented by trade union rules or artists individually.

A performer's rights, like the rights of copyright in a protected work, last for a specific period of time. The period is 50 years from the end of the calendar year in which the performance takes place. It appears there must be some degree of permanence about the performance for the rights to crystallise. In other words the consent right attaches for the 50 years to a recorded performance; it can hardly attach for that time to a mere actual "live" theatrical or concert performance or "live" broadcast performance.

Unlike the rights of copyright a performer's rights are strictly personal to the performer and cannot be assigned. However, the Act expressly declares the rights are transmissible on a performer's death so that the performer's personal representatives or the person to whom by will the rights have been given succeeds to the rights granted under the Act.

A Person Having Recording Rights

The rights of a performer outlined above are predicated on the simple and ordinary way of an individual giving a performance. Now under section 185 of the Act there emerges a third man, namely "a person having recording rights" meaning a person who is a party to and has the benefit of an exclusive recording contract.

An "exclusive recording contract" is defined as "a contract between a performer and another person under which that person is entitled to the exclusion of all other persons (including the performer) to make recordings of one or more of his performances with a view to their commercial exploitation." Commercial exploitation means "with a view to the recordings being sold or let for hire or shown or played in public." Bearing in mind the definition of "recording" as noted above it needs to be understood that recording rights are not limited to sound only but include film.

The Act prescribes qualifying conditions like those for performers but as regards a company or organisation, it further stipulates that the body must be one formed under the laws of a part of the United Kingdom or another qualifying country, and have a place of business at which substantial business activity is carried on.

A person having recording rights is invested with the same rights and for the same period of time as a performer. Those rights are infringed by a person who in relation to a performance without the consent of the person having recording rights or that of the performer, makes a recording of the whole or any substantial part of the performance otherwise than for his private and domestic use. Likewise if a person shows or plays in public or broadcasts the whole or any substantial part of a performance by means of a recording which was and which that person knows or has reason to believe was made without the appropriate consent. The infringement of rights by the importation of recordings or engaging in selling and hiring or distributing recordings noted above also applies.

The same qualifications to these rights being infringed where a person believed on reasonable grounds that consent to any of these activities had been given apply as do the rules on "fair dealing." A person having recording rights may assign or license them to another qualified person unless barred from doing so by the express terms of the contract. Any assignee or licensee is bound by the consents given by a performer.

Remedies

The remedies which the Act gives to performers and to persons having recording rights whose rights are infringed are the same. Apart from enacting offences and penalties, like those in the repealed Performers Protection Acts, the Act gives rights of civil redress, namely, damages and injunction as any breach of the rights is a breach of statutory duty. In addition an order for delivery up of illicit recordings can be sought and there is a right of seizure of illicit recordings found exposed for sale or otherwise immediately available for sale subject to prior notice being given to the police. These remedies and the the penal provisions of the Act correspond to those for infringement of copyright considered in Part 6, below.

Through the operation of its provisions the Act may protect the economic interests of a performer but it does not protect his personality, or his particular style or way of performance; it does not prevent another person from imitating or impersonating a performer. Redress for any unauthorised use of a performer's name or the appropriation of his reputation for the purposes of commerce can only be sought from the common law actions of passing off and unfair competition.

C. PERFORMANCES BY CHILDREN AND YOUNG PERSONS

The law relating to children participating in entertainment and performing is somewhat fragmented in as much as it is to be found in the general provisions of sections 22 to 30 of the Children and Young Persons Act 1933 and sections 37 to 43 of the Children and Young Persons Act 1963 and the Children (Performances) Regulations 1968 (S.I. 1968 No. 1728). Other later legislation concerning children and their employment does not impinge on their performing or participating in entertainment. (Children are persons under the age of 16; young persons are persons under the age of 18).

The 1968 Regulations established a uniform code of rules superseding the bye-laws of local authorities but their administration rests upon local authorities, or more particularly local education authorities. The Regulations apply to children up to the age of compulsory school attendance, *i.e.* up to and including the last day on which a child is subject to compulsory attendance. The provisions of the Acts of 1933 and 1963 dealing with performances abroad, with training and taking part in dangerous performances apply to young persons over the compulsory school age. The general restrictions on the employment of children under the age of 13 years and on the employment of children on a Sunday do not apply to employment in entertainment. However, the statutory control on child performances now established applies to virtually all kinds or forms of entertainment and performances and to both amateur as well as to professional performances.

THE LICENCE

By section 37 of the 1963 Act (as amended) it is necessary to have a licence granted by a local authority for a child to take part in a performance:

(a) in connection with which a charge is made (whether for admission or not); or

(b) in licensed premises (*i.e.* licensed under the Licensing Act 1964); or

(c) in any broadcast; or

(d) in any performance not falling within paragraph (c) above but included in a programme service within the meaning of the Broad-casting Act 1990.

A child is treated as taking part in a performance if he takes the place of a performer in any rehearsal or in any preparation for the recording of a performance. (By not mentioning the making of gramophone records it follows that strictly a child under 13 cannot be employed for the making of records and when above this age no licence is required).

Licences are not to be granted for a child under the age of 14 to perform unless the applicant declares there are special reasons for doing so. Briefly these are:

(a) the licence is required for acting and the part to be performed cannot be taken by an older child; or

(b) the licence is for dancing in ballet which does not form part of a general entertainment; or

(c) the nature of the child's part in the performance is wholly or mainly musical and either the performance is of this description or it consists of opera and ballet.

In two situations the need for a licence is dispensed with. The first is where in the six months preceding the performance the child has not taken part in any other performance of a type indicated above on more than three days. This dispensation applies to professional performances but rather it helps the situation of most amateur performances for if an amateur production with children runs for four nights a licence will not be needed unless it runs for longer with the same children. Even so, what may be called "the working conditions" prescribed in Part VI of the 1968 Regulations still apply in these circumstances.

The second exemption is when the performance is given under arrangements made by a school or body of persons approved by the Home Office or local authority and no payment in respect of the child's taking part in the performance is made to him or any person except to defray expenses. This covers the performance recognisably given for charity or as part of school activities. The Regulations have no application in this instance as any "working conditions" thought necessary would be contained in the approval given by the Home Office or local authority.

The Act does not define the meaning of the phrase to "take part in a performance" so that it must be construed in its ordinary meaning. It must include acting a part or role, performing in a manner which is directed, reciting a poem or the like, singing, dancing and playing an instrument. The place and circumstances of a performance are clearly relevant especially a performance on a stage or concert platform but the fact that a performance does not take place in public is not conclusive of whether a performance is subject to the law governing child perform-ances. The need for a licence for a child to perform may be avoided when either of the exceptions noted above can be applied—but the number of performances given by a child can be material in the aggregation of the total number of performances which are permissible within a 12 month period as mentioned below.

Power to License

The licensing powers of local authorities are to some extent discretionary as the 1963 Act requires an authority before granting a licence to be satisfied:

(a) that the child is fit to perform, that proper provision is made to secure his health and kind treatment, that arrangements are made to ensure that his education will not suffer, and that provision is made for any sums earned by the child to be protected; and

(b) that a licence can be granted in accordance with the rules contained in the Regulations.

Otherwise, if an application is properly made a local authority has no power to refuse a licence, for example, on the grounds that it does not approve of the role to be played or the performance generally. If an authority refuses a licence or revokes or varies a licence, then under the provisions of the Act it is required to give its reasons in writing. An appeal against such a decision or the imposition of a condition attaching to a licence (other than one which an authority is obliged to make) lies to a magistrates' court.

1968 REGULATIONS

The 1968 Regulations comprise 43 detailed rules and three schedules and reflect the principles laid down by the enactments for the welfare of children. The Regulations cover such matters as medical examination, the number of days in a week on which a child may perform and rehearse, the hours he can be away from home, rest periods between and the duration of performances and rehearsals, dressing room and like facilities accord-ing to age and sex, lodging accommodation and transport home, supervi-sion and control by a responsible person or "matron," school attendance and how earnings are to be dealt with. Part VI of the Regulations lays down the "working conditions" when no licence is required such as for amateur performances or otherwise as noted above.

The different circumstances under which performances take place in the present day world of entertainment are reflected in the Regulations. This is especially so in regard to filming and broadcasting where a certain flexibility is allowed over hours of work, night work and the like but within the limits laid down by the licensing authority.

Some restrictions and conditions apply for all licences whatever the age of the child or the type of performance. Thus a licence cannot be granted (except in a few special situations) for a child who, during the 12 months preceding the performance, has taken part in other performances on more than 79 days; for a child under 13 the number is 39 days. Again there is strict control over the granting of a licence for a performance which involves a child being away from his normal place of residence.

As for rehearsals, although these may not require a licence, a licensing authority must take rehearsal time within the 14 days prior to a performance into account when considering an application. Rehearsals on a performance day count in reckoning the hours of work and the number of performances allowed, and all rehearsals within a licence period count towards the total number of rehearsals and performances permitted in a week. The place of rehearsal, as much as the place of performance, is subject to approval by a licensing authority. Whether or not a performance is the subject of a licence, a child is not to be employed in any other form of employment or entertainment on the day on which the child performs or on the day immediately following. A child is deemed to be "employed" for this purpose if, even without receiving any reward, he assists in a trade or occupation carried on for profit.

Licensing Procedure

The licensing system set up by the 1963 Act and the 1968 Regulations requires an application to be made by the person generally responsible for arranging the production or performances and countersigned, by way of approval and support, by the child's parent or guardian. The form is detailed and comprehensive in that information is to be supplied about the performances and the arrangements for the child's welfare and schooling, other entertainment performances given by the child and other employment and earnings. Applications are submitted to the local (education) authority for the area in which the child resides. If the child resides abroad then the application is made to the authority for the area in which the applicant resides or has his place of business. Applications are required to be made 21 days before the day of the child's first performance.

Before granting a licence, a licensing authority can make what enquiries it considers necessary, for example, interviewing the applicant, parent and child, calling for a head teacher's report, having the child medically examined and enquiring about how the child's earnings from the engagement are to be dealt with (but not as to amount or adequacy of the fees payable) and the arrangements for his or her education or instruction during absence from usual school attendance. Where a licence is granted for performances which are to take place outside the area of the licensing authority, then particulars of the licence are sent by the licensing authority to the local authority for the area where the performances are to take place for that authority to see that the conditions of the licence are observed.

It is on the licence holder that the responsibility rests for complying with all the terms and conditions contained in the licence. For example, it is the licence holder who must ensure the approved arrangements for a child's education are carried out, that any injury or illness is notified to the parent and to the licensing authority; the duty does not rest on the teacher or the matron.

A licence holder is required to produce the licence at the place of performance on request to an authorised officer of a local authority or police officer. He can apply to the licensing authority for a variation of the licence should the need arise. The licence holder is also to keep certain records (in substance corresponding to the terms and conditions contained in the licence). These records must be retained for six months after the last performance to which a licence relates and produced on demand to an official of the licensing authority.

The enforcement of the law of child performances is secured by the powers of entry and inspection of premises conferred by the enactments on officials of local authorities and police officers. They are empowered to enter any place to which a licence authorising a child to perform or train relates, and to make enquiries about the child. Also these officials have a general power to enter broadcasting and film studios at any time to make enquiries as to children taking part in performances there. Other premises can be entered under the authority of a justice's warrant if there is reasonable cause to believe that employment is taking place or a child is performing or being trained in circumstances contrary to the law. If a person causes or procures a child, or being his parent allows a child to take part in a performance without a licence when one is required, or fails to observe any condition of a licence or knowingly or recklessly makes a false statement concerning an application for a licence, or being the licence holder fails to keep and produce the records required to be kept, then penalties of fines and imprisonment can be imposed by the courts.

Children Working Abroad

Provisions of the Children and Young Persons Act 1933 (as amended by the 1963 Act) govern performances for profit by children abroad and prohibit the training of children under 12 years for performances of a dangerous nature and restrict the training of young persons under 16 years for such performances without the licence of a local authority. A licence is personal to the young person concerned and is granted on terms and conditions after enquiry by the authority but it cannot be refused if the local authority are satisfied that the person is fit and willing to be trained and proper arrangements are made for his or her protection. There is a right of appeal to a magistrates' court respecting a licence and there are penalties for contraventions of the provisions of the Act. Dangerous performances are not defined except that they "include acrobatics and all performances as a contortionist."

As for children performing abroad except where a young person under 18 is only temporarily residing in this country, no person having charge or care of a person under 18 may allow him, and no person may cause or procure a person under 18 to go abroad (*i.e.* outside the United Kingdom) without a licence for the purpose of singing, playing, performing or being exhibited for profit, or taking part in any broadcast or performance which is recorded for use in a broadcast or in a film intended for public exhibition. A licence to perform abroad is granted by a police court magistrate, not a local authority. It can be granted for a person who is 14 but under 18 on such terms as are thought fit provided the licence is applied for by or with the consent of the parent or guardian, it is for a particular engagement, the person is fit, proper arrangements are made for his or her care, etc., while abroad, and the contract or document of engagement is understood by him or her. A licence can be granted for a child under 14 but only in the like circumstances as where a licence may be granted for a child under 13 to take part in a performance in the United Kingdom. Seven days notice of the intention to apply for a licence must be given to the police for the area in which the child resides to allow for the necessary enquiries to be made.

A licence cannot be granted for longer than three months at a time but it can be renewed; it can also be revoked or varied at the discretion of the court if reason is found for so doing. Security for the observance of the terms upon which the licence is granted can be required of the applicant by the court.

Contracts of Minors

The principles of the law of contracts of engagement have been outlined in Section A above, but it is appropriate to note the special considerations which apply to contracts for the engagement of young performers apart from the rules just reviewed. Contracts entered into with minors—persons under 18 years of age—provided they are generally beneficial to them are as binding and enforceable as if entered into with adults. It is not essential for the terms of a contract to be beneficial in every way as when considering a contract a court will view it as a whole weighing the onerous terms against the beneficial and decide on which side the balance lies. Because one term may be against a minor, such as a restriction on his appearances, that will not entitle a minor to repudiate his or her contract because he or she is a minor if it is shown that the term is a standard and reasonably justified term in all the circumstances.

Under the 1968 Regulations a parent is required to subscribe to the application for a licence and there must be shown to be satisfactory arrangements for safe-guarding the earnings of a child and there are other conditions to be satisfied. Thus a management engaging a child subject to the Regulations may be better protected from any question as to the enforceability of the contract than when engaging a minor who is above the age for the Regulations to apply to him or her. If the circumstances are that the engagement does not require a licence then as a precaution and to show that no unfair advantage has been taken of the child performer, either the contract of engagement should be countersigned by the child's parent or guardian, or the contract made with the parent for him to provide the services of the child.

D. EMPLOYMENT PROTECTION

In Section A the general principles of law affecting personal contracts were reviewed and in Sections B and C the statute law and regulations specifically governing the engagement and employment of performers. There is also the vast body of law enacted by Parliament, supplemented by regulations made by government departments, which is as much applicable to performers and others working in entertainment as it is to persons generally. This general law can be broadly classified as follows:

(a) the law as it affects the individual and in particular the contractual relationship which is formed when one person engages the personal services of another;

(b) the law concerning the status and recognition of trade unions, and employers' associations and the legal immunities conferred on their officials; industrial relations and the resources and procedures for conciliation; strikes and picketing;

(c) the law affecting discrimination in the selection, remuneration and conditions of employment offered to individuals;

(d) the law regulating working conditions and safety and health at places of work;

(e) the law of social security and compensation for industrial injuries.

In the following pages consideration is given to some aspects of the employment legislation which impinge on the engagement of performers and others in entertainment.

It has been mentioned earlier that a large proportion of persons engaged in entertainment are freelance and self-employed but it would be erroneous to conclude that therefore none of the law considered here has any relevance to persons who are not in every sense employees. The distinction between a contract of service (or contract of employment) and a contract for services is material for the application of much of the employment protection legislation, but it is immaterial for the purposes of the Equal Pay Act 1970, the Sex Discrimination Act 1975, the Race Relations Act 1976 and in regard to health and safety and environment laws.

The term "contract of employment" is defined by statute as "a contract of service or of apprenticeship, whether it is express or implied and (if express) whether it is oral or in writing." Furthermore let it be acknowledged that persons engaged in earning a living are workers whatever other titles or distinctions they may assume: as such they come within the scope of the Trade Union and Labour Relations Act 1974. Apart from a few technical exceptions, by this Act "worker" means "a person who works or normally works or seeks to work under a contract of employment, or under any other contract (whether express or implied, and, if express, whether oral or in writing) whereby he undertakes to do or perform personally any work or services for any other party to the contract who is not a professional client of his." However, it is chiefly an employee, meaning "an individual who has entered into or works under or, where the employment has ceased, worked under a contract of employment," who is given absolute rights and privileges by statute and in particular under the Employment Protection (Consolidation) Act 1978.

As apparent from its title the 1978 Act is an amalgamation of statutes but it has been further amended by later Employment Acts. So the 1978 Act deals with such matters as (a) the duty cast on employers to give written notification of the terms of employment; (b) the periods of notice required to be given to terminate an employment; (c) the rights of employees to guaranteed payments, redundancy payments, maternity leave and benefit; (d) the rules for the computation of an employee's continuity of employment, the calculation of normal working hours and a week's pay all of which can be material to an employee's entitlement to and assessment of payments which can be claimed under the 1978 Act.

Because of the scope and complexity of this legislation only those aspects of it dealing with (a) the notification of the terms of employment; (b) the giving of notice of termination; (c) redundancy; (d) unfair dismissal; and (e) fixed term contracts are outlined in the following pages.

Particulars of Terms of Employment

There is a statutory obligation on an employer not later than 13 weeks after the beginning of an employee's employment to give to the employee a written statement of the terms of the employment. The statutory notice is to specify:

(a) the parties to the contract of employment;

(b) the date of the commencement of the employment and if the contract is for a fixed term the date of expiration;

(c) whether any employment with a previous employer counts as part of the employee's continuous period of employment and if so, the date when the continuous period of employment began;

(d) the scale of remuneration or method of calculating it;

(e) the intervals at which remuneration is paid, namely, weekly, monthly, or by some other period;

(f) the terms and conditions relating to hours of work (including any terms and conditions relating to normal working hours);

(g) any terms and conditions relating to holidays, public holidays and holiday pay and entitlement to accrued holiday pay on termination of the employment, sickness or injury and any provision for sick pay, and pensions and pension schemes;

(h) the length of notice which an employee is obliged to give and is entitled to receive;

(i) the title of the job which the employee is employed to do;

(j) information about disciplinary rules, where these may be seen, how any grievance relating to the employment can be pursued and dealt with.

Any changes in the terms of employment must be notified in writing by not later than one month after the changes. There is a general exemption from the obligation to provide a written notice of the terms of employment to persons whose hours of employment are normally less than 16 a week.

In lieu of notifying employees individually of the detailed terms of employment an employer is permitted in the statement to refer an employee to some document containing these detailed terms but the document must be reasonably available or accessible to the employee in the course of his employment. Where persons are engaged on the standard contracts and conditions of the collective agreements considered in this book it can be said with some justification that these requirements of the 1978 Act have been met. Even so, as a further precaution by displaying general details of conditions of engagement on notice boards at places of employment the requirements of the 1978 Act will be met.

An employee has the right to be given at the time of the payment of his wages or salary an itemised statement in writing showing the gross amount of pay, details of deductions and the net sum due. When there is included with the amount such items as royalties or other like payments these must be shown separately.

Termination of Employment

There are minimum periods of notice prescribed for the termination of any contract of employment which has exceeded a month's continuous service. An exception is made for a contract for a specific task which is not expected to last more than three months unless the employee is employed continuously for longer than this period. Before the expiry of the one month period an employer can (subject to what is said below) dismiss an employee summarily, but thereafter an employee is entitled to receive not less than the period of notice prescribed by the 1978 Act. However, to overcome the device of issuing successive contracts for a fixed term of one month or less to avoid the need to give the prescribed notice the 1978 Act expressly provides that any such contract of a person who has been continuously employed for three months or more is to be treated and have effect as if it were for an indefinite period. The 1978 Act expressly preserves the right of the parties to treat a contract as terminable without notice by reason of such conduct by either party as would by law entitle the other party to terminate the contract, for example, the grave misconduct by the employee, or the failure of an employer to pay the wages or salary due.

The period of notice which an employer must give to an employee to terminate a contract of employment is:

(a) if the person has been continuously employed for one month or more but less than two years, one week's notice;

(b) if continuously employed for two years or more but less than 12 years, one week for each year of employment;

(c) if continuously employed for 12 years or more then not less than 12 week's notice.

The notice required to be given by an employee to his employer who has been continuously employed for one month or more is one week only. These rules of minimum notice apply to part-time employees whose hours of employment amount to 16 hours a week or more.

The above are the statutory minimum obligatory periods of notice but a longer period may be mutually agreed upon as a term of the contract of employment. When the contractual period is longer than the obligatory period the latter counts at the end of the contractual period of notice. Thus if the contractual period is four weeks and the obligatory period is one week the latter will apply to the fourth week, and if two weeks it will apply to the third and fourth week of the contractual period. The significance of this is that if the employer gives notice of termination then during the obligatory period the employee can give written counter notice to terminate the employment but still the termination is deemed to be that of the employer's. Even so the employer is then entitled to give counter notice to the employee requiring him in effect to work out the contractual period of notice. If the employee fails to comply with the request without good reason—such as that he is required to start very promptly in his new employment—that may justify an employer refusing to pay redundancy money. Such a refusal can be referred to an industrial tribunal for adjudication.

During the obligatory period an employee is entitled to his minimum remuneration irrespective of whether he or the employer has given notice of termination. When notice is given by the employer by reason of redundancy then if the employee has completed or will have completed two years of continuous employment when the notice expires, the employer must allow the employee a reasonable amount of time off without loss of pay to look for new employment or make arrangements for training for future employment.

Where an employer terminates an employee's contract of employment with or without notice or where an employee's employment is for a fixed term and the contract of employment is not renewed, then if on the effective date of termination the employee has been continuously employed for six months the employee is entitled to request a written statement giving particulars of the reasons for dismissal. Complaint can be made to an industrial tribunal by an employee if an employer refuses to provide the written statement, or on the grounds that the particulars given are inadequate or untrue. If the tribunal finds the complaint well founded it may make a declaration of its findings of the reasons for the dismissal and award the employee a sum equal to two weeks pay.

Hours of work are irrelevant to a person's claims based on any of the discriminatory enactments but they are relevant to qualifying for payments under the 1978 Act. There must be a minimum of eight hours worked per week for there to be any rights under any of the provisions of the 1978 Act. For a person who works at least eight but less than 16 hours per week the qualifying period to claim any payments under the 1978 Act is five years. It is only persons employed for 16 hours or more per week who qualify for redundancy payment or compensation for unfair dismissal subject to their having a minimum of two years' continuous service.

Redundancy

Redundancy arises where an employee is dismissed on account of either:

(a) an employer ceasing or intending to cease carrying on the business for the purpose of which the employee was employed or at the place where the employee was employed; or

(b) the requirements of the business for the employee to carry out work of the particular kind or at the particular place have ceased or diminished or are expected to do so.

In addition where the amount of an employee's remuneration depends on his being provided with work, as with piece-work and other manual occupations, but because of lay-offs or short-time working the employee suffers a loss of pay, then if the conditions prescribed by the 1978 Act are satisfied the employee can claim to have been made redundant. When a pregnant woman exercises her rights to return to her employment after confinement but is not permitted to do so by her employer, then she is to be treated as having been made redundant.

The basic qualification for entitlement to redundancy payment is for an employee to have been continuously employed by his employer for two years on the date the employment ceases. The rules for determining continuity of employment to establish an entitlement to redundancy payment and what constitutes normal working hours and weekly pay for the purposes of calculating the amount due to an employee are set out in the detailed schedules to the 1978 Act. An employee will not be entitled to redundancy payment in the following circumstances:

(a) he has attained the normal retiring age of 65 (60 for females);

(b) he has unreasonably refused the offer of alternative employment;

(c) he was engaged under a fixed term contract of one year or more and waived any entitlement to redundancy payment;

(d) his employment was terminated because of his misconduct.

When there are to be changes in working conditions or a re-organisation of work such as to affect a person's employment then before the changes are made an employer ought to offer to renew or re-engage the employee(s) concerned. The offer need not be in writing but there may not be gaps of more than four weeks between the ending of the present employment and the starting of the new. If the offer does not affect the capacity and place in which an employee is to be employed and the other terms and conditions of the employment do not differ from those of the previous contract, or if there is a difference but the offer is of suitable employment in relation to the employee, then in either case if the employee unreasonably refuses the offer he forfeits any entitlement to redundancy payment by reason of the termination of his employment.

When the terms of the new contract are different from the corresponding terms and conditions of the previous contract, or there is a change in the capacity and place in which an employee is employed there is automatically a trial period of four weeks or such longer period as mutually agreed in writing. If during the trial period either the employee or the employer terminates the contract by due notice the effect is that the employee's dismissal and termination of employment count as from the ending of the previous contract. If the employee unreasonably terminates the contract and trial period then, as if he had unreasonably refused the offer of the renewal or re-engagement of his employment, he will forfeit his entitlement to redundancy payment.

When there is a change of ownership of a business whether the change occurs by virtue of the sale of the business or operation of law, if the new owner renews the contract of employment or re-engages the employee then the same situation exists as when a present employer renews or re-engages an employee as noted above.

An employee who is engaged under a contract of employment of definite duration, *i.e.* for a fixed term, is entitled to redundancy payment if it is not renewed. Where the contract is for two years or more this entitlement can be waived in writing by the employee before the term expires. The waiver can be a term of the contract itself or made separately as when an employee agrees to accept a bonus or *ex gratia* payment in lieu of the redundancy payment. If such a fixed term contract is renewed or the employee re-engaged then any arrangement about waiving future redundancy payment must be re-affirmed as being applicable to the renewed contract or re-engagement.

Part IV of the Employment Protection Act 1975 prescribes the procedure for handling redundancies. Consultation with a recognised union is required at least 30 days before the first dismissal where 10 or more employees (90 days for 100 or more employees) are to be dismissed within a period of 30 days at one establishment. Notice of the intended dismissals must also be given to the Secretary of State for Employment; failure to do so may lead to a reduction in an employer's rebate from the redundancy fund. These requirements do not apply where the employees concerned are under a fixed term contract of 12 weeks or less, or are employed to perform a specific task not expected to last for more than 12 weeks unless in either case the employment does in fact continue for more than 12 weeks.

Unfair Dismissal

Protection against the unfair dismissal of employees was first conferred by the Trade Union and Labour Relations Act 1974 but now Part V of the 1978 Act applies. The right not to be unfairly dismissed is a statutory right and is distinct from wrongful dismissal meaning dismissal in breach of the terms of the contract of employment; even so the two may overlap. Unfair dismissal is separate and distinct from redundancy as except for discriminatory redundancy, redundancy confers no right of re-instatement or compensation but only the right to redundancy payment if the employee qualifies in the way outlined above.

The protection against unfair dismissal extends to virtually all employees, the important exceptions or qualifications being as follows:

(a) part-time workers serving less than 16 hours a week;

(b) a person who has attained the age of 65 for a male, or 60 for a female, on the effective date of termination or, if under this age, has attained the normal retiring age for persons employed by his employer;

(c) a person who works mainly overseas;

(d) a person who has not been continuously employed for one year ending with the effective date of termination.

Eligibility

To be eligible to present a complaint of unfair dismissal an employee must have been continuously employed for two years. By the Employment Act 1980 (as amended) a concession is made in favour of small undertakings. As a result the right not to be unfairly dismissed does not apply to an employee "if the period (ending with the effective date of termination) during which the employee was continuously employed did not exceed two years, and at no time during that period did the number of employees employed by the employer for the time being of the dismissed employee, added to the number employed by any associated employer, exceed 20." This qualification or condition for protection against unfair dismissal can be important where, for example, a theatrical or any other company has only a nucleus of staff and engages artists and the like freelance who do not count as employees but the condition about the period of time and number of employees needs to be underlined.

An employee is treated as dismissed for the purposes of the Act where his contract of employment is terminated:

(a) by the employer with or without notice; or

(b) where an employee is employed for a fixed term and the term expires without being renewed under the same contract (but subject to what is said below); or

(c) when an employee terminates the contract without notice where he is entitled to do so by reason of the employer's conduct, that is to say, constructive dismissal.

Constructive Dismissal

Constructive dismissal occurs when by the action of an employer it is impossible for an employee to continue with the contract of employment, as when an employer transfers a place of work to another location but by the terms of the contract of employment the employee is not automatically compelled to move to a new work place; or where the employer has so changed the conditions of work or employment as in effect to be in breach of the contract of employment such as to entitle the employee to treat the contract as repudiated by the employer and therefore at an end.

Fair Dismissal

It is against unfair dismissal that an employee is protected and so the onus is placed on the employer to justify the dismissal as being fair by showing it was on account of one or more of the reasons stipulated in the 1978 Act, or some other substantial reason of a kind such as to justify the dismissal of a person holding the position which the employee held. So a dismissal may be fair if it was on account of one of the following reasons expressly recognised by the 1978 Act; namely:

(a) the capabilities or qualifications of the employee to do the work for which he was employed meaning his skill, aptitude, health, physical and mental condition, or where relevant his holding of academic, technical or professional qualifications;

(b) the conduct of the employee;

(c) the employee becomes redundant so as a consequence can be treated in accordance with the rules of redundancy;

(d) to continue the employment would be a breach of duty or restriction imposed by any enactment.

Unfair Dismissal

Dismissal is declared to be unfair when it is for certain particular reasons namely:

(a) where under the rules prescribed in the Employment Act 1982 the dismissal arises from an employee's membership or non-membership of an independent trade union, or an employee taking part in the activities of his union outside working hours or within the working hours allotted for this purpose;

(b) a female employee is pregnant or for reasons connected with her pregnancy (but the 1978 Act qualifies this to some extent), or is not permitted to return to work when she has elected to do so;

(c) discriminatory redundancy.

Dispute Procedure

If the fairness or grounds for dismissal are disputed an employee must normally present a claim within three months of the effective date of the termination of his employment to an industrial tribunal. A conciliation officer will normally first endeavour to obtain a settlement of the issue but otherwise it will be dealt with by an industrial tribunal. It is for the employer to show that the reason for the dismissal falls within one of the categories listed above and that the dismissal was fair and justified. If on consideration of the circumstances and having regard to the equity and substantial merits of the case a tribunal considers that the employer did not act reasonably and the dismissal was unfair, the tribunal can award compensation to the employee. A tribunal has the power to order the re-instatement or re-engagement of the employee if he so requests unless the employer shows that it was not practical to delay engaging a replacement, or that a reasonable time had elapsed before engaging a replacement without the employer receiving a request from the employee to be re-instated or re-engaged. If an employer does not comply with such an order the dismissal becomes in a sense "aggravated" and provision is made in the 1978 Act for the award of considerably increased compensation to the employee.

The award of compensation for unfair dismissal made by a tribunal consists of a "basic" award which is assessed according to an employee's age, length of service and pay, and a "compensation" award. A tribunal has discretion over the amount of any award having regard to the loss sustained by the employee but subject to the limit imposed by the 1978 Act. There is no appeal from the decision of a tribunal except on a point of law.

The setting up of the industrial tribunals has provided the means for the simple and inexpensive settlement of issues over dismissal and the payment of compensation but the ordinary courts still have jurisdiction in some situations. Fine distinctions can be made over wrongful dismissal and unfair dismissal. There is a right of appeal to the courts on matters of law from the decision of an industrial tribunal and the courts have jurisdiction in those cases where the industrial tribunals have no power such as when issues arise over long fixed term contracts of employment and when persons are not protected by the 1978 Act against unfair dismissal. The amount of compensation which an employee may be justified in claiming in some circumstances may exceed the limits which an industrial tribunal can award so that the case must come before the courts. Moreover, in the sphere of entertainment issues may arise which would not fall within the competence of an industrial tribunal such as publicity, the right to accept other engagements, the extent of a management's or other employer's right to exploit the products of an artist's services.

Fixed Term Contracts

There are many aspects of the legislation which deserve more consideration than is possible here but fixed term contracts merit particular attention because of their special treatment under the 1978 Act. For a contract to be one of a fixed term within the meaning and for the purposes of the 1978 Act its duration must be fixed in point of time, its starting and ending must be certain even if it can be prematurely terminated by notice within the stated period. A contract which purports to fix the duration by reference to the happening of some future event although bound to happen, such as the end of a run of a play, or until the completion of some particular employment does not count. If a contract is to do a particular task or render some specific service when the task or service has been completed the contract is automatically spent; dismissal or redundancy do not arise.

A contract of employment terminable by either party giving a stated period of notice, for example one month, is clearly one of indefinite duration. Furthermore when considering the rules for the giving of notice of termination of employment it was noted that where a fixed term contract of one month or less is successively renewed for a continuous period of three months or more, the contract is to be treated and have effect as if the employment were for an indefinite period. Thus in neither instance can the rights and obligations set forth in the 1978 Act be avoided.

When a contract of employment is for a fixed term it does not follow that an employee cannot qualify for redundancy payment. The exception is the contract for a fixed term of one year or more and the employee has specifically agreed in writing as a condition of the engagement, or separately during its term, to waive his entitlement to payment. The non-renewal of a fixed term contract may constitute unfair dismissal but claims under the Act for unfair dismissal can similarly be waived if the contract is for one year or more and the dismissal consists only of the expiry of the contract without its being renewed.

The rationale of these provisions which permit a waiver of rights is that in the particular circumstances of the employment—and entertainment is an example—an employee is fully aware of his standing with an employer from the start of the employment and the agreed remuneration may be at a rate which takes account of these concessions. Even so the courts view cautiously any signing away of statutory rights and provisions purporting to forego rights will be construed strictly. Indeed, such provisions are likely to be construed less favourably for an employer than for an employee as the latter will more likely be regarded as at a disadvantage in any negotiations about the terms of his employment than the employer.

This strict and cautious approach has been highlighted in cases where the courts have had to consider successive contracts and decide whether there has been an extension or renewal of a contract, or a re-engagement and the consequences of the distinctions. Renewal imports continuity of employment on substantially the same terms as then prevailing, but if new terms are accepted (and still more if there is a break in the employment), then more likely there is a re-engagement. In the latter situation the employment and the rights and obligations under the 1978 Act will need to be considered wholly afresh. If the situation is one of extension or renewal then the provisions of the last and subsisting contract will govern the rights and obligations between the employer and employee. Only if the later contract is for a fixed term and of the requisite length of time can the issue of the waiver by an employee of his right to redundancy payment or claims for unfair dismissal become real. If any waiver of statutory rights in a present contract is to carry over and continue to apply to a new contract this needs to be made clear especially in regard to any waiver of redundancy payment. There can be little if any doubt that the courts will require the same certainty in regard to any waiver of rights in the event of unfair dismissal. The following case is illustrative of the difficulties.

A writer was employed on a three year contract which was carried on for another two years and then for one more year, so that apparently there were six years of continuous service. The court was prepared to accept that despite minor alterations there had been a renewal of the three year contract when it was extended by another two years. However, the contract for the last and sixth year was so different from the first as to be a wholly new contract and as this was for less than two years the court held that the writer was entitled to compensation when it was not renewed. (Note that the two years is now one year). The fact that the writer in the earlier contract had waived his right to compensation for unfair dismissal did not prejudice his entitlement to compensation as the two contracts were separate.

When an employee continues working beyond the date of expiration of his fixed term contract and without its being formally renewed, it will be inferred as a matter of law that the employment will have been renewed from week to week or month to month or other period corresponding to the frequency of payment of the employee's salary. As a consequence the contract of employment is one of indefinite duration and will be subject to the provisions of the 1978 Act conferring the right not to be unfairly dismissed and to redundancy payment in the event of redundancy.

E. INDUSTRIAL INJURIES AND SAFETY AT WORK

The statute law reviewed above deals with the "hiring and firing" of employees and the terms and conditions of their employment. Another vital aspect of employment is the protection of employees from the dangers and risks of accident, injury and illness which may be suffered in the course of their employment. The roots of an employer's obligations to protect employees and to pay compensation for injury suffered by them in the course of their employment lie in the principle formulated by the common law that an employer has the duty to carry out his operations and enterprise in a manner and with such care as not to expose his employees to unreasonable risks of injury or harm. This principle has been refined so that employers have a duty to provide:

(a) safe premises, plant and machinery;

(b) a safe system of working;

(c) adequate supervision and instruction; and

(d) competent fellow employees.

These duties are not absolute but must be performed and observed with all due and reasonable care.

Employer's Duty of Care

The fair and just application of these principles have at times been hampered by traditional concepts and ideas about the relationship between "master and servant"—the designation once general in the law of employment—but which are no longer supportable in present day working conditions and with the modern legal and business structure of industry and commerce. Parliament has by statute intervened to correct anomalies and impose additional duties on employers. Since the passing of the Law Reform (Personal Injuries) Act 1948 an employer cannot avoid liability for the breach of his duty of care on the grounds that the injury or damage suffered by an employee was due to the negligence or fault of a fellow employee even if the fellow employee was disobeying instructions. By the passing of the Employers Liability (Defective Equipment)

Act 1969 an employer is rendered liable for injury or damage suffered by an employee due to the defective state or condition of equipment, the expression "equipment" meaning "any plant, machinery, vehicle, aircraft and clothing." The liability is strict for it is not a question of whether the employer was negligent or not, or that the defect in the equipment was latent and not discoverable by the employer, or that the equipment was obtained from a reputable supplier. Any injury suffered in this way is deemed to be due to the negligence of the employer, but the defect must be attributable in whole or in part to the fault of a third party whether that party can be identified or not. These two Acts both expressly bar any contracting-out but do not affect the law relating to contributory negligence.

By the Law Reform (Contributory Negligence) Act 1945 a claim for compensation due to another's negligence can no longer be defeated because of the claimant being partly at fault through himself not having taken due care. So an employer cannot avoid liability for injury suffered by an employee although the injury was sustained in part by the employee's own fault or negligence but the amount of compensation will be reduced by an amount proportionate to the share of blame attaching to the employee.

The law requires employers in the discharge of the general duty of care and the observance of statutory duties to have regard not only for the careful man but also for the man who is inattentive to such a degree as can normally be expected of working men. The endeavour to get quick results, the likelihood of "cutting corners"—especially in the pressures which can arise in entertainment—need to be borne in mind. The number of accidents occurring from the use of electrical musical instruments and sound amplification equipment in places not purposely constructed as studios and theatres is perhaps a sombre demonstration of the lack of supervision and inattention to risks and dangers often due to haste.

Further Duties

Additional duties for the protection and safety and for the health and welfare of employees have now been imposed by statutes which have outpaced the limited provisions of past public health enactments dealing only with matters of cleanliness and sanitation. The most important of these are the Factories Act 1961 and the Offices, Shops and Railway Premises Act 1963. In many ways they complement each other in their scope and purpose and requirements for registration and powers of officials to make inspections. The condition and structure and maintenance of premises, the provision of washing and changing facilities, fire precautions, the guarding and operation of machinery, the provision of first aid are some of the matters covered although to a considerable extent the finer details and duties of employers are contained in the large number of regulations made under these enactments.

The Factories Act 1961 applies to premises in which persons are employed in manual labour for the making, repairing, alteration, etc., of articles and when the work is being carried on by way of trade or for the purposes of gain. But more relevant here is to note that among other provisions defining places to which the Act applies there are included the following:

(a) "any premises in which the making, adaptation or repair of dresses, scenery or properties is carried on incidentally to the production, exhibition or presentation by way of trade or for purposes of gain of cinematograph films or theatrical performances, not being a stage or dressing room of a theatre in which only occasional adaptations or repairs are made;" also

(b) "any premises in which the production of cinematograph films is carried on by way of trade or for purposes of gain, so however, that the employment at any such premises of performers and attendants on such performers shall not be deemed to be employment in a factory."

Thus places used for entertainment are subject to the provisions of the Factories Act if there is carried on there more than occasional adaptation and repair of costumes, scenery and properties. Film studios are clearly within the provisions of the Act but the artists performing there and their attendants are excluded from any rights or benefits otherwise conferred on employees by the Act. When a factory is set up there is a duty on the occupier of the premises to give notice of this to the district Factory Inspector. Various notices have to be displayed on the premises, records kept and returns made annually to the Factory Inspector. Various powers of entry are conferred on Inspectors to enter premises to see that the requirements of the Factory Regulations are being observed.

The Offices, Shops and Railway Premises Acts 1963 affects places used for entertainment as it applies to all offices. Any part of a building which is set aside for administration, the handling of money, operating telephones or clerical work is an office and so subject to the Act although the rest of the building with which the activities of the office are concerned such as a theatre, concert hall or club, is not subject to the Act. Premises which are exempt from the Act are those where the sum total of hours worked in any week is normally not more than 21. The administration of the Act rests with the district councils and Greater London Boroughs (not the Factory Inspectorate) but otherwise the scope and application of the Act corresponds with the factory legislation.

The general duty of care owed by employers to their employees formulated by the common law is therefore supplemented and expanded by numerous enactments and regulations any infringement of which can result in penalties being imposed by the courts. Although an employee cannot claim compensation for the mere breach by an employer of a statutory duty, if he suffers injury or harm and if there is established a causal connection between the infringement of a regulation and the injury suffered, then compensation for the injury will be recoverable irrespective of any question of negligence on the part of either the employer or the employee. The common law duty of care may itself sustain a claim for compensation since this forms a substratum to the whole question of liability, but where in the particular circumstances no negligence can be proved the alternative ground of liability for breach of a statutory duty may be supportable.

Health and Safety at Work Act 1974

The passing of the Health and Safety at Work Act 1974 (in what follows referred to as "the Act") brought about a major reform of the law respecting working conditions and the safety of employees. As a result of the implementation of the regulations referred to below some of the provisions and rules provided for in the enactments mentioned above will be superseded. The Act imposes on an employer a positive duty "to ensure so far as is reasonably practicable, the health, safety and welfare at work of all his employees." This is explained as meaning that "the time, trouble, cost and physical difficulty of taking measures to avoid risks are not wholly disproportionate to [the duty]. The size or financial position of the employer is not to be taken into account in this calculation."

The Act applies to all employment and it embraces welfare. It requires positive action for the achievement of its objectives and so confers on officials more far reaching powers of enquiry and inspection than under earlier factory legislation. Inspectors have powers to serve improvement notices to secure compliance with the statutory regulations, or prohibition notices to stop the carrying on of activities or prevent activities which involve the risk of serious personal injury. There is a right of appeal with regard to any such notices to an industrial tribunal and to the Court of Appeal.

It is by the detailed and technical regulations made under the Act that rules are prescribed about working conditions, for the safety of employees and their protection from the harmful effects of industrial processes. As a result of the need to implement European Community directives on health and safety at work a series of new regulations with codes of practice is being introduced. The duties about to be prescribed are not completely new but these regulations will repeal and amend certain existing rules and clarify and make more explicit what is in current health and safety law. Furthermore these new regulations will in some respects extend the duties of employers to members of the public who may be affected by the work being done. Also self-employed persons will have duties under the regulations to protect themselves and others.

The first of the new regulations is the Management of Health and Safety at Work Regulations 1992 (S.I. 1992 No. 2051) which set out some broad general duties which will apply to almost all kinds of work and are aimed mainly at improving health and safety management. An obligation is placed on employers to assess the risks to the health and safety of employees and anyone else who may be affected by the work activity carried on, and to make arrangements for putting into practice the preventative and protective measures that follow from the assessment. Where an employer has five or more employees these assessments and the arrangements must be written down. There are also included rules concerning consultation with employees on matters of safety, and for the supervision, training etc., of employees, including that of temporary workers. The regulations also place duties on employees to follow health and safety instructions and to report any danger.

Other regulations about to be introduced will prescribe detailed rules respecting work equipment safety, the manual handling of loads, work place conditions, personal protective equipment, and display screen equipment.

A person's civil rights at common law to recover compensation for accident, injury, illness or death arising in the course of employment are not affected by the Act. Indeed, it confers civil remedies for the breach of its provisions. There is further sanction given to the Act by its swingeing penal provisions which in some cases involves fines of unlimited amount and imprisonment. The shield of company anonymity is torn away because any executive, manager, secretary or other officer with whose consent or connivance or by whose neglect an offence or contravention of the Act is committed, is rendered personally liable.

The Act casts a general duty on an employee while at work to take reasonable care for the health and safety of himself and others who may be affected by his acts or omissions at work and to co-operate with his employer in the observance and compliance with any duty or relevant statutory provisions imposed on the employer. If an employee fails to discharge a duty he too is liable to a penalty under the Act; if due to his fault or negligence a fellow employee suffers injury or harm the civil liability of the employer for the misdeeds of the employee remains and is not affected by this provision of the Act.

Insurance

Generally employers and persons engaged in business or some enterprise will take the precaution of obtaining insurance cover. Now by the

Employers' Liability (Compulsory Insurance) Act 1969 an employer carrying on any business is compelled to insure against liability for personal injury or disease sustained by his employees in the course of their employment in Great Britain. The duty does not apply to employees who are close relatives of the employer or to employees who are not ordinarily resident in Great Britain; a few statutory undertakings are exempted from the Act. The obligation to insure applies to most employers as the expression "business" is defined as including "a trade or profession, and includes any activity carried on by a body of persons, whether corporate or unincorporated." Detailed regulations prescribe the amount for which an employer is to maintain insurance and what policy of insurance satisfies the general requirements of the Act. Certificates of insurance are required to be displayed at each place of business where employees whose claim may be subject to an indemnity under the insurance are employed and to be produced to inspectors. Failure to insure is a criminal offence and where the offence is committed by a corporation then if this has occurred with the consent or connivance of or facilitated by any neglect by a director, manager, secretary or other officer of the corporation, then that person is also liable to criminal proceedings and a fine.

Employee's Property

One last consideration is that of an employer's duty respecting the property of an employee. Both the Factories Act 1961 and the Offices, Shops and Railway Premises Act 1963 lay upon employers an obligation to provide suitable accommodation for the placing and storage of employees' clothing not required during the hours of employment. The risk or danger of theft has been held to be significant in deciding the suitability of the accommodation provided. Otherwise there is no general duty of care owed by employers to employees for the safety and care of their possessions and property brought to a place of work. The principle in fact rests on a case which concerned the theft of an actor's clothing and property from a dressing room.

F. DISCRIMINATION

The Equal Pay Act 1970, Sex Discrimination Act 1975 (as amended) and Race Relations Act 1976 can be considered in combination for they have as their purpose the elimination of discriminatory acts and abuses against persons because of their sex or marital status or race. The scheme of this legislation is not only to provide means for the redress of individual grievances but by the setting up of the Commission for Racial Equality and the Equal Opportunities Commission to provide means for detecting and eliminating unfair and discriminatory practices. These Commissions can make investigations into practices and issue non-discrimination notices requiring the recipient to cease doing the acts found to be unlawful acts of discrimination or potentially discriminating practices. Only those aspects of the legislation relating to employment are considered here.

Racial Discrimination

The Race Relations Act 1976 is about the treatment of people on "racial grounds," *i.e.* on grounds of "colour, race, nationality or ethnic or national origins," and the treatment of people as members of a racial group, meaning "a group of persons defined by reference to colour, race, nationality or ethnic or national origins." The Act is concerned with the discrimination of all persons meaning:—

(a) direct discrimination, as when one person treats another less favourably than he treats or would treat other persons on social grounds; and

(b) indirect discrimination, as when a person, although applying a requirement or condition to people of other racial groups, applies a requirement or condition to a considerably smaller proportion of the same racial groups that a person within that proportion cannot comply with it and it is to that person's detriment because he cannot comply with it; and

(c) discrimination by victimisation, *i.e.* by treating persons differently on account of their having asserted any rights under the Act or taken steps to ensure the enforcement of its provisions.

Thus to discriminate within the meaning of the Act means to treat a person in any of these ways.

The Act renders it unlawful for a person in relation to employment by him to discriminate against any person in the arrangement for selecting and offering employment, in the terms and conditions of employment, by refusing or deliberately omitting to offer employment, in the opportunities or facilities given for promotion, training or advancing a person's career, and in the dismissal of a person. For the purposes of the Act employment means "employment under a contract of service or of apprenticeships or a contract personally to execute any work or labour," so that freelance, independent performers and others employed in entertainment and the performing arts are covered by the Act.

There is a limited right of discrimination where being of a particular racial group is a genuine occupational qualification for a job. The jobs within the exceptions are very few but include where "the job involves participation in a dramatic performance or other entertainment in a capacity for which a person of that racial group is required for reasons of authenticity" or where the job involves "participation as an artist's or photographic model in the production of a work of art, visual image or sequence of visual images for which a person of that racial group is required for reasons of authenticity." Another like exception applies to places where food or drink is served to and consumed by members of the public in a particular setting. In deciding if a particular job is one for which race, colour or nationality is a genuine qualification it is sufficient if only some of the duties of the job fall within these job descriptions. Even so there is a refinement as these exemptions do not apply to the filling of a vacancy "when the employer already has employees of the racial groups in question," who are capable of carrying out the duties and who it would be reasonable to employ and where the number of employees is sufficient to meet the employer's likely requirements in respect of those duties without undue inconvenience.

A complaint of discrimination is normally dealt with by an industrial tribunal, but the Act also prescribes for a complaint to be referred to a conciliation officer to endeavour to resolve a dispute and avoid the complaint needing to be determined by an industrial tribunal. If the matter is dealt with by a tribunal and it finds the complaint well founded it can (a) award compensation for loss of earnings and for other losses including prospective earnings and injured feelings (but up to the limit a tribunal is empowered to award for unfair dismissal); and (b) make a recommendation to the employer to obviate or reduce the adverse affect of the discrimination. If the employer fails to comply the tribunal can increase the award but not beyond the limit as above.

Equal Pay and Sex Discrimination

The aims of the Equal Pay Act 1970 and the Sex Discrimination Act 1975 are to secure equal treatment in employment of men and women, "employment" having the same meaning as in the context of the Race Relations Act. The requirements of both the Acts are generally satisfied in the entertainment business by the uniform minimum rates of pay and the terms of the collective agreements negotiated by the management associations and trade unions. However, in the application of the various agreements to individuals and especially when above minimum rates are paid, breaches of the Equal Pay Act may occur. Differences in fees may clearly be justifiable on the grounds of the roles individuals are to perform or their professional standing, but any differences of pay or treatment of members of a chorus, troupe of dancers or rank and file orchestral musicians may not be so easily justified.

As for the discrimination under the Sex Discrimination Act 1975 in essence the same concepts of direct and indirect discrimination, and discrimination by victimisation are to be found. Similarly in relation to employment it is unlawful to discriminate against a woman or against a person on grounds of his or her marital status in virtually the same ways or under the same conditions as outlined above in considering specifically racial discrimination.

Exceptions to discrimination are recognised where a person's sex is a genuine occupational qualification. Thus exemption is permitted when the essential nature of the job calls for a man (or woman) for reasons of physiology (excluding physical strength or stamina), or in dramatic performances or other entertainment for reasons of authenticity so that in either case the essential nature of the job would be materially different if carried out by a person of the other sex. Clearly so far as the casting of male and female roles is concerned this provision unequivocally confers exemption. Probably it would also apply to choristers and dancers so that if the lines of chorus and dancers were not evenly matched there would be no case to answer of discrimination. How any exemption could be justified for instrumental musicians is perhaps an open question.

G. PERSONS FROM ABROAD—WORK PERMITS

Because of the extent to which entertainment and the performing arts are supported by the exchange and engagement of persons from overseas a very brief explanation of the basic principles of immigration control and the procedure for the issue of work permits is included here.

Until 1962 the system of control and the issuing of work permits applied only to aliens but then it was extended but now the control is governed by the Immigration Act 1971 and the rules of practice for the administration of the Act promulgated from time to time by the Home Secretary.

In principle a person who is a British citizen and who holds a United Kingdom passport, or a person who has a certificate of patriality issued by a British Government representative overseas or by the Home Office, has an absolute and unrestricted right of entry into the country but all other persons, that is to say "non-patrials," can enter only with permission. A person on arriving in the United Kingdom must produce to the Immigration Officer a valid national passport or other document establishing his identity and nationality and furnish to the Immigration Officer such information as may be required for the purpose of deciding whether the person entering requires leave to do so and, if so, whether and on what terms leave should be given. Leave to enter will normally be given for a limited time and any conditions attached stated on admission and entered in a person's passport or travel documents.

Persons entering as visitors must be bone fide and if there is reason to believe that a person's real purpose is to take employment then permission will be refused. Businessmen—and doubtless impresarios, producers and promoters of entertainment come within this category—admitted as visitors are free to transact business during their visit. Self-employed persons such as writers and painters and the like may be admitted if the Immigration Officer is satisfied that they can support themselves and their dependants and do not intend to do work for which a work permit is necessary. Thus they can pursue their profession as a writer or composer, etc., and publish, perform or exhibit their work but cannot enter into employment.

A person entering to take up employment, apart from a few special categories of persons, can do so only if in possession of a work permit issued by the Department of Employment. However, the permit is not itself an entry clearance as the Immigration Officer can still refuse entry if his examination reveals good reason for doing so on general grounds of public good, or where false representations have been made or material facts concealed to procure the work permit, or the holder's true age puts him outside the limits of employment, or he does not intend to take the employment specified or is incapable of doing so. If the period of validity of the permit has expired the Immigration Officer may admit the person concerned if satisfied that circumstances beyond his control prevented his arrival before the permit expired and that the job is still open to him. A person over 16 years of age who is a foreign national, *i.e.* not a Commonwealth citizen who is admitted to take up employment for longer than three months, or for the purpose of a visit or business or self-employment for longer than six months is required to register with the police.

There are two special categories of foreign nationals to be considered:

(a) Nationals of EC Countries
   A national from one of the member countries of the European Community may be admitted on production of a national identity card in lieu of passports when visits are for six months or less. No work permit is required as an EC national can enter to take-up or seek employment, to set up in business or work as self-employed;

(b) Visa Nationals.

Persons who are nationals of listed foreign countries namely, Eastern European countries, the Russian Federation and other republics of the CIS, all Asian countries other than a few such as Israel, Japan, Turkey, all African countries other than Algeria, Ivory Coast, Morocco, Tunisia and the Republic of South Africa, and Cuba are required to produce to the Immigration Officer a passport or other identity document endorsed with a United Kingdom visa. Normally they will be refused entry if they are without a current visa. Where the purpose of entry is to take up employment, very often the possession of a work permit is a pre-requisite of the local British Consulate to the issuing of a visa.

Work Permits

The practice and procedure of the Department of Employment respecting work permits has undergone a major revision in recent times. A separate sub-Section of the Overseas Labour Section of the Department handles applications for entertainers, sportspersons and models as a class apart from other applications. In this study reference is only to entertainers.

Applications are made by the prospective employer to the Overseas Labour Section of the Department located at Sheffield on the form provided (Form WP3). As the staff of the Section are few in number and as over 6,500 applications are handled in a year applications are but rarely processed in less than four weeks.

In the form of application there is required to be to set down particulars of the employer, and of the overseas person to be employed (including particulars of the person's employment and engagements and major achievements over the preceding two years), and a description of the work offered and the terms of employment, and a statement of the action taken to engage United Kingdom or European Community nationals. The application must be signed by the employer except that if the employer has no United Kingdom presence it may be signed by a solicitor. The application incorporates a declaration attesting the correctness of the particulars given and that no person who is normally resident in the United Kingdom or a national of the European Community will be displaced or excluded as a result of the employment of the overseas national named in the application. Requests for further information may be made by the Section and enquiries conducted by correspondence and interview.

Where a group of artists or musicians is to be employed provision is made for the listing of the persons in the one application. With groups of up to 19 members a permit is issued for each member. For groups of 20 or more a letter of permission is addressed to the employer/representative and the Immigration Office of the port of entry notified when the details of the time and place of arrival are confirmed.

When a permit is granted it is sent to the employer who is responsible for forwarding it to the person concerned as it will need to be produced to the immigration authorities on entry to the United Kingdom. For those countries for which there is a visa requirement the application will need to be produced to the British consul in the country concerned.

The system of work permits is directed to protecting the employment opportunities of persons resident in this country. For this reason the payment offered by an employer and conditions of employment are material factors in the consideration of an application. In principle permits are issued only for top class international performers or to those possessing some exceptional talent. For a performer not so placed or established there must be produced evidence of attainment of professional skill and reputation—evidence of actual qualifications, previous professional engagements, reviews and publicity, a published recording of a performance. In the process of considering applications the Department of Employment regularly consults the appropriate management association and the performers' unions but the decision regarding an application rests with the Department. Sometimes wider considerations are brought to bear in the withholding or granting of a permit, such as that by the issuing of a permit further employment opportunities will be generated—such as in the film industry and where there are international reciprocal opportunities for employment of United Kingdom subjects.

With the operation of the system of work permits as applied to entertainment there are a few other points to note. An employer does not have to be an employer in the strict sense of the term. A promoter or agent may make application provided both are established. Where there is shown to be a continuity of bookings then a single permit or "season ticket" may be issued for a period of time. Permits are granted for specific employment or engagements so if additional paid employment is to be undertaken the Department should first be notified. Personal appearances and interviews do not count provided the person concerned does not, for example if a singer, sing his latest hit.

Although confirmation should first be sought from the Department in each case, permits are not normally required for performers taking part in specified annual international arts festivals, in cultural seasons and in charity shows, but it is only for those exact purposes for which the dispensation is given. Similarly with persons entering the United Kingdom for auditions or trials, but if such persons are to perform before a fee paying audience then application for a permit must first be made.

Part 6

THE ELEMENTS OF COPYRIGHT

A. INTRODUCTION

There is a significant difference between the creative activity of a writer, composer, or artist from that of the performer in that the activity of the former yields a material product whereas the activity of a performer does not. So it is that the creator of a work of literature, drama, music, painting, photography, sculpture and design automatically acquires a proprietary right in his work which the law protects as copyright. As the first owner of the copyright in his work, the creator is free to deal with his work as he chooses like any other of his property; he can keep it, make a gift of it, sell it and he can destroy it. The works which are protected by copyright, how protection is secured and how the rights which the law confers on works can be dealt with are the subject matter of this Part 6.

Until the beginning of the present century only literary, musical and artistic works as products of individual creation were afforded copyright protection. As new means of artistic expression were discovered, the photograph, the sound recording, and then the cinematograph film, the law had to accommodate these phenomena. Moreover, it had to take account of their most often being the product of a collaboration of persons brought together or assembled by entrepreneurs, themselves often creatures of the law, namely, the corporate enterprise or company.

It is perhaps worthy of note that two concepts or ideas have dominated the scope and rationale of copyright law as revealed from a study of the history of the law in England and France. English law was late in acknowledging any proprietary interests in an artistic or intellectual work as distinct from the ownership in the tangible property or material in which the work was set down. The right of an author of an unpublished work to decide if and when it should be printed and published had been established as a tenet of natural law and was re-affirmed by the judges in 1774. The first statute covering what is now recognised as copyright was passed in 1709 "for the encouragement of learning by the vesting of copies of published books in authors or purchasers of such copies," but what was protected were books and not works as such. This pre-occupation of the law with "property" was but a demonstration of the principle that he who invests his time and energies or money in a "product" has the right to exercise control over it to the exclusion of others.

Under French law which was emerging at about the same time, works were regarded as essentially the product of individual creation and achievement and so an extension of an author's personality. Thus the law conferred on an author rights ("droit d'auteur") which not only protected his work from exploitation by others but also assured him rights of recognition and integrity when his work was used. (Such ideas have only now been accepted into English law as will be noted later). The cult of the personal quality or nature of authorship affected the development of the French copyright law, and the law of other Continental countries, by maintaining a narrow view of what works would be protected. Thus not until recent times have "mechanical" works such as records, films and videograms been accorded protection by analogy of "neighbouring" rights of copyright.

International Copyright Conventions

By the later part of the nineteenth century with the growth of learning, literature, music and the arts, the great advances in the techniques of reproduction and the means of communication, and borne along by expanding commercial and industrial interests, the European states came to agree on the need for the mutual recognition of rights of copyright in the works of their subjects. However, the difference of approach in the philosophy and rationale of copyright protection between the French and English legal systems made this task difficult. The first major step came in 1886 with the adoption of the Berne Convention for the mutual protection by European countries of the literary and artistic works of their subjects. This Convention is the root of the copyright laws of most nation states and has been revised from time to time, the latest being in Paris in 1971.

After the Second World War under the aegis of the United Nations Educational, Scientific and Cultural Organisation there was adopted the Universal Copyright Convention of 1952; it was revised in 1971. This second international convention to some extent reflects the criterion and way of copyright protection established in the USA (which was not then an adherent of the Berne Convention). Furthermore the Universal Copyright Convention was devised to cater for the special needs of the developing third world countries particularly educational needs.

Both the Berne and Universal Copyright Conventions prescribe the principles upon which subscribing nation states are to grant protection to the works of their nationals, and reciprocally to the works of foreign nationals. Nonetheless countries have their own separate national laws and so consequently what works are given protection, for how long, the extent of the protection and the formalities prescribed (if any) for securing protection will be found to differ from country to country. The majority of countries are today signatories to both Conventions. Of the major world powers it is noteworthy that the USSR signed the Universal Copyright Convention and that the Russian Federation alone has affirmed its adherence to the Convention but other members of the CIS have apparently tacitly confirmed their adherence. China is now a signatory to the Berne Convention but not to the Universal Copyright Convention.

The most important differences between the two Conventions to be noted are as follows:

(a) The Berne Convention stipulates a minimum term of protection for literary, dramatic, musical and artistic works of the life of the author plus 50 years; under the Universal Copyright Convention the term is the life of the author plus 25 years. For other works such as records, the term of protection is, respectively, 50 and 25 years from the date the work is first published or made available for exhibition.

(b) No formalities had to be observed for authors to acquire protection for their works in the European countries which established the Berne Union. Following this tradition, the Berne Convention does not prescribe any formalities. The laws of the USA and of some other countries whose copyright laws are modelled on those of the USA impose a system of registration as a condition for securing copyright protection. To bridge this difference the Universal Copyright Convention provides that it is necessary but sufficient to give notice of the claim to copyright in the way explained in the following Section dealing with international copyright protection.

There are other European and International Conventions which impinge on copyright law as they apply to the protection of works (such as records, films and broadcasts) which do not fall directly within the scope of the Berne and Universal Copyright Conventions. The Rome Convention of 1961 for the Protection of Performers, Producers of Phonograph and Broadcasting Organisations brought about for the first time rights of protection for performers. These Conventions have been signed by various countries who have absorbed their provisions into their domestic laws.

International Copyright Protection and the Treaty of Rome

The citizens of foreign and Commonwealth countries obtain protection for their works in this country on the grounds of either their satisfying qualifications for protection under the Copyright, Designs and Patents Act 1988 (considered below), or their work being first published in the United Kingdom or a country to which the Act extends.

By section 159 of the Act, the Government is empowered to order the application of the copyright laws to the works of authors who are citizens of other countries of the European Community or countries in membership of the Berne or Universal Copyright Unions. Otherwise before an order can be made the Government is to be satisfied reciprocal protection is given to owners of works protected under United Kingdom Laws. By section 160 of the Act a power is conferred whereby if the laws of any country fail to give adequate protection to British copyright works, then the Government can withdraw United Kingdom protection for the works of authors of the country in default.

The rights of copyright protection given to the works of British subjects abroad will depend upon the domestic laws of a country and the principle of reciprocity of treatment. The copyright laws of most of the Commonwealth countries and countries historically associated with Great Britain resemble those of this country. The laws of most foreign countries conform to the minimum requirements of the International Conventions but contain their own particular individual rules.

With the major exception of the USA few national laws require compliance with any formalities for a work to obtain protection. As briefly noted above the Berne Convention dispenses with such formalities. The Universal Copyright Convention declares that if the domestic laws of a Member State require as a condition for copyright protection compliance with some formality such as registration, then such a State "shall regard the requirements as satisfied with respect to all works protected in accordance with this Convention and first published outside its territory and the author of which is not one of its nationals, if from the time of the first [authorised] publication all copies of the work bear the symbol © accompanied by the name of the copyright proprietor and year of first publication placed in such manner and location as to give reasonable notice of claim of copyright." As a further assurance it has become an accepted practice to include the symbol as prescribed when works are published or made available for exhibition.

By Britain joining the European Community there has not come about any substantial change to the law of copyright but it has affected some dealings with works. The fundamental distinction between the copyright in a work and the rights of ownership and possession in the actual physical or tangible form in which the work is embodied is reflected in the Articles of the Treaty of Rome and the Regulations of the European Commission. This has been confirmed in pronouncements of the European Court of Justice for example, "The concept of copyright comprises the prerogatives of the author which are inalienable rights of distribution when there is a material medium, and of performance if there is no material medium." So there is recognised a distinction between the existence of a proprietary right and the exercise of that right, that is to say, the absolute right of an author to decide to exercise any of his rights of copyright and his prerogative to prevent others exercising them without his consent.

Moreover a distinction is drawn between rights of (public) perform-ance, broadcasting and rental which have no material medium, and rights of publication and reproduction which yield an actual material product. Whenever these two latter rights are dealt with and assigned it is crucial to bear in mind the rules of the Common Market respecting the free move-ment of goods. The intellectual property rights of nationals of member States are inviolable but merchandise knows no boundaries within the European Community.

Authors and owners of copyright in literary, dramatic and musical works can restrict the countries within the European Community in which their works can be publicly performed or broadcast; makers of cinematograph films of any description can do likewise. However, once the publication or reproduction of a work is authorised, that is, when a literary work is printed and published, or a musical work is made avail-able to the general public in the form of records or pre-recorded tapes, or similarly a film is released in the form of video cassettes, any provision of the licence which purports to limit the territories of the European Com-munity within which such merchandise can be distributed and sold will be void and of no effect. It will offend the basic rules of the Treaty of Rome which prohibit any restriction on the import and export of goods between Member States.

There are numerous examples of the application of this principle. When pre-recorded tapes were authorised to be manufactured and sold in the United Kingdom but not exported, the attempt to prevent their being exported to Belgium failed. Any like restrictions applied to dealings with books and video cassettes and to reproductions of artistic works would similarly fail. Even so it does not follow that the conditions of a licence could otherwise be flouted such as by exporting video cassettes in a dubbed or sub-titled version to suit the market of a Member State, or exercising a rental right when the licence is for the sale of cassettes. If an author licenses the publication of his work in the English language in England he cannot prevent the distribution of the publication in Common Market countries but he would not as a consequence forfeit his translation rights. These are the author's proprietary rights so that he could restrain any translation and publication of his work in a foreign language.

The Articles of the Treaty and the Regulations of the Commission because of their complexity have not gone unchallenged and the transac-tions of international conglomerates engaged in entertainment have given many opportunities for argument before the European Court of Justice about the interpretation and application of European Community law. Suffice it to mention two instances. The Court has recognised that Member States have established special corporate monopolies for broad-casting and so the Court has conceded that television broadcasting rights may be assigned and limited territorially so that any attempt by one broadcasting organisation to relay a transmission of a programme from one country to another would be an infringement of copyright if done without the consent of the copyright proprietor. As a second example, the limitation territorially of the right to exhibit films theatrically has not been held to contravene European Community rules. The specific object of a theatrical film distribution agreement is the showing of a film, *i.e.* the exercise of the performance right, a right which has no material medium. So there is no violation of the rules for the free movement of goods or services.

The European Commission is currently propounding for the greater harmonisation of copyright laws between Member States for the exploitation of works at the highest level. The developments in the technology of communication and access to works are seen as heralding profound changes in copyright law as happened at the turn of this century. The laws of copyright most sought to be harmonised are those relating to the duration of the term of protection, the extension of rental and reprographic rights, more effective rights to prevent the private copying of works, and for the uniform recognition and enforcement of moral rights. These are matters which lie in the future. In what follows in this Part 6 is an explanation of the copyright law as it now exists in the United Kingdom.

B. FUNDAMENTALS OF COPYRIGHT LAW

The modern law of copyright can fairly be said to date from the enactment of the Copyright Act 1911 which revised and consolidated the existing statutory copyright laws which variously protected literary and dramatic works, musical compositions, engravings, sculpture and fine arts. Of interest too is that the Act gave copyright protection for the first time to contrivances "by means of which sounds may be mechanically reproduced in like manner as if such contrivances were musical works," namely, the gramophone record. It was not until the Copyright Act 1956 that copyright protection was extended to cinematograph films and to radio and television broadcasts.

As a consequence of the revisions to the Berne and Universal Copyright Conventions and their ratification by the Government it was necessary to reform the law and make amendments to it following a detailed review of copyright law (the Whitford Report 1977) and representations for changes in the law made by industry and various organisations representing authors and providers of creative works of all kinds. Thus there was enacted the Copyright, Designs and Patents Act 1988. As the title indicates the Act deals with various aspects of intellectual property so only Part I covering copyright and those Parts of the Act covering related topics will be studied.

The Copyright, Designs and Patents Act 1988

Although as a generalisation it can be said the law of copyright is contained in the Copyright, Designs and Patents Act 1988—hereafter the Act will be referred to as "the 1988 Act" or simply "the Act"—it does not comprise the whole law. The Act contains interpretive sections, yet for the meaning of such ordinary concepts as "originality," "public performance," "copying" and what is a "literary work," it is necessary to refer to the judgments of the courts when disputes have arisen about these and many other words and provisions repeated from earlier enactments.

The 1988 Act has made changes to the law but rather it is a re-statement than a major reform of copyright law to take account of the progress in the means by which material is recorded or stored or copied.

So in section 172 it is declared that where a provision of the Act corresponds with the provisions of the previous law that provision is not to be construed as departing from the previous law merely because of a change of expression. Thus whereas in the Copyright Act 1956 one of the infringing acts was "reproducing" a work, now it is "copying" it. In the earlier Act the expression "cinematograph film" was taken to include the sounds embodied in any soundtrack associated with the film. In the new Act there is reference simply to "film," meaning "a recording on any medium from which a moving image may by any means be produced." These are but two instances of changes in expression which like others are not intended to bring about a change in the law. The section also underlines the importance of judicial decisions of the past by affirming they may be referred to in the application and construction of the new Act.

The Act came into force on August 1, 1989 but its application to works then in existence is set out in schedule 1 to the Act. For historical reasons the schedule is detailed and in parts complex as it deals with particular works such as films, the calculation of the term of copyright in certain works and the remedies available for infringement of copyright. However, in general the schedule establishes that works in which copyright subsisted under the 1956 Act have continuity of protection. Neither the copyright ownership of a work nor any dealings or assignments of interests in copyright made prior to the Act coming into force are affected. In principle the rights of copyright granted by the 1988 Act, the acts permitted by law which would otherwise be an infringement of copyright, the manner of dealing with the rights of copyright and their enforcement are the same for works existing at the time of the Act coming into force as for works created on and after August 1, 1989.

An innovation to English law brought about by the Act in compliance with the Berne Convention is the conferring of moral rights on authors of some works and on film directors. These rights are considered separately below. A second major innovation of the Act has been the granting to performers of rights in their performances corresponding to some extent to rights of copyright, and rights to persons having exclusive recording rights. The provisions of the Act setting out these rights are reviewed in Part 5. A third notable innovation has been the granting of a rental right in sound recordings, films and computer programmes.

Copyright versus Ownership and Possession

Copyright exists only in those works as defined in the 1988 Act. The owner of copyright has the exclusive right to do those things in relation to a work set out in the Act and designated as acts restricted by copyright. It is those acts which comprise the copyright in a work so if anyone else does any of them, such as copying or publishing, without the consent of the owner there is an infringement of his proprietorial rights. It is the author, the person who creates a work who (with some important exceptions), is the first owner of the copyright in the work. As owner and proprietor the author is at liberty to exercise any of the rights in his work and to deal with them as he chooses just as with any other of his property; and he can take legal action to protect his work and rights.

The copyright in a work is totally separate and distinct from the rights of ownership and possession of the text of a literary work, the score of a musical work, the negative of a photograph or film, the canvas of a painting, or the master tape of a sound recording. The person who owns or has possession of the physical material comprising a work does not necessarily own the copyright in the work. The loan, gift or sale of the material object—the book, print, canvas, sculpture, tape, etc.—will not of itself convey any rights or interest in the copyright in the work. This may be obvious with a published work such as a book but not so obvious with an unpublished work. The distinction was interestingly illustrated in a case which concerned the manuscript of an unpublished story entitled "The Life of Christ" which Charles Dickens wrote for his children. By his will, Dickens gave all his private papers to his sister-in-law Georgina Hogarth and the remainder of his property to other persons. The court decided—as the law stood then—that the gift by Dickens of his private papers did not automatically confer a gift of the copyright in them. The two gifts were separate and distinct so that the other persons acquired the copyright in the story "The Life of Christ" and Georgina Hogarth the ownership of the original manuscript.

This dichotomy between the ownership of the copyright in a work and the ownership and possession of the physical material can further be illustrated by a most ordinary and every day example of "a literary work," namely the writing and receiving of a letter. The writer has copyright in his letter and the recipient has an absolute right of ownership of the paper upon which the correspondence is written by the fact of the letter having been addressed and delivered to him. As owner of the paper the recipient is entitled to deal with it as he chooses for he has no duty to preserve it or return it to the writer. He can keep it, give it away, sell it or destroy it. What he is not at liberty to do is to publish it or otherwise deal with it in a way as to infringe the writer's copyright in the letter; and neither is anyone else into whose possession the letter (or paper) comes.

Where there is unity of ownership both of the copyright and of the material object there can be no conflict of interests in any dealings with a work but there may be when the ownership is separated. This can be especially important with commissioned works. If the entire copyright in a work is to be acquired by the person who commissions it, that person must as a consequence and by necessary implication acquire the right of ownership of the material object or substance. However no such simple conclusion can be made when only limited rights are to be acquired, such as the right of publication, first performance or exhibition. As the author will retain ownership of the residue of the rights of copyright then by implication he will normally retain the right of ownership of his script, or score or canvas. The issue can be important when organisations commission works from established authors and artists and the title to the ownership of the material object and access to it for further use or reproduction is disputed.

In the following pages much attention will be paid to infringement of copyright but it must not be overlooked that there are legal principles governing the ownership of a protected work as a material object or article. Any wrongful dealing or "conversion" of the work as a piece of physical property will be treated in the same way as any wrongful dealing with any other item of property. Thus it is relevant to consider briefly what obligations the law places on a person who has actual physical possession of a work but is not the owner of any of the rights of copyright in it.

There is first a duty cast on persons generally not to deal with another's property in a way as to deny his right and title to it; in legal parlance, not to convert it to his own use. This means that the person in possession must not sell the article or property, or deliver or pass it to another without permission save where a person in possession has a right of lien on property as, for example, a film laboratory over negative and prints for the payment of processing services. Secondly, there is a general duty of care of a person's property by taking those preventative steps which any reasonable mindful person could be expected to take if the property were his own. The first rule is absolute but the application of the second can depend on the particular circumstances. Thus where, for example, a manuscript or the like is given and received gratuitously perhaps for advice or review, liability on the recipient will arise only in circumstances of gross negligence in the care of the work. But where a work was delivered to a publisher it was held that by accepting the manuscript prospectively with a view to its being published the publisher thereby undertook the higher duty which the law imposes in such a relationship, namely to take reasonable care to prevent loss or damage to the work.

Where there is loss or destruction of the material substance, that is the script, the musical score, the canvas or plate or other fabric of an artistic work, the only redress which the law can give is an award of damages to the owner of the property. Any award is most likely to be measured according to the worth or value of the material substance not the likely value or revenues the work may earn in publisher's or box office or reproduction royalties. The extent to which the courts will compensate economic damage or loss (as distinct from loss or damage or injury to persons and physical property) depends on the relationship of the parties and there being a duty of care, the foreseeability of injury or loss arising from the failure to observe that duty, and the remoteness of the damages suffered as a consequence of the breach of the duty of care.

Qualifications for Copyright Protection

No formalities of any kind such as registration or notice are required for a work to have copyright protection. Copyright is acquired and subsists automatically in a work provided the qualifications as prescribed in sections 153 to 156 of the Act are satisfied.

A work qualifies for protection if at "the material time" the author was a qualified person. The expression "qualified person" means a person who is:

"(a) a British citizen, a British Dependent Territories citizen, a British National (Overseas), a British Overseas citizen, a British subject or a British protected person within the meaning of the British Nationality Act 1981; or

(b) an individual domiciled or resident in the United Kingdom or another country to which the relevant provisions of the Act extend; or

(c) a body incorporated under the laws of the United Kingdom or of another country to which the relevant provisions of this Part [of the Act] extend."

The expression "material time" means in relation to literary, dramatic, musical or artistic works:

"(a) [if the work is unpublished], the time when the work was made or, if the making of the work extended over a period, a substantial part of that period;
[Note that a work is made when "it is recorded, in writing or otherwise."]

(b) [if the work is published], when the work was first published or, if the author had died before that time, immediately before his death."

For other descriptions of work, namely records and films the material time is when the work was made. For broadcasts and cable transmissions, it is when the broadcast or transmission was made.

Works of joint authorship qualify for protection where any one of the authors satisfies the foregoing requirements.

A work (other than a broadcast) can qualify for copyright protection on the alternative ground of it being first published in the United Kingdom or in a country to which Part I of the Act extends. If a work is in fact first published abroad and then is published in the United Kingdom or in a country to which Part I extends, provided the second publication takes place within 30 days of the first, the publication will be treated as a simultaneous publication and so the work will qualify for protection. A broadcast qualifies for protection if it is made in or sent from a place in the United Kingdom or another country to which Part I extends.

The international aspects of copyright protection have been alluded to above. Thus it is that through the application of section 159 of the Act and Orders in Council made under it protection is accorded in the United Kingdom to the works of persons who are domiciled or resident in countries in membership of the Berne and Universal Copyright Conventions and to other countries when an Order so decrees.

The registration of works at Stationers' Hall in the City of London does not confer copyright in a work or give it any special protection. The service of registration provided by the Livery Company serves only to record a person's claim to be the proprietor of the copyright in a particular published work. When an application for registration is made a copy of the work is required to be filed and it is at the Registrar's discretion whether or not to make the registration. The registers are open for public inspection but the material deposited with an application is treated as private and under no circumstances is it disclosed to anyone. After seven years and unless a registration is renewed the material is destroyed.

C. WORKS PROTECTED BY COPYRIGHT

At the beginning of the 1988 Act in section 1 the works in which copyright can subsist are listed, namely:

(a) original literary, dramatic, musical or artistic works;

(b) sound recordings, films, broadcasts or cable programmes; and

(c) the typographical arrangement of published editions.

In sections 3 to 9 these three broad categories of works are described and defined but as pointed out above, the courts have played an important role in interpreting and applying the like words in previous copyright legislation so that the decisions of the courts are material to understanding what works are subject to copyright protection. This is particularly so in regard to the requirement for a literary, dramatic, musical or artistic work to be "original".

The description "original" has nothing to do with newness, inventiveness, inspiration, uniqueness, novelty and the like. What is required by law for a work to have protection is originality in the labour, skill and judgment of an author in expressing and reducing his ideas, thoughts, researches and the like to permanent form. The law does not protect the ideas, thoughts, researches, etc., themselves. Perhaps the classic judicial exposition on originality for the purpose of copyright protection is to be found in a case before the court in 1916 dealing with the copyright in examination papers when it was said: "The word 'original' does not in this connection mean that the work must be the expression of original or inventive thought. Copyright Acts are not concerned with the originality of ideas, but with the expression of thought, and in the case of 'literary work' with the expression of thought in print or writing. The originality which is required relates to the expression of the thought . . . But the Act does not require that the expression must be in an original or novel form, but that the work must not be copied from another work—that it should originate from the author."

The courts emphasise that what is protected is the material form in which thoughts and ideas are expressed or images recorded and not the thoughts and ideas and images themselves; were it otherwise intellectual and scientific advancement would be barred. Much of what passes for new or original is the product of accumulated knowledge and experience, or derived from the common currency or stock of ideas and a cultural inheritance. As was remarked in another case in 1923 concerning copyright in a compilation of literary works, "What is the precise amount of knowledge, labour, judgment or literary skill or taste with which the author of any book or other compilation must bestow upon its composition in order to acquire copyright ... cannot be defined in precise terms. In every case it must depend largely on the special facts of the case and must in each case be very much a question of degree." Similarly with other works such as paintings, sculptures, photographs, recordings or films. Painting Salisbury Cathedral, sculpting the human form, photographing Trafalgar Square, recording church bells, filming the landing of Concorde at Heathrow are not acts protected by copyright. The originality the law recognises lies in the particular painting, sculpture, photograph, record or film itself and it is that originality which is protected from being copied without permission.

Just as copyright protection is not dependent on a work's uniqueness so too a work's intellectual content and aesthetic appeal are immaterial. The law attempts no value judgment of the quality or usefulness of a work and so many works have been declared protected which might be thought hardly meritorious or worthy of copyright protection as works of literature, music or art.

LITERARY, DRAMATIC AND MUSICAL WORKS

Section 3 provides for literary, dramatic and musical works and these are defined as follows:

> " 'literary work' means any work, other than a dramatic or musical work, which is written, spoken or sung, and accordingly includes:
>
> (a) a table or compilation; and
>
> (b) a computer program.
>
> 'dramatic work' includes a work of dance or mime; and
>
> 'musical work' means a work consisting of music, exclusive of any words or actions intended to be sung, spoken or performed with the music."

One of the works within the rubric of "literary work" is a computer program. This is important as the 1956 Act did not directly provide for such works. Computer generated works were catered for in a special enactment which has been made redundant and repealed by this present Act.

Literary Works

The "literary" of the expression "literary work" refers to the nature of the work as distinct from, for example, a painting and not to its being a work of literature. Thus examination papers, traders' catalogues, trade advertisements, directories, time-tables, programme listings, rules of a game and a football coupon have been given protection.

On the other hand the courts have not given protection to the titles of works, or to common phrases or expressions for instance as used in advertisements because to do so would be an appropriation of the language. Furthermore, there was not found to be sufficient skill and effort and so originality for such kinds of work to have copyright. Even when a word was invented—"Exxon"—to establish a corporate identity for the furtherance of the company's trade and goodwill, the court did not concede copyright in it.

The inclusion of speech (and song) as part of the definition of "literary work" in section 3(1) is new to copyright law and is likely to produce difficulties of interpretation and application which will need to be resolved by the courts. Mere speech like a performance of any kind does not of itself acquire copyright protection. For a literary, dramatic and musical work to have copyright protection it is necessary to comply with the requirements laid down in subsection (2) where it is provided that copyright does not subsist in any of these works "unless and until it is recorded, in writing or otherwise."

"Writing" is widely defined for it "includes any form of notation or code, whether by hand or otherwise and regardless of the method by which, or medium in or on which, it is recorded, and written shall be construed accordingly." Shorthand, braille and morse are forms of notation as are musical notation, computer software and the products of such means of communication as facsimile and reprography. It will be for the courts to determine what permanent form will satisfy the requirement "or otherwise."

A sound recording such as the commonplace tape recording would appear to meet the requirement.

The time when a work is made is relevant for its qualifying for protection and by section 3(2) a work is regarded as having been made at the time when it was recorded. It is immaterial whether a work was recorded by or with the permission of the author, and if it was not recorded by the author that fact does not affect the question whether copyright subsists in the record as distinct from the work recorded.

If a speech, lecture, story, poem, dramatic dialogue or piece of music is delivered or performed from a prepared text or script, as the work is already recorded in writing it is protected and any copying, recording, public performance or broadcasting without the author's consent would be an infringement of his copyright. Where there is no prepared text or script and any work such as described above is delivered or performed extemporaneously the author's rights can be at risk as the means for recording the work "in writing or otherwise" are now readily available— the tape recorder being an obvious means.

If the recording of, for example, a speech is made by the author then the copyright in both the speech and the recording will be his. Difficulties arise when the recording is made by another person and without the author's knowledge and permission. The speech or work will gain copyright by virtue of its having been recorded and the record will have copyright protection as a sound recording. It has been argued that the person making the recording infringes the author's copyright but since not until a work has been recorded "in writing or otherwise" does copyright exist in it, is there at the time of the recording any copyright to infringe?

The problem is not new for when in 1900 a reporter made a shorthand report of a speech (which it appears was delivered extemporaneously) the report was accorded protection on the grounds that the shorthand report was a product of sufficient skill and labour to qualify for copyright protection. This decision has not gone unquestioned and it remains to be seen if it would be applied today to the making of an unauthorised tape recording by the push of a button.

Where a recording is made with the express or implied approval of the author and the purpose for its making made known to him there may not be the grounds for disputing the existence of two separately owned rights of copyright. It would require some written agreement between the persons concerned for the separate rights to be combined and belong to either of them.

The recording of speech of daily or passing interest may not be of any consequence but when what is recorded has serious meaning and substance then these issues are likely to be contentious especially if the recording was surreptitious. The matter spoken may, for example be important and valuable scientific or technical information, it may be confidential, a play may be improvised, and likewise music. A recording may be of an interview of the reminiscences of the great and the good (or the bad) which may have lasting interest. Further weight has been added to these issues since an author (but not the person making the recording) now has moral rights in his work and a performer rights in his performance. Some resolution of this problem is provided by section 58 of the Act which subject to certain conditions exempts from infringement the copyright in spoken words as literary works where the recording is made for the purpose of reporting current events or broadcasting.

A question currently exercising the minds of copyright lawyers is the status in law and protectability of formats for programmes and especially broadcast quiz and competitive shows. Some analogy is to be found in the rules of a game. Copyright creates a monopoly which may have an economic value but certainly precludes other persons using a protected work; for these reasons there must be certainty in the subject matter of the monopoly. What is open to doubt is whether recurring features and situations of a programme, the use of stock phrases, the presence of a celebrity and repeated scenic effects produce the unity required to constitute a work in a permanent form sufficient for such programmes to have protection in their own right and distinct from the parts—the scripts, music, graphics and other elements—which make up the programmes.

Dramatic Works

Dramatic work is defined as including "a work of dance or mime"; not very enlightening. The definition embraces scripted dialogue—a play, tragedy, comedy, farce, sketch and musical play. The intended manner of presentation is immaterial—theatrical, film, or broadcasting—as the mode of presentation does not change the work itself. What is open to question is whether scenic effect can be brought within the definition of a dramatic work.

Mere spectacle or character "get up" are not susceptible to copyright protection. Anyone who views a performance and follows the same manner or style of presentation does not infringe copyright. Despite a director giving life and vitality to the printed text to a dramatic work his creative contribution has no protection in law. Moral rights are given only to a film director. However, stage directions, a lighting plot, a cue sheet and the like if in a permanent form are copyright works like the script of the play itself. It should not be overlooked that a stage setting for a dramatic work may acquire copyright protection as an artistic work.

Musical Works

Musical work is defined as meaning "a work consisting of music, exclusive of any words or action intended to be sung, spoken or performed with the music." Music as such is not defined doubtless because of the difficulty of coping with the ingenuity of composers and musicians, the infinite possible combinations and kinds of sounds and permutations of beat and rhythm. But the definition puts beyond doubt that the lyrics of a song, the libretto of an opera and the book of a musical play are works separate from the music and as literary works have independent copyright protection.

It has already been pointed out that for a work to have protection it must be fixed, have permanent form and also that the time and place of the making of the work are material to its qualifying for protection. These considerations can lead to a vexatious argument when a work created by one person is recorded in writing or otherwise by another. The matter is perhaps especially acute with musical works since musical themes can be memorised and set down in score after being heard and the means for the unauthorised recording of a performance of music are now so readily available. The situation may arise in particular with "pop" groups whose music is often not written down but their spontaneous creation. The issue seems never to have been brought before the courts but the conclusion is—on the authority of leading writers on copyright law and not the author—that although a person who records a performance has copyright in his recording, even if unauthorised, a composer/musician is not deprived of his ownership of the copyright in his music. The score or recording is evidence of the musical work but it is the music itself which is the substance of the work and is to be protected.

ARTISTIC WORKS

By section 4(1) "artistic work" means:

"(a) a graphic work, photograph, sculpture or collage, irrespective of artistic quality;

(b) a work of architecture being a building or model for a building; or

(c) a work of artistic craftsmanship."

In subsection (2) there are definitions by way of further meaning:

" 'building' includes any fixed structure, and a part of a building or fixed structure;

'graphic work' includes—

(a) any painting, drawing, diagram, map, chart or plan; and

(b) any engraving, etching, lithograph, woodcut or similar work;

'photograph' means a recording of light or other radiation on any medium on which an image is produced or from which an image may by any means be produced, and which is not part of a film;

'sculpture' includes a cast or model made for the purposes of sculpture."

Although there is no great difference in the meaning given to an artistic work from that contained in the Copyright Act 1956, in this new Act a collage is included and the definition of a photograph allows protection to extend to new works akin to photography such as a hologram where nothing is visible until it is illuminated.

The phrase "irrespective of artistic quality" in regard to a graphic work, photograph, sculpture or collage endorses the tenet of copyright law that a work's usefulness, or intellectual merit or the presence or absence of uniqueness are immaterial to its being protected. Artistic works do not have to be gallery exhibits to acquire copyright. A work must be original in the sense it is the product of the author's skill and labour and not a copy of another's work, but the most simple or elementary drawing or painting or "snap" has protection.

As the phrase "irrespective of artistic quality" is not attached to the other artistic works listed it may be asked if a standard of quality applies to them. The question has exercised the minds of judges over works of no real artistic appeal whatsoever such as proto-types for furniture and protective babycot covering. It was pointed out that the subject of copyright is a "work of artistic craftsmanship" and not an "artistic work of craftsmanship." Lord Simon then remarked, "It is therefore misleading to ask, first, is this a work produced by a craftsman, and secondly, is it a work of art? It is more pertinent to ask, is this the work of one who was in this respect an artist-craftsman?"

RECORDS, FILMS AND BROADCASTS

Records

In common parlance records are considered protected by copyright but it is a sound recording which is protected. By section 5 of the Act " 'sound recording' means:

(a) a recording of sounds, from which the sounds may be reproduced; or

(b) a recording of the whole or any part of a literary, dramatic or musical work, from which sounds reproducing the work may be produced;

regardless of the medium on which the recording is made or the method by which the sounds are reproduced or produced."

Paragraph (b) of the definition covers those situations where, for example music is played on a synthesizer from which no sounds are emitted but by being connected to recording equipment music is recorded.

There is no bar to the making of a recording of any sound which may have been previously recorded; a musical work is a prime example provided that the work is out of copyright and no licence is therefore required. Moreover there is no legal obstacle preventing two or more persons making a recording of the same sound at the same time. The copyright in a sound recording resides in the produced recording and it is this which is protected rather than the records derived and manufactured from the produced recording.

Films

" 'Film' means 'a recording on any medium from which a moving image may by any means be produced.' " This simple description replaces the expression "cinematograph film" contained in the 1956 Act which alluded to sequences of visual images recorded on translucent material and capable of being shown as a moving picture.

The new definition puts beyond doubt that the modern means for reproducing visual images—the magnetic video tape and disc and other means which may be devised in the future—can render a product within the definition. Yet this new definition may not be so welcome for whereas the expression "cinematograph film" was taken to include the sounds embodied in any sound track associated with the film, now there exists two works, "a sound recording" and "a film" each having a separate copyright and conceivably separate copyright owners.

What has been said above concerning the making of sound recordings can be said of the making of films.

Broadcasts

Broadcasting and cable transmissions are separately defined in the Act. Section 6 is about broadcasting only, which is defined as "a transmission by wireless telegraphy of visual images, sounds or other information which—

(a) is capable of being lawfully received by members of the public; or

(b) is transmitted for presentation to members of the public;

and references to broadcasting shall be construed accordingly."

The definition does not make a distinction between a terrestrial and satellite or celestial transmission. If a satellite transmission is encrypted then for it to qualify as a broadcast by being "capable of being lawfully received by members of the public" the decoding equipment must have been "made available to members of the public by or with the authority of the person making the transmission, or the person providing the contents of the transmission," that is, the programme. The place from which a broadcast is made is, in the case of a satellite transmission, the place from which the signals carrying the broadcast are transmitted to the satellite.

The second part of the definition of a broadcast in (b) above—a transmission for presentation to members of the public—covers transmissions
of programmes and events which are not intended to be available to the
public at large but to the public only at selected places.

Although a broadcast may be received by telecommunication (that is by
cable), that does not alter the status of the broadcast as a broadcast within
the meaning of the section.

The general rule that an author is the first owner of the copyright in a
work applies to broadcasting. By section 9(1) it is the person making the
broadcast who is regarded as the author and who therefore is the first
owner of the copyright in the broadcast. The person making the broadcast
is the person as defined in section 6(3) as follows. "References to the
person making a broadcast, broadcasting a work, or including a work in a
broadcast are—

(a) to the person transmitting the programme, if he has responsibility
to any extent for its contents; and

(b) to any person providing the programme who makes with the
person transmitting it the arrangements necessary for its
transmission;

and references to a programme, in the context of broadcasting are to any
item included in the broadcast." Furthermore, by section 10 a broadcast is
to be treated as a work of joint authorship where more than one person is
to be taken as making the broadcast.

Thus for example as the BBC both provides and transmits programmes
it is the sole owner of the broadcast. With the ITC as it owns the transmitting equipment and has supervisory powers over the content of the
programmes supplied by a programme contractor, the ITC and the programme contractor together constitute the person making the broadcast
and so together own the copyright in the broadcast. It is the copyright in
the broadcast which is the subject of joint ownership. The ownership of
the copyright in the programme supplied for broadcasting whether original in the programme contractor or provided by an independent producer
for a contractor is not affected.

Section 7 is about cable transmissions. A cable programme service is
defined as "a service which consists wholly or mainly in sending visual
images, sounds or other information by means of a telecommunications
system, otherwise than by wireless telegraphy, for reception—

(a) at two or more places (whether for simultaneous reception or at
different times in response to requests by different users); or

(b) for presentation to members of the public;

and which is not, or so far as it is not, excepted by or under the provisions of this section."

The definition is wide enough to include teletext and such like services in addition to regular television and radio programmes. The exceptions referred to are communications not intended for general reception, *e.g.* two way private cable systems such as a telephone network, and closed circuit systems.

The ownership of the copyright in a cable programme as such is with the person (company or corporation) who provides the cable programme service to subscribers. The copyright in the programme supplied resides with the person who provides and licenses the programme to the operator of the cable programme service.

By section 14 the duration of the copyright in a broadcast is 50 years calculated from the end of the calendar year in which the broadcast was first made. No extension to the term of copyright is obtained by repeating a broadcast. There is no copyright protection for a broadcast which is repeated after the expiry of the term of copyright in the original broadcast. Nonetheless this does not affect the protection which the material or programme broadcast may still enjoy.

A broadcast must like any other work qualify for protection in accordance with the Act. Section 156 provides that a broadcast qualifies for copyright protection if it is made from a place in the United Kingdom or from another country to which Part I of the Act extends. By the operation of section 159 and any Government order (made as noted above when considering the international aspects of copyright), protection is extended to foreign broadcasts.

OTHER WORKS

Published Editions

A work which is apart from those reviewed above but in which copyright can subsist by section 8 is "the typographical arrangement of published editions." A detailed consideration of this class of work falls outside the ambit of this study but the existence of the protection should not be overlooked particularly where such a work is reproduced by way of illustration. What is protected is the appearance and presentation of text and material, the set up or layout of a published work but not the work itself. Much skill and labour may be expended in the creation of a new publication of a classic work of literature as well as in the first publication of a new work; likewise in the publication of a music score.

The Act gives published editions protection in particular against copying in any form save for the exceptions and privileges allowed for libraries in accordance with the Act. The protection is for 25 years from the end of the calendar year in which the edition was first published but copyright does not continue in the re-publication of the typographical arrangement of a published edition.

Adaptations of Works

Apart from the classes of works in which copyright may subsist as noted above copyright may also subsist in an adaptation. For an adaptation to acquire protection then like any other work it must be the product of independent skill, judgment and labour such as to render it substantially different from the original. Thus in section 21(3) of the Act an adaptation is defined as:

"(a) in relation to a literary or dramatic work, means—

    (i) a translation of a work;

    (ii) a version of a dramatic work in which it is converted into a non-dramatic work or, as the case may be, of a non-dramatic work in which it is converted into a dramatic work;

    (iii) a version of the work in which the story or action is conveyed wholly or mainly by means of pictures in a form suitable for reproduction in a book, or in a newspaper, magazine or similar periodical;

(b) in relation to a musical work, means an arrangement or transcription of the work."

As an adaptation of any other kind of work would be an interference with the original, it is not to be wondered at that only literary, dramatic and musical works are specified. What is surprising is that in regard to the representation of the version of a work pictorially no provision is made for an adaptation in the form of story board and animated film.

All rights of copyright attach to an adaptation like any other work. However, being a derivative work, if the original work is in copyright then to make the adaptation or do any act in relation to it without the consent of the owner of the copyright in the original work is an infringement of the latter's rights. If an adaptation is made of a work in the public domain then the author of the adaptation has unrestricted rights of copyright in his work. Instances of adaptations being accorded copyright are a new text or version of a play of Shakespeare, the pianoforte score of an opera, the abridgement of a book. The making of adaptations and their infringing copyright is considered further below.

Copyright in Infringing Works

Having made a survey of the works in which copyright exists it may be asked if copyright can subsist in a work which infringes another's copyright. If the infringing work is the product of the expenditure of time, skill and labour such as a translation or other kind of adaptation it seems the work will be protected but the copyright will be sterile. The owner of the copyright in the original work may sue for the infringement of his work and by injunction prevent the author of the infringing work exercising any of his rights, but it is not clear whether the owner of the original work acquires any copyright in the infringing work.

D. OWNERSHIP AND DURATION OF COPYRIGHT

The author of a work is the person who originates and creates it and very sensibly it is that person who by section 11 of the 1988 Act is designated the first owner and proprietor of the entire copyright in a work. That is the principle but there are exceptions as noted below.

The concept of authorship is varied in the Act for particular works. For sound recordings and films by section 9(2)(a) "the person by whom the arrangements necessary for the making of the recording or film are undertaken" is deemed the author and so the first owner of the copyright in the work. The "person" making the arrangements may be one actual person or persons working in partnership, or a number of persons working in combination as an incorporated company. For broadcasts and cable programmes special provisions of the Act apply as noted earlier.

Where a literary, dramatic, musical or artistic work is computer-generated, meaning "the work is generated by computer in circumstances such that there is no human author of the work," by section 9(3) it is "the person by whom the arrangements necessary for the creation of the work are undertaken" who is taken to be the author and therefore first owner of the copyright in the work.

Employer's Ownership

There are exceptions to the principle that the author is the first owner of the copyright in a work, the most important being works created in the course of employment. In section 11(2) of the Act it is provided that "where a literary, dramatic musical or artistic work is made by an employee in the course of his employment, his employer is the first owner of any copyright in the work subject to any agreement to the contrary." If there is to be an agreement to the contrary then the contract of service or employment needs to make this clear in writing since dealings in copyright need to be evidenced in writing.

The distinction between a contract for services, and a contract of service or employment has been examined in Part 5 and here is a demonstration of the legal significance of the distinction. The entire copyright in the work of a "staff" writer, script editor, composer or arranger, employed under a contract of employment by a theatrical, film, television, newspaper or publishing company or the like will belong to the employer as of right unless there is an express term to the contrary in the contract of employment.

However, it should be noted that the entitlement of the employer to the copyright in an employee's work is limited to works "made in the course of his [the employee's] employment." Whether a work is so made is a question of fact and interpretation of the contract, or the terms and conditions of employment. If an employer acquiesces in an employee pursuing some activity, even to the extent of defraying the expenses incurred by the employee in so doing, then unless the product or work is clearly within the scope of the work or duties for which the employee is engaged the employee will not forfeit his copyright in his work to the employer.

Commissioned Works

When a work is commissioned the author will still be the first owner of the copyright in it unless by the terms of the engagement (the contract for services) it is stipulated that the person commissioning the work is to acquire the whole or particular rights of copyright. As explained in Section G below, the Act makes provision for dealing with the copyright in a work yet to be created or produced. When the commissioned work is an adaptation of an existing work, or is to form a part of a compilation or a production to which other persons have contributed or are contributing it is important for the ownership of the commissioned work to be indisputable.

The copyright in a work as a proprietary right may reside with an author independently of the rights of the owner of the physical object or material in which the work is embodied. This distinction is particularly important for artistic works but it can be an issue with scripted works and musical compositions when the person commissioning a work is to retain possession of it. Thus in addition to providing for the ownership of the copyright in a commissioned work the right of ownership of the material embodying the work also needs to be assured.

The issues reviewed above apply also to commissioned sound recordings and to films with the further consideration that often the constituent parts of these works are themselves commissioned works.

If a work is commissioned without a formal written agreement that is not fatal but if the copyright ownership is disputed it will be for the person who commissioned the work to prove affirmatively his right of ownership, not the author. In the foregoing it has been assumed that the work created has been wholly that of one person or author, yet it may have been suggested or outlined by another. It is in this kind of situation that the basic principles and underlying concepts as to the nature of copyright outlined earlier have relevance. As there is no copyright in ideas, a person who suggests a plot or theme or an outline for a drawing or design cannot in law claim authorship or ownership of the copyright in the work produced by another. Unless it can be shown that a person is a mere amanuensis it is the person who originates the language and sets it down in a material form who in law is the author and so first owner of the copyright in the work. Where resort is had to a "ghost writer" then only by the terms of the contract of engagement can the "author" relating a story or memoirs secure the copyright in the work of the writer.

Joint Authors

Works of joint authorship and the separate rights of joint authors are recognised by the Act. By section 10(1) a work of joint authorship means "a work produced by the collaboration of two or more authors in which the contribution of each author is not separate from the contribution of the other author or authors." The collaborators must be authors in the sense just explained and not persons who merely contribute ideas. Works where the parts are separate and distinct such as a song, opera, musical play or ballet, where the lyrics, libretto, book and choreography are separate from the music are not therefore works of joint authorship. Each element of such a composite work can be dealt with by an author independently of any other author. When composite works are embarked upon it is appropriate for the authors first to agree mutually upon the extent, if at all, each can deal independently with the copyright in his contribution to the complete work otherwise any negotiations with a third party for the exploitation of the work could be impaired.

Crown Copyright

In addition to the exception to the basic rule of the ownership of copyright as noted above—namely works created in the course of employment—further exceptions are made by sections 163 to 168 of the Act for works subject to Crown and parliamentary copyright and works whose copyright vests in certain international organisations.

Where a work is made by an officer or servant of the Crown in the course of his duties, the work automatically qualifies for copyright protection and the Crown is the first owner of the copyright. The same rule applies to works created by or under the direction of the House of Commons or the House of Lords. Copyright protection can also be extended to original literary, dramatic, musical and artistic works made by an officer or employee of, or published by an international organisation as designated by the Government. This provision of the Act is to meet the very exceptional case of the work of an organisation not qualifying for protection under the rules of the international copyright conventions referred to earlier.

DURATION OF COPYRIGHT

The calculation of the term of copyright in a work has been greatly simplified by the 1988 Act. Whereas in the past the date from which the period of copyright was calculated depended upon the happening of certain events, now the general rule is that copyright subsists in a work for the life of the author plus 50 years. Even so the Act makes special provision for particular kinds of works including those in existence at the time the Act came into operation.

The copyright in a literary, dramatic, musical or artistic work by section 12 "expires at the end of the period of 50 years from the end of the calendar year in which the author dies." For works of joint authorship, normally the calculation of the 50 years is from the date of the death of the last of the authors to die.

Where a work is of unknown authorship "copyright expires at the end of the period 50 years from the end of the calendar year in which it is first made available to the public." Section 12 details what amounts to making a work available to the public—it "includes" amongst other activities performance in public, broadcasting and exhibition in public but presumably includes publishing the work. Furthermore one is left to presume the person first to do any one of these acts becomes the copyright owner of the work unless and until the identity of the author becomes known. In this event the author (or perhaps his successor in title) is fixed with the term as just described and not the basic rule (life plus 50 years) which could by chance be more beneficial.

If the work is computer-generated copyright expires at the end of the period of 50 years from the end of the calendar year in which the work was made.

The term of copyright in sound recordings and films is laid down in section 13. Copyright expires in these works:

"(a) at the end of the period of 50 years from the end of the calendar year in which it is made; or

(b) if it is released before the end of that period, 50 years from the end of the calendar year in which it is released.

A sound recording or film is 'released' when—

(a) it is first published, broadcast or included in a cable programme service; or

(b) in the case of a film or film sound-track, the film is first shown in public."

In determining whether a work has been released no account is to be taken of any unauthorised act.

Government publications are resorted to and used for many purposes but the provisions of the Act governing the scope and duration of Crown and Parliamentary copyright should not be overlooked. The provisions are elaborate and as the works concerned are in a class apart it is sufficient in this study to note that with regard to Crown copyright in literary, dramatic, musical or artistic works the term of copyright is 125 years from the end of the calendar year in which the work was made unless it is "published commercially" during the period of 75 years from the end of the calendar year in which it was made. In such an event the duration of copyright is 50 years from the end of the calendar year in which the work is first so published. For other works of Crown copyright the term of copyright is the same as for all other non-Crown copyright works.

The transitional provisions of the Act contained in schedule 1 and to which reference has been made earlier are particularly important with regard to the duration of copyright in works in existence at the time of the Act coming into force on August 1, 1989.

E. RIGHTS OF COPYRIGHT AND THEIR INFRINGEMENT

Copyright is about the exclusive right of an author to do certain acts in relation to his work. If anyone else does any of those acts without his permission there is an infringement of his copyright. It is under the 1988 Act that an author acquires these exclusive rights and his entitlement to obtain redress for any infringement of them. It is also under the Act that certain acts are allowed to be done in relation to a work which do not constitute an infringement of copyright. These permitted acts such as fair dealing are considered in the next Section.

The rights possessed by an author or copyright owner are listed in section 16 of the Act as, "the exclusive right to do the following acts in the United Kingdom—

(a) to copy the work;

(b) to issue copies of the work to the public;

(c) to perform, show or play the work in public;

(d) to broadcast the work or include it in a cable programme service;

(e) to make an adaptation of the work or do any of the above acts in relation to an adaptation."

It is these acts which are "the acts restricted by the copyright" and they extend to every description of work protected by copyright.

The section affirms that "copyright in a work is infringed by a person who without the licence of the copyright owner does, or authorises another to do, any of the acts restricted by the copyright." The section also declares that, "the doing of an act restricted by the copyright in a work is the doing of it:

(a) in relation to the work as a whole or any substantial part of it, and

(b) either directly or indirectly;

and it is immaterial whether any intervening acts themselves infringe copyright."

Copyright can now be infringed by a person who "authorises another" to do any of the acts restricted by copyright as well as by a person who himself does any of the acts. This is a new concept which apparently was introduced because of the advancement in the ways works of many descriptions can be copied or reproduced; it remains to be seen how the provision will be applied. Nonetheless there is a difference between providing the means whereby copyright can or might be infringed—the photo-copier, the recording equipment, the hiring out of a video-tape—from authorising a person to infringe copyright.

For an act to be an infringing act it need not be in relation to the whole of a work; it is sufficient for it to be in respect of a substantial part. What is a substantial part is essentially a matter of fact and degree. It will depend not merely on the perceived physical amount used but also on the significance of what is taken; on the quality rather than the quantity of what is taken. Works are frequently the result of an author's study of the ideas, thoughts, researches and creations of others and so the issue of infringement is often reduced to a consideration of the object or purposes of the use made of another's work, whether the use has been fair or amounts to an appropriation of the author's skill and labour, whether what has been taken diminishes the value of the original work so as to make it virtually redundant. There is a distinction between the appropriation and illicit use of a work and the "fair dealing" with a work as permitted by the Act.

It perhaps needs to be stressed that the rights of copyright in a work are mutually exclusive and this separateness is apt to be overlooked especially with works of the mechanical media. The copyright in a sound recording is distinct from the copyright in the recorded music; the copyright in a film is distinct from the elements which make up the film—the basic novel, script, music; the copyright in a broadcast is distinct from the copyright subsisting in the talk, story, play, music, record or film or other material which is broadcast. So the unlawful copying or public performance of any of these works is additionally an unlawful copying or public performance of the work embodied in the record, film or broadcast.

Infringement of copyright is divided into two classes, namely, primary and secondary. A primary infringement is the doing of any one of the five acts listed in section 16 as above and renders a person liable for breach of copyright regardless of whether he knew his action was an infringement of another's copyright. In such a case liability is said to be absolute. The acts of primary liability are considered next. Secondary infringements are acts such as the importation of copyright works or their sale in the course of business by a person knowing or having reasonable cause to believe his actions infringe copyright. For liability to attach to a person in such circumstances the required knowledge must be proved. This class of infringement is considered later.

PRIMARY INFRINGEMENTS OF COPYRIGHT

Copying a Work

By section 17 of the Act the copying of any description of a protected work is an infringement of copyright. In relation to literary, dramatic, musical and artistic works copying means "reproducing the work in any material form" and this includes storing the work in any medium by electronic means. With artistic works it also includes the making of a copy in three dimensions of a two-dimensional work, and of a copy in two dimensions of a three-dimensional work.

Copying in relation to a film, television broadcast or cable programme includes making a photograph of the whole or any substantial part of any image forming part of the film, broadcast or cable programme.

Copying in relation to the typographical arrangement of a published edition means making a facsimile copy of the arrangement, and this includes a copy which is reduced or enlarged in scale.

As a computer program is a work protected by copyright and its value is in its appearance or viewing on a VDU the concept of copying has been extended so that "copying in relation to any description of work includes the making of copies which are transient or are incidental to some other use of the work."

The literal copying of works such as printed matter, records, films and computer programs without the consent of the copyright owner is seldom now alone an issue for judgment as such an act is manifestly an infringement of copyright. For that reason little needs to be said here about such actual copying. Rather what else amounts to copying a work is of greater relevance in the context of this whole study and therefore merits special attention.

The underlying principles for deciding what constitutes the copying or reproduction of a work are well established in regard to literary, dramatic, musical and artistic works. These principles have been adapted and applied by way of analogy both to new works of the twentieth century which have acquired copyright protection and to the modern means for reproducing works. Allegations of plagiarism by the actual copying of a work are seldom disputed, but where an allegation is raised on account of a work's similarity to another, or whether the use of an existing work has been such as to amount to an infringement of copyright are often contentious issues. When works are based on traditional themes, or derived from a common source, or deal with actual events or the common situations of life it would be remarkable if similarities were not found to exist between two or more works.

The close similarity of incidents or situations or characters found in works, or of sounds in musical compositions or in the appearance of artistic works cannot alone substantiate a claim of plagiarism. In order to establish infringement by copying there must be shown to exist a causal connection between the copyright work and the allegedly infringing work. That is to say there must be shown to exist a sufficient degree of similarity between the works coupled with evidence of some opportunity or circumstances whereby copying could have occurred and leading to an inference of copying. When that inference arises the onus is on the alleged infringer to show affirmatively that his work is the product of his own independent research and study, his own labour and skill.

If there are many similarities of detail, of language, of scenes, and of features of a work but no explanation for these can be given then it will not be easy to refute an allegation of copying and plagiarism. This occurred with a film script written of a famous incident in history, the Charge of the Light Brigade. It was claimed the work was derived from common sources of literature and information but as the script was found in its structure, scenes and use of words to resemble so closely an existing copyright work, and as no explanation was forthcoming of when or how long it took the author to write the script, the claim of infringement of the original work was accepted by the court.

There is no monopoly in facts and information; it is the form or way in which material is expressed or presented which is protected. This principle was stressed in a judgment which has often been quoted concerning Palgrave's Golden Treasury of Poems:

> "In cases of works not original in the proper sense of the term, but composed of or compiled or prepared from materials which are open to all, the fact that one man has produced such a work does not take away from anyone else the right to produce another work of the same kind and in doing so to use all the materials open to him."

When a work of historical research combined with philosophical discussions and mysticism was used in the writing of a novel the court held it was legitimate to make use of the research but not to reproduce it and present it as if it were the work of the novelist. It is to be assumed that the author of a work of research of any description intends the information to be used by others otherwise the knowledge imparted would serve no purpose, but not that it should be used in such a way as to amount to an appropriation of his work and labour; in other words to steal his property.

A claim of subconscious copying as an explanation for the similarity between works, especially musical works, has caused anxiety where it has been advanced. Similarities between written works are less likely to be explained on this account, but with music actual copying is often less easily proved as musical themes can be buried deep in a composer's mind and subconsciously used and reproduced by a transposition of key, change of rhythm and the use of other techniques of musical composition. Furthermore, it has been remarked that the infringement of a musical work is not to be decided by a note for note comparison of the scores, but falls to be determined by the ear as well as by the eye. It was stated in a judgment concerning the so-called "Humming Chorus" in Puccini's "Madam Butterfly" that "the originality of a musical work is due not to the sequence of notes but to the treatment, the accentuation and the orchestration by Puccini; it is the music as a whole which is entitled to the protection afforded by the Act."

With paintings, drawings, graphic designs and like visual works again there may be resemblances, and with photographs a virtual identical likeness. If the works can be shown to have been independently produced, the coincidences or likenesses will be immaterial unless the special features found in one work—choice of view, perspective, design and layout—are found in the other work. Perhaps claims of subconscious copying may be advanced for abstract art where two such works show a marked resemblance. Then an enquiry into an artist's opportunity for seeing an existing work and into what work he has done in creating and developing his visual concepts and ideas may be justified.

The copying of an artistic work presents special problems as it can arise where there is a change in the form of the work. Copying includes the making of a copy in three dimensions of a two dimensional work, and the making of a copy in two dimensions of a three dimensional work. The conversion or reproduction of a painting, cartoon, drawing or the like in any material form without consent is an infringement of copyright. Thus when some cartoons which were published in "Punch" during the First World War were reproduced and performed on the stage as *tableaux vivants* in a revue it was held to be an infringement of the cartoons.

The manufacture without permission of objects representing the character "Popeye" featured in an animated cartoon film (which of course comprised many drawings) was held to be infringing copyright.

The exhibition in public of artistic works is not an infringement but the consent of the author or copyright owner is required for their reproduction and inclusion in any film or television broadcast or photograph unless on display in a place of public resort.

Technical drawings fall within the definition of artistic works and so are protected by copyright like drawings which are artistic but their use and copying for industrial purposes and the manufacture of articles are subject to special provisions of the Act covering design rights.

The copying and reproduction of a single frame of a film has been held to be an infringement of copyright. This occurred when a frame from one of the films in the series "Starsky and Hutch" was used for the making of photographs and posters without permission. Although the use of a single frame can hardly be regarded as a "substantial" copying of the film the decision can be justified by analogy with an unauthorised use of a "still" photograph. The provision of section 17 concerning the copying of films includes television broadcasts and so the principle applies to the taking of a photograph of an image of a television broadcast, unless the photograph is made for private and domestic use.

Adapting a Work

The making of an adaptation of a work, particularly of a literary or dramatic work, may be closely akin to copying it and many of the instances of infringement noted above could perhaps be viewed as acts of unauthorised adaptation. The distinction lies in the amount of originality, skill and labour expended in the making of an adaptation. For this reason, as noted earlier, an adaptation is a protected work with the adapter having all the rights of copyright in his work as any other author or copyright owner. However, being a derivative work then unless it is made with the consent of the owner of the copyright in the original work it will be an infringement of the latter's rights so that any exploitation of the adaptation could be restrained.

If an adaptation of a work is made with the licence and consent of the owner the licence should specify precisely the rights the adapter is at liberty to exercise in his adaptation and for how long. It may be made a condition of a licence that certain rights in the adaptation are reserved to the owner of the original work, or that on the expiration of the period during which the adaptation may be exploited all rights are to revert and pass to the owner of the original work.

As ideas are not protected by copyright it might seem that the plot of a work is not protected and could be used and adapted without risk of infringement. Even so since 1913 following a judgment about the dramatisation of an historical novel without permission it has been recognised and established that the taking for the purposes of a dramatic work of any substantial part of the combination of incidents in a copyright novel, even though none of the words are taken, is an infringement. In this instance the court remarked that the similarities and coincidences in the two works when taken in combination were such as to be entirely inexplicable as the result of mere chance coincidence.

In another case where two plays were much alike it was remarked in a leading judgment:

"In order to constitute an infringement [of the play by another play] it was not necessary that the words of the dialogue should be the same; the situations and incidents, the mode in which the ideas were worked out and presented might constitute a material portion of the whole play, and the court must have regard to the dramatic value and importance of what if anything was taken, even although the portion might in fact be small and the actual language not copied. On the other hand, the fundamental idea of two plays might be the same, but if worked out separately and on independent lines they might be so different as to bear no resemblance to one another."

Where a work is similar to another in that it draws on an existing work it is not always easy to decide if there has been an infringement of copyright especially when characters are developed, new relationships explored and new scenes and situations introduced. Certainly a change in the form of use or presentation of a work does not avoid an infringement of copyright as when Oscar Wilde's poem "The Nightingale and the Rose" was converted and presented as a ballet, the court recognised that the idea or plot of the poem itself was traditional and that allowance had to be made for the changed medium of the telling of the story, but taking the production as a whole the ballet was a substantial reproduction of the combination or series of dramatic events in the tale as told by Oscar Wilde. The conversion of a narrative work into dramatic form is an adaptation and its performance on stage or in a film without the consent of the copyright owner of the original work would be an infringement of copyright, that is unless the original work is in the public domain.

Section 21 of the Act expressly provides that the making of a version of a literary or dramatic work whereby the story or action is conveyed wholly or mainly pictorially in the form of strip cartoons, political cartoons and story book cartoons and graphics regardless of the absence of any words is an adaptation and so if produced without permission is an infringement of copyright. The same can be said of the making of an animated film version of a literary, dramatic or artistic work.

A parody and burlesque is less likely to be susceptible to a claim that it infringes a copyright for, as already amply demonstrated, just because a work is inspired by another it does not follow that the later work is an infringement of the original or earlier work. The test will be whether there has been bestowed in the creation of the parody that degree of independent work and labour as to make it an original work for the purposes of copyright.

Translations

The translation of a literary and dramatic work—and lyrics are literary works—is an adaptation and so if made without permission is an infringement of copyright. In this connection the international aspects of copyright and the protection afforded to the works of foreign nationals (as noted above) become relevant. The translation of a work in a foreign language into English as an adaptation can be an infringement of copyright just as much as the translation of a work in the English language into a foreign language.

Musical Arrangements

An arrangement or transcription of a musical work is an adaptation of the work and therefore if made without the licence of the composer or copyright owner is an infringement of copyright. What has been remarked above concerning the licensing of the making of adaptations of literary and dramatic works applies to musical works.

Where music is traditional or in the public domain then an arrangement, depending on the amount of individual skill and labour expended in its making, will constitute an original work and so be fully protected by copyright. Thus when John Gay's musical work "Polly" was revised and made into a new opera the new version was protected by copyright, but that did not prevent a recording company from having John Gay's airs again newly orchestrated and arranged for a recording of "Polly" so long as the particular features and style of the first arrangement were not copied. The making of a pianoforte score of an opera is an adaptation of the opera and likewise the making of an orchestral arrangement of the published piano accompaniment of a popular song. If these arrangements are made without consent being adaptations they are an infringement of copyright.

Publishing a Work

By section 18 of the Act the issue to the public by the putting into circulation for the first time in the United Kingdom of copies of any kind of protected work is an act restricted by copyright. Thus an author has the absolute right to decide upon releasing his work and making it available to the public. Once copies of a work have been lawfully issued then any distribution, sale, hire or loan of those copies (or their importation into the United Kingdom if first published abroad), does not constitute an infringement of copyright.

Under the Copyright Act 1956 the fact of a work being published or unpublished was material in determining the duration of the term of copyright protection as well as its qualifying for protection. As now by the 1988 Act the term of copyright is fixed for all works, the fact of publication of any kind of work (other than a broadcast or cable programme) is material only when the question of a work's qualifying for protection rests on the country where it was first published and not on the author being a British citizen or otherwise as noted earlier.

Publication is defined in section 175 as meaning the issue of copies of a work to the public and in the case of a literary, dramatic, musical and artistic work it includes making the work available to the public by means of an electronic retrieval system. The section also contains detailed provisions on what does not constitute publication; for example, the performance or broadcasting of a literary, dramatic or musical work, the exhibition of an artistic work, the playing or showing in public or broadcasting of a sound recording or film. This underlines that the rights of copyright are mutually exclusive; the exercise or licensing of one right such as publication does not convey the right to copy or publicly perform the work.

For a work to be published copies must be issued to the public but this does not mean the copies have to be sold; they can be distributed or otherwise made available for nothing. The Act stipulates that publication which is merely colourable and not intended to satisfy the reasonable requirements of the public does not count. Even so when, in order to comply with the rules for simultaneous publication for a work to qualify for protection, only a few copies of the song "You Made Me Love You" (which had first been printed and published in the USA) were put on sale in the heartland of London's music centre, it was judged to be sufficient to show there was an intention to satisfy the demands of the public if such demand should arise.

It follows that making copies of a script or musical score only for the purpose of the rehearsal and performance of a work does not amount to publication so that an author's right to choose to publish his work remains intact. Likewise the private printing and distribution of a limited edition of a literary or artistic work does not amount to publication within the legal definition.

By section 18 "the act of issuing [copies of a work] to the public includes any rental of copies to the public"; this is an innovation of copyright law. However, it is of limited application as it is only the owners of the copyright in sound recordings, films and computer programs who have the exclusive right to rent copies of these works to the public. There is nothing in the Act which confers on the authors of the works which are recorded or reproduced any rental right in their works, or any right to participate in the royalties or income derived from the exercise of the rental right by the producers of records, films or computer programs.

Rental is defined in section 178 as meaning "any arrangement under which a copy of a work is made available—

(a) for payment (in money or money's worth); or

(b) in the course of business, as part of services or amenities for which payment is made;

on terms that it will or may be returned."

The rental right hinges on the element of payment. If there is a charge by a library, or there is payment of a subscription to an association for the facility of hire then, like the payment for the hiring of a film from a high street video shop, if such activities are undertaken without the consent and licence of the copyright owners there is an infringement of the rental right. Through the associations representing the interests of record and film/video tape producers and libraries in particular, licensing schemes have been introduced which prescribe the fees and conditions on which records and videos may be made available for hire to the public. The schemes are still in their infancy. Section 66 of the Act makes provision for such schemes or agreements to be open to review by the Copyright Tribunal.

Public Performance of a Work

The public performance of a protected work is an act restricted by copyright. By section 19 of the Act only a literary, dramatic or musical work can be infringed by public performance. With a sound recording, film, broadcast or cable programme it is "the playing or showing of the work in public" which is an act restricted by copyright in any such work. A rather subtle distinction. The section provides that where a work is infringed by its public performance by means of apparatus for receiving visual images or sounds conveyed by electronic means, the person by whom the visual images and sounds are sent is not to be regarded as responsible for the infringement and likewise the performers of the work.

Section 19 defines "performance" in relation to a work in the following terms—

"(a) includes delivery in the case of lectures, addresses, speeches and sermons; and

(b) in general, includes any mode of visual or acoustic presentation, including presentation by means of a sound recording, film, broadcast or cable programme of a work."

It has been left to the courts to settle what is a public performance. A number of considerations have been taken into account: the place of performance, its accessibility to the public, the number of persons present, if an element of profit is present. It is not material whether any payment is or is not made by the public expressly for the purpose of viewing or hearing a performance, neither is it material whether the performance is an amateur or professional performance for the character or standing of the performers is of no importance. The performance of a stage play or musical work at a place of public entertainment is likely to fall within the description of a public performance if members of the public are present but not if they are excluded as for example during a rehearsal. A performance in a studio for the purpose of making a broadcast or producing records and tapes or filming is not of itself a public performance; it may be held to be so if members of the public are present.

One of the leading and guiding cases to have come before the courts on whether a performance was in public, concerned a performance given at a village Women's Institute. All the ladies present were members of the Institute who had paid a small annual membership subscription but they had not paid to attend the performance. It was held that although the attendance at the performance was confined to members of the Institute, as membership of the Institute was open to anyone this was not a performance on a domestic or quasi domestic occasion but was a public performance. In another case which concerned the relaying of music to workers in a factory, it was remarked that the question of whether or not a performance is in public is best considered by regarding the relationship of the audience to the owner of the copyright rather than that to the performers. More recently the playing of records in shops to attract members of the public to premises was held to be a public performance of music.

The need for the consent of the copyright owner to the "live" public performance of a dramatic or musical work can perhaps be more easily understood than when a work is performed publicly by means such as a record or film. The separateness of the rights of copyright in a work was remarked upon at the commencement of this Section and so it should be borne in mind there may be a pyramid or tier of copyright interests comprised in a work such as a record, film or broadcast. How the consent of copyright owners is obtained to the public performance and broadcasting of works generally is considered in Part 7.

Broadcasting a Work

The restriction on the broadcasting or inclusion in a cable programme service of protected works is prescribed in section 20. The restriction extends to literary, dramatic, musical and artistic works, and to a sound recording and film. A broadcast or cable programme being itself a protected work is brought within the scope of the section so that any re-broadcasting of a broadcast without the consent of the person making the broadcast is an infringement of copyright.

Sections 297/299 (as amended by the Broadcasting Act 1990) legislate for the fraudulent reception of broadcasts and cable programmes and for the imposition of criminal penalties for so doing. Civil rights of redress are enacted for copyright owners and persons who make charges for the reception of transmissions, or who send encrypted transmissions, against those persons who deal in or provide the means of, or facilitate the infringement of the copyright in a broadcast or cable programme.

SECONDARY INFRINGEMENTS OF COPYRIGHT

The importation of infringing copies of a work, dealing commercially with infringing copies, permitting premises to be used or providing the apparatus for the unlicensed public performance of a work are instances of secondary or indirect infringements of copyright. Unlike direct infringements where liability is absolute and irrespective of the presence or absence of a person's knowledge or intention to infringe copyright, with indirect infringements the onus is on the person alleging a breach of the copyright in his work to prove that the infringer "knew or had reason to believe" his action was an infringement of copyright.

What facts a defendant should be aware of to impute the knowledge goes to the heart of the issue. Where a person is engaged in business and it would be reasonable to expect him to be alert to the risks of infringement the imputation is the more likely to be sustained. A failure to make reasonable enquiries is of no avail. If a copyright owner is aware of the likelihood of the commission of an infringing act then a warning letter to the potential infringer will place the onus on the latter to show he did not have the required knowledge or grounds for belief his action would infringe copyright.

By Importation of Copies

By section 22 of the Act the copyright in a work is infringed by a person who, without the licence of the copyright owner, imports into the United Kingdom "otherwise than for his private and domestic use, an article which is, and which he knows or has reason to believe is, an infringing copy of the work." The person who imports the work must show it is for his private and domestic use but it is for the person alleging the infringement to show the importer had the knowledge or reason to believe the copy was an infringing copy. Knowledge that a work made abroad is an infringing copy when brought into the United Kingdom is not easy to prove or impute. The foregoing provision covers copyright works in general but certain works are given preferred treatment by sections 111 and 112.

These sections enable the owner of the copyright in published literary, dramatic and musical works to give written notice to the Commissioners of Customs and Excise requesting printed copies of specified works to be treated as prohibited imports for a stated period of time. This can be for up to five years but in any event not beyond the term of copyright in the work. There is a corresponding provision for sound recordings and films but the notice must be for works which are expected to arrive in the United Kingdom at a time and place which must be specified in the notice. These rigid requirements give but meagre assistance in combatting the importation of pirated copies of records and films. These provisions do not avail the author of the literary, dramatic or musical work which is the subject matter of the record or film for it is only printed copies of their works which can be treated as prohibited imports. Performers are in no better position. Authors and copyright owners of artistic works are not afforded the chance of preventing the illicit importation of infringing copies of their works by giving notice to the Customs and Excise but have to rely solely on section 22.

By section 27 "an article is an infringing copy if its making constituted an infringement of the copyright in the work in question." An article is also an infringing copy if "it has been or is proposed to be imported into the United Kingdom, and its making in the United Kingdom would have constituted an infringement of the copyright in the work in question, or a breach of an exclusive licence agreement relating to that work." This latter condition is made subject to the rules of the European Community for the free movement of goods.

By Commercial and Other Dealings

By section 23 of the Act "copyright in a work is infringed by a person who, without the licence of the copyright owner:

(a) possesses in the course of business,

(b) sells or lets for hire, or offers or exposes for sale or hire,

(c) in the course of business exhibits in public or distributes

an article which is, and which he knows or has reason to believe is, an infringing copy of the work." This section like the next is directed mainly at those who deal commercially with infringing copies of a work, the audio and video tape pirates of this world.

This form of infringement is not confined to persons in business as the section also provides that a person who otherwise than in the course of business and without the consent of the copyright owner distributes a work "to such an extent as to affect prejudicially the owner of copyright" infringes copyright in the work. In such a case then in addition to the need for the copyright owner to prove knowledge on the part of the alleged infringer the copyright owner must also show he has suffered loss from the distribution of his work.

As for exhibiting works in public—meaning, it seems, artistic works and not work such as films which are played or shown in public—it is the exhibition and distribution "in the course of business" of infringing copies which is a (secondary) infringement of copyright in the original work. It is not an infringement to exhibit in public in the course of business or otherwise an original work, or a copy of it provided the copy has been lawfully made.

Copyright in a work is also infringed under section 24 by the making, importation, possession in the course of business or sale or hiring of "an article specifically designed or adapted for the making of copies of that work, knowing or having reason to believe that it is to be used to make infringing copies." Merely to provide equipment whereby copyright can be infringed does not contravene the provision since the article such as a mould or plate or negative must be specifically made or adapted for copying a particular work without the copyright owner's consent. Manufacturers of audio and video cassette recorders are not liable as secondary infringers of copyright because although such equipment may be used in a way which infringes copyright, the equipment itself is not "specifically designed or adapted" for that purpose.

Another innovation of copyright law and which reflects the progress and diversity of the means of communication also arises under section 24. It is provided that "a person who without the licence of the copyright owner transmits the work by means of a telecommunications system (otherwise than by broadcasting or inclusion in a cable programme service), knowing or having reason to believe that infringing copies of the work will be made by means of the reception of the transmission in the United Kingdom or elsewhere" infringes copyright in the work. Telecommunications system is defined in the Act as "a system for conveying visual images, sounds or other information by electronic means." As this is a new provision of the law it remains to be seen how it will be applied and in what circumstances but certainly it embraces the modern telephone fax machine.

By Providing Premises for Public Performance

Where without the consent of the copyright owner a public performance of a literary, dramatic or musical work is given at a place of public entertainment, by section 25 any person "who gave permission for that place to be used for the performance is also liable for the infringement unless when he gave permission he believed on reasonable grounds that the performance would not infringe copyright." The liability is additional (secondary) to the primary liability of the person who performs the work in public.

A "place of entertainment" is not confined to a theatre or concert hall; the expression includes any premises which may be used for many purposes and only from time to time made available for hire for the purposes of public entertainment. Unlike the corresponding provision of the Copyright Act 1956 there is no exemption under section 25 from liability on the grounds the place of entertainment was made available without charge.

What are reasonable grounds for believing a performance would not be an infringement of copyright and thereby exonerate a person from liability, has not been well formulated in the few decisions of the courts where the issue has arisen. When permission was given for the use of premises for the performance of a specifically named work then because the work was named the person alleging infringement had less difficulty in establishing liability. Where a general permission is given and there is no immediate supervision or control of what works are performed, as for example with a concert of musical works or the showing of music videos at a discotheque, then it appears the courts will be more ready to accept a person having grounds for believing a performance would not infringe copyright.

When copyright in a work is infringed by being performed in public, or by the playing or showing of the work in public "by means of apparatus for playing sound recordings, showing films or receiving visual images or sounds conveyed by electronic means" then by section 26 the person who supplied the apparatus, the occupier of the premises who gave permission for the apparatus to be installed, and the person who supplied the sound recording or film may be liable for the infringement of the copyright in the work. As with all cases of secondary infringement it is necessary to show that such persons had the requisite knowledge or grounds for belief that their actions would be likely to result in an infringement of copyright.

F. ACTS PERMITTED WITHOUT INFRINGING COPYRIGHT

The 1988 Act enables certain uses to be made of protected works without the need for an author's consent or it even having first to be sought. The particular uses are prescribed and designated by the Act as "permitted acts" and so an author or copyright owner cannot prevent any person from doing any of the acts on the grounds of infringement of his copyright.

The permitted acts material to this study are:

(a) fair dealing for the purposes of research and private study;

(b) fair dealing for the purposes of criticism and review;

(c) incidental inclusion of a work in other works;

(d) uses and acts done in connection with education;

(e) copying done by librarians and archivists;

(f) uses in connection with public administration—parliamentary and judicial proceedings, public enquiries, public records.

Fair Dealing

By section 29 fair dealing for the purposes of research and private study does not infringe copyright in literary, dramatic, musical and artistic works. The objects of the research or private study are immaterial—the research can be for industrial and commercial purposes and so in the ultimate analysis for private gain—but only the person engaged in the research or private study can rely on the section in answer to an allegation of infringement of copyright.

The copying of works is a pursuit of those engaged in research and private study and as the facilities for copying are so much greater than in the past, section 29 takes account of this by in effect allowing only single copies of a work to be made. The copying can be done by a person on behalf of the researcher or student but the copying is not fair dealing if:

"the person doing the copying knows or has reason to believe that it will result in copies of substantially the same material being provided to more than one person at substantially the same time and for substantially the same purpose."

Fair dealing with all kinds of works without exception is permitted by section 30 for the purpose of criticism and review. The use may be of a number of works as where works are being compared, and the use may be for the criticism or review of performances of a work. Any such use of a work is conditional on its being "accompanied by a sufficient acknowledgement." The Act prescribes sufficient acknowledgement as meaning "an acknowledgement identifying the work in question by its title or other description, and identifying the author unless:

(a) in the case of a published work it is published anonymously;

(b) in the case of an unpublished work, it is not possible for a person to ascertain the identity of the author by reasonable enquiry."

Fair dealing with works for the purpose of reporting current events is similarly provided for but with the exception of photographs. The grounds for their exclusion is the difficulty of showing fair use when often the purpose of a photograph is for the reporting of news and current events. Where works are used for this purpose the requirement for a sufficient acknowledgement applies unless the reporting of current events is by means of a sound recording, film, broadcast or cable programme.

What proportion to the whole constitutes a fair use or dealing with a work can only be decided in the light of the circumstances of a particular case. Certainly the problem is more acute when works are used for the purpose of criticism, review or reporting current events as whatever is used will be more widely disseminated than when used for research and private study. This is particularly so with unpublished works when economic loss and detriment may more likely be suffered by an author than when it has already been published or otherwise exploited.

In many situations, and especially in the making of films and television programmes and the broadcasting of actual events, works which are protected by copyright will be audible and in vision simply as background or as part of a studio set or location. Provided the inclusion is incidental section 31 provides a defence: "Copyright in a work [without exception] is not infringed by its incidental inclusion in an artistic work, sound recording, film, broadcast or cable programme." The exploitation of such a work is not inhibited since it is also provided that the issue to the public of copies, or the playing, showing, broadcasting or inclusion in a cable programme service of such a work in which there is included incidentally a protected work, does not constitute an infringement of the protected work.

The section will not apply where works are featured, such as in a documentary film about the work of an artist. If a musical work, or spoken material, etc., is merely background and incidental to an actual happening—a sports event, public ceremony—then as "noises off" their inclusion in the filming or broadcasting of the event will not amount to an infringement of copyright. But where the music or other work is a programme item as, for example, the performance of music by a band appearing at an event, then the licence of the copyright owner is required for the inclusion of the music or other work in a film or broadcast.

Other acts permitted by the Act and considered below are either acts of less general scope than as above, or acts which are permitted only in respect of particular works or in particular circumstances.

Acts for the Purposes of Broadcasting

Broadcasting is by no means central to this study but it is fitting that those provisions of the Act which permit certain acts to be done in relation to the broadcasting of works without infringing rights of copyright in them should be considered at this juncture. In what follows, broadcasting is to be understood as including a cable programme service.

The first of the provisions is section 68 whereby a person who is licensed to broadcast a work may make a sound recording or film of it, or if the work is an artistic work make a photograph or make a film of it, or if the work is a sound recording make a copy of it. This recording of a work is permitted only for the purpose of making the broadcast and the recording is to be destroyed within 28 days of the broadcast. If the copyright owner's licence authorises a second broadcasting of the work then by implication—but not necessarily so—there is a right to retain the recording.

By section 69 of the 1988 Act as amended in part by the Broadcasting Act 1990, the copyright in a work is not infringed by the BBC or by the ITC or by a programme contractor in accordance with its obligations as a licensee of the ITC (and correspondingly the Radio Authority with regard to radio broadcasting) making a recording of a programme for certain purposes.

These are, briefly, for exercising control and supervision over programmes and enquiring into complaints made to the Broadcasting Complaints Commission and for enabling the Broadcasting Complaints Commission and Broadcasting Standards Council to discharge their functions under the Broadcasting Act. There is a like provision in section 75 which permits a body designated by the Secretary of State to record a broadcast for archival purposes without infringing any copyright in the broadcast or in any work included in it.

The hazards of using the spoken word which when "recorded in writing or otherwise" comes within the definition of a literary work have already been alluded to. As a protected work, the use of the spoken word is subject to the consent of the author but this can be dispensed with in broadcasting as laid down in section 58. The section also applies to "reporting of current events" so other media of information in addition to broadcasting have the benefit of the dispensation.

By section 58 if a record of spoken words is made in writing or otherwise for the purposes of broadcasting it is not an infringement of copyright in the words as a literary work to use the record or material taken from it for broadcasting provided the following conditions are met, namely:

(a) the record is a direct recording of the spoken word, that is the record is a wholly original recording;

(b) the making of the recording was not prohibited by the speaker and, where copyright already subsisted in the work, did not infringe copyright;

(c) the use made of the record or material taken from it is not of a kind which is prohibited by the speaker or copyright owner before the record was made; and

(d) the use of the record is by or with the authority of a person who is lawfully in possession of the record.

The prohibition and any prohibition concerning the use of the material mentioned in (b) and (c) above must it seems be actually expressed or implied at the time of the making of the record.

Public Readings

The reading or recitation in public by one person of any reasonable extract from a published literary or dramatic work is a permitted act under section 59 provided it is accompanied by a sufficient acknowledgement. The section also similarly permits the making of a sound recording, or the broadcasting of such a reading or recitation provided it is not the main content of the programme. So if works in the public domain are included in the reading, or if the programme content includes other material as well as the reading there would be no infringement of the copyright in the published literary or dramatic work.

Acts in Relation to Broadcasts

The rights of copyright in a broadcast and the acts which, if done without consent of the person making the broadcast would be an infringement of the copyright in the broadcast, are no different from those of other works. However in addition to the general exceptions allowed by law such as "fair dealing" there are other exceptions which apply solely to broadcasting.

The first arises under section 35 which enacts that the recording of a broadcast or cable programme by an educational establishment for its own use for educational purposes does not constitute an infringement of the copyright in the broadcast or cable programme, or in any work included in it. However, the section further provides that the exemption from infringement does not apply if and to the extent there is a licensing scheme in operation. There is such a scheme in operation so the immunity is in effect nullified.

The scheme is operated by the Educational Recording Agency (ERA) and is certified by the Government as required by section 143 of the Act and promulgated by regulation (Copyright (Certification of Licensing Scheme for Educational Recording of Broadcasts and Cable Programmes) (Educational Recording Agency Limited) Order 1990 (S.I. 1990 No. 879)). (A separate scheme sanctioned by regulation (Copyright (Certification of Licensing Scheme for Educational Recording of Broadcasts) (Open University Educational Enterprises Limited) Order 1990 (S.I. 1990 No. 2008)) exists for broadcasts of the Open University).

ERA represents the owners and controllers of the copyright in broadcasts and cable programmes and the works included in the programmes. So it acts on behalf of the BBC and the television broadcasting companies and the organisations representing authors and writers, the record industry, the music business and owners of artistic copyright and the performers' Unions.

On payment of an annual fee ERA grants in effect a blanket licence to educational establishments—schools, colleges, polytechnics and universities—the right to record broadcasts and cable programmes and to retain the recording indefinitely and make copies but only for use on the licensee's premises or residence of a teacher for the purposes of education. With schools and colleges under the jurisdiction of a local education authority it is normally the latter which is collectively licensed. After deducting an administration charge ERA apportions and distributes the revenues it receives to its members.

Under section 70 the making "for private and domestic use of a recording of a broadcast or cable programme solely for the purpose of enabling it to be viewed or listened to at a more convenient time" is not an infringement of any copyright in the broadcast or in any work included in it. If the broadcast programme comprises a sound recording or film, by recording the broadcast there is no infringement of the copyright in the sound recording or film as there would be if these works were copied or recorded directly. The vagueness and imprecision over the time of viewing is doubtless attributable to the difficulty of devising any form of words which could effectively restrict the viewing of a recording once made. However, any public viewing or performance of the recording would amount to an infringement of copyright in the broadcast and any sound recording or film included in the broadcast.

By section 71 the making for private and domestic use of a photograph of the whole or any part of an image forming part of a television broadcast or a copy of such photograph does not infringe any copyright in the broadcast or any film included in it. As the making is restricted to private use in effect it affirms the decision of the courts noted above that the photographic reproduction of a single frame from a film and its use, for example in any advertisement or publication without the consent of the copyright owner, is an infringement of copyright.

The public performance of a broadcast or cable programme (like the public performance of any other copyright work) without the consent of the person making the broadcast is an infringement of the copyright in the broadcast. Section 72 limits this rule by providing that the showing or playing in public to an audience who have not paid for admission to the place where the broadcast is to be seen or heard does not infringe any copyright in "the broadcast or in any sound recording or film included in it." Unlike any of the other above sections here the exemption does not extend to "any work included in" a broadcast. The reason for this and its consequences are perhaps a matter for speculation.

To distinguish a paying from a non-paying audience the section details the audiences to be treated as having paid for admission to a place, namely:

"(a) if they have paid for admission to a place of which that place forms part; or

(b) if goods or services are supplied at that place (or place of which it forms part)—

  (i) at prices which are substantially attributable to the facilities afforded for seeing or hearing the broadcast or programme, or

  (ii) at prices exceeding those usually charged there and which are partly attributable to those facilities."

There is also specified those who "shall not be regarded as having paid for admission to a place—

(a) persons admitted as residents or inmates of the place;

(b) persons admitted as members of a club or society where the payment is only for membership of the club or society and the provision of facilities for seeing or hearing broadcasts or programmes is only incidental to the main purposes of the club or society."

By section 73 the reception and immediate re-transmission of a broadcast included in a cable programme service is not an infringement of the copyright in a broadcast "if and to the extent that the broadcast is made for reception in the area in which the cable programme service is provided and is not a satellite transmission or an encrypted transmission." The section also provides that any work included in the broadcast is not infringed if and to the extent that the broadcast is made for reception in the area in which the cable programme service is provided. On the other hand the inclusion of a cable programme in a broadcast without the licence of the operator of the cable programme service and of the owner of the copyright in the cable programme itself would be an infringement of the two copyrights.

An innovation of copyright law is introduced in section 74 of the 1988 Act. This enables bodies (designated by the Secretary of State) for the benefit of people who are deaf or hard of hearing, or in other ways physically or mentally handicapped, to make and issue to the public copies of television broadcasts and cable programmes and to sub-title or otherwise modify the copies to suit the special needs of such persons without infringing the copyright in the broadcasts or the works included in the programmes broadcast. By the Copyright (Sub-Titling of Broadcast and Cable Programmes) (Designated Body) Order 1989 (S.I. 1989 No. 1013) the National Subtitling Library for Deaf People has been so authorised.

Acts in Relation to Sound Recordings

By section 67 it is not an infringement of the copyright in a sound recording to play it as part of the activities of, or for the benefit of, a club, society or other organisation if the following conditions are met:

"(a) the organisation is not established or conducted for profit and its main objects are charitable or are otherwise concerned with the advancement of religion, education or social welfare; and

(b) the proceeds of any charge for admission to the place where the recording is to be heard and applied solely for the purposes of the organisation."

The section exempts from infringement only the playing of the sound recording, it does not affect the rights of the owners of the copyright in any works such as music embodied in the recording. If, therefore, an audience is present the playing of the sound recording will be a public performance of the recorded work which if in copyright will need to be licensed for its performance in public.

There is no equivalent provision, that is to say no corresponding permitted act with regard to films.

Acts in Relation to Education and Libraries

The uses of copyright works for the purposes of education and by librarians and archivists which by law do not constitute an infringement of copyright are primarily the copying and particularly reprographic copying of works, and the publication of anthologies and so lie outside the scope of this study. But there are some other uses which should be noted. The right under section 35 to make recordings of broadcasts and cable programmes for educational purposes and the role of the Educational Recording Agency has been noted above.

By section 32 "copyright in a literary, dramatic, musical or artistic work is not infringed by its being copied in the course of instruction or of preparation for instruction, provided the copying—

(a) is done by a person giving or receiving instruction, and

(b) is not by means of a reprographic process."

There is a corresponding exemption from infringement of a sound recording, film, broadcast and cable programme by the making of a film or film sound-track of any of these works. These permitted uses extend to examinations. The section stipulates that the copies made cannot be dealt with in any way such as by hiring or sale.

By section 34 "the performance of a literary, dramatic or musical work before an audience consisting of teachers and pupils at an educational establishment and other persons directly connected with the activities of the establishment:

(a) by a teacher or pupil in the course of the activities of the establishment, or

(b) at the establishment by any person for the purpose of instruction,

is not a public performance for the purposes of infringement of copyright." Likewise the playing or showing of a sound recording, film, broadcast or cable programme.

The performance of a literary, dramatic or musical work need not be by a teacher or pupil; it can be by any person. A performance by a visiting theatre company or group of professional artists does not make their performance a public performance. On the other hand, the section provides that a person is not to be regarded as directly connected with the activities of an educational establishment simply because he is the parent of a pupil there. Thus concerts of music and other such end of term events at which parents and friends are present are public performances for the purposes of copyright law and if works in copyright are performed the performance will need to be licensed.

The expression "educational establishment" is defined in section 174 of the Act. It includes any school as generally understood and as defined in the principal Education Acts, and any other description of educational establishment specified for the purposes of the Act by Government order.

Acts in Relation to Public Administration

The sections of the Act providing for the use of works in connection with public administration, parliamentary and judicial proceedings, public enquiries and public records are detailed. What needs to be especially borne in mind is that although there is a mass of information and material which by law is required to be kept and entered in registers and made available for public inspection, in so far as it is factual information it may be copied. However, any wider dissemination of the information often requires the permission of the "appropriate person," meaning the person required by law to make the material open to public inspection, or the person maintaining the register. Company reports and returns made in accordance with the company laws, planning applications and plans with local authorities are examples.

Acts in Relation to Anonymous Works

With regard to acts done in relation to anonymous or pseudonymous literary, dramatic, musical or artistic works exemption from copyright infringement may be had under section 57. If at the material time it is not possible by reasonable enquiry to ascertain the identity of the author and as a result it is reasonable to assume that:

(a) either the copyright has expired, or

(b) the author died 50 years or more before the beginning of the calendar year in which the act is done,

then the act is not an infringement of copyright. When a work has been published then enquiry should be made of the publishers to ascertain the copyright status of the work.

Acts in Relation to Folk Songs

The recording of folk songs is the subject of a special provision of the 1988 Act. By section 61 the making of a sound recording of a song for archival purposes (maintained by designated bodies) is not an infringement of the copyright in the words and music provided that the words (but not the music) are unpublished and of unknown authorship at the time of the recording, the making of the recording does not infringe any other copyright, and the making of the recording is not prohibited by any performer. The Copyright (Recordings of Folksongs for Archives) (Designated Bodies) Order 1989 (S.I. 1989 No. 1013) has designated 12 such bodies which include for example, The Folklore Society and the National Sound Archive, the British Library. The Order prescribes that a person requiring a copy of a recording must satisfy the archivist that it is required for purposes of research or private study; no person may be supplied with more than one copy of the same recording.

Acts in Relation to Works of Architecture

It has already been noted that the incidental inclusion of an artistic work in a film, broadcast or cable programme is not an infringement of copyright in such a work. Section 62 of the Act goes beyond any incidental inclusion in respect of buildings, sculptures, models for buildings and works of artistic craftsmanship if permanently situated in a public place, or in premises open to the public. The copyright in such works is not infringed by:

"(a) making a graphic work representing it;

(b) making a photograph or film of it; or

(c) broadcasting or including in a cable programme service a visual image of it."

Furthermore the making and issuing to the public of copies of any of these works does not infringe the copyright in any of the above specified works. It should be noted that the exemption from infringement does not apply to all artistic works as defined in section 4 of the Act such as paintings and other graphic works and photographs.

While there may be no control over places of public resort—public gardens, squares and the like—that may not be so with premises open to the public whether on payment or not. If there are conditions for entry to premises and these are brought to the notice of the public unless there is strict supervision that may not stop the photographing of a work but it can be the grounds for legal action to prevent any exploitation or reproduction of an infringing copy of a work.

G. ASSIGNMENT AND LICENSING OF COPYRIGHT

Copyright can be dealt with like any other item of intangible or incorporeal property. The rights which a copyright owner has in a work can be dealt with collectively or separately. Copyright can be the subject of a gift in the life-time of the owner and it can be bequeathed by will. It can be bought and sold and used as security for the payment of a debt. The distinction between the rights of ownership of the copyright in a work from those in the material form embodying a work has been alluded to earlier. Here to be considered are dealings and transfers both voluntary and involuntary of the rights of copyright in a work.

Transfer on Death

For the purposes of this study the involuntary transfer of copyright can be dealt with briefly. On the death of an author the copyright in his works will pass to his executors or administrators and form part of his estate like all other of his personal property. The copyright will then by an Assent signed by his personal representatives (whose authority is derived from the grant of Probate or Letters of Administration issued from the High Court), be transferred to those persons named in the author's will to whom he has bequeathed the copyright in his works, or if the author has died intestate, then to his next-of-kin in accordance with the rules of intestate succession.

Where under a bequest a person is entitled to an original document or other original material in which a work is embodied and the work remains unpublished at the time of the testator's death, then by section 93 of the 1988 Act and unless a contrary intention is shown in the will, the bequest is to be construed as including the copyright in the work in so far as the testator was the owner of the copyright immediately before his death. When dealing with the copyright in the works of a deceased author the title of the person purporting to grant any rights in a work may require investigation. In the ordinary way the Probate granted to the personal representatives or their Assent in favour of the person beneficially entitled to the copyright is proof of that title.

Transfer on Bankruptcy

On the bankruptcy of an author the copyright in his published and unpublished works will automatically pass to the appointed trustee in bankruptcy to be dealt with and disposed of by him like all other of the bankrupt's property. So too if the owner or proprietor of the copyright in a work is a company or corporate body, on its compulsory liquidation or winding up the copyright will pass to the liquidator and fall to be dealt with and disposed of by him like all other assets of the company. All other dealings with copyright are therefore to be understood as being the voluntary act of the author or other owner of the copyright in a work and either gratuitous or for some valuable consideration, that is to say, resting on a contractual basis.

DEALINGS WITH COPYRIGHT

Assignments

Copyright in a work can be assigned wholly and entirely, or in part as when the individual rights which comprise the copyright in a work are dealt with separately. The transfer of ownership or a dealing by way of licence with copyright need not be of the entire copyright in a work but by section 90 can be limited in a number of ways so as to apply:

(a) to one or more, but not all, of the things the copyright owner has the exclusive right to do;

(b) to part and not the whole of the period during which copyright subsists in a work.

With the combined effect of the international copyright conventions and the operation of the Act, but subject to the rules of the European Community as explained at the commencement of Part 6, dealings can also be limited to specific countries.

Accordingly, for example, the publication right in a novel may be assigned and disposed of entirely world wide, or it may be granted in respect of certain countries in English alone and/or other languages for a limited period of time. In both instances the author or copyright owner retains all other rights in his work with liberty to deal with them as he chooses. A playwright may license the public performance of a play on the professional stage perhaps coupled with the right of publication of the script but will still retain all other of his rights in work. In such circumstances both the author of the novel and the playwright will be able to deal with the film or television rights in their works. By licensing the public performance of his music a composer does not lose control of the recording right. These principles of partial dealings apply to all rights in copyright works.

For an assignment of copyright to be binding in law whether made gratuitously or for some consideration, and whether entire or partial it must be in writing and signed by or on behalf of the assignor, meaning the author or other copyright owner. No particular form of words and no other formalities are prescribed by the Act. Even so the work, the subject matter of the assignment must be clearly identified and when less than the assignment of the entire copyright in a work is to be effected, that is when there is only a partial assignment, the rights to be assigned, the territorial limitation and the duration of the grant need to be clearly defined. There is no restriction on an assignment being made by a person under age but a contract entered into with an infant may be set aside on the grounds of undue influence or an assignee exercising an unfair advantage.

An agreement to assign copyright and an assignment are in law two different transactions. The agreement may be oral and if its existence or terms are disputed then the agreement will have to be proved affirmatively. Where a party goes back on an agreement the assignment may be accomplished by procuring a decree of the court for specific performance of the agreement. If in breach of a valid agreement a copyright owner effects an assignment of rights in favour of another person then that person will be the legal owner and proprietor of the rights assigned. The person to whom the rights should have been assigned, that is the other party to the contract, will have to seek redress by way of proceedings for breach of contract.

The legal significance of an assignment, and so the need for it to be in writing, is that it constitutes a transfer or conveyance of the ownership of copyright. Consequently the assignee, by acquiring the entire copyright in a work is entitled to deal or not to deal with it as he chooses subject to what is said below regarding an author's moral rights. If only a partial assignment is effected the same rule applies but only for the particular rights assigned. The assignee will be entitled to take proceedings for infringement and protection of the rights transferred to him on his own initiative and in his own name as by the act of assigning an author or other copyright owner divests himself of all rights and interests in a work as property. Furthermore the rights assigned will form part of the assignee's property and estate which he can deal with like all other of his property as explained above. If the assignee is a company or corporate body the same principles apply.

Future Copyright

Works which are commissioned are works yet to be created and can be the subject of agreement as to their future copyright. Section 91 defines future copyright as "copyright which will or may come into existence in respect of a future work or class of works or on the occurrence of a future event." The section also provides that a prospective owner of the copyright in a work on its coming into existence acquires the agreed rights of copyright automatically and without the need for further formalities. As with the transfer of copyright in an existing work any agreement about future copyright must be in writing. When the prospective owner is not to acquire the entire copyright in a work then the rights he is to acquire need to be stated, including their duration and territorial limits.

An option on an author's next work does not have the same legal effect as an agreement for the assignment of future copyright. An option agreement confers only a contractual right to elect to acquire the rights in a work as and on the terms set out. By exercising an option there is no automatic transfer of rights in a work for there must still be executed an assignment of copyright. Should an author fail to execute the assignment then as indicated above the author would be liable for breach of contract.

Licences

All or any of the rights of copyright in a work can be dealt with by way of licence in lieu of an assignment but the distinction is important. Whereas an assignment is a conveyance of rights, a licence (as once classically defined) "properly passes no interest in the property but only makes an action in respect of it lawful which without the licence would be unlawful." A licence or consent can be given quite informally, orally or in writing; it can also be implied as where an author knowing of a course of action assists with its execution or permits it to continue without objection. Because of the nature of a licence and lack of formality required for its granting none of the inherent rights of ownership attach to it as they do to an assignment so the courts will construe a licence strictly according to its terms. Not only in order to resolve any dispute about the fact of the granting of a licence but also to ensure certainty of its terms, a licence ought be in writing.

A mere permission or "bare licence" can be as easily withdrawn as it can be given, but a licence which rests on a contract as between an author or other copyright owner and another person cannot be so easily avoided. If there is a breach or default of the terms of the licence by either party the usual legal consequences and remedies will apply. Whether a licence can be passed on or sub-licensed by a licensee to another or is personal to the licensee is a matter of construction to be gathered from the terms of the licence. If it is personal then it will not be assignable to another without the permission of the licensor. Where a licence is assignable then the acts of the person who acquires the licence are deemed to be done with the permission of the licensor and of any other intermediary person upon whom the licence may be binding. Thus where an author or copyright owner makes an assignment of his rights in a work the assignee will take the rights assigned subject to any licence which may have already been granted to a third party.

The distinction between an assignment and licence has been stressed but just short of an assignment is the grant of an exclusive licence in respect of copyright works. An "exclusive licence" is defined in section 92 as meaning "a licence in writing signed by or on behalf of the copyright owner authorising the licensee to the exclusion of all other persons, including the person granting the licence, to exercise the rights which would otherwise be exercisable exclusively by the copyright owner." It follows that by granting an exclusive licence an author or copyright owner divests himself of the rights for the time and in the territories as specified in the licence.

An exclusive licensee has the same rights against a person who succeeds by way of assignment or otherwise to the copyright in a work, as against the person who granted the exclusive licence. In addition an exclusive licensee is given the power under section 101 of the Act to take proceedings and obtain the same remedies for an infringement of copyright in his own name as if the licence had been an assignment. However, these rights or powers are concurrent with those of the author or other copyright owner who therefore must be joined in any proceedings. The court is empowered to dispense with this requirement if an author is unwilling to be a party to the proceedings. In any proceedings a defendant can avail himself of any defence which he could have relied on had the action been brought by the person who granted the licence.

The words "assignment" and "licence" as applied to copyright or any other property transaction can be a trap for the unwary. They are legal terms of art with distinct meanings and consequences as has been demonstrated. They need to be used with precision as a transaction will not be effective as an assignment merely by being so called if, as a matter of law its true construction and meaning is a licence, and vice versa.

What has been said above about dealings with copyright needs to be understood as applying to dealings and transmissions made since the coming into operation of the Copyright Act 1956 on June 1, 1957. Under the earlier Copyright Act 1911 an assignment made by an author in his lifetime could not as a matter of law extend beyond 25 years after his death; at that point in time any copyright in a work which had been assigned reverted to the author's estate. The 1956 Act removed that limitation on assignment. Although with the passage of time this reversion of copyright is not often encountered it needs to be borne in mind because if the right of ownership rests on an assignment made by an author in his lifetime before June 1, 1957, it will be defective.

COLLECTIVE COPYRIGHT LICENSING

The right which by law authors and copyright owners have to control and license individually the use of their works is somewhat insubstantial when set against the reality of the means and opportunities in modern society for the illicit use of their works. This situation has led to the setting up of organisations with the resources to monitor and oversee on behalf of their members the proper and legitimate use of protected works and to take action against those who infringe copyright.

The music business was the vanguard in the formation of such organisations by founding the Performing Right Society and the Mechanical Copyright Society for the administration of the rights of public performance and reproduction of musical works. The rapid advance in the means and facilities for the copying of works has intensified the setting up of like organisations. Publishers have in fairly recent years established the Copyright Licensing Agency with the object of licensing the copying of extracts from books, journals and periodicals; provisions of the 1988 Act respecting reprography have enhanced the means for their so doing. The producers of sound recordings, films and videos have their associations for the protection and administration of the rights in their works and which now under the Act includes a rental right. As the recording of broadcast programmes by educational establishments is subject to control under the Act, the Educational Recording Agency undertakes the licensing of such recording as the agent of the broadcasting companies and owners of copyright works.

It is apparent from the foregoing that there has evolved a concentration of power and authority in a few organisations having the right to grant licences and to decide the terms and conditions of licences for the use of a significant range of copyright works. In order to prevent the abuse of this concentration of power the Act provides in two ways the means for this power to be subject to independent review. First by establishing the Copyright Tribunal to adjudicate on issues relating to particular kinds of licences, and secondly by empowering the Government to certify licensing schemes. As this latter procedure arises in only a few situations it can most fittingly be considered first.

Under section 143 a person operating or proposing to operate a licensing scheme may apply to the Government to certify the scheme. An application is entirely voluntary but is confined to schemes for particular purposes: the recording by educational establishments of broadcast programmes, the rental of sound recordings, films (and computer programs), the provision of sub-titled or otherwise modified copies of television programmes for the deaf or hard of hearing, and the reprographic copying of published works by educational establishments.

The effect of certification is to identify the works covered by the scheme and confirm the charges payable and the terms to attach to licences. A scheme has legal sanction by a statutory instrument made under the Act and thereby becomes a matter of law as any other provisions of the Act itself. Certification does not attest the reasonableness or fairness of a scheme and should this become an issue the matter can be referred to the Copyright Tribunal.

The Copyright Tribunal

The Copyright Tribunal is constituted under the Act and its functions and powers laid down in the Act. It comprises a Chairman and two deputy Chairmen, who are all required to be legally qualified, and a panel of eight other members. At any proceedings the Tribunal is to consist of a Chairman (who must be one of the legally qualified members) and two or more of the ordinary members. If a decision of the Tribunal is not unanimous then a decision can be taken by majority vote, the Chairman having a second casting vote if the voting should be equal.

The Tribunal has no right or power as a matter of course to intervene in any dealings with copyright as between individuals or organisations representing copyright owners. It is not a court for determining disputes relating to copyright. The Tribunal's primary function is to adjudicate on issues referred to it by interested or affected parties concerning (a) licensing schemes, and (b) licences granted by licensing bodies. (The Tribunal's jurisdiction over applications for consents on behalf of performers is considered in Part 5 above). The Act prescribes in sections 129/134 certain factors to be brought to bear by the Tribunal in its consideration of certain specified licences but otherwise it has a general discretion in arriving at its decisions. There is an obligation placed on the Tribunal when hearing all references and applications to have regard to the terms of other licences for like purposes where these exist, and to ensure there is no unreasonable discrimination between licensees and prospective licensees.

Licensing Schemes

A licensing scheme is defined in section 117 and can be one of three categories, namely:

(a) licensing schemes operated by licensing bodies for the copying or public performance or broadcasting of literary, dramatic, musical and artistic works, and of films;

(b) all licensing schemes in relation to the copyright in sound recordings (other than film sound-tracks when accompanying the film), broadcasts, or the typographical arrangement of published editions;

(c) all licensing schemes in relation to sound recordings, films or computer programs so far as they relate to licences for rental of copies to the public.

A licensing body is defined in section 116 as "a society or other organisation which has as its main object, or one of its main objects, the negotiating or granting, either as owner or prospective owner of copyright or as agent for him, of copyright licences, and whose objects include the granting of licences covering the works of more than one author." The organisations briefly mentioned above are licensing bodies.

A scheme is not of itself a licence but rather a statement or tariff or memorandum setting out the terms and conditions on which the operator of the scheme is willing to grant particular rights of copyright to prospective licensees. Most often a licensing scheme is operated by a licensing body but this is not necessarily so, in which event the scheme can be certified under section 143 as noted above.

When a licensing body proposes to introduce a licensing scheme then an organisation which is representative of those persons who will be affected by the scheme can have the scheme referred to the Copyright Tribunal for consideration and adjudication of its reasonableness.

Where a scheme is already in operation and a dispute arises between the operator of the scheme and a person (or an organisation representing a number of persons) who requires a licence covered by the scheme, the dispute can be referred to the Tribunal. The scheme remains in force until the proceedings before the Tribunal are concluded. If a person is refused a licence as provided for in a scheme or the licensing body fails to grant a licence within a reasonable time of its being requested, the person affected can refer the matter to the Tribunal for review and adjudication.

Separate from licensing schemes are copyright licences granted by licensing bodies for specific purposes or to cover exceptional circumstances, or which are required by a particular user or enterprise not covered by a published tariff or licensing scheme. Under sections 124/128 the terms on which a copyright licence is proposed to be granted or renewed by a licensing body can be referred to the Tribunal by the prospective licensee. The so-called "blanket licences" granted by the Performing Right Society to the BBC and the independent television companies are examples of a licence granted by a licensing body which, falling outside a licensing scheme, is open to review under these provisions of the Act.

It is only licensing schemes and copyright licences granted by licensing bodies which are referable to the Tribunal. It has no jurisdiction over licences granted individually such as by an author or copyright owner to another person. The terms and conditions of such licences are matters of negotiation solely as between a licensor and licensee and any dispute which arises over such a licence is subject to proceedings before the courts like any other civil dispute.

H. REMEDIES FOR INFRINGEMENT

As a result of the ease with which many kinds of works can be copied, especially printed material and the products of the entertainment industry, how to prevent illicit copying and how to compensate those who suffer as a result of the infringement or "theft" of their work were issues much debated during the passage through Parliament of the 1988 Act. The reforms to the law under the Act enable copyright owners to take swifter action than in the past to combat trading in pirated copies of protected works, and have increased the criminal offences which attach to copyright infringements and the penalties which can be imposed by the courts on conviction. It is not appropriate in this study to examine the niceties of legal procedures in actions for infringement of copyright but the following is an outline of the legal remedies available and the principles upon which they are granted.

Because of its intrinsically abstract nature clearly copyright cannot be "repossessed" when it is wrongly appropriated but apart from this copyright is as much protected by the law as any other form of property such as land, possessions and money. This principle is confirmed by section 96 of the Act where it is provided that infringements of copyright are actionable by a copyright owner and who may be awarded "all such relief by way of damages, injunctions, accounts or otherwise [as may be available to persons for] the infringement of any other property right."

Normally the right to take proceedings for infringement rests only with the copyright owner, but there are a few exceptions on record. If an author disposes of his entire copyright in a work by assignment he divests himself of the right to take steps for infringement of his work; it will be for the new owner or assignee to protect the copyright in the work. Where an author makes only a partial assignment of copyright, for example the right of publishing or public performance of a work, then the assignee as owner of the particular right will be entitled to take action to protect it. The author will be entitled to protect such of the rights in his work as he has retained. An exclusive licensee is also expressly granted powers under the Act to take proceedings in the same way as an assignee is entitled to do, but a mere licensee has to rely on the licensor, that is the copyright owner, to institute proceedings for infringement. The time within which legal proceedings must be brought for the protection of copyright is six years from the date of the alleged infringement.

Although an infringement may have been committed innocently and unintentionally, perhaps as the result of a mistake about the ownership of copyright or because permission was given by a person not entitled to do so, that will not alter a person's liability for the wrong doing. Any infringement is an unlawful interference with another's property so consequently the person affected has a right to compensation for the damage suffered. As was remarked in the course of a judgment delivered long ago, "The right of the owner of a copyright is not determined or measured by the amount of actual damage to him by reason of the infringement; copyright is a right of property and he is entitled to come to the court for the protection of that property even though he does not show or prove actual damage."

It is unwise to assume without question a work is not protected because, for example, the author's name is omitted, or there is no printed reservation of copyright, or that the term of copyright has expired. Under section 97 if in an action it is shown that at the time of the infringement a person did not know and had no reason to believe copyright subsisted in a work, then an author or other copyright owner will not be entitled to an award of damages. However, an author is not deprived of any other legal remedy which may be available to him such as an injunction to restrain any continuation of the infringing act and an account of profits.

Where there is a direct infringement of a work, such as by copying or public performance, this defence is not readily accepted unless a defendant can show that the circumstances were exceptional. With secondary infringement the position is reversed since the onus is on the plaintiff alleging infringement to prove the defendant knew or had reason to believe his action would be an infringement of copyright.

Self Help

To prevent infringement or to obtain redress for infringement of copyright generally recourse has to be had to legal proceedings. Self help is made possible under the Act but this is very limited and of doubtful value. The importation of infringing copies of a work can perhaps be prevented by invoking the provisions of section 111 of the Act and giving notice to the Commissioners of Customs and Excise as already noted. Section 100 permits a copyright owner or person authorised by him to seize infringing copies of a work found exposed or otherwise immediately available for sale or hire; in effect the right is restricted to street trading. Moreover, the right is so hedged with procedural rules, such as first giving notice to the police, that by the time a copyright owner has complied with them the person trading in pirated copies of photographs, audio and video tapes, etc., will most likely have closed up his bag and moved on to the next shopping precinct.

Injunction

When an author or other copyright owner discovers an infringement or plagiarism of his work the immediate need is to stop and prevent its continuation, or if there is a known positive threat of infringement to stop it happening. Thus the first and most usual step is to seek an injunction which is an order of the court directing a person to do, or more often refrain from doing a certain act. Properly an injunction is granted only when an issue has been fully tried in the courts in the presence of both parties *inter partes*, and a claimant has established his right of ownership and proved the actual or threatened infringement. Concurrent with the order for injunction is usually an award for damages, or order for enquiry into damages.

Often in the initial stages of an action for infringement interlocutory relief in the form of an interim injunction *ex parte* (meaning without the presence of the defendant) will be sought before the full trial of the action. Because this relief is discretionary the court must be fairly satisfied in the light of the facts adduced of the claimant's entitlement to the rights of copyright he alleges are at risk and the nature of the infringement. In the exercise of its discretion the court has to strike a balance of convenience between the parties and take into account a number of factors. What is material is the seriousness or gravity of the harm or damage either one of the parties may suffer by an order being granted or withheld; whether the act complained of will amount to an infringement especially if the issue turns on there being a substantial copying; whether the act complained of is but a fair dealing with a work. Also of importance is the consideration that once the issue is finally brought to trial and assuming the infringement is proved, whether an award of damages will be an adequate remedy and compensation for the injury inflicted, and whether the offending party will have the means to pay damages. Thus, for example, a claim may be advanced that a film or the like in the course of production is an infringement of a literary work and so until the issue is adjudicated the court may grant an interim injunction on terms such as that the production may continue but the film is not to be exhibited until the rights and claims of the parties have been determined.

A form of urgent and immediate injunctive proceedings *quia timet* is available when there is a real and substantial threat or likelihood of an infringement occurring, such as by the publication or performance of a work without permission and where prevention is better than cure. A critical consideration of the court when such an order is sought is the ability of the plaintiff to pay damages to the person who will be affected by the injunction if it should transpire that that person has done no wrong.

Damages

Damages are recoverable on proof of copyright infringement even if the circumstances preclude the granting of an injunction, for example, because of undue delay in bringing the action. Even so a wrong will not be permitted to continue simply because the offending party can pay by way of damages for the injury he inflicts. The principle of law upon which damages are awarded is that the injured party is to be paid such sum of money as will compensate him for the loss and damage inflicted by the action of the offending party. Thus the first consideration is an assessment of the amount or value of the depreciation suffered by a work's infringement—loss of sales or royalties or profits. There may also be reckonable the loss suffered because as a result of the infringement the value of the work has been permanently debased.

Generally damages are assessed only on the loss suffered by the injured party and no account is taken of any advantage or profit which the offending party may have gained. However, by section 97 a court is empowered in the light of the circumstances of a case and particularly having regard to the flagrancy of the infringement, or the benefit which has accrued to the offending party by his infringement, to award such additional damages as are justified. So the court is authorised to award exemplary damages when merited additional to the damages awarded according the the usual criterion in civil proceedings.

Account

A third remedy which the court can grant is for an account of profits. As its name suggests it ensures that an infringer compensates an owner by the amount of the profit or gain reaped by his action. Often an order for account of profits will be linked to an injunction but the order will not apply where damages are awarded on the principles as just outlined. Where only part of a protected work has been infringed the remedy is hardly practical and damages are more likely to be awarded, but when there has been an infringement of an entire work such as by reproduction or publication or performance, enquiry can be made of the resulting profit. Where an order is made there must be a full disclosure and the defendant will be required to produce his accounts and records to the court.

Delivery up of Infringing Copies

Until the coming into operation of the 1988 Act infringing copies of works were treated in law as the property of the copyright owner and so by being in possession of them the person who infringed copyright was also liable for conversion damages. This head of damages has been abolished by the Act and with it the rule that the infringing copies were deemed to be the property of the copyright owner. In its place section 99 enables a copyright owner to apply to the court for an order:

(a) for the delivery up of an infringing copy of a work by a person who has such a copy "in his possession, custody or control in the course of business;" and

(b) for the delivery up of "an article specifically designed or adapted for making copies of a particular copyright work" which a person has in his possession, custody or control "knowing or having reason to believe that it has been or is to be used to make infringing copies."

An order cannot be obtained if more than six years have elapsed since the infringing copy or article was made unless the copyright owner was under a disability at the time, or there was some fraud or concealment which prevented a copyright owner applying for an order in due time. When an order for delivery up is granted the court may also by section 114 order the forfeiture or destruction of the infringing copies or article for making copies. An order for delivery up and forfeiture cannot be had as of right. In making any order the court must consider whether the other remedies available in an action for infringement of copyright would be adequate compensation and protection of the interests of the copyright owner. Also the person in possession of infringing copies or an article for their making must be given notice of the order and may appeal against it. Thus an award of damages continues to be the major redress to which a person is entitled for infringement of copyright.

The civil remedies summarised above are not inconsiderable yet it is one thing to have remedies but quite another to have the means for pursuing and enforcing them. The residual powers of the court, which lie outside the Act, have been developed to assist in the prevention of copyright infringement by means of orders known as Anton Piller orders. These compel the disclosure of information so as to trace illicit trafficking and enable persons to enter premises and seize pirated articles. The sanction behind these orders may be limited because of the rules of privilege against self incrimination enjoyed by any person subjected to such an order. Allied to an Anton Piller order is a "Mareva" injunction whereby the assets of a person who infringes copyright can be prevented from being sold or removed to avoid the payment of damages.

Other branches of the general law which may be invoked to restrain infringement of copyright and plagiarism where the circumstances or conditions allow, are common law conspiracy, the Theft Act 1968 and the Trades Descriptions Act 1968.

Criminal Liability

The criminal liability for infringement of copyright is provided for in section 107 of the Act. It covers all kinds of works and lists a wide range of activities which if pursued without the consent of the copyright owner can lead to a criminal offence resulting in a fine or imprisonment. The main ingredient of an offence is the doing of any one of the prohibited acts in regard to an article "which is, and which [a person] knows or has reason to believe is, an infringing copy of a copyright work."

In all proceedings brought under penal enactments actual proof of the commission of the offence as defined by law is essential; so the knowledge or reason for the belief as required by the section will have to be proved affirmatively and beyond reasonable doubt. The weight of the section bears on a person infringing copyright in the course of business so a person who infringes copyright for his own private and domestic purposes will not be likely to have committed an offence but be civilly liable for a breach of copyright.

In addition to the offences connected with dealing in infringing copies or making articles especially intended for making infringing copies, section 107 also covers performances of a work. "Where copyright is infringed (otherwise than by the reception of a broadcast or cable programme):

(a) by the public performance of a literary, dramatic, or musical work; or

(b) by the playing or showing in public of a sound recording or film,

any person who caused the work so to be performed, played or shown is guilty of an offence if he knew or had reason to believe that copyright would be infringed."

Corresponding to the Anton Piller orders which may be obtained in civil proceedings, section 109 of the Act provides for the issue by local justices of search warrants. With a warrant a constable can enter and search premises (which are widely defined) and seize articles which may be evidence of the commission of an offence under section 107.

I. MORAL RIGHTS

The most radical of the innovations to copyright law brought about by the 1988 Act has been the introduction of moral rights for authors and film directors. The concept of moral rights was first established as an enforceable right under French law to underline the special regard had for literary, dramatic, musical and artistic works as the fruits of the mind of their creators and a reflection of their personality. In the nineteenth century the concept was adopted into the laws of other continental European countries and in Latin America. Moral rights were set out in the Berne Convention of 1886 but they have no place in the Universal Copyright Convention save for a provision made respecting the treatment of works in translation.

The concept of moral rights has rested on three principles:

(a) the right of publication—the right to decide whether a work is to be made public;

(b) the right of paternity—the right to claim and be identified as the author of a work;

(c) the right of integrity—the right of an author to object to any distortion or alteration or other derogatory treatment of his work which would be prejudicial to his honour or reputation.

Until the passing of the 1988 Act these rights hardly existed under English law but principles of law had been formulated—and which are still relevant as noted below—to protect material disclosed by one person in confidence to another, and to prevent a person gaining an unfair advantage by using surreptitiously the reputation of an author by passing off his work as that of another author.

Moral rights as legal and enforceable rights came into existence with the coming into operation of the 1988 Act on August 1, 1989. The rights apply to works coming into existence after that date and, with some qualification, they apply to works which were in existence on that date. Moral rights in a work subsist for so long as copyright subsists in the work.

The rights of copyright in a work, as has been noted earlier, are property rights which can be dealt with as and on what terms the owner chooses. Moral rights are quite separate and independent of copyright and are personal to the persons on whom they are conferred. The rights are transmissible on death to a person's successors in title but being personal they are not assignable. For that reason if an author assigns and disposes of part or the whole of his copyright in a work his moral rights remain with him unless he expressly waives them as a term of the assignment.

Because of the philosophical basis upon which the idea of moral rights rested, the Berne Convention has never acknowledged their existence for the mechanical or composite works of modern times, namely sound recordings and films. This principle has been adhered to in the 1988 Act but it does confer moral rights on the director of a film. There is no statutory definition of film director so the term has to be construed as in the film industry. "Film" is defined as meaning "a record on any medium from which a moving image may by any means be produced." Thus whether a production is on film negative or magnetic videotape is immaterial. So too is the kind of product—feature film, advertising film or promotion video, etc. If a distinction is made between the sound recording and photography of a film, the moral right extends to both elements of a film.

The Right of Paternity

By section 77 of the Act the author of a copyright literary, dramatic, musical or artistic work, and the director of a copyright film has the right to be identified as the author of the work or director of the film. The right is not limited to the work or film as originally produced; it applies to any adaptation (and to the exploitation of the adaptation) which may be made under any licence or assignment. If a dramatic version is made of a novel for any purpose then the author of the novel has the right to be identified—to be accorded credit—with the writer of the dramatic version. The right applies in relation to the whole or a substantial part of a work, and in deciding whether there has been a substantial use of a work presumably the courts will apply the same criterion as for a substantial infringement of copyright.

This right of paternity varies according to the type of work and the circumstances in which it is used or exploited. With a literary work (other than words intended to be sung or spoken with music) or a dramatic work, an author has the right to be identified whenever:

"(a) the work is published commercially, performed in public or broadcast or included in a cable programme service; or

(b) copies of a film or sound recording including the work are issued to the public."

The composer of a musical work, or a literary work consisting of words intended to be sung or spoken with music) has the right to be identified whenever:

"(a) the work is published commercially;

(b) copies of a sound recording of the work are issued to the public; or

(c) a film of which the sound-track includes the work is shown in public or copies of such film are issued to the public."

It is for practical reasons that the right does not apply to the public performance or broadcasting of music. Even so that does not preclude there being written into any licence for the performance of a musical work—especially a first performance—that the composer be identified as the author of the work.

The author of an artistic work has the right to be identified whenever:

"(a) the work is published commercially or exhibited in public, or a visual image of it is broadcast or included in a cable programme service;

(b) if it is featured, as distinct from being included incidentally, in a broadcast or a film which is shown to the public or copies of which are issued to the public."

The director of a film has the right to be identified "whenever the film is shown in public, broadcast or included in a cable programme service or copies of the film are issued to the public."

An author and film director each has the right to specify the form in which he is to be identified such as by the use of a pseudonym or initials; otherwise any reasonable form of identification may be used. The entitlement is to be identified clearly and reasonably prominently. If there is a commercial publication of a work, or the issue to the public of copies of a film or sound recording, the right is to be identified in or on each copy. If that is not appropriate then an author's or director's name is to be announced in some other manner likely to bring his identity to the notice of a person acquiring a copy of the work. In any other kind of situation the right is to be identified in a manner to bring the identity of an author or director to the attention of a person seeing or hearing the performance, exhibition, showing or broadcasting of a work.

The right to be identified has to be asserted by an author or director and unless or until it is asserted a person's exploiting a work in any of the above ways does not infringe an author's or director's right of paternity. It is open to question whether in fact it is sufficient for an author or director to affix his name to a work by way of assertion.

Section 78 provides that the right may (not must) be asserted generally, or in relation to any specified act or description of acts on an assignment of copyright in a work by a statement of assertion in the assignment, or by instrument in writing signed by the author or director. So it would seem a licensing of any right of copyright, if signed by an author or director, would fulfil the requirement of the section.

With the public exhibition of artistic works the right may also be asserted when the author or other first owner of copyright parts with possession of the original or an authorised copy of the artistic work, the author is identified on the original or copy, or on a frame, mount or other thing to which it is attached. Alternatively the right may be asserted by including in a licence authorising the making of copies of the work a statement signed by or on behalf of the person granting the licence that the author asserts his right to be identified in the event of the public exhibition of a copy made in pursuance of the licence.

There are technical rules concerning who is fixed with notice of an author's or film director's assertion of the right. Where the assertion is made in an assignment, the assignee and anyone claiming through him is deemed to have knowledge of the assertion. If it is made simply in writing, as when rights are granted by way of licence only, a person must be shown to have notice of an author's assertion of the right for him to be liable for its infringement.

Exceptions to the Right

By the provisions of section 79, the right of paternity does not apply to all works and in all circumstances when a work is used. It does not apply to a computer program or any computer-generated work. It is particularly noteworthy that the right does not apply to an author whose work was created in the course of employment as the copyright vests in the employer; similarly with the employment of a film director.

The right is not infringed where use is made of a work which is permitted by law *i.e.* fair dealing so far as it relates to the reporting of current events by means of a sound recording, film or broadcast, or the incidental inclusion of an artistic work in any of these works. The right does not apply to any work made for the reporting of current events. The right does not apply to a literary, dramatic, musical or artistic work made for purposes of publication in a newspaper, magazine or similar periodical, or in an encyclopaedia or other work of reference, or is made available for such purposes with the consent of the author. There are also exceptions for Crown copyright.

The Right of Integrity

The second of the moral rights of authors and film directors is to object to the derogatory treatment of a work. This is defined in section 80 as follows:

"(a) 'treatment' of a work means any addition to, deletion from or alteration to or adaptation of the work, other than—

   (i) a translation of a literary or dramatic work, or

   (ii) an arrangement or transcription of a musical work involving no more than a change of key or register; and

(b) the treatment of a work is derogatory if it amounts to distortion or mutilation of the work or is otherwise prejudicial to the honour or reputation of the author or director."

The right subsists in relation to the whole or any part of a work protected by copyright and the right exists throughout the term of copyright in the work.

By section 80 the right is infringed: "In the case of a literary, dramatic or musical work by a person who—

(a) publishes commercially, performs in public, broadcasts or includes in a broadcast or cable programme service a derogatory treatment of a work; or

(b) issues to the public copies of a film or sound recording of, or including, a derogatory treatment of the work.

In the case of an artistic work the right is infringed by a person who—

(a) publishes commercially or exhibits in public a derogatory treatment of the work, or broadcasts or includes in a cable programme service a visual image of a derogatory treatment of the work,

(b) shows in public a film including a visual image of a derogatory treatment of the work or issues to the public copies of such a film, or

(c) in the case of—

   (i) a work of architecture in the form of a model for a building,

   (ii) a sculpture, or

   (iii) a work of artistic craftsmanship,

   issues to the public copies of a graphic work representing, or of a photograph of, a derogatory treatment of the work.

In the case of a film, the right is infringed by a person who—

(a) shows in public, broadcasts or includes in a cable programme service a derogatory treatment of the film; or

(b) issues to the public copies of a derogatory treatment of the film,

or who, along with the film, plays in public, broadcasts or includes in a cable programme service, or issues to the public copies of, a derogatory treatment of the film soundtrack."

It remains to be seen how the courts will interpret and apply this embracing new law. From amongst all the fine detail it needs to be appreciated that it is the treatment of a work which must first be in issue and then whether the treatment is such as to be prejudicial to an author's honour and reputation. Treatment is the changing of a work and no matter what views or opinions an author or critic may have of the manner of any use, interpretation, performance or display of work such activities are not a treatment within the meaning of the section. The parodying of a work may arguably be a derogatory treatment but the greater the parodying the less can the parody be associated with the original work.

The Secondary Infringement of the Right

Like copyright there can be a primary or secondary infringement of the right not to have a work subjected to derogatory treatment. The person who is primarily liable is the person who publishes commercially, publicly performs or broadcasts a derogatory treatment of a work, or a photograph or other visual image of such a treatment of an artistic work. It is also a person who issues to the public copies of a film or sound recording incorporating a derogatory treatment of a work. It is also a person who exhibits in public or broadcasts a derogatory treatment of a film or who issues copies of such a film to the public—film in this context including any soundtrack associated with the film. The presence of absence of intention to infringe the right is immaterial; the liability is absolute.

Secondary infringement arises on the part of a person who—

"(a) possesses in the course of business; or

(b) sells or lets for hire, or offers or exposes for sale or hire; or

(c) in the course of business exhibits in public or distributes; or

(d) distributes otherwise than in the course of business so as to affect prejudicially the honour or reputation of an author or director

an article which is and which he knows or has reason to believe is, an infringing article," that is, a work or copy of a work which has been subjected to derogatory treatment as defined above. Liability rests on proof of a person's actual knowledge or reason to believe an article is an infringement of the right.

The right conferred on an author and director also extends to any adaptation of their work if the adaptation or treatment is attributed to or is likely to be regarded as the work of the author or director. An author may consent to the making of an adaptation of a work but the fact that the adaptation is not the author's must be made clear in any use or exploitation of the adaptation.

Exceptions to the Right

Concerning anonymous and pseudonomynous works, if any act done in relation to such works does not amount to an infringement of copyright as permitted under section 57 (see above), then there can be no infringement of moral rights in such works.

The right to object to the derogatory treatment of a work does not apply in relation to works made for the purpose of reporting current events. It does not apply to the publication of a literary, dramatic, musical or artistic work made for publication in a newspaper or periodical, or for inclusion in an encyclopaedia or like collective work of reference; it does not apply to such works made available for such purposes with the consent of the author. The right does not apply to a computer program or to any computer generated work.

With a work created by an author or director in the course of his employment and in which the copyright thereby belongs to his employer (and with works in which Crown or Parliamentary copyright exists and works the copyright in which belongs to certain international organisations as designated by the Government), the right of objection does not apply to anything done in relation to such works by or with the authority of the copyright owner provided the author or director is not at the time of the relevant act, or has not previously been identified in or on published copies of the work. Where these conditions are not observed, an employee author or director does not lose the right to object to the derogatory treatment unless there is a sufficient disclaimer. This means there must be a clear and reasonably prominent indication that the work has been subjected to treatment of the kind indicated above, to which the author or director has not consented.

There is a general provision in section 81 which affirms that the right of integrity is not infringed by anything done in relation to a work to avoid the commission of an offence or to comply with a duty imposed by any enactment. Even so where the author or director is identified at the time, or has been identified in or on copies of the work which have already been published then there must be a sufficient disclaimer as noted above.

The provision is clearly intended to permit alterations to a work to avoid any criminal offence under such enactments such as the Official Secrets Acts, the obscenity laws, the Video Recordings Act 1984 and such like laws; also to enable compliance with duties imposed under enactments such as the Theatres Act 1968 and the Broadcasting Act 1990 respecting performances and the content of programmes. What is open to doubt is whether the right is infringed where an alteration is made on the grounds of a risk of a work being defamatory. If an alteration is made on the grounds of a work being defamatory then, just as much as if the alteration were made on account of infringement of copyright, the treatment could hardly be said to be prejudicial to the honour or reputation of the author or director despite it amounting to a distortion or mutilation of the work.

Joint Authorship

Special provision is made in section 88 for the application of moral rights to works of joint authorship or where a film has been directed jointly. Each author has the right to be identified as joint author but each must assert the right. Each has a right to object to the derogatory treatment of a work and each can consent to the treatment of a work, but the waiver of the right of integrity by one author does not affect the right of any other joint author of a work.

Waiver of Moral Rights

Whereas a consent to the doing of an act in relation to a work can be given informally—but advisably it should be obtained in writing—by section 87 a waiver of moral rights must be in writing and signed by the person foregoing the rights. The waiver can be in respect of a specific work or class of works, or relate to existing and future works. The waiver may be conditional or unconditional and it may be expressed to be revocable. Where the waiver is in favour of the owner or prospective owner of the copyright in a work—such as when a work is commissioned—the waiver extends to the licensees and successors in title of the copyright owner unless the contrary is provided for in the signed document waiving the right.

The moral rights conferred on authors and film directors are not absolute and so their value is much depreciated when set against the power of commercial interests to require a waiver of the rights as a pre-condition of an engagement or agreement for any dealing with a work. By careful drafting the extent of any waiver may be curtailed as provided for in section 87.

False Attribution of Authorship

Allied to moral rights are two other rights. The first is to prevent works being falsely attributed to an author; this existed under the Copyright Act 1956. The second, but one which is an innovation of copyright law, is to protect privacy in certain photographs and films. The duration of each of these rights is different but an infringement of either of them is actionable as a breach of statutory duty. Like moral rights these rights are personal to the person entitled to them and therefore neither is assignable but passes on the death of the person concerned to his beneficiaries or personal representatives.

Section 84 confers on an author the right not to have expressly or impliedly any work or any part of a work falsely attributed to him. The right continues to subsist until 20 years after a person's death. Film directors have a corresponding right with regard to films. The right is infringed in relation to such works by issuing copies to the public, or exhibiting in public an artistic work or a copy of such a work. Falsely representing an adaptation of a work as the work of the original author is an infringement of the right. There is a secondary infringement of the right by a person who performs a work or shows a film in public or broadcasts a work knowing or having reason to believe that the attribution of authorship or directorship is false.

This right of the author of an artistic work is further infringed by a person who in the course of business deals with the work (or a copy of it) after the author has parted with possession of it as being his unaltered work, knowing or having reason to believe the work has been altered. There is also an infringement of the right by the issue to the public or a public display of material containing a false attribution of authorship or directorship, as for example by issuing a misleading advertisement.

Privacy of Private and Domestic Photographs

A person who commissions the taking of a photograph or the making of a film for private and domestic purposes is granted by section 85 the right not to have copies of it issued to the public, or for it to be exhibited or shown in public or in a broadcast. The right is for the duration of the copyright in the work. It is independent of any rights of copyright in the photograph or film and like other moral rights it is a personal right but one which passes to the commissioner's successors in title. If anyone does or authorises any of the above acts respecting these works without the appropriate consent there is an infringement of the commissioner's right. However, the right is not infringed by the incidental inclusion of a work in an artistic work, film or broadcast, or by its use for judicial and such like purposes, or where by section 57 of the Act the use of an anonymous or pseudonymous work is permitted on the reasonable assumption the copyright in the work has expired, or the author is deceased.

The right does not belong to the persons included in the photograph or film. Neither does it belong to the creator or author of the work despite his being by law the owner of the copyright in it, unless otherwise agreed between the author and the person commissioning the work. Even where the author reserves his copyright in the work the agreement of the person who commissioned it will be required for the exercise of any of the rights as described above. It should be noted that this right conferred by section 57 does not apply to other works such as a painting or sculpture commissioned for private and domestic purposes.

The Enforcement of Moral Rights

The infringement of any of the rights described above is a breach of statutory duty, that is a duty owed to persons entitled to the right or privilege conferred by statute. A person affected can take civil proceedings for damages. Actual loss does not have to be proved on account of the infringement (any more than it has to be proved for infringement of copyright), but it remains to be seen if the court will award special damages where there is a flagrant breach of the right.

Delay in asserting the right to be identified as the author of a work is a factor the court is required to have regard to in considering any award of damages for infringement of the right. In proceedings for breach of the right of integrity of a work the court may, if it considers it an adequate remedy in the circumstances, grant an injunction to restrain the act unless a disclaimer is made in such terms and manner as approved by the court dissociating the author (or film director) from the derogatory treatment of the work.

No action done in relation to a work before August 1, 1989 is actionable as an infringement of moral rights. For works in existence on August 1, 1989 the rights of paternity and integrity are not enforceable if the author of a work died before that date, or if a film was made before that date. Where before August 1, 1989 an author assigned or licensed rights in a work, or where rights in a work vested in a person other than the author (such as a commissioned work), no action for infringement of moral rights can be brought on account of anything done in the exercise of the rights assigned. The right to privacy granted to photographs and films as above does not apply to such works made before the commencement of the Act.

Droit de Suite

It is perhaps appropriate to conclude this survey of moral rights by mentioning another right provided for in the Berne Convention—the *droit de suite*. Authors and creators of many kinds of work derive benefit from the success of their work by having a continuing entitlement to royalties or participation in the profits derived from the exploitation of their work. An artist does not have this advantage but *droit de suite* enables him to benefit from an increase in the value of his work. When after the initial sale of a work there is a subsequent sale an artist becomes entitled to a percentage of the increased value. Under English law there is no *droit de suite*.

RELATED RIGHTS AND THEIR PROTECTION

Despite the introduction into English law of moral rights there are other principles of law outside the province of copyright which may need to be invoked for the protection of a work and the reputation of its author. Moral rights may be waived—they may be required to be as a condition of a contract—but that will not displace or prejudice other rights where they exist.

Confidentiality

As there is no copyright in ideas and as a work must have permanent form for it to gain copyright protection the question may be fairly asked what redress has an author of a dramatic plot, or composer of a musical theme, or an artist with outline sketches who having divulged his ideas to a producer/director, publisher, agent or the like finds such a person has surreptitiously reduced his work to writing or some permanent form and claims the copyright in it? There are two possible solutions. The first is that there may be found to exist a contractual relationship between the persons concerned so that any unauthorised dealing with the material or matters disclosed would amount to a breach of an express or implied term of the contract.

The second alternative solution is the principle of confidentiality and trust which the law recognises as subsisting between particular persons and according to the circumstances. The principle was explained by Lord Denning in 1967 in a case which concerned the disclosure of information respecting an industrial process where he said, "The law on this subject does not depend upon any implied contract. It depends on the broad principle of equity that he who has received information in confidence shall not take advantage of it. He must not make use of it to the prejudice of him who gave it without obtaining his consent." The information imparted must have the quality of confidentiality and it must be revealed in circumstances imposing or reasonably understood as imposing an obligation of confidence. Liability arises when the information is used without authority to the loss or detriment of the person concerned. The party who was given the information and uses it surreptitiously is liable to have to account for the secret benefit thereby gained.

Apart from the kinds of situations which might arise as indicated above, the principle of breach of confidence has been applied to the disclosure of family matters, private correspondence and diaries, and to the use of drawings and photographs. The principle was applied in 1894 and an injunction given by the court when a press critic was allowed to view a rehearsal of "His Excellency" by W. S. Gilbert and in breach of confidence he sought to publish a review prematurely and in so doing reveal the plot. Where there is established a breach of confidence on the grounds either of breach of contract or abuse of a special confidential relationship the court is likely to grant an injunction to stop the contin-uation of the breach by the wrongdoer and perhaps give an award of damages. It is still open to doubt if any wider restriction or action would be sanctioned by the court against a person who, for example, innocently published a work which was the product of a breach of copyright.

Passing Off

This body of law is primarily concerned with the protection of a person's business connection and his goodwill. Although copyright may not exist in the title of a work, as a result of the development of the law of passing off, the copying of the title of a work, like the mis-use of a performer's name, may be prevented. This aspect of the law is considered in the Introduction to Part 8.

Part 7

THE COMMISSIONING AND USE OF COPYRIGHT WORKS

A. INTRODUCTION

In the preceding Part (Part 6) the principles of copyright laws have been reviewed in a somewhat detached and academic way. In this Part the practical application of those principles will be considered in the context of the agreements for the writing of original dramatic and musical works, and licences for the public performance, broadcasting, and reproduction of existing copyright works.

Artistic creation is a very personal and often lonely pursuit so the services required of creative persons cannot be so neatly and conveniently prescribed by fixed hours of work and conditions of employment as for performers. Even so and especially in the broadcasting and mechanical media of entertainment, production schedules, the resources at the disposal of a producer, and the likely scope or potential for the exploitation of a work are factors which affect and influence the terms upon which authors are commissioned or rights are acquired in existing works.

As for performers, so too for writers there has evolved by custom and practice, but still more so in modern times by collective agreements, standard conditions upon which dramatic works are commissioned and licensed for performance and exploitation. In this development the Writers' Guild of Great Britain has served a major role. The Guild was established over 30 years ago and is recognised by the entertainment industry's management associations as the principal representative of professional writers for negotiating the minimum fees and terms for the writing and exploitation of dramatic works.

Membership of the Writers' Guild is open to any professional writer although full membership is subject to a writer qualifying according to a points system for his works published and/or performed as prescribed in the rules of the Guild. The activities of the Guild rest with its Executive Council, elected annually by the full members of the Guild, with the assistance of specialist committees and salaried General Secretary and staff.

In addition to collective agreements with the BBC the Writers' Guild has negotiated agreements with the associations representing the independent television programme companies, the cinema and television film producers, and also the Theatres National Committee representing the professional stage managements. The collective agreements variously prescribe the minimum conditions for the engagement of writers' services, and the minimum fees payable according to the rights acquired in existing or commissioned works. It has never been and is not a term of any of the collective agreements that commissions are to be offered only or mainly to members of the Guild, but that writers will not be engaged on terms less favourable than those contained in the applicable collective agreement.

B. LICENCES FOR THEATRICAL PRODUCTIONS

Licences for the production and public performance on the professional stage of plays, musical plays, operas, ballets, revues and other presentations are individually negotiated by a management with authors and composers (or most often their agents), or other copyright owners such as publishers. There are no minimum terms or fees prescribed for the licensing of plays on the commercial stage of the West End but there are collective agreements prescribing minimum royalty rates and terms and conditions of licences for the national companies and subsidised repertory theatre.

The detailed terms of stage licence agreements in addition to authorising the public performance of a play will frequently provide for the issues already remarked upon such as an author's freedom to deal with the residual rights in the play so as not to put at risk the investment in the production. Furthermore a management may secure a participation in the income generated from the exercise by an author or other copyright owner of the residual rights in a play, the value of which will be enhanced by the production and successful run of the play. When an established copyright work is licensed, or an author of high professional reputation licenses a new play a right of participation might not be conceded, but when a management commissions a play or tries out a new play a right of participation could be important as a means of lessening the impact of any loss and as compensation for the risk borne by a management.

WEST END THEATRE LICENCES

There is no standard agreement for the performance of plays and musical plays on the commercial stage of the West End although a fairly regular form or way of licensing exists. A sum as an advance on box office royalties will be negotiated and payable on the signing of the agreement and a management will have up to six months within which to assemble, produce and commence the run of the play in the West End but often with a right to a pre-opening provincial tour. Failure to open in the West End within the agreed time will result in the forfeiture of the advance paid and the licence unless a further payment to extend the option is agreed upon.

If the West End run is commenced within the prescribed time and conditional upon there being a consecutive run in the West End of a minimum number of evening performances, usually 21 but excluding paid preview performances, a management will have the right to produce the play in the English language throughout the United Kingdom, the Republic of Ireland, and English speaking territories of the British Commonwealth (excluding Canada).

Normally a licence will be for a fixed number of years but in each year not less than a specified number (usually 50) of regular paid public performances must be given. If less than the stipulated number is given then in order to retain the licence a sum will be payable to compensate for the short-fall in revenues, the amount due being calculated by reference to actual average box-office receipts during a stated period. Alternatively a minimum fixed sum representing a guaranteed income or share of box office takings may be a condition for the retention of the licence for its allotted span of years.

Author's Royalties

Material to the terms of a licence is the scale of royalty payments to be made to an author so the definition of net box-office revenues or receipts for the calculation of the amounts to be paid must be clear. The percentage of net box-office revenues payable is likely to be on a rising scale but the higher rates may be conditional on a management recouping the capital costs of the production. It is likely that the director, choreographer and designer will in part be remunerated from a share of box office revenues so it is important to be consistent in the definition of net box-office revenues to ensure the equitable application of the scale of royalty rates agreed with these persons. Provisions need also to be included whereby an author, and others with rights of participation in box-office revenues, are entitled to receive weekly financial statements, regular payments of the share due and properly audited accounts in order to verify the payments made.

In the past the definition of net box-office revenues for the purpose of assessing the sums due to any author was simple, as normally allowance was made only for "library" or theatre ticket agents' commissions and an allocation of "house" seats. Today the definition has tended to become more elaborate especially as apart from the author other persons are affected. So provision may be made for special reduced rates for previews and other particular occasions, for costs directly attributable to promoting and stimulating ticket sales, such as travel and restaurant commissions and other tie-ups. These somewhat special deductions will not normally apply in accounting for net box-office revenues from performances outside the West End but always allowance must be made for value added tax.

When in addition to royalties an author (or the like) is to share in the net profits from the production then as in all situations where a sum is to be paid from amounts designated as "profit" the meaning of profit must be carefully and adequately defined. What payments are to come within the scope of capital or production costs to the point of curtain up on the official first night, what items of expenditure are to comprise running costs and so be a first charge on box-office revenue, how any surplus is to be applied first in the accumulation of a reserve and then in the repayment of production costs are items which need to be adequately described. Furthermore in accounting for the profits and losses of a production there may also have to be reckoned any subsidiary income which may arise such as revenues from any post-London tour, revenues from a cast record album and revenues from the following subsidiary rights.

Subsidiary Rights

In addition to the basic right to produce the play in the West End but conditional upon the minimum number of performances having been given as noted above, a management will usually have other rights and interests in the play in particular:

(a) an option on the professional stage rights for the USA and Canada on the terms as specified in the licence agreement exercisable within a stated period after the "official" first night West End performance;

(b) an entitlement to participate in the author's royalties received from licences granted for repertory and amateur performances of the play within a stated number of years (usually five) following the end of the West End run; and

(c) an entitlement to participate in up to 20 per cent. of the author's receipts from the sale of the film and television rights in the play within a stated number of years (usually five) following the end of the West End run; and similarly if the USA professional stage option is exercised and the prescribed minimum number of consecutive performances given on Broadway with the result that it is possible for a management's participation to amount to 40 per cent. from these sources but no more.

From the point of view of a management the validity of the licence must be assured, that is to say the author (or other person purporting to grant the licence) must warrant the ownership of the copyright in the play and that by granting the licence no other person's prior overriding rights or interests are affected. If the play is an adaptation of a protected work then the author must warrant his right to make the adaptation and to license the production. Warranties regarding the accuracy of the content of the play and that nothing is included in it which if performed would be in breach of the Theatres Act 1968 (as amended by the Public Order Act 1986) or which is defamatory of any person need also to be included in the licence agreement. Furthermore provisions may be included restricting an author's exercise of the residual rights in the play so as not to impair a management's investment in the production. From the commencement of the licence until the end of the West End run and possibly for a period of time following there will be a bar on an author exercising the repertory and amateur stage rights and on the exercise of the television and film rights.

Depending on the circumstances and perhaps the standing of an author other terms may need to be negotiated. The prominence or style of credit to be accorded in the publicity of the play and in programmes may need to be specified in relation to the publicity to be accorded to a leading star or director. Other matters which may need to be provided for are, for example, an author's approval of the appointment of the director, musical director, choreographer, designer and principal members of the cast, of the choice of opening theatre, of the selection and use of extracts from critics' reviews in the promotion of the production, of the making and release of any cast record album and the apportionment of the record royalties.

THE THEATRES' NATIONAL COMMITTEE COLLECTIVE AGREEMENT

The Collective Agreement between the Theatres' National Committee and the Writers' Guild of Great Britain and the Theatre Writers' Union (jointly) made in October 1979 prescribes the minimum terms and conditions upon which authors may be commissioned to write plays, or the stage rights in existing plays may be acquired by the Royal National Theatre, the Royal Shakespeare Theatre and the English Stage Companies. The expression "writer" includes any adapter, composer, lyricist, librettist, or personal representative or successor of a deceased writer. The basic fees and other financial provisions are revised periodically and in their application allowance is made for the category of the theatre, the box-office capacity according to an auditorium and the length of a play.

By individual negotiation between the parties concerned improved terms may be agreed upon but the Agreement stipulates that within two weeks of any verbal agreement being reached a written contract adhering to the minimum terms and incorporating any especially agreed terms is to be issued by a producer. Unless the contract is returned signed by the author within four weeks of its receipt the contract becomes null and void.

There is payable to an author an initial fee. When a play is commissioned one half of the fee is due on the signing of the contract. The play is to be delivered within the ensuing 12 months and on delivery three-eighths of the fee becomes payable. Within three months of receiving the finished play a producer is to inform the writer of his decision to acquire the stage rights by paying the final one-eighth instalment of the fee, otherwise all rights in the play revert to the author and the monies paid are forfeited by the producer. For the stage rights in an existing non-commissioned play the entire initial fee is payable to an author on the signature of the contract. By the payment of the initial fee a producer is under no obligation to produce the play, and by entering into the licence agreement an author's copyright in the play remains unaffected save as expressly provided for by the terms of the Agreement.

No changes may be made to the text of a play without the author's permission if he is reasonably available for consultation. With a commissioned play a producer is entitled to require alterations to be made as necessary to avoid the producer facing legal action. An author can refuse to make the changes and withdraw the play by repaying the monies received for the commissioned work.

An author is entitled to attend all rehearsals of the play. Provided the author places himself fully at the disposal of the producer for the duration of the rehearsal period, the author is entitled to a fee for each week of the rehearsal period. If an author attends rehearsals only at the express wish of a producer a single attendance fee is payable.

The production and presentation of the play, its casting and the appointment of the director, designer, musical director and choreographer are subject to mutual agreement or understanding between an author and producer consistent with the artistic resources of the producer. Provided he is reasonably available an author is entitled to be consulted about the programme and all publicity material relating directly to the play which is under the control of the producer. An author is entitled to the equivalent of the credit accorded to the director and leading artists. A writer may use a *nom de plume* provided it is specified in the contract. An author is entitled to receive six copies of the rehearsal script and one "prompt" copy.

Upon the payment of the last instalment of the initial fee for a commissioned play, or the whole of the fee for an existing non-commissioned play, a producer acquires the exclusive right and licence to produce and perform the play in the United Kingdom excepting theatres in the West End of London. The first performance must be within 12 months of the payment of the initial fee but this period can be extended by up to two consecutive periods of six months by the payment for each extension of 50 per cent. of the initial fee. The continuation of the licence is conditional on there being given at least 26 paid performances (which may include not more than five fully paid or reduced price previews) in each 12 months counting from the date of the first paid performance of the play. The producer's rights become non-exclusive on and after the expiry of one year from the producer's first paid performance of the play.

Author's Royalties

An author is entitled to a proportion of box office income by way of royalty for each performance calculated on a somewhat complex formula and for which the following definitions are relevant. "Net box office receipts" means the sums received at the box office less VAT and other deductions such as library, credit card and other sales commissions, special discounts offered in accordance with a producer's established custom and practice, for example, for previous stand-by sales, sales linked to the offer of other goods and services, or as otherwise especially agreed with an author. "Net house cash capacity" means "the total revenue (less VAT or any other tax but without any other deduction) which would have been received by the box office for the sale of admissions for a performance if all admissions therefor had been sold at the advertised price."

The royalty payable is a percentage of a proportion of net box office receipts expressed as a percentage of net house cash capacity. On the first 25 per cent. of receipts so expressed, 10 per cent. is payable to an author by way of royalties; on the next 25 per cent.—5 per cent., on the next 25 per cent.—7.5 per cent., and on the final 25 per cent.—10 per cent. The Agreement provides for a producer to supply accounts of box-office receipts and royalty payments within 14 days from the end of each month during which performances of an author's play are given, but reasonable time is to be allowed for receipt of accounts and payments for performances given overseas. From the royalties due to an author there is set off the initial payment referred to above except for productions in certain of the smaller auditoria of the three Companies.

From the date of the licence agreement and continuing until the expiration of 12 months from the date of a producer's first paid performance of a play—an author may not license or assign to any third party any rights in the play in respect of the United Kingdom without the prior written consent of the producer. Any other dealings with the rights in a play must not detract from the options as noted below and granted to a producer as part of the consideration for the initial fee.

On and after the expiry of six months from the producer's first paid performance of the play in London an author is at liberty to license the production and performance of the play in a subsidised theatre. (There is a qualification to this provision for a play produced by the Royal Shakespeare Company at Stratford-upon-Avon). Unless a producer exercises the option for a West End theatre presentation as noted below, after the expiration of 12 months from the date of the first paid performance of a play the producer's rights under the licence agreement become non-exclusive but that does not avoid the commitment to cause the minimum of 26 performances to be given in each of 12 months in order to retain the licence.

Producer's Options

Coupled with the grant by an author of the basic and initial right to produce and perform the play, a producer obtains three separate options to give or cause to be given performances of the play, in theatres in the West End, in the USA (but not Canada), and in the rest of the English speaking world (including Canada but excluding the United Kingdom and the USA). The right to exercise any of these options is conditional upon the producer:

(a) having produced and performed the play within the time prescribed as noted above: as no minimum number of performances is prescribed it follows that one paid performance is sufficient;

(b) giving notice of the exercise of the option for performances in the West End within six months of the first paid performance but for the other two options within eight months;

(c) paying the prescribed sum for each option exercised on account of the royalties payable.

By exercising an option the producer obtains the exclusive right to perform the play at theatres:

(i) in the West End within 12 months from the expiry of six months from the date of the first paid performance (or by a second payment of the option money within 18 months);

(ii) in either the USA or the other English-speaking territories as above within 18 months from the expiry of eight months from the date of the first paid performance for performances.

The terms and conditions of the licences for these optional performances in the various territories are open to negotiation between the parties when the initial contract is signed as the Agreement does not prescribe them. However it is stipulated that if the option for performances in the

USA is exercised, the producer shall consult the author prior to authorising a production, presumably in regard to any required textual changes and way of presentation. In addition if the producer acquires the rights in the play for USA or Canada then the provisions of the Dramatist Guild Incorporated Minimum Basic Contract are to apply to all the rights in the play other than the "live" United Kingdom theatrical rights.

Producer's Participation

Corresponding with the practice in the commercial theatre the Agreement confers on a producer the right to participate in the royalties or revenues an author receives from the wider exploitation of a play. The entitlement is conditional on a producer having given 25 performances of the play pursuant to the terms of the licence agreement. Any disposition by an author during the term of the agreement of the television broadcasting and film rights in the play in any part of the world is subject to his first consulting the producer and to the terms of any disposition having been negotiated in good faith.

The share which an author must account for is of the gross revenues he receives less agent's commission not exceeding 10 per cent. The Agreement provides for an author to supply to a producer statements of gross revenues received within 14 days of each 12 month period from any disposition of rights. The percentage share of gross revenues payable are as follows but subject as provided below:

(a) Stage Rights: 20 per cent. of gross revenues from licences issued for professional performances of the play in the United Kingdom (excluding the West End) throughout the period a producer has the right to perform the play in the United Kingdom but not beyond five years from the date of the first paid performance.

(b) Television and sound recording rights: 20 per cent. of gross revenues from any disposition of these rights in any part of the world within five years from the first paid performance of the producer's production of the play in the United Kingdom (excluding the West End); if there is a first class production in the USA and provided not less than 21 performances are given (including not more than three reduced price performances) a further 20 per cent. of such revenues is payable.

(c) Cinematograph film rights: if within five years from the expiry of eight months from the first paid performance of the producer's production of the play in the United Kingdom (excluding the West End) an author licenses or assigns or disposes of these rights in any part of the world there is to be accounted for and paid to the producer a proportion of the gross revenues received by the author. The proportion is a percentage of the gross revenues. This percentage increases according to the amount of the gross revenues as set out in the Agreement; for example, £5,001 but less than £10,000—10 per cent. In addition the same percentage share is to be held in escrow for should the producer produce or cause to be produced the play in the USA.

There are two further qualifications of general application to be noted. In addition to the basic condition that a producer must have given 25 performances of a play to be entitled to participate in gross revenues as above, the entitlement is liable to abatement. If within the duration of the licence less than 50 performances are given only a quarter of the share of the gross revenues otherwise payable to a producer becomes payable; and if more than 50 but less than 75 performances then only a half. Even so an author is obliged to retain the differences in escrow so that in the event of the higher qualifying number of performances being given during the lifetime of the licence agreement the producer receives the difference withheld. Furthermore, the Collective Agreement stipulates that an author is entitled first to receive in any one year a prescribed minimum amount of gross revenues from the exploitation of the rights in the play as above before actually accounting for the share thereof payable to a producer.

Platform Plays

There is a supplement to the Collective Agreement for the production of platform plays by the three Companies at their auditoria. This category of play is defined as "a short play given by itself without decor at a time of day other than that of the presentation of the main evening bill or of regular matinee performances, or elsewhere at any time, under the producer's management, using a small cast with minimal costumes and properties, but does not mean a reading, whether of a play or not, recital or other performance of a non-dramatic work."

Like the main Agreement provision is made for minimum basic payments and rights of performance. A producer has the exclusive licence to produce and perform a play within six months of the payment of the basic fee and to perform it during the six months from the date of the first performance. The fee for a commissioned play is payable as to five-eighths on the signing of the contract but only if the producer accepts the play and desires to perform it as above is the balance of the fee payable. The whole of the basic fee for an existing non-commissioned play is payable on the signing of the contract.

The basic fee paid to an author is on account of the other sums payable by a producer, namely, a royalty of 10 per cent. of box-office receipts (as defined in the main Agreement), or a standard fee for each performance, whichever sum is the greater.

At any time within six months following the first paid performance a producer has the right to choose to deal with the platform play as a short play and to treat it as subject to the provisions of the main Agreement. On exercising this option a sum on account of future royalties is payable to the author and the licence is deemed to commence on the date of the payment.

Other of the general provisions of the main Agreement such as the rights to the copyright in a play, attendance at rehearsals, changes to the text, the credit to be accorded to an author and consultation respecting the production of the play apply to platform plays.

THE THEATRICAL MANAGEMENT ASSOCIATION COLLECTIVE AGREEMENT

The enterprise of many subsidised repertory theatre companies by presenting new plays on the professional stage has much increased in modern times so that in June 1986 the Collective Agreement was concluded between the Theatrical Management Association (TMA) and the Writers' Guild, the Theatrical Writers' Union and Scottish Society of Playwrights (jointly) in terms which resemble the Theatres' National Committee Collective Agreement. It provides for the payment of a basic fee in instalments and royalties to a writer, for a manager to have options to extend the scope of the licence and entitlement to participate in the income a writer receives from the wider exploitation of a play.

The TMA Collective Agreement applies to contracts entered into by a writer with a manager in membership of the TMA for the world premiere presentation of a play in the United Kingdom (excepting theatres in the West End) for performance by artists engaged under the Equity/TMA Standard Contract for Subsidised Repertory. There is excepted from the ambit of the Agreement the managements and companies subject to the Theatres' National Committee Collective Agreement, but there is included plays produced for children and young persons in auditoria under a manager's auspices but excludes plays for Theatre in Education. For the purposes of the Agreement the expression "writer" is defined very broadly so as to include a translator, composer, lyricist, writer of the book of a musical play.

Minimum Terms

The minimum terms and conditions are set out in the standard form contract annexed to the Agreement where it is stipulated that while a writer may obtain more favourable terms than those specified, no provision may be waived by a writer in consideration of more favourable terms under any other of the provisions of the standard contract. It follows that any special term or variation to the standard conditions should be expressly written into the contract.

A scale of minimum basic fees is prescribed with amounts fixed for each one of the four gradings under which a theatre or company may operate in accordance with the practice of the subsidised repertory theatre. (These fees and other fixed sums as provided for in the Agreement are subject to annual revision). With commissioned plays the basic fee is payable in three instalments; five-eighths is payable on signature of the contract, one-eighth on delivery of the script (the date to be specified) which is on account of royalties, and two-eighths on acceptance of the play since a manager may require alterations to be made to the script within 60 days following its delivery (or 90 days if requested by the writer). This final instalment is a non-returnable advance against royalties. If the play is not accepted by a manager the final instalment of the fee is not payable but all rights revert to the writer.

With a non-commissioned play, that is an existing play, three-quarters of the basic fee is payable on the signing of the contract a prescribed amount of which is deemed to be on account of royalties. If the play was in fact one first commissioned and paid for by another manager in accordance with the Agreement or the Theatres' National Committee Collective Agreement then only one-quarter of the basic fee is payable on the acceptance of the script as suitable for production. A manager is entitled to require alterations to be made to the play within 60 days of the signing of the contract and only on its acceptance does the final (or only) one-quarter instalment of the basic fee become payable and which is a non-returnable advance against royalties. If the play is not accepted all rights revert to the writer.

By paying the basic fee a manager acquires the right and licence for the period beginning on the date of the contract and continuing until the expiration of nine months from the date of the first performance, to present on tour and/or at a specified place performances of a world premiere production of the play. For a manager to have an exclusive licence, a standard additional fee is payable to the writer on the acceptance of the play. The first performance of the play is to be given not later than the date specified in the contract, or alternatively within 12 months from the date specified for the delivery of the completed script (save for any variation for the making of alterations required by the manager), or 18 months from delivery if later than such time. (Provision is made for deferring the first performance due to events beyond a manager's control). There is no obligation on a manager to present the play but to inform the writer promptly if he decides not to present the play. In any event if the play is not produced and presented in the contractual period the rights granted to the manager revert to the writer.

In respect of all performances of the play an agreed percentage of the net box office receipts is payable to the writer by way of royalties. Minimum royalty rates are prescribed and the minimum amount to be guaranteed by the manager. Although some instalments of the basic fee are recoverable from a writer's royalties as just noted, by the terms of the Agreement no deduction from royalties can be made unless and until the amount of the minimum guaranteed royalty has been paid to an author.

Manager's Options

Provided a manager presents the play within the prescribed time a manager has exclusive and separate options to perform the play or cause it to be performed (a) in the rest of the United Kingdom excepting the West End, (b) in the West End (including a pre-London tour not exceeding eight weeks for a straight play or 12 for a musical), (c) the USA, and (d) the rest of the world (excepting South Africa) for English-speaking productions. The options are exercisable at any time before the expiration of three months from the date of the last performance of the play pursuant to the contract by notice in writing to the writer and the payment of the prescribed standard sum on account of the royalties payable. It is for the parties to agree upon the duration and terms of the exclusive licences for the performances of the play which become effective upon the exercise of any of the options. Properly, and as a matter of law, these terms and conditions should be negotiated at the time of the making of the contract particularly the royalties payable.

Manager's Participation

A manager's entitlement to participate in the financial rewards accruing to the writer from the exploitation of the play (excluding of course the payments due to the writer by virtue of the terms of the contract and the manager's exercising all or any of the above four options), is conditional first on the manager having presented the play for at least 17 performances in accordance with the contract. Secondly the entitlement is subject to the writer receiving an income from the exploitation of the play of an amount in excess of "the threshold" as specified in the contract (but subject to the prescribed minimum sum) in each "qualifying year," meaning the 12 months commencing from the date of the first performance of the play given pursuant to the contract and each anniversary thereof.

For a period of four years from the date of the last paid performance of the play by the manager the writer is to ensure the manager receives the following amounts in excess of the threshold:

(a) a percentage as agreed but not more than two per cent. of the net box office receipts in respect of any further professional productions of the play in the United Kingdom (other than productions presented directly by or in association with the manager or productions mounted by a manager using artists engaged under the Equity/TMA Standard Contract for Subsidised Repertory);

(b) a percentage as agreed but not more than 12.5 per cent. of the writer's fees from the sale of film and television rights in the play.

Agent's fees not exceeding 10 per cent. are deductible before calculating the payments due to a manager. The sums due are payable not later than 60 days following their receipt by the writer or his agent, and accompanied with a certified statement of account. It is also provided that if the circumstances arise a manager shall waive the participation for the same period and in the same ratio as the writer and all other royalty participants (except artists) who shall have waived their royalties.

A manager is also entitled to be given credit if the play is performed and/or published otherwise than by the manager. The Agreement stipulates that a writer is to require to be printed in the programme and/or at the beginning of the printed version, the words: "first performed at . . ." followed by the date of first performance. In the event of the play being presented on television, film, radio or other media, a writer is to require there is included in the credits at the end, the statement: "first performed at. . . .". The Agreement does not expressly limit a manager's entitlement to this credit to four years like the entitlement to participate in a writer's additional income from the play but this might be inferred.

Other General Provisions

Other more general provisions of the Agreement provide that the choice of the director, designer and actor are subject to agreement fairly and reasonably arrived at between the writer and manager. A writer has the right to attend all rehearsals but is to pay due consideration to the manager's authority at the place of rehearsal. An attendance allowance is payable to the writer for up to 12 days during the rehearsal period and for any additional days of attendance at a manager's request. Any other expenses of the writer if incurred in connection with the preparations for the presentation of the play and with a manager's prior approval are to be reimbursed by the manager.

The Agreement further provides that a writer is to be accorded credit of similar prominence to that accorded to directors and leading actors in all the major advertising of the play and in programmes. The right is reserved for the writer to use a *nom de plume* provided this is specified in the contract when signed.

By the terms of the Agreement a writer warrants he is the sole author of the play and sole owner of all copyright in all languages throughout the world and is in full control of the rights granted to the manager; also that to the best of his belief the play contains no defamatory matter. Other warranties to apply as appropriate are that the play has not been previously performed or licensed, or else performed and licensed as specified in the contract, and that the writer has or has not received, a commission fee in respect of the play. Where a play is a work of joint authorship or a collaborative work then both authors should be joint parties to the contract and agree between themselves the division of the fees and royalties arising under the terms of the contract.

If a play is not wholly original but is a derivative work such as a translation or adaptation of an existing copyright work, then it is for the writer to secure all the necessary rights from the owners of the copyright in the source material and to agree with them what share of the fees and royalties paid by the manager under the contract is to be accounted for by the writer to such persons. An exception is made for incidental and interpolated music where the right of public performance is controlled by the Performing Right Society. In this instance it is for the manager to effect the necessary clearances and make payment of the fees due.

The Agreement provides that any dispute arising from the contract is to be referred to a Joint Committee comprising three representatives from each of the parties to the Agreement. Failing any settlement the issue is to be referred to a single arbitrator to be mutually agreed (or failing agreement then as appointed by the Secretary of State for Employment), and whose determination is to be final and binding.

THE INDEPENDENT THEATRE COUNCIL COLLECTIVE AGREEMENT

In April 1991 the Collective Agreement was made between the Independent Theatre Council and the Writers' Guild and Theatre Writers' Union (jointly) setting out the terms and conditions and minimum rates payable to writers for plays commissioned by and given premiere presentation by an Independent Theatre Council approved manager, and for the production of existing plays not already professionally performed but similarly first presented.

The Agreement makes provision for the creation of a play otherwise than in the rather conventional way of a prepared scripted dramatic work but by alternative working methods. Thus a writer and a manager may agree a schedule for the working out of material and devising of a play. Special provisions are also included concerning the copyright interests of persons who contribute to the devising of a play, or whose material is incorporated into a play. Only one fee is payable for a play and where a play is the product of co-writers it is for them to agree amongst themselves on the apportionment of the fee. If material is included in a play which is protected by copyright it is for the writer to secure the necessary clearances and make whatever payments may be due to the copyright owner; there is an exception to this for musical works as noted below.

Minimum basic fees are prescribed for plays of full length and for shorter plays, that is, of less than 70 minutes ordinary performance time. Where a play is the product of a previous commission or written by virtue of a writer having received a grant or the like then only a proportion of the basic fee is payable in accordance with the formula as set out in the Agreement. The basic fee for a play is payable in instalments—one-half on the signing of the contract, one-quarter on the delivery of the script of the play but the payment of the final quarter's instalment is conditional on a manager's decision to produce the play.

A standard form contract is annexed to the Agreement for the insertion of the negotiated terms and original fee, the completion of an alternative work-method where applicable and production schedule.

Manager's Rights

During the six weeks following the date of the delivery of a commissioned script a manager has the right in consultation with the writer to decide what amendments and changes are to be made to a script before deciding to produce the play. If no re-writing is required a manager is bound to inform the writer within three weeks of the delivery of the script of his decision; if any re-writing is required and allowing time for a writer to carry out the re-writing, the decision whether or not to produce the play must be given by a manager within 18 weeks of the delivery of the script. With a non-commissioned play, that is an already existing play, the writer and manager must agree and stipulate in the contract the date by which the manager is to decide on the production of the play. If the decision is not to proceed, the final instalment of the basic fee is not payable and all rights revert absolutely to the writer.

By the payment of the basic fee a manager acquires the exclusive right to present the play in its original production, that is, with substantially the same cast, director, design and other significant elements, in the United Kingdom (other than theatres in the West End excepting the Arts Theatre, Donmar Warehouse and Royal Court (downstairs) Theatre), for one year from the date of the manager's decision to produce the play. The right to present the play abroad is subject to the venues being named in the tour schedule issued on an agreed date as stated in the contract.

Following the one year's exclusive licence a manager has a consecutive non-exclusive licence of six months during which to present the play. This licence can be converted to an exclusive one for up to six months by the payment of half a per cent. of the original fee for each additional four weeks (and pro rata for less than four weeks) of the extended exclusive licence. A manager can also extend the period of the six month's non-exclusive licence for a maximum of five years calculated from the date of the decision to produce the play, by the payment of one per cent. of the original fee for each additional four weeks (and pro rata for less than four weeks) of the extension.

The basic fee entitles a manager to present the play for a total of 21 weeks (but not necessarily consecutive weeks) within the period of the exclusive, non-exclusive and extended non-exclusive licence without payment of performance or royalty fees. This right is subject to a manager presenting the play for at least 15 performances during the first 18 months following the decision to produce the play. If this qualifying number of performances is not attained then any extension of the 18 months period is subject to agreement between the writer and manager.

When a manager wishes to present the play beyond 21 weeks or during an extended period of a non-exclusive licence a weekly fee of two per cent. of the original fee is payable but there is no limitation on the number of performances which may be given in the week.

"Performance" for the purposes of the Agreement means a presentation of the play including previews and open rehearsals before a paying audience, or where a manager has been paid for the presentation of the play to an audience, *e.g.* performances in schools and youth clubs.

A manager may remount the original production after the periods mentioned above but within five years of the date of the decision to produce a play, with the agreement of the writer. Any licence is on a non-exclusive basis and subject to the payment to the writer of one per cent. of the original fee for an initial period of four weeks and thereafter pro rata per week up to the expiration of the maximum five years.

West End Option

A manager does not have an automatic option on the West End theatre stage rights and if this is required a supplementary standard fee is payable to the writer in addition to the fee payable on the signing of the contract. By such payment a manager has the option to acquire the West End rights in the play for one year, the option to be exercised within three months of the last scheduled performance of the play or by the end of the period of the exclusive licence, whichever date is the later. On the exercise of the option 50 per cent. of the original fee is payable to the writer as a non-returnable advance on the royalties payable for the West End run—the royalties being a matter for negotiation between a manager and writer at the time of the signing of the contract. A manager may extend the West End rights for another year by the payment of a further 50 per cent. of the original fee before the expiration of the first year.

If prior to a manager's exercising the option a third party makes a definite offer to the writer for the West End theatre rights and which the writer wishes to accept, the writer is entitled by giving written notice to the manager of the offer to require the manager to exercise his option within the following month or else forfeit the option.

Right to Record

A manager has the right, but subject to the written permission of the writer, to record the play on video or otherwise in rehearsal or performance for the purposes of research, archival and other private use of the manager (or a third party authorised by the manager with the writer's consent), and for promotional purposes but not for broadcast use. Short excerpts may be broadcast for promotional purposes in news, magazine and such like programmes provided the manager does not receive any income from this use and no extract is used in a manner detrimental to the writer's reputation. Longer excerpts may be broadcast in documentary and educational programmes subject to the writer's permission (not to be unreasonably withheld) and to his receiving payment for the broadcasting of the excerpt.

General Conditions

The general conditions of an engagement and licence for the performance of a play under this Agreement correspond closely with those of the TMA Collective Agreement. Although not always in identical terms, such matters as a writer's warranties and title to the copyright in a play, his entitlement to be consulted about the cast and director, to attend rehearsals and to an attendance fee, to be accorded credit and for the reversion of rights if the play is not presented, are provided for in the same way as in the TMA Agreement. This is so with the provisions concerning a manager's entitlement to be accorded recognition for the first performance of the play in any published version and on the giving of other performances of the play, a manager's obligation to clear music rights, the making of changes to the text of a play and the making of copies of the script for the purpose of the presentation of the play.

A manager is entitled to participate in a writer's income from the further use and exploitation of a play. The right is conditional on a manager having presented the play for at least 15 contracted performances (including performances which were planned and publicised but did not take place due to circumstances beyond a manager's control), within 18 months after the decision to produce the play. The entitlement lasts for five years from the end of the period of exclusive rights or a manager's last scheduled performance of the play, whichever is the later.

In addition to the five-year period, if further use occurs before a manager's last scheduled performance a manager has participation rights in the further use.

A manager's participation is also conditional upon a writer first receiving income from the further use and exploitation of the play of an amount equal to 50 per cent. of the minimum fee (at the rate prevailing at the material time), the amount being "the writer's income threshold." The income is calculated and to be accounted for yearly by a writer and once the threshold is passed a manager is then entitled to receive 10 per cent. of the writer's income from theatrical productions of the play (except productions by other Independent Theatre Council managers), and 10 per cent. from the sale of the film, television, radio or other media rights in the play. There is to be brought into account the income from all theatrical performances and from all sales of rights for other media during the period of the right of participation.

Any dispute which arises under the Agreement is to be settled in accordance with the Recognition and Procedural Agreement made between the parties.

REPERTORY AND AMATEUR RIGHTS

Licences for professional repertory performances are not often complicated especially when established works are to be performed, the period of the licence and royalty rates being the material terms. Exceptionally there may be included terms to ensure that no licence is given by an author or copyright owner to another repertory company or for any amateur performance in a way to unfairly prejudice the licensed performances. However, when a repertory or subsidised management presents a new play then the terms of the licence agreement may not be so simple. As a condition of its undertaking to produce and present the play an author may be required to undertake to pay or procure the payment to the management of a share of the author's box-office royalties if the production is transferred to the West End. A right to participate in the royalties and revenues obtained by the author from the wider exploitation of the play may be negotiated by a management but it is not usual for the right to extend to royalties or other revenues arising beyond two years from the date of the last performance given by the repertory management under its licence.

Amateur rights of public performance of a play may not always be available because by the terms of the licence agreement for the first professional stage production an author may be committed to withhold them for a certain period of time. Plays may be published but that does not confer a right of public performance under any circumstances. If the amateur rights are available then frequently their licensing will be handled by a central organisation acting on behalf of the author or copyright owner. Samuel French Ltd., being a world-wide organisation, may be regarded as the leading agent for the administration of amateur rights. The grant of a licence is usually to a named society or amateur group with permission to give a number of public performances of a work within a period of time at a place all as expressly stated. Payment for the licence may be either (a) a fee of a fixed amount, or an amount fixed according to the seating capacity of the venue, which is payable for each performance, or (b) a stated percentage of the gross box office receipts. The licensees have an obligation to deliver to the licensors within 21 days of the last performance of the production a certified statement of the box office receipts together with the share shown due, and to provide one copy of the programme.

Often a licence contains detailed stipulations about the giving of credit to authors and composers, to there being no alterations or additions to a work, and for there to be announced in all advertising matter that the production is by a company of amateurs.

With dramatico-musical works, often music publishers will own or control professional and amateur stage rights together with all other "grand rights" such as for the television broadcasting of the work or its production as a film. Licences for all these uses and performances will be individually negotiated between the copyright owners and producers.

C. AGREEMENTS FOR BROADCASTING AND FILMING COPYRIGHT WORKS

Any agreement for the acquisition of rights in protected works for use and exploitation in the mechanical media is apt to be somewhat detailed. Unlike the theatre and other forms of live entertainment where simply the right of public performance is the essence of the licence, in the mechanical media there is also involved rights of reproduction and often adaptation.

Because of the range of uses to which the various products of the mechanical media can be put authors and copyright owners, like performers, are concerned about the manner of the exploitation of their work, the period of time and the territories of exploitation. The Writers' Guild and to a lesser extent the Society of Authors on behalf of their members negotiate collective agreements setting out the basic terms and conditions for the commissioning of original dramatic works or the adaptation of existing works for broadcasting and film production; these agreements are considered in the following pages. The right of public performance and broadcasting of musical works and their reproduction and mechanical use, and similarly of existing recordings of musical works are normally licensed by societies constituted to administer these separate rights on behalf of their members as explained in the later Sections of this Part.

The financial outlay incurred in film and television programme production has led producers, like publishers, to be alert to the opportunity of mitigating costs by claiming a stake in the revenues or royalties an author may receive independently from the wider exercise of the rights in his work, such as publishing. Having borne the costs of production and enabled the work to gain prominence and publicity the bonus of a share in such additional income is considered to be justified. Conversely it is now usual for an author of a commissioned work to receive additional fees or a share of revenues or profits from the wider exploitation of a production as provided for in the collective agreements between the Writers' Guild and the BBC and the associations representing the independent broadcasting and film production companies. Whereas with commissioned works there are standard terms and minimum rates this is not quite so with agreements for the acquisition of rights in existing published works. The terms will depend upon the reputation of the author, the standing of the work but the amount of the payment for the rights is likely to be negotiated as a capital sum only, or a combination of a sum plus agreed residuals.

In modern times through the rise of the film industry coupled with the undoubted flair of the Americans for publicity and advertising, there has come to be recognised a new dimension to intellectual property, namely "merchandising rights." No such rights formally exist in English law in the way that copyright exists but they have evolved from common law principles for protecting the reputation and goodwill attaching to a trader's name and business connection, for protection against unfair competition, and by registration under the design copyright and trade mark laws.

The expression "merchandising rights" has been adopted into the jargon of the entertainment, publishing and advertising industries to mean the right to manufacture and sell goods which are reproductions of characters, drawings, cartoons and scenes derived from copyright works. Also to use these items and any names associated with them in the naming and packaging of merchandise and in the promotion and advertising of merchandise and services. There is no copying of a literary or dramatic work in the meaning and context of copyright law but rather an assumption or appropriation to a totally different mode of expression of an author's ideas and imaginative skills. However the use and application of original artistic works to merchandise involve rights of copyright and likewise the use of artistic works derived from original literary and dramatic works.

Frequently characters and designs are especially devised or invented for the promotion of goods and services but those which have gained acceptance into daily living in the wake of the publicity and exposure world wide of films and now of television programmes are often preferred. For this reason the control of merchandising rights and the division of revenues derived from this form of exploitation of works commissioned or acquired for performance are important considerations in the negotiation of rights.

Not all literary and dramatic works have potential in the context of merchandising rights so that in making agreements for acquiring or commissioning such works a realistic view needs to be taken. The potential is obviously greatest with works for films and programmes designed especially to appeal to children and for family entertainment when "spin-offs" in the form of toys, character reproduction and the application of slogans and names are most likely. Even so the potential from literary material especially prepared for programmes featuring hobbies and particular interests and where commercial tie-ups are feasible should not be overlooked.

With any grant of merchandising rights the scope of the rights and the duration and territorial extent of the licence need to be clear. Provisions should be included for the right of inspection of the quality of merchan-

dise produced, for the supply of information about marketing and exploitation, and for the rendering of accounts and royalty statements.
Normally the actual exploitation of merchandising rights will be undertaken by entrepreneurs so that any franchise agreement sub-licensing the
rights must reflect the basic agreement made between a producer and an
author or other copyright owner. In addition there must be cast on an
entrepreneur the obligation to take steps to protect the rights to the extent
allowed under trade mark law and when applicable, for patent and
design copyright registration.

WRITERS' COLLECTIVE AGREEMENTS FOR TELEVISION

There are two series of collective agreements made by the Writers' Guild
one with the BBC and one with the programme companies of the Independent Television Commission (ITC) for the commissioning of freelance
writers to write dramatic works for broadcasting by television. These
agreements do not apply to writers who are engaged as editors or in such
like capacities, or who are employees or "staff" writers of the broadcasting organisations.

Both series of agreements comprise three separate collective agreements for the commissioning of the following kinds or categories of
dramatic works, namely:

(a) Original Teleplays: works being original single plays written
expressly for television regardless that the plays may be presented
and broadcast under a generic title or as part of an anthology of
plays;

(b) Series and Serials: scripts for episodes of television series meaning
any group of programmes comprising a number of episodes having
a continuous theme, similar basic situation, format and continuing
characters, and a serial comprising a number of episodes with a
continuing story and characters;

(c) Dramatisations and Adaptations: scripts being either a conversion
of a narrative work—novel or story into dramatic form, or an
adaptation of an existing work or script in dramatic form—a stage
play, or radio or film script—for television broadcasting.

Each of the agreements prescribe minimum fees or "going rates" but
the amounts are subject to a number of factors in particular:
(a) the writer being an "established" writer, meaning:

(i) a writer who has been commissioned to write original tele-plays, scripts for television plays in the specific form of drama-tisations or adaptations, or episodes for television series or serials, with an aggregate slot length of not less than two hours under any of the series of collective agreements with the BBC and the programme companies; or

(ii) a writer who has written or had produced cinema screenplays either totalling two hours material or one single piece exceed-ing 90 minutes;

(b) the writer being new to television but a full member of the Writers' Guild with an established reputation as a writer for theatre, radio and books;

(c) the writer being a "new writer" meaning a writer who is not within any of the above descriptions;

(d) the slot length of the programme for which the script is commissioned;

(e) whether the writer commissioned to write the script for an episode also provides the story line;

(f) whether the writer is commissioned to write all the scripts of the episodes for a series or serial;

(g) the particular kind or category of programme (not being a regular drama programme for adult viewing) for which the script is commis-sioned, such as children, or educational or religious programme;

(h) whether the programme for which the script is commissioned is for regional or network transmission.

Many of the provisions of the collective agreements between the Writers' Guild and the BBC and the programme companies dealing with the more general issues attaching to an engagement are in like terms and so are considered together later. The provisions dealing with the crucial issues such as the writing, delivery and acceptance of scripts, the pay-ment of fees and the rights acquired are reviewed first and separately for each of the networks.

BBC Drama Commissions

There are no standard form contracts appended to any of the Collective Agreements between the Writers' Guild and the BBC. As the Agreements have been much amended and supplemented over the years it has become the practice of the BBC to issue contracts setting out virtually all the conditions of a writer's engagement (but based on the applicable Agreement) with provisions included appropriate to the kind of script commissioned—a single drama, episode of a series or serial, or adaptation.

In each contract the title of the commissioned script is specified (together with the programme title), the duration of the script, the date for its delivery and the initial fee. The initial fee is payable as to 50 per cent. on the signature of the contract and 50 per cent. on the acceptance of the script as suitable for television broadcasting.

Ordinarily within one month of the delivery of a script the writer is to be notified whether it is acceptable or if alterations are required. Where alterations are required they are to be carried out by the writer during a period of 56 days from the date of the delivery of the script. Where the alterations come to be made after the 56 day period then the writer is entitled to ask for payment of a further 25 per cent. of the initial fee. If a script is not accepted the final instalment of the initial fee (50 per cent. or 25 per cent. as the circumstances may be) is not payable and all rights in the script revert to the writer. These procedures may vary where a writer is commissioned to write more than one script.

Rights Acquired

By the payment of the initial fee the BBC has the exclusive right to broadcast a performance of the script once live or recorded simultaneously or non-simultaneously from all or any of the BBC's transmitters which serve BBC 1 or BBC 2 channels. (For Welsh language programmes transmissions may be from the ITC's transmitters for the Fourth Channel in Wales). The exclusive right is for two years from the date of the delivery of the script, or where more than one script has been commissioned from a writer the date of the delivery of the last of the scripts.

The two-year period can be extended to three years provided notice is given to the writer before the expiration of the initial two years and is paid the sum equal to 10 per cent. of the initial fee paid for the commission, and provided also that when the notice is given rehearsals have begun or are scheduled to commence and do commence before the expiry of three months from the end of the initial two-year period. Otherwise 20 per cent. of the fee is payable when the notice is given for the further year. If the script is not broadcast within the two year period (or as extended) then all rights in the script revert to the writer.

Provided the script is broadcast within the qualifying period then for the duration of the copyright in the script the BBC has the right of unlimited repeat transmissions in the United Kingdom. A writer is entitled to a fee for each repeated transmission. If the repeat is within three years of the date of the first broadcast 75 per cent. of the initial fee is payable. When the repeat is more than three years after the first initial broadcast the 75 per cent. fee is calculated on "an adjusted initial fee." This is assessed pursuant to the formula in a writer's contract so that the repeat fee is relative to the writer's rate current at the time of the repeated broadcast.

Subject to a script being first broadcast within the time as explained above, the BBC has the exclusive right for the full period of copyright in the script to license, or rather to authorise BBC Enterprises to make sales of programmes which include performances of the script without restriction throughout the world and whereby the programme can be delivered in any medium of television, including standard television and non-standard television, including (but not by way of limitation) any form of cable or satellite television broadcasting. Coupled with this right is the right of non-theatric exploitation throughout the world without restriction. For these rights there is payable to a writer 5.25 per cent. of the receipts of BBC Enterprises from all such sales. Special provisions govern the calculation of receipts by BBC Enterprises when programmes are co-produced by the BBC with a third party.

Videogram Rights

Videogram rights are the subject of a separate Collective Agreement, namely the Videograms Minimum Terms Agreement of 1989 (as amended) between the BBC, BBC Enterprises and the Writers' Guild. By virtue of this Agreement there is automatically included in a writer's contract the grant of an exclusive option for BBC Enterprises to acquire videogram rights. The option is exercisable at any time within seven years of the date of the first broadcast of the script (or last of the scripts if one of a series). The right to distribute, sell and hire to the general public videograms of a performance of a script is exclusive for the period of 10 years from the date of the exercise of the option and thereafter non-exclusive. On the first publication of a videogram of the script there is payable to the writer a non-returnable advance of an amount and on account of future royalties at rates and according to scale all as prescribed in the Videograms Minimum Terms Agreement.

In addition to the rights and options outlined above there is included in a writer's contract the right for the BBC without further payment to make recordings of scripted works for archival and record purposes, for use of excerpts in historic and like programmes, in trailers and for showing at festivals. Translation rights for the purposes of dubbing and sub-titling programmes for overseas exploitation are also acquired.

BBC Agreement for Sketch Material

There is a separate Collective Agreement between the Writers' Guild and the BBC for the commissioning of sketch material, quickies or news items specially written for a television light entertainment programme known as "LE Material." The contracts commissioning such material correspond closely with those for drama scripts but there are differences.

The principal differences are (a) a writer qualifies as an "established writer" for the purposes of the level of fees payable with 30 minutes of original LE Material as an alternative to the criteria outlined above, (b) the minimum and "going rates" are fixed by the minute, (c) for the sale of overseas television rights, non-standard television broadcasting rights and non-paying or non-theatric rights, there is payable a percentage of a writer's initial fee (or adjusted initial fee) at rates according to scales which distinguish both the territory and the rights licensed. The Videograms Minimum Terms Agreement referred to above, but with minor modifications, applies to light entertainment material.

The contracts and the terms and conditions for the commissioning of scripts by the BBC reviewed above apply to scripts commissioned for the main stream programming of the BBC. There are other general agreements but of particular note is one for commissioning complete and original dramatic material from freelance writers for educational television, whether schools or further educational programmes, and being of not less than 15 minutes' duration.

Although the terms and conditions on which such scripts are commissioned are in general as above there are important differences. The fee payable is calculated on minutage—a minimum rate per minute is prescribed—and 50 per cent. of the fee is payable on signature of the contract and 50 per cent. on acceptance of the script. With this payment the BBC has the exclusive right for the period of two years from the date of the delivery of the completed script to perform and broadcast the work once; two transmissions within 12 days count as one transmission. With repeat transmissions (the 12 day provision still applies) 75 per cent. of the initial fee is payable but not until seven years from the date of the first broadcast of the script does the formula for an adjusted fee mentioned above take effect.

Drama Scripts for Independent Television

The series of Collective Agreements comprising the Dramatisations and Adaptations Agreement, the Original Teleplays Agreement, and the Series and Serials Agreement between the Writers' Guild and the programme companies was much revised in 1989. There are no standard form contracts annexed to these Agreements so the contracts made by the programme companies with writers incorporate the provisions of the applicable Agreement and specify the programme for which a script is commissioned, the required duration, the time for its delivery, the basic fee and other terms as may be especially negotiated with a writer or the practice of a programme company to include.

In each of the Collective Agreements minimum basic fees are prescribed but at rates according to a writer's status as described above. The basic fees or "going rates" specified are for network transmissions. If a regional programme company commissions a script for transmission in its own area only, then 50 per cent. of the appropriate basic fee is payable. If subsequently the transmission is over any or all of the other regional companies' transmission areas a further 25 per cent. of the basic fee becomes payable.

The basic fee for a script is payable in instalments, the first of 50 per cent. being payable on the signing of the contract. A further instalment of 25 per cent. is payable when a writer delivers the script but the obligation to make payment of the final instalment depends on the circumstances.

Generally as soon as practicable, but in any event within 48 days of a writer delivering a script, a programme company must notify the writer whether the script is acceptable for transmission, or that reasonable alterations are required, or that the script is not acceptable and is rejected. If the script is accepted the remaining 25 per cent. of the fee is then payable, but if the script is rejected no further payment is due and all rights revert to the writer.

Where revisions are required then within two months of the writer delivering the amended script (but for an original teleplay within two months from the date of the writer first delivering the script), a programme company is to inform the writer of the acceptance or rejection of the revised script. If the script is accepted the remaining 25 per cent. of the fee is then payable. If the revised script is rejected the last instalment of the fee is not payable unless a programme company fails to give notice of the rejection within the prescribed time. In such an event the script is deemed to have been accepted and therefore the final instalment will remain payable.

With scripts commissioned under the Dramatisations and Adaptations Agreement and the Series and Serials Agreement there is a refinement to the foregoing in that a programme company may notify a writer that the script is not acceptable without revision by another writer or writers. In such circumstances the final instalment of the fee is not payable but the 75 per cent. of the basic fee paid constitutes the fee upon which repeat fees are to be calculated. Any other exploitation fees which may become payable in respect of the script are shared proportionately between the writer and the other writer(s) of the script as accepted and performed.

Rights Acquired

The payment of the basic fee entitles a programme company to broadcast a script by television once only live or recorded simultaneously or non-simultaneously over all the areas covered by the ITC transmitters or one transmission on Channel 4, unless only regional rights have been acquired as noted above. A programme company also acquires repeat rights and options as variously provided in each of the Collective Agreements unless otherwise especially agreed with a writer.

Under the Original Teleplays Agreement a programme company acquires only the exclusive right to perform and broadcast a play once but subject to the first transmission being within two and a half years of the date of the delivery of the final script. This period can be extended by a year provided notice is given to the writer three months before the expiration of the initial period and is paid the sum equal to 10 per cent. of the writers' fee. A programme company is entitled to repeat the broadcasting of the play within three years of the date of the first broadcast by the payment of 100 per cent. of the writer's fee for each repeat transmission. Overseas television broadcasting and other additional rights are subject to the payment within 18 months of the first transmission of the play of option monies as a non-returnable advance on additional payments.

With scripts commissioned under the Dramatisations and Adaptations Agreement a programme company acquires the exclusive full and unrestricted television rights throughout the world for the full period of copyright together with the additional rights as described below, subject to the payment of repeat fees and royalties as noted below.

The Series and Serials Agreement provides that the extent of the copyright to be acquired in a script is subject to agreement between a programme company and a writer. The entire copyright may be acquired, or the limited rights as in the Dramatisation and Adaptations Agreement and subject to the like further payments. The important exception is where all the episodes of an original series or serial with a finite length are written by one writer. The Agreement provides that in this case a programme company acquires the exclusive right to transmit a recording of the work overseas during the period of five years from the date of the first transmission in the United Kingdom subject to the payment of royalties as noted below. It appears that repeat rights are similarly limited to the five year period. There is no automatic entitlement to the additional rights.

Although in principle for each repeated performance and transmission of a script 100 per cent. of a writer's fee is payable the Collective Agreements make concession for repeats after peak viewing hours and for repeats of schools and educational programmes.

For repeats commencing at or after 11.30 p.m. there is payable to a writer one-third of the repeat fee otherwise applicable to the programme. However, where such a reduction would result in a payment of less than one-third of the going rate current at the time of the repeat, then the maximum reduction is one-third of the going rate, (or one-sixth if the original commission was made by a regional company and based on 50 per cent. of the going rate). Where the original fee was less than one-third of the current going rate (or one-sixth in the case of a regional production), no reduction may be made. This situation is likely to arise particularly with programmes made some years ago.

With schools programmes additional fees are due as follows:

(a) no additional fee is payable in respect of one repeated transmission within the same school term as that in which the original transmission took place or for a second repeat of one programme from a series of schools programmes transmitted as a preview showing to teachers;

(b) by the payment to a writer of 100 per cent. of the original fee a programme company has the right to a further two transmissions in all areas under the same terms and conditions as (a) above;

(c) by the payment to a writer of a further 100 per cent. of the original fee a programme company may acquire the right to two additional transmissions in all areas under the same terms and conditions as (a) above.

(d) the possible total of three series of transmissions—possible by the payment of the initial fee and the additional fees as above—may be spread over five years.

In respect of educational programmes, for a repeat after 12 months from the date of the original transmission of a programme the repeat payment due to a writer is based on the going rate current at the time of the repeat rather than on the original fee.

Additional Rights

Other rights of exploitation of recorded performances of scripts which may be acquired are compendiously defined in all the Agreements as "all media" rights and which expression embraces "any and all means of distribution, transmission or exploitation now known or hereafter developed including (but not by way of limitation) cable television, videograms, satellite broadcasting, terrestrial broadcasting non-theatric use and showings by closed-circuit television to captive audiences whether in the United Kingdom or overseas, excepting only original transmissions and repeats on ITV and Channel 4 and theatric rights." Subject to what is said below these all media rights are exercisable world wide and throughout the term of copyright in a script.

From the exercise of any or all of these rights there is accountable and payable to a writer a royalty of 5.6 per cent. of the gross receipts from programme sales. Where a script is commissioned from more than one writer the individual payments to each of the writers is calculated by dividing the total payment of 5.6 per cent. of gross receipts pro rata to their original fee.

The foregoing represents in principle the extent of the additional rights of exploitation in programmes made on or after January 1, 1988. However, the Agreements expressly stipulate that if the application of these royalty payments would be inappropriate for a particular pro-gramme it is open for a programme company and writer to discuss alternative arrangements in advance of the production. Unless a pro-gramme company has acquired the entire copyright in a script, or a special restriction has been inserted in a writer's contract, a writer is free to exercise any of the rights in his work which do not fall within the above definition of additional or "all media" rights.

Some General Conditions

Many of the general terms and conditions for the engagement of writers included in the Collective Agreements of the Writers' Guild with the BBC and the programme companies or in the individual contracts with writers are alike and so can be considered together. However, there is a general provision included in the BBC contract which is not included in the Collective Agreements of the programme companies but ought to be included in a writer's contract, namely warranties by a writer with regard to his script.

Warranties

Except where a script is based on a format or other material supplied to a writer upon which to base his work, it should be stipulated as a term of a writer's engagement that the script will be his original work and not infringe any person's copyright or other rights. Where any copyright material is used and incorporated in a work the written consent of the owner to the inclusion of the material and therefore to its broadcasting and exploitation needs to be obtained. One further warranty to attach to a writer's work is that it will not contain any defamatory matter. This warranty is normally qualified so that a writer is not liable for defamatory matter which in the opinion of the broadcasting organisation was included in the script without negligence or malice on the part of the writer. A libel may be perpetrated innocently but not so the copying of another's work and infringement of his copyright.

Credit Provisions

The Agreements variously provide for a writer to be accorded screen credit at the beginning or end of the transmission of a programme. If a precise form or style of credit is to be accorded it will need to be made a special term of the contract. If a writer elects not to be credited with the authorship of a work this is required to be notified prior to the making of the credit captions. Provision is made for the giving of credit in the announcement and advertising of a programme but in terms that no liability attaches to a broadcasting organisation for the omission or default of a third party in the giving or printing of the credit due.

Alterations to Scripts

The right to make alterations to a script is usually a matter of concern to a writer and may therefore need to be the subject of special stipulation in the contract. Also if a writer desires that no change be made to the title of a work this should be stipulated in the contract.

The Collective Agreements of the programme companies provide for the right to make reasonable alterations as may be considered necessary in the interests of television production, or for the purpose of complying with any requirements of the ITC if a writer is unwilling or unable to carry out the alterations himself. The Original Teleplay Agreement further provides that if a writer objects to the making of the required alterations, then unless a programme company has incurred legal obligations to a third party the writer has the right to buy back the rights in the play by repaying 50 per cent. of the fees already paid to him.

Under the terms of the BBC contracts it is provided that when alterations are required they will be discussed with the writer and if possible mutually agreed upon. However, the right to make minor alterations is reserved by the BBC and the right to make such other alterations as in the opinion of the BBC are necessary in order to avoid involving them in legal action or bringing them into disrepute. After a script has been accepted no alterations are to be made by the BBC unless when asked to do so the writer is unwilling to make them and the writer has had the opportunity—if he so requests and the BBC agrees that time permits—to make representations about the proposed alterations. For this purpose there is to be a meeting within 48 hours of the request (excluding weekends) and at which the writer may be represented by the Writers' Guild, or if he is not a member of the Guild by his agent. Failing agreement on the alterations the final decision rests with the BBC.

Apart from the foregoing the BBC undertakes not to make any structural alterations as distinct from minor alterations without the consent (not to be unreasonably withheld) of a writer or his agent. Where for any reason a writer is not immediately available for consultation at the time which the BBC regards as the deadline for the making of alterations (such as on account of the production being in rehearsal or recorded), then in such circumstances the alterations can be made.

There is included in the contracts of the BBC a provision whereby a writer asserts his right to be identified as the author of a work. Subject to the BBC's observance of the terms of the Collective Agreements relating to credits and alterations of scripts, then the BBC has a defence to a claim by a writer that his moral rights have been infringed. There is no moral rights provision included in the Collective Agreements of the programme companies so that provision should be made in a writer's individual contract.

The Agreements provide for a writer's entitlement to attend a read-through of a script and one rehearsal when standard attendance fees are payable at rates agreed with the Writers' Guild. If a writer is requested to make extra attendances then his reasonable expenses are payable in addition to the attendance fee.

Story-line

When only a story-line is commissioned it is normally on the basis of a non-returnable payment to a writer of 10 per cent. of the fee prospectively payable for the completed script. If a story-line is not to be developed the copyright in the work reverts to the writer but if a script is commissioned the 10 per cent. payment counts towards the initial fee as it becomes due.

Right of Publication

No right of publication of a script is automatically acquired by a broad-casting organisation under any of the collective agreements. However, the BBC Collective Agreements stipulate that for the year following the first transmission of a script a writer is not to grant rights of publication to a third party without first consulting the BBC. Where the publication or "novelisation" rights in a script are desired, particularly with scripts for series or serials, or with major co-productions, these rights should be negotiated with a writer at the time of the commission. Unless the entire copyright in a script is acquired as an express term of a commission, then apart from the exceptional circumstances which may arise as noted above, no right of publication is likely to be implied by law simply from the grant of television broadcasting rights.

Rejection of Work and Dispute Procedure

It has been noted that a commissioned script may be rejected as unaccept-able and payment of the last instalment of the fee avoided. The grounds for doing so must be based on a reasoned and objective judgment of the writer's professional competence and the quality of the work produced. The obligation to pay the final instalment of the fee cannot be avoided by a decision to change the format of a serial, or by a change of cast or other circumstances arising extraneous to the commissioning of a script. A broadcasting organisation has no obligation to perform and broadcast a commissioned work but unless a writer fails to fulfil his professional commitment the obligation to pay the agreed commissioning or basic fee remains. Where a script is rejected and the rights revert to the writer it needs to be borne in mind that if the script is not wholly original—being an adaptation of another's copyright work, or an episode of a series with the format supplied to the writer—it will be a derivative work and the reversion of rights to the writer in his work will have little if any economic value.

The Collective Agreements make provision for dealing with disputes concerning their interpretation, or the interpretation of an individual contract between a writer and a broadcasting organisation. Generally a dispute is referable to a Joint Committee comprising representatives of the broadcasting organisation and the Writers' Guild. Failing a settlement the dispute is then to be referred to a single arbitrator mutually acceptable to both sides who is to determine the issue and whose decision is to be binding on both sides.

WRITERS' AGREEMENTS FOR BBC RADIO BROADCASTING

The Collective Agreement of February 1992 made between the BBC, the Society of Authors and the Writers' Guild sets out revised minimum terms and conditions for the commissioning of original plays and other dramatic works, and adaptations of other works (excepting works already in dramatic form), primarily for broadcasting in the BBC's domestic radio services.

Each contract with a writer is to name the title of the script and the programme for which it is commissioned, the duration of the script, the date for its delivery and the initial or basic fee. The initial fee is settled by individual negotiation between the BBC and a writer; the fee is calculated at a rate per minute of the length of the commissioned script, subject to final adjustment should the need arise. Half the initial fee is payable within 14 days of the exchange of the contract and the balance on the acceptance of the script.

The minute rate payable depends on a writer being either an "established writer" or "a beginner". The former is defined as one who within a period of three years has satisfactorily completed the specified output of radio works, or is an established writer within the meaning of the television broadcasting collective agreements relating to writers outlined above. Minutage rates as agreed between the BBC, the Society and the Writers' Guild are set out in the Agreement, namely, a per minute "going rate" for established writers, and a minimum per minute rate for beginners. These two rates are the norm and so 100 per cent. is payable for a play or a series or serial when the format and the characters are provided by the writer. For scripts for episodes of a series or serial for which the format and characters are provided by the BBC or a third party only 75 per cent. of the applicable minute fee is payable. With dramatisations the percentage ranges from 65 per cent. to 85 per cent. according to the amount of original work required for the writing of a dramatisation.

Ordinarily within 30 days of the delivery of a script a writer is to be notified whether it is acceptable or if alterations are required. Where alterations are required they are to be carried out by the writer during the period of 56 days from the date of the delivery of the script. If further alterations are required after the 56 day period a writer is entitled to payment of a further 25 per cent. instalment of the initial fee. If a script is not accepted the final instalment of the initial fee (50 per cent. or 25 per cent. as the circumstances may be) is not payable and all rights in the script revert to the writer. These procedures are modified for plural script contracts, that is, when a writer is contracted to write more than one script.

Rights Acquired

By the payment of the initial fee the BBC has the right to broadcast a script live or recorded simultaneously or non-simultaneously from all or any of the BBC's transmitters which serve the BBC's domestic radio services. This right, and the subsidiary rights as noted below, are conditional on the script being first broadcast within two years from the date of its acceptance, or the date of acceptance of the last of the scripts (not exceeding 13) where a writer has been commissioned under a plural script contract. If the broadcast does not occur within the two-year period the BBC's rights in the script lapse.

Provided the script is first broadcast within the qualifying period the BBC may at any time repeat the performance and broadcasting of the script without further payment. For the third and any additional broadcast of a script in the BBC's domestic radio services there is payable an amount equal to 44.5 per cent of the writer's "adjusted initial fee." In accordance with the formula included in the Collective Agreement a writer's initial fee is adjusted so that the calculation of the repeat fee is based on the "going rate" for the writer applicable at the time of the repeated broadcast.

Simultaneously with the first two transmissions of a script in the domestic radio services the work may be broadcast in the BBC's World Service when no additional fee is payable. Otherwise in order to obtain the right to broadcast the script in the World Service in the English language before the second broadcast in the domestic radio services there is payable an amount equal to 29.5 per cent. of the writer's initial fee for each World Service cycle, a cycle being four transmissions within a seven day period. When a broadcast in the World Service takes place after the second broadcast in the domestic radio services the 29.5 per cent. fee is calculated on the writer's adjusted initial fee. At any time after the first cycle of broadcasts further cycles may be broadcast by the payment for each cycle of an amount equal to six per cent. of the writer's initial fee, or when the cycle is broadcast after the second broadcast in the domestic radio services six per cent. of the writer's adjusted initial fee.

If a broadcast in the World Service is in a foreign language a supplementary fee is payable to the writer. For two broadcasts in any one foreign language 15 per cent. of the writer's initial fee is payable. Where the broadcasts occur after the second broadcast of the work in the domestic radio services the 15 per cent. is calculated on the writer's adjusted initial fee.

Included in the terms on which a work is commissioned is the right of the BBC at any time after the broadcasting of the script in the domestic radio services to include the work in the BBC's Transcription Service. For this right there is payable to a writer a percentage of his initial fee according to the scale of percentages for the territories of the world and the number of broadcasts authorised all as set out in the Agreement. When the right is exercised after the second broadcasting of the work in the domestic radio services the percentage payments are calculated on the writer's adjusted initial fee.

In addition to the rights and options outlined above, the BBC has the right to broadcast excerpts of a work after the first broadcasting of the script in the domestic radio services on payment of a proportion of the initial fee. Also the BBC has the right without further payment to make recordings of scripted works for archival and record purposes, for use of excerpts in historic and like programmes or in trailers, and for inclusion in cable programme services so long as the script is included via the transmission of the programme simultaneously with the BBC's own broadcast. The BBC also has translation rights for the purpose of exercising its various broadcasting rights in a script.

The radio broadcasting rights which the BBC has in a script are non-exclusive and revert unconditionally to a writer if the script is not broadcast within the time as noted above. Once a script has been accepted and the initial fee paid a writer may not prior to the first broadcasting of the script authorise any other radio or television broadcast or public performance of the script in the United Kingdom. The BBC reserves the right to match any offer made to a writer for the right to broadcast a script (or an adapted or changed format version) on television, this matching right being exercisable between the date of the signing of the contract and the end of the period one month following the date of the first broadcast of the script, or of the last script if one of a number commissioned under a plural script contract.

Furthermore, a writer also undertakes not for the year following the first broadcasting of the script in the BBC's domestic radio services to grant rights of book publication or commercial recording in the script to a third party without first notifying the BBC in writing. If the BBC or BBC Enterprises fails to respond within 21 days of the notice the writer is free to dispose of the rights as he chooses.

Warranties

A writer is required to warrant (except where a script is based on a format or other material supplied to a writer) that the script will be his original work and not infringe any person's copyright or other rights. Where any copyright material is used and incorporated in a work by the writer the written consent of the owner to the inclusion of the material and therefore its broadcasting and exploitation must be supplied to the BBC. A further warranty is that the script will not contain any defamatory matter. This warranty is qualified in that a writer will not be held responsible for defamatory matter which in the opinion of the BBC was included in the script without negligence or malice on his part. A libel may be perpetrated innocently but not so the copying of another's work and infringement of his copyright.

Alterations to Scripts

When alterations are required to a script normally they are to be discussed with the writer and if possible mutually agreed upon. However, the BBC reserves the right (a) to make minor alterations, (b) to make alterations to a script if it is one of a series to which other writers have contributed in order to achieve stylistic conformity, and (c) to make such other alterations as in the opinion of the BBC are necessary in order to avoid it being involved in legal action or bringing the BBC into disrepute.

After a script has been accepted alterations of the kind in (c) above are not to be made by the BBC unless when asked to do so the writer is unwilling to make them and the writer has had, if he so requests and the BBC agrees that time permits, an opportunity to complain about the proposed alterations. For this purpose there is to be a meeting within 48 hours of the request (excluding weekends) at which the writer may be represented by the Writers' Guild, or the Society of Authors, or if the writer is not a member of either, then by his agent. Failing agreement about the alterations the final decision rests with the BBC.

Apart from the foregoing the BBC undertakes not to make any structural alterations as distinct from minor alterations without the consent (not to be unreasonably withheld) of the writer or his agent. Where for any reason a writer is not immediately available for consultation at the time which the BBC regards as the deadline for the making of alterations (such as on account of the production being in rehearsal or recorded), then in such circumstances the alterations can be made.

If a writer wishes to make adherence to the title of the script a condition of the contract this must be asserted either by notice in writing when delivering the script or on the signature of the contract, whichever is the later. Otherwise if a change of title is required by the BBC it is to be discussed with the writer (if available) but the final decision rests with the BBC.

There is included in the contract a provision whereby a writer asserts his right to be identified as the author of a work. Subject to the BBC's observance of its obligations relating to credits and alterations of scripts, then the BBC has a defence to a claim by a writer that his moral rights have been infringed.

A writer does not have rights of consultation respecting the production of a work, or attendance at its rehearsal and recordings. However, the Agreement provides for consultation between the BBC and a writer on production depending on the standing and availability of a writer and the constraints of time. When a producer requests a writer to attend a rehearsal or recording, his travel expenses and a subsistence allowance are payable by the BBC.

Non-Dramatic Works

The radio broadcasting of published prose, poetry and dramatic works in their entirety, or of extracts, is generally in accordance with the terms agreed by the BBC with the Publishers Association and the Society of Authors. Minimum rates are prescribed but fees are negotiable and are paid on the minutage of a broadcast work, but for poetry on the half minutage.

With commissioned works 50 per cent. of the fee is payable on the signature of the contract and 50 per cent. on the acceptance of the work as suitable for broadcasting. The BBC has the non-exclusive right under the licence to broadcast the work within two years of the signing of the contract "live" or recorded once in the BBC's domestic radio services and in the BBC's World Service. There may be an unlimited number of repeated broadcasts in the domestic radio services during the two years following the initial broadcast of the work subject to the payment of 100 per cent. of the initial fee for each additional transmission. For the right to broadcast the work separately in the World Service an additional fee is payable and which payment is for a cycle of five transmissions within a period of seven days. If the work is translated and broadcast in a foreign language a further supplement is payable. Any extension of the two years of the licence period is subject to further agreement.

The broadcasting rights which the BBC acquires in published material are also usually non-exclusive and if a work is not first broadcast within two years of the signing of the contract the rights lapse. With contracts licensing the broadcasting of existing plays a concession is made whereby a writer by giving reasonable advance notice prior to the first broadcasting of the play can revoke the licence.

WRITERS' COLLECTIVE AGREEMENT FOR FILMS AND TELEVISION FILMS

In October 1990 a much simplified Collective Agreement was made between the Producers Association and the Independent Programme Producers Association and the Writers' Guild for the engagement of freelance writers to write screenplays for cinema films, television films and videograms. With effect from February 1992 the Agreement, as revised, is between the Writers' Guild and the Producers Alliance for Cinema and Television (PACT). The Agreement does not apply to persons engaged as script editors or in like capacities but only to writers commissioned to write specific scripts for performance by artists.

Standard form contracts for the commissioning of writers to write scripts for single films and for films comprising a series or serial are annexed to the Agreement and incorporate by reference the general conditions of engagement contained in the Agreement. Special terms, but not less favourable ones, may be negotiated between a writer and producer and recorded in a writer's contract. The forms provide for the insertion of the times and stages of work commissioned and the amount of the various instalments of the fee payable at each stage. In this connection certain of the definitions set out in the Agreement need especially to be noted:

"Treatment"—an outline or synopsis in narrative form of an entire story indicating the fuller structure and development and characterisation of the plot.
"First Draft"—the full development of the treatment or in its absence a definition in terms of visual action and dialogue suitable as a production for cinema and/or television exhibition.
"Second Draft"—the second complete draft of the screenplay as requested by the producer, which, if accepted, shall become the script as next defined.
"Principal Photography Script"—the approved and finally accepted version of a shooting script for principal photography with individual

scenes, and full dialogue incorporating all alterations and amendments required by the producer.

The fees payable for the services of a writer at each of the stages are individually negotiable but minimum rates are prescribed; each of the fees is payable in two instalments, namely on the commencement of a stage and on the delivery of the material. If as often happens a total or combined composite fee is agreed, it follows that the fee may not be less than the total of the minimum payments prescribed in the Agreement for each of the above stages. After the payment of the fee for the principal photography script, for certain films, as noted below, an "additional use pre-payment" is automatically payable and so part of the total negotiated fee may need to be apportioned to this payment and which forms part of the total guaranteed payment or fee.

General Provisions

By the general provisions of the Agreement a writer affirms his commitment to the writing and delivery of the script and warrants that it will be his original work and not infringe the copyright of any person, or to the best of his knowledge and belief contain matter defamatory of any person. Furthermore a writer undertakes to render his services in a professional manner and carry out adequate research for the writing of the script, to deliver it in the stages and at the times as specified in the contract—time being of the essence of the contract—and with due despatch to make incidental and minor revisions as reasonably requested by the producer. Ordinarily following the delivery of a script a producer is to notify a writer within 30 days either of its acceptance or to request revisions. Any revisions are to be completed by a writer within 14 days of their being notified and within the next following 14 days a producer is to signify the acceptance or rejection of a script.

A writer also undertakes to attend meetings as reasonably required for the planning and writing of the script. If this entails travel beyond 30 miles of the place where the writer normally works his travel and additional expenses necessarily incurred are to be reimbursed provided the expenses are first authorised by the producer. If after acceptance of the final draft of a script a writer is specifically requested by a producer to attend further meetings, a daily attendance allowance is payable to the writer.

A writer is entitled to be given notice of the time and place and to attend the showing of the "rough cut" of the production and to be informed of the final screen title of the production should this not be as stated in the writer's contract. On completion a producer is to provide the writer with a videotape copy of the production.

If the commissioned script is to be based upon or includes material supplied by the producer there is an indemnity on the latter's part for any loss the writer may incur by the inclusion of the material. This is especially relevant where the commissioned screenplay is a dramatisation or adaptation of a copyright work as the rights for the making of the dramatisation and the exploitation of the film will need to have been acquired by the producer from the copyright owners. Should the writer of the screenplay also be the author of the original published work a formal grant of these rights in the original work to the producer will still be needed.

Acquisition of Copyright

Although the total of the payments for a writer's services is required to be inserted in the contract even so under the terms of the Agreement a producer has a right of "cut-off" at any one of the stages. Only if a writer completes all these does the principal photography payment become due. The copyright in a writer's script material passes to a producer only as and when payment is made for the stage in respect of which the services are rendered. Any sums due after the payment of the principal photography payment on account of the uses and exploitation of a film in accordance with the Agreement, are recoverable from a producer (or his assignee) only as an ordinary debt.

Where a writer is commissioned to write an original treatment but which is rejected only the fee due on commencement is payable but all rights remain vested in the writer. Where a writer is commissioned to write a treatment based on ideas or a format provided by a producer if the treatment is rejected both instalments of the whole fee are payable but all rights of copyright remain with and vest in the producer. Where at other stages the material written by a writer is rejected then provided all instalments of the fees due up to the point of rejection have been or are paid, for example, with a second draft script both the commencement and delivery payments on the dates specified in the writer's contract, then the copyright in the material passes and vests in the producer.

Where a script is wholly original to a writer then if after two years from the date of its delivery the principal photography of the film has not commenced the writer is entitled to retrieve the copyright in his work by the payment of 50 per cent. of the fees paid to him by the producer. Where a script is based on another's work or the format of a series or serial supplied by the producer this buy-back right may need to be especially provided for in the contract of engagement.

Although the entire copyright in a script vests in a producer the Agreement provides that the right to publish a script is open to negotiation between a writer and producer. It is a matter of importance if a novelisation of the screenplay is likely or the script is one for a series or serial film production and likely to be used in any published story version. The

Agreement also acknowledges that merchandising rights may be of material interest to the parties and so are reserved for separate negotiation.

Rights of Exploitation

The extent to which a producer may exploit a film which incorporates a writer's work depends first on the category of film (whether made on film or tape) for which a script is commissioned and the amount of the total guaranteed payment, and secondly on the purchase as and when a producer may decide, of additional rights or uses. The categories of films, the amounts of the total guaranteed payments, the basic minimum rights acquired and the fees payable for specific additional uses or rights of exploitation are all set out in the Agreement.

The categories of films and the rights of exploitation secured are as follows:

No. 1—feature films budgeted in excess of £2 million all rights except free television broadcasting rights and videogram rights.

No. 2—(a) feature films budgeted between £750,000 up to £2 million; and

(b) television films budgeted at £750,000 and above and not subject to any ceiling:

either:
(i) world theatrical rights; or

(ii) two UK network television transmissions and a limited theatrical release in the UK over a period of three months in not more than 10 cinemas and not all of the same circuit, the release to be within a period commencing nine months before the first television transmission in the UK and terminating three months after.

No. 3—films budgeted below £750,000—either:

(i) world theatrical rights; or

(ii) two UK network television transmissions.

No. 4—television series and serials with the format provided other than by the writer—one UK network television transmission.

The Agreement requires that on the first day of principal photography of a feature or single television film a producer is to submit to a writer a certified statement of the budget as approved by the financiers. If the amount is in excess of the budget limit set for the category of film for which the script was commissioned, the minimum payments due are amended accordingly.

When a script is commissioned for a film in category No. 1 or 2 the minimum prescribed total guaranteed payment includes a minimum "additional use pre-payment" which is a payment on account of the amounts due if and when a producer opts to exercise any of the listed additional rights. This additional use pre-payment is customarily paid to a writer not later than the first day of principal photography of the film.

Additional Uses

The additional rights of exploitation which may be purchased for minimum amounts as prescribed in the Agreement according to the category of the film and the uses being acquired, are as follows:

(1) theatrical rights:

> UK—(subject to negotiation);
>
> US—(subject to negotiation);
>
> Rest of the world;

(2) UK television for seven years by payment of a fee for each transmission subject to the payment for a minimum of three transmissions;

(3) if two UK transmissions are first acquired for films in categories Nos. 2 and 3—additional UK transmissions by an additional payment for each transmission;

(4) US network Prime Time;

(5) US network Non-prime Time;

(6) US Public Broadcast Service;

(7) US other television;

(8) rest of the world free television;

(9) US major pay television;

(10) US and the rest of the world pay television;

(11) videogram world wide.

The UK television rights include simultaneous European cable transmissions. Apart from the limitations on the number of UK transmissions as above, the payment for each one of the uses gives unlimited rights of transmission and without limit of time. Non-theatric rights as usually understood in the film and television industry are automatically acquired by a producer with the payment of the total minimum payment for a script.

Television Series and Serials

The Agreement makes special provision for scripts commissioned for films within category No. 4—Television Series and Serials. The total minimum and total guaranteed payments are assessed and paid differently from other commissions. (The terms do not apply to twice-weekly serials).

A total minimum payment or script fee is prescribed which is payable in equal instalments up to the time of acceptance of the second draft of the script as provided for in a writer's contract. This total minimum payment is for one UK network television transmission. However, on the first day of principal photography of the production a producer must either pay a further 100 per cent. of the script fee and thereby acquire worldwide television rights (except those listed below), or alternatively affirm that the production is solely for UK domestic transmission. In this event only a further 75 per cent. of the script fee is payable and a producer thereby acquires the right to one repeat UK network transmission. Thus the total minimum payment or script fee together with the additional percentage payment is the total guaranteed payment due to a writer.

There is a further refinement in that if the alternative payment of 75 per cent. of the script fee is made and subsequently the series is offered for sale abroad, that is apart from the excepted sales as below, the 100 per cent. worldwide buy-out payment will (additionally) become due on the date, whichever is the earlier, the programme is first licensed to a foreign buyer or transmitted by a buyer.

The excepted rights referred to above and for which use fees as a percentage of the total minimum payment are payable are:

UK network television second repeat	50 per cent.
UK network television third and each subsequent repeat transmission	25 per cent.
US network television Prime Time	100 per cent.
Non-prime Time	50 per cent.
US Public Broadcast Service	15 per cent.
US other television	15 per cent.
US major pay television	20 per cent.
Other US and rest of the world pay television	10 per cent.
Videogram rights	7.5 per cent.

Other General Provisions and Disputes Procedure

A writer is entitled to retain any monies paid to him direct under any collective agreements negotiated by a recognised foreign or domestic collecting society, but may not claim against a producer for any default of such a society to make any payment as may be due to a writer.

The Agreement confirms the right of a producer to assign the benefit of a writer's contract and all rights in the work written by the writer, but a producer is not thereby relieved of his obligations to the writer. The writer or his agent should be informed of an assignment.

The Agreement makes provision for dealing with any dispute arising from its operation and interpretation. The matter is to be referred to a Standing Joint Committee to consist of not more than three representatives of the Writers' Guild and three of PACT not involved in or who could stand directly to benefit from the dispute in any way.

The Committee is normally to meet within 72 hours (three working days) of the matter being referred to the two organisations and be presided alternatively at each meeting by a representative of the two organisations but who may not vote. If the Committee reaches an agreed decision on any issue the decision constitutes a settlement which is to be accepted by the parties. In the event that the Committee fails to agree on any issue, a further meeting of the Committee is to be convened and presided over by an independent person with power to settle the matter. The decision of the independent person is final and binding on both parties. The Advisory, Conciliation and Arbitration Service (ACAS) may be consulted on the appointment of the independent person to preside at the Committee. This provision for dealing with disputes does not affect or restrict the rights of either party to apply to the courts for equitable relief.

THE SCREENWRITING CREDITS AGREEMENT

There is no provision respecting moral rights but a writer is entitled to screen credit in accordance with the terms of the Screenwriting Credits Agreement of 1974, as amended, annexed to the Agreement. The entitlement is to either a "main" or "subsidiary" writing credit defined as follows:

(a) The only Main writing credits permitted are:

    (i) "BY. . ." where a writer has written both the story and the screenplay and when the producer, at his sole discretion, decides that such credit immediately follows the main title credit.

    (ii) "WRITTEN BY. . ." where the writer has written both the story and the screenplay and such credit appears elsewhere in the film.

      (iii) "SCREENPLAY BY..." where a writer has made a substantial contribution to the writing of the screenplay.

    (b) The only Subsidiary writing credits permitted are:

      (i) "STORY BY..." or "SCREENSTORY BY..." (as the case may be) where a writer contributes by providing either the story or screenstory upon which the screenplay is substantially based.

      (ii) "NARRATION BY..." where the writer's contribution is in the form of narration.

      (iii) "ENGLISH SCREENPLAY VERSION BY..." where the writer has written the English version of a foreign language screenplay or story.

The maximum number of writers permitted to share in each of the two categories is three unless the circumstances are exceptional such with an omnibus or episodic film. A source material credit may also be included as a separate item in the same card devoted to the writing credits. The Agreement contains detailed provisions regarding the size and position of screen credits and that the credits are to be on the negative of the completed film and the positive copies made for exhibition.

The obligation to give writers credit in advertising and publicity is limited to writers entitled to a Main writing credit and when credit is accorded to the director, and the advertising is issued by or under the direct control of the producer. The customary industry exceptions for the giving of advertising credit apply—such as "teaser" and trailer—but if a director is accorded credit in any such excepted advertising then if the writer is entitled to a sole main writing credit the writer is to be accorded credit.

A writer is entitled to forego credit either by notice expressly at the time of the engagement or by written notice within 48 hours after the screening of the "rough cut" of the film. As soon as practical after completion of principal photography a producer is to notify every person who has been engaged to contribute to the screenplay, and the Writers' Guild, of the proposed Main and Subsidiary credits. Unless objections (if any) are made within 14 days of the notifications, the credits become final and binding on the parties. Procedures for resolving disputes over credit entitlements are prescribed in the Agreement, and for a producer to procure from a third party an undertaking to observe the credit obligations which if given and delivered to the writers absolves the producer from liability for any breach of the credit obligations.

D. THE ADAPTATION OF LITERARY AND DRAMATIC WORKS

Stage plays and television and film scripts are often adaptations of works such as a novel, story or dramatic work, and so it is important to consider the legal implications of the making and exploitation of an adaptation of such works. An adaptation whether of a classic work in the public domain or of a protected work, possesses all the rights of copyright as if it were a wholly original work. The copyright in an adaptation will belong to the adapter unless it is commissioned and the contract of engagement provides that the future copyright in the adaptation is to belong to the person commissioning the work. The collective agreements considered above variously specify the terms and conditions on which writers are engaged to undertake adaptations of works.

Most professions and businesses have their jargon—the lawyers of course are the worst offenders—but the expression "changed format rights" has come to be used especially in the broadcasting and film industries. It is often applied when the characters and situations in, for example, a series of comedy programmes are changed for the series to be produced and exploited in a new medium or market, and for when a game show is altered or changed for it to be marketed and sold in a different country. Such rights of alteration and change are, in law, adaptation rights.

The making of an adaptation of a copyright work—including a translation—is one of the acts restricted by copyright. As an adaptation is a derivative work it follows that the written permission and agreement of the copyright owner of the original protected work to the making of the adaptation must be obtained by the adapter, or the person commissioning the adaptation. It therefore follows that the rights which can be exercised in the adaptation will be governed and controlled by the terms and conditions of that agreement.

There are no standard agreements for the making of adaptations of protected works but any such agreement needs to define precisely the medium of exploitation of the adaptation—stage, broadcasting, film, videogram and any combination of these—and the territories where performances in the medium can be given, transmitted, distributed or sold and the duration of the licence.

Depending on the nature of the work there may be other issues to be covered in an adaptation agreement. If there is to be a change of title for the production and performance of the dramatic version of the work this should be provided for as well as agreement on the credits to be accorded to the author of the original work and the adapter. In the advertising and promotion of a dramatisation a brief synopsis will normally need to be published and so the right to make and publish a synopsis of a specified number of words should be provided for; if the work is already published it should be ascertained that the synopsis right does not contravene any publishing agreement. Depending on the nature of the work it may be appropriate to agree an option for the acquisition of the equivalent rights in any sequel which the author of the original work may write; merchandising rights may also be a factor in the negotiations.

The consideration for the right to make and exploit the adaptation must be part of the licence agreement. It may be a single capital payment on the signing of the agreement, or a payment on account of royalties or other monies arising from the exploitation of the adaptation. What monies and when due and payable need to be defined and specified. Where payments are derived from revenues and a share of profits there must also be included provision for the keeping of accounts and the furnishing of financial statements and rights of inspection of records to verify the statements and payments made.

If the licence is for a limited purpose, such as for the making and performance of a stage play, or for the adaptation of a work as a film script, it may be a condition of the licence that all residual rights of copyright in the adaptation or script are to be reserved to the owner of the original work and not retained by the adapter. In this way the owner of the original work also secures complete control of the adaptation.

The licence to make an adaptation will most likely be personal to the adapter. Ordinarily the right and title of the ostensible copyright owner of the work proposed to be adapted to authorise and license the adaptation should be investigated. Where other rights in the work have already been granted to third parties, such as publishing rights, or licences for the making of other versions, these also need to be investigated to ensure there is no conflict of interests to prejudice or inhibit the exploitation of the adaptation.

In order to maximise the opportunities for an adaptation to earn royalties or other revenues there may need to be included in a licence agreement some limitation on the right of the author or copyright owner to exploit the original work. The copyright owner may undertake for a specified period of time not to authorise the performance of his work, or the making and performance of another version of his work, such as would compete with the exploitation of the adaptation and diminish its value. Thus where the right is granted for the conversion of a novel into a dramatic version for performance on the stage, the right to license any version or other use of the novel in another media may need to be restrained. If a licence is granted for the adaptation of a dramatic work into a musical play, performances of the original drama may be restrained to protect the value of the new version.

The moral rights of authors created by the Copyright, Designs and Patents Act 1988 are proprietary rights and therefore are important terms of adaptation agreements. The right of paternity, the right to be identified as the author of a work, must be asserted and so as mentioned above, the form or style of credit to be accorded to the author of the original work and to the adapter respectively needs to be provided for in the licence agreement.

As for the right of integrity, for an author not to suffer the derogatory treatment of his work, any comment here can only be speculative in the absence of any reported proceedings brought under the new laws. Unless there is a stipulation in the licence agreement respecting moral rights, such as an author reserving a right of (reasonable) approval of an adaptation, where the licence is for a mutually agreed purpose, and still more so if the right to make the adaptation is granted for valuable consideration, it remains to be seen what view the courts would take of an author's complaint that an adaptation was a derogatory treatment of his work.

Footnote for "the quickie"

In the preceding pages dealings with literary and dramatic works have been highlighted but it should not be overlooked that advertising copy, sketches, monologues, comic patter "gags" and "quickies" are as much capable of copyright protection as the most earnest drama. It follows that the use of such material both in theatrical performance and variously in the mechanical media requires to be licensed by the author or copyright owner. The actions of the comic who on the stage drops his trousers at the moment of a "black-out"—usually still to the laughter of the audience—and other like pantomime routines can be copied by others, but the lines and patter he speaks might be original in him and therefore protected by copyright.

E. COMPOSERS AND MUSIC PUBLISHING AGREEMENTS

The rights of copyright in musical works are the same as in literary and dramatic works but the way in which they are dealt with and exploited bears little comparison. Clearly it is performance which matters and it is the enterprise of music publishers to achieve the performance of a musical work live or by mechanical means or by broadcasting which goes to the root of the terms of publishing agreements.

In the past representatives of music publishers laboriously for many weeks by personal demonstration promoted the sale of copies of compositions to secure their performance in homes, in concert halls, music and dance halls, variety palaces, tea rooms and such like places. Today and especially with pop music the musical score has rather given way to the "demo tape" of the singer/songwriter and the thrust of promotion is directed towards securing the recording of a work and a place for it in the charts. Thus a music publisher has to have the resources, organisation and flair to match composer, lyric-writer, performer, band or group leader and record producer, and to perceive and respond to changing modes and fashions in music rather in the same way as a producer of merchandise. All this can involve a considerable investment of money which can be as much a speculation by a publisher as the time and concentration expended in the creative efforts of composers and lyricists.

In the past the terms on which publishers accepted musical works for publication were very standardised, but that is no longer so as more regard is now paid to the reputation and economic worth of a composer/ lyricist. In addition, changes to publishing agreements have been brought about through consultations between the organisations representative of composers and lyricists, and of publishers. The Composers' Guild of Great Britain serves to promote and help the professional interests of composers of serious music and the commissioning and performance of new music. The British Academy of Songwriters, Composers and Authors (formerly the Songwriters' Guild) performs the same functions in the field of light and popular music by ensuring that British composers and songwriters are given the fullest opportunity for the promotion and performance of their works, and by organising festivals and awards for these purposes. Neither of these organisations is directly involved in the negotiations of minimum rates or conditions of engagement although both have available standard publishing agreements.

The Composers Joint Council which is the collective representative body for composers' organisations engages in negotiations on rights and makes recommendations on fees payable for the services of composers. The Musicians' Union negotiates rates for the arranging and copying of music. The Music Publishers' Association is similarly concerned to advance the interests of its publisher members and engages in the promotion of all music and in all media.

The music publisher of the nineteenth century emerged as the successor to the music patron of classical times. Because of his total involvement in the promotion and exploitation of a work, the publisher came to acquire the entire copyright in it for a single payment. Although publishers have continued to acquire the entire copyright in musical works (save for the rights of public performance and broadcasting as explained below), with the establishment of royalty collecting societies royalty payments have replaced a lump sum payment thereby ensuring that composers receive compensation commensurate with the success of their individual works. (The payment which may be made to a composer on the commissioning of a work is a separate consideration). The publication of music in the more literal sense of the printing of copies produces only a minor contribution to royalties. It is the income from the exploitation of the separate rights of public performance, broadcasting and mechanical reproduction and how this income is to be divided between publisher and composer/lyricist which is crucial in publishing agreements.

PUBLISHER'S RIGHTS

For many years it has been a standard practice and term of publishing agreements for a composer/lyricist to assign the ownership of his work to a publisher for the duration of the period of copyright and throughout the world, and for the royalties from its exploitation to be divided equally between writer and publisher. These terms no longer apply as a matter of course, certainly not with the publication of pop and light musical works. Changes have come about through the cult of personality of composer/ songwriters and their earning power from appearances and recordings, and as a result of the rulings of the courts respecting the onerous terms of publishing agreements and the unfair advantages taken by a few unscrupulous publishers or managers.

Thus the assignment of rights may be limited to a specific number of years, or restricted to certain territories, or conditional upon a publisher fulfilling certain obligations respecting the exploitation of a work. These are likely to be the procuring or generation of a minimum royalty income within a specified time. More likely, the obligation will be for a publisher to secure within two years of the date of the publishing agreement the release to the public of a commercial recording of the work through a bona fide record company, or its inclusion and synchronisation in a film or television film or other audio-visual production. If there is a failure to fulfil these obligations there is an automatic reversion to the writer of the rights in the work.

As the owner of the copyright in a musical work the publisher will have control of the licensing and negotiation of royalties for the public performance, broadcasting and reproduction of a work. But except for staged performances of opera, ballet, musical plays and dramatic performances of certain works this is an over-simplification. As explained in the following Sections the Performing Right Society has a material role in the licensing of the public performance and broadcasting of musical works, and the Mechanical-Copyright Protection Society in the licensing of the reproduction of works. The apportionment of the royalties from the exploitation of these rights as between publisher and composer/lyricist has normally been 50:50 but this is no longer invariable. The more preferential division of royalties in favour of the composer/lyricist under the rules of the Performing Right Society is being adhered to rather than the minimum of 50:50 which is permitted under the Society's rules. The share of royalties from the exploitation of mechanical rights is similarly now more negotiable so that a composer/lyricist may receive 60 per cent. where a single work is published but 75 per cent. where a composer/lyricist has an on-going commitment to a publisher. The division of royalties should be set out in a publishing agreement as a record of what is agreed.

The publication of contemporary serious music is conducted on more traditional lines and so rights will be acquired for the duration of the term of copyright and the division of royalties 50:50, except for operatic and other works given stage performances or otherwise performed dramatically. A modern work may be commissioned by a society or sponsor but a concert performance of the work with a good critical acclaim is likely to be the inducement for its publication.

The outlay incurred in the actual printing and publication of a work—particularly an orchestral work—can be considerable and as a work may not have wide appeal it follows that the recoupment of costs will take much longer than is likely with pop and light music. It is also on account of printing costs that despite the classical repertoire being in the public domain, still the printing of and publishing of editions of musical works and the hiring of scores is confined to a few long-established music publishing houses. Such editions may have copyright protection as compilations. In addition a special protection under the Copyright, Designs and Patents Act 1988 may be available as the making by any photographic or similar process of a reproduction of the typographical arrangement of a published edition is an act restricted by copyright. The protection is for 25 years from the end of the calendar year in which the edition is first published. The hiring of scores or parts is an important function and source of income of a classical music publisher and for as long as a work is in copyright a share of the hire income is normally accounted for and paid to the composer.

Moral Rights

By assigning his copyright a composer divests himself of the ownership and control of his work. This is often underlined in music publishing agreements by it being expressly stated that a publisher has the right to make adaptations, arrangements and alterations to the music and/or lyrics of a work and to change the title, as well as to further assign and deal with all or any of the rights acquired in the work as the publisher chooses. Once it could be said these were absolute and unqualified rights but that may not be so any longer so by virtue of the personal moral rights of authors created by the 1988 Act as noted in detail in Part 6 above.

The right of paternity, that is, the right to be identified as the author of a work, has to be asserted and the place for this is ideally the publishing agreement. Music publishing agreements have not provided for the announcement of the name of a composer or lyricist on published copies of a work—doubtless as this is accepted as a matter of course—but if a composer requires his work to be published and exploited under a pseudonym then this should be stipulated in the publishing agreement.

As for the right of integrity, that is the right of a composer not to have his works subjected to derogatory treatment, it remains to be seen quite what effect the right has on such clauses as above. A recent case can be regarded as indicative of the approach of the courts to the protection of the moral rights of authors and composers and underlines the need for the inclusion of a provision making clear the right of a publisher or any third party to make adaptations or arrangements or alterations to a work, or to change the title of a work, or alternatively a provision whereby an author or composer waives his moral rights wholly or in part.

The case arose from the intended release of a recording of a medley made of a composer's songs when the lyrics were in part altered and also the music of other composers was interspersed in the recording. The court ruled there was an arguable case that the treatment of the composer's songs was a distortion or mutilation such as to be a derogatory treatment and infringement of the composer's moral rights. Also there was an arguable case that the making of the medley was an adaptation of the compositions, within the meaning of the 1988 Act, and having been made without the consent of the copyright owner was an infringement of copyright. The court further ruled that the defendants had not proved that the licence (of the Mechanical-Copyright Protection Society) to reproduce the compositions included the right to adapt them for the purposes of the recording.

These proceedings were for an injunction to prevent the release of the recording which the court granted in the exercise of its discretionary powers. The composer's moral rights were at risk and the view of the defendants that any damages to the composer could be mitigated by the publication of a disclaimer on the records in question was rejected on the grounds that any disclaimer would not reach the eyes or ears of the people who heard the record performed in public or over the radio. The issues were not fully adjudicated upon as they would have been at a trial, hence the rulings that they were "arguable". This being so the judgment of the court cannot be regarded as final.

Commissioned Works

When a composer is commissioned to write original music such as a concert work, or music for a stage production, or for a film, or for a television or radio programme, or a jingle for a "commercial," the services to be provided and the rights of copyright in the commissioned work need to be specified in the contract of engagement. If it is a condition of the commission that the publishing rights in the music are to belong to the organisation or company commissioning the music (or its nominee) as often happens when music is commissioned for films and television programmes, then the rights will be contained in the publishing agreement made collateral to the commissioning agreement and the issues considered above in regard to music publishing agreements will arise.

The fee payable for a commissioned work will be negotiable but there may need to be reckoned the cost of copying of parts especially if a large orchestral work is being commissioned. Similarly the cost of orchestration may need to be taken into account especially with music composed for the stage, film or television when the pressures and demands can be acute compared with those likely to arise with a concert commission. Furthermore, a composer as part of his engagement especially for films and television programmes may be required to conduct the performance and recording of the music and this service is also reckonable in negotiating the total fees.

When music is commissioned for a film there will normally be included in the composer's agreement either expressly or by implication the right to record the music in the soundtrack of the film—the synchronisation right. If a record or audio cassette of the soundtrack recording of the film, or a videogram of the film is manufactured and issued to the public, a mechanical royalty will be payable to whoever is the copyright owner of the music. The same principle applies to the like use of music commissioned for a television or radio programme. As the publisher will usually be the copyright owner, the royalties from such exploitation of the music—usually collected by the Mechanical-Copyright Protection

Society—will be shared with the composer as provided for in the publishing agreement made collateral with the agreement commissioning the music.

If the composer is engaged to conduct the performance at the recording of the music a conductor's royalty will also be payable to him on the sale of the records and audio cassettes of the recording.

F. THE PUBLIC PERFORMANCE AND BROADCASTING OF MUSICAL WORKS

The output of musical works of all kinds and the extent of their perform-ance is so enormous that in most countries of the world there exists societies to organise and license the public performance and broadcasting of copyright music. The Performing Right Society Limited which was established in 1914 performs this service in the United Kingdom. Further-more, by its affiliations with corresponding societies in other countries the works of British composers and lyric writers are made available for performance abroad and likewise the works of foreign writers are made available for performance here. Over the years the Society has become a large organisation representing 24,000 members but through its affiliates 750,000 composers, lyric-writers and music publishers, and controlling a repertoire of about two and a half million registered works. Currently it has an annual revenue of about 90 million pounds from licences granted for the public performance and broadcasting of music in this country and of over 40 million pounds from its affiliated societies in respect of per-formances of the works of its members abroad. In 1991 over 107 million pounds of the society's revenue was distributed to its members.

The system whereby the Society acquires the right of public perform-ance in the works of its members and therefore has a virtual monopoly over the licensing of the public performance and broadcasting of copy-right musical works has its critics. Yet no other means suitable to present day conditions have been devised whereby on the one hand composers and lyric writers are protected from the illicit use and public performance of their works, and on the other hand countless music users ranging in size and function from broadcasting organisations to village halls can obtain from one licensing source permission to publicly perform any work from the vast repertoire of available copyright music and songs. However as will be seen the Society does not in all circumstances license the performance of musical works; for example the performance of pro-tected operas and musical plays is reserved and controlled by the owners of such works.

By the terms of the constitution and rules of the Society its members decide on the tariffs or royalties charged for the performance of their music and the distribution of revenues received and so it can fairly be asked to what extent can prospective music users question the fees charged? The Society is very aware of its monopoly position and in deciding its tariff charges whenever practical it negotiates with officials or organisations such as trade associations, societies and the like who represent various classes or categories of music users. In this respect the Music Users' Council plays an important role. Moreover, the Society is not the sole or final arbiter of licence fees. It is a "licensing body" and its tariffs are "licensing schemes" within the meaning of section 116 of the Copyright, Designs and Patents Act 1988, and its "blanket" licences with certain particular organisations fall within section 124 of the Act. Thus organisations representative of music users and persons and organisations who are licensees of the Society can refer any issue regarding the fairness of any tariff or licence, or the refusal of a licence to the Copyright Tribunal whose functions and powers are reviewed in Part 6, above. It is to the credit of the Society that little recourse has been had to the Tribunal since its creation under the Copyright Act 1956 apart from the references initiated by the broadcasting organisations.

Membership of the Performing Right Society

The Society is a company limited by guarantee and governed by its full and associate members in general meeting. Its main objects are to license the right of public performance and broadcasting of the works of its members and the works of members of its affiliated societies, to collect the royalties and revenues derived from licences granted by it and after deducting administration costs, to distribute the remainder to its members and affiliated societies. Except for those matters which by law or the Society's constitution are reserved to be exercised by members in general meeting, the management of the Society is vested in the General Council which is elected by full and associate members. The administration of the general affairs of the Society is undertaken by the Executive Council whose members are appointed by and from amongst the members of the General Council, and a permanent staff supervised by the Chief Executive appointed by the General Council. Membership of the Society is open to composers and lyricists and to publishers of musical works. There are three categories of membership, namely provisional, associate and full, and under the Society's Articles of Association the General Council is empowered to lay down the qualifications for admission to each class. On admission to the Society entry is as a provisional member. The conditions for admission to the Society and advancement to associate and full membership are as follows.

(a) Provisional Membership:

Qualifications for admission:

(i) composers and lyricists—three works which must each have been either:

(a) commercially recorded, or

(b) broadcast within the past two years, or

(c) performed in public on at least 12 occasions within the past two years, and commercially published.

Alternatively the writer-applicant can be:

(a) A writer who has had one work in the Top 50 of a popularity chart recognised by the PRS, within the past 12 months.

(b) A writer who has written the theme or opening/closing music for a film which has been publicly exhibited or for a series of three or more episodes broadcast on network television or network radio.

(c) A classical composer or lyricist who has achieved a network broadcast lasting five minutes or longer.

(d) A classical composer or lyricist who has had two performances, each lasting five minutes or longer, at a concert or recital of classical music licensable by the Society.

An application must be accompanied by suitable evidence such as a copy of the record or sheet music, or a printed concert programme. In the case of a public performance, where there is no evidence on a printed programme that a performance has taken place, some other form of corroboration will be required, *e.g.* a copy of the engagement contract. Every applicant must also submit a birth certificate.

(ii) publishers—a catalogue of 15 works of which at least 10 have been commercially published or commercially recorded. In addition:

(a) The writers of the 15 qualifying works must be members of PRS, or of one of its affiliated societies.

(b) The publisher must have acquired rights in at least 10 of the works for a territory within the EC.

(c) In a case where the catalogue of works consists entirely of works recorded on the soundtrack of films then:
(i) such catalogue must not consist only of works recorded on the soundtrack of one film, and

(ii) the works must be of not less than 30 minutes' duration in aggregate as recorded on such soundtrack.

A copy of the record or sheet music must be submitted in support of the application; copies of all assignments between the applicant and the writers in respect of the works concerned must also be supplied. Individual applicants must also submit a birth certificate.

An admission fee of £50 for writers and £250 for publishers (both inclusive of VAT) is payable with the membership application and this is refunded if an application is unsuccessful.

The rights of membership are to receive the reports and accounts of the Society.

The following definitions apply to the admission criteria:

"Broadcast" means:

transmission by a television or radio broadcasting station (excluding community or hospital radio) and/or inclusion in a cable programme.

"Film" is defined as in section 5 of the Copyright, Designs and Patents Act 1988. It thus includes videograms (whether in the form of cassettes or discs) as well as films in the narrower sense.

"Commercially published" means:

made available to the public by sale or hire in graphic form.

"Commercially recorded" means:

(i) the work has been released to the public on a record label listed in the Music Master or Gramophone catalogues, or

(ii) the work has been recorded and made available to the public by inclusion in a catalogue of a recorded music (*e.g.* background or mood music) library, or

(iii) the work has been recorded and transmitted by a television or radio broadcasting station or included in cable programme, or

(iv) the work has been recorded on the soundtrack of a film which has been released for public exploitation.

"Network Radio" means:

BBC Radio 1, 2, 3 or 4, (including Radio Scotland, Radio Wales, Radio Ulster or RTE).

(b) Associate Membership:

Qualifications for admission: One year's membership as a provisional member; also the member must have aggregated PRS earnings within a period of three years of £780 if a writer member, and £3,900 if a publisher member earned over a period not exceeding three years.

The rights of membership are: to receive the reports and accounts of the Society; to attend general meetings and to vote on a show of hands or on a poll or postal ballot.

(c) Full Membership:

Qualifications for admission: The member must have the minimum PRS earnings in at least two of the three years concerned of—

(i) if a writer member £4,330 in 1989, £4,890 in 1990 and £5,470 in 1991;

(ii) if a publisher member £21,650 in 1989, £24,430 in 1990 and £27,350 in 1991.

The rights of membership are: to receive the reports and accounts of the Society; to attend general meetings; to seek election to the General Council; to one vote on a show of hands, 10 votes on a poll or postal ballot. Full members whose earnings in a number of years reach a further criteria as laid down by the General Council have an additional 10 votes.

Note that the earnings criteria as above are automatically adjusted each year in line with the changes in the total revenue distributed to members.

Other Rules of Membership

Advancement to associate and full membership status is automatic once the prescribed qualification has been attained. The new status is notified to a member and is not lost by any subsequent decline in earnings below the level of the criteria current at the time of the notification.

If no royalties are credited to a provisional writer over a three-year period, and if the royalties of a provisional publisher member do not exceed an aggregate of £250 over three years their membership will normally be terminated by the Society. An associate membership is terminated after a period of five years in which no royalties whatsoever have been credited.

Membership cannot be transferred but the rules of the Society provide for the termination of membership on the death of a member, on liquidation (applicable when a member is a limited company or firm), by resignation, by the expiration of the copyright in a member's works and by resolution of the General Council. Because a member must assign and transfer to the Society the rights in his works which it is to administer (as explained below), the rules governing cessation of membership are as important as those for admission. A member can resign his membership by three months' written notice but by the Society's rules resignation can be effected only at three-yearly intervals counting from the date of first admission.

When termination arises on the death of a member the rights vested by him in the Society during his life-time continue to remain so vested and controlled by the Society for a period ending on December 31, in the seventh year following the member's death. The payments to which the member would have been entitled during this period are paid to his personal representatives. Under the rules of the Society an executor or other legal personal representative or beneficiary of a deceased member may at the discretion of the Society, and provided the amount of the aggregate royalties of a member in the three years preceding his death amount to £250, be admitted to the category of successor membership in the class of the deceased member. In such circumstances the rights vested in the Society by the deceased member then remain with the Society for so long as the successor member remains in membership of the Society and royalties are accounted for to the successor member.

If a member is a limited company or a firm its membership ceases upon its liquidation (other than a voluntary liquidation for the purpose of reconstruction), and for a firm on its ceasing to carry on business. The rights already vested in the Society remain so vested and controlled until December 31 of the seventh year following the year of liquidation or cessation of business. During this period any payments due as if to the company or firm were still a member are paid to the persons entitled for the time being to receive payment of debts due to the company or firm.

The Rights Administered by the Society

The rights in the musical works of its members which the Society on their behalf is empowered to control are defined in the Society's Articles of Association as follows:

  (i) the performing right;

  (ii) for writer members only, the film synchronisation right in every work composed or written by the member primarily for the purpose of being recorded on the soundtrack of a particular film or films in contemplation when such work was commissioned;

  (iii) such other rights, or such parts of the rights mentioned above as the General Council may direct, for the whole world or such part or parts of the whole world as the General Council may direct, in all or any works or parts of works present and future, of which the member is the writer, publisher or proprietor.

On admission to the Society as a matter of course a member is required to sign and return the Deed of Assignment vesting and transferring to the Society these rights in a member's existing and future works. If the member fails to return the Deed to the Society within one year from the date of his admission his membership is terminated.

It needs to be stressed that the rights attach not only to a writer's works in existence at the time of his admission but also to his future works. Thus where a composer or lyric writer is commissioned to compose an original work there must always be included as a term of the commissioning agreement a provision reserving to the Society the performing right in the work. The same principle applies to a writer who is an employee of a company. As it is a condition of membership that the performing right in a member's work shall be invariably reserved to the Society, if a member fails to comply with this rule he is in breach of his contract of membership. In such circumstances the Society is free to take proceedings against the member or a third party by way of injunction and a claim for damages for infringement of the rights which belong to it by virtue of the Deed of Assignment.

The precise scope of the rights administered by the Society is set out in the directives of the General Council and they are reproduced below with the permission of the Society. The following is first an outline of their scope but also some definitions which need to be noted.

"Musical work" is defined as including:

(a) any part of a musical work,

(b) any vocal or instrumental music in films,

(c) any musical accompaniment to non-musical plays,

(d) any words or music of monologues having a musical introduction or accompaniment,

(e) any other words (or part of words) which are associated with a musical work (even if the musical work itself is not in copyright, or even if the performing right in the musical work is not administered by the Society).

"Performing right" means in relation to a musical work, the right to do, or authorise other persons to do, any of the following acts:

(a) to perform the work in public,

(b) to broadcast the work, or include it in a cable programme service, insofar as such rights subsist under the law relating to copyright in the

United Kingdom, and includes such corresponding rights as subsist under the laws relating to copyright in all other countries of the world as in force from time to time.

"Film Synchronisation right" in respect of any musical work means the exclusive right in any part of the world to record the work in the sound-track of a film. (The term "film" has the same meaning as it has under the 1988 Act).

"Dramatico-musical work" means an opera, operetta, musical play, revue or pantomime, insofar as it consists of words and music written expressly therefor.

"Ballet" means a choreographic work having a story, plot or abstract idea, devised or used for the purpose of interpretation by dancing and/or miming, but does not include country or folk dancing, nor tap dancing, nor precision dance sequences.

The performance in places of public entertainment and elsewhere, that is where as a matter of law a performance is deemed to be in public, of most modern classical or serious music, light music and pop music whether orchestral or instrumental and with or without vocal parts, will fall within the ambit of the Society's administration. Moreover, this will be so whether the performance is given by professional or amateur musicians present at the performance, or by mechanical means—by the playing of records, audio cassettes, compact discs, or by the playing of juke-boxes or by the exhibition of any film or videogram, or by the reception of a broadcast transmission or music relay service. However, there are some works which may not be administered by the Society in particular dramatico-musical works and ballets.

Grand Rights and Small Rights

In the music business there has evolved a distinction for dramatico-musical works and ballets between "grand rights" and "small rights" performances and according to whichever kind of performance is given the performing right in the work will be administered by the copyright owner or the Society. Grand rights are not as a general rule administered by the Society but by the copyright owner; it is the exceptions to this rule which are indeed complicated. When dramatico-musical works and ballets are performed by means of films made primarily for exhibition in cinemas and when the films are broadcast by television, the performing right is administered by the Society. Special rules also apply to broadcast performances of these works.

The performance on stage or otherwise dramatically of the whole, or an excerpt from a dramatico-musical work or a ballet is an exercise of the grand rights and will be administered or licensed by the copyright owners. Where a performance of an entire dramatico-musical work is given "in concert," that is, non-dramatically, it is an exercise of the grand rights and will be licensed by the copyright owner. When only an excerpt (or excerpts) of a dramatico-musical work is performed and the perform-ance is non-dramatic then if the duration of the performance exceeds 25 minutes the performance will be licensed by the copyright owner, but otherwise the performance rights will be administered by the Society. If a performance of a ballet is given complete or in excerpt non-dramatically, that is without any visual representation, the rights will be administered by the Society.

The distinction between grand rights and small rights is often a fine one especially when only an excerpt is performed. Any dressing-up of the performance such as appearance in period costume or the like for the presentation of even a single item (an extract) from a musical play may, for example, be regarded as a dramatic performance and therefore an exercise of the grand rights. In an endeavour to help determine into which category a performance will fall the Society has provided guide-lines the text of which is as follows:

1. If an excerpt from a dramatico-musical work is performed on televi-sion or on stage it will be deemed to be dramatic if it is accompanied by any dramatic action, whether acted, danced or mimed, and thereby (and/or through the use of costume, scenery or other visual effects) gives a visual impression of or otherwise portrays the writers' original conception of the work from which the excerpt is taken.

2. It follows (by way of example) that a performance will **not** normally be deemed to be a dramatic performance if in the case of an excerpt not clearly to be regarded as "dramatic" under 1:

   (a) the excerpt is presented on a fixed set which is not based on the set of the original dramatico-musical work. (A "fixed set" would be one which is used for the whole or a substantial part of the television or stage show); or

   (b) the performer(s) is/are wearing a costume which is not a cos-tume from or based on the original dramatico-musical work; or

   (c) scenic effects are limited to the use of either a single prop, and/or a backcloth or a piece of scenery (whether physically present or created by technical means, *e.g.* lighting effects) provided that the use thereof is not combined with costume from or based on the dramatico-musical work from which the excerpt is taken.

Directives

The text of the Society's directives referred to above and which are effective from January 1, 1992 are as follows:

For Public Performance:

The performing right in every musical work of which the member is the writer, publisher or proprietor, except:

1. A dramatico-musical work whether staged or otherwise; provided that the rights administered by the Society do nevertheless include the right to perform in public:

    (a) a dramatico-musical work or an excerpt or excerpts from a dramatico-musical work performed by means of a film or by means of a radio or television set used for the purpose of giving a public performance of broadcast programmes;

    (b) a non-dramatic excerpt or excerpts from a dramatico-musical work (however performed) the total duration of which in the course of the same programme is 25 minutes or less and which excerpt or excerpts—
    (i) are not a "potted" version of the work, or
    (ii) are not or do not cover a complete act of the work.

2. The whole or any part of any music and of any words associated therewith composed or used for a ballet if accompanied by a visual representation of such ballet or part thereof; provided that the rights administered by the Society do nevertheless include the right to perform in public any such music and words so composed or used and accompanied by such visual representation when performed by means of—

    (a) a film; and/or

    (b) a television set used for the purpose of giving a public performance of broadcast programmes.

3. Any musical work specially written for a *son-et-lumière* production when performed in or in conjunction with that production.

4. Any musical work (being a musical work which is not a dramatico-musical work or part of a dramatico-musical work) specially written for a production of a dramatic work in a theatre when performed in or in conjunction with that dramatic work.

For Television Broadcasting (otherwise than by microwave distribution):

The broadcasting right in every musical work of which the member is the writer, publisher or proprietor, except:

1. A dramatico-musical work whether staged or otherwise; provided that the rights administered by the Society do nevertheless include the right to broadcast on television:

   (a) a dramatico-musical work or an excerpt or excerpts from a dramatico-musical work broadcast by means of a film made primarily for the purpose of public exhibition in cinemas or similar premises; and

   (b) a non-dramatic excerpt or excerpts from a dramatico-musical work (by whatever means broadcast)—the total duration of which in the course of the same programme does not exceed 20 minutes and which excerpt or excerpts—
   (i) are not a "potted" version of the work or
   (ii) are not or do not cover a complete act of the work.

Note

At the option of the member who is the owner of the copyright in a dramatico-musical work PRS may administer the broadcasting right in a dramatic excerpt or excerpts from the dramatico-musical work broadcast in a documentary programme where non-dramatic excerpts from the dramatico-musical work also appear in the same programme and where the total duration of all the excerpts in the course of the programme does not exceed 20 minutes.

2. The whole or any part of any music and of any words associated therewith composed or used for a ballet if accompanied by a visual representation of such ballet or part thereof; provided that the rights administered by the Society do nevertheless include the right to broadcast on television any such music and words so composed and used and accompanied by such visual representation when

   (a) a ballet or part or parts thereof are performed by means of a film made primarily for the purpose of public exhibition in cinemas or similar premises; or

   (b) a ballet or parts thereof, having been devised for the purpose of a broadcast on television, have a total duration in the course of the same programme not exceeding five minutes; or

   (c) a part or parts (being less than the whole) of a ballet, not having been so devised, have a total duration in the course of the same programme not exceeding five minutes.

Note

At the option of the member who is the owner of the copyright in a ballet PRS may administer the broadcasting right in a part or parts (being less than the whole) of the ballet broadcast in a documentary programme where the total duration of all the parts in the course of the programme does not exceed 20 minutes.

3. Words written for the purpose of a commercial advertisement unless such words are sung to music specially written for a commercial advertisement or to non-copyright music and the sung performance has a duration of not less than five seconds.

For Radio Broadcasting (otherwise than by microwave distribution):

The broadcasting right in every musical work of which the member is the writer, publisher or proprietor, except:

1. A dramatico-musical work; provided that the rights administered by the Society do nevertheless include the right to broadcast on radio an excerpt or excerpts from a dramatico-musical work the total duration of which in the course of the same programme does not exceed 25 minutes or 25 per cent. of the total length of the work whichever shall be the shorter and which excerpt or excerpts—

   (i) are not a "potted" version of the work or

   (ii) are not or do not cover a complete act of the work.

2. Words written for the purpose of a commercial advertisement unless such words are sung to music specially written for a commercial advertisement or to non-copyright music and the sung performance has a duration of not less than five seconds.

For inclusion in a Cable Programme Service and for Broadcasting by microwave distribution:

The right to include in a cable programme service or to broadcast by microwave distribution every musical work of which the member is the writer, publisher or proprietor except words written for the purpose of a commercial advertisement unless such words are sung to music specially written for a commercial advertisement or to non-copyright music and the sung performance has a duration of not less than five seconds.

Film Music

Music which is commissioned and composed expressly for a film or films is subject to special rules for it has been noted above that in addition to the performing right in such music the Society controls the synchronisation right of writer members.

The assignment of the synchronisation right by a writer member on admission to the Society is subject to the express condition that at the request of a composer or author the Society will assign or license the synchronisation right to the film producer or other person who commissioned the work. Any such assignment or licence is subject to the Society obtaining from the film producer an agreement in a form satisfactory to the Society for the payment to the Society of such fees either by way of a lump sum, or share of receipt of royalties, or otherwise as the Society may require, in respect of any exhibition of the film embodying the commissioned work in cinemas (motion picture theatres) in the USA.

The acquisition of the synchronisation right and introduction of the above rule was brought about because of the different system operating in the USA for the payment of performing fees for synchronised film music. In the USA when a composer is commissioned to compose original music for a film, the fee for his services is negotiated to take account of the licence granted by the composer, as a term of his engagement, for the synchronisation of the music in the film and for its public performance by means of the exhibition of the film in motion picture theatres.

The Ad hoc Release of the Performing Right

The rules of the Society provide for a special procedure whereby at the request of a member the Society can return the whole or any part of the performing right in any of his works to the member to enable him to license certain performances in particular circumstances. The prior agreement of the Society is required and is conditional on the licence for the dramatic performance of the work being exclusive to the specified licensee in a defined context and charged at a royalty rate not less than the appropriate tariff rate. Examples of the works when this procedure may be invoked are:

(a) Compilation shows—when there is a dramatic presentation featuring the works of a particular composer and/or lyricist, or where works are used to feature the career of a famous performer, or a particular period of time, or a particular type of music. The musical works will seldom have been written for the compilation show but on the contrary will most often be items from existing dramatico-musical works or compositions not originally intended for dramatic performance.

(b) Interpolated music in plays—music not specially written for a theatrical production, which is performed by, or intended to be audible to, a character or characters in the production.

(c) Music theatre—meaning contemporary classical pieces of music which employ an element of drama in their presentation. The works are usually capable of being performed with or without dramatic action and so not classified by the Society as dramatico-musical works.

(d) Cantata musicals—dramatico-musical works designed for perform-ance in schools where the works can be sung in concert simply as canta-tas, or can be accompanied by acting or mime, scenic effects or the like.

(e) Specially written music to accompany silent films.

The Division of Royalties Between Writers and Publishers

The terms and conditions contained in music publishing agreements are fairly standard, although not necessarily so, and make provision for the reservation to the Society of the right of public performance and broad-casting of a work. To carry this into effect the Society has by its rules established a procedure for the notification of works and prescribes the minimum percentage to which all writer members are entitled of the share of the royalties from the exploitation of the performing right in their works.

Notification of Works

The procedure and forms for the notification of works have been devised jointly by the Society and the Mechanical Copyright Society and so avoid a duplication of notices to both organisations. In addition to the title of the work and the names of the writer(s) and publisher there is to be notified details of the kind of musical work, distinguishing in particular music for films and advertising jingles; the division of the royalties between a writer(s) and a publisher, and when applicable the sub-division between a composer and lyricist of the writers' share of the royalties; particulars of split copyright interests as where there are sub-publishing arrangements between publishers for particular territories. These forms also serve to identify the works of authors internationally and thereby ensure the collection and accounting of royalties by the Society's overseas agents and affiliated societies.

Both writer and publisher members are required to comply with the notification procedure. With published works it is the publisher member who is responsible for giving the notification but which must be counter-signed by the writer member unless the writer member is a party to an exclusive songwriter agreement with the publisher and details of the agreement have previously been lodged with the Society.

Writer members must give notice of all unpublished works when a specific performance is known about and when an unpublished work is commercially recorded. If a writer member assigns rights in his work to a foreign publisher, or to a British publisher who is not a member of the Society a copy of the contract is to be provided with the notification.

All works commissioned for cinema, television, radio and video productions should be notified by the writer whether or not the work is published. Where the music is commissioned by a film company for inclusion in a feature film, for the reasons noted above, a copy of the contract needs to be supplied to the Society for it to license the performance of the music by the exhibition of the film theatrically in the USA. When the film is a television film then only if the film is released for theatrical exhibition in the USA need the commissioning contract be supplied to the Society, as for a feature film.

When music is an arrangement of a work still in copyright it will not be accepted into the Society's repertoire as a work separate or independent of the original for the purpose of sharing performing right royalties. Continental societies recognise the arranger of a copyright work as being entitled to some share of these royalties.

With an arrangement of a musical work out of copyright the degree of originality has to be assessed and the arrangement graded before it can be accepted into the Society's repertoire and treated as a work protected by copyright. The assessment is based on a scale of ratings, the highest being for original arrangements where the arranger's contribution is very substantial and distinctive, the lowest being for simple transcriptions such as minor additions or subtractions, or simple figured base realisations for use in an orchestral work. According to the rating awarded to an arrangement it shares in the distribution of royalties like a wholly original work.

Because of the quantity of musical arrangements made initially for broadcasting the grading of a work is often based on information supplied to the Society. If a grading is disputed a composer/arranger can submit the score or other material for a review of the assessment by the Society's Music Classification Committee. Lyrics are similarly dealt with. The value of alterations and additions to a work in the public domain are assessed; the grading is less difficult as the quantity or extent of the changes is more readily apparent. Wholly new works will be treated like any other original lyrics of a vocal work.

Division of Royalties

Under the rules of the Society the standard division of royalties is eight-twelfths to the composer and four-twelfths to the publisher; if there is a lyric writer to share in the royalties the division is equal, that is four-twelfths to all three persons. Even so the rules permit flexibility in the division of royalties but subject to the absolute and invariable rule that a publisher cannot receive more than six-twelfths of the royalties. So it follows that a writer member having assigned the performing and broadcasting rights in his work to the Society on admission cannot receive less than six-twelfths of the royalties earned (or when the work includes a lyric then three-twelfths for the composer and three-twelfths for the lyricist). Where apart from a publisher a copyright owner has an interest in the royalties, then the latter's participation or share of the royalties must be from the publisher's share and not the writer's share. In the area of light and pop music, publishers have taken advantage of the permissible six-twelfth division of royalties but now the trend is for the division to be weighted more in favour of composers and lyric writers. If there is a variation of the standard division of royalties it must be notified to the Society.

There are some details of the application of the scheme for the allocation of royalties which need special mention.

(a) If only the lyrics of a work are non-copyright then the share of royalties which would otherwise be payable to the lyric writer is paid to the composer, but subject to (f) below. If the music is an arrangement of a work in the public domain and the lyrics are also non-copyright the lyrics will be ignored and the arrangement will be treated in the same way as an instrumental arrangement and according to the grading of the work as mentioned above.

(b) When a composer or lyric writer is not a member of the Society his share will be paid to the copyright owner/publisher.

(c) When a publisher is not a member his share will be allocated to the composer or allocated equally between the composer and lyric writer, unless the publisher has assigned his rights to a member.

(d) When a work which was originally a vocal work is performed only instrumentally that still does not affect the lyric writer's entitlement to share in the royalties earned from the performance of the instrumental version of the work.

(e) When a work which was originally instrumental has words added subsequently, instrumental and vocal performances are separated for the purpose of the sharing of royalties; the lyric writer receives his share only for vocal performances. In such circumstances the vocal version of the work will usually be published under a new title and thereby enable performances of the two works or versions to be more easily identified.

(f) The translator of non-copyright words, or the author of new words replacing original non-copyright words, receives a normal lyric writer's share of royalties. If the translation or new words should fall out of copyright during the subsistence of copyright in the music the composer will receive the translator's or new writer's share of the royalties.

(g) When under a sub-publishing agreement the original words are translated or so adapted as to amount to a new lyric, the lyric writer will normally receive a share of two-twelfths of the royalties and which will be taken equally from the shares of the composer and the original lyric writer.

(h) A sub-publishing agreement between publishers cannot affect the invariable rule that a publisher cannot receive more than six-twelfths of the royalties from performances of a work.

With published arrangements of non-copyright music the division of the royalty between publisher and composer/arranger is first governed by the rating of the work as explained above. There is an elaborate scale for the sharing of the royalty earned by the work between publisher and arranger, and lyric writer if applicable. It has to be borne in mind that the costs to a music publisher of the printing and publication of an arrangement are no different from those of a wholly new composition.

Because film producers and television companies often stipulate as a condition for the engagement of a composer to compose original music for a film that the composer assign the publishing rights in a work to a music publisher nominated by the company, the Society has amended its rule respecting the division of royalties arising for such works. As from July 4, 1991 the publisher's share of performing right royalties may not exceed three-twelfths unless the publisher has undertaken to use all reasonable endeavours to exploit the commissioned work for the benefit of the writer(s) by means additional to the inclusion of the work in the sound-track of the film for which it was commissioned and the public performance or broadcasting of the film in question or its inclusion in a cable programme service.

The Licensing of the Performing Right by the Society

The person who without the permission of the owner of the copyright in a protected work performs the work in public infringes copyright. Furthermore, a person who permits a place of public entertainment to be used for such a performance also indirectly infringes copyright. In order to satisfy these two principles of law the Society's system of licensing is geared mainly to licensing the owners and occupiers of premises where music is performed rather than the countless numbers of persons who actually perform musical works in public. In this way a considerable if not complete uniformity of treatment is accorded to music users of a like kind or class.

Performers and promoters of entertainment are not normally licensed by the Society unless a performance is to take place on premises seldom used for public entertainment. This kind of situation can arise when a major pop festival is held in an open area or where an occasional concert or other entertainment is arranged and held on premises not normally used for public entertainment. There is a special licensing agreement between the Society and the National Federation of Music Societies which caters for the public performances of music by music societies and clubs affiliated to the Federation given in places not normally used for public entertainment. Performances given by music societies on premises regularly used for public entertainment will be covered by the licences issued by the Society for the premises.

Licences are granted by the Society to persons and organisations without discrimination on terms and subject to the payment of royalties at rates prescribed in the Society's tariffs. The tariffs are negotiated by the Society with organisations representative of music users but application can be made to the Copyright Tribunal for an adjudication where the terms and rates prescribed are disputed.

It is only copyright musical works which come within the Society's repertoire and licensing system. Works in the public domain—the classics, traditional music—can be publicly performed and broadcast without any restriction or licence. However, if the classic or item of traditional music is in fact an arrangement which qualifies as a new and separate copyright work then it is very likely that the arranged or transcribed classic will be in the Society's repertoire and therefore its performance will need to be included in a programme return when a return is required to be made.

With few exceptions the Society's licences are blanket licences authorising the public performance of the entire repertoire of musical works controlled by the Society on behalf of its members and its affiliated societies world wide. Even so it needs to be remembered that the Society's licences cover only the exercise of the performing right which it administers in musical works as outlined above. Thus the exercise of the grand rights in dramatico-musical works and ballets is subject to the consent of the owner of the copyright of such works.

Tariffs and Royalties

There are over 40 standard tariffs covering the numerous places and conditions under which music is performed live or relayed or made available to the public in a mechanical medium. So there are tariffs for theatres, concert halls, dance halls, community halls, clubs, pubs, bingo halls, cinemas, for hotels, restaurants, shops, industrial premises, for premises owned by local and public authorities, for open air places and sports stadia, and for motor coaches, trade fairs by way of example.

Royalty rates are based upon a number of factors, such as the capacity and potential for box office takings of the premises, the actual total expenditure on musical entertainment and the potential number of listening audience. But the overriding consideration is whether the music is "featured," meaning that it is the dominant part of the entertainment as at concerts, dance halls or discotheques—or merely background music. The fact that no charge is made for admission to a place of public performance, or the performance is a general amenity of the premises does not of course absolve a music user from the obligation to pay royalties for the performance or relaying of music.

Licences are granted for a year and the royalties payable assessed in the light of the information supplied by a licensee of the anticipated kind and extent of music usage. If there is a reduction or increase in the amount of use it should be reported to the Society to effect an adjustment of the royalty rate. This is especially so where royalties are calculated as a percentage of turnover or of the musical budget of a place of entertainment, or on the number of employees at factory or office premises, or on a substantial and fluctuating number of dances or other functions with music. Where only background music is played at premises or where only a small fixed number of functions occur on premises an annual flat charge is made with adjustment to take account of inflation.

In some instances licences are individually negotiated by the Society such as with the broadcasting organisations and the proprietors of major concert halls and art centres. Also where music festivals are arranged, or a commissioned work is to be first performed, or where music is to be performed under exceptional circumstances special licences may be negotiated. Music performed to patients in hospitals and homes and music performed during services in churches and other places of worship is not charged for, but the performance of music in cathedrals and churches at other times is subject to the Society's licence regardless of whether a charge is made for admission. The use of music in the course of curricular studies in primary and secondary schools like other copyright works is subject to special exempting rules under the 1988 Act as noted above, but otherwise performances of music will be subject to the Society's administration even if they may be beneficial to education.

The Making of Returns of Music Performed

The supply of information by licensees of the performance of musical works is obviously crucial to the Society for it to be able to distribute fairly to its members the royalty payments received. On the other hand it is recognised as being quite impractical and unrealistic to require all the thousands of licensees to make regular returns of the music performed at licensed venues. Accordingly for the purpose of its recording details of performances of copyright music the Society distinguishes licences for broadcast performances and those for general public performance.

Normally it is a condition of the blanket licences granted to the broadcasting organisations that they regularly supply complete returns of all music used. Local radio stations are not required to make returns of music broadcast by the use of commercial recordings or stock records.

For other music users the Society has from time to time adopted schemes for obtaining programme information but both their effectiveness and cost have been questioned especially as regards live performances. Following consultations with associations representative of composers and publishers the Society has beginning in 1992 adopted a new scheme to cover performances of live music. In place of the programme collection policies for classical events and popular events of the past there is a new live distribution policy based on programme information from a representative list of 550 venues and 50 major festivals spanning all genres of music. It is the licensees of the listed venues and festivals who are required as a condition of the Society's licence to make detailed returns for every live music performance in the main auditoria of the venue, and of every musical event at a listed festival. In addition programme returns are required for single events and tours, such as pop concerts and tours which generate a royalty payment to the Society of £500 or more, whether or not an admission charge is made.

For assessing other live public performances of music, reference is made to the radio logs supplied to the Society by the BBC and the local radio stations. As for the public performance of music by mechanical means wherever performed and whatever the kind of music the assessment is based on statistical data which reflect contemporary patterns of music use such as monthly record sales charts, disco sales or performance charts and data supplied by background music contractors and broadcasting organisations. Film performances in cinemas are recorded from returns of films exhibited at cinemas and the music cue sheets of film producers.

The Distribution of Royalties to Members

The system operated by the Society for the allocation of its disposable licence income to its writer and publisher members is complex. This is perhaps inevitable when the objective of attaining the most fair and equitable apportionment of royalties is set against the many factors which have to be reckoned—the extent and diversity of music making, the number and kinds of places in which music is performed or heard in public, the vast repertoire of works and the fluctuations in the popularity and frequency of performances of works during the term of a work's copyright protection. Furthermore account must be taken of the income received by the Society from its affiliated societies overseas for the performance of members' works overseas; and conversely the payment of royalties to the affiliates for the performance of their members' works in this country.

The basis for a member's participation in a distribution of revenues is the accumulation or aggregation of points awarded for performances of his work. There is no discrimination between works or their performance other than as laid down in the scheme. The basic classification of performances—between broadcasting and general public performance—is applied for the distribution of revenues and within each of these classes there are sections. A scale of points is devised for each section and from the analysis of the programme information and returns received by the Society, works are identified and a member's accumulation of points recorded for his participation in the periodical distributions of revenues.

In principle works are treated alike so the basis for the award of points is the minutage duration of a work, or extract of a work and the number of performances. Where it has been considered appropriate to make distinctions criteria are applied to differentiate the values or points allotted. So with broadcasting there is a weighting of points according to the scale of value set against each of the listed stations and networks. With television the points are according to whether the music is featured, or background, or a signature tune or the like.

In the class of general public performances there are three sections. First with live performances, in addition to the points award based on the minutage of a work as usual, the points are multiplied by a factor representing audience capacity when performances take place at the listed venues and festivals. Secondly, with performances by means of film or videogram, the points awarded for the duration of the music are distinguished for featured and background music as shown on the cue sheets. Thirdly, that is all other public performances of recorded music, generally the award of points is by reference to the statistical data such as record sales charts as mentioned above.

Apart from distributions on the basis outlined above, as only relatively few out of the total number of licensees are required to make returns—for reasons touched on above—the scheme makes allowance for works performed but not reported by distributing an allotted share of revenues to writer and publisher members for unlogged performances. A member qualifies to participate in an allotment by having received at least one programme credit in the two years preceding the year of the distribution. The sum allotted depends on a member's programme fee earnings in the year preceding the distribution but subject to his receiving a minimum sum. These allotments are paid in July of each year.

A writer member may also qualify for a distribution or allowance under the Society's Earnings Equalisation Scheme which applies to members who have reached 50 years of age and completed 25 years of membership.

G. THE RECORDING AND REPRODUCTION OF MUSICAL WORKS

The recording and mechanical reproduction of all protected musical works needs to be licensed by the copyright owner irrespective of the manner or purpose for which a recording is made. The recording of a song, instrumental or orchestral work, or jingle for the making of audio tapes or records for performance in private or in public, or for sale and hire to the public, or for the purpose of broadcasting, or for inclusion in the sound-track of a film, videogram or commercial, are instances of the exercise of the right of reproduction and need to be licensed.

The reproduction right as a constituent of copyright law has not always existed. The reproduction of musical works by means of perforated rolls, discs and cylinders which began in the late nineteenth century was not regarded as "copying" music and an infringement of copyright. So the manufacturers of the forerunners of the compact disc and audio cassette were able to reproduce musical works without any legal restraint. This situation was reversed by the Copyright Act 1911 which enacted that copyright in a literary, dramatic or musical work included the right "to make any record, perforated roll, cinematograph film, or other contrivance by means of which the work may be mechanically performed or delivered." So the right of mechanical reproduction was established by law and ensured that authors and composers would be compensated for the use of their works.

The 1911 Act also broke new ground by recognising a sound recording as a work itself to be protected by copyright. Furthermore, whilst the 1911 Act deprived record producers of the total freedom to reproduce works, it conferred on them a statutory right to record and reproduce a musical work for the purpose of making records for retail sale to the public. The right was conditional on a work's having previously been recorded with the copyright owner's consent, to notice of the intended recording being given to the copyright owner, and to the payment of the statutory royalty introduced under the 1911 Act.

Following the growth of the record industry there came the "talkie" film whereby a musical work could be "mechanically performed or delivered," in the words of the 1911 Act in synchronisation with the filmed visual action. So there emerged what has become to be known in the music business and film industry as the synchronisation right for the reproduction of musical works in the soundtrack of films.

Mechanical-Copyright Protection Society Limited

With the increasing use and commercial value of the mechanical right organisations representing music publishers and composers were established to oversee the operation of the new statutory recording right and the collection of royalties, and to administer the synchronisation right. As a result of the merging of the organisations in the past into the Mechanical-Copyright Protection Society Limited (MCPS) the MCPS has become the principal organisation which on behalf of its members administers the right of reproduction of musical works in the United Kingdom and, through its associated organisations, in overseas countries. With the enactment of the Copyright, Designs and Patents Act 1988 the statutory recording right was totally abolished. As a consequence the role of MCPS as a central organisation from which record companies, broadcasting companies, film producers and other music users can obtain licences for the recording of musical works has increased in importance.

MCPS is owned by the Music Publishers' Association which itself is a members' association. Membership of MCPS is open to composers and music publishers alike and is not necessarily conditional on an applicant having already produced, performed or published a minimum number of works. The conditions of membership are set out in a standard Membership Agreement coupled with annexed Terms and Conditions of Business. MCPS undertakes to use its best endeavours to protect the rights in works from being infringed; not to discriminate between members in the exercise of its powers save as expressly provided for in the Agreement; to collect royalties and duly account for them. Another of its principal undertakings is to ensure that the terms and conditions of all licensing schemes, blanket licences and standard licences are in the best interests of members generally and where necessary to defend them before the Copyright Tribunal.

A member is required to warrant his right to enter into the Membership Agreement and to grant to MCPS the rights and powers prescribed. On admission and thereafter during his membership, a member is required to notify MCPS of all musical works controlled or administered by him and in doing so to warrant that the rights mentioned below in the works are controlled by him. A member undertakes not to exercise any of the rights in the works which by virtue of his membership he has empowered MCPS to exercise. A member also undertakes to indemnify MCPS for any liability arising from any breach of these warranties and undertakings. Membership is for an initial one year and thereafter, apart from exceptional circumstances, it continues until either party gives to the other six months' written notice of termination.

Terms and Conditions of Business

The general terms on which MCPS undertakes to its members to license and deal with the rights it controls are contained in three schemes of Terms and Conditions of Business annexed to the Membership Agreement. The first scheme is for product licensing, that is, for the manufacture and retail sale of audio records and tapes and videograms. The second is for blanket licensing and embraces the licensing of broadcasting organisations and other music users such as providers of background music services and juke-box suppliers. The third scheme covers other licences such as licences required for the recording of works by public authorities and by independent users where recordings are not for sale, but for specialist purposes, licences for the synchronisation of works in films, and licences for the use of library music (production music) in areas not covered by a blanket licence scheme.

These three schemes are statements of the principles on which MCPS devises the licensing schemes and codes of practice for licensing the reproduction of the musical works and for negotiating blanket licences for the use of members' works. They are also an explanation of the basis on which royalties are collected and distributed to members and the rates of commission charged by MCPS to members. All the costs of the negotiation and licensing of rights and all expenses of management are borne by MCPS out of the accrued commissions.

The forms and procedure for members to give notice of works to be administered by MCPS have been devised jointly with the Performing Right Society to avoid needless duplication. As most often but not invariably a publisher by the terms of the publishing agreement acquires all rights of copyright in a work, except the rights of public performance and broadcasting, it will be the publisher who will make the returns and supply information of each work. There is no MCPS rule of membership which requires a minimum percentage of royalties to be paid to a composer. The entire royalty due in respect of a work is paid to the publisher member and it is for the publisher to account to the composer for whatever share of the royalty may be due to him as negotiated and provided for in the publishing agreement. Where a composer is in membership of MCPS then in respect of his unpublished works—for which there is a separate form for notification—it follows the royalties due in respect of his works are paid to him direct.

Rights Administered

The MCPS does not take an assignment of any rights of copyright but upon the registration of membership MCPS becomes the sole and exclusive agent of the member for the management and administration of certain rights in his works. The principal right which MCPS is empowered to exercise is "to make or authorise the making in the Territory of Sound-Bearing Copies of the Works for the purpose of the use or exploitation thereof in any manner or media now known or hereafter invented." The expression "Sound-Bearing Copies" means "each and every recording of the whole or any part of a work from which sound reproducing the work or part thereof may be produced directly or indirectly regardless of the medium on which the recording is made or the method by which the sounds are reproduced or produced, and whether or not visual images or other works may be reproduced or produced from such recording." The "Territory" is the United Kingdom and subject to qualifications, other territories of the world.

Coupled with the above right is the right for MCPS to issue or authorise the issue to the public of copies of sound-bearing copies of works, and to import or authorise the importation of sound-bearing copies of works into the territory. With these combined principal rights the MCPS is able to authorise the recording of works by all manner of means and for all purposes and to authorise the multiplication and distribution of copies of recordings including copies of those recordings legally imported.

Licensing Schemes

Based on the Terms and Conditions of Business referred to above, MCPS has devised various licensing schemes and codes of practice to satisfy the main purposes for which musical works are recorded. The licensing schemes contain details of the procedures for obtaining individual licences for the recording of particular works for specific purposes. Tariffs of royalty rates are prescribed, the methods of calculation and the time for payment. Where no licensing scheme is applicable then the terms of a licence will be individually negotiated with a music user and account taken of the purposes for which a work is required to be recorded.

Blanket licences operate differently as by the payment of an annual sum a licensee, such as the BBC or the television programme companies, is permitted to record without restriction works from the entire repertoire of MCPS for inclusion in programmes made by, or commissioned but owned by, the licensee. Music cue sheets and reports of sales or exports of programmes are required to be supplied to MCPS at regular intervals and based on these, distributions of the annual licence fee are made proportionately to members less commission. In principle, programmes can be exploited without limitation world wide by radio and television, and non-theatrically. Any other use such as the retail sale of programmes requires to be licensed separately, for example, in accordance with MCPS's licensing scheme for videograms.

Because of the standing of MCPS and with the abolition of the statutory royalty the terms upon which MCPS licenses the reproduction of the musical works in its repertoire is a matter of great concern to the record industry and other music users. The MCPS is a licensing body and the terms on which it licenses reproduction right are licensing schemes within section 116 of the 1988 Act. As noted in Part 6 above it is open to any affected person to refer any issue regarding a licensing scheme to the Copyright Tribunal for adjudication. Recently the British Phonographic Industry on behalf of the record industry joined issue with the MCPS before the Copyright Tribunal respecting the royalty payable for the recording of works and other of the conditions prescribed by MCPS in its record licensing schemes.

After an extensive review of the issues and a comparison with the rates prevailing in other countries, particularly continental Europe—the Copyright Tribunal concluded as "a value judgment rather than the result of any precise mathematical calculation" that the royalty payable should be at the rate of eight and a half per cent. of PPD—in broad terms the price published by the record companies for sales to dealers, or six and a half per cent. of the retail price of a record. Relevant to this ruling are other elements of the licensing schemes relating to the issuing of copies or the distribution of records which were considered by the Tribunal. There is no variation to the rate, it is uniform regardless of the kind or quality of music recorded or the format of the recording. There is no minimum amount of royalty payable to allow for differences in prices between full and budget price records or marketing arrangements. No account is taken of the number of tracks on a record although the royalty may be shared between a number of composers. Where only part of a record contains a copyright work then the amount of the royalty payable is in the proportion the duration the copyright work bears to the duration of the whole record.

At the time a member registers his work he can elect to limit the exercise by MCPS of the rights it otherwise acquires over his works. Thus a member can elect to make the grant of a licence for the first recording of a work for the making of records for sale to the public subject to his consent; he can elect under certain circumstances to receive record royalties direct from record companies. A member can elect to exclude from the control of MCPS the right to license the making of a particular kind of sound-bearing copy, that is the making of any particular recording, other than a recording which may be made by virtue of the grant to a third party of a blanket licence such as granted by MCPS to the BBC and the television programme companies. For example, a member can choose to reserve for himself the licensing of the synchronisation right for films for theatrical release and for independent television programmes. A member can also elect to exclude any overseas country from the scope of the authority of MCPS if he is already a member of another corresponding society.

Without consulting a member it is not the practice of MCPS to license complete dramatico-musical works (including ballets) or excerpts from such works unless the excerpt does not exceed 20 minutes, does not involve a complete act, or a "potted version" of the complete work, and the excerpt is not presented in a dramatic form.

The licence which MCPS grants to any person or company is only to record a work; the licence does not carry with it any other right of copyright such as to perform the work in public or broadcast it. If the person making the recording wishes to make any adaptation or arrangement of the work then the consent of the copyright owner, or MCPS if it has been authorised to give it by a member, must first be obtained. However, under the terms of the Membership Agreement there is one exception to this rule. Unless a member at the time of registration has stipulated that his consent is required to the first making of a commercial record or audio tape of his work, MCPS is empowered, as part of the terms of any licensing scheme or standard licensing agreement for the manufacture and sale of commercial records, to permit the making of any modification to a work which does not "alter the character of a work." The moral rights of authors are material in the application of this permission so it is crucial that any modification or arrangement does not amount to a derogatory treatment of a work.

The licensing of mechanical rights is conducted by MCPS on behalf of its members in overseas territories either directly or through local societies. It has reciprocal agreements with over 50 such societies. MCPS is affiliated to BIEM (Bureau International des Sociétés Gerant les Droits d'Enregistrement et de Reproduction Mécanique) an international organisation which serves as the representative of the interests of copyright owners in the negotiations with the International Federation of the Phonographic Industry (the international trade association of the record industry), respecting the licensing of mechanical rights for the production of regular records and tapes.

H. THE REPRODUCTION AND PUBLIC PERFORMANCE OF SOUND RECORDINGS

The copyright protection conferred by the Copyright, Designs and Patents Act 1988 on a sound recording is wholly separate from that which may subsist in the musical or other work embodied in the recording. If the musical or other work which is recorded is in the public domain then public performance and broadcasting rights and mechanical reproduction rights considered in the two preceding Sections have no place. It is the recording alone which is protected by copyright.

A sound recording for the purposes of the Act embraces any kind of recording of sounds from which sounds may be reproduced; the medium on which the recording is made or the method by which the sound may be reproduced or produced are immaterial to the recording being a work protected by copyright. Thus in addition to records in the ordinary accepted sense (including the modern versions of audio tapes and compact discs), the sound-tracks of films and videograms are within the protection as sound recordings.

Reproduction of Sound Recordings

The copyright in a sound recording is first owned by the person who creates it, meaning the person by whom the arrangements necessary for its making are undertaken. The rights of copyright and their primary and secondary infringement are considered in Part 6 above, but the rights to be considered here are those of copying or reproducing a recording, and the public performance and broadcasting of a recording.

The dubbing or synchronisation of a sound recording in another work such as a film or videogram, or in another sound recording or "sampling" is an act of copying and requires the consent of the copyright owner of the sound recording. There is another factor to bear in mind, namely the rights and interests of the performer of the work recorded. By the terms of the contract of engagement between the producer of the sound recording and the artist or musician a limitation may be placed on the manner or extent to which the recording may be exploited. Although the proprietary ownership of the copyright in the recording will not be affected the contractual restrictions cannot be avoided. In reviewing in Part 3 above the collective agreements for the recording services of musicians, the importance of the scope of any consent was noted. Furthermore, a performer has rights in his performance and a person having exclusive recording rights in a performer has rights under Part II of the 1988 Act as noted in Part 5 above. Any extended use of a recording without their consents may be an infringement of their rights and actionable as a breach of statutory duty.

The British Phonographic Industry grants or negotiates on behalf of those of its members by whom it is empowered to do so, licences for broadcasting organisations and other enterprises to dub commercial records in programmes and compilation discs. Ordinarily for the inclusion in any audio or audio/visual production of a recorded work the licence and consent of the owner of the copyright in the recording must be obtained, and if the work itself is in copyright also that of the copyright owner.

Production Music

Production music (or "library" music) is music which is especially composed and/or arranged and recorded with the object of its inclusion primarily in audio/visual productions such as advertisements, instructional, educational, documentary and entertainment films and videotapes, and in broadcast programmes of all kinds. The licensing of recordings in the production music library catalogues is administered by MCPS on behalf of its producer members. A code of conduct exists for the procuring of licences and the payment of royalties either directly by the maker of the audio/visual work or by the facilities house undertaking the dubbing. The tariff of royalties caters for the different kinds of production and their uses and the extent of their exploitation.

Public Performance and Broadcasting of Recordings

Of rather more importance to the owner of the copyright in a sound recording in economic terms are the rights of public performance and broadcasting. These rights in commercial recordings are usually controlled by Phonographic Performance Limited on behalf of record producers and manufacturers. This organisation serves much the same function for its members as by way of analogy the Performing Right Society does for composers, lyric writers and music publishers.

Phonographic Performance Limited (PPL) is a company limited by guarantee the principal objects of which are to exercise and enforce on behalf of its members all rights and remedies of proprietors under the 1988 Act in respect of the public performance and broadcasting of records.

Any person who is the owner of the performing and broadcasting right in a sound recording or who is entitled to the benefit of or has an interest in this right is eligible for associate membership but the membership of PPL comprises mainly established record producers and record companies regularly engaged in the making and manufacture of records in the United Kingdom. A British registered subsidiary of a foreign record company manufacturing records in the United Kingdom is eligible for election and a foreign record producer which authorises the importation of records into the United Kingdom may be admitted to membership if in his own country there are reciprocal rights of protection for the recordings made by British producers.

On election to membership a record producer is required to assign to PPL the performing and broadcasting rights and related dubbing rights in his recording which he then owns and which may subsequently come into his ownership during his membership of PPL. By virtue of his membership a record producer grants to PPL the sole power and authority in the United Kingdom:

(a) to authorise or permit or forbid the exercise of all performing rights in respect of records or sound recordings, the performing right in which is or does become vested in the member during his membership;

(b) to grant licences on his behalf for the exercise of any such performing right;

(c) to collect fees and subscriptions and all monies whether for the performance of any of the records the performing rights in which are vested in or controlled by PPL, or by way of damage or compensation for unauthorised performances;

(d) to take proceedings against all persons infringing the performing rights, defend or oppose any proceedings taken against a member in respect of such rights and generally deal with all disputes concerning the performing rights vested in and controlled by PPL.

A record producer's membership ceases on his death or, if a company, on its winding up but the rights of PPL continue in being until the end of PPL's current financial year and then lapse. Membership also ceases on the expiration of the copyright in the records of a member in respect of which he is entitled to participate in the licence revenues received by PPL. Members can resign by giving six months notice and the directors of PPL can terminate a member's membership by 21 days notice in writing, but a member is entitled by counter-notice to require the question of the continuation of his membership to be decided by PPL as a whole at an extraordinary general meeting.

Licensing Schemes

Like other of the collecting societies PPL in the management of its licensing operations distinguishes broadcast performances from public performances. Thus it has negotiated with the BBC, the programme companies of the ITC, the independent local radio companies and cable and satellite radio and television operators licences for the blanket use of PPL's repertoire. Licensees pay an annual fee which may be a fixed sum, or a royalty calculated according to a licensee's use of recordings or revenue income. Licensees are required to make regular returns to PPL of broadcast performances of records. There are other agreements with student and hospital radio stations and special event radio broadcasters which involve nominal or zero charges.

The licensing of the public performance of records is based on tariffs many of which are settled by negotiation between PPL and representatives of trade associations and other organisations representative of various music users. PPL is a licensing body and the tariffs and terms on which it licenses its repertoire are licensing schemes within the meaning of section 116 of the 1988 Act—as noted in Part 6 above. Thus the terms of its licence agreements can be brought before the Copyright Tribunal for review by any persons affected. In the report of the Monopolies and Mergers Commission of December 1988 into the collective licensing of the public performance and broadcasting of sound recordings, it was remarked that the tariffs and terms of licences had most often been negotiated by PPL with representatives of licensees without the need for recourse to an adjudication by the Tribunal so no reason was found to interfere with the agreements.

The issues which count in the assessment of royalties and the terms of public performance licences are the size of premises, the potential listening audience, the particular kind of use or circumstances in which music is performed, such as commercial, public amenity, instructional, and whether the performance is "featured" or background. These considerations are reflected in the number and range of tariffs as there are tariffs, for example, for specially featured entertainment being performances at discotheques and clubs; for background music performances at hotels, public houses, shops and other places of general public resort; for performances in professional theatrical productions and amateur societies; for music performances in places of public resort such as shopping precincts and parks; for performances in exhibition areas. Licences are generally issued to organisers of entertainment rather than to proprietors or managers of premises. This is especially so with background music so that it is the providers of juke-boxes and compilations of recordings who are licensed by PPL.

Licences are usually issued on an annual basis for the blanket use of PPL's repertoire, which is the accumulation of the repertoires of its member record producing companies as notified by them in accordance with the conditions of membership. In addition to specifying the royalties payable and other general conditions of the licence, there is a stipulation for the making of returns of performances if required by PPL. Normally only those licensees engaged in some special activity or who use a rather specialised repertoire are required to make returns of performances.

Session musicians are paid a single fee for their services; other performers—featured artists, groups etc. are more likely to receive royalty payments from the manufacture and sale to the general public of recordings of their performances. Only very exceptionally does a performer by the terms of his recording contract have any entitlement to participate in the revenues a record company receives from the broadcasting and public performance of a recording. This has been a matter of contention by the Unions representing performers. As noted in the survey of the various collective agreements, performers are entitled to residual or other royalty payments for any extended use of any recording of their performance in broadcast programmes and films. Moreover, the Rome Convention of 1961 for the protection of performers, producers of records and broadcast organisations provides for producers and performers to receive equitable remuneration in respect of the broadcasting and public performance of recordings. Although the United Kingdom has ratified the Convention no legislation has been enacted to ensure compliance with this obligation. The situation has been left to be resolved on a voluntary basis.

By the terms of its constitution PPL is empowered to make payments to and for the benefit of copyright owners, artists, performers and any body of persons representing any of them. Accordingly PPL sets aside 20 per cent. of its net royalty income for payment to named performers and 12.5 per cent. for the services of unidentified session musicians. This latter percentage is paid to the Musicians' Union which it keeps in a special fund and apart from its general income.

The Report of the Monopolies and Mergers Commission remarked upon the absence of adequate arrangements for a register of performers and of their recorded performances to ensure they individually benefited from the revenues set aside by PPL. Apart from the returns required from a very small minority of specialist licensees the public performance of records is not monitored. Only the radio broadcasts of the BBC and some of the independent radio stations are monitored. The Commission judged these returns to be inadequate for assessing the full extent of the use or performance of artists' recordings and for ensuring they received individually what should be due to them. PPL is currently revising its procedures in order to identify more accurately the diverse broadcasting of recorded performances so that revenues are distributed more effectively and particularly to specialised types of performers.

PPL is a non-profit making organisation and after the payments as outlined above and making allowance for the cost of management and administration, its revenues are distributed to its members according to the use of sound recordings as reported for radio broadcasts and the returns of those licensees required to make returns.

I. FILM PRODUCTION AGREEMENTS

Despite the recurring lamentation about the state of the British film industry there is still a considerable output of films and videograms of many kinds and for many purposes so that this study would be incomplete without a review of the general structure and provisions of film production agreements. These agreements may vary in their terms and complexity according to the kind of film—cinema feature film with a star cast, television film, documentary or instructional film, or advertising and promotional film—but the core essentials are the same. Many of the topics and issues already and to be considered in this study have relevance in the planning of a production and may need to be reflected in the provisions of a production agreement. In what follows attention is directed to the two party agreement, that is, between a company commissioning a film and a producer undertaking its making and delivery, as distinct from the making of a film "in house" where the organisation engaged in its making also engages in its exhibition and exploitation.

It may appear to be stating the obvious but an agreement should begin by stating and defining what is to be produced including the technical specification. It should specify the elements of the film in the sense of the script upon which it is to be based, the principal artistic and other creative personnel, the location(s), the duration or running time, the primary purpose and medium of exploitation, the time for delivery and what is to constitute the actual completion and delivery of the film and so the fulfilment of the commission.

Rights to be Acquired

By entering into a production agreement a producer assumes legally binding and enforceable obligations but these do not begin and end simply with the photographing and recording of the action. There has to be co-ordinated and in place commitments with third parties to procure the constituent parts which make up the whole of the production, and the resources and facilities required for the completion of the enterprise. Moreover many of the agreements with third parties must themselves be in terms as will enable the producer to comply with his obligations and satisfy the terms and conditions of the production agreement. The most common issues can be demonstrated by a few simple examples.

The rights owned by or licensed to a producer in any source material and in the script upon which the film is to be based must correspond with the rights to be exercised in the completed film, that is, according to the medium of exploitation, territorially and for the full period of copyright unless a shorter period is adequate. This same point arises with any copyright protected works or material to be incorporated in the film—artistic works, music, library or other recorded music and sounds, and library footage.

The engagement of artists and musicians, of the production team and technicians will normally be in accordance with industry practice and the terms of their engagement subject to the industry collective agreements. Artistic and other creative persons may have continuing rights beyond the period of actual engagement—entitlement to credit, the payment of royalties—and these matters need to be anticipated in the devising of the terms of a production agreement.

The agreements for the provision of services and facilities, such as for the hire of costumes and properties and the like, for the hire of equipment and studios and the use and access to locations are not likely to be significantly affected by the terms of the production agreement since they will be spent in their operation. More critical are the arrangements for the conveyance, processing and storage of film negative. A laboratory will have a lien on the material in its possession for the payment of its charges. Furthermore, on the completion of the film and the acquisition of the copyright in the film by the company commissioning the production (as noted below), the company must be able to assert its superior rights of ownership.

Budget and Finance

As with most enterprises the matter of expenditure and budgets is para-mount. Direct costs are identifiable and usually quantifiable with amounts set aside for overheads, interest charges, insurance premiums and guarantor's fees. There may also need to be brought into account the fees, if any, to be paid in advance to those persons entitled to receive residual or other payments according to the exploitation of the film. Depending on the circumstances, a contingency sum may be written into the budget. The consequences of a production exceeding the agreed cost, that is, the treatment of overcost both as respects who must bear it and how it is to be recouped should be made certain.

The amount of the agreed budget represents the commitment on the part of the company to advance the monies and for the producer to complete and deliver the film within the agreed cost, inclusive of the production fee as agreed between the parties. The arrangements for the advancing of the cost of production, the opening of a separate bank account, the drawing down of monies, the accounting and audit of the production accounts should be provided for in the agreement. Ideally the budget like the finally approved script as the two crucial identifiable elements of the agreement should be initialled by the parties and annexed to the agreement.

As a means of ensuring the financial stability of the enterprise and to deal with any contingency which may arise (apart from any losses which may be recoverable under the terms of the production insurance policy), in addition to the two party production agreement there may be joined as a third party a completion guarantor. In consideration of the payment of a fee or premium, the guarantor underwrites the obligations of the producer by undertaking to take over and complete the production in accordance with the production agreement in certain eventualities, for example, if the budgeted cost is exceeded, the producer is in serious breach of the production agreement, or the producer fails in business. The completion guarantor in order to protect his interests and limit his liability normally exerts a searching and critical scrutiny over the entire project; the copyright and the terms of contracts entered into by the producer and the budget will be examined and the right reserved to oversee and be advised of the progress of the production.

In order for the company commissioning the production to protect its investment it may be a condition of the production agreement that a legal charge is taken by the company over the enterprise. The production at all stages with all the elements as they accrue in the making of the film together with the producer's rights and interests in all agreements with third parties conferring rights, or for services or facilities, and the completed film as a copyright property, are set apart from all other of the property and assets of the producer as a security (*i.e.* a charge) for the repayment or realisation of the monies advanced or loaned for the production. Because of this charge no third party can lay claim in priority to the production for the payment of any debt or in satisfaction of a claim against the producer, even one arising out of the production of the film. On the completion and delivery of the film and by the acquisition by the company of the copyright in the film, the legal charge is automatically extinguished. It is usually a term of a completion guarantee that the guarantor acquires a second charge over the production in the event of his advancing monies to complete the production. The guarantor thereby secures a preferential right to the recoupment of the sums he advanced once the company which commissioned the film has first recouped its outlay.

Insurance

The obligation to effect and maintain insurance cover is normally placed on a producer but subject to the amount and extent of the cover being approved by the company. In Part 10 of this study the elementary principles of insurance and the need for insurance are touched on, and the issues which affect theatrical and other live performances. With film production the issues can be complex due to the many variable circumstances and conditions under which a production may take place, and the potential dangers which attach to film production. The services of specialised insurance brokers should not be overlooked for advice on the cover to be effected. Special considerations can arise over cast insurance and the loss of their services, indemnity cover for liability for loss or damage to the property of third parties, to chattels used in the course of production or to buildings and land occupied on location, the insurance of personnel and crew in transit and when on location overseas in compliance with the terms of the Union collective agreements, and the insurance of the film negative in transit and the film as a completed product.

Copyright in a Film

With the range of executive and managerial functions and responsibilities attaching to the business of film production it seems that the law, or rather Parliament, by the provisions of the Copyright, Designs and Patents Act 1988 has correctly legislated that the authorship and therefore the first ownership of the copyright in a film lies with "the person by whom the arrangements necessary for the making of the film are undertaken." The producer of the commissioned film is such a person and so the first owner of the copyright in it. The ownership evolves as the production proceeds, in all takes, clips, recordings cut outs and the like as well as at the point of the final editing and completion of the film for exhibition. Accordingly the production agreement will stipulate that on completion the copyright in the film (and all takes etc.) passes to the commissioning company. The terms of the agreement may be sufficient to achieve the assignment but the agreement may stipulate for the execution of such documents as may be necessary to assure and vest in the company the legal and beneficial ownership of the copyright in the film.

At this point the producer is divested of all proprietary rights in the film and so coupled with the assignment there needs to be formal notice and authority addressed to the laboratory or whoever has custody of the film, thereafter to deal with the commissioning company as the owner of the film. As owner the company has the absolute right to deal with and give directions concerning the disposition of all or any rights in the film and the making and supplying of prints save only as may be stipulated in the production agreement. It has been noted that usually the producer contracts with third parties for the acquisition of all elements to be incorporated into the film and for the engagement of all persons and services required for its production and completion. In most instances the undertakings of the producer to such third parties are fulfilled by the payment of whatever fees or charges have been agreed. However, often there are continuing obligations to third parties, such as to accord screen and advertising credit to writers, performers, the director and others, and to pay additional fees or royalties as the film is exploited. There may also be contractual limitations which may affect the manner or extent of the exploitation of the film. In law the producer remains liable for the observance of any such continuing obligations. Therefore the production agreement should stipulate for the company to undertake to perform these continuing obligations and for the producer to be indemnified in the event of the company failing to do so.

THE COMMISSIONING OF INDEPENDENT TELEVISION PROGRAMMES

Much of what has been said above about film production applies to the making by independent producers of films primarily intended for television broadcasting. As the Government policy requiring the ITC and the BBC to engage and commission independent producers to make programmes for television broadcasting has become a statutory imposition it is fitting to note in a little more detail the legal and contractual issues surrounding the commissioning of independent productions.

By sections 16 and 186 of the Broadcasting Act 1990 it is required of both the ITC and the BBC "that in each year not less than 25 per cent. of the total amount of time allocated to the broadcasting of qualifying programmes in the service is allocated to the broadcasting of a range and diversity of independent productions." This percentage may after due consultation with the ITC and the BBC be varied by the Government by an order made pursuant to section 16. The expressions "qualifying programmes" and "independent productions" are given somewhat elaborate meaning and definitions in the Broadcasting (Independent Productions) Order 1991 (S.I. 1991 No. 1408) and summarised below. The expressions need to be understood as applying to a "relevant broadcaster," meaning the person who provides the television broadcasting service and who is therefore bound by the requirement for a percentage of qualifying programmes to be independent productions.

Definitions

A "qualifying programme" is one:

(a) made by the relevant broadcaster or by a person commissioned by him;

(b) made by the relevant broadcaster together with any other person, or by a person commissioned by the relevant broadcaster together with any other person provided not less than 25 per cent. of the actual cost of the production of the programme has been borne or provided by the relevant broadcaster; and

(c) a programme consisting of live coverage of an event provided the coverage does not exceed 75 per cent. of the duration of the programme and the remainder of the programme is made by the relevant broadcaster or a person commissioned by him.

There is excluded from the definition of qualifying programmes the repeat transmission of programmes, news programmes and other sundry programmes, and advertisements, or any separate item whose duration is two minutes or less.

An "independent production" is a programme:

(a) which falls within the definition of a qualifying programme;

(b) if the elements of a programme of a live event, such as commentary and the like, is provided by an independent producer;

(c) with regard to the making (but not the use) of a number or series of commissioned programmes, then if the contractual obligations of a broadcaster and producer may run in excess of five years it is open to either party to terminate the obligations at intervals of not more than five years.

(d) which has not been commissioned on terms and conditions which require the independent producer to use the production facilities of the broadcaster or not to use the production facilities of some other broadcaster.

An "independent producer" is a producer:

(a) who is not an employee (whether or not on temporary leave of absence) of a broadcaster;

(b) who does not have a shareholding greater than 15 per cent. in a broadcaster; and

(c) which is not a body corporate in which the broadcaster has a shareholding greater than 15 per cent.

Network Arrangements

The provisions of the 1990 Act governing the arrangements for the supply of network programmes on Channel 3 take effect on January 1, 1993. The 15 regional licensees have appointed and engaged the Independent Television Association (ITVA) to serve as the conduit for the making or obtaining of programmes for the network and for their being made available to the regional licensees for showing in their regions. A detailed agreement has been entered into jointly by each of the regional licensees with the ITVA respecting the management of the functions and business of the ITVA in regard to the networking arrangements in accordance with the Statement of Principles approved by the ITC in April 1992. The agreement includes provision for the contributions by the regional licensees to the total of the monies to be expended for the making of network programmes in return for the right to broadcast the programmes in their regions. The production of each programme is made the subject of a separate network programme licence agreement between the ITVA and the individual regional licensee setting out a specification of the programme, the time for delivery and the licence fee.

What programmes are made and which of the regional licensees is to undertake their production is decided in consultation amongst all the regional licensees. The ITVA does not itself make or own programmes as it is the agent of the regional licensees. The ownership of the copyright and the rights of exploitation in a network programme belong entirely to the particular regional licensee which has undertaken to produce or commission the production of the programme and be responsible for making it available to the network. As regards the role of the independent producer it is for a regional licensee to decide to commission and fund such a production. If an independent production is sought or intended for network transmission it is for a regional licensee to propose through the system of consultation that the project is adopted and brought into the networking arrangements like any other network programme. Even so it is envisaged that independent producers will have access to the Network Centre staff to solicit support for their projects. The network arrangements are subject to review by the Director General of the Office of Fair Trading. The Report of the Director General published in December 1992 is critical of the arrangements and especially as regards the access to the network by independent producers. It remains to be seen what changes are made to the networking arrangements once the further references and enquiries possible under Schedule 4 of the 1990 Act have been made.

The Channel Four Company has led the way in creating a sustained output of independent productions and by doing so has set the precedents for the terms and conditions of upon which productions are commissioned. In recent years the ITVA and the BBC have each published statements of practice and procedures and terms of trade for the commissioning of independent productions. The regional licensees each have terms of trade but these are substantially alike as they are based on the guidelines of the ITVA and the codes referred to below.

Production Agreement

The form and terms of the agreement between a broadcaster and an independent producer for the making and delivery of a programme or film are not so different from that of a film production agreement as outlined above regardless of whether the project is one initiated by the producer or the broadcaster, that is, a regional licensee or the BBC.

Although a broadcaster may dispense with the need for a completion guarantor, the personal commitment and warranty of the individual producer will be required by way of endorsement of the obligations expressed to be undertaken by the production company. When a project initiated by an independent producer needs to be expanded and developed for it to be judged suitable for production and broadcasting, a budget and terms may first be agreed by letter, or by a formal development agreement for a producer to undertake the required preparation. Such an agreement will normally stipulate that all rights in the project are assigned to the broadcaster so when the project proceeds the development agreement is merged into the production agreement. It is usually provided that if the project is abandoned the producer remains free to find alternative sources of finance and means for the production of the film and by repaying the expenditure incurred by the broadcaster on the development all rights in the project will revert to the producer.

In undertaking a production a producer will be required to seek to obtain all rights, permissions and consents whereby the film can be exploited in all media throughout the world for the full term of copyright without restriction; any limitation to this principle will need to be provided for in the production agreement. The entire copyright in the completed film will pass to the broadcaster but when a project is to be funded entirely by the broadcaster (as is most often the case) the production agreement may also stipulate for the broadcaster to participate in any revenues which may arise from any subsidiary rights or uses remaining with the producer or a third party in the material upon which the programme or film is based. Likewise the agreement may provide for the producer to have a continuing interest or stake in the film with an entitlement to receive a share of the revenues from its wider exploitation. As a result a distinction is often made between primary, secondary and reserved rights.

Primary rights are rights of exhibition of the film in all forms and media—broadcasting, theatrical, non-theatrical and videogram. By the payment of the commissioning fee specific rights will be exercisable by the broadcaster but from the income it receives from the other forms of exploitation and exhibition a stated share may be payable to the production company. Secondary rights are those rights generated by or arising from the production but which are exploitable apart from the broadcasting or exhibition of the film itself. Secondary rights exist for example in specially composed and recorded music, in the script in the form of book publication rights, and merchandising rights in the characters, names and title of the production. However, whether such rights pass to the broadcaster and if so to what extent and on what terms they can be exploited by the broadcaster will depend upon the contracts made by the producer for the services of performers and others and for the acquisition of rights in the material incorporated in the film. It is these factors which justify the broadcaster having a right of approval of contracts entered into by the producer. It is a matter for negotiation as to what share the producer is to have of the profits arising from the exploitation of these secondary rights.

Reserved rights are all those rights in underlying literary, dramatic, musical or artistic works upon which a programme is based but which are not incorporated or exhausted by the making of the film; rights such as sequel rights, re-make rights, rights of adaptation and performance in another medium. Any control exercisable by the broadcaster over the disposition of such rights will, as with the secondary rights, depend on the terms of the contracts made with third parties.

Apart from the general principles of law which affect any entertainment or production—plagiarism, defamation, obscenity, racial hatred and the like—both the BBC by the terms of its Charter and the licence whereby it broadcasts programmes, and the ITC, the regional licensees and the Channel Four Company by virtue of the Broadcasting Act 1990 are subject to rules affecting what may be broadcast. In compliance with its statutory duties the ITC in January 1991 produced the Programme Code and the Code of Programme Sponsorship, also the Code of Advertising Standards and Practice and the Rules for Advertising Breaks. The regional licensees are directly responsible for the observance of these Codes, any contravention of them and the terms of the licence under which they are licensed to broadcast in their allotted region can have serious consequences. In order to meet its commitments as a broadcaster the BBC has instituted a set of Producers' Guidelines, not rules.

The Codes and Guidelines cover all aspects of broadcasting and programme content, in particular they provide for matters of good taste, decency, and the portrayal of violence in programmes, for the means or devices exercised for the gathering of information, for the conduct of interviews, the recording of public events, for the broadcasting and presentation of party politics, industrial disputes and religious affairs, and the conduct of competitions and award shows and charitable appeals. It follows that the essence of these codes is reflected in the provisions of production agreements and result in a broadcaster reserving to itself rights of approval at various stages of a production and to view negatives, and the right of final editorial control over the produced film or programme.

J. POSTSCRIPT FOR AUTHORS OF ARTISTIC WORKS

The definition of artistic works for the purposes of copyright law and the protection given to them have been briefly considered in Part 6 above. It is beyond the scope of this study to consider the protection these works may have as designs applied to articles or merchandise but by way of post-script to what has been written about literary, dramatic and musical works, a few comments need to be made about the creation and use of artistic works in entertainment.

Copyright Protection

Paintings, drawings, sketches created for sets or costume designs, or for scenery or studio backcloth have copyright protection as much as other works in accordance with the Copyright, Designs and Patents Act 1988. The principle is that the creator of a work is the first owner of the copyright; the one exception is for works created in the course of employment when by law the copyright automatically vests in the employer. Where a work is produced "freelance" the ownership of the copyright in a commissioned work and the rights exercisable therefore need to be the subject of written agreement.

Authors of artistic works have moral rights like authors of other works and the scope and enforceability of these rights are explained in Part 6 above. These rights are personal to an author and cannot be dealt with separately from the work but they can be waived—as may be stipulated in a contract commissioning a work.

The 1988 Act has brought about an important change in the law regarding artistic works of portraiture. The presumption which existed in law that the person who commissioned a portrait was the owner of the copyright in it has been repealed. For the purposes of copyright and the enjoyment of moral rights portraiture is treated like other artistic works. However, a person who for private and domestic purposes commissions the taking of a photograph or making of a film has overriding rights respecting the issuing of copies of the work to the public and its exhibition or showing to the public.

The Act resolves a doubt about who in law is the author and therefore first owner of the copyright in a photograph. The creator of a work is in law the author and a number of persons might lay claim to the creation of a photograph—the person responsible for its composition, or for its actual taking, or for its development or printing. It seems that the person who takes a photograph by exposing the film is its creator and author and so first copyright owner. This conclusion is based on section 4 which defines a "photograph" as meaning "a recording of light or other radiation on any medium on which an image is produced or from which an image may by any means be produced, and which is not part of the film."

In the taking of photographs in connection with entertainment, front-of-house and such like photographs of theatrical productions and artists, "stills" for film and television productions a number of issues can arise. Because of the contractual obligations to artists under Equity collective agreements considered above, and as special stipulations about the taking, selection and publishing of photographs may be included in the contracts of star artists in any branch of entertainment, a management or producer needs to ensure control over the copyright in commissioned photographs, at least control of the rights of reproduction and publication.

Use of Artistic Works

By accepting a commission to create an artistic work for a theatrical presentation, film or other production there is granted if not expressly then by implication, the right for the work to be copied and reproduced for the purposes of the presentation, performance and exploitation of the production. However, any more extended use may need to be expressly provided for as a term of an artist's engagement. The mere display or exhibition of an artistic work is not an infringement of copyright but its reproduction and publication in theatre programmes, souvenirs and the like without the licence of the author will be an infringement of his copyright.

The inclusion of an artistic work in a television broadcast is restricted by copyright, but its inclusion in a television broadcast or film by way of background or otherwise only incidentally is not an infringement of the copyright in the work.

The use of artistic works as featured works of art in broadcasts or films requires the consent of the copyright owner. The terms and conditions upon which such consent is given, the fees payable and especially if any videogram of the broadcast or film is released for sale to the public, are all negotiable matters. However, if the use of the work is for the purposes of criticism or review and the use can be said to be a fair dealing with the work and is accompanied by a sufficient acknowledgement to the author, then no such formal consent is needed. For the use of artistic works no longer protected by copyright, a royalty may be indirectly obtained by the owner charging a fee for the loan of the works, or for the provision of facilities for the making of the broadcast or the filming at a gallery, museum or the like.

The so-called "merchandising rights" derived from the titles, characters and scenes in films and television programmes especially have evolved and become of great commercial value in modern times. It follows that the terms upon which artistic works are commissioned for the purpose of exploiting merchandising rights and the ownership of these works are issues which merit as much consideration and negotiation as the commissioning and ownership of the film or television script.

Part 8

THE PERFORMANCE

In the preceding Parts of this study attention has been given to both the law and to the customary practices of the entertainment business as they affect the engagement of performers and the rights in their performances, and as they affect authors, composers and producers and the protection of their works. There remains to be considered the law, both civil and criminal, concerning what is or can be performed and the manner of performance.

Provisions of the Theatres Act 1968 are material to what is performed on the stage as noted in Section C below. The exhibition and release to the public of films and videograms are subject to the Cinemas Act 1985 and the Video Recordings Act 1984 which are considered in Part 9 below. In broadcasting it is the terms of the BBC's Charter and notably the Broadcasting Act 1990 under which broadcasting organisations are constituted and licensed to operate which govern what may be transmitted by radio and television. These Acts directly affect entertainment but otherwise the legal restraints on the freedom of expression of thought, ideas, feelings and conduct are no different for entertainment than for any other pursuit where meaning is conveyed by writing, speech, sounds, pictures or gestures.

The law as it affects freedom of speech and freedom of expression is to be found in the laws of obscenity, blasphemy, sedition, indecency, criminal libel, contempt of court, breach of parliamentary privilege, official secrets, public order and discrimination to name a few. Each of these laws is rooted in the common law or statute law and variously empower the courts to impose fines, terms of imprisonment and confiscate property. All these laws fall within the province of the criminal law so that proof of any offence charged rests wholly on the prosecutor and where the burden of proof required is greater than in civil proceedings.

There are aspects of the civil law which impinge on performers and their performances apart from the rights in performances considered in Part 5 above. In some countries the idea of the unlawful appropriation of a personality for the purposes of gain has secured recognition. Under English law the wrong of unjust enrichment through the improper use of a person's name or likeness has evolved from the law of "passing off" which exists to protect a person's business connection and goodwill. It is a body of law which serves to prevent unfair competition between persons engaged in a common field of activity. It may be invoked where through the use of another's name, or the way in which a business is conducted, or the way in which merchandise is produced and marketed, members of the public may be confused and misled into believing that the business of merchandise is that of another, that is, of the person instituting the proceedings. In more recent times these principles have been applied to the illicit use of an another's professional name and reputation.

The courts have intervened by injunction and an award of compensation where the rights infringed do not amount to a breach of contract or interference with rights of ownership of property. Instances of the courts granting redress on the grounds of unjust enrichment are, when a pop group used the name or style of another existing group and thereby infringed the latter's goodwill and business reputation. When the name of the group "Abba" was applied to goods without their consent, although no merchandise had already been licensed or produced using their name, the unilateral action was held to be an interference with their reputation. An injunction was granted by an Australian court to stop the reproduction on the sleeve of a record of the photograph of professional dancers without their consent and in such a manner as to suggest they were sponsoring or recommending the recording. The use of the name of a chain store trading predominantly in goods for infant care as part of the title of a book on the subject of infant care was restrained.

Although copyright protection may not extend to a title or invented word, protection has been secured on the grounds of unjust enrichment where the title chosen for a film was the same as that of an already published novel although the works were not alike. Where a film was exhibited in a way calculated to mislead the public into believing it included a renowned sketch but did not, the owner of the sketch who was not in the film was granted an injunction to restrain injury to his reputation and property.

The pirating of works protected by copyright can be restrained but the law has been slow to prevent the piracy of a personality otherwise than as just noted. There is no proprietary right or copyright in a performance as such. The personal right a performer has to prevent the recording or broadcasting of his performance without his consent is a different matter. There is no monopoly in the manner of presentation of any act or entertaiment so that the copying of the style, or manner of a performance cannot be restrained.

However, when the distinctive voice of a famous actor was simulated and impersonated in a "voice over" for a television commercial advertisement, the court acknowledged the proposition that an actor has a business or professional reputation in his performance of dramatic and musical works and that his goodwill lay in his performances. The court made no final pronouncement on the point as no evidence was adduced that the actor had suffered damage from the deceptive impersonation. Even so the conclusion must be that for one person by imitation to confuse the public about another artist's performance is to put that artist's goodwill at risk. No confusion arises where there is a straight or obvious impersonation as in a variety act or the like so then there cannot be a right of action.

Mere spectacle is not protected by copyright. What is protected is a dramatic work which is not defined but includes "dance or mime." Scenic effects, characters, "get up" alone do not appear to be protected but with the advance in stage technology and the making, for example, of elaborate lighting plots the use of such works, like the use of a stage set, without consent may be an infringement of artistic copyright.

B. DEFAMATION

The civil wrong or tort of defamation is difficult to explain succinctly as it is beset with fine distinctions and procedural rules touching freedom of speech. The law of defamation may be regarded as an intrusion on this freedom but its scope is the protection of a person's reputation, not his character, which is not the same thing. A person has the right not to have his reputation disparaged or impugned without justification just as much as a person has the right not to be physically assaulted. However, the law does not confer on any one a right to the esteem of others so if a person is mimicked or caricatured to the extent his feelings are offended, then unless such mimickry or ridicule is so far-fetched as to amount to a positive reflection on his reputation the law affords him no redress.

Definition

Many attempts have been made to define what constitutes defamation but they have been found wanting in precise meaning. In the report of the Faulks Committee's enquiry into the law of defamation a statutory definition was proposed, namely "Defamation shall consist of the publication to a third party of matter which in all the circumstances would be likely to affect a person adversely in the estimation of reasonable people generally." Attempts to lay down an objective test generally founder because people's attitudes change. The attribution to a person or organisation of some personal conduct or life-style, or of some belief or allegiance, or of some way of professional conduct or business dealings might in one decade bring opprobrium but not in another. As one writer has aptly observed, it may be easier to show what a person has said is wrong, than to show that a person was wrong to say what he said.

It is the form of the expression of the defamation which distinguishes libel and slander. If the defamation is spoken it is slander, but if it is in a fixed or permanent form it is libel; the difference has important legal consequences. In order to succeed in an action for slander, with few exceptions there must be proof of actual damage suffered as a result of the slander. With libel no such pre-condition of proof of damage is required as compensation is automatically recoverable in the form of an award of damages.

It is not only words a such which may be defamatory as section 16 of the

Defamation Act 1952 provides that the expression "words" includes "pictures, visual images, gestures and other methods of signifying meaning." Moreover, some forms of expression or publication are by statute declared to constitute libel and so the legal consequences as just noted apply.

Publication

By section 4 of the Theatres Act 1968 the publication of words in the course of the performance of a play is to be treated as publication in permanent form and therefore a libel. "Play" is expressly defined in the Act (see page 591, below), so that words spoken on stage otherwise than in the course of the playing of a role, for example, by an entertainer appearing in person, would seem to fall outside the section. Exemptions from the rule prescribed by section 4 are given under section 7 of the Act for performances given "on a domestic occasion in a private dwelling," and for performances given solely or primarily for the purposes of rehearsal, or to enable a record or cinematograph film to be made of the performance, or for it to be broadcast. These refinements are likely to have little consequence as most often performers will have been using scripted material and so the defamatory matter will have already been published in permanent form by the fact of the existence of the script and its distribution to performers and other persons.

By section 166 of the Broadcasting Act 1990 the publication of words in the course of any programme included in a programme service is publication in permanent form.

Defamatory matter visible to the eye as in a photograph, print, cartoon, painting or sculpture is publication in permanent form just as publication in the more conventional sense of printed text. The same applies to film and videogram. There is no decided authority whether the publication of defamatory matter by means of a record or audio-tape is publication of a libel or slander. The assumption is that the publication would be a libel as a precedent has been set by a decision of the courts that the speech recorded in the sound-track of a film was a libel.

Any person can be defamed and companies and organisations can be defamed if a statement is damaging to their property or goodwill. An action by a person defamed does not survive the person's death and from this rule follows the rule that a deceased person cannot be defamed so his or her next of kin have no redress in law for any statement allegedly defamatory of the deceased person. Moreover an action by a person defamed does not survive the death of the person who utters the defamation unless the matter has been brought to judgment.

Action for Defamation

An action for defamation must be in respect of a particular statement and a plaintiff must prove that the statement complained of is defamatory, that it is defamatory of him, and that it has been published to a third party. It is for a judge to decide as a matter of law if the words complained of are capable of bearing a defamatory meaning in the particular circumstances of their publication. The test is whether a reasonable man reading the publication complained of would discover in it matter defamatory of the plaintiff. If two meanings are possible, one defamatory and one not, then the sense in which they were uttered must be left to the jury since it is for the jury to decide on the evidence adduced if the words are defamatory of the plaintiff.

Words will be construed in their ordinary meaning and if this is plain and understood literally then that is sufficient and the plaintiff can rely on the words as uttered. But if the meaning is doubtful or concealed, as where the words are uttered in a context or in circumstances which require their being specially construed, then the burden rests on the plaintiff to allege an innuendo and demonstrate that the words have a particular meaning and are capable of being understood by reasonable men in the special sense or meaning propounded and were so understood and received.

For a defamatory statement to be actionable a plaintiff must show that the words complained of refer to him. The plaintiff need not be expressly named but when his identity depends on inference then the test which the law applies is an objective one: would a reasonable person reasonably believe or conclude that the words or statement refer to the plaintiff? It matters not whether the person making the statement intended it to be defamatory, or intended it to refer to someone else, or that fictitious names or other means were used to avoid any implication or suggestion that the statement referred to an actual person. It is enough if the plaintiff can show he was sufficiently identified in the statement that persons who knew him would have understood the words as referring to him and that he was the person meant. It is this rule which has confounded novelists, playwrights, publishers, film producers, broadcasters, etc., where due to the most incredible co-incidences through similarities of name, description or other circumstances it has transpired that a story, script or production has been understood as referring to an actual person and as defamatory of him.

Liability

It is the publication or uttering to a third person of defamatory material which is the basis of the cause of action and every person who takes part in the publication or dissemination of defamatory material may be liable for the consequences. The maker of a defamatory statement is not liable for its repetition unless authorised by him, or repetition was the natural or probable consequence of the original publication or utterance, such as an arranged interview or meeting. Every repetition of a defamatory statement gives rise to a cause of action against the person who makes the repetition. Liability for an unauthorised defamation or repetition of a defamatory statement may attach to a person on the grounds of his vicarious liability for the action of another as arises from the relationship between employer and employee or a person who is the agent of another.

A person's innocence or good intentions in the making or repetition of a defamatory statement does not avoid liability. Thus for example when the play "Soldiers" by Rolf Hochhuth (which had aroused controversy because it connected the late Sir Winston Churchill with allegations of his involvement in a plot to kill General Sikorski, the Polish Prime Minister) was presented by a prominent theatrical management, the point of view that there was a public duty to allow the presentation of a controversial matter did not avail and relieve the management from the proven libel against the pilot who had piloted the plane which crashed and resulted in the death of the General. Moreover the management's reasonable action in obtaining an undertaking from those producing the play that any reference to persons which might be libellous had been or would be cut from the play, and which undertaking was not observed, did not absolve the management from liability. Sir Winston Churchill being dead his next of kin or estate could bring no action, but the pilot being alive was able to do so.

Newspaper proprietors, printers, publishers and broadcasting organisations, and by way of analogy presumably exhibitors of defamatory matter such as a film, videogram or photograph, are jointly and severally liable with the author or originator of the defamatory material as publishers of the libel. A person such as an amanuensis or a performer in a play, who is an innocent intermediary in the dissemination of a defamation can avoid liability if he proves he did not know the item contained a libel or was likely to do so, and that this absence of knowledge was not due to any want of care on his part.

Defences

As has been noted above, the fact that a person did not intend to libel another makes no difference to his liability at law. Statements such as "all the characters in this work are imaginary and fictitious and have no resemblance to actual persons" are immaterial to the question of liability although such statements may tend to support a contention that the defamation was unintentional and innocent, which can be highly relevant to the question of damages. There are various grounds of defence to an action for defamation but their application is highly technical. The principal defence where there is a wholly innocent libel is that provided by section 4 of the Defamation Act 1952 but still the rules are strict.

Innocent Libel

For section 4 of the 1952 Act to apply the words must have been published "innocently," meaning that either the publisher did not intend to publish them of and concerning the other person and did not know of circumstances by virtue of which they might be understood to refer to him, or that the words were not defamatory on the face of them and the publisher did not know of circumstances by virtue of which they might be understood to be defamatory of the other person. But in either case the publisher must show that he, including any servant or agent of his concerned with the publication, exercised all reasonable care in relation to the publication.

If these conditions are satisfied then a publisher may make an offer of amends expressly under the section, meaning an offer to publish a suitable correction of the words complained of with sufficient apology. Where the defamatory statement has been printed and distributed a publisher must also take such steps as are reasonably practical to notify persons who may have received the defamatory words that the words are alleged to be defamatory of the person aggrieved. If the steps cannot be agreed by the parties an application may be made to the High Court to settle the terms of the correction, the apology and the mode of distributing or publishing the correction. With the offer of amends there must be a sworn statement specifying the facts relied upon as establishing the innocence of the publication, that is, an explanation of the action taken before publication to verify that the statement did not or could not reasonably be construed as referring to the plaintiff. If the offer of amends is accepted then no further proceedings can follow but if it is refused and proceedings are commenced the publisher has a defence if he proves that the words complained of were published innocently of the plaintiff and the offer of amends was made as soon as practicable. However, the publisher cannot rely on any other facts to establish his innocence apart from those set out in the statement made at the time of his offer of amends.

When works are performed or used in the course of entertainment if checks have been made so far as reasonably possible to ensure that there are no actual persons corresponding to the fictional characters, or that the situations or incidents depicted could not be held to refer to actual persons, then the writer and any third party responsible and liable as the publisher of a defamatory statement would very likely be able to establish his innocence and thereby take advantage of the section. But if words are published in any circumstances without proper prior research and enquiry then other grounds of defence to a claim for damages for defamation will need to be relied upon.

When a person takes proceedings against another for defamation he does not have to prove the statement is false as this is presumed in his favour where the words are prima facie defamatory of him. If the statement has been published by the defendant otherwise than innocently under section 4 then to defeat a claim he must succeed under one of the common law defences the chief of which are justification, privilege and fair comment.

Justification

This is a plea of truth and the onus of proof rests on the defendant. Should it be that not every detail of the statement is true that will not destroy the defence provided the words not proved to be true do not materially injure the plaintiff's reputation having regard to the substantial truth of the statement. If distinct or separate parts of the statement are true but some are false then alternative grounds of defence may be relied upon in respect of those which are false.

The defence of justification or truth is absolute and total and is maintainable regardless of the motivation or purpose for the publication. Publication may be in bad taste or considered an invasion of privacy but the law protects only a person's reputation and not generally his privacy so that no compensation can be obtained for embarrassment or annoyance or loss suffered by the revelation of the truth about someone.

Absolute Privilege

This defence is, put briefly, confined to statements in Parliament and Parliamentary papers, statements in the course of and in reference to judicial proceedings and communications between officials of Government. Fair and accurate reports of judicial proceedings if published contemporaneously are also regarded as within this ground of defence.

Qualified Privilege

This is a defence which the law allows where there exists some public or private duty whether legal or moral on the part of the person making the statement which justifies his communicating it to a person who has a corresponding duty or interest in receiving the statement. Exposure of mis-conduct or improper dealings and the giving of testimonials are particular examples of the application of the principle. Whether the duty exists is a question of law to be tested in the light of the particular circumstances.

As the defence is not absolute it will not prevail where the statement has been made with malice, meaning that the person who made the statement did so with the object of securing some personal advantage rather than in pursuance of a duty or some legitimate interest. If a statement is made recklessly and without regard to its substantial truth then malice on the part of the person who made it may be inferred.

By sections 7 and 9 of the Defamation Act 1952 the defence of qualified privilege was extended to the press and broadcasting media in the publication of fair and accurate reports of public affairs, proceedings, enquiries and the like and reports relating to the affairs and proceedings of public organisations and associations, and the publication of extracts from public records open to the public. Reports of public meetings held lawfully and in the course of which there is discussion of matters of public concern are also privileged but subject also to the defendant at the request of the plaintiff having published a statement by way of explanation or contradiction.

Fair Comment

This is a defence which is applicable to statements made in good faith and without malice about public affairs and matters of public interest, and about matters which are brought to the notice of the public and subject to public review or criticism, such as entertainment and artistic works of all kinds. Government and public institutions and organisations, public figures in relation to their public duties and matters which directly concern or relate to their performance of their public duties come within the scope of matters of public concern, but the extent to which comment may be made about the private affairs of public individuals is open to question.

It is permissible to comment and express opinions about persons but not to make false statements and although often difficult to separate, the opinion must be distinguished from the false statements. The comment may be prejudiced or exaggerated but that does not necessarily detract from its integrity provided the comment is based on facts and can be regarded as likely to have been made by any fair-minded person. But if it is proved that the comment was malicious, that the maker did not believe in its truth or was really indifferent to its veracity and given to spite the plaintiff, or was not given to benefit and inform the public the defence fails. The maker of the statement has the onus of proving that the matter is one of public concern, the facts on which the comment is based are true, and the comment is such as a reasonably fair-minded man might make. It is for the plaintiff to prove malice on the part of the maker so as to destroy the privilege but it is for the judge to decide as a question of law if the subject matter of the comment is, or the occasion was one of public interest or concern.

Remedies

The award of damages for loss of reputation is the usual way a person is compensated for a defamatory statement or publication. General damages, meaning compensation for the loss or harm the law assumes a person to have suffered, will automatically be awarded but special damages or compensation for particular loss will only be awarded if such a loss is shown to have been suffered. A defendant's belief in the truth or fairness of his statement, the extent of its publication, the motivation for the publication are all relevant to the court's determination of the amount of general damages to be awarded to a plaintiff.

The remedy of injunction is granted by the High Court at its discretion when a person's legal rights have been infringed or there is a distinct likelihood they will be. It is available where a defamatory statement has been published but rather more often an injunction is sought where publication is about to occur or is continuing. As at this stage the issue of whether or not the publication is defamatory will usually not have been fully tried before the court, the person seeking such an injunction will be required to satisfy the court on a number of points: that there is a serious question or issue to be tried, that there is a distinct balance in his favour that his action will succeed and that damages will not be a full and adequate compensation as the injury to his reputation is likely to be severe. As already remarked a balance often has to be struck between maintaining freedom of expression and protecting a person's reputation so that an interlocutory injunction will very rarely be granted where a defendant announces his intention to rely on the defence of justification.

Criminal Libel

This is an offence at common law. The essence of criminal libel is the tendency of a publication to cause a breach of the peace. Truth is no justification unless it can be proved the publication was for the public benefit. The rule of civil libel that no action can be brought for defamation of a deceased person or a group of persons very generally described, does not apply to prosecutions for criminal libel. Prosecutions for criminal libel are very rare for although there may be no reason in law why a libel for which damages have been awarded could not also be the subject of a criminal prosecution, only the most extreme and serious libel is likely to be the subject of a public prosecution.

C. THE BOUNDARIES OF PERFORMANCE

The law as it affects performances live on stage, or in the medium of film, videogram or broadcasting, is part of an amorphous body of law governing freedom of expression, expression not only by speech and writing but also by any other manner in which meaning is conveyed. It embraces laws on obscenity, blasphemy, sedition, indecency, racial hatred and criminal libel.

The evolution of these laws owes much, for better or worse, to the pronouncements of judges which have reflected their attitudes or prejudices in their assumed role as protectors of public morals, right thinking and good peaceable behaviour. Many of these laws have been supplanted by legislation but the loose and imprecise drafting of many of the enactments has resulted in paradoxes and inconsistencies in their application and made more intense arguments over the legitimacy of many provisions of the law. The moral certainties of times past are no longer so certain as social attitudes change with the greater awareness and currency in ideas brought about by the very fact of modern communication. Laws to protect persons from injury, and to protect property, even if imperfectly administered are accepted whereas laws which seek to control what persons may say, exhibit or perform, what persons may read, see or hear will always be contentious. Persons engaged in the performing arts often have strong views which they wish to propound or express without restrictions. The following is an outline of the salient parts of public law which impinge on the performing arts and entertainment.

OBSCENITY

For those engaged in the business of entertainment perhaps the first concern is not to get embroiled with the laws on obscenity. The Theatres Act 1968 provides for the offence of obscenity but only in the context of the public performance of plays. It is the Obscene Publications Act 1959 (as amended in 1964) which enacts the substantive laws of obscenity and so has been the focus of attention and interpretation. Not only are printed and published works within its scope but through supplementary amendments films, videograms and broadcasting are made subject to its provisions. As the law affecting severally the performance of plays, the making and exhibition of films and videograms, and broadcasting are but variations of the principles laid down in the 1959 Act, attention is first directed to these principles.

Definition

For a matter to be obscene it must satisfy the statutory definition set out in section 1 of the Obscene Publications Act 1959, namely that "an article shall be deemed to be obscene if its effect or (where the article comprises two or more distinct items) the effect of any one of its items is, if taken as a whole, such as to tend to deprave and corrupt persons who are likely, having regard to all the relevant circumstances, to read, see or hear the matter contained or embodied in it."

In the past isolated incidents or items included in a work could be enough to render a work obscene but now a work has to be considered as a whole. What is in issue is no longer a single scene but the overall and dominant impression created by a work. It must be shown to tend to deprave and corrupt and this today is perhaps the most severe test. A work may cause offence, be shocking, vulgar, lewd, but such features even if dominant are not of themselves enough. Deprave and corrupt are read as synonymous and the word "corrupt" has been regarded as implying a powerful and corrosive effect going far beyond a tendency to lead persons morally astray.

A further obstacle is to identify the persons who are likely to be depraved and corrupted. The law's "reasonable man" has no place in this context for instead there has to be reckoned all the relevant circumstances. It is not only the totally innocent who are to be protected but also the less innocent. What can be material to the issue of obscenity is proof of the class or kind of persons to whom the material is aimed. The law has sensibly shifted away from regarding a work as obscene simply because it may be seen by a child. More regard is had to how a work is exploited and made available, and to whom. Even then the question arises of what is the number of persons to be affected? In dealing with this hurdle the courts have interposed on the Act a test that there must be a significant proportion of those into whose hands the material comes who would be led into corruption.

Juries are left to rely and judge from their experience and general awareness of acceptable standards of what material is depraving and corrupting. As Geoffrey Robertson and Andrew Nicol in their book "Media Law" have succinctly deduced from a survey of the cases, "the effect of publication must be to produce real social evil, going beyond immoral suggestion or persuasion, and constituting a serious menace to the community."

Obscenity is not confined to matters of sex and pornography as the courts have taken the view that obscenity embraces encouragement in the taking of drugs and encouraging violence. Factual information about drugs has been accepted, but not a work which sensationalises and highlights only the favourable affects of drugs. Violence may be held to be obscene when material depicting violence is directed towards the very young. Brutality in sexual encounters has been viewed as obscene.

The intention of a writer or creator of a work does not count. A work may be intended to enlighten or entertain, to be a contribution to art and learning; on the other hand it may avowedly be intended to shock, to excite or gratify some perceived emotional needs. The intention, the purpose of the work makes no difference as the offence of obscenity is absolute. If the material is found to be obscene no excuse or explanation can make it otherwise. The material is to be judged on its own and not by comparison with other works.

Defence of Public Good

However, although material may prima facie be obscene, section 4 of the 1959 Act establishes the defence of public good. A person cannot be convicted of an offence under the Act or an order made for the forfeiture of material, "if it is proved that publication of the article in question is justified as being for the public good on the ground that it is in the interests of science, literature, art or learning [in the sense of scholarship], or other objects of general concern." The onus of proof rests on the defendant but the burden of proof is less than that which the criminal law imposes on the prosecutor alleging a work is obscene.

The opinion of experts may be admitted in evidence to uphold or rebut the defence. The evidence of witnesses is as to the merits of the work such as to justify its publication, not as to its being inoffensive or offensive. It is for a jury to decide whether the publication was for the public good.

Prosecution

Liability to prosecution falls on the person who whether for gain or not publishes the material, that is, who distributes, lends, gives or sells the material to another, or where the article is one which contains or embodies material to be looked at or heard, who shows, plays or projects it. Mere possession of obscene material is not an offence, but where a person has possession of obscene material for publication for gain, and regardless of whether the gain or profit is for himself or another, that person is liable to prosecution. Such a person has a defence by proving he had no reasonable cause to suspect the material in his possession was obscene, as for example, when in possession of a sealed package or reel.

A prosecution for obscenity may not be commenced more than two years after the commission of the offence. This rule has been a trap as the commission may not simply occur once as by the act of first publication, but by continuous distribution. The penalties provided by the Act are forfeiture of the obscene material and fines and imprisonment.

Police Powers

Powers are conferred on the police under a warrant issued by a local justice or magistrate to search premises and seize material believed to be obscene. The occupier of the premises may be summoned to show cause why the material should not be forfeited. The owner, author, maker or distributor of the material also has the right to explain why the material should not be forfeited. If the court decides the articles seized are obscene and is satisfied they were kept for publication for gain, the court can order them to be forfeited. There is a right of appeal to the Crown Court and the articles may not be destroyed until the expiration of the time within which an appeal may be entered and the issue finally adjudged. If material is ordered to be destroyed the matter ends there as no penalty can additionally be imposed.

Films and Broadcasts

There are refinements to the Act with regard to films and sound-tracks.

(a) The defence of public good applies if the publication is justified as being in the interests of drama, opera, ballet or any other art, or of literature or learning. A factual film is most likely to have a good defence and an entertainment film which has a certificate of the British Board of Film Classification likewise.

(b) Proceedings under the Act can only be instituted with the consent of the Director of Public Prosecutions where the article is a moving picture film of a width of not less than 16mm and the publication was or took place in the course of a film exhibition. It follows that films of eight mm width are subject to the full effect of the Act.

(c) A warrant for the search and seizure of material by a constable as mentioned above must have the sanction of the Director of Public Prosecutions.

Videograms are treated as films for the purposes of the Act but are also subject to the Video Recordings Act 1984 as more particularly reviewed in Part 9 below.

By section 162 of the Broadcasting Act 1990 the exemption accorded to television and sound broadcasting from the offence of publishing an obscene article given under the 1959 Act ceases to have effect. In view of the responsibilities laid upon the ITC, the Radio Authority and their regulatory powers under the Broadcasting Act, the presence of the Broadcasting Complaints Commission to receive and consider complaints about programmes, and the duty of the Broadcasting Standards Council to draw up codes relating to broadcasting standards which are to be adhered to, one may wonder at the need for this change in the law.

Put briefly, matter in a programme which is included in a programme service is treated as publication for the purposes of the 1959 Act. The consent of the Director of Public Prosecutions is required to the institution of any prosecution. The defence of public good can be invoked on the grounds that the matter included in a programme was justified in the interests of drama, opera, ballet, or any other art, or in the interests of science, literature or learning or any other objects of general concern. A person may not be convicted of an offence under the 1959 Act in respect of the inclusion of any matter in a relevant programme if he proves he did not know and had no reason to suspect the programme would include matter rendering him liable to be convicted of an offence of publishing obscene material. There are other procedural technical provisions concerning suspected offences.

Obscenity and the Theatre

The Theatres Act 1968 abolished the historical powers of the Lord Chamberlain to censor the public performance of plays. The Act expressly declares in section 1(2) that in granting, renewing or transferring any licence for the use of premises for the public performance of plays, "the licensing authority shall not have power to impose any term, condition or restriction as to the nature of the plays which may be performed under the licence or as to the manner of performing plays thereunder." (An exception is made for demonstrations of hypnosis).

Censorship as through a side door was attempted in 1981 without success by a private prosecution under the Sexual Offences Act 1956 with regard to a scene in the play "The Romans in Britain" presented by the Royal National Theatre Company. By section 28 of the Local Government Act 1988 it is provided that a local authority shall not intentionally promote homosexuality. It remains to be seen if this provision erodes the principle established under the 1968 Act as above respecting the manner in which licensing authorities may exercise their powers. However, as section 28 stipulates that in any proceedings brought concerning the application of this provision a court is to draw such inferences as to the intention of the local authority as may be reasonably drawn from the evidence before it, it seems hardly likely a prosecution respecting a general policy of subsidising the theatre would be successful.

In place of the Lord Chamberlain's censorship of the theatre, the Theatres Act 1968 enacted three offences in connection with the performance of plays, namely obscenity, incitement to racial hatred, and provoking a breach of the peace. The provision on racial hatred has been replaced by provisions in the Public Order Act 1986 as noted below.

With regard to obscenity, section 2 of the 1968 Act provides that "a performance of a play shall be deemed to be obscene if, taken as a whole, its effect was such as to tend to deprave and corrupt persons who were likely, having regard to all the relevant circumstances, to attend it."

Section 3 provides that a person may not be convicted of an offence under section 2 "if it is proved that the giving of the performance in question was justified as being for the public good on the ground that it was in the interests of drama, opera, ballet or any other art, or of literature or learning." The opinion of experts as to the artistic, literary or other merits of a performance of a play may be admitted either to establish or negative the ground of the defence. It is the merits of the performance which count.

Other Offences in the Performance of Plays

It is fitting at this point in the consideration of the Theatres Act 1968 to note two other offences which may possibly be committed in the giving of a performance of a play as some general provisions of the 1968 Act apply to their enforcement as they apply to the provision on obscenity.

Racial Hatred

Incitement to racial hatred by the giving of a public performance of a play was an offence under section 5 of the Act, but this provision has been replaced by section 20 of the Public Order Act 1986. This provides that "if a public performance of a play is given which involves the use of threatening, abusive or insulting words or behaviour, [such as to stir up racial hatred] the person who presents or directs the performance is guilty of an offence." It is further provided that if such a person is shown not to have intended to stir up racial hatred, it is a defence for him to prove he did not know and had no reason to suspect that:

(a) the performance would involve the use of offending words or behaviour, or

(b) the offending words or behaviour were threatening, abusive or insulting, or

(c) the circumstances in which the performance would be given would be such that racial hatred would likely to be stirred up.

The nature of racial hatred and offences under the 1986 Act are considered below.

Breach of Peace

The third of the offences is that of provocation of a breach of the peace and is set out in section 6 of the Act. "If there is given a public performance of a play involving the use of threatening, abusive, or insulting words or behaviour any person who (whether for gain or not) presented or directed that performance shall be guilty of an offence under this section if:

(a) he did so with intent to provoke a breach of the peace, or

(b) the performance, taken as a whole, was likely to occasion a breach of the peace."

Some general comments need to be made about these offences.

1. The provisions enacting these offences are specific in that the offences arise in the performance of a play. Section 18 of the Theatres Act 1968 defines a play as meaning:

"(a) any dramatic piece, whether involving improvisation or not, which is given wholly or in part by one or more persons actually present and performing and in which the whole or a major proportion of what is done by the person or persons performing, whether by way of speech, singing or action, involves the playing of a role; and

(b) any ballet given wholly or in part by one or more persons actually present and performing, whether or not it falls within paragraph (a) of this definition."

The core of the definition is the playing of a role, so if a performance falls outside this definition, such as a variety act, strip-tease or personal appearance, an offence cannot be charged under the above provisions. In such situations common law offences may be charged such as that the performance or what was said or done was obscene, indecent, offensive, disgusting or injurious to morality, or an indecent exhibition, or as regards incitement to racial hatred an offence under other provisions of the Public Order Act 1986.

2. In proceedings brought under the Theatres Act or the Public Order Act, if a performance is based on a script, the actual script on which the performance was based is admissible as evidence of what was performed and the manner of performance and unless the contrary is shown by evidence the performance can be taken to have been given in accordance with the script. "Script" means the text of the play—words, music or

other notation—together with any stage or other directions for the performance and whether or not contained in a single document. Section 10 of the Theatres Act empowers a superintendent of police if he has reasonable grounds for suspecting that an offence under these enactments has been committed or is likely to be committed by any person in respect of a performance of a play, to order the actual script (if one exists) upon which the performance was or, will be based to be produced to a police officer and allowed to be copied; the copy so made can be produced in proceedings as if it were the actual script. Any order made under this section must be in writing and name the person to whom it relates and describe the performance in a manner sufficient to enable the performance to be identified.

3. The offence of giving an obscene performance is committed whether or not it is given in public or private. Thus a private performance at a theatre club or the like is subject to the law of obscenity but an exception is expressly made for "a performance of a play given on a domestic occasion in a private dwelling." The offences of incitement to racial hatred and provocation of a breach of the peace are only committed if a performance of a play is in public. But none of these offences are committed where a performance of a play is given solely or primarily for the purposes of rehearsal, or for the making of a recording of a performance, or for it to be broadcast provided it is proved that only persons directly connected with the giving of the performance were present at the performance.

4. It makes no difference whether a performance is given for gain or not. It is the person who presented or directed the performance who is liable to proceedings and a penalty regardless of whether or not he was present during the performance. A performer or artist who performs under the direction of another person is not liable on account of his taking part in the performance unless without reasonable excuse he performs otherwise than as directed; also he cannot be accused of aiding or abetting the commission of an offence.

5. As remarked above, if a work is judged to be obscene the offence of obscenity is absolute. With the offences of incitement to racial hatred and provoking a breach of the peace, intent on the part of the accused is a necessary ingredient of these offences and the intent must be proved affirmatively by the prosecution.

6. No proceedings for any of these offences under either of the Theatres Act or the Public Order Act can be brought in England and Wales except by or with the consent of the Attorney General.

INDECENCY

The obscenity laws are concerned with material likely to deprave and corrupt persons; the laws about indecency are about conduct or displays which in the circumstances are neither sought nor anticipated and therefore likely to cause public outrage. Both concepts are somewhat insubstantial. It is in relation to sexual matters and publications depicting sexual acts or poses that the indecency laws have been invoked especially the importation of material or its despatch through the Post Office.

Indecency in public is variously proscribed in civic enactments but the display of indecent matter is subject to the Indecent Displays (Control) Act 1981. Section 1 makes it an offence for any person to display, or cause or permit the public display of indecent matter. "Matter includes anything capable of being displayed, except that it does not include an actual human body or any part thereof." "Indecent" is not defined but has to be determined objectively in regard to the matter itself and the surrounding circumstances. The placement of other matter with the particular matter, or the persons likely to view the matter may be material factors.

The absurdities of the law and its administration, certainly in the past as applied to works of art and the performing arts, have largely been overcome since the Act exempts matter displayed or included in certain situations. Thus no offence is committed under the Act in relation to any matter:

(a) included in any broadcasting service or television programme service;

(b) included in the display of an art gallery or museum and visible only from within the gallery or museum;

(c) displayed by or with the authority of, and visible only from within a building occupied by, the Crown or any local authority;

(d) included in a performance of a play (within the meaning of the Theatres Act 1968);

(e) included in a film exhibition as defined in the Cinemas Act 1985 and in accordance with the provisions of that Act.

There are perhaps two points of special note arising from the above exemptions. As regards live entertainment, it is a display in the course of the performance of a play which is exempted and not a display given in any other kind of live entertainment. The display to the public outside or in the foyer of any place of entertainment to which the public have access, of any photograph or the like of any form of entertainment, or any "still" from a film, if indecent would not likely fall within the above exemptions.

The Act confers on the police the power under a warrant to enter premises and seize material suspected of being indecent, and empowers courts to impose fines or imprisonment or both on persons convicted of an offence under the Act.

If a company or other incorporated body is convicted of an offence, then if the offence was committed with the consent or connivance of, or was attributable to any neglect on the part of, any director, manager, secretary or other person purporting to act in such a capacity, that person may also be prosecuted.

Children and Indecency

Whatever opinion there may be about the laws of obscenity and indecency, few persons will question the need for a law in the endeavour to protect children from harm and still more their use and involvement in the making of material purposely salacious and certainly of material which is obscene. It is in the sphere of photography and film production and exploitation where this issue of indecency is most likely to arise; it might conceivably affect live entertainment.

The Indecency with Children Act 1960 provides that any person who commits an act of gross indecency with or towards a child, or who incites a child to commit such an act with that person or another, is liable to imprisonment. Of more general concern is the Protection of Children Act 1978 which makes it an offence:

(a) to take, or permit to be taken, any indecent photograph of a child— meaning under the age of 16; or

(b) to distribute or show such indecent photographs; or

(c) to have in his possession such indecent photographs, with a view to their being distributed or shown by himself or others; or

(d) to publish or cause to be published any advertisement likely to be understood as conveying that the advertiser distributes or shows such indecent photographs, or intends to do so.

Section 7 of the Act provides that references to a photograph are to both the negative and positive versions; and the references include a film and an indecent photograph comprised in a film; also film includes any form of video-recording.

It must be concluded that it is the indecent posed or contrived pose of a child and by way of sexual indulgence which is the substance of the offence and not a photograph of an actual and real situation which involves a child. The situation may be extreme but if it is taken as a record of an happening for a legitimate reason, such as for a documentary film, then no offence is committed by virtue of the defence allowed by the Act.

The offence of taking an indecent photograph is absolute, but no offence is committed if it is established that the distribution and possession of photographs was for "a legitimate reason," or that the accused had not himself seen the photographs and did not know and had no cause to suspect they were indecent. The offence of advertising under (d) above, can affect titles and the way in which a film or videogram or other product is promoted. Although the film or videogram may not contain indecent material, if it is advertised in such way as to highlight or suggest the inclusion of indecent material involving children an offence may be committed.

As with the indecency laws as noted above, the Act provides for powers of entry and search of premises. Where a company is convicted of an offence its officers and managers may be liable to prosecution.

RACIAL HATRED

Various kinds of offence of racial hatred are covered in Part III of the Public Order Act 1986. Racial hatred is defined in section 17 as meaning "hatred against a group of persons in Great Britain defined by reference to colour, race, nationality (including citizenship) or ethnic or national origins." The offence of racial hatred can occur:

(a) by the use of threatening, abusive or insulting words or behaviour, or display of such written material;

(b) by the publication or distribution of written material which is threatening, abusive or insulting;

(c) by the public performance of a play—as has been noted in the review above of the Theatres Act 1968;

(d) by the distribution, showing or playing of a recording of visual images or sounds which are threatening, abusive or insulting;

(e) by the broadcasting of or inclusion in a programme service of threatening, abusive or insulting visual images or sounds;

(f) by the possession of racially inflammatory material with a view to its propagation.

With all these offences an intent to stir up racial hatred must be proved. If the intent is absent then the conduct or action on the part of the accused must be such "as having regard to all the circumstances racial hatred is likely to be stirred up thereby." In this event an accused may still not be guilty of an offence under the Act if he shows he did not intend his words or behaviour to be, and was not aware it might be threatening, abusive or insulting.

Except within a private dwelling, the offence of using threatening, abusive or insulting words or behaviour, or of displaying such written material can occur in any situation. Thus in the world of entertainment it can arise in any kind of live entertainment by words, song, gesture or other display, as well as by the publication and distribution of the offending material. With regard to the distribution, showing or playing of a recording which incorporates offending material, section 21 provides that recording means "any record from which visual images or sounds may, by any means, be reproduced." It follows that only sound recordings, films and videograms are subject to the Act. The distribution, showing or playing must be to the public or a section of the public but it need not be for gain for an offence to be committed. It is a defence for a person to prove he was not aware of the content of the recording and did not suspect, and had no reason to suspect the recording contained material which was threatening, abusive or insulting.

Despite the extent of the supervision of broadcasting already alluded to, section 22 of the Act renders a programme broadcast or included in a programme service (as defined in the Broadcasting Act 1990) subject to the Act. The persons liable are the person providing the broadcast or programme service, any person who produced or directed the programme, and any person using the offending words or behaviour. The intent to stir up racial hatred must be proved; the defences as noted above apply to any of these persons whereby they may be absolved from an offence under the Act.

The mere possession of racially inflammatory material is not an offence. But if the possession is with a view to such material being displayed, published, distributed, shown, played or included in a programme service and the ingredients of an offence as noted above are present, an offence is committed. It is a defence for an accused to prove he was not aware of the content of the written material or recording and did not suspect, and had no reason to suspect the recording contained material which was threatening, abusive or insulting. This defence could be of particular importance to distributors and the like who have possession of films and videograms merely as merchandise in the course of trade.

Section 24 of the Act empowers a constable in possession of a justice's or magistrate's warrant to enter and search premises (using reasonable force if necessary) where a person is suspected of possessing inflammatory material. Where a person has been convicted of an offence under the Act, a court may order the forfeiture of the offending material but the material may not be destroyed before the expiration of the time within which an appeal may be entered against the conviction, and if an appeal is instituted before the issue is finally determined.

If a company or other incorporated body is convicted of any of these offences then if the offence was committed with the consent or connivance of a director, manager, secretary or other person purporting to act in such a capacity, that person may also be prosecuted. A conviction under the Act can result in a fine or imprisonment or both. No proceedings for any of the offences under Part III of the Act can be brought in

England and Wales except by or with the consent of the Attorney General.

BLASPHEMY AND BLASPHEMOUS LIBEL

These common law offences are defined as the publication orally or in writing (respectively) of matter which vilifies or is contemptuous of or which denies the truth of the Christian religion, or the Bible, or the book of Common Prayer. The mere denial of the truth of religion, or to question the existence of God, or to express opinions hostile to religion do not amount to blasphemy. It is when such views or opinions are expressed and couched in indecent and scurrilous or offensive terms such as to outrage the feelings of the general body of Christian believers that the offence is committed.

This is a province of the law which has been in limbo since 1922 when a public prosecution for blasphemy was last brought. The prosecution of "Gay News" in 1977 in respect of the publication of a poem was a private prosecution. In a report of the Law Commission in 1981 it was questioned whether only the Christian religion should be protected. If other beliefs are to be upheld the Commission doubted if any effective definition of the beliefs to be protected could be devised upon which to convict a person for the offence of blasphemy.

PROPERTIES

The rules and regulations to be observed in the installation and use of equipment and machinery and of scenery, properties, stage effects and so on at theatres and other places of entertainment are part of the general law. They are often underlined by the special technical regulations included as part of the conditions of the licence granted by a local licensing authority for the use of premises for the public performance of plays as explained in Part 9 below. However, safety precautions need also to be considered from the point of view of the performers themselves and others working behind the scenes. The principles of the law relating to the duty of care to employees and the operation of the Health and Safety at Work Act 1974 were touched on in Part 5. However, there are some points of law which should be noted relevant to the use of equipment and the accoutrements of a performance.

Uniforms

By the Uniforms Act 1894 and other relevant enactments the wearing of uniforms of any of the naval, military or air forces, or of the police or of a

uniformed chartered association is permitted in the course of the performance of a stage play at a place licensed for the public performance of
plays. It is also permitted in the course of a music hall or circus performance, in the course of a bona fide military representation and in the
production of a film. It is provided that uniforms are not to be worn or
used in such a manner or under such circumstances as to bring them into
contempt.

Weaponry

The possession of firearms is controlled by the Firearms Acts 1968–1988
and these enactments distinguish between firearms and prohibited
weapons. The former are defined as a lethal barrelled weapon of any
description from which any shot, bullet or other missile can be discharged; the latter as firearms of a kind whereby missiles can be continuously discharged and a weapon designed for the discharge of any
noxious liquid, gas or other thing and designed to inflict bodily harm.
Ammunition is also defined in relation to these various categories of
weapons.

It is an offence for a person to have in his possession or to purchase or
acquire a firearm without a certificate or as authorised by the certificate
where required by the Act, and similarly to be in possession of ammunition. Shot guns with a barrel not less than 24 inches in length, air weapons
and ammunition for these fall outside the requirements of the Act as
regards the holding of a certificate as also do blank cartridges not more
than one inch in diameter measured immediately in front of the rim or
cannelure of the base of the cartridge. Antique firearms which are sold or
possessed as a curiosity or ornament are exempted.

Prohibited weapons and ammunition are controlled by the Home
Office and from where authority must be obtained if these are to be used
for any purpose in the production of any stage drama or for the purposes
of filming. Certificates are normally issued to the producer or other
responsible person in charge of a performance and are conditional on the
firearms being kept safe and secure when not in actual use; any loss or
theft must be reported to the police. It is by section 12 of the Firearms Act
1968 that a person who is taking part in a theatrical performance or
rehearsal thereof, or in the production of a film may for these purposes
have a firearm in his possession without holding a certificate as otherwise
required by the Act.

Animals

The special rules of law and of liability for injury suffered by persons or
damage to property as a result of the keeping or escape of animals cannot

be included here, but attention needs to be given to the enactments respecting the training and use of animals in performances. By the Performing Animals (Regulations) Act 1925 it is provided that no person is to exhibit or train any performing animal unless registered under the Act. The meaning of exhibit in this context is the use or performance of an animal at any entertainment to which the public are admitted whether on payment or otherwise; training is to be understood as training for the purpose of such exhibitions. The Act provides for local authorities to keep registers and issue certificates as required by the Act and confers on local government officials and the police powers of entry to inspect premises to ensure that the conditions attaching to the certificate of registration are being complied with, and the training or exhibition of performing animals is not being carried on cruelly. Even so the Act expressly stipulates that officials and police officers cannot go on or behind the stage during a public performance of performing animals. Under the Act the courts have a residual power to make an order against a person prohibiting or making conditions for the training or exhibiting of animals.

The general law which protects animals and which applies to both domestic and wild animals if in captivity or confined or subject to restraint by some appliance or means, is contained in the Protection of Animals Act 1911 and later statutes dealing with particular creatures and their use. There is a general provision to protect animals from cruelty, abuse or injury and therefore it is under this Act that proceedings can be taken for alleged cruelty and inflicting suffering on animals when the 1925 Act would be inappropriate because the entertainment is not one to which the public are admitted, such as when animals perform in studios or on locations for film productions or television or other photography. The Act was invoked for the protection of a gold fish in a bowl as when in the course of the action of a play the bowl was smashed and the goldfish left to gasp for breath this was held to be cruelty within the limits of the Act.

Maltreatment of animals in the course of the production of films is indirectly made an offence by the effect of the Cinematograph Films (Animals) Act 1937. This prohibits the exhibition in public or the supply for public exhibition of any cinematograph film (whether produced in Great Britain or elsewhere), which in its production involved the cruel infliction of pain or terror on any animal, or the cruel goading of any animal to fury. A court can infer from the film as exhibited to the public that its making involved cruelty.

Hypnosis

Exhibitions, demonstrations and performances of hypnotism given at or in connection with any entertainment to which the public are admitted are subject to control of the licensing authorities under the Hypnotism

Act 1952. Performances of hypnotism given in the course of the perform-ance of a play within the meaning of the Theatres Act 1968 are exempted from the licensing requirements of the 1952 Act.

Delivery of Scripts to the British Library Board

Section 11 of the Theatres Act 1968 prescribes that when there is given in Great Britain a public performance of a new play, being a performance based on a script, a copy of the actual script on which that performance was based is to be delivered to the Trustees of the British Museum free of charge within one month following the date of the performance. The British Library Act 1972 established the British Library Board and it is to the Board that in practice a copy of a script is delivered and which gives a receipt on behalf of the Trustees as required by the section. The responsi-bility for the delivery of the copy of the script rests on the person who presented the performance as it is he who is liable to a fine for failing to comply with the section.

The requirement applies only to a play not previously performed in public (whether for gain or not) in Great Britain, but not to one based substantially on a play previously performed in public or based sub-stantially on a text of a play which has been published in the United Kingdom. The script of a play produced solely or primarily for rehearsal, or for the making of a record, videogram, film or broadcast is disregarded for the purposes of the section. Should the play later be performed before a public audience a copy of the script would need to be deposited with the Board unless by then the play had been published in the United Kingdom when a copy would have been deposited by the publisher.

Part 9

THE LICENSING OF PLACES OF ENTERTAINMENT

A. ADMINISTRATION

The need for premises to be licensed for public entertainment of one kind or another, the authority empowered to issue, vary or cancel a licence, the arrangements and procedures for any applications regarding licences, and the conditions upon which licences can be granted are all matters of law and depend on legislation enacted by Parliament. Although there are numerous statutes covering the various kinds of entertainment—theatre, cinema, music, dancing, exhibitions—the administration of the legislation is cast upon local government authorities. Police and fire authorities have duties and powers in regard to the superintending of licences which have been issued, but the granting, withholding and revocation of licences fall to be decided by local authorities as administrative and executive functions of government. This is quite separate and distinct from and unlike the administration of the liquor licensing laws where all matters respecting the licensing of premises for the sale and consumption of intoxicating liquor are decided by local justices sitting at sessions especially convened for the purpose.

The powers conferred on local authorities over the licensing of entertainment—or more accurately the premises used for entertainment—are granted primarily in the interests of public safety and for the avoidance of injury to persons and damage to property by fire and other hazards. Only in a few instances does the legislation prescribe the conditions on which licences are to be granted. Otherwise local authorities have a discretion over the administration of the licensing Acts and the exercise of their powers as they consider appropriate to local needs and circumstances. The power to grant or withhold a licence affects both community and private rights and its exercise impinges on economic and commercial interests both public and private, and on local amenities. The precise conditions on which a licence is granted may be as crucial as the granting or withholding of a licence. The central government has no power to interfere with local authorities in the exercise of their powers but the legislation confers on applicants for licences rights of appeal to the courts.

Local government in England and Wales underwent major reform and re-organisation with the passing of the Local Government Act 1972 and similarly in Scotland by the passing of the Local Government (Scotland) Act 1973. More recent enactments have brought about further changes to the structure of local government; the details are not material for this study. It is sufficient to note that in England and Wales it is the district councils (but in the Greater London area the London borough councils), and in Scotland it is the island and district councils which, under the various enactments now to be considered, are designated as licensing authorities with the power to license premises for entertainment and to enforce the terms and conditions upon which licences are granted.

Local Authority Powers and Obligations

Local authorities are empowered to arrange for the discharge of many of their functions by a committee or a sub-committee or an officer of the authority. So in practice local authorities delegate their licensing powers to a committee and prescribe its rules and standing orders. Where an authority comprises a large urban area the licensing committee may be sub-divided for the easier flow of business.

It will depend upon an individual council's standing orders whether the powers allotted to a committee are "referred" or "delegated" powers. The precise wording of the standing orders and this distinction can be important. Referred powers are such that the decisions of a committee require confirmation by the council before having effect, whereas with delegated powers a committee's decision takes immediate effect. A council can withdraw the delegated power at any time but that cannot be done to the prejudice of persons who may have been affected by a decision already made by a committee. By this wide power of appointment of committees where legislation requires a council to enquire into or to investigate or to be satisfied as to some matter before making an order or granting a licence or the like, then an enquiry conducted by a committee becomes in law that of a council's. Similarly the decision of a committee under powers delegated to it by a council such as to grant or withhold a licence, to impose conditions or restrictions, to vary or revoke a licence, are the decisions of the council and for which the council is answerable.

One of the few specifically enacted obligations of members of local councils is to disclose any pecuniary interests direct or indirect in any contract or proposed contract or other matter under consideration at a meeting and to refrain from any discussion or voting on the issue. The scope and application of this rule has been the subject of much review by the courts but they have not sought to interpret it rigidly, holding that its purpose is to prevent members from being exposed to temptation or even the semblance of temptation in the performance of their duties. Thus the phrase "pecuniary interest" is not confined to a personal pecuniary interest, but by the Local Government Act 1972 it now embraces indirect pecuniary interest by virtue of membership of a company or other body, partnership or employment where the company or body, partner or employer has a direct pecuniary interest.

Section 97 of the 1972 Act prevents the basic principle being applied in a far-fetched and absurd manner by discounting the rigour of the rule when a council or committee member is the owner of a small fraction of the shares of a company (provided there is still a disclosure of the small shareholding), or is a council tax payer or inhabitant of the area affected, or a person entitled to participate in any service offered to the public, or where a member's interest is "so remote or insignificant that it cannot reasonably be regarded as likely to influence a member." In other words, because a local councillor frequents a local dance hall or theatre that of itself would not disqualify him from membership of the committee considering and hearing an applicaiton for a licence, whereas having a substantial shareholding in a company or having some standing in a body or association interested in an application would do so. If a councillor or committee member fails to disclose an interest which by law he should have disclosed it appears that his vote will render void any decision on the grounds that the committee, acting in a quasi-judicial capacity, will have acted in disregard of the tenets of natural justice.

In exercising their licensing powers local authorities are acting in a quasi-judicial capacity as they are determining issues which affect the rights and interests of individuals. In their consideration of applications they must adhere to the principles of natural justice to ensure that matters in issue are dealt with fairly and justly. The procedures for hearing and determining applications are left to the discretion of local authorities for as was remarked by Lord Parmoor in a case before the House of Lords in 1915:

> "Where the question of the propriety of procedure is raised in a hearing before some tribunal other than a court of law, there is no obligation to adopt the regular form of legal procedure. It is sufficient that the case has been heard in a judicial spirit and in accordance with the principles of substantial justice."

It follows that local authorities must be ready to hear not only an applicant but also other persons whose interests may be affected by the decision of the authority. Applications have to be considered after hearing the representations of both sides and without bias. However, it is open to a local authority to have a general policy regarding the exercise of a licensing power provided the policy is a reasonable one and which it is fair to apply. What the courts have ruled as not permissible is for a policy to be applied rigidly and inflexibly and without allowing an applicant to state his case. Reasons may be advanced by an applicant urging that a policy should be changed or not applied in the particular instance, but so long as an authority affords the opportunity for a point of view to be stated orally or in writing, an authority is entitled to apply its general policy to the particular application or issue under consideration as to any other.

Licensing Procedures

As local authorities recognise the importance of giving proper and systematic consideration to applications for the grant, renewal or transfer of a licence and the issues which impinge on their decisions persons having an interest in an application are supplied with written information about the conduct and procedures adopted by licensing committees at a hearing.

The procedures can be adopted according to local needs and circumstances as the enactments under which licences are granted do not lay down procedures in detail. The actual form and content of licences are devised by licensing authorities except when by statute certain conditions are required to be incorporated. Thus, for example a licensing authority can prescribe the form and amount of advertising it requires for the making of an application, such as announcements in local newspapers and the affixing of notices to the premises involved. It can also prescribe the time within which notices of objection to an application must be given, the documents and plans required in support of an application or its opposition. Applications for the grant, renewal or transfer of licences which are straightforward and unopposed are usually dealt with administratively. Even opposed applications may be settled by consultation and conciliation between the interested parties and the licensing authority.

When opposition to an application is not settled administratively then the hearing resembles that of court proceedings. Usually it is the party making objections who will be heard first with any witnesses; then in turn will follow the applicant and any supporting witnesses. Witnesses are open to cross-examination by opposing parties and to questioning by members of the committee, as obviously are the parties themselves. The parties can elect to be legally represented. Although the rules of evidence do not apply to hearings before licensing authorities as they apply to proceedings before the courts, all parties as well as the committee should have the opportunity of seeing copies of statements, documents, plans, photographs and letters intended to be adduced as evidence before the committee. Where a document is first produced at a hearing by one party it is usual for the committee Chairman to ascertain if the other party has seen it or objects to its sudden production, but its acceptance as evidence is determined by the Chairman.

The enactments provide for a right of appeal to the courts by an applicant who is refused a licence or is aggrieved by the terms and conditions upon which a licence is granted. A party who opposes an application has no right of appeal against the decision of the licensing authority granting the licence. In such a situation the objection will have to be raised again at the time when the application for the renewal of the licence is made.

It has been remarked that an applicant is entitled to the licence sought unless there are good and sufficient grounds for refusing it, or for granting it but only on special conditions which have not been agreed to by an applicant. So it follows that an applicant is entitled to know the objections he has to overcome and the reasons for any refusal of a licence, or the imposition of special conditions. The failure of a licensing committee to explain fairly and reasonably its reasons for refusing a licence or for its imposing special conditions could constitute grounds for challenging and questioning whether the council (on whose behalf the licensing committee acted) had properly discharged its duties and responsibilities.

B. THE LEGISLATION

The Acts of Parliament requiring premises used for entertainment to be licensed are considered in detail in the following Sections but a few general comments by way of introduction are appropriate. The body of general planning law and regulations which govern the building of theatres, cinemas, concert halls, arts centres and the like, or the conversion of an existing property to any of these uses is outside the scope of this study; also the Theatres Trust Act 1976 under which is constituted the Theatres Trust for the protection of theatres for the nation. The law governing the sale and consumption of intoxicating liquor and the licensing of premises for these purposes is also excluded as although such liquor may enhance entertainment—indeed our lives generally—this province of the law is not directly relevant to entertainment.

The enactments which prescribe what premises and places used for public entertainment must be licensed are:

(i) Theatres Act 1968;

(ii) Cinemas Act 1985;

(iii) Local Government (Miscellaneous Provisions) Act 1982;

(iv) Civic Government (Scotland) Act 1982—for Scotland only;

(v) London Government Act 1963 (as amended) and London Local Authorities Act 1991;

(vi) Private Places of Entertainment (Licensing) Act 1967—for England and Wales only.

None of these enactments apply to Northern Ireland. The law governing Sunday entertainment is considered in a later Section. Other enactments relevant to entertainment are referred to in the text.

The licences granted by local authorities under the above Acts are mutually exclusive and allow premises to be used only for the kind of entertainment described in the licence. For example, a music licence granted under the Local Government (Miscellaneous Provisions) Act 1982 does not extend to the exhibition of films or videos. Thus if more than one kind of entertainment is to be provided at premises then a separate licence will be required for each form of entertainment. However, as will be seen some concession is allowed by the terms of the relevant Acts for the performance of incidental music in theatres and cinemas.

Public Entertainment

Although some kinds of entertainment given in private and for gain may be subject to the licensing laws the above Acts are principally concerned with public entertainment. What constitutes public entertainment is not as simple as might be assumed as the legislation does not define it. The fact of payment being or not being demanded for admission to any form of entertainment is not conclusive of its being or not being public. The crucial test is whether any member of the public has a right to enter premises and be admitted to an entertainment. The remarks of Lord Chief Justice Parker made in 1961 in the course of his judgment in a case concerning the admission of the public have been often cited as he said:

> "[the test is] not whether one, two or three or any particular number of members of the public were present, but whether on the evidence, the proper inference is that the entertainment was open to the public in the sense that any reputable member of the public on paying the necessary admission fee could come into and take part in the entertainment."

Many clubs exist to provide entertainment which is not for the general public but some are set up simply with the object of avoiding the licensing laws. Nonetheless, whether an entertainment is public or private is a question of fact to be decided on the evidence. The ease with which membership of a club can be obtained is a material consideration when the objective is put to the test. If there is no real formality or selection process or no meaningful interval of time between the making of an application for membership and attaining the status of member of a club, then it will be hard to resist the conclusion that the club designation is but a sham and an attempt to avoid the licensing laws. This was the conclusion of the court recently despite a card check on membership being made at the entrance to an acid house party at which over 7,000 members were present.

If proprietary clubs and members' clubs and societies are properly conducted with rules for the admission and election of members and the introduction of guests, then any entertainment which is provided by the club for the benefit of its members and guests is provided for a particular description of person and so is not public entertainment.

Apart from the enactments listed above there is also the general body of statutory and regulatory law for the supervision of premises and places of public resort which is of course applicable to premises used for entertainment. Moreover, theatres, cinemas, dance halls and the like are places of employment so that the general law relating to employment must not be overlooked, in particular as it affects actual working conditions as provided for in the Offices, Shops and Railway Premises Act 1963 and the Health and Safety at Work Act 1974.

Because of the powers given to local licensing authorities and the thoroughness of the enquiries and inspections usually carried out preparatory to the granting and renewing of licences it will be found that the general requirements of the law covering such matters as public health, the provision for disabled persons, the safety of buildings, and the environment are reflected in the terms and conditions upon which licences are granted. Be that as it may the following statutory powers and provisions merit special attention by persons providing entertainment.

Children's Entertainment

The Children and Young Persons Act 1933, section 12 applies where entertainment is provided for children under 14 or where children predominate. If the number of children on the premises exceeds 100 there is a duty on the persons providing the entertainment to have sufficient adult attendants who are properly instructed in their duties to prevent the presence of more persons than the building can properly accommodate, and who can exercise control of the movement of children and other persons admitted to the building and generally take all other reasonable precautions for the safety of children. If the occupier of premises for hire or reward permits them to be used for entertainment the occupier has a duty to take all reasonable steps to ensure that these rules are observed.

Anyone on whom the duty rests to observe or ensure the observance of the rules but who fails to do so is liable to a penalty. If the premises are licensed as a place of public entertainment and there is infringement of these rules the licence can be revoked by the local licensing authority. The Act provides that a constable may enter any building in which he has reason to believe an entertainment is being, or is about to be given to ascertain if the above requirements are being complied with. An official authorised by a licensing authority has the like power for the like purpose to enter premises which are licensed by that authority. The duty of enforcing these provisions of the Act rests on the licensing authority when the premises are licensed but otherwise it is for the police to take proceedings. The section may be regarded as a heavy underlining of the licensing legislation generally which contains provisions for the special care and protection of children at places of entertainment.

Fire Certificate

The provisions of the Fire Precautions Act 1971 requiring certain premises to have a fire certificate issued by the local fire authority do not apply to premises used for entertainment. It would seem that the extent of the licensing powers of local authorities and the way they are exercised renders any more certification and formalities unnecessary. Even if there is no express requirement under a licensing enactment for notice of an application for a licence to be given to the local fire authority, usually a local authority will require notice of the application to be so given; at least it will consult with local fire officers about fire risks at premises before granting a licence. Moreover, the licensing enactments variously empower fire officers to enter premises licensed for entertainment to check the fire precautions and ensure that the conditions of a licence regarding safety and the means of escape are being observed.

Entertainment in Sports Grounds

Pop concerts and festivals are a feature of present day public entertainment and are subject to the entertainment licensing laws considered below. In addition when such events take place in stadia and sports grounds their organisers and managers need to take account of the safety requirements imposed under the Safety of Sports Grounds Act 1975 as amended by the Fire Safety and Safety of Places of Sport Act 1987 and the conditions of the certificates which are granted by local authorities as required by these Acts.

These combined Acts apply to sports grounds generally and not only, as in the past, to large and perhaps prestigious stadia. A local authority in whose area is situated a sports ground which by statutory order is made subject to these enactments, is empowered to issue general or special safety certificates according to the activities to be allowed and the number of events to be permitted. In carrying out these powers a licensing authority can make detailed enquiries about the qualifications of the management of such places and can impose conditions for the granting of safety certificates with rights of entry to ensure compliance with the conditions.

There is a residual power whereby if a licensing authority is of the opinion that the admission of spectators to a sports ground or any part of a sports ground involves or will involve a risk to them so serious that, until steps have been taken to reduce it to a reasonable level, the admission should not be permitted, the local licensing authority can issue a prohibition notice. There are rights of appeal against the conditions on which a safety certificate may have been granted and against the issue of a prohibition notice.

Infringement of Licensing Legislation

Persons who infringe the licensing legislation or who contravene the terms and conditions upon which licences are granted or renewed commit a criminal offence which on conviction can result in the imposition of heavy fines and in some cases imprisonment as variously prescribed by the Entertainment (Increased Penalties) Act 1990. In addition if the holder of a licence is convicted of an offence a licensing authority may revoke the licence—a penalty of perhaps graver consequence than the imposition of a fine for if a licence is withdrawn the premises cannot then be used for the purposes intended.

Some offences are absolute, such as using premises without their being licensed as required by law. Offences arising from contravening the terms of a licence are not absolute since, in order for a person to be convicted, there are pre-conditions which a prosecution must show to have existed when the offence was committed. Variously the legislation provides that it is a person who "knows" or who "has reasonable cause to believe or suspect" in the existence of some circumstances or state of affairs who is liable to conviction. In some instances defences are written into the penal provisions of the enactments such as that a person "exercised all due diligence" to prevent some occurrence, or "took all reasonable precautions" to avoid the commission of an offence. Where such a defence is allowed the burden of proof resting on an accused is not as onerous as that which rests on the prosecution to prove the offence. The legal textbooks are replete with examples of the interpretation and application of such phrases. Much depends on the evidence and facts of a particular case and the objects of the statute under which an offence is created.

Food Safety

As an addendum to this outline of licensing legislation there needs to be mentioned the Food Safety Act 1990. The Act is a comprehensive enactment about food production, manufacture, importation and supply generally so most of its provisions are not material to this study.

The Food Premises (Registration) Regulations 1991 (S.I. 1991 No. 2825) require certain premises to be registered in accordance with the prescribed rules. In principle no person may use any premises for the purposes of a food business on five or more days, whether consecutive or not, in a period of five consecutive weeks unless registered. "Premises" are widely defined and include stalls and vehicles. A food business is defined as "any business in the course of which commercial operations with respect to food are carried out." Food offered as a prize or reward or given away in connection with any entertainment to which the public are admitted whether on payment or not, and food provided for the purposes of advertisement or the furtherance of any trade or business, is brought within the scope of the Regulations. The expression "entertainment" includes "any social gathering, amusement, exhibition, performance, game, sport or trial of skill."

The Regulations prescribe the form of application to be completed by the proprietor of the food business and for the application to be made to the Registration Authority constituted under the Act, namely the local district councils and the London borough councils. Particulars of the registration are open to public inspection. The failure to comply with the registration requirements and the use of premises without their being registered is a criminal offence. Powers are conferred on the police and officials of the local authority to enter premises to check on the compliance with the Act and the Regulations.

There are exempted from the Regulations premises where the retail sale of food is by means only of automatic vending machines, and premises where the supply is only of beverages, or biscuits, potato crisps, confectionery or other similar products and which sale is ancillary to a business whose principal activity is not the sale of food.

C. THEATRES

The Theatres Act 1968 ("the Act") regulates the licensing of premises for use as theatres, prescribes the licensing procedure, and confers powers of entry to premises and the enforcement of the Act on licensing authorities and the police. Those provisions of the Act respecting the performance of plays are considered in Part 8.

No premises may be used for the public performance of any play except under and in accordance with the terms of a licence granted by the licensing authority for the area in which the premises are situated. The need for premises to be licensed under the Act depends upon whether the critical words "play," "premises" and "public performance" as defined in section 18 of the Act apply in any given situation.

"Play" is defined as meaning—

"(a) any dramatic piece, whether involving improvisation or not, which is given wholly or in part by one or more persons actually present and performing and in which the whole or a major proportion of what is done by the person or persons performing, whether by way of speech, singing or acting, involves the playing of a role; and

(b) any ballet given wholly or in part by any one or more persons actually present and performing, whether or not it falls within paragraph (a) of this definition."

This definition is not without problems of meaning and construction although so far no issues have been raised before the courts about its interpretation. Opera and operetta are not expressly mentioned but as singing is and in view of the inclusion of ballet and as both singing and ballet normally have musical accompaniment it must be assumed that "play" includes opera and operetta. Improvisation is expressly included if it involves the playing of a role. If a person appears as himself "in person," as in variety and cabaret, performing songs and patter but not performing material which involves the playing of a role the performance will fall outside the definition and so the Act will not apply but instead the legislation covering music and public entertainment will be relevant.

By section 12(3) of the Act music which is played by way of introduction to the performance of play, during any interval and at the conclusion of a performance, or in the interval between two performances, is treated as part of the performance of the play provided the total playing time amounts to less than a quarter of the performance time of the plays performed at the premises on any one day.

"Premises" are defined as including "any place"; not very enlightening! It seems to ensure the application of the Act to conditions where there is a public performance of a play in a temporary structure such as a marquee, or in the open such as in a field or garden or courtyard. The word "premises" connotes buildings of all kinds—halls, barns, cellars, churches, school or college buildings and the like, that is buildings which are not purposely built as a theatre in the ordinary sense of the word.

"A public performance" is defined as including "any performance in a public place within the meaning of the Public Order Act 1936 and any performance which the public or any section thereof are permitted to attend, whether on payment or otherwise." The meaning of "public place" referred to in the 1936 Act has in fact been revised by the Criminal Justice Act 1972 which in section 33 defines "public place" as including "any highway and any other premises or place to which at the material time the public have or are permitted to have access whether on payment or otherwise." Thus put briefly, if a play is performed in any place such as just described and although the amenities and facilities are minimal and regardless of there being no charge, if the public or any section of the public are at liberty to view the performance then there is a public performance.

Licensing Powers and Procedures

A licensing authority is empowered to prescribe what information it requires to have furnished for it to consider any application and what other notices it requires to be given in regard to an application. A licensing authority can impose any term, condition or restriction it considers necessary in the interests of physical safety and health (and for controlling demonstrations of hypnosis). However, section 1 of the Act expressly declares that no term, condition or restriction may be imposed by a licensing authority for the grant, renewal or transfer of a licence concerning "the nature of the plays which may be performed or the manner of their performance."

Not less than 21 days' notice of the intention to make the application for the grant or transfer of a licence is required to be given to the licensing authority and to the chief officer of police for the area in which the premises are situated. An application for the renewal of a licence requires not less than 28 days' prior notice to the licensing authority. An application for an occasional licence, or renewal of an occasional licence, requires only 14 days' prior notice to the licensing authority. It is open to a licence holder at any time to apply for a variation of the terms, conditions or restrictions upon which a licence has been granted.

Licences are normally granted for a year, that is unless an application is for a shorter period, or for one or more particular occasions only. When a licence is granted to a person, if requested it can be transferred by the licensing authority to another person thereby overcoming the anomaly which would arise where for example, there is a change of house manager. If a licence holder dies the licence automatically continues in favour of his personal representatives for up to three months from the date of death but the period can be extended by a licensing authority.

As compliance with the Act and the terms of a licence and the liabilities or penalties for non-compliance rest mainly on owners and occupiers of premises used for the public performance of plays, it follows that such persons will normally be applicants for the grant or renewal or transfer of a licence. There is no requirement corresponding to that in the repealed Theatres Act 1843 that a licence may be granted only "to the actual and responsible manager for the time being of the theatre." A corporate body or association just as much as an individual can apply for a licence but often a licensing authority will stipulate for the house manager of a theatre to be the nominee of a corporate licence holder. It is premises which are required to be licensed under the Act so any licence granted to a person or organisation is for the premises as specified and is applicable only to those premises. If an organisation, for example an amateur dramatic society is presenting a public performance of a play, or if a touring company is presenting public performances of plays at successive venues then it is important to establish that the premises used for the performances are licensed under the Act.

A licence can be granted in respect of premises in the course of construction or which are undergoing extensive alterations subject to the condition that it shall not have force until the work to be undertaken has been completed to the satisfaction of the licensing authority.

Licensing authorities are empowered to impose such reasonable fees as they may determine—in effect the costs of the administration of the Act—for most applications made pursuant to the Act. No fee is payable for the grant or transfer of a licence for one or a number of particular occasions (that is for occasional licences), for the public performance of plays if the licensing authority are satisfied that the performances are of an educational value or other like character, or the performances are for a charitable or other like purposes.

There is a right of appeal against the refusal of a licensing authority to grant or renew or transfer a licence and against the refusal of an application for the variation of the terms of a licence. A licence holder also has a right of appeal regarding the terms upon which a licence is granted and against the revocation of a licence by a licensing authority. Any appeal lies to the magistrates' court (in Scotland to the Sheriff), acting for the area within which the premises are situated. The appeal must be brought within 21 days of the notice of the decision of the licensing authority appealed against. If an appeal is made against the refusal of an application for the grant or transfer of a licence, notice of the appeal must also be given to the chief officer of police and other persons who under the licensing procedure of a local authority are to have notice of such applications.

The decision of a magistrates' court is automatically binding on a licensing authority but an applicant has a further right of appeal against the decision of a magistrates' court to the Crown Court. Where an appeal is made against the revocation of a licence or the refusal of an application for the renewal of a licence, the licence is deemed to remain in force during the period within which an appeal may be brought and until the determination of the issue or the appeal is abandoned.

Theatres which operate by letters-patent of the Crown are exempt for the requirement to be licensed under the Act but this is in effect the only privilege of such theatres. The licensing authority for the area in which such a theatre is situated can impose any requirements concerning the theatre as it would be entitled to impose in the ordinary way of licensing premises under the Act.

Premises licensed under the Act or by letters-patent for the public performance of plays are, by the combined operation of section 19(1) of and schedule 2 to the Act and to the Licensing Act 1964 (as amended), relieved of the necessity to obtain a justices' licence for the sale of intoxicating liquor provided the proprietor of the premises, meaning presumably the licence holder, gives notice to the clerk of the local licensing justices of the intention to sell intoxicating liquor at the theatre. By being deemed licensed premises under the 1964 Act it follows that a theatre must observe the local permitted hours for the sale of intoxicating liquor but a theatre is not restricted to selling liquor at the times when public performances of plays are taking place. However, because of the strict interpretation of the combined effect of the Licensing Act 1964 and the Theatres Act 1968 it has been ruled that the simple formalities available under the 1964 Act for acquiring an extension of hours cannot apply to a theatre as a theatre proprietor does not hold a justices' licence but enjoys only a concession or dispensation (under the 1968 Act) from the need to have an ordinary or regular local justices' licence to sell intoxicating liquor. The moral is that theatres regularly operating at late hours and desiring to serve refreshments and intoxicating liquor after locally permitted hours should have a justices' licence granted in accordance with the liquor licensing laws, or else obtain a special licence when late service is exceptional.

Powers of Entry and Enforcement

The powers of entry and inspection of premises to ensure compliance with the Act are contained in section 15. If a justice of the peace (in

Scotland the Sheriff) is satisfied by information on oath there are reasonable grounds for suspecting that any premises are being used for the public performance of a play without a licence, he can issue a warrant enabling a police officer or authorised officer of the licensing authority to inspect the premises to establish if the Act is being contravened. Where premises are licensed under the Act then an authorised officer of the licensing authority may on showing his authority, at all reasonable times inspect the premises to ensure that the terms and conditions or restrictions upon which the licence has been granted are being complied with. A police officer similarly has the power of entry and inspection of licensed premises, also an authorised officer of the local fire authority if that authority is different from the licensing authority. Any person who wilfully obstructs a person authorised to carry out any of these inspections is liable to criminal proceedings.

If a public performance of a play is given at any premises not licensed under the Act then by section 13(1)—

(a) any person concerned in the organisation or management of the performance; and

(b) any other person who knowing or having reasonable cause to suspect that the performance would be given at premises for which no licence is in force allows the premises to be used for the giving of the performance, or who lets the premises or otherwise makes them available to any person for the giving of the performance,

is guilty of an offence.

By section 13(2) it is provided that if any of the terms, conditions or restrictions on or subject to which a licence is held are contravened or not complied with:

(a) the holder of the licence; and

(b) any other person who knowing or having reasonable cause to suspect that the premises would be used otherwise than in accordance with the terms of the licence, allows the premises to be so used, or lets the premises or otherwise makes them available to any person by whom the premises are to be so used,

is guilty of an offence.

If the holder of a licence is charged with an offence under this provision it is a defence to prove the contravention took place without the holder's consent or connivance and that he exercised all due diligence to prevent it. No such special defence extends to any other person who is charged with an offence under section 13(1).

A person guilty of any offence under section 13 is liable to a heavy fine or imprisonment or both. If the holder of a licence is convicted then in addition the licensing authority may revoke the licence. This cannot occur unless the time (21 days) within which a licence holder can appeal against the conviction has expired without an appeal having been brought, or if brought has either been abandoned or resulted in the conviction being upheld.

The cover of virtual anonymity of the corporate licence holder does not avail when an offence is committed under the Act. Section 16 provides that where it is proved that an offence was committed with the consent or connivance of or attributable to any neglect on the part of any director, manager, secretary or other similar officer of the body corporate, or any person purporting to act in any such capacity, then any such person as well as the corporate body is liable to be proceeded against and incur the due penalty.

D. CINEMAS AND FILM EXHIBITIONS

The Cinemas Act 1985 consolidated and amended the law governing the licensing of premises used for the exhibition of films by repealing the Cinematograph Acts of 1909, 1952 and 1982. In addition to the rules about licensing there are also the detailed technical rules contained in the Cinematograph (Safety) Regulations 1955 (S.I. 1955 No. 1129) as amended in 1958 (by S.I. 1958 No. 1530) which, although made under the repealed legislation, are deemed to be made under section 4 of the Act. Being statutory regulations they automatically and without exception or variation form part of the terms and conditions upon which premises are licensed. The regulations provide for the safety of equipment, the safe storage and handling of film and other technical rules appertaining to film exhibitions.

The Celluloid and Cinematograph Film Act 1922 combined with the regulations made under it, deals with matters of safety and fire precautions and the registration of premises where quantities of raw celluloid (as defined) and of cinematograph films are stored or processed, or dealt with in the course of the actual production of a film. The Act is directed at premises used for film production, editing and handling; it does not apply to premises licensed under the Cinemas Act 1985.

Section 1 of the Cinemas Act 1985 (in what follows referred to as "the Act"), enacts that no premises shall be used for film exhibitions without being licensed for the purpose unless the exhibition falls with the category of an "exempted exhibition" as provided for in sections 5 and 6. The management of film exhibitions is also subject to the detailed Home Office Regulations which have statutory force as they are made pursuant to powers conferred on the Secretary of State under section 4 of the Act to make regulations about safety and related matters.

"Film exhibition" is defined as meaning "any exhibition of moving pictures." No longer is there any reference to cinematograph film, or to moving pictures "produced on a screen by means which include the projection of light." As a consequence all exhibitions of moving pictures in whatever medium—film, video, television—appear to come within the scope of the Act unless expressly exempted. The definition expressly excludes an exhibition which is produced by the simultaneous reception and exhibition of programmes included in a programme service within the meaning of the Broadcasting Act 1990.

As for video programmes of whatever kind, and video games, it seems that whether the premises are required to be licensed will depend on the circumstances. At discotheques and such places where the musical entertainment is supplemented with music videos and where concerts of "karaoke" are given the premises may need to be licensed under both the Act as well as under the enactments governing places used for music, dancing and singing. The issue came before the courts with regard to video game machines in public places—arcades, shops, etc.—when it was affirmed that an "exhibition of moving pictures" denoted the showing of moving pictures to an audience rather than a display of moving objects on a video screen. The conclusion is that where the means or facilities provided for the viewing of a video or moving picture are virtually for individual viewing the Act will not apply, but where there is an audience the premises will need to be licensed.

Apart from the special category of exempted exhibitions (considered below), the requirement for premises to be licensed is mandatory. There are no pre-conditions such as that a film exhibition must be in public, or in a particular description of place or premises, or that the film must be of a specific width or gauge. "Premises" is not defined but must be construed more widely than as meaning simply a permanent building as special provision is made for the licensing of "a building or structure of a movable character."

By section 7 premises used only occasionally and exceptionally for film exhibitions—community halls, assembly rooms, leisure centres and the like—then provided the use is limited to six days in any one calendar year the premises are exempted from the need to be licensed. Even so the occupier of the premises must give to the local licensing authority, the fire authority and the chief officer of police of the area where the premises are situated not less than seven days' prior written notice of an intended exhibition. In addition the occupier must comply with the Home Office Regulations and any conditions notified to him in writing by the licensing authority. Any exempted film exhibitions (as noted below) do not count against the six days mentioned above.

If an exhibition is given in "any building or structure of a movable character" then it is not necessary to have a licence from the licensing authority for the area where the exhibition takes place provided the owner of the building or structure holds a licence of the licensing authority for the area in which he ordinarily resides. However, section 8 under which this concession is granted, requires the person intending to give the exhibition to give two days' prior written notice to the licensing authority, the fire authority and to the chief officer of police of the area where an exhibition is to take place. The Home Office Regulations must be complied with and any conditions notified in writing by the licensing authority of the area where an exhibition is to take place.

Although music, dancing and singing are included in a film, section 19 avoids the need for the premises where the film is exhibited also to be licensed under the legislation governing premises used for public music, singing or dancing. Furthermore, music played as an introduction to, or during intervals, or at the conclusion of a film exhibition is similarly disregarded provided the total playing time of such music on any one day is less than a quarter of the total running time of the film exhibition(s) given in the premises on that day.

Licensing Powers and Procedures

An application for the grant of a licence under section 1 of the Act for premises to be used for film exhibitions, and for a consent under section 2 (for exhibitions specifically for children) is made to the licensing authority in whose area the premises are situated. An applicaton for the renewal or transfer of a licence is similarly so made. The forms and procedures for applications are prescribed by the local licensing authorities save as expressly provided in the Act.

Not less than 28 days prior notice of the intention to make an application must be given to the licensing authority, to the fire authority (meaning the authority discharging the functions of fire authority under the Fire Services Act 1947) and to the chief officer of police for the area in which the premises are situated. When a licence is currently in operation then provided before its expiration application is made within the prescribed 28 days for its renewal (or transfer), the licence is deemed to continue in force (with any necessary modifications) until the application is determined by the licensing authority, or is withdrawn.

Fees are payable for the various applications as prescribed by the local licensing authorities but within the limits of the amounts laid down in the Act or as varied by statutory regulations.

Under section 1 licensing authorities are empowered to grant licences "to such a person as they think fit" to use any premises specified for the purpose of film exhibitions "on such terms and conditions and subject to such restrictions as they may determine." In the exercise of these powers a licensing authority must always have regard to the Home Office Regulations and have concern for the well-being of children attending film exhibitions. In addition when considering applications, licensing authorities are required to have regard to any observations submitted to them by the fire authority or the chief officer of police. Licences can be granted for up to but not beyond 12 months at any one time.

There is a right of appeal to the Crown Court, or in Scotland to the Sheriff, within 21 days of the decision of a licensing authority respecting the refusal of a licence, or on account of the terms and conditions or restrictions on which it is granted, or on account of the revocation of a licence. There is a right of appeal from a licensing authority's refusal of an application for the renewal or transfer of a licence. Notice of the appeal must normally also be given to the fire and police authority. When a licence is revoked, or its renewal or transfer refused the licence is deemed to remain in force during the period within which an appeal may be brought. If an appeal is brought then the licence continues to have effect with any necessary modifications until the determination of the appeal or its abandonment.

Licensing powers were first conferred on local authorities by the Cinematograph Act 1909 with the object of their overseeing the safety of the public in cinemas. However, because of the generality in which the powers were expressed local Watch Committees (who with the borough councils were the forerunners of the present day licensing authorities), as guardians of public order took upon themselves the previewing of films and approval of their content rather by way of analogy with the powers of the Lord Chamberlain over the public performance of stage plays under the Theatres Act 1843. Herein lies the genesis of the controversial powers of censorship exercisable by local authorities.

In order to achieve some consensus on what was not considered by the many local authorities to be suitable for public viewing, in 1913 the film industry established the British Board of Film Censors, now the British Board of Film Classification. It was given the duty "to induce in the minds of the licensing authorities and of those who have in their charge the moral welfare of the community generally," that films certified by the Board had been examined responsibly. Nonetheless, local authorities maintained their independence and right of approval of films for public exhibition and this was endorsed in cases brought before the courts. Moreover, when one licensing authority sought to make it a condition of a licence that no film not passed by the Board for public exhibition could be shown, it was held that the condition was invalid as it amounted to an unlawful delegation of a power exercisable only by the licensing authority.

Although today licensing authorities usually accept the certificate of the Board it is not always so. A licensing authority may of its own volition—usually as a result of local opinion—view a film and pronounce upon it; it may even grant a certificate or classification withheld by the Board. The Board is not a public body but is acknowledged by licensing authorities as a means for the orderly and systematic classification of films. As noted below the Board has been designated as the competent authority for the purpose of classifying videos in accordance with the Video Recordings Act 1984.

The classifications or categories adopted by the Board were revised in 1982 and are as follows—

U—UNIVERSAL Suitable for all

Uc—UNIVERSAL Particularly suitable for children

PG—PARENTAL GUIDANCE General viewing, but some scenes may be unsuitable for young children

12—Suitable only for persons of 12 years and over

15—Suitable only for persons of 15 years and over

18—Suitable only for persons of 18 years and over

There is also a "Restricted 18" classification to apply to films shown under special licence and with the consent of the local licensing authority pursuant to the Local Government (Miscellaneous Provisions) Act 1982 referred to below. The classification is—

RESTRICTED 18—For restricted distribution only through specially licensed premises to which no one under the age of 18 is admitted.

Control of Film Exhibitions for Children

The Act makes special provision for when children—persons under the age of 16—are present at film exhibitions. Under section 1(3) of the Act a duty is cast on licensing authorities in the granting of licences—

"(a) to impose conditions or restrictions prohibiting the admission of children to film exhibitions involving the showing of works designated, by the authority or by such other body as may be specified in the licence, as works unsuitable for children; and

(b) to consider what (if any) conditions or restrictions should be imposed as to the admission of children to other film exhibitions involving the showing of works designated, by the authority or such other body as may be specified in the licence, as works of such other description as may be so specified."

Although premises may be licensed for film exhibitions when a film exhibition is organised wholly or mainly for children then additionally by section 2 of the Act the exhibition requires the consent of the licensing authority. In granting the consent the authority is empowered to impose special conditions or restrictions.

Section 4 of the Act empowers the Secretary of State (the Home Office) to make special regulations for the health and welfare of children in relation to attendance at film exhibitions. Like the regulations referred to above these regulations—the Cinematograph (Children) (No. 2) Regulations 1955 (S.I. 1955 No. 1909) form part of the terms of a licence granted by a local authority. Also they are of general application and not confined to the special kind of film exhibitions for children mentioned above.

The general duty under the Children and Young Persons Act 1933 (see page 587) for persons providing entertainment for children to take special care for their safety applies to film exhibitions licensed under the Act.

Exempted Film Exhibitions

When legislation was first enacted regulating the showing of films the cinema was in its infancy and "the talkie" was nearly two decades away. In time films gained recognition as works having aesthetic merit and organisations of many kinds were founded with the object of enabling films to be viewed selectively. Furthermore, films were being made not only for entertainment but for purposes of education and instruction. In 1952 and 1982 the law was reformed to exempt non-profit making film exhibitions given by societies and clubs, exhibitions given for the purposes of education and instruction, and exhibitions in places of public resort such as museums and the like from the need to be licensed. These reforms have been consolidated in the Act.

Section 5 exempts any film exhibition given in a private dwelling-house to which the public are not admitted and the exhibition is either not promoted for private gain, or the sole or main purpose of the exhibition is to demonstrate any product, to advertise any goods or services or to provide information, education or instruction. The Home Office Regulations do not apply to such exhibitions and if the premises are already licensed under the Act none of the terms and conditions of the licence apply to the exhibition.

For a film exhibition at a place other than a private dwelling house to be exempted the following conditions prescribed by section 6 must be satisfied:

(a) either the public are not admitted, or if admitted are admitted without payment, or

(b) the exhibition is given by an exempted organisation.

For both kinds of exhibition there are two further conditions to be satisfied, namely—

(a) the exhibition is not promoted for gain, or

(b) the sole or main purpose of the exhibition is to demonstrate any product, to advertise goods or services or to provide information, education or instruction.

The permutations are considerable.

An "exempted organisation" is a society, institution, committee or other organisation which at the time of the exhibition is the holder of a certificate from the Secretary of State certifying it is not conducted or established for profit. Application for a certificate can be made at any time and for which a fee is payable. The issue of a certificate is discretionary as an organisation may neither promote film exhibitions for private gain, nor may its objects consist of or include the giving of film exhibitions to which the public are admitted.

Consistent with these statutory requirements, an application for certification as an exempted organisation is made to the Home Office supported with information about the constitution of the society and the conduct of its affairs. A certificate is normally granted for five years.

By section 20 an exhibition is promoted for private gain "if, and only if—

(a) any sums paid for admission to the exhibition, or

(b) any other sums (whenever paid) which in all the circumstances can reasonably be regarded as paid wholly or partly for admission to the exhibition, or

(c) where the exhibition is advertised (whether to the public or otherwise), any sums not falling within paragraph (b) above which are paid for facilities or services provided for persons admitted to the exhibition, are applied wholly or partly for private gain."

The section contains additional provisions concerning matters of proof when, in any proceedings, whether an exhibition was promoted for private gain is in issue. Merely dispensing with admission charges will not suffice if any charges are made for services such as food and drink. These may be attributed or treated as payment for the viewing and thereby render the exhibition as one promoted for profit. The publicity for the exhibition is a material consideration.

The effect of a film exhibition being exempted is that the premises used are not required to be licensed in accordance with section 1. If the premises are in fact already licensed then the conditions or restrictions which would otherwise apply, such as that the films exhibited must be approved by the licensing authority, will be avoided although the Home Office Regulations may still apply.

Although where the provisions of section 6 are satisfied exemptions are permitted there are two overriding qualifications to be borne in mind. The first is that there cannot be an unlimited succession of exempted exhibitions at one place. By section 6(4) if on more than three out of the last preceding seven days premises have been used for exempted film exhibitions then the concession becomes exhausted.

Secondly exhibitions organised solely or mainly for children are still subject to special rules. A consent under section 2 is not required simply on account of the exempted exhibition and if in respect of the premises where the exhibition is given a consent is in force none of the conditions or restrictions attaching to it apply to the exhibition. However, if such an exhibition is for children who are members of a club or society and whose principal object is their attendance at film exhibitions (and irrespective of there not being any element of private gain), the exhibition will not qualify as an exempted film exhibition unless it is given in a private dwelling-house or as part of the activities of an educational or religious institution.

Powers of Entry and Enforcement

General powers are conferred on constables, authorised officers of licensing authorities and fire authorities by section 13 of the Act to enter premises licensed under the Act, premises which are used only occasionally for exhibitions, premises which are licensed when they are used for an exempted exhibition, and exhibitions in movable buildings or structures to ensure compliance with the terms of licences granted and the provisions of the Act, which include the Home Office Regulations. Any official of the licensing authority or of the fire authority exercising the powers of entry under the Act must produce his authority at the request of the occupier of the premises. Any person who intentionally obstructs any of the officials in the exercise of their powers of inspection is guilty of an offence.

Fire officers have authority on giving 24 hours' notice to the occupier to enter the premises in respect of which a licence is in force, and premises and structures notified to be used for occasional exhibitions, to ensure that the fire precautions are adequate and the rules on fire precautions are being observed.

The right to enter any premises not licensed under the Act to ascertain if they are being used in contravention of the Act can only be exercised by a constable or authorised officer of a licensing authority with a warrant issued by a justice of the peace. If a constable has reasonable cause to suspect that a person has committed an offence under the Act he can require that person to give his name and address. Only if this request is refused or the address is reasonably suspected of being false may a constable arrest that person without a warrant; this power does not extend to Scotland. Where premises are entered on the authority of a justice's warrant a constable or authorised official of a licensing authority may remove apparatus and equipment or other property on the premises relating to any alleged offence under the Act.

Section 10 sets out the offences which may be committed under the Act and the persons liable for any infringement. An offence is committed where premises which are required to be licensed under the Act are used for an exhibition without a licence, where an exhibition given for children (which requires consent under section 2) is given without the consent, where premises are used otherwise than in accordance with the terms of any licence or consent and the regulations, or where there is a breach of section 6 governing exempted film exhibitions. The person liable is the person concerned in the organisation and management of the exhibition, and where a licence is in force the holder of the licence.

If premises are used for an exhibition without being licensed the person concerned can incur a heavy fine. Lesser fines can be imposed for other offences under the Act. A person who knowing or having reasonable cause to suspect that premises would be used in contravention of the Act allows the premises to be so used, or lets or makes them available, commits an offence and is also liable to incur a fine.

Section 10 allows a general defence for any person charged with any of the offences to prove that he took all reasonable precautions and exercised all due diligence to avoid the commission of the offence.

When an offence is committed by a corporate body and it is proved to have been committed with the consent or connivance of, or to be attributable to any neglect of any director, manager, secretary or other officer, or any person purporting to act in such a capacity, then that person as well as the corporate body is guilty of the offence and liable to incur a penalty as prescribed.

If the holder of a licence granted under section 1 is convicted of any offence under section 10, or an offence under section 12 of the Children and Young Persons Act 1933 for failing to provide for the safety of children as mentioned above, the licensing authority may revoke the licence.

Special Licences Under the Local Government (Miscellaneous Provisions) Act 1982

In Part II of this Act provision is made for the control of sex establishments including "sex cinemas" which, stated briefly, are defined as any premises, vehicle, vessel or stall used to a significant degree for the exhibition of films (and videos) which are concerned primarily with sexual activity. There is expressly excluded from the definition a dwelling-house to which the public is not admitted.

These provisions are to cover film exhibitions which can be perhaps described as "soft pornography" and so would normally fall outside the purview of the general licensing of cinemas and film exhibitions. Premises used for these purposes have to be especially licensed by a local authority for which a detailed procedure and conditions are laid down in schedule 3 to this Act. The rules do not apply unless and until a local authority by an affirmative resolution adopts them as being applicable to the area. Similar rules apply in Scotland under the Civic Government (Scotland) Act 1982.

E. VIDEO RECORDINGS FOR SALE TO THE PUBLIC

As a consequence of cinema films being made available on videotape for sale and hire to the general public the Video Recordings Act 1984 ("the Act") was enacted to satisfy the need felt for videos to be classified for their suitability for domestic viewing and especially in the presence of children. The Act is not about the licensing of premises but it is fitting that it should be reviewed at this point in the study of the legislation affecting entertainment.

The Act empowered the Home Secretary to appoint persons to undertake the classification of videos and the British Board of Film Classification was designated to perform this function. Although in its origins the Board was the creature of the film industry, by its composition and structure it stands apart from the creative and production arm of the industry. The Board is an independent body and its designation under section 4 of the Act rests on the approval of the arrangements and procedures it instituted, including a right of appeal against a classification. As a non-profit making corporation the Board meets the cost of its operations solely from the tariff of charges it levies for classification certificates, the tariff being subject to government approval.

It is a misconception to regard the Act as an instrument of censorship. A videotape or videodisc like any other publication is liable to censorship if it falls foul of the Obscene Publications Acts 1959 and 1964 or infringes other provisions of the criminal law. Then the censoring body is the court. Accordingly the Board is enjoined not to classify films which may be in conflict with the law. The Act is essentially about classifying and labelling videos principally for the protection of children and to distinguish the suitability of a work for particular age groups. When the Act was before Parliament the question of restricting the freedom of adults to obtain videos of the kind of films classified as R18 in order to prevent their being seen by children was earnestly debated. The solution found was for such videos to be available only in licensed sex shops, that is sex shops licensed under the Local Government (Miscellaneous Provisions) Act 1982 referred to above.

Video Classification

Unlike the classification by the Board of cinema films—which as explained above has no statutory foundation but is usually adopted by licensing authorities—the classification and labelling of videos is a requirement of the law. There is a specific obligation and duty cast upon the Board by section 7 of the Act that the certificates issued must contain—

(a) a statement that the video work is suitable for general viewing and unrestricted supply (with or without any advice as to the desirability of parental guidance) with regard to the viewing of the work by young children or as to the particular suitability of the work for viewing by children; or

(b) a statement that the video work is suitable for viewing only by persons who have attained the age (not being more than 18) specified in the certificate and that no video recording containing that work is to be supplied to any person who has not attained the age so specified; or

(c) the statement mentioned in (b) above together with a statement that no video recording containing that work is to be supplied other than in a licensed sex shop.

The categories of classification and the symbols devised by the Board reflect these statutory requirements and are as follows:

U—UNIVERSAL Suitable for all

Uc—UNIVERSAL Particularly suitable for children

PG—PARENTAL GUIDANCE General viewing, but some scenes may be unsuitable for young children

15—Suitable only for persons of 15 years and over

18—Suitable only for persons of 18 years and over

RESTRICTED 18—To be supplied only in licensed sex shops to persons of not less than 18 years.

The category Uc was introduced so as to distinguish works intended particularly for young children from those marketed for the whole family. The category Restricted 18 attaches to videos which for the reasons noted above are judged suitable for sale only through licensed sex shops.

The labelling of both the actual video and the case or container is prescribed by statutory regulations made pursuant to section 8 of the Act. These specify the categories of classification as above and accompanying symbols and their size and placement on cassettes and include provisions to prevent the concealment or obscuring of a classification.

The procedure for the submission of works for classification is for a supplier to send the work together with the Board's submission form and other material as prescribed and payment of the fee of an amount according to the running time of the work. A work is viewed by at least two examiners in the light of the Board's established criteria and if cuts are required these are specified so that the work can be re-submitted and re-examined. On the basis of the work as approved by the Board an interim clearance form is issued on which is entered the Board's intended category of classification. When counter-signed by the applicant then the classification certificate is issued. The Board provides an on-screen category card similar to that issued for cinema films. Although the inclusion of such a card is not a statutory requirement, its inclusion in a video is considered to be a means of further assurance to the public that the work has been classified.

Where an applicant disputes the Board's classification as notified in the interim clearance form it may be resolved by informal discussion with officials of the Board. If the dispute is not settled an applicant has a right of appeal within 42 days of the receipt of the written notice of the Board's decision to the Video Appeals Committee in accordance with the procedure as prescribed.

A classification certificate is a legal requirement and so should be kept by an applicant as evidence that a work has been classified. The certificate specifies the title of the work, the classification given, the registration number in the Board's register and date of registration, the precise running time of the approved version, and a list of its component parts if these are individually named. A classification certificate is valid for a video only in the form in which it has been classified so that if subsequently the work is varied or changed by the deletion of material or insertion of additional material the new version will, unless submitted to the Board, be an unclassified work and so be in breach of the Act.

Offences and Exemptions

The Act provides that it is an offence for anyone to supply a video recording of a work without its bearing a classification certificate unless either the video work is an "exempted work" or the supply of a video recording is an "exempted supply." Supply for the purposes of the Act embraces not only sale and hire but also exchange and loan whether or not for reward.

The definitions are material to the application of the Act and should be noted:

A "video work" means—any series of visual images (with or without sound) produced electronically by the use of information contained on any disc or magnetic tape and shown as a moving picture.

A "video recording" means—any disc or magnetic tape containing information by the use of which the whole or a part of a video work may be produced.

A video work is an exempted work if taken as a whole—

(a) it is designed to inform, educate or instruct;

(b) it is concerned with sport, religion or music; or

(c) is a video game.

A video work is not an exempted work for the above purposes if to any significant extent it depicts—

(a) human sexual activity or acts of force or restraint associated with such activity;

(b) mutilation or torture of, or other acts of gross violence towards humans or animals;

(c) human genital organs or human urinary or excretory functions;

or if it is designed to any significant extent to stimulate or encourage anything falling within (a) above, or, in the case of anything falling within (b) above is designed to any extent to do so.

Section 3 of the Act defines "exempted supplies." In summary these are, for example, where the supply is neither for reward nor in the course of or furtherance of a business; where the supply is for exhibition in cinemas and other places licensed by a licensing authority as explained earlier in this section, or for broadcasting by the BBC or the ITC; where the supply is in the ordinary and normal course of the actual production and processing of video recordings. Other exemptions include video recordings supplied for medical and related uses.

Subsection 5 of the section caters for the private or home movie in that a supply is exempted where the supply is of a video work which is a record of an event or occasion for persons taking part in the event or occasion, or are connected with the persons taking part in the event or occasion recorded. The exemption is conditional on the video work not breaching to any significant extent the basic tenets noted above regarding sexual activity, violence, etc.

The issue whether a video work is an exempted work, or a supply is an exempted supply is a question of law and therefore to be decided by the courts. These are not in any way issues for determination by the Board. Furthermore it needs to be borne in mind that it is not only entertainment videos as such which are subject to the Act; a trailer, advertisement and music video are self contained works and so fall within the Act.

The Act does not require premises and places where video recordings are sold or hired to be licensed by local authorities. By an amendment to the Act by the Criminal Justices Act 1988 the enforcement of the Act is vested in a Local Weights and Measures Authority combined with the powers granted under the Trades Descriptions Act 1968 which confers powers on officials to make test purchases and to enter premises and inspect and seize goods and documents. In addition, section 17 of the 1984 Act empowers a justice of the peace on being satisfied by information given on oath that there are reasonable grounds for suspecting that an offence under the Act has been or is being committed on any premises, and that evidence that the offence has been or is being committed is on those premises, may issue a warrant authorising a constable to enter and search the premises within one month from the date of issue of the warrant. A constable may seize anything found on the premises which may be required to be used as evidence in any proceedings for an offence under the Act.

Various offences are created under the Act to secure the observance of its provisions, adherence to the rules on classification and the labelling of video recordings, and to prevent the falsifying of a classification certification, including falsification by altering a video work after the issue of a certificate. In addition to penalties by way of fines, the courts have power to forfeit video recordings.

F. MUSIC AND DANCING AND ENTERTAINMENT

Until 1982 the licensing of premises for public entertainment was the responsibility of local authorities or local licensing justices. With the enactment of the Local Government (Miscellaneous Provisions) Act 1982 and in line with the legislation governing the licensing of theatres and cinemas a consistent system of licensing was established for England and Wales. The licensing powers and procedures adopted under the 1982 Act were pre-dated by the London Government Act 1963 which, as amended, provides for the licensing of public entertainment in the Greater London area. As there are only minor differences between the 1982 Act and the legislation specific to the Greater London area in so far as they relate to entertainment licensing in the following comments reference is made only to the 1982 Act. The licensing of public entertainment in Scotland is considered separately at the end of this section.

The licensing of public entertainment is prescribed by section 1 of the 1982 Act but the operative provisions concerning what and when premises and places are to be licensed, the licensing procedures and the powers of entry and enforcement are all contained in the first schedule ("the Schedule") to the Act. The requirement for any premises or place to be licensed depends on the kind of entertainment provided and where it is given.

No public dancing or music or any other public entertainment of a like kind may be provided at any place except under and in accordance with the terms of a licence granted by the licensing authority for the area in which the place is situated. This rule does not apply in the following circumstances—

"(a) to any music performed in a place of public religious worship, or if performed as an incident of a religious meeting or service;

(b) to an entertainment held in a pleasure fair; or

(c) to an entertainment which takes place wholly or mainly in the open air."

A place of public religious worship means "one which belongs to the Church of England or to the Church of Wales (within the meaning of the Welsh Church Act 1914), or one which is for the time being certified as required by law as a place of religious worship."

The fact that no charge is made for admission to the entertainment, or that the premises or place are used only occasionally for an entertainment does not dispense with the need for the premises to be licensed. Whether the entertainment is given by professional or amateur performers is also immaterial.

The music performed can be of any kind and performed by any number of persons. If in place of performances by musicians actually present the music is provided by means of a broadcast or wired relay, or by the use of pre-recorded audio-tapes, juke-box or disco record apparatus (with or without the services of a disc-jockey) that does not avoid the need for the premises to be licensed in accordance with the Act unless the following applies.

By section 182(1) of the Licensing Act 1964 premises which are licensed for the sale of intoxicating liquor are exempt from the requirement for a music licence under the 1982 Act, provided the entertainment is restricted to the relaying of radio and television broadcasts, or to the mechanical reproduction of music, or to performances by not more than two persons or sometimes in one of these ways and sometimes in another. A combination of recorded sound and one or two live performers playing at the same time—as for example with "karaoke"—would appear to breach this concession so that in such cases the premises would need also to be licensed under the 1982 Act.

When music video-tapes are used in the course of public dancing or musical entertainment then being film exhibitions within the definition of the Cinemas Act 1985 the premises will also need to be licensed under that Act. This is because as remarked earlier, licences granted in accordance with the various enactments are mutually exclusive and for only the particular kind of entertainment specified. However, provided the video-tape exhibitions are incidental to the main activity carried on at the premises and are merely to accompany the dancing then usually the terms of the licence and in particular the technical regulations will be less stringent than those imposed for premises licensed as cinemas.

Dancing may be dancing which is performed before an audience—ballet, chorus, small groups or solo—or performed by the public present such as ballroom and disco dancing. In cases before the courts it has been held that a school of dancing is not required to be licensed where the public are not admitted. Music performed at an ice skating rink to which the public are admitted has been held to come within the scope of the Act so that the premises needed to be licensed.

Public entertainment is not defined but the words have to be construed in their natural and ordinary meaning. Public lectures, addresses and political speeches can hardly be considered as entertainment; they may be amusing. Performances by comedians, conjurers and acrobats, "Punch and Judy" shows, circuses and exhibitions of hypnosis are within the intendment of the Act. Entertainments such as displays or contests of boxing, wrestling, judo, karate and other indoor sports are subject to separate licensing rules under the Act but as amended by the Fire Safety and Safety of Places of Sport Act 1987.

In the exercise of their licensing powers licensing authorities are empowered to make regulations prescribing standard conditions setting out the terms and conditions and restrictions of general application which will be deemed to apply to a licence unless expressly excluded or varied at the time its being granted, renewed or transferred. Where such regulations have been made a licensing authority must make them available to the public on payment of a reasonable fee.

The waiver noted at (c) above of the need for a licence for entertainment which takes place in the open air has been much curtailed by the fact that most local authorities have adopted the special powers exercisable under paragraphs 3 and 4 of the schedule. These paragraphs provide that public musical entertainment held wholly or mainly in the open air on private land may not be given except in accordance with a licence granted by the appropriate authority. A licence may be granted (or renewed) only in respect of one or more particular occasions at the place as specified in the licence.

A licence granted under these special powers may be on such terms and conditions and subject to restrictions imposed for all or any of the following purposes but no others: to securing the safety of performers and other persons present at the entertainment, to securing access for the police and emergency services, to ensure the provision of adequate sanitation, and to prevent persons in the neighbourhood from being unreasonably disturbed by noise.

There are a few additional points concerning the application of these two paragraphs of the schedule to be noted. It is provided that "entertainment is musical if music is a substantial ingredient". Land is private "if the public has access to it (whether on payment or otherwise) only by the permission of the owner, occupier or lessee." These special powers do not apply to "a garden fete, bazaar, sale of work, sporting or athletic event, exhibition, display or other function or event of a similar character, whether limited to one day or extending over two or more days, or to a religious meeting or service, merely because music is incidental to [the event]."

Licensing Procedures and Enforcement

The procedure for applications for the grant, renewal or transfer of a licence, the powers of local authorities to prescribe the terms and conditions upon which licences are to be granted, and the powers of enforcement of the licensing law correspond closely with the rules for theatre and cinema licences. There must be given 28 days' notice of an application for the grant, renewal or transfer of a licence and it must be given to the local district council of the area wherein the entertainment is to take place, and to the chief officer of police and the fire authority. Information as required by the licensing authority must be supplied by an applicant and the licensing authority is enjoined to have regard to the observations made by the police and fire authorities respecting an application.

A licensing authority is empowered to prescribe reasonable fees for the grant, renewal or transfer of entertainment licences. It is also empowered to remit the fees otherwise chargeable where a licensing authority is of the opinion the entertainment is of an educational or other like character or is given for a charitable or other like purpose. Fees are not payable if an application is for a licence for an entertainment at a church hall, chapel hall or other similar building occupied in connection with a place of public religious worship, or at a village hall, parish or community hall or other similar building.

Licences are normally in force for one year unless a shorter period is prescribed, or the licence is only for one or more particular occasions. During the period a licence is in force application can be made to the licensing authority for a variation of its terms. If during the period of a licence the holder dies the person carrying on the functions at the place licensed is deemed to be the holder until legal personal representatives of the deceased have been appointed, or the licence is transferred to some other person. When a licence is currently in operation then provided before its expiration application is made within the prescribed 28 days for its renewal (or its transfer to another person), the licence will continue in force (with any necessary modifications) until the application is determined by the appropriate authority or is withdrawn.

If the application for the grant, renewal or transfer of a licence is refused by a licensing authority, or the application for the variation of any term is refused, or if a licence holder is aggrieved by any term, condition or restriction under which a licence has been granted, or if a licence is revoked by the licensing authority, there is a right of appeal to the local magistrates' court within 21 days of the date the decision is notified to the person concerned. An appeal from the decision of the magistrates court may be made to the Crown Court. Where any appeal is pending then a licence remains in force until the appeal is determined or it is withdrawn.

Powers of entry to premises licensed under the Act to ensure compliance with the terms of a licence are conferred on a constable, an authorised officer of the local licensing authority, and an authorised officer of the fire authority; this general power is exercisable only at a time when an entertainment is being or is about to be given at the place licensed. A fire officer by giving not less than 24 hours prior notice to the occupier of a place in respect of which a licence is in force can enter the place to ascertain the adequacy of the fire precautions and to ensure that the conditions of the licence respecting fire precautions are being observed.

A constable or authorised officer of a licensing authority in possession of a warrant granted by a justice of the peace may enter any place which he has reason to suspect is being used for the provision of public entertainment without being licensed for the purpose. The officials making inspections if required to do so by the occupier must produce their authority and any person who without reasonable excuse refuses to permit an inspection to be carried out commits a criminal offence.

If any public dancing, or music, or any other public entertainment is provided at any place in respect of which a licence is not in force, (a) any person concerned in the organisation or management of the entertainment, and (b) any other person who, knowing or having reasonable cause to suspect that such an entertainment would be so provided at the place, either allowed the place to be used for that entertainment, or let or otherwise made the place available to any person by whom an offence in connection with that use of the place has been committed, commits an offence and is liable to severe penalties. If the holder of a licence, or any other person as described in (b) above contravenes the terms or conditions of a licence an offence is committed and such person is liable to a fine. If the holder of the licence is convicted of an offence the licensing authority is empowered to revoke the licence but subject to the holder's right of appeal.

Where a person is charged with any offence as just noted, it is a defence that he took all reasonable precautions and exercised all due diligence to avoid the commission of the offence. Furthermore no offence is committed by using premises contrary to the terms and conditions of the licence if a special order of exemption has been granted under section 74(4) of the Licensing Act 1964 for the premises (or part of the premises) and the use is within the permitted hours on such special occasion or occasions as specified in the order.

Licensing in Scotland

The Civic Government (Scotland) Act 1982 prescribes for the licensing of premises in Scotland used for public entertainment and confers the licensing powers on the district councils and island councils. Even so for the licensing provisions and powers to apply the material section 41 of and schedule I to the Act must first be affirmatively adopted by resolution of a local council.

Section 41 enacts that a licence is required for the use of premises (and it appears also vessels and vehicles) as a place of public entertainment meaning—"any place where on payment of money or moneys worth to which members of the public are admitted or may use the facilities for the purpose of entertainment or recreation." There are detailed exemptions to this general rule as follows:

(a) an athletic or sports ground while being used as such;

(b) an educational establishment within the meaning of the Education (Scotland) Act 1980 and universities and theological colleges;

(c) premises belonging to or occupied by any religious body while being used wholly or mainly for purposes connected with that body;

(d) premises licensed under the Theatres Act 1968 and the Cinemas Act 1985 or Part II of the Gaming Act 1968;

(e) premises in respect of which there is a permit under section 16 of the Lotteries and Amusements Act 1976 while being used in pursuance of the permit;

(f) licensed premises within the meaning of the Licensing (Scotland) Act 1976 in which public entertainment is being provided during the permitted hours within the meaning of the Act;

(g) premises in which machines for entertainment or amusement are being provided incidentally to the main purpose or use of the premises where that main purpose or use is not a place of entertainment.

The detailed rules set out in schedule I to the Act about the making of applications, the conditions attaching to licences, the powers of entry on premises and penalties for the breach of a licence or using premises without one when a licence is required, correspond closely with the rules described with regard to licensing in England and Wales; but there are important differences and refinements. For example, the times within which a local authority must consider an application for the grant or renewal of a licence and reach a final decision are prescribed; if a decision is not reached within these times the application is to be deemed to have been approved. The procedure for making and hearing applications is laid down in precise terms including the requirement for a notice of the making of the application to be displayed on the premises concerned for 21 days and for objections to be submitted in writing.

Although a general discretion is conferred on local authorities in the exercise of their powers regarding the conditions and restrictions upon which a licence is granted, the schedule is explicit about the matters to be noted and considered—how an activity is to be conducted, the character of the persons who will manage the activity, the location of the premises, the number and persons likely to use the facilities, nuisance and public order.

Normally licences are granted for three years unless a shorter period is prescribed by the licensing authority. Appeals concerning the refusal of the grant or renewal of a licence, the terms imposed or the revocation of a licence lie to the Sheriff within 28 days of notice of the decision. A right of appeal on a point of law can be made to the Court of Session.

Private Places of Entertainment

To complete the topic of licensing premises used for public entertainment it is necessary to mention the Private Places of Entertainment (Licensing) Act 1967 as amended by the above main 1982 Act. The 1967 Act has no application to any area unless it is adopted by a district council; it does not apply to Scotland.

The 1967 Act requires premises used, apparently on any occasion, for dancing, music or any other entertainment of the like kind which is not a public entertainment but is promoted for private gain to be licensed. This requirement is avoided where:

(a) the premises are licensed under the 1982 Act for public dancing and music, and the private entertainment takes place during the hours permitted by the "public" licence;

(b) the premises are licensed premises, or are a licensed canteen within the meaning of the Licensing Act 1964, or are premises in respect of which a club or other body is registered under Part II of the Licensing Act 1964;

(c) the premises are licensed under the Theatres Act 1968 or are used for an entertainment which is provided there for the purpose of being broadcast for general reception;

(d) the entertainment is promoted by and for the general benefit of a society or an association or club which is not established or conducted as a commercial undertaking, or is established for the purpose of participation in or support of athletic sports or athletic games.

Although the Act has received scant recognition and could be regarded as superfluous in view of the scope of the legislation considered above and the licensing of premises under the Licensing Act 1964, its operation must not be overlooked in those areas where it has been adopted by a local authority.

G. THE TERMS AND CONDITIONS OF LICENCES

All the enactments which have been considered conferring licensing powers provide that licences may be issued by licensing authorities on such terms and conditions and subject to such restrictions as may be thought fit, or words to that effect. To supplement the comments made at the start of this Part 9, the following is an indication of the criteria adopted by the courts in their examination of the reasonableness and fairness or validity of the conditions imposed by licensing authorities.

Local Authority Responsibility

Parliament has conferred on democratically elected local councils the task and responsibility for administering these Acts so that local circumstances, local knowledge, local needs and local opinion or wishes can be taken account of in considering applications of one kind or another and deciding on the terms and conditions upon which licences are granted. The courts will not substitute their opinion or views for those of a licensing authority unless the decision is so far-fetched and so unreasonable as to be unsupportable. Their role and function is to see that the powers conferred on licensing authorities are properly exercised in accordance with the relevant statute and the general law and that all matters material to the issues under review have been given due weight and that nothing extraneous has been allowed to affect a decision.

There is nothing in the enactments which requires an applicant to show affirmatively his bona fide intention to carry on the activity for which a licence and permission are sought. The fitness of the applicant to hold a licence and the suitability of the premises are properly matters of enquiry but if no objections can be made on either of these counts, then within the bounds of their discretion it is open to a licensing authority to grant the application on such conditions as they may think fit.

The making of a general rule respecting the terms on which licences will be granted has been held to be an abdication of the very discretion conferred on a licensing authority. The distinction between a rule and a policy may be a fine one but it is not open to a licensing authority to make decisions by rule of thumb. Every application is required to be considered on its merits in the light of a proper hearing and the opportunity given to an applicant to show why a policy may not be applicable in a particular case, or that the terms and conditions proposed are inappropriate to the case. By the same token because a licence has been regularly renewed without question or any variation of its terms that does not itself prevent the making of changes by a licensing authority if the changes can be justified although this may result in a loss of business. It has been held that a licensee has a legitimate expectation that a licensing authority will act consistently and fairly when the renewal of a licence is sought. In such circumstances a licensing authority must review the whole situation and give rational reasons for its decision, that is, reasons properly relevant to the grounds for refusing the renewal of a licence.

In granting licences an authority has no power to limit or restrict activities which are lawful and do not require to be licensed. Thus to purport to prohibit the mere spoken word (as distinct from rehearsed or contrived dialogue which may constitute a play within the meaning of the Theatres Act 1968), in a licence for music and dancing would lie outside the powers of a licensing authority. On the other hand a theatre licence may be granted on condition that there shall be no sale of intoxicating liquor despite the concession allowed by the Theatres Act 1968. A licence for music and dancing, or for film exhibitions may be granted but only on the condition that no application is made for a licence to sell intoxicating liquor on the premises. Because of the powers of inspection and supervision conferred on licensing authorities and the police, the condition that a licence is to be held by a named person as the representative of a company or association rather than by an impersonal legal entity appears to be valid. Restrictions on the hours when children under a specified age may be present at an entertainment and whether or not accompanied by an adult have variously been upheld. A total bar on the admission of children to Sunday entertainments has been held to be valid.

Because a condition is included in a licence which exceeds or is contrary to the powers vested in a licensing authority that does not totally invalidate or nullify the licence. The control which the Lord Chamberlain exercised over the performance of plays was abolished by the Theatres Act 1968 and so a licensing authority has no right or power to impose any terms or conditions or restrictions as to the content or manner of performance of plays which may be performed under a theatre licence, an authority's powers being confined to matters of physical safety and health and the control of exhibitions of hypnosis.

Under the licensing legislation local authorities are legally entitled to promulgate rules of management and technical regulations for places of public entertainment as they see fit. In the past there have been divergences between licensing authorities in their requirements which has often been a source of inconvenience and needless expense especially to touring companies. In recent years as the result of joint consultation between representatives of local authorities, the professional institutes and the Home Office, guide-lines on fire precautions and related matters have been adopted and so brought about a greater uniformity in the technical regulations.

Health and Safety Legislation

Places of entertainment are also places of work and so the Health and Safety Executive plays an important part in the co-ordination of the rules of management. In this connection after consultation with representatives of employers and employees within the broadcasting, film and video production, theatre and allied sectors of the entertainment industries the Executive has set up a new Joint Advisory Committee to be known as the Broadcasting and Related Industries JAC. The Committee is to serve as a forum for the discussion of the application and implementation of health and safety legislation, to disseminate information and promote good practices in the industry and to raise the concerns of the industry with manufacturers, suppliers and installers of equipment used in the industry.

Rules of General Management

The following is a brief outline of the kind of matters covered by the rules of general management and the technical regulations for places of entertainment prescribed by most licensing authorities.

The general rules of management apply according to the particular circumstances and provide for: the hours of opening and closing of premises; the identity of the person to be in charge of and responsible for the premises; the maintenance of good order and conduct and the avoidance of nuisances or undue inconvenience to the immediate neighbourhood especially by the amplification of music; the suitability, display and content of poster advertisements, photographs and programmes displayed or sold; overcrowding; the inspection and certification of ceilings; the use of scaffolding and plant when carrying out repairs and maintenance to the premises when remaining open to the public.

More particular and precise rules cover: the keeping of entrances clear and still more so all exits, gangways and corridors free of obstruction and notices about exits of sufficient size and prominence; the arrangement of closely-seated audiences and seating plans of premises not regularly used for a closely-seated audience; the general arrangements for and the marshalling of audiences, *i.e.* standing enclosures, waiting and queuing areas; fire precautions and the assignment of duties to be performed by members of the staff; fire drill and the recording of the holding of fire drills and the inspection of appliances generally; the storage and standards of fire prevention risks required for scenery, properties, curtains and furnishings; the provision of dressing rooms and staff rooms and sanitation.

Special conditions may apply to entertainment especially for children as distinct from entertainment which may particularly appeal to children, for example, pantomime. Even with pantomime and other entertainments, if children are likely to comprise the greater part of the audience the duties imposed by the Children and Young Persons Act 1933 will need to be observed.

With theatres and other premises used for stage presentations it is a usual condition of a licence that not less than seven days prior notice in writing is given to the licensing authority of the date on which a production will first be presented and publicly performed. This is in order that, if considered advisable, an inspection can first be carried out by the licensing authority to check the safety to the public of any part or aspect of the performance. Where any action in the course of a production takes place or extends into the auditorium—flying wires and the like—additional safety precautions may be prescribed. The use of materials and equipment for special effects, and of explosive and highly inflammable substances are subject to special regulations. Additional rules may apply to premises having a separate stage when prescribed in the technical regulations.

The general rules of management are extended and amplified for premises used for film exhibitions. The technical regulations made under section 4 of the Cinemas Act 1985 referred to in Section D above are automatically incorporated and the rules concerning children's attendances at cinemas. These comprise rules for the admission of children by barring a child under five from a children's film exhibition, and barring a child under seven to any cinema exhibition unless in either situation the child is throughout the exhibition accompanied by an adult bona fide in charge of the child. The sale or consumption of intoxicating drinks is not allowed on premises during film exhibitions. This restriction may not apply if the exhibition forms only a small part of the entertainment and the sale or consumption of intoxicating liquor is not otherwise prohibited by the conditions attaching to the licence for any other kind of entertainment at the premises.

H. SUNDAY ENTERTAINMENT

Of the many Acts of Parliament affecting entertainment there is perhaps none which for so long has been a source of controversy and argument as the Sunday Observance Act 1780, for despite reforms it remains the basis of the restrictions on Sunday public entertainment. With its quaint yet somehow resourceful language—section 2 begins: "And whereas, by reason of the many subtle and crafty contrivances of persons keeping such houses, rooms or places as aforesaid it may often be difficult to prove who is the real owner or keeper thereof," the Act is not easily avoided by devices such as increasing the prices of refreshments on a Sunday, concealing the identity of the "keeper" of the premises or obtaining payment for tickets by subscriptions or contributions. The principle of the Act of 1780 is that no house, room or place is to be opened and used for public entertainment or amusement or for publicly debating any subject to which persons are admitted on payment or by tickets sold for money. "Place" has been widely construed so that where a motor cycle scramble was held in a park, that part which was set aside for the event was held to be a "place." The increasing of prices on a Sunday for food and refreshments is deemed to constitute payment for the purposes of the Act.

The persons held to account and the extent of their liability is according to their involvement in the event and the order of culpability is the keeper of the premises and the ostensible keeper, the person who is conducting or managing the entertainment or acting as master of ceremonies, the moderator or president or chairman of a meeting or debate, the doorkeeper, servants and other persons who collect or receive money for tickets, and the person advertising or causing any of these events to be advertised.

The Act being prohibitive is construed strictly, so that if the entertainment is not public but is private the payment of money for admission will not make it unlawful. Accordingly performances at Sunday theatre clubs and the like, dances, dinners and such functions for which a charge is made are not within the Act so long as the public are not admitted. If the Sunday entertainment or amusement is open to the public but no charge is made for admission there is no infringement of the Act, but it may be a condition of a licence where one is required by law that the entertainment shall not take place on a Sunday or only under special conditions. If the activity can be said to fall outside the scope of entertainment or amuse-

ment then even if there is a charge to the public there can be no infringement of the Act. There is no statutory definition of public entertainment
or amusement but the Sunday Entertainments Act 1932 removed the
ambiguity to the extent of enacting that no offence is committed under the
1780 Act by persons who manage, conduct, or otherwise take part in or
attend any museum, picture gallery, zoological or botanical garden or
aquarium, or any lecture or debate.

Sunday Entertainments Act 1932

Cinemas were first allowed to be opened on a Sunday by the enactment of
the Sunday Entertainments Act 1932 but now section 9 of the Cinemas Act
1985 governs the use of premises and the exhibition of films on a Sunday
in England and Wales. If a licensing authority has licensed the premises
for film exhibitions under section 1 of the 1985 Act it is empowered to
allow them to be opened on a Sunday on such terms and conditions as it
thinks fit. Provided premises are so licensed then no person can be guilty
of an offence under the Sunday Observance Act 1780 by reason of his
having managed or otherwise been concerned with any film exhibition at
the premises.

There is an overriding condition prescribed by section 9 of the 1985 Act
which attaches to any such licence as it affects employment. No person
may be employed by any employer on a Sunday in connection with a film
exhibition, or any other exhibition or entertainment given with a film
exhibition, who has been employed on each of the six previous days by
that employer in any occupation, or by any other employer in connection
with similar exhibitions or entertainments.

The section allows for emergencies such as where staff are required on
account of the illness of a skilled person or the breakdown of equipment
and no alternative or substitute person is available. The circumstances
must be reported to the licensing authority within 24 hours of the occurrence, and the employee given a day's rest in lieu of the Sunday worked.
It is also provided that there is no contravention of the condition if an
employer having made due enquiries had reasonable grounds for believing an employee had not been previously employed as to lead to a breach
of the condition. If there is a contravention of any of the conditions under
which a licence for Sunday film exhibitions is granted the holder of the
licence is liable to a fine but a licensing authority is not empowered to
revoke the licence.

The Sunday Entertainments Act 1932, which applies only to England
and Wales, also relaxed the restrictions on the giving of musical entertainments. The licensing authorities which have authority to license premises
kept or ordinarily used for public dancing, singing, music or other public
entertainment of the like kind are by the Act also empowered to grant

licences on terms as they may decide for musical entertainments on a Sunday. Musical entertainment is defined as "a concert or similar entertainment consisting of the performance of music, with or without singing or recitation." It has been held to be an infringement of the Act for an artist to deliver patter and imitations with special piano accompaniment for Lord Chief Justice Goddard remarked in a case in 1953 that "If a music-hall artist is sent on stage to give an entertainment consisting really of patter, than merely because there is somebody at the back of the stage playing a piano ... that entertainment cannot by any stretch of imagination be called a musical entertainment in the nature of a concert."

Sunday Theatres Act 1972

When the Theatres Act 1968 was enacted no alteration was made to the law concerning Sunday performances but the Sunday Theatres Act 1972, which applies only to England and Wales, in effect waives any offence under the Sunday Observance Act 1780 by persons who are concerned in the performance of a play on a Sunday at premises which are licensed under the Theatres Act 1968 or by authority of letters patent. The 1972 Act does not in any way alter or add to the powers of licensing authorities over the granting of licences under the Theatres Act 1968 but it does provide that premises are not to be used for the public performance of any play on a Sunday between 3 a.m. and 2 p.m. if the premises are in the inner London area and between 2 a.m. and 2 p.m. elsewhere. The public must be clear of the auditorium by 2 a.m. and not admitted before 2 p.m. If there is any breach of these conditions the holder of the licence or letters patent is liable to a fine or imprisonment or both. There are no statutory rules about the employment of persons at theatres on a Sunday in the way as applicable to cinemas under the Sunday Entertainments Act 1932.

Conclusions

It follows therefore that entertainment which continues beyond midnight on a Saturday and is of a kind within the Sunday Observance Act 1780 is unlawful unless there is some exempting legislation. The public performance of a play after midnight on a Saturday would appear to be exempted so long as the performance ceases before 3 a.m. in the Inner London area and 2 a.m. elsewhere by reason of the provisions of the Sunday Theatres Act 1972. As for cinematograph exhibitions, subject to observing the provisions of the Sunday Entertainments Act 1932 concerning the employment of persons on a Sunday there is no statutory bar to late night Saturday performances continuing into the early hours of Sunday

Even so a licensing authority may impose a restriction or condition about late Saturday night performances.

With public dancing, singing, music and other like entertainment which continues after midnight only where the premises are already licensed for any of these purposes in the ordinary way and are also licensed under the Licensing Act 1964 and for which a special hours certificate has been granted, can the entertainment continue into the early hours of a Sunday. The granting of the special hours certificate under the 1964 Act removes any infringement of the Sunday Observance Act 1780. In any other circumstances any such kind of entertainment which continues beyond midnight on a Saturday which is public and for payment would conflict with the 1780 Act unless it were strictly a musical entertainment and a licence for such entertainment on a Sunday was also in force. If the entertainment were public but without payment still it could not continue beyond midnight on a Saturday unless it were solely a musical entertainment as a licensing authority has no power to license any other form of entertainment under section 3 of the Sunday Entertainments Act 1932.

In Scotland the licensing of Sunday entertainment at theatres, cinemas, concert halls and other public places is subject to the discretion of the licensing authorities under their general powers in accordance with the principal licensing enactments.

Part 10

PREMISES AND PEOPLE

A. AGREEMENTS FOR THEATRES AND HIRE OF PREMISES

THEATRE AGREEMENTS

The agreement made between a theatre management and a production company for the use of a theatre can perhaps be regarded as a compromise of their somewhat separate interests. A theatre management is concerned to maximise the use and income to be derived from the ownership of a fixed asset and the profits to be had from the ancillary services which are part of the business of theatre management. When a theatre is "dark" recurring expenses of rates and general maintenance continue and the blight of prolonged periods of closure can lead to the loss of prestige. Accordingly the choice of productions such as will attract and serve local needs and maintain local goodwill rests on the judgment of a theatre management which will therefore be concerned about the content, style and quality of a presentation, the star attraction and publicity attaching to it, the number of performances and the box office appeal.

A non-resident production company on the other hand has a rather different approach as inevitably its interest in a theatre is transistory compared with its concern to ensure continuity of performances and profitability for a particular production. The standard of general management for a theatre, its local standing and scope for publicity, its technical facilities, its seating capacity, and its potential box office revenue are of prime concern to a theatrical producer as it is from a producer's share of box office takings that running expenses—salaries, hiring charges, travel and subsistence, royalties—must first be paid and then the capital cost of a production recouped. The gradual adjustment of these respective interests of managers and producers has led to there being a fairly common form of theatre agreement. It has to be said that its terms rather favour the management but then that is no different from most other situations where owners let or hire out their premises or property.

A theatre agreement does not confer on the production or touring company any legal rights or interests in the theatre. It may be that misguidedly words are used such as a "letting" or "lease" of the premises, but the use of such formal expressions will not alter the fundamental legal character of the relationship of the parties namely that of licensor and licensee. Seldom in the making of a theatre agreement is it intended to create the relationship of landlord and tenant with all the legal consequences which ensue from that relationship.

By the making of a theatre agreement there is granted a licence or permission to use premises (or parts of premises) for particular purposes at particular times and on certain specified conditions. If the licence is revoked by the theatre management without justification and in breach of the agreement then the production company, that is the licensee, will be entitled to sue for damages as for the breach of any other contract. If an improper revocation or other material breach of a contractual licence is threatened the party affected may take proceedings to obtain from the courts an injunction or order for specific performance to prevent the threatened action. So too if the terms are imprecise or incomplete the courts will within the very limited discretion they allow themselves to imply terms in an agreement, seek to give effect to the presumed intention of the parties. If for example no provision has been made specifying the period of notice either party is to give to the other to terminate a contractual licence, then a period of notice will be implied of such length as in all circumstances the court considers fair and reasonable.

Some of the factors which are likely to affect the content and terms of theatre agreements are considered below, but always it needs to be borne in mind that if one party desires to protect itself from the legal consequences of its inability to perform its obligations, or to cast on a defaulting party liability for some exceptional loss which it may suffer from the other's default, then provisions to meet these situations will need to be mutually agreed upon and made a part of the contract. The occurrence of some event wholly outside the expectation of the parties may discharge them both from their obligations, but because due to some unexpected course of events or circumstances, or even misfortune, it becomes more difficult, more onerous or more costly for one party to perform its undertakings this does not relieve that party of its obligations. The non-appearance of a principal artist, the breakdown of equipment, the non-availability of costumes or stage properties and scenery, the failure of public services preventing the operation or supply of services and facilities to be provided by a theatre management, are examples of happenings which ordinarily will not automatically absolve a party unless there is an express stipulation relieving it from liability.

If there is default by one party then the amount of damages which will be recoverable will only be such sum as fairly compensates the injured party for the loss naturally and directly arising in the particular circumstances. If wider considerations are to apply for the assessment of the amount of the indemnity for the loss, or more extended grounds are to justify the recovery of compensation then these need to be spelt out and expressly stated in the agreement. Thus following these general principles a theatre management will often expressly avoid liability for loss suffered by a production company from the closure of a theatre due to circumstances beyond its control and loss suffered from its inability to provide services and facilities due to circumstances beyond its control.

For the professional stage fairly standard forms of theatre licence agreements exist and those well practised in theatre administration are doubtless familiar with their provisions and the issues which can arise concerning their application. Having noted the underlying general legal principles affecting theatre licence agreements, some of the salient features and matters for possible negotiation commonly encountered are considered in the following paragraphs.

Scope and Duration of the Licence

The essence of most theatre agreements is that the proprietor or theatre management has and retains possession and control of the entire premises, a theatrical producer or other promoter of an entertainment being given permission and licence—but not necessarily exclusively—to use and have access to specified parts of the theatre. The description of these parts may be particular or general and if the latter then the extent of the licence must be construed in the light of the object and purpose for which the theatre licence agreement is entered into. Generally it will be implied that the licence extends to the whole of the stage area, dressing rooms, scenery dock, control boxes or consoles, orchestra pit, green room. If there are special needs such as use of offices, workshops and construction areas, additional storage space, then these extra requirements perhaps need to be provided for in the agreement. Unlike a "fourwalls" agreement where for a rental of the entire premises their running and management are given over to a licensee, the usual theatre agreement confers only the very limited rights of use and access to the particular parts of the theatre as detailed in the agreement, with the management retaining absolute control of the auditorium, bars, cloakroom, house staff and so on.

The times when access is to be given to the theatre may need to be expressly agreed upon especially where the theatre has alternative uses, as for example, film exhibitions or concerts, or when the licence spans a busy season such as Christmas or during a festival when other shows may be presented. Unless a licence is expressed to be exclusive then like the owner of any premises a theatre management is entitled to use the theatre and allow others to do so at times when the theatre is not contractually required to be available to the production company. The use may be for whatever purpose the management may decide so long as it is not in direct conflict or competition with the object and purpose of the agreement made with the production company.

The number and times of performances in a week—and the opening night where this is not at the start of the agreement—need to be specified. If special facilities are required prior to opening, or during a run such as for rehearsals and the like, then provision for these should be made and the liability for the additional house costs made clear.

As most theatre agreements are made with a company or other corporate legal entity constituting the production company, the persons who will come within the scope of the licence to use and have access to parts of a theatre will be those who are the servants, agents, and representatives of the company, and its contractors. This must be so unless the agreement is personal to named artists or performers. Other persons who come upon the theatre premises and who may be connected with the business of entertainment and interested in the production for some reason—authors, union representatives, artists' agents, costumiers, press and public relations representatives—enter more likely with the tacit consent of the theatre management and not strictly by virtue of the theatre agreement. The legal consequences of this distinction are dealt with in Section D below.

The period of time during which a theatre is to be licensed and made available is usually fixed. If the duration of a licence is indefinite but subject to termination on the happening of certain events or to the giving of notice of termination, then the events or length of notice and the manner of service of the notice need to be stated precisely.

Facilities and Services to be Provided

A specification of the stage equipment, lighting and sound systems and other production facilities available may be provided by a theatre management as a matter of business practice. It will be implied, if not expressly stipulated, that the equipment is in good working order and suitable for the purposes intended to the extent that reasonable care and diligence can be expected to reveal defects at the commencement of the licence; but there needs to be an express undertaking that the management will maintain the equipment in good working order and renew it as necessary. To the extent that the equipment is insufficient for the needs of a production then provision must be made to make certain the responsibilities and obligations for providing additional equipment and special effects and for bearing any additional expense. When extra equipment is brought in then wider considerations can arise expecially if it is provided by an outside contractor; special hiring terms may be applicable.

The smooth and orderly turnaround of touring productions may be hampered because of local regulations, the physical and technical resources of a theatre and the particular requirements of a production. With foresight and planning these obstacles of "get in" and "get out" are normally overcome. When exceptional difficulties or hazards may be encountered such as could delay the opening of a production or result in incurring additional costs to avoid such a happening, these contingencies should be provided for in the agreement.

Allied to the provision of stage and other equipment are the services to be provided by a theatre management particularly the availability of stage staff. The personnel required and the bearing of the cost of wages and salaries needs to be clear. Some costs may be apportioned and others set against the share of box-office revenue payable to the production company as for example the excess time worked on "get-in" and "get-out," and additional rehearsals. Also of importance in this context is the demarcation of authority and control over the actual use of equipment. The theatrical producer may give directions concerning the manner and extent of the use of equipment but its actual operation will normally be undertaken by the house staff.

When a performance is to be broadcast or filmed, the theatre management, the production company and the organisation undertaking the broadcast relay or filming need to agree on the facilities required and the obligations of the parties. A specification of the equipment, the arrangements for its installation and removal and its operation should be made clear, and the liability for the payment of any additional services provided or costs incurred by a management. Provisions should made to ensure compliance with safety regulations and extended indemnity insurance cover.

Safety and the Theatres Act 1968

The responsibility for safety and compliance with the statutory laws and regulations governing health and safety at work, the prevention of fire and other hazards and the protection of the public and visitors to theatres and such like places, falls primarily on the theatre management as the occupier of the premises. Thus it is legitimate for a theatre management to lay down rules and procedures and require strict compliance with them in order to minimise both the risk of injury and infringement of the law. Obligations respecting insurance cover are material in this connection but this topic is treated separately below.

As explained in Part 9 above the licences issued to a management under the Theatres Act 1968 are granted subject to detailed conditions of management and technical rules concerned with safety and such like matters. The observance of these conditions is secured by statutory powers of entry and inspection of licensed premises by authorised officials and a breach of the conditions can lead to the loss of a licence. So it follows that the conditions attaching to a licence granted under the Theatres Act 1968 must be reflected in a theatre agreement and a contractual undertaking secured from a production company that it will comply with the requirements of a licensing authority respecting the precautions to be taken against fire and other hazards and any other conditions upon which a licence has been granted in so far as they apply to the conduct of a performance.

Conversely a production company as the person responsible for the organisation or management of a public performance of a play, is entitled to be satisfied that a theatre management is in possession of a valid licence granted under the Theatres Act 1968 for the theatre or other place of performance. If no such licence is in force a production company will be guilty of an offence under section 13(1) of the Act. In the ordinary course of business if no express warranty is given by a theatre management that a licence under the Act is in force for the theatre, then probably such a warranty would be implied but in other circumstances such an assumption might not be supportable. If an express warranty or undertaking is given or could be fairly implied but in fact no licence is in force, a right to damages for the loss suffered by the production company having to abandon the performance would arise. On the other hand, even the giving of an express warranty by a theatre management respecting a licence would not seem to excuse a production company from the offence of giving a public performance of a play in premises not licensed under the Act for the offence is an absolute one and not qualified in any way.

The Performance and the Performers

What is to be performed, the artists who are to appear, the identity of the director, music director and such like creative persons, the numbers of chorus, dancers, and accompanying orchestral musicians, the design, appearance, manner and standard of presentation are all matters which are likely to be fundamental in negotiating a theatre agreement. The extent to which these matters are especially covered in an agreement will rather depend upon the particular circumstances and the policy of the parties making the agreement.

(i) Approvals

When a currently staged production is booked by a management there can hardly be reserved a right of approval of its content and presentation. Rather there is an obligation on the part of the production or touring company to produce the entertainment at the theatre as currently billed, staged and presented; any material deviation from that obligation would constitute a breach of the producer's undertaking.

When a new production is being planned and rehearsed then there may be included in the agreement provisions giving a management a right of cast and script approval, etc., and conferring a right to require the exclusion of a song or speech or dialogue or other material or feature of a production or programme, as a precaution against infringement of the Theatres Act 1968 and claims for legal liability such as defamation. Even so such provisions need careful scrutiny to ensure there is no scope for abuse of the right of approval or veto in a way which goes beyond their legitimate object. To overcome the problem of doubts or disputes arising as to whether any material to be performed does or might infringe the Act or otherwise expose either party to legal liability, a provision can usefully be incorporated whereby both parties agree to take professional advice and to accept the advice tendered.

(ii) Copyright Licences

For public entertainment the possession of licences from copyright owners for the public performance of literary, dramatic and musical works is essential and therefore undertakings respecting the granting of licences where works are in copyright and the payment of royalties due are important provisions of a theatre agreement. Where a licence is required for the public performance of a play, a musical play, opera or operetta the responsibility for procuring the licence and paying the royalties will usually rest on the production company.

When musical items are to be publicly performed live or by means of records or tapes either as programme material or simply as theatre overture, interval or the like background music, then ordinarily such performances will come within the scope of the licences which a theatre management should hold and warrant it has from the collecting societies which represent the owners of copyright music and records. When the musical works to be performed do not come within the scope of a management's regular licence from the Performing Right Society then it should be a condition of the theatre agreement that the production company or other user of the premises will provide a proper return of the music performed and pay the royalties due.

(iii) Union Agreements and Legal Matters

A mutual undertaking by a theatre management and a production company to observe the minimum working conditions and rates of pay in accordance with the various collective agreements between the management associations and the entertainment Unions can be fairly implied as a term of a theatre agreement, if not expressly stated. The Employment Act 1990 does not bar collective agreements but makes unlawful a refusal to employ a person on account of his not being a member, or refusing to become a member, of a trade union. When additional chorus or accompanying orchestral musicians or stage extras are needed and recruited locally their rates of pay and conditions of employment will usually be in accordance with the applicable collective agreement.

If the whole or an excerpt of a performance is to be broadcast or filmed or recorded, the prior approval of the performers and others concerned must be obtained. This is most likely to be the concern and responsibility of a production company or promoter and in compliance with the terms of the Union collective agreements. Moreover, without the consent of a performer any such action is an infringement of the rights conferred on performers under Part II of the Copyright, Designs and Patents Act 1988 as outlined in Part 5 above. The right is personal to a performer and is not limited to professional performers. There is nothing in the 1988 Act to suggest a person may be liable as an aider and abetter for the infringement of a performer's rights. If in the attempt to prevent illicit or "bootleg" recordings of performances, a manager inserts in programmes or displays a notice drawing attention to the rights of performers, it can hardly be doubted that no blame could attach to a management for such recordings.

When children are to perform the circumstances may be such that a valid licence may be needed in accordance with the Child Performance Regulations as outlined in Part 5 above. The licence should be applied for by a producer or promoter but a theatre management should be aware of the powers of entry of officials of local authorities and of the police to ensure compliance with the law concerning performances by children and young persons and the conditions attaching to a licence.

(iv) Barring Clauses

As both parties to an agreement have an interest in the maximisation of box office revenues, restrictions may be sought to be imposed by one party on the activities of the other. To be enforceable a restriction should be no more onerous than is necessary to protect the legitimate interests of a party. Thus there may be imposed an undertaking on a production company or promoter not to present the contracted performance at another place within a specific radius of the theatre within a specified time. Conversely, a theatre management may be required to undertake not during a stated period of time to present or permit the presentation of a production of a kind as would compete with the production company's presentation.

Publicity and Promotion

The general arrangements for the publicity and promotion of a production ought to be agreed so that responsibilities can be clearly assigned and costs controlled. The extent and content of advance publicity, the date for it to be launched, the medium of publicity, the date when copy is required and approvals given to bills and programmes if a right of approval is reserved by a management, are matters which according to the circumstances may need to be settled between a theatre management and a production company.

The form and layout of billing and programmes may often be conditioned by the credit obligations undertaken in contracts with artists, authors and other persons contributing to the production—including perhaps the backers or sponsors. Where these contractual obligations have been entered into they must be followed through and reflected in agreements with theatre managements, programme compilers and publicity contractors. Copyright clearances may be required for the inclusion of photographs, synopses, reviews and other material in programmes and souvenir books. The sale of programmes and souvenir books will normally form part of the business of theatre management so that if any costs or revenues are to be shared or commission paid provisions about these matters need to be incorporated into the theatre agreement.

Special provisions may also need to be included for other matters such as receptions, charity performances, previews, critics and opening nights and front of the house displays of photographs, quotes from critics reviews, record albums, books and so on.

Box-office and Accounting

As the agreement between a theatre management and a production company is essentially a business transaction, the provisions regulating the control of revenues and expenditure, the keeping of accounts and the sharing of box office receipts need to be exact for in their application lies the measure of the fulfilment of the enterprise—apart from any aesthetic or cultural objectives. Normally all front of the house activities and the proceeds from these are exclusively reserved by a theatre management so the only source of income or revenue of concern to both management and producer is that received at the box-office.

A theatre agreement usually stipulates that the theatre management is to manage and control the box office and receive all payments made for admission to the theatre. This implies the acceptance of obligations and responsibilities by a management as was remarked upon in a recent case before the court. In the course of the judgment it was stated:

"The contractual undertaking of a theatre management to run and manage the box office imports the obligation to run it efficiently by providing a reasonable standard of service to the production company, ticket agencies and the general public. That is a standard below perfection. Allegations of inefficiency raise issues of scale and degree since the occasional failure to deal promptly with enquiries or isolated mistakes in the form of double booking especially at peak times do not constitute inefficiency."

It is important to understand that the monies received at the box office belong to the theatre management; they are not received by a management as the agent of the production company or as a trustee. The legal consequences of this are that the payments due to the production company in accordance with the terms of the theatre agreement are but ordinary debts owed by the management.

A production company has no preferential rights or claims over other creditors of the management although it will very likely be relying on the payment of its due share of box office takings to meet its obligations, such as the payment of artists' and musicians' salaries, royalties and other expenses of production and the recoupment of capital outlay. Thus provision needs to be made for the rendering of weekly statements of box office takings and running expenses and for the prompt payment to the production company of the net amount of takings due. A producer should have access to the records and accounts to be audited at the end of a run.

Most often a theatre management will retain the sole right to fix seat prices and therefore the amount of the total revenue (less VAT) which can accrue from one or a week's performance can be ascertained. Against this figure may need to be set allowances for house seats or other like concessionary or complimentary tickets, agency commission, special rates for previews and block bookings—all of which ought to be provided for in the theatre agreement.

Many of the detailed provisions of a theatre agreement will inevitably be reflected in the accounts and financial results of a production, as the deductions which can be made or set off by a theatre management from the box office takings can be only those items of running expenses of the theatre and of the production which it has been agreed shall be deductible. For example, stage expenses and salaries of stage staff and overtime paid for extra rehearsals and for "get-in" and "get-out"; advertising, printing and promotion expenses; front of house expenses, salaries and house costs for lighting and heating; the cost of premiums for additional insurance cover where needed. When by arrangement a theatre management makes payment of production expenses on behalf of a production company—artists', musicians', and stage management staffs' salaries, author's royalties, hire charges for scenery, sets, costumes, properties and the like—these payments will need to be reflected in the weekly statements and the outlay set off against the share of box office revenue due to the production company.

A guarantee of minimum box office takings given by either of the parties to the other may be a term of a theatre agreement. It may be given by a theatre management to induce a production or touring company to perform at a theatre. In these circumstances a management can fairly make the guarantee conditional on being supplied with a detailed break-down of a company's weekly operating costs as normally it will only be the amount of these costs which will be guaranteed. If the box office takings fall below this figure the amount of the difference combined with the total of the theatre's weekly running expenses will be the true loss to a management.

Conversely the guarantee may be given by a production or touring company in order to continue the run of a production despite poor attendances and to defer a management's notice of termination when there is a short fall in box-office takings beyond a fixed number of consec-utive weeks. Moreover, often to underwrite the financial obligations of a production company another individual or company may be joined as a party to the theatre agreement as guarantor of the payment of the guaran-teed sum and any other costs, expenses or liabilities recoverable from a production company, as where for example a theatre management bears the costs of salaries and fees for artists, musicians, etc., when a producer defaults.

It is perhaps especially when a production runs into a loss that the terms of a theatre agreement are most earnestly considered whereas the time for a critical examination is at the making of the agreement. The circumstances and conditions which are to exist for either party to be entitled to call on the other to honour an obligation of guarantee need to be most carefully drawn both in legal and accounting terms: what items of cost are to be brought into account, the limits on expenditure on particular items, the party to bear particular costs. The weekly statement or "contra" account must reflect the provisions of the theatre agreement and show the crediting of receipts and the debiting of expenses allowed or admitted and the balance then apportioned and/or carried forward in the way as stipulated in the agreement. The number of weeks of notice of termina-tion on either side should be fixed: the break even figure or minimum box office receipts to be maintained to prevent notice being given need to be specified or capable of being indisputably calculated. If a shortfall in box office receipts is allowed then the number of consecutive weeks which may elapse before notice can be given should be specified and how the resulting cumulative deficit is to be recouped and recourse had to guaran-tees need to be made clear in the agreement.

The precarious state of the theatre and the need to make provision for losses should not totally inhibit the contemplation of profit and provision being made for its sharing. A theatre management's participation in profits is likely to rise only where there is a long run of a production and then the sharing is usually of the profit accruing to the production com-pany and not the theatre management. When a theatre agreement con-fers on a theatre management an entitlement to participate in the profits of the production, accounting provisions must be included to secure first the recoupment of capital costs and management expenses incurred by the production company as well as the running expenses. In addition to the profits derived from the presentation at the particular theatre, the profits or net revenues arising from any transfer or tour of the production and from any cast record album, broadcasting or other wider exploitation of the production might also be brought into account.

The foregoing is no more than a general survey of the terms and issues which arise in the negotiation and settlement of theatre agreements. The relevance of some of the points made or the need to introduce and provide for others must depend upon the attitudes and policies of those concerned and the infinite variety of conditions and circumstances surrounding the making of a theatre agreement. Thus the managements in membership of the Society of West End Theatre are required to observe the Society's standing recommendations and these need to be reflected in theatre agreements. The matters covered are, for example the due observance of union agreements, newspaper classified advertisements, press and preview nights and charity collections in theatres.

AGREEMENTS FOR OTHER PREMISES

The legal and commercial issues considered above apply in much the same way to the management of concert halls, dance halls, assembly rooms, community halls and club premises. In many respects the issues apply as much to amateur performances as to professional performances and whether the use and hire of premises is for a period of time or a one night stand.

With arts centres and concert halls the turnover of bookings is inevitably much greater than for the average theatre. Premises may be put to different uses even at the same time in different parts of the premises. Perhaps depending on the prestige of the venue a management may be selective of the kind of entertainment presented and its promoter.

Sponsorship can be a matter of concern as conflicts of interests can arise especially if an arts centre or the like has the on-going support of a local sponsor. The identity and business of the sponsor of an event should be known to a management when the hiring of premises is negotiated, and the form and extent of the publicity to be accorded to the sponsor considered in joint consultation if special facilities are required for exhibitions or demonstrations.

As remarked in Part 9 above, where the system of the licensing of places of entertainment is explained, the conditions upon which licences are granted reflect the regulations of government departments and local authorities which are mainly concerned with public safety and the prevention of fire and other hazards. It is therefore essential for a management to retain paramount rights and powers of supervision of the premises and the general conduct of the entertainments and events presented at a venue. Accordingly licence agreements should incorporate provisions whereby hirers undertake to observe all the rules and regulations appertaining to the entertainment being presented and the regulations governing the use of the premises laid down by the local authority and for a management to be able to take prompt and effective steps if there is a material breach of the undertaking by the hirer. It is crucial for a management not to put at risk the licence granted for the premises and moreover it must ensure that the conditions of the licence are observed otherwise it could be in breach of the conditions of the insurance protection and indemnity and so prejudice any claim.

Very often the organisations and persons hiring premises are not in the business of entertainment and are not alert to the risks and dangers inherent in their activities or generally informed about safety regulations. It follows that a management ought to make full enquiries about the purpose of the hiring and the entertainment being presented with a view to assessing potential risks. This is especially so if stage and other like equipment are to be brought on to the premises and if special effects, lighting and sound amplifiers are to be used. Only exceptionally should persons who are not members of the staff of the premises be permitted to operate equipment likely to cause injury or damage. A management ought also to be satisfied, particularly for discotheques and concerts by celebrity groups that there will be adequate arrangements for maintaining good order on the premises and for the supervision of audiences both on entering and leaving the premises.

If an entertainment is primarily for children the special rules under the Children and Young Persons Act 1933 about the number of children who may be admitted and for the presence of qualified persons to supervise and have control of the children need to be borne in mind.

Central to a hiring agreement is the purpose of the hire for as the licence from the local authority for the premises must be one which covers the kind of entertainment to be provided, otherwise the hiring must be made conditional on a licence being granted. If alcoholic drinks are to be available then the premises must also have in force the appropriate justices' licence under the Licensing Acts. Concert halls and the like do not have the benefit of the concession accorded to theatres licensed under the Theatres Act 1968 whereby the need for a justices' licence is avoided if alcoholic drinks are served during normal licensing hours. The provisions of the Food Act 1990 affecting the supply of food and the requirement for premises to be registered should not be overlooked, as briefly noted in Part 9 above.

Terms of Licence Agreement

A hiring or licence agreement should adequately describe the parts of the premises to which the hirer and public are to have access. The day or period of booking must be specified and in this connection also the days and times when access is to be given for such purposes as rehearsals, the delivery and installation of equipment and the like required for the event or entertainment. What equipment is to be made available and by whom it is to be operated need to be specified, likewise the provision of house staff. Where premises are to be used for music and dancing entertainment, for example for a discotheque, the number of persons to be admitted should be specified.

The charge for the hiring must be clear and when payment is due. An amount may be payable as a deposit on the signing of the agreement and the balance on or before the day of the event or as otherwise stipulated. If the hire charge comprises a fixed sum and a percentage of the box office income, then if costs or deductions are to be allowed these need to be defined otherwise the percentage will be calculated and due on the gross revenues. It may be appropriate to make provision for a right of cancellation by the hirer within a certain time, subject to (or without) forfeiture of the deposit. A management may wish to reserve the right to cancel the hire and terminate the agreement if any instalment of the charges or fees is not paid on the due date. A third party may be joined to the agreement as guarantor for the payment of the hire charges and any other expenses incurred and for the payment of compensation for damage caused to the premises due to the fault or negligence of the hirer and recoverable by the management.

Where box office facilities exist the conditions upon which management will provide them must be precise and clear. The method and times for accounting for box office takings, the right to deduct commission and the rate of commission, and the right of a management to set off all charges and expenses recoverable from the hirer for the use of the premises and the supply of services and facilities before paying over the net box office receipts also need to be covered.

If a management requires a promoter or organisation presenting a concert or other entertainment to include in programmes, posters, advertising and tickets, details of the management and other information, such a requirement should be made an express term of the licence agreement. Similarly if any services are to be provided by a management in the way of front of the house publicity or other display on or about the premises, or by the provision of advertising and mailing lists the conditions on which such services are offered and the obligation of a promoter to deliver the promotional material in due time should be expressly dealt with in the agreement.

When the entertainment being presented includes material protected by copyright, such as a play, musical work, film, record or video recording, it is important that there is included in the licence agreement a warranty by a promoter that the consent of the copyright owners for the public performance of the material has been or will be obtained. Because of a management's potential liability for infringement of copyright it can legitimately require the licence to be produced where one is needed and to look to a promoter for an indemnity for any costs and charges incurred by a management as a result of the breach of the warranty. Where the premises are licensed by the Performing Right Society for the public performance of music in its repertoire the benefit of that licence will normally extend to a hirer. Where a return of the music performed has to be made to the Society a management must require the hirer to supply details of the music performed: similarly with the public performance of records if required by Phonographic Performance Ltd.

B. HIRING AGREEMENTS

As theatrical productions and many other entertainments are often assembled for short periods of time and the places of performance are frequently changing, the use of sets, costumes, properties and much technical equipment is likely to be only temporary and therefore managements and producers have to deal with contracts of hire perhaps almost as much as contracts of engagement. Similarly equipment installed in premises may be hired or "leased"—special plant, sound and lighting equipment, musical instruments, relay equipment, additional furnishings, automatic vending machines, towel and toilet equipment, fire extinguishers. Many enactments of modern times confer rights on and give protection to consumers of goods and services whereas in the past consumers have had to rely mainly on express contractual terms. The Consumer Protection Act 1974 and the Supply of Goods and Services Act 1982 confer rights and provide for certain basic terms to be implied in hiring agreements.

The essence of a hiring agreement is that goods or equipment hired are and remain throughout the period of the hire the property of the supplier. Accordingly most hiring agreements specify the duties of hirers respecting the use, care, handling, maintenance and installation of the equipment coupled with a right for the owner or supplier to have access to the premises where the equipment is to be kept in order to carry out inspections, to service it and to repossess it at the termination of the period of hire or sooner if there is any default by the hirer. The hirer is entitled to assume that the supplier, the person letting out the equipment, is the owner of it or is entitled to make the hiring; also that provided the hirer pays the hire charges or rental and observes his undertakings he can have quiet and uninterrupted possession of the equipment for the duration of the agreed period of hire. If the supplier makes default in either of these expressed or implied undertakings he is liable in damages to the hirer for the loss sustained by his being deprived of the equipment and the expense of obtaining its replacement. Where equipment is delivered to the hirer but is not in accordance with the agreement the hirer must give notice of the default or else he may be deemed to have affirmed the hiring. There is no obligation on the hirer to return the equipment but he should take reasonable steps to guard and protect it from wilful damage or harm until it is repossessed by the owner or supplier.

Implied Terms

In the absence of any express terms there is implied in contracts of hire a warranty that the equipment or goods hired are of merchantable quality, that is, free from defects which reasonable care and skill could reveal, as distinct from latent defects. If the defects are drawn to the attention of the hirer, or if the hirer examines the goods and the defects ought to be apparent on inspection, the term will not be implied. There is no implied term about the fitness of goods for a particular purpose unless in the course of negotiations a hirer expressly or by implication makes known the purpose for which the goods are hired. The term will then be implied irrespective of whether the purpose is one for which the goods are commonly supplied unless the circumstances are such that it would be unreasonable for the hirer to rely on the skill or judgment of the supplier. If a hirer specifies the sound or lighting equipment to be supplied he cannot complain if it does not fulfil his purposes or satisfy his expectations, but he can complain if it is defective or useless because of its faulty construction which reasonable care or skill could have revealed. There is no general implication of law that the supplier of equipment hired will service it for this is a matter of agreement. Such a term is the more likely to be implied when the equipment is installed by the owner, where its construction is especially complex and still more so where there is an express prohibition on the hirer tampering with the equipment.

There is a duty on the hirer to exercise reasonable care and diligence for the safety and protection of the equipment hired and the onus rests on him to show that there was no negligence on his part such as to have led to its loss or damage. The test of reasonableness in this context is objective for it is not enough for a hirer to show that he exercised the same standard or degree of care for the hired equipment as he exercised for his own, but that he exercised the care which in all the circumstances could be reasonably expected. A hirer of equipment is not normally a guarantor of its safe keeping but when it is not in use a hirer should not leave equipment exposed to the risk of deterioration or damage or theft when reasonably prudent action could prevent this.

A hirer has a duty to return equipment to the supplier or otherwise deal with it as directed by the owner at the end of the hiring but there is uncertainty—in the absence of an express term—whether the duty also implies an obligation to return the equipment in the same condition as when hired. Whether "fair wear and tear" can be reasonably regarded as an implied term may depend upon the circumstances of the hiring. The hiring of scenery and costumes must obviously entail greater wear even in the short run than the hiring of a grand piano or sound amplification equipment or an antique or oil painting used on the stage set.

When equipment is defective or dangerous and results in physical damage to other property of the hirer, or causes injury or loss to the hirer, the owner or supplier may be liable under the terms (or implied terms) of the contract. A supplier is not an insurer against all defects but is liable for defects which skill and care can guard against and so liability may arise where there is a failure to exercise this standard of care. The owner may expressly exclude or limit liability on the grounds of negligence or indeed in respect of liability on any basis, but all such exempting clauses are strictly and critically construed by the courts. Moreover, exemption clauses will not avail the supplier against claims by a third party who suffers injury or damage as a result of his negligence if that person comes within the boundaries of the common duty of care which the law imposes on suppliers. The persons likely to come within the bounds of this duty are employees of the hirer and persons reasonably foreseeable as likely to be near where the equipment is installed.

If the owner or supplier does not retain control of the equipment or render any interference with it impossible except by some wilful or deliberate act of another, then he has a duty to warn the hirer of any unusual dangers. When such warning has been given the hirer has the duty and responsibility to warn and prevent harm to third parties. Where the owner hires out his workmen to operate equipment the inference is that he has retained control of it and so the risks and liabilities will attach to him, yet the workmen may be so much under the direction and supervision of the hirer that the inference might not be supportable. The distinction appears to lie between giving directions on where and when equipment is to be installed and operated, and giving instructions about its assembly, operation and dismantling. Even so where workmen are hired out with equipment, the onus is on the owner or supplier to show that his workmen have become the servants or employees of the hirer.

Liability for Breach

If there is a breach of the terms of a contract of hire the party in default will be liable for the damage suffered by the other. If the hirer suffers from the delay or default of the supplier the amount of the damages recoverable will not likely be more than the cost and expense of obtaining the equipment from an alternative supplier. It would require the inclusion in the contract of express undertakings by the supplier for him to be liable for special damages suffered due to his delay or default in the performance of the contract if time is of the essence of the agreement. The loss of box office receipts or profits due to performances having to be cancelled because of the non-delivery or defective state of hired equipment would not generally fall within an award of damages, whereas the direct running costs—theatre rental, salaries, etc., may perhaps come within the calculation of the damages suffered.

Likewise with any default by the hirer, the damages awarded to a supplier will be based on general principles of law. When the hiring is for a term or period and on the basis of the regular payment of hire charges, if there is such a delay or non-payment of rental which amounts to a repudiation of the hiring, then the agreement may be terminated. In this event the supplier is entitled to be put, by the award of damages, in the same position as if the contract had been performed, subject to the duty which the law always attaches to all claims for damages for breach of contract, to take reasonable steps to mitigate the loss. If there is a readily available market or alternative demand for the equipment so that it can be hired out again the hirer will be bound to pay only the actual loss suffered by the supplier. If because of the special design or other special feature of the equipment ordered there is no alternative demand the position will be different and the supplier will be entitled to be put in the position as if the contract had been performed by the hirer.

C. INSURANCE

When the management of any business or owner of premises has to decide upon the contingencies to be covered and the cost of doing so (in the form of premium payments), two dominant issues emerge. First there has to be considered the potential liabilities to third parties on account of the very nature and conduct of the enterprise or ownership of a particular property and the extent to which this liability may be alleviated by insurance. Secondly there has to be considered the amount which an entrepreneur or property owner is prepared to set aside or risk by way of actual loss in order to satisfy claims without recourse to an indemnity from insurers. Nonetheless it has to be borne in mind that by law some insurances are compulsory, such as employers liability insurance.

These general speculations apply to entertainment which can be a hazardous undertaking because of the various conditions and circumstances in which it is provided, the number and kinds of people engaged and the presence of an audience. The risks to be covered and the amount of indemnity required will depend on many factors: whether the entertainment is a single event, a run of a production at one place or on tour and a series of events such as a festival; the likelihood of personal injury or damage to property due to the very nature of the entertainment; the professional competence and professional standing of the persons engaged to perform; the value of the "physicals" used in the production; the terms of the hiring of properties, costumes, etc.; the size and likely conduct of the audience; the investment in the enterprise; the running costs of the production and the consequential loss flowing from a cancellation or postponement of the production. These considerations are crucial for any professional management but some are just as relevant to an entertainment presented by an amateur organisation or society.

The law relating to contracts of insurance is somewhat distinctive from that governing other commercial transactions and so some rudimentary principles need to be noted. The first is that for a policy of insurance to be enforceable, *i.e.* for a claim to be supportable, there must have been a disclosure of all material facts by the insured in answer to the enquiries of the insurer (usually set out in the form of proposal), prior to the issuing of the policy. Facts are deemed material if they would influence an insurer whether to accept the risk at all, or if accepted then on what conditions and for what premium. Once the risk has been accepted an insurer cannot avoid liability under the terms of the policy. However, if circumstances change during the period of the cover so as to increase the risk or there is a material alteration of the conditions under which the risk was accepted and the policy issued, the assured is bound to disclose them; not to do so may jeopardise any claim.

Policies of insurance are contracts of indemnity for loss suffered or liability incurred in certain eventualities which in essence are unwanted or unexpected due to accident, negligence, disaster or some supervening occurrence beyond the insured's control. Loss of or damage to property due to ordinary wear and tear, from something inherent in the thing itself as distinct from something from without, will not normally come within the ambit of insurance cover. Where property is insured against loss or damage that will be the limit of the cover and liability. Nothing will be recoverable for loss of use, for the inconvenience or consequences arising from the insured being deprived of the property unless these consequences are specifically covered in the policy.

Only the actual material loss suffered by the insured will be compensated and this is likely to be assessed upon the market value of the property at the time and place of the loss. This result can be avoided with a policy issued on a full replacement basis, "new for old," when a insurer's liability will be for the cost of obtaining property of a similar quality to that lost, or alternatively where the amount of the indemnity is expressly agreed upon at the time of the making of the policy, meaning a "valued policy." If there is damage as distinct from loss, then the amount of the indemnity will be assessed according to the cost of repair. An insured cannot recover more than the amount or sum of the insurance cover. As for premises insurance, if the property is under-valued then if the insurance policy includes an "average" clause the insured will be deemed to be his own insurer for the amount of the shortfall. This means that if the property has been insured for less than its re-instatement value the insured will not be entitled to recover more than a proportionate part of the loss.

When insurers accept a claim for indemnity they have a right of subrogation, that is, to seek to recover from whoever was responsible, the amount of the loss incurred or the cost of making good the damage suffered. With this right insurers stand in the place of the insured and so the latter is bound to assist the insurers in the enforcement of this right. It is for this reason that there is an obligation on persons insured to make a full disclosure of all matters and circumstances affecting any loss or damage suffered and not to negotiate with third parties any settlement or waiver of the right to compensation otherwise the right of indemnity and recourse of the insurers may be prejudiced.

Ordinarily the compensation payable under a policy of insurance is paid only to the insured so that the sum paid becomes part of the insured's assets. Should it be that the insured is insolvent then the insurance monies would be liable to be seized for the payment of unpaid debts. However, where such circumstances arise the interests of third parties such as members of the public and employees in the compensation paid under a third party liability insurance are protected by the Third Parties (Rights Against Insurers) Act 1930. By this Act if before or after the event which gave rise to the liability the insured becomes bankrupt or makes a composition or arrangement with his creditors, or being a company is wound up (unless voluntarily for the purpose of reconstruction or amalgamation), then all rights of the insured to the compensation recoverable are transferred to the third party.

Theatre Management Insurance

In the usual way of business a proprietor or manager of a theatre concert hall or other premises will have comprehensive cover for the premises against damage or destruction from fire and other disasters and for public or third party liability on account of the Occupiers Liability Act 1957 and the Defective Premises Act 1972 as explained in the following Section. There will usually be included in the policy for the premises cover the stage machinery, lighting, sound and other equipment but there may be a separate and special insurance cover for the heavy theatrical and stage equipment such as the safety curtain, revolving stage and main lighting circuits against not only loss or damage to the equipment itself but also an indemnity for consequential loss due to the operational failure of the equipment.

The contract for the use and hire of the theatre or concert hall or the like will normally impose an obligation on the production company or promoter of the entertainment not to use the premises in such a way as to increase the risk of damage to the premises and equipment or cause injury to persons, or otherwise impair the properietor's or management's right of indemnity from his insurers. If there is a one-off situation on account of the particular nature or hazard from the event or entertainment, or because of the size or type of audience, or the provision of additional facilities on the premises, such as for filming, special cover should be obtained.

Furthermore although usually (but not necessarily so) the stage and theatrical equipment installed on the premises will be covered by insurance of the premises, the equipment, scenery, properties and costumes brought on to the premises by production companies and promoters or their contractors or employees are not likely to come within a management's insurance. The particular kind of entertainment to be presented may affect the cover. Contentious issues over liability can also arise when damage or injury is caused by the negligence or fault of stage or other house staff operating equipment at the direction of a production company or promoter of an entertainment and whether the liability falls to be treated as an employer's liability, or as public or third party liability.

Both theatre management and production companies have an insurable interest in box office takings and other forms of "money" as often defined in a policy of insurance and so should have protection against their loss although the liability will in fact fall where the money rests (as explained above in considering the provisions of theatre agreements). Furthermore because of their joint involvement, both a management and a producer should consider the need to have cover against liability for unintentional defamation, breach of copyright and other such legal liability.

Policies for "consequential loss," meaning loss of profits, may be taken out by a theatre management to cover loss of box office revenues and profits from bars and other usual front of the house activities. The cover is normally assessed on an annual basis and according to whether the revenue is derived from a share of box office receipts or a specific rental. Compensation will be payable upon the happening of any of the usual risks. A special indemnity insurance may also be had for loss of profit or revenue due to performances not being given on account of such causes as failure of public services, the failure of the safety curtain or such like equipment and a compulsory closure or "denial of access" due to government intervention or national event. The period in respect of which the indemnity is given can vary according to the particular occurrence which is covered. For fire or other major damage resulting in a long period of closure the indemnity may be for a period of 18 months or two years, whereas the indemnity period for the loss of performance due to the failure of the safety curtain could be counted in days.

Producers' and Promoters' Insurance

The insurance cover needed by a production company or promoter of an entertainment will depend very much upon the type of entertainment provided and the size of the enterprise. The risk of damage and liability to others arising from the presentation of a regular "straight" stage play, club variety performance, or ordinary gig or concert performance is not likely to be as great as from the presentation of a theatrical spectacular, a production with technical effects, a production supported with amateur performances, a pop festival, tournament or carnival. Similarly the amount of cover for loss or damage to property, scenery, costumes, properties, equipment and musical instruments will also depend upon the particular circumstances. The needs of a touring theatrical or ballet company or symphony orchestra for insurance cover are likely to be greater than those of a small company of performers, an ensemble or a group of singers or musicians.

The distinction between a contract of employment and a contract for services has been considered in earlier parts of this study and an instance of the significance of this is to be found in the context of insurance law. When artists, peformers, stage management, production, road staff and the like are contracted as employees then insurance must be effected in accordance with the requirements of the Employers Liability (Compulsory insurance) Act 1969. Where persons such as leading artists, international celebrities and directors, for example, are engaged then separate contracts of indemnity for liability arising from any injury illness or death they may suffer during or arising from their engagement may need to be negotiated.

As the management of theatres, concert halls and the like usually expressly disclaim liability for any loss suffered because of the closure of the premises due to causes outside their control, insurance indemnity for a producer's or promoter's financial loss may be prudent. The loss particularly to be considered is that arising from the outlay incurred to meet the running expenses and continuing outgoings in order to keep a production going during a period of interruption or until a production is terminated or abandoned. Where there is uncertainty about the length of a run the period of cover for this kind of loss is likely to be short. Insurance protection for running expenses should also be considered where a production is being toured to meet any contingent liability due to delayed opening because of late delivery of scenery, etc., as well as cover for actual loss or damage to the "physicals" in transit.

Protection for the financial consequences of the postponement or cancellation of a production or entertainment through accident, illness or other misfortune befalling performers, or an unexpected happening may be essential because of commitments entered into with others. Where a galaxy of stars is cast for a production if one star drops out for any reason and is replaced by an understudy the loss may not be so acute as public support may not be so much affected; where a production or lavish spectacular is built around a single star the position is likely to be very different. Where an entertainment of whatever kind is a single event and rests on the appearance of a particular performer or group, the financial loss ensuing from the collapse of the production or non-appearance of the star attraction may be such as to need to be underwritten by insurance. Where cancellation or non-appearance insurance is taken out both management and producer can insure for the loss of their respective shares of box-office takings but normally the amount of an insurer's indemnity will be based on box-office records or a reasonable forecast of takings. Often with cast insurance there is a two day excess for illness but with non-appearance from other causes the indemnity applies immediately.

Another risk which may need to be covered is the loss of the capital outlay expended on a production. Capital costs and investment in the setting up and rehearsing and preparation of a production can be colossal yet due to some disaster or supervening event a production could fail to open and have to be abandoned. The risk covered is solely a "prior to opening" risk and serves to protect investor's money so that a single premium will be negotiated and payment out of the insurance money will be due only in the events covered. This situation must be distinguished from the cover given against the risk of postponement or interruption of a production when the amount of the insurance will be based on the likely running costs and not the capital cost of the production.

Artists performing solo or in groups should have regard to third party liability especially if there is an element of danger in their act or performance. Liability due to the defective state of equipment needs to be borne in mind particularly by musicians and variety artists using electrical and other potentially dangerous equipment. Insurance cover for loss or damage to the personal belongings of performers, to their equipment, costumes, musical instruments as well as personal insurance against their injury, illness or accident is also of concern to the freelance and independent performer. Equity and Musicians' Union both have insurance schemes to meet these contingencies.

D. LIABILITY FOR INJURY TO PERSONS AND DAMAGE TO PROPERTY

The risk of accidents occurring at places of entertainment causing personal injury and liability to pay compensation, coupled with potential liability for damage to property are matters of concern to any responsible management or owner of premises. The legal ramifications can be considerable because of the innumerable circumstances which can arise and affect claims. First the premises used for entertainment range from a theatre or arts centre to a local community hall and the entertainment can be of many kinds. Secondly these premises are "public" in the sense that all kinds of persons may lawfully enter and remain on them for different reasons or purposes—as a paying or non-paying member of the audience, as a mere enquirer at the box-office, as a performer, as a member of the house staff, as a contractor or employee of a contractor engaged to render some service on the premises or make a delivery of supplies, or as an official to carry out an inspection. Thirdly, consider whose act or omission to act may be the cause or indirect cause of an injury or damage suffered—the management of the premises, an employee of the management, an artist or other person performing at the premises, an independent contractor, or other persons legitimately or perhaps improperly on the premises.

These are but examples of the kinds of considerations which can arise and because of their complexities it will perhaps be understood why no simple statement of the law of liability is possible. What follows is offered as an indication of the legal issues likely to emerge when claims are made or defended for personal injuries or damage to property, particularly those arising from loss suffered due to the state of premises or happenings on premises.

Occupiers' Liability Act 1957

The law governing the liability of occupiers and others for injury or damage resulting to persons or goods lawfully on land or other property underwent a major reform by the passing of the Occupiers' Liability Act 1957. The Act did not make radical changes to the substantive law but removed some anomalies and established one single common duty of care. The Act does not contain any concise definitions of "occupier," "premises," or "visitor," but on the contrary retains the rules of the common law as to their meaning and application. The defences to claims for alleged breaches of the duty of care such as contributory negligence, assumption of the risk and the giving of warning remain unaffected. Thus a mere reading of the Act alone will do little to enlighten the reader about the liability or entitlement to claim damages.

Liability for injury to persons—and to a lesser extent for damage to property—suffered due to the defective condition of premises, or due to things done or omitted to be done on premises, rests primarily on the occupier. An owner is not necessarily the occupier and very often a chain of landlord and tenant relationships may be interposed between the freehold owner of the property and the person in actual possession and occupation. The fact that an owner or superior landlord has an obligation to repair and maintain property does not make such a person the occupier. The test which the common law has evolved to identify an occupier is to establish who is in control of the premises; who it is who can decide and know what persons may come on to the premises; who it is who knows, or ought to know, of the state of the premises so as to be aware of dangers whether concealed or not and can remedy them, or who can at least take steps to give warning of danger to those who are invited onto the premises or are likely to enter them.

Control denotes power to admit or exclude persons from premises but this power may not exist where possession is not exclusive, as with premises in multiple occupation when common parts are retained by a landlord and a number of leases are given in respect of separate parts of premises. In such situations where foyers, corridors, stairs, lifts and lavatories remain in the possession of the owner of the premises, under the Occupiers' Liability Act the duty of care owed to persons who lawfully enter and use the common parts is cast upon the owner or landlord of the premises. This factor of control is very important where only parts of premises are given over as with theatre agreements, concert hall lettings, the setting aside and licensing of an area or a booth for serving refreshments or for the sale of books, records, etc. In all these kinds of situations the question arises whether or not the person in possession of the premises has effectively divested the control of them. Where only a licence to use premises has been given as with the hire of a dance hall or concert hall for a precise purpose and at specified times, the licensor cannot be said to have divested control. Likewise where a licence to use parts of premises is given either for a definite or indefinite time as with theatre agreements or an agreement permitting the setting up of a booth or the like. Usually the very essence of all such agreements is the retention by the owner or leaseholder of control and supervision and management of the entire premises.

Duty of Care

The duty of care prescribed by the Act is in respect of the occupation of premises but the meaning of premises has received a wide interpretation by judges. Thus it has been defined as "a term which embraces places and structures of all sorts on which persons may be invited to come." Obviously the term includes land and buildings in the ordinary sense and the fixtures attached to property, but the term has also been held to include less permanent structures such as a grandstand, scaffolding, staging—and even a diving board. In all these instances there has been a fair degree of annexation or securing of the structure to the land or building. Section 1(3) of the Act expressly extends liability to persons "occupying or having control over any fixed or movable structure."

An occupier of premises does not necessarily occupy or possess the chattels on them so as to render him liable for any injury or damage suffered by any use made of them. Thus fine distinctions may emerge over liability, for example, for fixed or movable seating, temporary staging which is put up by contractors in a hall or at a fête or festival, and equipment and plant installed on premises. The significance of many such refinements and distinctions is to apportion primary and secondary liability and to enable recourse to be had to alternative sources of indemnity on alternative grounds of liability.

The duty of care owed to all lawful visitors is defined in section 2(2) of the Occupiers' Liability Act 1957 as "a duty to take such care as in all the circumstances of the case is reasonable to see that the visitor will be reasonably safe in using the premises for the purposes for which he is invited or permitted by the occupier to be there." An important feature of the statement of the duty is that it applies only in respect of a person's presence on premises for the purposes for which he is invited by the occupier to be there. A member of a theatre audience who goes back stage, a visitor to a club who goes into the kitchens or service areas, a visitor to a gallery who enters a storage place (by way of random example) would not generally be on those particular parts of the premises by invitation of the management. However the courts have been very indulgent towards persons who have gone astray in search of a lavatory, but on the other hand they have not been lenient where persons have abused their use or presence on premises as where instead of walking down a stairway a person slides down the bannister rail. Also material to deciding whether a person's presence on premises is legitimate is the time or duration of the visit.

Trespassers

Persons who enter premises unlawfully, as trespassers, cannot complain if by doing so they suffer injury. However, as trespassers are not necessarily rogues the Occupiers Liability Act 1984 casts on occupiers a duty of care towards the uninvited. The duty is to prevent a trespasser suffering injury from a danger on the premises of which the occupier knows, or ought to know, and the risk is one which in all the circumstances it is reasonable to expect the occupier to take precautions to prevent. Dangerous machinery, exposed cables, building repairs and the like, need to be fenced. The equipment and paraphernalia especially of the business of entertainment are an allurement and attract the duty of care, but not one of total assurance, against injury being suffered by a person who is just curious—*i.e.* a trespasser.

Compliance with Duty

Whether the common duty of care has been observed and performed is very much dependent on the facts and circumstances of a particular case. As the leading textbook on the law of tort (Clerk & Lindsell on *Torts*) succinctly summarises the problem:

> "In determining whether what was done or not done by the occupier was in fact reasonable, and whether in the particular circumstances of the case the visitor was in fact reasonably safe, the court is free to consider matters that have proved relevant in the past such as the obvious nature of the danger, warnings, lighting, fencing, the age of the visitor, the purpose of his visit, the conduct to be expected of him and the state of knowledge of the occupier."

Occupiers are not insurers of the safety of visitors for it has frequently been acknowledged that visitors themselves must keep a reasonable look out for their safety. The gravity of risks involved may have to be weighed against the work to be done or the activity or purpose of a visitor's presence. Yet the fact that there never has been an accident, that what is done (or not done) is common practice is not necessarily a sufficient answer to an allegation of a breach of the duty of care. Broken glass is obviously dangerous and there is a duty to see it is swept away once the danger is perceived, but if a glass is knocked from a bar counter and smashes and at the same time a visitor falls and in doing so by mischance cuts his hand on the glass there is not necessarily a breach of the duty of care on the part of the occupier. So too where premises are rendered unsafe by the acts of vandals such as the removal of light bulbs and so on.

The circumstances may be such that no negligence can be attributed to an occupier if he has kept a reasonable lookout and inspected the premises for possible hazards. Some guidance on this kind of problem is to be found in a judgment of the High Court when it was remarked: " 'Reasonable care' involved consideration of the nature of the danger, the length of time that the danger was in existence, the steps necessary to remove the danger and the likelihood or otherwise of injury being caused."

The scope of the duty of care and the need to take extra precautions according to the presence of special circumstances or persons who need to be considered, is underlined by the 1957 Act which expressly requires occupiers to be prepared for children to be less careful than adults; this reflects the decisions of the courts which have recognised that children are susceptible to being allured by natural childish curiosity into dangers which adults would avoid. Places of entertainment are obviously open to this kind of added risk. Conversely the 1957 Act expressly recognises the situation of persons being on premises in the exercise of their special skills. Persons carrying out maintenance work or performing some technical services are expected to appreciate and guard against any special risks ordinarily incident to the exercise of their particular calling. Thus an electrician must be alert to faulty wiring and so on but not necessarily to a concealed trap or hidden danger not reasonably to be expected to be encountered in the course of his work.

The duty of care may be discharged by giving warning of danger but then the adequacy of the warning is apt to be questioned. A mere notice may not be sufficient for the circumstances may justify additional measures, such as extra lighting and fencing. Merely to give notice of a hole in the ground or of defective stairs is not likely to be a sufficient performance of the duty of care to guard against injury.

What is particularly to be borne in mind is that the duty of care cannot in the ordinary way be delegated to others. However, the 1957 Act covers the situation where, as with highly technical plant and equipment which requires expert attention for its construction and maintenance, the occupier must rely on others for the effective discharge of the duty of care. So the 1957 Act absolves the occupier from the liability if a qualified and competent contractor has been engaged to carry out the required work and a visitor suffers damage due to the neglect or fault of the expert in carrying out the work. Even so, it is still encumbent on the occupier to show that he used care in the selection of a competent contractor and took such steps as reasonably ought, to satisfy himself that the work had been properly done. The obvious examples are the maintenance and repair of lifts, safety curtain, stage mechanism, boilers and heating apparatus. If regular inspections are not carried out or action taken to see they are carried out or if defects become apparent then the occupier clearly has the duty to take steps to give warning of possible danger or even eliminate the use of whatever may give rise to the risk of injury.

Duty to Third Parties

In the past where the owner of property granted a lease of premises to a tenant for a term of years and was neither in possession nor occupation of the premises no duty of care was cast on the landlord by the common law towards his tenants' visitors. Section 4 of the 1957 Act first changed this rule and section 4 of the Defective Premises Act 1972 has brought about further drastic reform in the law. Where premises are let under a tenancy which puts on the landlord an obligation to the tenant for maintenance or repair of the premises, the landlord also owes a duty to all persons who might reasonably be expected to be affected by defects in the state of the premises, to take such care as is reasonable in all the circumstances to see that they are reasonably safe from personal injury or from damage to their property caused by a "relevant defect." A relevant defect is defined as meaning "a defect in the state of the premises existing at or after the material time [meaning broadly when the tenancy commences or possession is acquired if earlier] and arising from, or continuing because of, an act or omission by the landlord which constitutes or would if he had had notice of the defect, have constituted a failure by him to carry out his obligations to the tenant for the maintenance or repair of the premises."

The duty is owed if the landlord knows of the defect as the result of being notified by the tenant or otherwise, or if he ought in all the circumstances to have known of the defect. There may be a chain of leases respecting the premises but that does not affect the liability of an intermediate or superior landlord who has undertaken the obligation to maintain and repair the premises. Moreover the provision applies where the relationship of landlord and tenant rests only on agreement for a lease or tenancy agreement, or on a tenancy at will or on sufferance, as where a tenant holds over and continues in occupation after the expiration of the term of the lease.

Section 4 of the 1972 Act further extends the liability of a landlord to third parties where premises are let under a tenancy which expressly or impliedly gives a landlord a right of entry to carry out any maintenance or repair. This liability arises from the time the landlord is first in a position to exercise the right of entry to make good the defect which he knows about by notice or otherwise. In such circumstances if the tenant fails to carry out his repairing obligations the landlord cannot shield himself from liability to a third party, but the legal obligations as between the landlord and the tenant remain unaltered.

In its general application section 4 of the 1972 Act therefore attaches to landlords who undertake to maintain and repair premises a duty of care not only to the tenant but to all persons who might reasonably be expected to enter or use the premises. However the section does not relieve the occupier of the common duty of care. If there is a defect or risk of injury the tenant/occupier still has the duty to take reasonable steps to prevent harm and to give warning of danger in the ordinary way. The section does not alter the fundamental principle and shift the duty of care to the landlord but rather it affords the person who suffers injury an alternative party from whom to seek redress. Where either the landlord or the tenant is in breach of his obligations, the one may have a claim against the other for an indemnity for the amount of the damages awarded and paid to the injured third party.

Extent of Liability

The Occupiers' Liability Act 1957 has not altered the common law rules respecting the kinds of damage for which an occupier in breach of the duty of care is responsible. Certainly the liability extends to personal injury and to the personal effects of the injured person, but the extent of the liability for damage to property alone on the grounds of the breach of the duty of care (as distinct from liability on other grounds such as nuisance) is uncertain. With the main exception of a landlord's duty and liability towards third parties as explained above, the Act does not create liability where none existed before. The common law has never placed on an occupier of premises as such, liability for the theft of a visitor's property, for example where permission is given, or can be presumed, to leave a car or cycle in an area, and it is difficult to see how liability can attach for mere damage to property. As will be seen in Section G different considerations arise where property is received by a person not as occupier of premises but as a bailee of goods.

Contract Terms and Conditions

Contractual relationships can materially affect the question of an occupier's liability. In the first place, where an occupier contracts with another and the performance of the contract necessitates the other party entering or having access to the premises, it is open to the occupier to lay down special terms and conditions respecting the use of the premises and thereby limit his duty of care and the extent of his liability for any injury or damage the other party might suffer resulting from his being on the premises. Even so the limitation of both the duty and the liability can only be as between the actual parties to the contract for, by the provisions of section 3 of the 1957 Act, the occupier is prevented from relying on special exempting provisions of a contract to avoid the statutory duty of care owed to persons generally and who are "strangers" to the contract. However, if by the terms of the contract the occupier has undertaken duties towards the contractor greater than the common duty of care then the "strangers" to the contract can also take advantage of those special terms and obligations.

These rules are material to contracts engaging theatrical companies, visiting orchestras, and performers in many situations. If the contract made by a management being the legal occupier of a theatre or concert hall or club premises purports to limit liability to the theatrical company or promoter of an entertainment this limitation cannot prejudice the rights of the individual artists or performers as they are not a party to the contract. But if by the terms of the contract greater obligations are undertaken by a theatre or other management being the occupier of the premises, these obligations benefit not only the theatrical company or promoter but also the individual artists or performers whose services are being supplied.

Until recent times owners and occupiers of premises—apart from a few very special exceptions—have had complete freedom to decide upon the terms and conditions upon which persons may enter and use their premises. The changes in the law about the duty of care owed to visitors and especially as just noted in regard to "strangers" to a contract reflect society's awareness that in modern times and conditions this total freedom is no longer acceptable. The freedom may be justified where the parties are on equal footing or where the circumstances or use of premises are exceptional but in the vast majority of situations there is no negotiation about the terms and conditions of access or use of premises. On entering a theatre or other place of entertainment one does not stop to negotiate such matters. A ticket of admission may constitute a written contract but then often terms will need to be implied as respects the matters here under consideration or perhaps the ticket holder will be referred to a detailed written statement of terms and conditions of admission. Be that as it may, where the contract is silent as to the duty of care and responsibilities undertaken by the occupier respecting the premises, then by section 5(1) of the 1957 Act it is to be automatically implied that the occupier has undertaken to observe the common duty of care. This provision is further made to apply to fixed and movable structures as it applies to premises and so highlights what has been said above about grandstands, stages and the like.

With the passing of the Unfair Contract Terms Act 1977 avoidance of the general duty of care is rendered still more difficult. One of the objects of this Act is to control a person's power to exclude or restrict his liability both contractually or on the basis of negligence arising in the course of business. In other words the liability or duty arising (a) from the occupation of premises used for business purposes by the occupier, or (b) from things done by a person in the course of business—whether his own business or another's business.

A person cannot by the terms of a contract or notice given to persons generally or to a particular person, exclude or restrict his liability for death or personal injury resulting from negligence. Claims or liability for damage or loss suffered to property, to goods and to chattels may be excluded or restricted but the term or notice of exclusion must be judged by the criterion of reasonableness according to the particular circumstances. Included in the 1977 Act are guidelines by which to apply the test of reasonableness: the bargaining strength of the parties, the inducement to accept the terms and whether knowledge of the excluding terms can fairly be imputed to a customer.

The 1977 Act further provides that it is immaterial whether any liability in negligence, that is any breach of the duty of care, arose from an inadvertent or intentional act or arose directly or vicariously, meaning due to the fault of another. Furthermore where a contract or notice purports to exclude or restrict liability for negligence a person's agreement to or awareness of it is not of itself to be taken as indicating his voluntary acceptance of any risk.

Liability for Activities

The Occupiers' Liability Act 1957 deals with liability due to the state of premises "or to things done or omitted to be done to them." This alternative has led to the questionable conclusion that because an occupier has the power and authority to control or supervise what is done on the premises he is therefore under a duty of care to persons respecting all the activities taking place on them. In other words the Act applies not merely to the physical condition of the premises but also to the activity carried on there. The activity might be that of the occupier or of a third party such as a touring company, a visiting troupe or group or performer. Any liability arising from an activity might alternatively rest simply on the grounds of negligence and a breach of the general duty of care.

The genesis of the modern concept of legal liability for negligence is to be found in the classic—even hallowed—statement of Lord Atkin in a case before the House of Lords in 1932 when he said:

"The rule that you are to love your neighbour becomes in law, you must not injure your neighbour; and the lawyer's question, Who is my neighbour? receives a restricted reply. You must take reasonable care to avoid acts or omissions which you can reasonably foresee would be likely to injure your neighbour. Who, then in law is my neighbour? The answer seems to be—persons who are so close and directly affected by my act that I ought reasonably to have them in contemplation as being so affected when I am directing my mind to the acts or omissions which are called in question."

Liability for acts or omissions cannot of itself arise unless there is proof of actual injury or damage which is the result of another's failure to take the care or take the precautions which can reasonably be expected having regard to the foreseeability of the risk of injury being suffered.

Like the liability which is cast on an owner or occupier for injury suffered from a failure to maintain and repair premises so too under the 1957 Act, liability may be cast on the occupier for injury suffered due to the activities of other persons carried on at the premises. The technicalities are considerable and perhaps best left to the insurers and the lawyers as leading authorities have variously argued whether the Act which decrees a statutory duty of care has displaced liability on the grounds of negligence as noted above. The issue is apt to be further complicated and confused where a contractor who is admitted to premises to engage in some activity is required by the occupier to undertake to indemnify him for damages and claims arising from any fault or wrongdoing by the contractor. A few instances of liability to members of the public in the context of entertainment may help to shed light on the extent of the problem.

An actor who was a member of a touring company which was engaged by the lessee of a theatre, in the course of his act fired a pistol and in so doing a loose cartridge was also discharged which hit a member of the audience. As the lessee knew that firearms were to be used the court held that there was an obligation on the lessee to take reasonable care that the pistols were so loaded as not to be dangerous. The court ruled that the lessee of the theatre owed a duty of reasonable care to see that members of the audience were not exposed to unusual dangers which he either knew of or ought to have known of. But the court also commented that the obligation on the lessee did not necessarily impose on him a liability for every unexpected act of negligence on the part of one of the actors. Each case rests very much on its facts and so this case can be contrasted with another where a dancer's shoe flew off and hit a member of the audience and it was held that there had been no negligence particularly as the performance was not intrinsically dangerous.

The earlier case is also instructive as in the course of his judgment Lord Justice Bankes remarked:

> "It seems obvious to me that the duty of an invitor in a case like the present is not only confined to the state of the premises, using that expression as extending to the structure merely. The duty must to some extent extend to the performance given in the structure, because the performance may be of such a kind as to render the structure an unsafe place to be in whilst the performance is going on, or it may be of such a kind as to render the structure unsafe unless some obvious precaution is taken. As an illustration under the latter head I would instance a case where a tight-rope dancer performs on a rope stretched over the heads of the audience. In such a case the provision of a net under the rope to protect the audience in case the performer fell seems so obvious a precaution to take that in the absence of it the premises could not be said to be reasonably safe."

A more recent case involved the death of a spectator at a motor racing meeting and where the court held in favour of the organisers of the meeting on the grounds that they had given by display warning of the dangers and clearly disclaimed liability for any injury or damage howsoever suffered. (Note that the cause of action arose before the passing of the Unfair Contract Terms Act 1977.) It was stressed that people may well take risks by attending events such as motor racing or taking part in dangerous activities but people do not take on the risk of injury due to the defaults of organisers or promoters of dangerous activities. If there is negligence then there is liability. But if everything is done which is reasonable in the circumstances then visitors to premises attending an event cannot complain and hold organisers liable for any injury they may suffer, as where at a motor racing meeting a car crashes and flies into the air and falls in to a crowd kept back to a distance from the track as is prudent.

This case can be contrasted with one when a spectator at an ice hockey match who was standing in the aisle next to the side boards suffered an eye injury caused by an ice hockey stick. As the risk of injury was foreseeable then side boards of a suitable height or other protection should have been installed. As a consequence of the failure of the management to take this precaution the spectator suffered injury and so was awarded damages.

E. THE RISK OF NUISANCE

In the preceding Section attention has been focused on the liability of an occupier for injuries suffered by visitors to the premises. Other grounds of liability can arise from the ownership and occupation of property but a consideration of all these would go beyond the scope and purpose of this study. However, as one potential cause of liability, namely common law nuisance, is very relevant to the business of entertainment a brief explanation of the principles applicable is appropriate.

Everyone is entitled to do on his own land or property anything which does not interfere with other persons in the ordinary enjoyment of life or the ordinary modes of using property. Inevitably there has to be a balance struck between the right of one person to do what he likes on his own land and the right of another not to be deprived or restricted in the use and enjoyment of his property. A nuisance is not excused because the activity pursued by one occupier is beneficial to the public, or no other place can be found where it can be carried on. Similarly an occupier cannot on account of some extraordinary or special requirement of his trade or business, or due to some susceptibility, prevent another using his property in a lawful manner or restrict another in his use and enjoyment of his property. The conflict of interests can be demonstrated from two contrasting situations. Where premises were used as an experimental laboratory and its activities carried on were affected by external noise and vibration, an adjoining occupier of premises could not on that account be restrained from the ordinary use and enjoyment of his property. But where a trader regularly parked large vans outside his premises but in such a way as also to block the entrance to the adjoining cafe which resulted in the cafe proprietor suffering a loss of customers, the trader was held liable for damages as he had no right in the pursuit of his business to cause a nuisance to an adjoining occupier of premises. Only by agreement between the persons affected, or by virtue of some statutory power, can a person be deprived of the use and enjoyment of the amenities of his property by another.

Nuisance as Applied to Entertainment

Applying these principles to the entertainment business it follows that no legal action can be maintained because due to the legitimate and proper use by the occupier of adjoining premises rehearsals and performances in a theatre or studio may be affected. Conversely, theatres and other premises used for entertainment must be managed and conducted so as not to cause a nuisance to occupiers of adjoining properties. Queues which cause obstruction and prevent access to adjoining premises have been particularly disliked by the courts; queues must be controlled by the theatre management and not left to be supervised by the police. On the other hand, the courts have clearly acknowledged that it does not necessarily follow that because some activity or event attracts a large crowd it is therefore a nuisance. Because people congregate to look at an attractive shop window display or the arrival of a celebrity that does not make these activities a nuisance; and if people go in large numbers to a place of entertainment, a circus or a boxing contest for example, this does not make these events a nuisance. However, the nuisance can arise from the action of crowds which can fairly be anticipated and if brought about by or directly attributable to the way an enterprise is conducted or managed; hence the attitude of the courts to queues. Another example is of proprietors of club premises who were held to have caused a nuisance by arranging and continuing events and entertainments into the small hours although nothing illegal or improper as such was being done or carried on at the premises. When club members and guests left the premises they regularly caused considerable annoyance and disturbance in the neighbourhood and this was judged to be directly attributable to the way the club was managed. Rather like issues of negligence, the determination of issues of nuisance depend very much on the particular facts of a case.

Where by the act or omission of an occupier of premises physical damage, for example from flooding or explosion is inflicted on another's property, an action for common law nuisance will be supportable but liability may alternatively rest on rules of law of strict liability for the "escape" of dangerous things. Liability for nuisance more often arises from a continuous state of affairs, where by the act or omission of an occupier there is an unreasonable and substantial interference with another's use and enjoyment of his property and as a result of which he suffers damage or loss. The reasonableness of a person's conduct is very material to proving, or perhaps disproving, the existence of a nuisance, and it will be judged in the light of such considerations as the time, duration and frequency of the occurrences causing the nuisance, the extent of the operations or activities being carried out, the means used to avoid or minimise the nuisance or disturbance and whether the act although trifling in itself is done maliciously. Building operations are notoriously a nuisance but they do not constitute actionable nuisance if all reasonable skill and care are taken to avoid annoyance and injury. Rehearsal room activities and violin lessons can be an annoyance to neighbours but they are not a legal nuisance if conducted and managed with due consideration for adjoining occupiers, particularly as to the time the rehearsals or lessons begin and end.

There is no catalogue of nuisances but noise, vibration, encroachment, offensive odours, noxious vapours, filth and garbage, obstruction and crowds, have variously come under scrutiny. Today the location, construction and management of places and premises and the activities, processes and undertakings carried on at premises have become subject to statutory control—and entertainment is an example of this as already explained in Part 9—so that actions for common law nuisance particularly as regards interference with the enjoyment of property have tended to be supplanted by proceedings under the town and country planning laws and such regulatory legislation.

Liability for Nuisance

As the law of nuisance serves to protect the use and enjoyment of property, generally an action can only be brought by the person in possession and occupation of the affected property. An absent landlord may take action if the nuisance is such as to inflict some permanent damage to the property, for example from flooding or vibration, or interference by encroachment on the property, but not if the activity is merely to result in the loss of tenants or render the letting of premises more difficult. It is doubtful if a person not having exclusive possession of property could bring an action for a private nuisance. Thus the owner or lessee of premises used for entertainment or as a studio, is the one most likely to have a right of action rather than a visiting company performing at a theatre or studio.

The person liable to be sued for nuisance is normally the occupier of the property from which the nuisance emanates for he is presumed to have control of the property and therefore responsibility for what goes on. So an occupier will be liable for the acts of his employees and agents on the principle of vicarious liability; also for the acts of his independent contractors as an occupier is obliged to see that contractors in carrying out their undertakings use means which will not cause a nuisance to others. Always the person who creates the nuisance is primarily liable irrespective of whether he is or ever was in actual occupation of the property from which the nuisance emanated such as an independent contractor, or is able to abate the nuisance. A landlord who creates a nuisance, or expressly or impliedly permits his tenant to do so, or who lets premises with a nuisance upon them which he has knowledge of or can be imputed to have knowledge of, or who undertakes to maintain and repair the property or has the right to enter and inspect it, is deemed to have control of the property and therefore can be held liable for a nuisance. The tenant's liability as occupier does not diminish but both the landlord and the tenant may be liable jointly and severally so the person affected may have alternative sources from which to obtain compensation. Whether or not the landlord or tenant is held liable to pay compensation, the one may have a right of contribution from the other towards payment of the damages awarded.

Remedies

The remedies for nuisance are an injunction and damages. The courts have a discretion over the granting of an injunction the effect of which is to restrain or perhaps stop the performance or continuation of the act or omission constituting the nuisance. The general principle is that the courts will not grant an injunction if the award of damages is a sufficient compensation for the harm suffered or likely to be suffered. However, judges have remarked particularly concerning wrongful acts which are a nuisance, that acts are not to be indirectly permitted or bought at a price by the award of damages. Where it is proved that the nuisance existed at the time the action was commenced then generally an injunction will lie, but if meanwhile the nuisance has been abated that will not necessarily prevent the complainant seeking an injunction if the nuisance recurs. Depending on the circumstances often an injunction will be in terms to curtail or restrain the offending activity rather than impose a total prohibition. Self-help or abatement is open to an occupier where this can be done without entry on to the offending property unless there is a real emergency. In other circumstances the remedy is beset with technicalities of procedural notices and if in the act of abating the nuisance any unnecessary harm is done the liability for this falls back on the person seeking to stop the nuisance. Moreover the remedy of self-help is of little value where the nuisance is an impairment to the use and enjoyment of property rather than actual physical damage.

Public Nuisance

Public nuisance is a separate and distinct ground of liability; it goes beyond ordinary nuisance in that it causes damage or inconvenience or annoyance to the public at large. The nuisance must materially affect the reasonable comfort and convenience of life of a class of people such as a neighbourhood. But the number of persons to comprise a class is a question of fact in each case for the number can be quite small depending on the circumstances. If a nuisance is widespread or indiscriminate in its effect so as to affect a community or number of persons it is likely to be considered a public nuisance. An act or omission which is trifling and not a private nuisance may by its cumulative effect amount to a public nuisance. Furthermore unlike a private nuisance there does not necessarily have to be a state of affairs or degree of permanence; a single event may be sufficient. This is often the situation with pop festivals, fair grounds and open air activities. The principle was established in the last century for when an excessive amount of explosives was used in quarrying which resulted in a wide scattering of rocks, it was held there did not have to be a number of repetitions of such a hazard so as to bring about a state of affairs to constitute a nuisance: one blast was enough!

Statutory Nuisance

A further classification of nuisance as a statutory nuisance has come about as the result of the enactment of numerous statutes regulating modern living conditions; statutes dealing with public health, highways, pollution, noise, dangerous substances and processes and the environment generally. The administration and enforcement of much of this legislation rests with local government authorities. Because of the wide scope of this regulatory law the concept of public nuisance has tended to be over-reached and superceded by statutory nuisance, the committing of which leads to intervention by public authorities and the imposition of a fine.

Of especial relevance is the Environmental Protection Act 1990 which enables both local authorities and private persons to take summary proceedings where a statutory nuisance exists. Where a local authority is satisfied a statutory nuisance, for example, the state of premises is such as to be prejudicial to public health, or noise nuisance exists or is likely to occur or recur, it is empowered to serve an "abatement notice" on the person responsible for the nuisance, or if he cannot be found on the owner or occupier of the premises. The notice can impose conditions requiring the abatement of the nuisance and prohibiting or restraining its occurrence or recurrence; it may also specify work to be done and within what time to abate the nuisance. If the person concerned without reasonable excuse contravenes or fails to comply with the notice he is guilty of an offence and can incur a heavy fine.

The person on whom the notice is served has a right of appeal to the magistrates court within 21 days of the service of the notice. Various defences are permitted under the Act. For example, where noise is caused in the course of a trade or business, it is a defence to prove that the best practical means have been used for preventing or for counteracting the effect of the noise.

A private person in occupation of premises can make complaint to a magistrates court of a statutory nuisance. Proceedings are against the person responsible for the nuisance, or if that person cannot be found, against the owner or occupier of the premises concerned. Notice of the intention to take the proceedings must first be given by the complainant to the offender; not less than three days' notice if the nuisance is noise, otherwise not less than 21 days. The same defences as above are available to the offender. If a court is satisfied the nuisance exists, or although abated is likely to recur, it can make an order requiring the defendant to abate the nuisance, or prohibiting its recurrence. If the order is not complied with the court can impose a heavy fine.

Under the Control of Pollution Act 1974 local authorities are empowered to designate all or any part of an area as a noise abatement zone and to specify the classes of premises within the area subject to regulated noise levels. There are very technical rules for the measurement of noise levels. A public register of premises classified and the permitted noise levels has to be maintained. When the levels are exceeded on classified premises the local authority is empowered to serve a notice requiring strict observance if the level of noise emanating is unacceptable, reduction is practical at a reasonable cost and the public would benefit. If such a notice is served six months must be allowed for compliance; there is a right of appeal against the notice to a magistrates' court. Whilst these provisions may be viewed by some as onerous and restrictive for outdoor entertainment and especially open air pop concerts it should not be overlooked that they could be invoked in the interests of entertainment where other commercial or industrial activities are conducted in a way as to cause annoyance or interfere with an entertainment.

Street noises are particularly covered in the 1974 Act. A loudspeaker is not to be operated in the street (subject to certain special exemptions) between 9 p.m. and 8 a.m. for any purpose, or at any other time for the purpose of advertising any entertainment, trade or business. A street is defined as a highway and any road, footway, square or court which is for the time being open to the public. If the loudspeaker is not in the street but on premises then if the noise which emanates constitutes a nuisance then the situation will fall to be dealt with by a local authority under its powers under the 1990 Act mentioned above or this Act as noted above, or by the occupier of neighbouring premises who is aggrieved by the noise. The section of the Act covering street noises makes special provision for loudspeakers used in connection with the sale of foods and the like so that for example an ice cream van can operate between 12 noon and 7 p.m. provided no annoyance is caused in a locality.

F. AUDIENCES AND VISITORS

Although in this study the performer and the creative person have received the most attention, the public also needs to be considered. Rather perhaps depending on the circumstances and kind of entertainment offered, a person present on premises or other place of entertainment may variously be designated or referred to as a member of the audience, a spectator, a patron or customer but the title or appellation will make no difference in law. From the legal standpoint persons are either licensees or trespassers—the former are admitted, the latter are not; licensees are distinguished as "bare" licensees and contractual licensees. In the context of this study other classifications serve no purpose and especially so since as already noted the law appertaining to personal injuries sustained on premises has been reformed.

On numerous occasions and in numerous circumstances people enter "public" places and premises or perhaps more accurately the public parts of premises: Their presence is with the tacit or presumed consent or permission of the owner or occupier, as when persons enter a theatre foyer to see "what's on," or a gallery to view an exhibition or to visit an arts centre, a library or shop, or enter other places such as public gardens or car parking areas or other premises where conveniences and facilities are available. In all these instances as a matter of law persons so using the premises are bare licensees and as such they are entitled to remain just for so long as the owner or occupier allows and until they are asked to leave. Where persons are admitted for payment or other legal consideration then they are contractual licensees for they will have been admitted for a mutually contemplated purpose—such as to see a performance or view an exhibition or for refreshment.

Contract by Ticket of Admission

The person who enters a theatre or concert hall, discotheque or other place of entertainment upon payment of the price of a seat or ticket is admitted by virtue of an agreement, *i.e.* a contract, normally with the occupier or proprietor of the premises where the entertainment takes place. If for any reason the performance does not take place, or if the billed artists do not perform, or there is any omission in the performance as a result of which the ticket holder does not get what he bargained for,

the liability falls on the proprietor or management of the place of entertainment and not for example, on a visiting touring company, artist,
concert promoter or distributor of a film. However this may not always be
so as where premises are hired out and the sale of tickets is by the
presenter of the entertainment such as an independent promoter or
amateur society.

In the ordinary course of events the contract is formed at the point
when a person makes an offer to attend a performance or entertainment,
normally by tendering the price of a ticket, and a management or organ-
iser of the entertainment accepts the offer by issuing a ticket of admission,
or a voucher is handed over when a ticket is purchased from a ticket
agency acting on behalf of a management. If a member of the public is
induced to attend a performance and purchases a ticket that person is at
liberty to take legal proceedings for any default by a management just as
much as for the breach of any other contract. Accordingly it is important
for the terms and conditions to be established at the time when the
contract is formed for these cannot be altered or varied or added to later,
for example, by notice in a programme given away or sold later.

If tickets are sold subject to conditions such as the right of a management to make changes in the cast or alterations to the programme then
this must be made plain and preferably on the face of the ticket. If the
conditions take up more space than the average sized ticket, then attention should be drawn to the existence of the special conditions and
directions given as to where they can be read without difficulty or inconvenience. The person seeking entertainment is not likely to be much
concerned or interested in "the small print" of this ticket of admission
unless he has an accident when his failure to do so could well be his loss.
Even so the basic principles outlined above need to be borne in mind
especially over such matters as changes of times of performance, of cast
and of programme. If there is any default in regard to these matters it is
difficult to conceive of circumstances where a refund of the price paid for
the ticket would not absolve the management from further liability. The
disappointment suffered by the ticket holder or any expense incurred by
him in attending would not come within the measure of damages or loss
for which a court would award compensation.

Discrimination on the Grounds of Race

With the passing of the Race Relations Act 1976 a more positive control
and right of redress have been enacted in regard to direct and indirect
discrimination in the provision of goods, facilities and services as well as
of employment as noted in Part 5 above. The Act makes special mention
of the provision of facilities for entertainment, recreation or refreshment,
and under the general provisions of section 20 it is unlawful for any

person concerned with the provision of these facilities for the public or a section of the public, whether for payment or not, to discriminate against a person who seeks to obtain or use the facilities or services. The offence lies in refusing or deliberately omitting to provide them, or by refusing or deliberately omitting to provide them to a person in the like manner or on the like terms as they are provided to other members of the public or other members of a section of the public of which the person is a member. Discrimination is given a statutory meaning and embraces direct and indirect discrimination but the discrimination is essentially one grounded on a person's colour, race, nationality or ethnic or national origins. Admission to public entertainment and recreational facilities cannot be denied on racial grounds but it does not follow that refusal of admission cannot rest on other substantial grounds, such as that the person is a critic whose presence is not welcome by a management or is a known trouble-maker in the sense of causing annoyance or offence to other persons present on the premises.

The Act confers on a person who is unlawfully discriminated against a right to bring civil proceedings for the recovery of damages and the award by a court can include compensation for injured feelings. The Commission for Racial Equality has powers to investigate complaints of discrimination and if satisfied that a person is committing or has committed an unlawful discriminatory act, can issue a non-discrimination notice. There is a right of appeal against the issue of such a notice. If during the period of five years beginning on the date on which a binding non-discrimination notice is served on a person it appears to the Commission that the discriminatory acts are persisted in, it can apply to the court for an injunction for the discontinuance of the acts.

Conduct of Audience

A ticket holder has a general right to enter and remain on the premises and to occupy the seat reserved or place allotted to view the whole performance or entertainment, or to be present at the event (or discotheque or whatever) so long as he conducts himself properly and complies with the conditions of entry. The conduct to be expected of an individual member of an audience is that he will behave with due regard for the comfort and convenience of other members present. He is entitled to react to a performance and show excitement and approval, or disapproval—to applaud or jeer—but not to act so as to impede or obstruct the performance. If a person disapproves of or dislikes a performance then he must leave quietly.

Persons who make a nuisance of themselves or cause annoyance such as in all the circumstances is not to be tolerated by reasonable people, and persons who are drunk or whose behaviour is contrary to law, are in breach of an express, or more often implied condition of admission. If the misconduct is serious a management is entitled to terminate the contract and require the person concerned to leave—and if necessary escort the person from the premises by or in the presence of a senior member of the staff.

Where more serious disorder occurs, as when a person uses threatening, abusive or insulting words or behaviour or disorderly behaviour such as to cause harassment or alarm, or to lead to the belief that immediate unlawful violence will be used, these constitute offences under the Public Order Act 1986 and usually justify police intervention.

Where a person has been given an implied or express permission to enter premises open to the public, as with the examples above of a bare licence and a contractual licence, if the licence is terminated then whenever possible a formal request ought to be made for the person to remove himself and the reasons for the request given. The person must be given time to withdraw but if he fails to do so, as he then is no longer present with the licence and consent of the management he becomes a trespasser and can be dealt with as such. A person who enters parts of premises which are not open to the public is a trespasser on those parts. A person is also a trespasser if his entry or use of the premises is illicit such as gaining access and deliberately avoiding payment to view a performance, or by coming in off the streets to use the conveniences. If a management is faced with a trespasser, or a person who in law becomes a trespasser, who does not promptly remove himself when asked to do so, it is legitimate to use such degree of force as is reasonable in order to prevent the person entering or to control his movement or secure his exit. If a person deliberately enters another's premises or recklessly interferes with another's property, he takes on himself the risk of being restrained and must suffer the consequences of his being reasonably restrained or ejected; but he is not presumed to take on the risk of a savage blow or restraint out of all proportion to the circumstances of the occasion. Moreover, the right so to deal with a trespasser is that of the occupier of the premises (and his employees and agents) but not others—except of course the police.

Trespass

"Trespassers will be prosecuted" is a meaningless statement because trespass is not a crime (apart from a few specific statutory exceptions), but a trespasser lays himself open to civil proceedings for the recovery of damages. It may be that proceedings are not often brought by private persons when simply only a wrongful entry has been made as no more than nominal damages are likely to be awarded. However, where actual damage is suffered and inflicted then general damages will be recoverable but the amount will depend very much on the facts of a particular case; a person is not necessarily answerable in law for all the loss which flows from the damage he inflicts on others whether due to negligence or done wilfully. The person who does a wrongful act is liable only to those persons whose rights are thereby violated even if the consequences of the action may seriously affect other persons. If a trespasser interferes with some equipment as a result of which a performance is prevented the damages recoverable will be measured in regard to the damage directly inflicted on the equipment and the cost of its repair or replacement, not the consequential loss such as box-office revenue. If the entry and damage were shown to have been deliberate with the very purpose of preventing a performance special damages may be awarded for the loss directly suffered from the wrongful act, but not for the loss of potential profits or prestige or injured feelings.

Criminal Actions

All that has been said above about the presence of individuals on premises and the right of a management to admit or refuse admission, or having admitted a person to require him to leave must be understood as falling within the province of the civil law. Any dispute about the legality of any such action falls to be dealt with in the civil courts. Only when a serious disturbance occurs such as to justify resort to the police or where there is serious damage or interference to property or assault on persons do such actions become the subject of the criminal laws to be dealt with by prosecution in the magistrates' courts.

Crimes relating to personal property such as active stealing or which involve deception and in general terms amount to stealing are covered principally by the Theft Act 1968. An additional offence particularly noteworthy in this study is one constituted as the result of some notorious instances of art thefts at exhibitions. Section 11 of the Act provides that where the public have access to a building in order to view the building or a part of it, or a collection or part of a collection housed in it, anyone who unlawfully removes from the building any article or part of an article displayed or kept for display to the public in the building or in its grounds is guilty of an offence. The scope and application of the section have yet to be tested but it does eliminate some of the prerequisites of the crime of larceny or theft such as particularly the need for proof that the person charged with the offence took the property with the intention of permanently depriving the owner of it. The section clearly aids all organisations and museums providing exhibitions of art and other objects but it is also a valuable protection for managements of theatres and concert halls and the like which mount exhibitions from time to time in support of a current production, a local appeal, a local society or association.

Overt and malicious damage to property is governed by the Criminal

Damage Act 1971. Where a person unlawfully damages or destroys any property belonging to another intentionally or treats property recklessly, meaning that some act is done deliberately and knowing there is a risk of damage and damage and destruction do result, that person commits a serious offence under the Act; the offence is aggravated when the intentional act can also endanger life. If the damage or destruction is perpetrated by fire, the crime is arson as distinct from mere criminal damage and involves a graver penalty. Threats to damage or destroy property are also offences under the Act and can be committed against not only the actual owner of property but also against the person having custody or control of it.

Serious crimes such as those described above may justify the arrest of the offender but the powers of private persons to make an arrest are subject to very technical rules contained in the Police and Criminal Evidence Act 1984 and whether an offence is an "arrestable offence" according to the particular statute under which an offence has been created. If a person who is suspected of some criminal offence can be persuaded "to come to the manager's office" while enquiries are made (and probably the police are called), that is very likely to be the more discreet and prudent course of action. Because a person is taken to a manager's office for questioning and for proceedings perhaps to be sanctioned by a management official, it has been ruled that that does not necessarily amount to false imprisonment.

Police powers of arrest without a warrant are much greater than those of private persons. So where a police constable has reasonable cause to suspect an arrestable offence has been committed or is about to be committed, he can without a warrant arrest the person he reasonably suspects of being guilty of the offence, or about to commit the offence. Moreover, if an individual requests a police constable to take another person into custody having alleged that such other person has committed an arrestable offence or inflicted a grievous wound, the police constable is empowered by common law to arrest the person concerned if the charge or allegation is reasonable and made by a person deserving of credence. If the charge proves unfounded, however, the person making it and not the police constable will be responsible for the false arrest.

G. HATS AND COATS

What to do with hats and coats etc. is a problem which afflicts both management and members of the public (if not for the same reasons) as the legal issues which can arise from what in itself is a minor though necessary facility provided by good management can be complex. Hang a coat on a peg, leave an article in a room, or a car in a parking space and at the most a ticket or token may be handed out. When a ticket is given out, does it constitute a contract or is it merely a receipt for the payment made for the mere licence or permission to deposit an article or park a car? The rights and liabilities of the parties affected may rest solely on the principles of the common law of bailment, for the essence of a bailment is the handing over or delivery of possession and custody of an article by the owner, "the bailor," to the recipient, "the bailee," with the intention that the article will be re-delivered to the bailor. On the other hand the basis of the rights and liabilities of the parties may be contractual, especially when a payment is involved, when the terms of the contract may override the principles of the common law of bailment which would otherwise automatically apply.

Accepting that the ticket constitutes the contract—the conditions may be printed on the ticket or displayed on the premises—there have been many instances where the courts on the particular facts of a case have held that the printed conditions and disclaimers of liability have been rendered inapplicable by the actual promises or representations of attendants or other employees. Thus to cite one instance by way of example: a customer was about to park his car in a car park as he had regularly done locked in accordance with the notices displayed but was induced by the attendant "on the instructions of the management" to leave the car unlocked despite the customer telling the attendant there were valuables in the car. The "instructions" were wholly false and when the valuables were found to be missing the management was held liable for the loss. The customer had been affected by the representation of the attendant and as the attendant had ostensible authority to make the representation on behalf of the management the latter was liable to the customer.

An article or indeed any article or chattel cannot be foisted on a person. For one person to assume responsibility for another's property there must be a delivery by the bailor and an acceptance by the bailee with the common intention that possession of the article should be transferred from the one to the other. If an article is left by its owner on premises where he has no right to be at all, or at the time when the article was left he had no right to be, there cannot be said to be an acceptance of possession by the owner or occupier of the premises. If a person who is legitimately on premises leaves or places an article in such a position as no reasonable person could fairly and sensibly assume that the article would be taken into possession by the owner or occupier, he cannot complain of its loss. Where racks or stands are placed in a public area this does not of itself necessarily imply an intention or representation by a management that it accepts possession of the articles placed on the stands. However, if the management by a member of its staff receives the articles and even where that member receives the articles although such action is not strictly a part of his normal or regular duties, then the management may be held to have voluntarily accepted possession of the articles; how much more so then when the articles are taken and placed in a separate private area or room.

Duty of care

When a person takes possession of articles or goods as a bailee he assumes a duty of care for their safe keeping irrespective of whether a charge is made. The standard of care required to satisfy the duty will depend on the circumstances and not entirely on whether or not the bailment was gratuitous. The kind of premises and their usual function, the kind of persons regularly using the facilities and the kind of articles reasonably to be expected to be deposited are reckonable factors. The criterion of the duty is the exercise of the care to be expected of a reasonable man in the particular circumstances, not the care with which the bailee keeps his own goods and chattels. If an uncommon or unexpected danger arises then reasonable efforts must be made to avoid the risk of harm to the goods deposited and reasonable steps taken for their protection. Even if the bailment is gratuitous still the duty prevails although what would constitute reasonable efforts might be judged less severely. Once the fact of bailment is established then regardless of whether it was gratuitous or for payment, if articles or goods are lost or damaged during the deposit an inference of negligence on the part of the bailee automatically arises and the onus is on him to show that reasonable and proper care was taken for the safe keeping and re-delivery of the property. If the duty can be shown to have been discharged, a bailee is not obliged to show how the loss or damage in fact occurred without any negligence on his part. The display of a notice in such terms as "all goods left at customer's risk" will not avail if the duty of care cannot affirmatively be shown to have been discharged. Where the bailment rests on a contract then only if there is an unequivocal express term avoiding or limiting liability in negligence will the liability be avoided.

Very often the bailee is an employer, for example a theatre management, and so is responsible for the acts and omissions of the staff which are within the scope of their employment. Acts of negligence, conversion of property and theft are not to the layman within the scope of a person's employment but in law, as has often been remarked, the improper carrying out of duties by an employee does not relieve the employer of liability from the consequences of the impropriety—as in the above example of the car park attendant. If a duty of care exists by law and its observance is entrusted to another then the one on whom the duty rests is answerable for the manner in which it is carried out. If an employee or agent is entrusted with property but is careless so that it is damaged or lost or stolen by an employee or agent or even by a stranger, the employer is liable for the consequences. Even so in the ordinary way a bailee is not an insurer of the safety of goods deposited with him and therefore is not liable for accidents or loss which are not attributable to his negligence or to the negligence of another which in law attaches to him such as an employee.

Because of the legal consequences which result from the acceptance even gratuitously of articles for deposit and safe keeping, it is not easy to be certain about what to do with hats and coats. The provision of the simplest facilities for the placing of articles may best protect a management from responsibility and liability so long as it cannot be held to have accepted or taken possession of the articles. The facility so provided implies nothing more than a mere licence so to place the articles; likewise the provision of an open area adjacent to premises for the parking of cars by users of the premises. The reception of articles by attendants is constructively acceptance by the management and the giving of a ticket for receipt and checking out on re-delivery are sensible precautions and tending to show the discharge of the duty of care. The acceptance of articles merely upon payment of a charge and the handing over of a ticket can be equivocal. If it is intended to establish a special contractual relationship this must be apparent at the time and the ticket must contain a statement of the terms and conditions upon which the articles are accepted for deposit, or clearly make reference to those terms which must be easily ascertainable. Moreover if the purpose of the ticket is to give notice of the limitation of liability for loss or damage the conditions must be sufficiently comprehensive and explicit to make clear this limitation. If this precaution is taken it should not then be rendered of no effect by some oral representation or other conduct by the management or by its employees waiving the conditions.

H. LOST PROPERTY

It is generally assumed that the finder of a lost article is entitled to keep it unless the true owner is found. Yet the application of this principle can be much affected by a number of considerations: the place of the finding; the status of the finder, that is, whether he is a private individual or employee at the place of the finding; the legal standing of the person in occupation or possession of the premises or place where the finding occurred; whether the article was simply lying on the property (*e.g.* on the floor) or was attached to it in the sense of being secreted or purposely concealed. However as the problems of finding lost property are likely to arise only in the ordinary way of members of the public attending at places of entertainment, the more esoteric considerations which sometimes can arise—or might have been raised when Faust's Marguerite found a casket of jewels—will not be pursued.

The owner or person in occupation of land and premises is presumed to intend to exercise such control over his property that things which may be upon it, or in it or under it, if found by an employee or stranger are deemed to be in his possession. On the other hand when articles are left merely lying on land or on premises for example, in a foyer, auditorium, dressing room, restaurant, or shop floor, the view is that such a person cannot be presumed to have knowledge of the presence of the articles with the intention of exercising control over them and being in possession of them. The distinction is rather artificial but perhaps it is practical.

If an attendant or other employee of the management of premises finds an article in the course of his employment it is clearly established that the possession (by finding) of the employee is deemed to be the possession of the employer. Where a visitor or customer at the premises finds an article this legal principle does not apply so the finder has the right of possession.

Where an article is found in a public place such as in the street and outside a theatre or the like, the finder is under no absolute duty to take charge of it. If he does he thereby assumes a duty to take care for its safe custody and to return it on demand to the rightful owner and cannot claim any compensation for any trouble or expense incurred in looking after the article.

The principle that a person although not the owner of an article can have a right of possession superior to the person who is in actual possession of the article can be demonstrated by the circumstances of a management in control of a cloakroom. The management would have such a prior right of possession as against the finder of an article deposited in a cloakroom by its owner. However, if the owner could not be traced or did not seek to recover the article and enforce his title to the property, then the finder would succeed to the ownership of the article by the act of finding. If an article is wrongly handed over by an attendant that may be construed as a finding by the recipient.

The possession of an article by a finder is and continues to be lawful unless and until the owner demands its return. Taking possession of a lost article is not wrong unless the finder dishonestly appropriates it with the intention of depriving the lawful owner of possession. Where a finder believes that by taking reasonable steps the owner could be discovered then by law the finder has a duty to take those steps to search for the owner; reporting the loss to the police is an obvious step. The failure to take such steps constitutes theft by finding under the Theft Act 1968.

For the purpose of the law of finding, the owner of an article is no more than the person with a better title to it than other claimants. If an owner can establish his title for example by showing his name on the article or identifying some special characteristic or feature known to him, or otherwise proving his ownership or overriding right to have possession of the article, he can recover it from the finder. The true owner can always recover his property from anyone into whose hands it comes unless he can be held to have abandoned it, or the period of limitation within which to take proceedings for the recovery of the property—six years from the time of the loss—has expired, or the property has been sold in the special circumstances of "market overt."

The accumulation of property lost on premises to which the public are admitted can be an inconvenience and embarrassment to managements but resulting from the passing of the Torts (Interference with Goods) Act 1977 and by following the procedure as laid down this need not remain so. In effect if lost property has been safeguarded for a reasonable time and after making reasonable enquiries it has not been possible to trace the owner or make any communication with him, or the owner fails to give instructions about its disposal the property can be sold. The seller is liable to account for the proceeds of sale less any costs of selling reasonably and fairly incurred. Where there is an accumulation of lost property a management ought to advertise the proposed sale in the local press and allow a reasonable interval of time within which owners can have the opportunity to recover their property. However when rather valuable property is involved the procedures prescribed by the Act should be strictly adhered to, or alternatively application made to the county court or High Court for an order under section 13 of the Act for the sale of the property.

Part 11

AGENTS AND PERSONAL REPRESENTATION

A. THE BASIC RULES OF AGENCY

As those familiar with contracts for the engagement of artists, writers, directors, etc., will know, there is usually included at the end of the contract a provision whereby all fees due to the artist and all notices given to him are to be remitted to his agent. This placing last of the mention of the agent is hardly a fair reflection of the importance of the role often performed by theatrical and literary agents but perhaps it can be excused on the grounds of expedience. Following this custom and with the same sentiment, it is fitting that this study should be concluded with a short explanation of the role of agents and personal managers and their legal standing.

A personal representation is usually undertaken by an express agreement between an artist and an agent made orally or in writing. Some agents prefer to rely on a general understanding with their clients. This may be unobjectionable in law as no formalities are essential to bringing about the relationship but as will be seen below, there is now a statutory obligation on agents to provide clients with a written statement of their current terms of business and to furnish these details to the Department of Employment.

Agent's Authority

An agent performs a personal service for his client. He represents him and acts for him so that he can acquire rights and incur obligations on his behalf. Because of the personal nature of the relationship it follows that without permission an agent cannot delegate to another the authority given to him or the duties assumed by him. Where an agency is organised as a company or firm then this principle is often maintained by nominating a particular person to act and perform the functions of agent.

The nature and extent of the authority a person confers on his agent is the core of the relationship. Where an express or general authority is conferred there is coupled with it an implied authority to do all incidental but necessary acts required to bring about what is to be done or accomplished. This can be construed as entitling an agent to incur expenses on behalf of his client. If in carrying out his assignment or functions an agent does what is usual or regular according to a profession or business then his client or "principal" will be bound by the commitment or obligation made with a third party on the client's behalf. The same legal principles apply to the actions of employees acting as agents of their employers, or by officials acting on behalf of companies or corporate organisations. Authority will be imputed to an employee or official to negotiate and to do all those things reasonably to be expected of a person having the status accorded to him by the employer or organisation.

Normally an agent in consultation with his artist client will negotiate an engagement, settle its duration, the fees or salary payable and the special stipulations to meet the particular circumstances. In the ordinary way a written contract will be issued by the engaging company and the negotiations confirmed by the artist's signature. If there is a dispute about the terms of the contract then whether or not there is a concluded deal between an artist and a company will fall to be decided on the legal principles outlined above in considering contracts of engagement. Where an artist starts an engagement then by so doing he will most likely be deemed to have ratified the engagement as negotiated by his agent.

Agent's Obligations

The assumption of the role of agent carries particular obligations. Paramount is the duty of a agent to act within the scope of his authority and to observe the instructions of his principal. If an agent exceeds his authority and in consequence his client suffers loss or liability the agent will be answerable to his client; alternatively he may be liable to others for breach of warranty of authority. An agent must act with care and skill and perform his duties with the diligence, prudence and judgment to be expected of a person pursuing the business or profession in which he is engaged. If an agent so conducts the affairs of his client and has acted in a manner as in all the circumstances can fairly and reasonably be expected, the agent cannot be held responsible if his efforts are not successful or do not achieve the results desired.

Duty of Fidelity

The standing of an agent rests on confidence and trust and so the law imposes on him a duty of fidelity to his principal. This duty is the basis of the rule that an agent must not let his own interests conflict with those of his client; his dealings with others must not be such as to cast any shadow on the integrity of his judgment in his handling of the affairs and business of his client. An agent must not make a secret profit or secure some preferment for himself by virtue of his acting for his client. If an agent uses property such as copyright material which is entrusted to him, or uses information given by his client or acquired for the benefit of his client and turns such information to his own account to obtain a secret profit, then the agent is accountable for that profit. It is the taint of secrecy which is the fault so if a client is informed about the activities by his agent and consents to them or raises no objection the secrecy is removed. Unlike the perpetrating of some fraud or the taking of a bribe, the making of a secret profit will not necessarily deprive an agent of his rights against his client if these should be disputed but he can be called to account for the profit.

An agent has the duty to pay over all money received on behalf of his client and this duty applies regardless of any claims of other persons to the money received and to any amount which may be due to the agent himself except as mentioned below. If an agent receives money as the result of some mistake of fact or which has not been earned, or is paid under a void contract, then only if the agent has notice of the error before the time for him to account to his client for the money can an agent legitimately withhold payment. Coupled with this duty to account is the duty of the agent to keep his client's property and money separate from his own and from other people's. So an agent must keep proper accounts and produce them when required. If an agent fails to make due and timely payments a client can bring an action for account for money had and received to the principal's use, as well as sue for breach of contract or pursue an action at common law.

Payment of Commission

The duty of a client is to pay the remuneration or commission to his agent as agreed. In the normal way of business the assumption of the role of agent is not gratuitous and if nothing has been expressly agreed about the commission payable then the payment will be recoverable on a basis of what is reasonable in the circumstances. This will be assessed in the light of the custom and usage of a business or profession in which an agent is engaged. Commission is due when earned by the agent, when he has brought about the event or situation for which he was engaged. It is immaterial that the event or result is not as profitable or beneficial to the client as he had expected as, for example, when an engagement is cancelled or when royalties or shares of profits are not as high as expected.

The right of an agent to recover expenses from his client will depend upon the contractual terms of the agency but otherwise upon the expenses having been incurred with express or implied authority of the client and in the course of the agent's performance of his services. Where there is a right to recover expenses an agent is entitled to set off his expenses before accounting for any money due to his client. An agent also has a lien, that is a power to retain the property of his client which has come into his possession in the course of his acting as agent, to enforce the payment of commission earned and expenses which he is entitled to recover.

Difficulties and disputes can arise where a client acts on his own behalf as a term will not readily be implied in an agency agreement that a client may not do so. Put another way, an agent must show as a term of the agreement that by acting on his own behalf a client has deprived the agent of the opportunity for him to earn remuneration. By appointing an agent as "sole agent" this does not of itself bar a person acting on his own account. On the other hand there must be a very clear term obliging a client to perform or carry on with his enterprise or business or profession so as to enable an agent to act and earn commission. If an agency is for a fixed term then if it is broken by a client the usual consequences of a breach of contract will follow, as where an artist leaves one agent for another. But it is open to question if damages could be secured for loss of opportunity to earn commission because an artist decides to leave or give up his profession.

Contract Resulting from Agent's Negotiations

In the ordinary course of events an agent will not be a party to the contract resulting from his negotiations. The contract will be as between his client and the company engaging the artist's services. The rights and obligations to be enjoyed and performed under the contract will be those of the actual parties to the contract and the agent will have no standing in regard to them. On the other hand if an agent has pursued negotiations without authority he will be liable to a person who suffers loss as a result of having relied on the agent's misrepresentation even if the misrepresentation was made innocently. If such a person has notice of the absence of the agent's authority, or where by custom or usage he would accept the agent was not warranting his authority, then he could not claim to have been misled by the misrepresentation. Where a loss has been sustained on the grounds of an agent's breach of warranty of authority then usually the measure of damages will be the loss suffered as if the contract had been made and then repudiated.

Revocation of Agency

It is a rule of the law of agency that a client can revoke the authority of his agent by notice at any time. Only in a few exceptional and rather technical situations does the law deprive a person of the right to take back the power he has conferred on another to act for him. Correspondingly an agent can renounce his authority and relinquish his representation of his principal at any time. Such unilateral action by either party if not consented to by the other and if in breach of the terms of the contract of agency will automatically confer a right of action for damages against the defaulting party. The authority of an agent also automatically ends by the death, insanity or bankruptcy of either the principal or the agent.

B. AGENTS' AND PERSONAL MANAGERS' AGREEMENTS

The general principles of law just reviewed form the foundation of representation agreements regardless of whether or not they are written. Even so a written contract is to be preferred as then the internal arrangements between an agent and his client can be expressly agreed and set down and in this way the implications of law avoided which would otherwise apply to their relationship but which might be contrary to their real intention.

The scope of an agent's authority and the duties he is to perform will depend upon the kind of representation undertaken and the particular profession his client is pursuing—actor, singer, musician, director, playwright, author, designer, etc., and perhaps the client's standing. A representation agreement may provide simply for an artist to receive advice and guidance about his professional career and for the agent to secure engagements for him suitable to his talents. A management agreement entails a greater commitment in the way of continuously supervising, moulding and directing an artist in his performance and managing the conduct of his business and professional affairs. Thus such an agreement is likely to include even control over the works of an artist especially pop artists and groups.

The role which agents perform in initiating productions and their involvement with promoters, managements and executives in matching creative people and selling the services of their clients may be seen as conflicting with the duty of fidelity mentioned above. This involvement of agents is inherent in the entertainment business and must be acknowledged by artists and others; indeed it is likely to be desired and expected. Similarly a client must accept the real possibility of his agent representing other clients who like himself are seeking opportunities, even perhaps the same engagement. These kinds of situations are to be distinguished from where an agent acts at one and the same time for an artist client and a producer or manager client when negotiations for an engagement can lead to a conflict of interests. In such circumstances there is a duty of disclosure to both parties and a need for their consent to the agent acting for both of them. Furthermore, for an agent not to reveal a personal interest or stake in a production or presentation to a client whose work or sevices of some kind he is representing for that production would obviously be a breach of the duty the law imposes not to make a secret profit from acting for a client.

The terms of representation agreements which need to be covered include a proper statement or description of what the agent is to do and the manner of his carrying out his duties; in other words the nature and extent of his authority. A client may require to be represented in only a particular area of entertainment or only in respect of a particular talent or pursuit or only in this country. The obligation of a client to report offers for his services needs to be clear so that a client is not entitled to act on his own account. Where an agent or management is a corporate body the officials designated to carry out the duties of representation should be named and the effect of their ceasing to be part of the organisation made clear, otherwise if the agency continues in being a client will have no automatic right to seek alternative representation.

The right to commission, the amount and manner of its calculation, when it is due, and the right to deduct it before accounting for fees and royalties received should all be made certain. The expenses which can be incurred and any limitation on them need to be expressly stated. This is especially so with management agreements for pop artists and groups when a management may engage various supporting services—road managers, booking agents, publicists, music arrangers and copyists. The obligation to recover VAT in addition to the fees payable for an artist's services and social security payments and the payment of VAT by an artist on the services rendered by the agent to him are additional matters which may be covered in a representation agreement.

The duration of the period of representation should be stated or provision made for due notice of termination to be given by the parties. If either party desires to reserve a right to curtail the duration of a long-term agreement, for example if the fees earned fall short of a stipulated minimum, or a client elects to discontinue his profession or an agent to discontinue in business, then provision ought to be made accordingly. Material to the termination or expiration of an artist's representation is an agent's entitlement thereafter to commission on fees or royalties or share of profits accruing from engagements contracted during the period of representation but received after the termination. As no firm rule can be applied to this kind of situation then the representation agreement ought to make clear the rights and liabilities of agent and artist.

C. THE EMPLOYMENT AGENCIES ACT 1973

The Employment Agencies Act 1973 ("the Act") has not altered the law of agency but made obligatory the adoption and observance of some of the principles noted above by employment agencies and employment businesses. The Act was amended by the Employment Protection Act 1975 as regards the system of registration of employment agencies and businesses and was brought into operation on July 1, 1976. It is supplemented by Statutory Instruments made under the Act dealing with the procedures for applications for the grant and renewal of licences, the fees chargeable and the detailed rules to be observed in the conduct of employment agencies and businesses.

The legislation has established a national code of licensing and regulation under the Department of Employment so that with a few very special exceptions it is an offence for any person to carry on at any premises an employment agency or employment business without a licence from the Department authorising that person to carry on such agency or business at the named premises.

Licence Application, Grant and Renewal

The procedure for applying for a licence is that for not less than 21 days before making an application a notice of the intended application must be legibly displayed to the public on or near the premises where the agency or business is to be carried on and notice of the application advertised in a newspaper approved by the Department. A copy of the newspaper containing the advertisement must accompany the application. The information and particulars to be supplied are considerable: precise details about the applicant and his affairs, or if the applicant is a company about the company and its directors and officers; particulars of the persons to be employed by the agency or business in a managerial capacity; details of membership of any professional body or trade association; the names of three referees; details of the premises where the business is to be carried on; the class or classes of employment to be covered by the agency or business; with a employment agency, particulars of its services if these are to extend to persons from abroad seeking employment in the United Kingdom and to persons seeking employment abroad, and with an employment business particulars if it is intended to send persons abroad.

There are 12 classes of employment listed in the Employment Agencies and Employment Businesses (Applications for Licences) Regulations 1976 (S.I. 1976 No. 712) and an agency or business can be carried on only in those classes of employment for which application has been made and the licence granted. One of the 12 designated classes is for "performers and other occupations in the entertainment industry."

If during the currency of a licence there are changes in the particulars given these must be notified in writing within one month to the Department. The procedure for the renewal of a licence is much simpler provided any changes in the particulars first given when application was made for the licence have been notified. The application for the renewal of a licence does not need to be publicised. If the holder of a licence dies it is deemed transferred on his death to his personal representative but if the licence is held by persons jointly then it is deemed transferred to the survivor.

Licences are granted for a year or such longer period up to three years as may be specified and are similarly renewable; the fee payable is at the rate of £114 per annum. Applications for licences and their renewal are made to the local Employment Agency Licensing Office of the Department of Employment.

An application for the grant or renewal of a licence can be refused on the grounds as set out in section 2(3) of the Act such as that the applicant is under 21. More importantly the grounds for refusal are that the applicant is a person who on account of misconduct or for any other sufficient reason is unsuitable to hold a licence for the class of employment agency or business covered by the licence. An application can be refused if any person who is or is to be concerned with the carrying on of the agency or business is similarly so regarded as being unsuitable to be associated with the business. Other grounds for refusal are that the premises where the business is conducted are unsuitable or that the agency or business has not been properly conducted. If a licence is refused or if it is revoked written notice and the reasons for this must be given by the Department. The Act makes provision for appealing and making representations against such a decision within 21 days of the decision being notified.

Powers of Department of Employment

Section 9 of the Act confers powers on the Department through its duly authorised officers to enter premises used or to be used for any agency or business and to inspect them. It also empowers officials to inspect records and other documents required to be kept in pursuance of the Act and the regulations made under it. Officials are also empowered to request they be furnished with information reasonably required to ensure that the Act and the regulations are being duly observed, but a person cannot be required to answer any question tending to incriminate himself, or if the person is married his wife (or her husband). When offences committed under the Act and regulations are committed by a company then not only will the company be liable to a penalty but a director, manager or secretary of the company will also be liable if the offence is proved to have been committed with the consent or connivance of or to have been attributable to the neglect of such a person.

Conduct of Agencies

It is section 5 of the Act which permits regulations to be made to secure the proper conduct of agencies and businesses and to protect the interests of persons availing themselves of their services. The Conduct of Employment Agencies and Employment Business Regulations 1976 (S.I. 1976 No. 715) have been made under this section and embody the meticulous rules to be observed by employment agencies and employment business. There are 12 detailed regulations and six schedules and these cover in addition to rules of general management, such matters as the records to be maintained, for safeguarding clients money, advertising, fees and the terms of business and information about these to be given to persons using the services of agencies and employment businesses, the services provided respecting persons under the age of 18, and the control, management and accounting for clients' money. The holder of a licence is required to display the licence on the premises to which the licence relates with a copy of any regulations under the Act which apply to the employment agency or business.

One of the features of the Act is that by section 6 a person carrying on an employment agency or employment business cannot demand or directly or indirectly receive from any person a fee for finding him or seeking to find employment for him; contravention of this provision can result in a fine. Employment for the purpose of the Act includes "employment by way of a professional engagement or otherwise under a contract for services." Charges for services can therefore only be made to employers. The Act does allow exceptions to be made to this rule and such an exception has been made by the Employment Agencies Act 1973 (Charging Fees to Workers) Regulations 1976 (S.I. 1976 No. 714) in respect of a person carrying on an employment agency in the entertainment industry. The scope of the exception is governed strictly by the definitions contained in the Regulations and the classes of persons or occupations specified namely:

"entertainment industry means the production and presentation of films, television and sound broadcasts, and recordings, and of plays, operas, ballets, musical and variety performances, and other similar means of entertainment whether taking place in theatres, concert halls, dance halls, clubs, or any other places of public or private entertainment."

The persons or occupations covered are:

"(a) actors, singers, musicians, dancers and other performers;
(b) composers, directors, assistant directors, production managers, assistant production managers, lighting cameramen, camera operators, make-up artists, film editors, action arrangers and co-ordinators, costume and production designers, recording engineers, hairdressers, property masters, film continuity personnel, sound mixers, and still photographers."

Authors and script writers are excluded from the list so the basic rule will apply to their employment but not to dealings in their own works.

The Regulations do not permit an agent to charge a fee to an artist etc., when a fee is charged to the employer, or where on the date the artist etc., commences the employment the agent and employer are connected with each other, that is to say:

(i) the agent, or partner of his, or, where the agent is a company, a director of that company, is also the employer;

(ii) the employer is a company controlled by any of the persons referred to in (i) above;

(iii) the employer, or partner of his, or where the employer is a company, a director of that company, is also the agent;

(iv) the agent is a company controlled by any of the persons referred to in (iii) above; or

(v) the employer and the agent are both companies of which a third person has the control.

For the purpose of these rules "a company is controlled by a person if he exercises, or is able to exercise, or is entitled to acquire control (whether direct or indirect) over the affairs of the company and, in particular, but without prejudice to the generality of the foregoing, if he possesses, or is entitled to acquire the greater proportion of the share capital or voting power of the company."

It was pointed out above that it is not essential for a contract of agency to be in writing and the Act has not altered this principle. Even so the Regulations require that before an agent takes on the representation of a client he must supply a written statement containing details of his current terms of business if these are not embodied in a proper written representation agreement.

Arising from what has just been said about the exemption for employment agencies from the rule governing the making of charges for finding persons employment and generally about the operation of the Act and the regulations made under it, two definitions in the Act require particular notice, namely:

(a) "employment agency—means the business (whether or not carried on with a view to profit and whether or not carried on in conjunction with any other business) of providing services (whether by the provision of information or otherwise) for the purpose of finding workers employment with employers or of supplying employers with works for employment by them";

(b) "employment business—means the business (whether or not carried on with a view to profit and whether or not carried on in conjunction with any other business) of supplying persons in the employment of the person carrying on the business, to act for, and under the control of, other persons in any capacity."

Fines can be imposed for breaches of the Act and the Regulations but that does not recompense persons who have suffered loss, especially of their earnings, as a result of the malpractice of an agent. Despite its meticulous detail the legislation has not achieved the purposes for which it was designed as there is little monitoring of agents. Some reform of the Act and Regulations is likely in the future but of immediate interest to the entertainment industry is the proposed amendment to the Regulation (S.I. 1976 No. 714) referred to above. The new Regulation will make certain that an agent may only charge a person a fee after he has secured that person employment, and that any fee or commission is only payable out of that person's earnings from the particular engagement or employment. This amendment is intended to overcome the practice of some agents charging clients a registration fee as a condition of their agreeing to act as agent.

INDEX to COLLECTIVE AGREEMENTS

(between Managements and Trade Unions for the services of
Performers and Writers)

Collective Agreements for Performers

Commercials—Television Advertisements

GENERAL INDEX

(See also Index to Collective Agreements)

Dramatic works—*cont.*
  public performance, stage rights for, 443, 460–461
  public readings, 404
Droit de suite, *See* **Moral rights**

Educational Recording Agency, 405, 416
Employers' liability and insurance, 339–344
Employment,
  contracts of, 299–300
   fixed term, 337–338
  discrimination, 345–347
  employees' property, duty regarding, 344
  health and safety, 339–343, 623
  notice of terms of, 328–329
  protection, 327–338
  redundancy, 331–333
  termination of, 329–331
  unfair dismissal, 333–336
Entertainment Agents Association, 88, 96
Equity. *See* **British Actors' Equity Association**
Equipment,
  hire of. *See* **Hire of equipment**
  safety of, 340–343, 623, 624
Esher Standard Contracts, 21, 81.
European Broadcasting Union, 202–203

Fight directors. *See also* **Stunt arrangers/performers**
  theatre engagements, 79–80
Film Artists Association, 253
Film directors,
  moral rights, 429, 432
Film production agreements, 533–537
Films,
  exhibition of. *See* **Cinemas**
  sale and hire to the public, 607–611
  separate copyright in, 374, 536
Firearms. *See* **Weapons**
Fire certificates and precautions,
  places of entertainment, at, 587–588, 623–624
Folk songs,
  protected recordings of, 409–410
Food regulations, 589
Foreign artists,
  taxation of, 310–312
  work permits, 349–352

Gags and quickies,
  copyright in, 491

Hire of equipment,
  agreements for, 647–650
  defective, 648–649
  hirer, duties of, 648